IN DEPTH
ESSAYISTS FOR OUR TIME

Carl H. Klaus
University of Iowa

Chris Anderson
Oregon State University

Rebecca Blevins Faery
Mount Holyoke College

HBJ
Harcourt Brace Jovanovich, Publishers
San Diego   New York   Chicago   Austin   Washington, D.C.
London   Sydney   Tokyo   Toronto

Preface

In making this collection, our primary goal has been to provide some of the best essays we could find by twenty-five outstanding and richly varied essayists—Woody Allen, Francis Bacon, Russell Baker, James Baldwin, Bruno Bettelheim, Joan Didion, Annie Dillard, Loren Eiseley, E. M. Forster, Ellen Goodman, Stephen Jay Gould, Ernest Hemingway, Edward Hoagland, Martin Luther King, Jr., Margaret Mead, George Orwell, Jonathan Swift, Lewis Thomas, Henry David Thoreau, Barbara Tuchman, Mark Twain, Alice Walker, E. B. White, Tom Wolfe, and Virginia Woolf. Each author is represented in depth—by four or five pieces—resulting in a collection of more than 100 essays.

This collection includes the most current essayists as well as writers from earlier periods whose work continues to speak to the interests and issues of our time. Likewise, it provides essays both by well-known literary figures and by authors who are best known for their work in the sciences, social sciences, and public affairs. So, the anthology as a whole offers an opportunity to read the essays of twenty-five distinguished writers and thinkers ranging widely across various subjects and fields of human concern.

We have organized the collection alphabetically, by author, because this arrangement provides the handiest means of quickly locating individual essayists and their work, while leaving the material free to be organized as anyone might wish. This organization also serves to remind one of how diversified the essay can be by producing such striking juxtapositions as Bacon and Baker, Goodman and Gould, Tuchman and Twain, or Wolfe and Woolf. But we also recognize the value of studying essays in terms of their rhetorical patterns and their thematic relationships to each other. So, a topical guide to the essays follows the table of contents, and a rhetorical index and an author-title index appear at the back of the book.

To provide a framework for thinking about the essay as a form of reading and writing, our general introduction focuses on the most distinctive aspects of the essay as defined or commented on by essayists who appear in the collection. Though essays can, of course, be understood in and of themselves, they are so directly related to the experience and outlook of their authors that it seems useful to know more than just a handful of facts about the persons who have written them. So, our introductions to each of the essayists provide detailed information about their lives, careers, accomplishments, interests, and ideas, as well as their thoughts about writing.

To encourage a careful study of the essays, our questions following each selection explore a sequence of interrelated issues. These questions, referred to as "Lines of Inquiry," are not separately listed and numbered as in a quiz or examination, but are grouped in paragraphs because they are intended to stimulate lines of thought or investigation bearing on important aspects of each essay. In each case, the Lines of Inquiry contain three paragraphs of questions: the first focuses on aspects of form; the second on aspects of content; and the third on the relationship of the piece to personal experience and ideas, to contemporary culture and thought, or to other essays in the collection. So, the Lines of Inquiry, like the introductions, are meant to stimulate thoughtful reading, discussion, and writing—to lead one in depth through essays and essayists for our time.

For their helpful reactions to the table of contents, the introductions, and the Lines of Inquiry, we are grateful to Professors Laura Julier, Drake University; Charles Schuster, University of Wisconsin-Milwaukee; and Jeffrey L. Spear, New York University. For their expert work in bringing this book into print, we are grateful to the staff of Harcourt Brace Jovanovich: especially Marlane Miriello, our current English editor, and Thomas Broadbent, our former English editor, for their advice and support; as well as Cheryl Hauser, production editor; Eleanor Garner, permissions editor; Gina Sample, designer; Vicki Kelly, art editor; and Sarah Randall, production manager, for their contributions to the book.

C.H.K.

C.A.

R.B.F.

Contents

Preface   *iii*

Topical Guide to the Essays   *ix*

Introduction: On the Essay   *1*

Woody Allen   *8*

    Spring Bulletin   *12*
    My Speech to the Graduates   *16*
    A Brief, Yet Helpful, Guide to Civil Disobedience   *19*
    The Early Essays   *22*

Francis Bacon   *26*

    Narcissus; or Self-Love   *30*
    Of Youth and Age   *32*
    Of Studies   *35*
    Of Negotiating   *37*

Russell Baker   *40*

    The Cruelest Month   *44*
    A Visit with the Folks   *47*
    Marriage à la Mode   *50*
    Completely Different   *53*

James Baldwin   *56*

    Autobiographical Notes   *61*
    Stranger in the Village   *66*
    A Fly in Buttermilk   *77*
    If Black English Isn't a Language, Then Tell Me What Is?   *85*

Bruno Bettelheim   *90*

    Joey: A "Mechanical Boy"   *95*
    Growing Up Female   *106*
    The Ignored Lesson of Anne Frank   *122*
    Some Comments on Privacy   *133*

Joan Didion   *144*

    John Wayne: A Love Song   *149*
    Georgia O'Keeffe   *157*
    On the Mall   *161*
    On the Road   *166*
    On Keeping a Notebook   *171*

Annie Dillard   *178*

　The Death of a Moth   *183*
　Living Like Weasels   *186*
　The Deer at Providencia   *190*
　Singing with the Fundamentalists   *194*

Loren Eiseley   *204*

　How Flowers Changed the World   *209*
　The Bird and the Machine   *218*
　The Long Loneliness   *226*
　The Hidden Teacher   *232*

E.M. Forster   *244*

　The Game of Life   *248*
　My Wood   *251*
　What I Believe   *254*
　Anonymity: An Enquiry   *262*

Ellen Goodman   *272*

　Anxiety Is the Class Uniform   *276*
　Protection from the Prying Camera   *278*
　Sinking the Relationship   *281*
　In the Male Direction   *283*

Stephen Jay Gould   *286*

　A Biological Homage to Mickey Mouse   *290*
　Women's Brains   *299*
　On Heroes and Fools in Science   *305*
　Darwin's Dilemma: The Odyssey of Evolution   *309*

Ernest Hemingway   *314*

　The Three Acts of a Bullfight   *318*
　A New Kind of War   *321*
　The Clark's Fork Valley, Wyoming   *326*
　Monologue to the Maestro: A High Seas Letter   *329*

Edward Hoagland   *336*

　A Run of Bad Luck   *340*
　Dogs, and the Tug of Life   *343*
　The Problem of the Golden Rule   *352*
　What I Think, What I Am   *362*

Martin Luther King, Jr.   *366*

　An Experiment in Love: Nonviolent Resistance   *370*
　Letter from Birmingham Jail   *375*

I Have a Dream   *390*
Black Power   *394*

Margaret Mead   *422*

A Day in Samoa   *426*
Warfare: An Invention—Not a Biological Necessity   *430*
Adolescents   *436*
New Superstitions for Old   *446*

George Orwell   *452*

A Hanging   *456*
Shooting an Elephant   *461*
Marrakech   *468*
Some Thoughts on the Common Toad   *474*
Politics and the English Language   *478*
Why I Write   *490*

Jonathan Swift   *496*

A Meditation upon a Broomstick   *500*
An Essay upon the Art of Political Lying   *502*
Hints Towards an Essay on Conversation   *507*
A Modest Proposal   *514*

Lewis Thomas   *522*

The Iks   *529*
On Cloning a Human Being   *529*
The Tucson Zoo   *533*
The Corner of the Eye   *536*
The Art of Teaching Science   *540*

Henry David Thoreau   *548*

My House   *553*
Where I Lived, and What I Lived For   *561*
War of the Ants   *571*
Civil Disobedience   *574*

Barbara Tuchman   *592*

"Perdicaris Alive or Raisuli Dead"   *596*
Mankind's Better Moments   *609*
Is History a Guide to the Future?   *624*
History by the Ounce   *633*

Mark Twain   *644*

"S-t-e-a-m-boat a-comin'!"   *648*
Corn-Pone Opinions   *651*
Was the World Made for Man?   *656*
"The Turning Point of My Life"   *661*

Alice Walker   *670*

Beauty: When the Other Dancer Is the Self   *675*
The Civil Rights Movement: What Good Was It?   *682*
The Black Writer and the Southern Experience   *690*
Am I Blue?   *695*

E.B. White   *700*

Once More to the Lake   *704*
The Ring of Time   *710*
The Age of Dust   *718*
A Slight Sound at Evening   *720*
The Essayist and the Essay   *728*

Tom Wolfe   *730*

O Rotten Gotham—Sliding down into the Behavioral Sink   *734*
The Pump House Gang   *745*
Honks and Wonks   *759*
The Right Stuff   *772*

Virginia Woolf   *784*

The Death of the Moth   *788*
On a Faithful Friend   *791*
Thoreau   *795*
Women and Fiction   *802*
The Modern Essay   *809*

Rhetorical Index   *823*

Author-Title Index   *831*

Topical Guide to the Essays

Autobiography and Personal Experience

Russell Baker   The Cruelest Month   *44*
Russell Baker   A Visit with the Folks   *47*
James Baldwin   Autobiographical Notes   *61*
James Baldwin   Stranger in the Village   *66*
Joan Didion   On the Road   *166*
Joan Didion   On Keeping a Notebook   *171*
Annie Dillard   The Death of a Moth   *183*
Annie Dillard   Singing with the Fundamentalists   *194*
Loren Eiseley   The Bird and the Machine   *218*
Edward Hoagland   A Run of Bad Luck   *340*
George Orwell   Shooting an Elephant   *461*
George Orwell   Why I Write   *490*
Henry David Thoreau   My House   *553*
Henry David Thoreau   Where I Lived and What I Lived For   *561*
Mark Twain   "The Turning Point of My Life"   *661*
Alice Walker   Beauty: When the Other Dancer Is the Self   *675*
E. B. White   Once More to the Lake   *704*

Biography and Portraiture

Francis Bacon   Narcissus; or Self-Love   *30*
James Baldwin   A Fly in Buttermilk   *77*
Bruno Bettelheim   Joey: A "Mechanical Boy"   *95*
Joan Didion   John Wayne: A Love Song   *149*
Joan Didion   Georgia O'Keeffe   *157*
Stephen Jay Gould   A Biological Homage to Mickey Mouse   *290*
Ernest Hemingway   Monologue to the Maestro: A
   High Seas Letter   *329*
Alice Walker   Am I Blue?   *695*
E. B. White   The Ring of Time   *710*
Virginia Woolf   On a Faithful Friend   *791*
Virginia Woolf   Thoreau   *795*

Conflict, Violence, and War

Woody Allen   A Brief, Yet Helpful, Guide to Civil
   Disobedience   *19*
James Baldwin   A Fly in Buttermilk   *77*
Bruno Bettelheim   The Ignored Lesson of Anne Frank   *122*
Ernest Hemingway   The Three Acts of a Bullfight   *318*

Ernest Hemingway   A New Kind of War   *321*
Edward Hoagland   The Problem of the Golden Rule   *352*
Martin Luther King, Jr.   An Experiment in Love:
   Nonviolent Resistance   *370*
Martin Luther King, Jr.   Letter from Birmingham Jail   *375*
Martin Luther King, Jr.   Black Power   *394*
Margaret Mead   Warfare: An Invention—Not a
   Biological Necessity   *430*
George Orwell   Some Thoughts on the Common Toad   *474*
Henry David Thoreau   War of the Ants   *571*
Henry David Thoreau   Civil Disobedience *574*
Barbara Tuchman   "Perdicaris Alive or Raisuli Dead"   *596*
E. B. White   The Age of Dust   *718*
Tom Wolfe   O Rotten Gotham—Sliding down into the Behavioral
   Sink   *734*
Tom Wolfe   The Right Stuff   *772*

Contemporary Experience

Woody Allen   My Speech to the Graduates   *16*
Russell Baker   Completely Different   *53*
Russell Baker   Marriage à la Mode   *50*
Bruno Bettelheim   Joey: A "Mechanical Boy"   *95*
Joan Didion   On the Mall   *161*
Joan Didion   On the Road   *166*
Annie Dillard   Singing with the Fundamentalists   *194*
Loren Eiseley   The Bird and the Machine   *218*
Ellen Goodman   Protection from the Prying Camera   *278*
Ellen Goodman   Sinking the Relationship   *281*
Edward Hoagland   The Problem with the Golden Rule   *352*
Martin Luther King, Jr.   Black Power   *394*
Lewis Thomas   On Cloning a Human Being   *529*
Tom Wolfe   O Rotten Gotham—Sliding down into the Behavioral
   Sink   *734*
Tom Wolfe   The Pump House Gang   *745*
Tom Wolfe   Honks and Wonks   *759*

Culture and Society

Woody Allen   My Speech to the Graduates   *16*
James Baldwin   Stranger in the Village   *66*
Annie Dillard   The Deer at Providencia   *190*
Edward Hoagland   The Problem of the Golden Rule *352*
Margaret Mead   A Day in Samoa   *426*
Margaret Mead   Warfare: An Invention—Not a Biological
   Necessity   *430*
Margaret Mead   Adolescents   *436*
George Orwell   Shooting an Elephant   *461*

George Orwell   Marrakech   *468*
Lewis Thomas   The Iks   *526*
Lewis Thomas   The Tucson Zoo   *533*
Henry David Thoreau   War of the Ants   *571*
Barbara Tuchman   Mankind's Better Moments   *609*
Mark Twain   Corn-Pone Opinions   *651*
Alice Walker   The Black Writer and the Southern Experience   *690*
Tom Wolfe   O Rotten Gotham—Sliding down into the
   Behavioral Sink   *734*
Tom Wolfe   The Pump House Gang   *745*
Tom Wolfe   Honks and Wonks   *759*

Education, Learning, and Schooling
Woody Allen   Spring Bulletin   *12*
Francis Bacon   Of Studies   *35*
Russell Baker   The Cruelest Month   *44*
James Baldwin   A Fly in Buttermilk   *77*
Annie Dillard   Singing with the Fundamentalists   *194*
Loren Eiseley   The Hidden Teacher   *232*
Ellen Goodman   Anxiety Is the Class Uniform   *276*
Ernest Hemingway   Monologue to the Maestro: A High
   Seas Letter   *329*
Lewis Thomas   The Art of Teaching Science   *540*
Henry David Thoreau   My House   *553*
Tom Wolfe   Honks and Wonks   *759*

Literature and the Arts
James Baldwin   Autobiographical Notes   *61*
Joan Didion   John Wayne: A Love Song   *149*
Joan Didion   Georgia O'Keeffe   *157*
E. M. Forster   Anonymity: An Enquiry   *262*
Ernest Hemingway   Monologue to the Maestro: A High
   Seas Letter   *329*
Edward Hoagland   What I Think, What I Am   *362*
George Orwell   Why I Write   *490*
Mark Twain   "The Turning Point of My Life"   *661*
Alice Walker   The Black Writer and the Southern Experience   *690*
E. B. White   A Slight Sound at Evening   *720*
E. B. White   The Essayist and the Essay   *728*
Virginia Woolf   Thoreau   *795*
Virginia Woolf   Women and Fiction   *802*
Virginia Woolf   The Modern Essay   *809*

Nature and Natural Experience
Annie Dillard   The Death of a Moth   *183*
Annie Dillard   Living Like Weasels   *186*

Loren Eiseley   How Flowers Changed the World   *209*
Loren Eiseley   The Bird and the Machine   *218*
Loren Eiseley   The Long Loneliness   *226*
Loren Eiseley   The Hidden Teacher   *232*
Ernest Hemingway   The Clark's Fork Valley, Wyoming   *326*
Edward Hoagland   Dogs, and the Tug of Life   *343*
Margaret Mead   A Day in Samoa   *426*
George Orwell   Some Thoughts on the Common Toad   *474*
Lewis Thomas   The Tucson Zoo   *533*
Henry David Thoreau   Where I Live and What I Lived For   *561*
Henry David Thoreau   War of the Ants   *571*
Alice Walker   Am I Blue?   *695*
E. B. White   Once More to the Lake   *704*
E. B. White   A Slight Sound at Evening   *720*
Virginia Woolf   The Death of the Moth   *788*

Politics and Government

Woody Allen   A Brief, Yet Helpful, Guide to
   Civil Disobedience   *19*
E. M. Forster   What I Believe   *254*
Martin Luther King, Jr.   An Experiment in Love: Nonviolent
   Resistance   *370*
Martin Luther King, Jr.   Letter from Birmingham Jail   *375*
Martin Luther King, Jr.   I Have a Dream   *390*
Martin Luther King, Jr.   Black Power   *394*
George Orwell   Shooting an Elephant   *461*
George Orwell   Marrakech   *468*
George Orwell   Politics and the English Language   *478*
George Orwell   Why I Write   *490*
Jonathan Swift   An Essay upon the Art of Political Lying   *502*
Jonathan Swift   A Modest Proposal   *514*
Henry David Thoreau   Civil Disobedience   *574*
Barbara Tuchman   "Perdicaris Alive or Raisuli Dead"   *596*
Alice Walker   The Civil Rights Movement: What Good
   Was It?   *682*

Psychology and Human Behavior

Francis Bacon   Narcissus; or Self-Love   *30*
Francis Bacon   Youth and Age   *32*
Bruno Bettelheim   Joey: A "Mechanical Boy"   *95*
Bruno Bettelheim   Growing Up Female   *106*
Bruno Bettelheim   The Ignored Lesson of Anne Frank   *122*
Joan Didion   On Keeping a Notebook   *171*
Annie Dillard   Living Like Weasels   *186*
Annie Dillard   Singing with the Fundamentalists   *194*

Loren Eiseley   The Bird and the Machine   *218*
Loren Eiseley   The Long Loneliness   *226*
Ellen Goodman   Anxiety Is the Class Uniform   *276*
Ellen Goodman   In the Male Direction   *283*
Stephen Jay Gould   Women's Brains   *299*
Edward Hoagland   The Problem of the Golden Rule   *352*
Margaret Mead   Adolescents   *436*
Margaret Mead   New Superstititions for Old   *446*
George Orwell   A Hanging   *456*
George Orwell   Shooting an Elephant   *461*
Jonathan Swift   A Meditation upon a Broomstick   *500*
Lewis Thomas   The Iks   *526*
Lewis Thomas   On Cloning a Human Being   *529*
Barbara Tuchman   Is History a Guide to the Future?   *624*
Mark Twain   Corn-Pone Opinions   *651*
Mark Twain   "The Turning Point of My Life"   *661*
Alice Walker   Beauty: When the Other Dancer Is the Self   *675*
Tom Wolfe   O Rotten Gotham—Sliding down into the Behavioral
   Sink   *734*

Race and Racism
James Baldwin   Autobiographical Notes   *61*
James Baldwin   Stranger in the Village   *66*
James Baldwin   A Fly in Buttermilk   *77*
James Baldwin   If Black English Isn't a Language, Then Tell Me
   What Is?   *85*
Bruno Bettelheim   The Ignored Lesson of Anne Frank   *122*
Martin Luther King, Jr.   An Experiment in Love: Nonviolent
   Resistance   *370*
Martin Luther King, Jr.   Letter from Birmingham Jail   *375*
Martin Luther King, Jr.   I Have a Dream   *390*
Martin Luther King, Jr.   Black Power   *394*
George Orwell   A Hanging   *456*
George Orwell   Shooting an Elephant   *461*
George Orwell   Marrakech   *468*
Henry David Thoreau   Civil Disobedience   *574*
Alice Walker   The Civil Rights Movement: What Good
   Was It?   *682*
Alice Walker   The Black Writer and the Southern Experience   *690*
E. B. White   The Ring of Time   *710*

Science and Technology
Russell Baker   The Cruelest Month   *44*
Loren Eiseley   How Flowers Changed the World   *209*
Loren Eiseley   The Bird and the Machine   *218*

Stephen Jay Gould Women's Brains *299*
Stephen Jay Gould On Heroes and Fools in Science *305*
Stephen Jay Gould Darwin's Dilemma: The Odyssey of
  Evolution *309*
Lewis Thomas On Cloning a Human Being *529*
Lewis Thomas The Art of Teaching Science *540*
Henry David Thoreau My House *553*
Barbara Tuchman Is History a Guide to the Future? *624*
Mark Twain Was the World Made for Man? *656*
E. B. White The Age of Dust *718*
Tom Wolfe O Rotten Gotham—Sliding down into the Behavioral
  Sink *734*

Values and Beliefs

Woody Allen My Speech to the Graduates *16*
James Baldwin Stranger in the Village *66*
Bruno Bettelheim The Ignored Lesson of Anne Frank *122*
Annie Dillard Living Like Weasels *186*
Annie Dillard Singing with the Fundamentalists *194*
Loren Eiseley The Bird and the Machine *218*
E. M. Forster The Game of Life *248*
E. M. Forster What I Believe *254*
Edward Hoagland The Problem of the Golden Rule *352*
Martin Luther King, Jr. An Experiment in Love: Nonviolent
  Resistance *370*
Martin Luther King, Jr. I Have a Dream *390*
Martin Luther King, Jr. Black Power *394*
Margaret Mead New Superstitions for Old *446*
Jonathan Swift A Meditation upon a Broomstick *500*
Henry David Thoreau Where I Lived and What I Lived For *561*
Henry David Thoreau Civil Disobedience *574*
Mark Twain Corn-Pone Opinions *651*
Mark Twain Was The World Made for Man? *656*
Mark Twain "The Turning Point of My Life" *661*

Women and Women's Experiences

Bruno Bettelheim Growing Up Female *106*
Joan Didion John Wayne: A Love Song *149*
Joan Didion Georgia O'Keeffe *157*
Joan Didion On Keeping a Notebook *171*
Annie Dillard The Deer at Providencia *190*
Ellen Goodman Anxiety Is the Class Uniform *276*
Ellen Goodman In the Male Direction *283*
Stephen Jay Gould Women's Brains *299*
Margaret Mead Adolescents *436*

Alice Walker   Beauty: When the Other Dancer Is the Self   *675*
Virginia Woolf   Women and Fiction   *802*

Writing, Language, and the Essay

Woody Allen   The Early Essays   *22*
James Baldwin   Autobiographical Notes   *61*
James Baldwin   If Black English Isn't a Language, Then Tell Me
   What Is?   *85*
Joan Didion   On Keeping a Notebook   *171*
E. M. Forster   Anonymity: An Enquiry   *262*
Ellen Goodman   Sinking the Relationship   *281*
Stephen Jay Gould   Darwin's Dilemma: The Odyssey of
   Evolution   *309*
Ernest Hemingway   Monologue to the Maestro: A High Seas
   Letter   *329*
Edward Hoagland   What I Think, What I Am   *362*
George Orwell   Politics and the English Language   *478*
George Orwell   Why I Write   *490*
Barbara Tuchman   History by the Ounce   *633*
Alice Walker   The Black Writer and the Southern Experience   *690*
E. B. White   The Essayist and the Essay   *728*
Tom Wolfe   Honks and Wonks   *759*
Virginia Woolf   Women and Fiction   *802*
Virginia Woolf   The Modern Essay   *809*

Introduction: On the Essay

*The principle which controls it is simply that it give pleasure; the
desire which impels us when we take it from the shelf is simply to
receive pleasure. Everything in an essay must be subdued to that
end.*

In this uncompromising
statement from "The Modern Essay," Virginia Woolf reminds us that
before essays became the solemn business of English courses, people
read them "simply to receive pleasure." People have also written them
for pleasure, as E. B. White makes clear by describing the essayist as
someone "who thoroughly enjoys his work." In citing these passages
from essays and essayists in this collection, we don't mean to suggest
that the essay is a trivial kind of writing—far from it. Indeed, if you
look at Woolf's "The Death of a Moth" or White's "The Age of Dust,"
you'll see that in these very short pieces, as in their longer essays, they
engage quite serious aspects of experience. Yet they do so in a way that
people have often found pleasurable to read and that they evidently
found pleasurable to write. So, it seems useful to begin by considering
what essayists mean by the pleasure of the essay and how it can go
hand in hand with a serious approach to experience and ideas.

By looking into the way that essayists describe the pleasure of the
essay, you can also discover something about the nature of the essay.
For example, in writing about what "delights him" as an essayist, White
alludes to the origin of the word "essay," which comes from the French
verb *essayer,* meaning literally to attempt or to try.

> Each new excursion of the essayist, each new "attempt," differs from the
> last and takes him into new country.

In keeping with the root meanings of the word, many essayists have
looked upon the essay as a means of trying things out or attempting
something new in writing. So, too, it has often come to be regarded as
a type of writing that is particularly amenable to exploration, to "excursion," to a kind of mental journeying that takes the writer—and the
reader—"into new country." If you look, for example, at Joan Didion's
"On the Road," you'll see that while it seems to focus primarily on her
experiences and impressions during a cross-country series of radio and
television interviews, it also takes account of her mental journey during
that trip as she tried to answer a single question—"Where are we heading?"—a question that echoes hauntingly from the first to the last line
of the essay.

In some sense, of course, every kind of writing—essay, sonnet, or
scientific report—is an adventure, if only because a writer never knows

exactly what a piece is going to say or exactly how it's going to work out until it is completely written. So, you're far from being alone whenever you wonder exactly how you're going to finish a piece of writing. The uncertainty and the discovery that come from writing are probably best captured in the well-known question that has been attributed to many writers: "How do I know what I think until I see what I've said?" But some kinds of writing involve more foreknowledge or prestructuring than others. The author of a scientific article knows exactly what data it will include before the writing begins, just as the author of a sonnet knows the fourteen line structure that it will follow before the writing begins. Essayists usually prefer to take a less predetermined, more venturesome, approach to writing.

The adventurous impulse of most essayists has led the essay, in turn, to become an unusually varied kind of writing, as you can see just by looking at the work of the first two writers in this collection—at the deadpan comic wit of Woody Allen and the epigrammatic wisdom of Francis Bacon. Throughout this collection, in fact, you will find equally striking contrasts as you move from one author to the next, or one piece to the next. In her first piece, for example, Margaret Mead offers a vivid and evocatively detailed description of a typical day in a primitive Samoan fishing village; in her second, by contrast, she offers a closely reasoned argument against the inevitability of war. In short, the essay is an open form. It gives a writer the freedom to travel in any direction, even on occasion to reverse direction in midcourse, or to make some very surprising turns, as Eiseley does in "The Bird and the Machine." So, too, it gives a reader the pleasure of being taken on an engaging, and often surprising, mental journey.

Given such freedom, it's hardly surprising that essayists celebrate "the extraordinary flexibility" of the essay, as Edward Hoagland does in "What I Think, What I Am." Flexibility, according to Hoagland, is what has enabled the essay "to ride out rough weather and hybridize into forms that suit the times." So you will find that the essays in this collection embody a wide range of forms: stories, parodies, meditations, impersonations, parables, portraits, and interviews. They rely, too, upon numerous ways of explaining and defending ideas, from straightforward description and illustration to elaborate modes of argument and logic. And they are written in every possible style, from casual to formal, from earthy to airy, from plain and simple to ornate and highly oratorical. The essay is an open invitation to you to "hybridize into forms that suit the times."

A successful hybrid is the product of careful cross-breeding. So, essayists have always faced a special challenge—not just to run rampant, like an unchecked weed, but to flourish and flower and bear fruit in ways that are disciplined, yet not mechanically predictable. Lacking preset or prescribed structures, such as the who, what, when, where, and why of a news report, essayists feel compelled to develop their own structures, their own means of achieving coherence. As White puts it, "the essay, although a relaxed form, imposes its own disciplines, raises its own problems, and these disciplines and problems soon become apparent . . . to anyone wielding a pen merely because he entertains random thoughts or is in a happy or wandering mood." In a similar vein, Hoagland observes that "though more wayward or informal than an article or treatise, somewhere it contains a point which is its real center, even if the point couldn't be uttered in fewer words than the essayist has used."

Pointedness, as Hoagland implies, is perhaps the essayist's most important source of discipline, the quality that gives an essay "its real center," its authentic sense of coherence, even when it may lack most conventional forms of surface continuity. For example, George Orwell's "Marrakech" may at first glance appear to consist of five completely separate and unrelated segments, each of which offers a snapshot-like description of a different scene in and around Marrakech. But if you look at the essay closely, you'll see that those snapshots provide a progressively more disturbing picture of the colonial world at work at Marrakech. Similarly, Russell Baker's "Completely Different" at first glance seems to be a disconnected sequence of sentences, but a close examination of those sentences reveals that they are connected to each other by their critique of contemporary American society. Without such a clear sense of purpose, of pointedness, even the most carefully organized piece of prose would be a hollow bit of writing. So, while affirming the importance of pleasure, Woolf also takes pains to note that the art of the essay "has for backbone some fierce attachment to an idea."

If pointedness were the hallmark of the essay, however, it would be difficult to distinguish from a newspaper editorial or a scholarly article, both of which are also attached to issues and ideas. So, you might wonder exactly what it is that sets the essay apart from these other forms of writing. Hoagland suggests some of its most important distinguishing qualities in this contrast of the essay and the article:

> Essays don't usually boil down to a summary, as articles do, and the style of the writer has a "nap" to it, a combination of personality and originality and energetic loose ends that stand up like the nap of a piece of wool and can't be brushed flat. Essays belong to the animal kingdom, with a surface that generates sparks, like a coat of fur, compared with the flat, conventional cotton of the magazine article writer, who works in the vegetable kingdom, instead.

By putting his contrast in terms of an extended and richly suggestive metaphor, rather than in terms of a straightforwardly literal statement, Hoagland clearly echoes the qualities of the essay that he defines in this passage. As an essayist, Hoagland seeks to display the very "original-ity" and energy that distinguish the essay, as he sees it, from the "con-ventional" and methodical ways of the article.

What Hoagland calls originality, others might refer to as artfulness, and still others might define as a concern for the craft of writing, or the "magic of writing," as Woolf puts it in "The Modern Essay." What-ever terms they use to talk about this aspect of the essay, essayists clearly see it as a means of conveying their ideas in striking, evocative, and engaging ways. In some pieces, such as Hoagland's, this special quality may show itself in a vivid and suggestive metaphor; in others, such as Didion's "On the Road," it may come from variations upon a haunting and evocative question or statement; in others, such as Mead's "A Day in Samoa," it may result from a richly detailed description; in others, such as Eiseley's "The Bird and the Machine," it may come from a well-turned story of personal experience; and in others it may come just from "the impact of one sound on another" or "the firmness of good prose," as Orwell says in "Why I Write." Wherever it comes from, this special quality must be responsible for at least part of the pleasure that Woolf attributes to the essay and part of the power that she claims it has to "lay us under a spell," "to fix us in a trance which is not sleep but rather an intensification of life."

Still, the magic of good writing alone, while it might be capable of laying us under a spell, is surely not sufficient in and of itself to produce what Woolf refers to as "an intensification of life." Something else about the essay must be responsible for that, much as something else about it must be responsible for Hoagland's assertion that "essays belong to the animal kingdom" rather than "the vegetable kingdom" of the article. The only thing that could, in fact, account for both of their claims is what both of them refer to as "personality" in the essay—the sense of a human presence that you can hear and feel and see at work whenever you are reading an essay and giving it your sole attention. Listen, for example, to this sentence from Alice Walker's essay on the civil rights movement, in which she tries to convey how it affected her, and you will get a sense of what we mean by talking about a human presence in the essay:

> I have fought and kicked and fasted and prayed and cursed and cried myself to the point of existing.

That single sentence conveys both the intensity of her past experi-ence and the continuing intensity of her feelings about it. Walker pro-duced the intensity in part by piling up all those plain and simple but forceful verbs, each of which denotes a quite different yet equally in-tense kind of activity. You can feel the intensity, too, in the way she

moves from one verb, one action, to the next by means of the conjunc-
tion "and," which gives each of those verbs much more emphasis than
if she had strung them out in the more usual way with commas:

> I have fought, kicked, fasted, prayed, cursed, and cried myself to the
> point of existing.

You can also sense how extraordinary she considers the outcome of all
those actions by the surprising way in which she ends the sentence, not
by crying herself to sleep but by crying herself "to the point of existing." That, surely, is what Woolf means by "an intensification of life"
in the essay, or what Hoagland means when he speaks of essays as
having "a surface that generates sparks, like a coat of fur. . . ."

The essay, as you can see, allows for the presence of personality in
a way that technical articles do not. Indeed, personality is so important
an aspect of the essay that Woolf considers it "the essayist's most proper
. . . tool." Yet she also considers it a "most dangerous and delicate
tool." It is dangerous, because it can be overdone to the point of being
self-conscious, and delicate because it entails perhaps the most difficult
of all balancing acts in writing: "Never to be yourself and yet always
[to be yourself]." How is it possible, you might wonder, both to be
yourself and not be yourself? If you think about the matter, you'll realize soon enough that whatever you write can never fully convey yourself
in all its flesh-and-blood complexity. Because an essay consists of words,
it embodies an essentially fictional version of yourself. Besides, some
aspects of yourself you'd probably just as soon not display in writing.
The best you can hope for, then, in any piece of writing is to be true
to some aspect of yourself that bears on whatever you are writing about
at that moment.

Just to see how an essayist's mood or outlook can change from one
essay to the next (or one passage to the next), look at this sentence from
"Beauty: When the Other Dancer Is the Self," an essay in which Walker
writes about the experience of having lost the sight in one of her eyes
and at this moment is trying to convey the worry and embarrassment
she has felt about the possibility of people detecting her damaged eye:

> At night in bed with my lover I think up reasons why I should not appear
> on the cover of a magazine.

This sentence is just as frank as the other, indeed is much more personal
and intimate in the details that it reveals. Yet it is by no means as intense as the other, if only because it does not engage in any kind of
stylistic heightening. It seems by contrast to be a coolly matter-of-fact
statement, in which Walker almost seems to be poking fun at herself
for worrying about how her eye might look on the cover of a magazine

when she is not at all worried about how it looks when she is in bed with her lover. And now to hear yet another side of Walker, a more formal, intellectual, and culturally critical aspect of her self, listen to this stylistically complex sentence from "The Black Writer and the Southern Experience":

> Outcasts to be used and humiliated by the larger society, the Southern black sharecropper and poor farmer clung to his own kind and to a religion that had been given to pacify him as a slave but which he soon transformed into an antidote against bitterness.

The play of personality that you have witnessed in these few sentences by Walker typefies what you will find within the writing of virtually every essayist in this collection. As E. B. White says, "The essayist . . . can pull on any sort of shirt, be any sort of person, according to his mood or his subject matter—philosopher, scold, jester, raconteur, confidant, pundit, devil's advocate, enthusiast." In that long list of possible roles, White suggests what may ultimately account for the special pleasure and power of the essay. To the writer, it offers an inexhaustible set of possibilities for giving voice to experience, thought, and belief in an artful and authentically human way. To the reader, it offers equally rich possibilities for witnessing other minds, other personalities, in action. By enabling such a humane give and take of ideas, the essay satisfies one of the most enduring and significantly human desires. So it is that people continue to get pleasure from the essay.

Woody Allen
1935—

Not only is there no God, but try getting a plumber on the weekends.

The universe is merely a fleeting idea in God's mind—a pretty uncomfortable thought, particularly if you've just made a down payment on a house.

In these one-liners from an essay entitled "My Philosophy," Woody Allen demonstrates why he has been called the "cerebral comedian," "Camus with a sense of humor." In his essays as in his movies, he reflects on philosophical questions, speculating about the existence of God and the identity of modern man. But in the next breath he undercuts his own abstractions, reducing the philosophical to the physical, the serious to the ridiculous, or rather, he holds the serious and the ridiculous in tension, so that even while we're laughing at the joke we're thinking about its larger context.

The son of a jewelry engraver, Allen was born in Brooklyn, New York, named Allen Stewart Konigsberg, and raised as "a religious Jew." He legally changed his name to Heywood Allen as a young man. (According to his father he got the nickname of "Woody" because he always brought the stick to the stickball game.) Not particularly bookish or intellectual at first, he graduated from high school with a C− average, then went to New York University, where he was expelled for bad grades, and then to the City College of New York, where he dropped out after a few classes. "I loathed every day and regret every day I spent in school," he said in an interview. "I never had a good teacher who made the least impression on me." Yet at some point in his youth Allen became "a voracious reader," delving into philosophy and literature on his own. "You have to read to stay alive," he said in another interview. Early on, he also showed such talent as a writer that his teachers frequently read his essays aloud as examples of grace and organization.

While still in high school, Allen began exploiting his way with words, selling gags and one-liners to New York columnists and celebrities. At 17 he went to work as a regular staff writer for the National Broadcasting Company, creating jokes and comic routines for such popular comedians of the time as Sid Caesar, Art Carney, Buddy Hackett, and

Gary Moore. When he was just 22, he won the Sylvania Award for the best comedy script of 1957. Dissatisfied with the way other people were reading his lines, he then went on the road himself as a stand-up comic, and after several years of learning and struggle was also writing and starring in his own plays and movies.

During the last twenty years he has made more than a dozen widely praised, as well as widely criticized, films, and has become one of the most successful and influential filmmakers in America. His early movies, like *Take the Money and Run* or *Play It Again Sam* (1972), are antic, slapstick stories about a hapless "schlemiel" or dolt victimized by the physical world and inept with women. In *Love and Death* (1975), Allen began exploiting more serious themes for his comedy, parodying Russian literature and the films of Ingmar Bergman. In 1977 he wrote, directed, and starred in *Annie Hall,* a partly autobiographical film examining the relationship between a neurotic intellectual and a beautiful young woman who finally grows beyond him. It won Academy Awards for best picture, best director, and best screenplay. Since *Annie Hall* Allen has often experimented with darker themes and more innovative cinematic techniques in movies like *Interiors* (1978), *Manhattan* (1979), *Stardust Memories* (1980), *Radio Days* (1987), and *September* (1988). He has also continued to display his comic vision of experience in such films as *A Midsummer Night's Sex Comedy* (1982), *Zelig* (1983), and *Hannah and Her Sisters* (1986).

Varied though his films have been, the heroes of Allen's movies are often pessimistic and guilt-ridden, often uneasy about their Jewishness, always obsessed with sex and death, rarely able to find fulfillment, compulsively sharing with us and with their filmic companions the intimate details of their personal lives. Underneath the humor is anxiety; underneath the farce, confessional. Some cultural observers, such as Joan Didion, have attacked Allen for being excessively self-absorbed, convinced that "adolescence can extend to middle age." Others have defended him as a satirist who turns the clichés and preoccupations of contemporary life back onto themselves, subtly making fun of his own characters and the narcissism of our culture.

These tensions also characterize Allen's essays and short stories, which he has been publishing from the beginning of his career in the *New Yorker, Playboy,* and other magazines. They are collected in three books: *Getting Even* (1971), *Without Feathers* (1975), and *Side Effects* (1980). Some of these short pieces, like the early movies and the stand-up routines, are loose narratives laced with one-liners, a stitching together of gags and what Allen calls "verbal cartoons," in which he describes his reactions to absurd physical situations or juxtaposes concrete images in surrealistic ways. Yet many of the short stories have a tight narrative structure. For example, "The Kuglemass Episodes" won the O. Henry

Award for the best short story of 1976–77. And his essays often balance humor and reflection with the sophistication of his finest movies.

In his essays as in his movies, Allen tries to amuse us while also exploring the frustrations and anxieties of contemporary life, to depict both our human incapacity and our intellectual drive:

> Once again I tried committing suicide—this time by wetting my nose and inserting it into the light socket. Unfortunately, there was a short in the wiring, and I merely caromed off the icebox. Still obsessed by thoughts of death, I brood constantly. I keep wondering if there is an afterlife, and if there is will they be able to break a twenty?

Here, as in many of his prose pieces, he combines comic improbability with philosophic anxiety, the humor of the wet nose in the light socket with the "brooding" and the "wondering," and the thoughts of death. Allen's strategy is to put these levels of meaning together, not so much in one-liners as in what we might think of as two-liners: first the serious ("I keep wondering if there is an afterlife"), then the absurd undercutting ("and if there is will they be able to break a twenty?"). So he portrays himself as a bumbler and incompetent yet at the same time parodies intellectual pretention. He makes us laugh but in the same instant helps us to see ourselves more clearly.

However casual or spontaneous he might sometimes seem, Allen has "absolutely Prussian self-discipline when it comes to writing." He is "driven"—as a writer of screenplays, fiction, and essays—to get the words right, to sharpen his commentary on American culture. "If I don't write every minute," he says, "I have this terrible guilt. It's like— I don't know—if I don't write, I'll be sorry someday."

Spring Bulletin

The number of college bulletins and adult-education come-ons that keep turning up in my mailbox convinces me that I must be on a special mailing list for dropouts. Not that I'm complaining; there is something about a list of extension courses that piques my interest with a fascination hitherto reserved for a catalogue of Hong Kong honeymoon accessories, sent to me once by mistake. Each time I read through the latest bulletin of extension courses, I make immediate plans to drop everything and return to school. (I was ejected from college many years ago, the victim of unproved accusations not unlike those once attached to Yellow Kid Weil.) So far, however, I am still an uneducated, unextended adult, and I have fallen into the habit of browsing through an imaginary, handsomely printed course bulletin that is more or less typical of them all:

Summer Session

Economic Theory: A systematic application and critical evaluation of the basic analytic concepts of economic theory, with an emphasis on money and why it's good. Fixed coefficient production functions, cost and supply curves, and nonconvexity comprise the first semester, with the second semester concentrating on spending, making change, and keeping a neat wallet. The Federal Reserve System is analyzed, and advanced students are coached in the proper method of filling out a deposit slip. Other topics include: Inflation and Depression—how to dress for each. Loans, interest, welching.

History of European Civilization: Ever since the discovery of a fossilized eohippus in the men's washroom at Siddon's Cafeteria in East Rutherford, New Jersey, it has been suspected that at one time Europe and America were connected by a strip of land that later sank or became East Rutherford, New Jersey, or both. This throws a new perspective on the formation of European society and enables historians to conjecture about why it sprang up in an area that would have made a much better Asia. Also studied in the course is the decision to hold the Renaissance in Italy.

Introduction to Psychology: The theory of human behavior. Why some men are called "lovely individuals" and why there are others you just want to pinch. Is there a split between mind and body, and, if so, which is better to have? Aggression and rebellion are discussed. (Students particularly interested in these aspects of psychology are advised to take one of these Winter Term courses: Introduction to Hostility; Intermediate Hostility; Advanced Hatred; Theoretical Foundations of Loathing.) Special consideration is given to a study of consciousness as opposed to unconsciousness, with many helpful hints on how to remain conscious.

Psychopathology: Aimed at understanding obsessions and phobias, including the fear of being suddenly captured and stuffed with crab-meat, reluctance to return a volleyball serve, and the inability to say the word "mackinaw" in the presence of women. The compulsion to seek out the company of beavers is analyzed.

Philosophy I: Everyone from Plato to Camus is read, and the follow- 5 ing topics are covered:

Ethics: The categorical imperative, and six ways to make it work for you.

Aesthetics: Is art the mirror of life, or what?

Metaphysics: What happens to the soul after death? How does it manage?

Epistemology: Is knowledge knowable? If not, how do we know this?

The Absurd: Why existence is often considered silly, particularly for 10 men who wear brown-and-white shoes. Manyness and oneness are studied as they relate to otherness. (Students achieving oneness will move ahead to twoness.)

Philosophy XXIX-B: Introduction to God. Confrontation with the Creator of the universe through informal lectures and field trips.

The New Mathematics: Standard mathematics has recently been rendered obsolete by the discovery that for years we have been writing the numeral five backward. This has led to a reëvaluation of counting as a method of getting from one to ten. Students are taught advanced concepts of Boolean Algebra, and formerly unsolvable equations are dealt with by threats of reprisals.

Fundamental Astronomy: A detailed study of the universe and its care and cleaning. The sun, which is made of gas, can explode at any moment, sending our entire planetary system hurtling to destruction; students are advised what the average citizen can do in such a case. They are also taught to identify various constellations, such as the Big Dipper, Cygnus the Swan, Sagittarius the Archer, and the twelve stars that form Lumides the Pants Salesman.

Modern Biology: How the body functions, and where it can usually be found. Blood is analyzed, and it is learned why it is the best possible thing to have coursing through one's veins. A frog is dissected by students and its digestive tract is compared with man's, with the frog giving a good account of itself except on curries.

Rapid Reading: This course will increase reading speed a little each day until the end of the term, by which time the student will be required to read *The Brothers Karamazov* in fifteen minutes. The method is to scan the page and eliminate everything except pronouns from one's field of vision. Soon the pronouns are eliminated. Gradually the student is encouraged to nap. A frog is dissected. Spring comes. People marry and die. Pinkerton does not return.

Musicology III: The Recorder. The student is taught how to play "Yankee Doodle" on this end-blown wooden flute, and progresses rapidly to the Brandenburg Concertos. Then slowly back to "Yankee Doodle."

Music Appreciation: In order to "hear" a great piece of music correctly, one must: (1) know the birthplace of the composer, (2) be able to tell a rondo from a scherzo, and back it up with action. Attitude is important. Smiling is bad form unless the composer has intended the music to be funny, as in *Till Eulenspiegel,* which abounds in musical jokes (although the trombone has the best lines.) The ear, too, must be trained, for it is our most easily deceived organ and can be made to think it is a nose by bad placement of stereo speakers. Other topics include: The four-bar rest and its potential as a political weapon. The Gregorian Chant: Which monks kept the beat.

Writing for the Stage: All drama is conflict. Character development is also very important. Also what they say. Students learn that long, dull speeches are not so effective, while short, "funny" ones seem to go over well. Simplified audience psychology is explored: Why is a play about a lovable old character named Gramps often not as interesting in the theatre as staring at the back of someone's head and trying to make him turn around? Interesting aspects of stage history are also examined. For example, before the invention of italics, stage directions were often mistaken for dialogue, and great actors frequently found themselves saying, "John rises, crosses left." This naturally led to embarrassment and, on some occasions, dreadful notices. The phenomenon is analyzed in detail, and students are guided in avoiding mistakes. Required text: A. F. Shulte's *Shakespeare: Was He Four Women?*

Introduction to Social Work: A course designed to instruct the social worker who is interested in going out "in the field." Topics covered include: how to organize street gangs into basketball teams, and vice versa; playgrounds as a means of preventing juvenile crime, and how to get potentially homicidal cases to try the sliding pond; discrimination; the broken home; what to do if you are hit with a bicycle chain.

Yeats and Hygiene, A Comparative Study: The poetry of William Butler Yeats is analyzed against a background of proper dental care. (Course open to a limited number of students.)   20

Lines of Inquiry
"Spring Bulletin"

In the opening paragraph of this piece, Allen claims that his "imaginary . . . course bulletin" is "more or less typical of them all." What aspects of its visual layout, its organization, and its prose style seem typical to you? What aspects of its content do you think typical? In what respects are its form and content exaggeratedly typical? In what respects are its form and content atypical? Examine one or two of the course descriptions closely to see how the interplay among typical, exaggeratedly typical, and atypical elements of form and content produce its humorous effects.

The target of a satiric essay may or may not be the same as its nominal subject. For example, to what extent do you think this piece is intended to poke fun at college bulletins? To what extent does it seem instead to be mocking "adult-education come-ons"? To what extent does it seem to be ridiculing college education itself? Does Allen's humor have a potentially serious side to it? Based on this "imaginary" but "typical" bulletin, how does Allen seem to be portraying and evaluating the purposes, contents, and methods of college courses?

How do you think your response to this piece was affected by the fact that you are presently enrolled in college courses? How do you suppose someone who has been out of college for several years might respond to this piece? How do you suppose someone who had never been to college might respond to it? In other words, what kind of experience and knowledge does a reader have to bring to this piece in order to understand it and enjoy it?

My Speech to the Graduates

More than any other time in history, mankind faces a crossroads. One path leads to despair and utter hopelessness. The other, to total extinction. Let us pray we have the wisdom to choose correctly. I speak, by the way, not with any sense of futility, but with a panicky conviction of the absolute meaninglessness of existence which could easily be misinterpreted as pessimism. It is not. It is merely a healthy concern for the predicament of modern man. (Modern man is here defined as any person born after Nietzsche's edict that "God is dead," but before the hit recording "I Wanna Hold Your Hand.") This "predicament" can be stated one of two ways, though certain linguistic philosophers prefer to reduce it to a mathematical equation where it can be easily solved and even carried around in the wallet.

Put in its simplest form, the problem is: How is it possible to find meaning in a finite world given my waist and shirt size? This is a very difficult question when we realize that science has failed us. True, it has conquered many diseases, broken the genetic code, and even placed human beings on the moon, and yet when a man of eighty is left in a room with two eighteen-year-old cocktail waitresses nothing happens. Because the real problems never change. After all, can the human soul be glimpsed through a microscope? Maybe—but you'd definitely need one of those very good ones with two eyepieces. We know that the most advanced computer in the world does not have a brain as sophisticated as that of an ant. True, we could say that of many of our relatives but we only have to put up with them at weddings or special occasions. Science is something we depend on all the time. If I develop a pain in the chest I must take an X-ray. But what if the radiation from the X-ray causes me deeper problems? Before I know it, I'm going in for surgery. Naturally, while they're giving me oxygen an intern decides to light up a cigarette. The next thing you know I'm rocketing over the World Trade Center in bed clothes. Is this science? True, science has taught us how to pasteurize cheese. And true, this can be fun in mixed company—but what of the H-bomb? Have you ever seen what happens when one of those things falls off a desk accidentally? And where is science when one ponders the eternal riddles? How did the cosmos originate? How long has it been around? Did matter begin with an explosion or by the word of God? And if by the latter, could He not have begun it just two weeks earlier to take advantage of some of the warmer weather? Exactly what do we mean when we say, man is mortal? Obviously it's not a compliment.

Religion too has unfortunately let us down. Miguel de Unamuno writes blithely of the "eternal persistence of consciousness," but this is no easy feat. Particularly when reading Thackeray. I often think how comforting life must have been for early man because he believed in a powerful, benevolent Creator who looked after all things. Imagine his disappointment when he saw his wife putting on weight. Contemporary man, of course, has no such peace of mind. He finds himself in the midst of a crisis of faith. He is what we fashionably call "alienated." He has seen the ravages of war, he has known natural catastrophes, he has been to singles bars. My good friend Jacques Monod spoke often of the randomness of the cosmos. He believed everything in existence occurred by pure chance with the possible exception of his breakfast, which he felt certain was made by his housekeeper. Naturally belief in a divine intelligence inspires tranquillity. But this does not free us from our human responsibilities. Am I my brother's keeper? Yes. Interestingly, in my case I share that honor with the Prospect Park Zoo. Feeling godless then, what we have done is made technology God. And yet can technology really be the answer when a brand new Buick, driven by my close associate, Nat Zipsky, winds up in the window of Chicken Delight causing hundreds of customers to scatter? My toaster has never once worked properly in four years. I follow the instructions and push two slices of bread down in the slots and seconds later they rifle upward. Once they broke the nose of a woman I loved very dearly. Are we counting on nuts and bolts and electricity to solve our problems? Yes, the telephone is a good thing—and the refrigerator—and the air conditioner. But not every air conditioner. Not my sister Henny's, for instance. Hers makes a loud noise and still doesn't cool. When the man comes over to fix it, it gets worse. Either that or he tells her she needs a new one. When she complains, he says not to bother him. This man is truly alienated. Not only is he alienated but he can't stop smiling.

The trouble is, our leaders have not adequately prepared us for a mechanized society. Unfortunately our politicians are either incompetent or corrupt. Sometimes both on the same day. The Government is unresponsive to the needs of the little man. Under five-seven, it is impossible to get your Congressman on the phone. I am not denying that democracy is still the finest form of government. In a democracy at least, civil liberties are upheld. No citizen can be wantonly tortured, imprisoned, or made to sit through certain Broadway shows. And yet this is a far cry from what goes on in the Soviet Union. Under their form of totalitarianism, a person merely caught whistling is sentenced to thirty years in a labor camp. If, after fifteen years, he still will not stop whistling, they shoot him. Along with this brutal fascism we find its handmaiden, terrorism. At no other time in history has man been so afraid to cut into his veal chop for fear that it will explode. Violence breeds more violence and it is predicted that by 1990 kidnapping will be the dominant mode of social interaction. Overpopulation will exacerbate problems to the breaking point. Figures tell us there are already more people on earth than we need to move even the heaviest piano. If we do not call a halt to breeding, by the year 2000 there will be no room to serve dinner unless one is willing to set the table on the heads of strangers. Then they must not move for an hour while we eat. Of course energy will be in short supply and each car owner will be allowed only enough gasoline to back up a few inches.

Instead of facing these challenges we turn instead to distractions like   5
drugs and sex. We live in far too permissive a society. Never before has pornography been this rampant. And those films are lit so badly! We are a people who lack leaders and coherent programs. We have no spiritual center. We are adrift alone in the cosmos wreaking monstrous violence on one another out of frustration and pain. Fortunately, we have not lost our sense of proportion. Summing up, it is clear the future holds great opportunities. It also holds pitfalls. The trick will be to avoid the pitfalls, seize the opportunities, and get back home by six o'clock.

Lines of Inquiry
"My Speech to the Graduates"

In writing this imaginary speech, Allen relies on a number of playful stylistic maneuvers, which you can see by examining a segment of it in detail. For example, make a list of the clichés and trite expressions that he uses in the first paragraph. Then make a list of the nonsequiturs that appear in the first paragraph. Then make a list of the other disjunctive and surprising passages that appear in the first paragraph. To what extent does this humorous blend of elements seem to prevail in each of the subsequent paragraphs?

The title of this piece suggests a parody of a typical graduation speech. In what respects might it also be understood as a playful engagement with some very disturbing aspects of contemporary culture? In what respects might it even be considered as expressing a genuine sense of the absurd in the contemporary world? In other words, how seriously do you take Allen's discussion of science in the second paragraph, religion in the third paragraph, and government in the fourth?

You've probably sat through a long-winded graduation speech or sermon at some point in your life, so you know how boring it can be for listeners when a speaker runs on too long. But Allen is clearly poking fun at something more than just the length of such talks. What is it about such talks that leaves them open to the kind of mockery that is at work in this piece?

A Brief, Yet Helpful, Guide to Civil Disobedience

In perpetrating a revolution, there are two requirements: someone or something to revolt against and someone to actually show up and do the revolting. Dress is usually casual and both parties may be flexible about time and place but if either faction fails to attend, the whole enterprise is likely to come off badly. In the Chinese Revolution of 1650 neither party showed up and the deposit on the hall was forfeited.

The people or parties revolted against are called the "oppressors" and are easily recognized as they seem to be the ones having all the fun. The "oppressors" generally get to wear suits, own land, and play their radios late at night without being yelled at. Their job is to maintain the "status quo," a condition where everything remains the same although they may be willing to paint every two years.

When the "oppressors" become too strict, we have what is known as a police state, wherein all dissent is forbidden, as is chuckling, showing up in a bow tie, or referring to the mayor as "Fats." Civil liberties are greatly curtailed in a police state, and freedom of speech is unheard of, although one is allowed to mime to a record. Opinions critical of the government are not tolerated, particularly about their dancing. Freedom of the press is also curtailed and the ruling party "manages" the news, permitting the citizens to hear only acceptable political ideas and ball scores that will not cause unrest.

The groups who revolt are called the "oppressed" and can generally be seen milling about and grumbling or claiming to have headaches. (It should be noted that the oppressors never revolt and attempt to become the oppressed as that would entail a change of underwear.)

Some famous examples of revolutions are:

The French Revolution, in which the peasants seized power by force and quickly changed all locks on the palace doors so the nobles could not get back in. Then they had a large party and gorged themselves. When the nobles finally recaptured the palace they were forced to clean up and found many stains and cigarette burns.

The Russian Revolution, which simmered for years and suddenly erupted when the serfs finally realized that the Czar and the Tsar were the same person.

It should be noted that after a revolution is over, the "oppressed" frequently take over and begin acting like the "oppressors." Of course

5

by then it is very hard to get them on the phone and money lent for cigarettes and gum during the fighting may as well be forgotten about.

Methods of Civil Disobedience:

Hunger Strike. Here the oppressed goes without food until his demands are met. Insidious politicians will often leave biscuits within easy reach or perhaps some cheddar cheese, but they must be resisted. If the party in power can get the striker to eat, they usually have little trouble putting down the insurrection. If they can get him to eat and also lift the check, they have won for sure. In Pakistan, a hunger strike was broken when the government produced an exceptionally fine veal cordon bleu which the masses found was too appealing to turn down, but such gourmet dishes are rare.

The problem with the hunger strike is that after several days one   10
can get quite hungry, particularly since sound trucks are paid to go through the street saying, "Um . . . what nice chicken—umm . . . some peas . . . umm . . ."

A modified form of the Hunger Strike for those whose political convictions are not quite so radical is giving up chives. This small gesture, when used properly, can greatly influence a government, and it is well known that Mahatma Gandhi's insistence on eating his salads untossed shamed the British government into many concessions. Other things besides food one can give up are: whist, smiling, and standing on one foot and imitating a crane.

Sit-down Strike. Proceed to a designated spot and then sit down, but sit all the way down. Otherwise you are squatting, a position that makes no political point unless the government is also squatting. (This is rare, although a government will occasionally crouch in cold weather.) The trick is to remain seated until concessions are made, but as in the Hunger Strike, the government will try subtle means of making the striker rise. They may say, "Okay, everybody up, we're closing." Or, "Can you get up for a minute, we'd just like to see how tall you are?"

Demonstration and Marches. The key point about a demonstration is that it must be seen. Hence the term "demonstration." If a person demonstrates privately in his own home, this is not technically a demonstration but merely "acting silly" or "behaving like an ass."

A fine example of a demonstration was the Boston Tea Party, where outraged Americans disguised as Indians dumped British tea into the harbor. Later, Indians disguised as outraged Americans dumped actual British into the harbor. Following that, the British disguised as tea, dumped each other into the harbor. Finally, German mercenaries clad only in costumes from *The Trojan Women* leapt into the harbor for no apparent reason.

When demonstrating, it is good to carry a placard stating one's po-   15
sition. Some suggested positions are: (1) lower taxes, (2) raise taxes, and (3) stop grinning at Persians.

Miscellaneous methods of Civil Disobedience:

Standing in front of City Hall and chanting the word "pudding" until one's demands are met.

Tying up traffic by leading a flock of sheep into the shopping area.

Phoning members of "the establishment" and singing "Bess, You Is My Woman Now" into the phone.

Dressing as a policeman and then skipping.

Pretending to be an artichoke but punching people as they pass.

Lines of Inquiry
"A Brief, Yet Helpful, Guide to Civil Disobedience"

Look closely at the first paragraph and try to figure out the source(s) of humor, if any, in each sentence. How do you react, for example, to the notion of trying to identify a fixed number of "requirements" for "perpetrating a revolution," to the specific requirements that Allen defines, and to the style in which he defines those requirements? Does the second sentence, about "dress . . . time and place," work in a similar or different way? And how about the third sentence? Compare the second paragraph to the first to see if you can discern a similarly comic process at work. Can you discern a pattern of humor at work in these and subsequent paragraphs, or does it arise unpredictably?

Here, as in his other pieces, Allen challenges us to pinpoint the object(s) of his ridicule. In what respects do you think this piece intends to mock the idea of civil disobedience? In what respects does it seem to be mocking revolutionaries themselves? In what respects does it seem to be mocking the methodical format of guidebooks, handbooks, textbooks, and the like? To what extent does it seem to be having fun for the sake of fun itself? To what extent does the humor have a serious side to it, as in the observation that "after a revolution is over, the 'oppressed' frequently take over and begin acting like the 'oppressors' "?

How do you suppose the timing of this piece, which was first published in 1972, affected the initial response of readers? Consider, for example, how it might have been received by readers during the civil rights marches of the mid-sixties, or the campus demonstrations of the late sixties? How are your understanding of this piece and your response to it affected by a reading of Thoreau's "Civil Disobedience" or King's "An Experiment in Love: Nonviolent Resistance"?

The Early Essays

Following are a few of the early essays of Woody Allen. There are no late essays, because he ran out of observations. Perhaps as Allen grows older he will understand more of life and will set it down, and then retire to his bedroom and remain there indefinitely. Like the essays of Bacon, Allen's are brief and full of practical wisdom, although space does not permit the inclusion of his most profound statement, "Looking at the Bright Side."

On Seeing a Tree in Summer

Of all the wonders of nature, a tree in summer is perhaps the most remarkable, with the possible exception of a moose singing "Embraceable You" in spats. Consider the leaves, so green and leafy (if not, something is wrong). Behold how the branches reach up to heaven as if to say, "Though I am only a branch, still I would love to collect Social Security." And the varieties! Is this tree a spruce or poplar? Or a giant redwood? No, I'm afraid it's a stately elm, and once again you've made an ass of yourself. Of course, you'd know all the trees in a minute if you were nature's creature the woodpecker, but then it would be too late and you'd never get your car started.

But why is a tree so much more delightful than, say, a babbling brook? Or anything that babbles, for that matter? Because its glorious presence is mute testimony to an intelligence far greater than any on earth, certainly in the present Administration. As the poet said, "Only God can make a tree"—probably because it's so hard to figure out how to get the bark on.

Once a lumberjack was about to chop down a tree, when he noticed a heart carved on it, with two names inside. Putting away his axe, he sawed down the tree instead. The point of that story escapes me, although six months later the lumberjack was fined for teaching a dwarf Roman numerals.

On Youth and Age

The true test of maturity is not how old a person is but how he reacts to awakening in the midtown area in his shorts. What do years matter, particularly if your apartment is rent-controlled? The thing to remember is that each time of life has its appropriate rewards, whereas when you're dead it's hard to find the light switch. The chief problem about death, incidentally, is the fear that there may be no afterlife—a depressing thought, particularly for those who have bothered to shave. Also, there is the fear that there is an afterlife but no one will know where it's being held. On the plus side, death is one of the few things that can be done as easily lying down.

Consider, then: Is old age really so terrible? Not if you've brushed your teeth faithfully! And why is there no buffer to the onslaught of the years? Or a good hotel in downtown Indianapolis? Oh, well.

In short, the best thing to do is behave in a manner befitting one's   5
age. If you are sixteen or under, try not to go bald. On the other hand, if you are over eighty, it is extremely good form to shuffle down the street clutching a brown paper bag and muttering, "The Kaiser will steal my string." Remember, everything is relative—or should be. If it's not, we must begin again.

On Frugality

As one goes through life, it is extremely important to conserve funds, and one should never spend money on anything foolish, like pear nectar or a solid-gold hat. Money is not everything, but it is better than having one's health. After all, one cannot go into a butcher shop and tell the butcher, "Look at my great suntan, and besides I never catch colds," and expect him to hand over any merchandise. (Unless, of course, the butcher is an idiot.) Money is better than poverty, if only for financial reasons. Not that it can buy happiness. Take the case of the ant and the grasshopper: The grasshopper played all summer, while the ant worked and saved. When winter came, the grasshopper had nothing, but the ant complained of chest pains. Life is hard for insects. And don't think mice are having any fun, either. The point is, we all need a nest egg to fall back on, but not while wearing a good suit.

Finally, let us bear in mind that it is easier to spend two dollars than to save one. And for God's sake don't invest money in any brokerage firm in which one of the partners is named Frenchy.

On Love

Is it better to be the lover or the loved one? Neither, if your cholesterol is over six hundred. By love, of course, I refer to romantic love—the love between man and woman, rather than between mother and child, or a boy and his dog, or two headwaiters.

The marvelous thing is that when one is in love there is an impulse to sing. This must be resisted at all costs, and care must also be taken to see that the ardent male doesn't "talk" the lyrics of songs. To be loved, certainly, is different from being admired, as one can be admired from afar but to really love someone it is essential to be in the same room with the person, crouching behind the drapes.

To be a really good lover, then, one must be strong and yet tender.   10
How strong? I suppose being able to lift fifty pounds should do it. Bear in mind also that to the lover the loved one is always the most beautiful

thing imaginable, even though to a stranger she may be indistinguishable from an order of smelts. Beauty is in the eye of the beholder. Should the beholder have poor eyesight, he can ask the nearest person which girls look good. (Actually, the prettiest ones are almost always the most boring, and that is why some people feel there is no God.)

"The joys of love are but a moment long," sang the troubadour, "but the pain of love endures forever." This was almost a hit song, but the melody was too close to "I'm a Yankee Doodle Dandy."

On Tripping Through a Copse and Picking Violets

This is no fun at all, and I would recommend almost any other activity. Try visiting a sick friend. If this is impossible, see a show or get into a nice warm tub and read. Anything is better than turning up in a copse with one of those vacuous smiles and accumulating flowers in a basket. Next thing you know, you'll be skipping to and fro. What are you going to do with the violets once you get them, anyhow? "Why, put them in a vase," you say. What a stupid answer. Nowadays you call the florist and order by phone. Let *him* trip through the copse, he's getting paid for it. That way, if an electrical storm comes up or a beehive is chanced upon, it will be the florist who is rushed to Mount Sinai.

Do not conclude from this, incidentally, that I am insensitive to the joys of nature, although I have come to the conclusion that for sheer fun it is hard to beat forty-eight hours at Foam Rubber City during the high holidays. But that is another story.

Lines of Inquiry
"The Early Essays"

In his mock-prefatory remarks, Allen comments on these essays in the manner of a literary editor, noting that "like the essays of Bacon, Allen's are brief and full of practical wisdom." If you were writing a prefatory note to these pieces, what other aspects of them would you call to your readers' attention? For example, how would you describe their structure, their style, their tone of voice, and their subject matter?

Allen's mock preface together with the essays that follow it suggest that he is mocking several things simultaneously. To what extent do you think he is poking fun at Bacon's essays? At personal essays? At very brief essays? At essays in general? At scholarly interest in the early writing of well-known authors and public figures? At essay collections, or other textbook anthologies, such as the one you are reading right now?

Like his other pieces in this collection, "The Early Essays" involves a burlesque or parody of a particular kind of writing. In what respects do all of these pieces use similar comic techniques? In what respects does each of them use a different and distinctive comic strategy?

Francis Bacon
1561–1626

*The inquiry of truth which is the love-making or wooing of it,
the knowledge of truth which is the presence of it, and the belief
of truth, which is the enjoying of it, is the sovereign good of
mankind.*

So Bacon wrote in
1625, shortly before his death, and throughout his life he did, in fact,
work on an elaborate plan to reform existing methods for the discovery
of truth in every area of learning. But for most of his life he dedicated
himself to the acquisition of political influence and power—first in the
court of Queen Elizabeth I, then in the court of her successor King
James I. So he lived a divided existence, continually engaged in the
public affairs of a lawyer and statesman, while also pursuing his private
interests as a philosopher and essayist.

The youngest of eight children, he was born in London to a well-
connected family, attended Cambridge University from 1573 to 1575,
turned to the study of law in 1579, and was formally qualified as a
barrister in 1582. By 1584 he had taken a seat in Parliament, by 1585
he was writing letters of political advice to the queen, and by 1591 he
had allied himself with the Earl of Essex, a young favorite of the queen.
Like any aspiring statesman of his time, Bacon knew that only by gaining access to the court could he hope to win political appointments and
to influence the course of his country's affairs. But neither his perenially
good advice, nor his friendship with Essex, nor even his hand in pros-
ecuting Essex for an attempted revolt against the queen in 1601
was sufficient to help Bacon gain advancement during Elizabeth's
reign. Though she respected his mind and trusted his allegiance, she
rarely acted on his advice, and apparently never forgave him for once
having voted against a special military tax that she had requested
from Parliament.

Not until the accession of James in 1603 did Bacon's services and
connections begin to pay off, though somewhat more slowly than he
expected. Still, despite thinking in 1605 that he was "fitter to hold a
book than play a part," he had evidently learned the statesman's part

well enough to acquire positions and titles of increasing influence and status—King's Counsel in 1604, Solicitor-General in 1607, Attorney-General in 1613, Privy Councillor in 1616, Lord Keeper in 1617, Lord Chancellor in 1618, Baron Verulam in 1618, and Viscount St. Albans in 1621. But by 1621, Bacon's close connection with the court had made him a suspect figure in the eyes of Parliament which was then fiercely at odds with the King. Parliament, therefore, was delighted to receive petitions against Bacon charging him with bribery—in particular, with accepting gifts from persons whose cases he was adjudicating. Though Bacon claimed that he had not ever allowed such gifts "to pervert justice," he did "confess that in the points charged against me . . . there is a great deal of corruption and neglect." Accordingly, he was fined, imprisoned briefly, dismissed from the office of Chancellor, and declared ineligible ever to hold public office again. So he retired to his family home and turned full time to the philosophic and literary projects that he had been working at for more than twenty years.

Chief among these projects was Bacon's ambitious plan to create a new philosophy of scientific investigation. At the opening of the seventeenth century, when Bacon was working on this project, science still relied very heavily upon abstract reasoning, ancient authority, *a priori* assumptions, and occult beliefs. Bacon, by contrast, believed that scientifically reliable truths could only be derived from repeated observation, systematic investigation, and coordinated experimentation. Bacon, in short, anticipated modern scientific research by recognizing the need to establish and sustain a careful inductive method. So, he set himself the task of preparing an elaborate treatise that would survey existing sciences, expose all the errors and sources of error in human knowledge, expound a new method of interpreting nature, and provide a comprehensive record of natural phenomena to be interpreted by this method. Though he could not possibly have completed this extraordinary project, he did write a number of works related to it, most notably *The Advancement of Learning,* 1605, *Novum Organum* (literally, the new method), 1620, and *The New Atlantis,* 1624, a piece of utopian fiction in which he envisioned an ideal state based on the principles of his new philosophy.

Of all Bacon's literary works, the most carefully wrought are unquestionably his *Essays,* three different editions of which were published during his lifetime—in 1597, 1612, and 1625—each successive edition reflecting a marked growth in the range of Bacon's interests and experience. So, the collection of essays grew from ten in the first edition, to thirty-eight in the second edition, to fifty-eight in the third edition. The breadth of their subject matter gradually increased to focus not only on such worldly topics as "Of Counsel," "Of Ceremonies and Respects," "Of Expense," "Of Negotiating," and "Of Regiment of Health," but also to engage a rich array of psychological, social, and ethical topics, such as "Of Anger," "Of Boldness," "Of Envy," "Of Friendship," "Of Goodness and Goodness of Nature," and "Of Marriage and Single Life." So whereas the title of the first and second editions refers to the pieces as simply *Essays,* the title of the third edition quite appropriately gives them the much more expansive name of *Essays or Counsels, Civil and Moral.* Not only did Bacon add new essays to each edition, but he also revised the essays that he carried over from one edition to the next, making them successively more cohesive, detailed, and weighty.

As the first essayist in English, the ever-ambitious Bacon unquestionably wanted to leave his mark on the form, and he did so by writing essays that clearly differed from those of his predecessor in France, Michel de Montaigne (1533–92). Whereas Montaigne made himself the centerpiece of his essays, and thus is usually regarded as the creator of the personal essay, Bacon carefully worked to exclude any appearance of himself from his essays, and thus scholars often regard him as originating a formal tradition in the essay. Whereas Montaigne thought of the essay as a tentative form of writing, a means of exploring his thoughts and feelings, in keeping with the meaning of the French verb *essayer* (literally, to try out, or to test), Bacon conceived of his essays as "counsels," "as grains of salt," as aphorisms that would contain "some good quantity of observation," and thus "come home to men's business and bosoms."

Given his background as a lawyer and statesman and his desire to give good counsel, Bacon's essays often convey a markedly cautious, prudential, and even calculating view of experience, especially when he is dealing with subjects that touch upon the world of public affairs and business:

> It is generally better to deal by speech than by letter, and by the mediation of a third than by a man's self. Letters are good when a man would draw an answer by letter back again, or when it may serve for a man's justification afterwards to produce his own letter, or where it may be danger to be interrupted or heard by pieces.

But given his enduring commitment to the advancement of truth, Bacon's essays just as often cut to the heart of a matter in memorably pointed prose:

> If you would work any man, you must either know his nature and fashions, and so lead him; or his ends, and so persuade him; or his weakness and disadvantages, and so awe him; or those that have interest in him, and so govern him.

Narcissus; or Self-Love

Narcissus is said to have been a young man of wonderful beauty, but intolerably proud, fastidious, and disdainful. Pleased with himself and despising all others, he led a solitary life in the woods and hunting grounds; with a few companions to whom he was all in all; followed also wherever he went by a nymph called Echo. Living thus, he came by chance one day to a clear fountain, and (being in the heat of noon) lay down by it; when beholding in the water his own image, he fell into such a study and then into such a rapturous admiration of himself, that he could not be drawn away from gazing at the shadowy picture, but remained rooted to the spot till sense left him; and at last he was changed into the flower that bears his name; a flower which appears in the early spring; and is sacred to the infernal deities,—Pluto, Proserpine, and the Furies.

In this fable are represented the dispositions, and the fortunes too, of those persons who from consciousness either of beauty or some other gift with which nature unaided by any industry of their own has graced them, fall in love as it were with themselves. For with this state of mind there is commonly joined an indisposition to appear much in public or engage in business; because business would expose them to many neglects and scorns, by which their minds would be dejected and troubled. Therefore they commonly live a solitary, private, and shadowed life; with a small circle of chosen companions, all devoted admirers, who assent like an echo to everything they say, and entertain them with mouth-homage; till being by such habits gradually depraved and puffed up, and besotted at last with self-admiration, they fall into such a sloth and listlessness that they grow utterly stupid, and lose all vigour and alacrity. And it was a beautiful thought to choose the flower of spring as an emblem of characters like this: characters which in the opening of their career flourish and are talked of, but disappoint in maturity the promise of their youth. The fact too that this flower is sacred to the infernal deities contains an allusion to the same thing. For men of this disposition turn out utterly useless and good for nothing whatever; and anything that yields no fruit, but like the way of a ship in the sea passes and leaves no trace, was by the ancients held sacred to the shades and infernal gods.

Lines of Inquiry
"Narcissus; or Self-Love"

Bacon structured this essay like Aesop's fables or Christ's parables: it begins with a story that is followed by a moral interpretation of it. How did you react to this basic structure? How might you have reacted to the story of Narcissus had Bacon not provided any commentary on it? How might you have reacted to an essay on the dangers of self-love without the story of Narcissus? What do you consider to be the benefits and the limitations of combining story and commentary in this basic two-part structure?

The full story of Narcissus is much longer than Bacon's version of it—five pages of verse rather than one brief paragraph of prose, as you can see by looking it up in a translation of Ovid's *Metamorphoses*. What details has Bacon omitted? What details has he changed? How has he altered the story to fit the purposes of his moral point? How would you alter Ovid's story to make it suit a moral point of your own about the dangers of narcissism in our own time?

Bacon is not the only essayist in this collection to combine story and commentary in a morally pointed way, as you can see by looking at Baldwin's "Stranger in the Village," Bettelheim's "The Ignored Lesson of Anne Frank," Dillard's "Living Like Weasels," Orwell's "A Hanging," Swift's "A Meditation upon a Broomstick," Walker's "Am I Blue?" or Woolf's "The Death of the Moth." Read one or two of these essays on your own, and then consider how—and why—they differ from Bacon's in their use of story and commentary.

Of Youth and Age

A man that is young in
years may be old in hours, if he have lost no time. But that happeneth
rarely. Generally, youth is like the first cogitations, not so wise as the
second. For there is a youth in thoughts as well as in ages. And yet the
invention of young men is more lively than that of old, and imaginations stream into their minds better, and as it were more divinely. Natures that have much heat, and great and violent desires and perturbations,
are not ripe for action till they have passed the meridian of their years:
as it was with Julius Caesar, and Septimius Severus. Of the latter of
whom it is said, *Juventutem egit erroribus, imo furoribus, plenam:*[1] and yet
he was the ablest emperor, almost, of all the list. But reposed[2] natures
may do well in youth. As it is seen in Augustus Caesar, Cosmus, Duke
of Florence,[3] Gaston de Foix,[4] and others. On the other side, heat and
vivacity in age is an excellent composition[5] for business. Young men
are fitter to invent than to judge, fitter for execution than for counsel,
and fitter for new projects than for settled business. For the experience
of age, in things that fall within the compass of it, directeth them, but
in new things abuseth[6] them. The errors of young men are the ruin of
business; but the errors of aged men amount but to this, that more
might have been done, or sooner. Young men, in the conduct and
manage[7] of actions, embrace more than they can hold; stir more than
they can quiet; fly to the end, without consideration of the means and
degrees; pursue some few principles which they have chanced upon absurdly; care not to innovate,[8] which draws unknown inconveniences;
use extreme remedies at first; and, that which doubleth all errors, will
not acknowledge or retract them; like an unready horse that will neither
stop nor turn. Men of age object too much, consult too long, adventure
too little, repent too soon, and seldom drive business home to the full
period,[9] but content themselves with a mediocrity of success. Certainly

---

[1] He passed a youth full of folly, or rather of madness (from Spartianus,
Life of Severus, II).
[2] Calm, settled.
[3] Cosimo de' Medici, d. 1574.
[4] Duke of Nemours, nephew of Louis XII of France; he died at the battle of
Ravenna in 1512.
[5] Temperament.
[6] Misdirects.
[7] Management.
[8] Are not careful about changing things.
[9] Completion.

it is good to compound employments of both; for that will be good for the present, because the virtues of either age may correct the defects of both; and good for succession, that young men may be learners while men in age are actors; and, lastly, good for extern[10] accidents, because authority followeth old men, and favour and popularity youth. But for the moral part, perhaps youth will have the pre-eminence, as age hath for the politic. A certain rabbin, upon the text, *Your young men shall see visions, and your old men shall dream dreams,*[11] inferreth that young men are admitted nearer to God than old, because vision is a clearer revelation than a dream. And certainly, the more a man drinketh of the world, the more it intoxicateth; and age doth profit rather in the powers of understanding than in the virtues of the will and affections. There be some have an over-early ripeness in their years, which fadeth betimes. These are, first, such as have brittle wits, the edge whereof is soon turned; such as was Hermogenes the rhetorician,[12] whose books are exceeding subtle, who afterwards waxed stupid. A second sort is of those that have some natural dispositions which have better grace in youth than in age, such as is a fluent and luxuriant speech, which becomes youth well, but not age: so Tully[13] saith of Hortensius,[14] *Idem manebat, neque idem docebat.*[15] The third is of such as take too high a strain at the first, and are magnanimous more than tract[16] of years can uphold. As was Scipio Africanus,[17] of whom Livy saith in effect, *Ultima primis cedebant.*[18]

Lines of Inquiry
"Of Youth and Age"

The title of this essay suggests that it is a comparison and contrast. In what respects is it organized like a comparison and contrast of youth and age? In what respects is it organized, instead, like a string of associated thoughts that have to do with youth and age? In what respects is it organized, instead, like a meditation on youth with references as necessary to age? In what respects is it

---

[10] External.

[11] Joel 2.28. The *rabbin*, or rabbi, is Abravanel.

[12] Greek rhetorician of the second century A.D. He is said to have lost his memory at the age of twenty-five.

[13] Cicero.

[14] Roman orator, at one time a rival of Cicero.

[15] He remained the same when the same (style) no longer became him (Cicero, *Brutus,* XCV).

[16] Length.

[17] Roman general, d. 183 B.C. According to Livy, *History,* XXXVIII.53, Scipio was more suited to war than the peaceful times of his later years.

[18] His last actions were not equal to his first (from Ovid, *Heroides,* IX.23).

organized, instead, like a meditation on age with references as necessary to youth? Exactly how would you define the focus and organization of this essay?

In the sixth sentence of his essay, Bacon says, "Natures that have much heat, and great and violent desires and perturbations, are not ripe for action till they have passed the meridian of their years. . . ." But in the tenth sentence, he says, "On the other side, heat and vivacity in age is an excellent composition." Why does Bacon look upon "heat" as a defect in one instance and an asset in the other? Similarly, why does he somewhat later criticize "young men" for their tendency to "fly to the end, without consideration of the means and degrees," yet also fault "men of age" because they "consult too long" and "adventure too little"? How do you account for these apparent contradictions? Exactly where does Bacon stand in his judgments of youth and age? What criteria does Bacon seem to be using in his judgments of each?

When you think about youth and age, what qualities of each are uppermost in your mind? What differences between the two do you consider to be most important? What do you believe to be the benefits and limitations of each condition? How does your thinking on this subject compare with that of Bacon? With that of your parents? With that of popular contemporary attitudes?

Of Studies

Studies serve for delight, for ornament, and for ability.[1] Their chief use for delight, is in privateness and retiring;[2] for ornament, is in discourse; and for ability, is in the judgement and disposition of business. For expert men[3] can execute, and perhaps judge of particulars, one by one; but the general counsels, and the plots and marshalling of affairs come best from those that are learned. To spend too much time in studies is sloth; to use them too much for ornament is affection; to make judgement wholly by their rules is the humour of a scholar. They perfect nature, and are perfected by experience, for natural abilities are like natural plants that need proyning[4] by study; and studies themselves do give forth directions too much at large, except they be bounded in by experience. Crafty[5] men condemn studies, simple men admire them, and wise men use them; for they teach not their own use; but that is a wisdom without them and above them, won by observation. Read not to contradict and confute; nor to believe and take for granted; nor to find talk and discourse; but to weigh and consider. Some books are to be tasted, others to be swallowed, and some few to be chewed and digested: that is, some books are to be read only in parts; others to be read, but not curiously;[6] and some few to be read wholly and with diligence and attention. Some books also may be read by deputy, and extracts made of them by others, but that would be only in the less important arguments, and the meaner sort of books; else distilled books are like common distilled waters, flashy[7] things. Reading maketh a full man; conference a ready man; and writing an exact man. And therefore, if a man write little, he had need have a great memory; if he confer little, he had need have a present wit;[8] and if he read little, he had need have much cunning, to seem to know that he doth not. Histories make men wise, poets witty,[9] the mathematics subtle, natural philosophy deep, moral grave, logic and rhetoric able to contend. *Abeunt studia in mores.*[10]

---

[1] To make men able.

[2] Seclusion.

c[3] Men who have learned only from experience, not study.

[4] Cultivating.

[5] Practical (but also, cunning).

[6] With great care.

[7] Insipid.

[8] Ready mind.

[9] Ingenious.

[10] Studies go to make up a man's character (Ovid, *Heroides,* XV.83).

Nay, there is no stond[11] or impediment in the wit[12] but may be wrought out by fit studies, like as diseases of the body may have appropriate exercises. Bowling is good for the stone and reins;[13] shooting[14] for the lungs and breast; gentle walking for the stomach; riding for the head; and the like. So if a man's wit be wandering, let him study the mathematics; for in demonstrations, if his wit be called away never so little, he must begin again. If his wit be not apt to distinguish or find differences, let him study the Schoolmen,[15] for they are *cymini sectores*.[16] If he be not apt to beat over matters,[17] and to call up one thing to prove and illustrate another, let him study the lawyers' cases. So every defect of the mind may have a special receipt.[18]

Lines of Inquiry
"Of Studies"

Throughout this essay, Bacon tends to break down topics into three parallel parts, as in his opening sentence—"Studies serve for delight, for ornament, and for ability." What benefits and what drawbacks do you find in this form of writing? As a means of evaluating the form, try out a few different ways of revising Bacon's opening sentence: drop one of the three parallel phrases, add a fourth of your own choosing; rearrange the three, rewrite the sentence completely to put Bacon's ideas in your own words. How does each of your revisions affect the coherence, development, meaning, and rhythm of the sentence? How would you have to revise the second sentence to make it fit your revisions of the first?

Judging from the various uses of studies that Bacon discusses, what do you suppose he considers to be the most important purpose of education? Judging from the various methods of learning he discusses, what do you suppose he considers to be the most effective method of education? How do you suppose he would react to the educational ideas that Eiseley discusses in "The Hidden Teacher" or that Thomas proposes in "The Art of Teaching Science"?

In what respects do Bacon's educational ideas strike you as being out of date? In what respects do they appear to be up to date? How does the range of subjects that he surveys in his essay compare to the range of coursework in your own academic experience? In Woody Allen's "Spring Bulletin"? In what respects do you agree, in what respects do you disagree, with Bacon's ideas of education?

---

[11] Obstacle.
[12] Mind.
[13] Playing bowls is good for the bladder and kidneys.
[14] Archery.
[15] Medieval theologians and academics.
[16] Hair-splitters.
[17] Cover the ground thoroughly.
[18] Prescription (for remedy).

Of Negotiating

It is generally better to deal by speech than by letter, and by the mediation of a third than by a man's self. Letters are good when a man would draw an answer by letter back again, or when it may serve for a man's justification afterwards to produce his own letter, or where it may be danger to be interrupted or heard by pieces. To deal in person is good when a man's face breedeth regard, as commonly with inferiors, or in tender[1] cases, where a man's eye upon the countenance of him with whom he speaketh may give him a direction how far to go; and generally, where a man will reserve to himself liberty either to disavow or to expound. In choice of instruments, it is better to choose men of a plainer sort, that are like to do that that is committed to them, and to report back again faithfully the success,[2] than those that are cunning[3] to contrive out of other men's business somewhat to grace themselves, and will help the matter in report for satisfaction sake.[4] Use also such persons as affect[5] the business wherein they are employed, for that quickeneth much; and such as are fit for the matter, as bold men for expostulation, fair-spoken men for persuasion, crafty men for inquiry and observation, forward and absurd[6] men for business that doth not well bear out itself. Use also such as have been lucky and prevailed before in things wherein you have employed them; for that breeds confidence, and they will strive to maintain their prescription.[7] It is better to sound a person with whom one deals afar off, than to fall upon the point at first, except you mean to surprise him by some short question. It is better dealing with men in appetite,[8] than with those that are where they would be. If a man deal with another upon conditions, the start or first performance is all;[9] which a man cannot reasonably demand, except either the nature of the thing be such which must go before; or else a man can persuade the other party that he shall still need him in some other thing; or else that

---

[1] Delicate.

[2] Outcome.

[3] Who know how.

[4] Report the outcome as better than it really is (in order to please their employer).

[5] Like.

[6] Unyielding.

[7] Their claim to be considered lucky.

[8] Keen for advancement.

[9] All-important.

he be counted the honester man. All practice is to discover, or to work.[10] Men discover themselves in trust, in passion, at unawares, and of necessity, when they would have somewhat done and cannot find an apt pretext. If you would work any man, you must either know his nature and fashions,[11] and so lead him; or his ends, and so persuade him; or his weakness and disadvantages, and so awe him; or those that have interest in him, and so govern him. In dealing with cunning persons, we must ever consider their ends, to interpret their speeches; and it is good to say little to them, and that which they least look for. In all negotiations of difficulty, a man may not look to sow and reap at once, but must prepare business, and so ripen it by degrees.

---

[10]The purpose of all smart dealing is to find out things about men, or to manipulate them.

[11]Habits.

Lines of Inquiry
"Of Negotiating"

In this essay, unlike his others in this collection, Bacon uses both the indicative and imperative mode—sometimes making assertions that "it is better" to do this or do that, sometimes making commands. What tone of voice and personality do you associate with each mode? How do you account for the frequency and location of each mode? Bacon also combines different forms of address in this essay—sometimes using the third person indirect address, sometimes using the second person direct address (you), and sometimes using the first person plural (we). Again, what effects do you associate with each form of address, and how do you account for the points at which he uses each form? What connections, if any, do you see between his shifting mode, shifting form of address, and his overall subject and purpose in this piece?

What kinds of negotiations do you suppose that Bacon is referring to in this essay? Why do you suppose he considers it better in these situations "to deal by . . . the mediation of a third than by a man's self"? What criteria does he seem to be using in his choice of persons to do the negotiating? Given his advice about choosing negotiators and carrying on negotiations, what do you infer about Bacon's idea of negotiating? About his view of human nature? About his ethical standards?

Think about a recent negotiating experience of your own. Did you do the negotiating yourself or did you use someone else to do it for you? Was the negotiating carried on by letter, in person, or in some other form? What issues did you take into account in deciding how to carry on your negotiations? How did your method of negotiating compare with Bacon's? How was your method of negotiating influenced, if at all, by your views of human nature? By your ethical standards? By contemporary styles of negotiating? By twentieth-century technologies that influence the process of negotiating?

Russell Baker
1925—

I don't suppose that anybody can make it through a whole lifetime here in the twentieth century twilight zone without an occasional suspicion that he is living in a global booby hatch.

For over twenty years, writing in his thrice weekly "Observer" column for *The New York Times*, Russell Baker has been voicing his suspicions about the "booby hatch" of contemporary American life. His stance in these columns is that of a simple, down-to-earth man trying to hold onto his sanity in the face of technological progress, social change, and the pressures of the big city, someone longing for the family values of the past. The world has become too complex, he said in an interview, and "no individual really controls his own destiny." Baker responds to this situation, not with despair or nostalgia, but with humor. Week after week he parodies contemporary excesses and his own frustrated yearnings, describing with dry, understated wit "the ironies of the public condition."

Baker was born in Morrisville, Virginia, during the Depression, and in early childhood lived the simple, rural life of another time. After his father died he moved from relative to relative with his mother and sister, living in New Jersey and finally Baltimore while his mother struggled both to make a living and to make "a good man" out of his passive, dreamy son. She was a strong-willed woman, as Baker describes her in his autobiography *Growing Up* (1982), determined to give him the "gumption" he needed to make it in the world. As a schoolboy, he dreamed of becoming a writer because he envied "the ease of the writer's life." "What writers did," he thought then, "couldn't even be classified as work." His first real experience of the pleasure, and the hard work, of writing came in high school when he wrote a theme on "The Art of Eating Spaghetti." The idea of writing an essay didn't interest him at all at first—"of all forms of writing, none seemed so boring as the essay"—but suddenly, sitting sprawled on the sofa, he recalled "the warmth and good feeling" of his family eating spaghetti around the kitchen table. "Suddenly I wanted to write about that," he recalls. "I wanted to put it down simply for my own joy," not for the teacher. The result was an A$^+$ and the beginning of Baker's characteristically personal, engaged prose style.

After earning a B.A. in English at Johns Hopkins University in Baltimore, with a brief interruption in the Navy, Baker went to work as a reporter for the *Baltimore Sun*. He had wanted to write a novel, to become the next Hemingway, but his experience as a journalist convinced him that "the world I was living in was so much more interesting than the world I was capable of conceiving." Eventually he became the *Sun*'s London reporter and then in 1954 went to work for the *New York Times* in Washington, D.C., covering congressional politics. Political reporting challenged Baker at first, but he became disillusioned and bored after a few years. Congress was a "pocket of tedium." All he seemed to do was "sit in the lobby and listen to the older reporters breathe." Besides, people and events interested him most, not ideas or policies. "I've always been weak on political theory," he admits.

In 1962 he was given the chance to refurbish the "Observer" column for the *New York Times* and began writing more open-ended, informal pieces, developing his gift for humor. He continued to deal with political subjects at first, but gradually shifted to more personal, domestic topics and more literary forms, particularly after moving from Washington to New York. Over the last two decades, writing three times a week—140 pieces a year, nearly 100,000 words a year—Baker has become one of America's most respected columnists, essayists, and humorists. His columns have been collected in a number of books, including *All Things Considered* (1965), *So This Is Depravity* (1980), and *The Rescue of Miss Yaskell and Other Pipe Dreams* (1983). In 1979 he won the Pulitzer Prize for commentary, and in 1982 won the Pulitzer again for his autobiography, *Growing Up*, regarded by many as a classic of the genre.

In his political columns Baker writes about the pretentions and absurdities of big government, from waste and fraud in the Pentagon to self-delusion in the imperial presidency to the "fat" and deliberate vagueness of bureaucratic rhetoric. One of his favorite strategies is to invent absurd hypothetical situations—the Pentagon delivering a state-of-the-art tank on his doorstep, a disgruntled scientist appearing in his office carrying an atomic bomb. He also likes to take shots at the hypocrisies of Congress. "There's a natural affinity," he says, "between a used car salesman and a congressman. Neither one wants you to know what's under the hood." As he moved away from strictly political themes Baker continued to draw upon the basic forms of satire: as he puts it, "dialogues, fantasies, hoaxes, parodies, burlesques." He imagines the Lone Ranger in a lawyer's office being stripped of his hero's status. He imagines watching contemporary movies with Gary Cooper at his side, fantasizing about Cooper's angry responses to the modern anti-hero.

More recently Baker has gone from satire "back to the essay form," writing more directly about his concerns. In what might be called his "city essays," he describes the rudeness of cab drivers in New York, the impossibility of finding a parking place, the ceaseless noise, portraying himself as an ordinary man victimized by a society that has become too big for any individual to change. "As things become bigger and bigger," he says, "the results become smaller and smaller." He is especially interested in the anxieties of the middle-class consumer, and often writes about the implications of television and television commercials. "I am shaving and it worries me," he says in one essay. "It has become too complicated. . . . Nowadays you don't have a razor anymore. You have a shaving system. I am always nervous in the presence of systems."

In his "country essays," by contrast, Baker describes his early childhood in rural Virginia, growing up in a large family without the burden of material wealth, as well as his visits to Virginia as an adult and his recent purchase of a farm outside the town where he was born. In the simple, natural world of the country—lying in bed at night with the window open, watching "a fattening moon glide imperceptibly toward the mountain behind the raspberry patch"—he has the time and the quiet "to pause and try to make sense of things." In these pieces, too, Baker worries that the pace of modern life has taken us away from basic values. As he said in an interview, "I tend to be very strongly in favor of family, continuity of family relationships, like things the way they are, am very slow to accept change." It was his belief in the importance of family and tradition that led him to write his acclaimed autobiography. He wanted his children "to know that they were a part of a long chain of humanity extending deep into the past and that they had some responsibility for extending it into the future."

Understatement, concreteness, and compactness characterize Baker's prose. Convinced that most readers of the *Times* were bored or intimidated by the paper's polysyllabic, Latinate style, he set out in his columns to "simplify the diction," to evolve a more "casual," conversational style that would "hook people and get them to read." He sees humor as the most effective of these "devices" for communicating a moral, but his humor is not slapstick, nor dependent upon one-liners. It develops more from the subtle ironies of the situations he describes— a blending, in a sense, of Woody Allen's sharpness and sense of the ridiculous with the whimsy and descriptiveness of E. B. White. He causes us to chuckle, not to laugh. "My aim," he says, "is really to sneak up on some pretty dense skulls and just insert a little needle in and let in a little daylight."

The Cruelest Month

The third week of September has always been a grisly time for schoolchildren. It is then that the romance of education, sparked by the back-to-school excitement of fresh books, new teachers, virginal fountain pens and notebooks unstained by ink blots and baffling mathematical formulas, begins to yield to reality.

And what is that reality? It is knowledge. Knowledge that it will be nine long months before summer vacation rolls around again. Knowledge that the geography teacher dislikes you. Knowledge that the gym instructor finds your physique absurd. Knowledge that you are never going to understand at least three of the subjects with which you are saddled and are going to suffer horribly for months as you sink into the quagmire of F's recording the progress of your ignorance.

It was Jean Shepherd, I believe, who said that after three weeks in chemistry he was six months behind the class. This is a common experience, this sensation of being locked forever in the starting gate while the rest of the class is galloping for the back stretch, and it leaves many people scarred for life.

A woman I know, though financially well-heeled, still refuses to set foot in Italy because in seventh-grade Latin she became aware, after three weeks in the classroom, that she would never be able to conjugate the verb *esse* to Cicero's satisfaction. Assurances that Cicero is no longer to be encountered in Rome do not comfort her. She associates the Italian peninsula with personal humiliation.

I myself have always avoided Germany since discovering in 10th grade that German has two dozen ways of saying "the." I could be wrong about this, since I was wrong about everything else in German. Nevertheless, there is the fact. That memory of a third week in September when classmates began hooting about my tendency to use the dative feminine singular form of "the" when the accusative neuter plural was called for—this memory has created a lifelong barrier between Germany and me.

Schools do not concede that it is ridiculous to require every student to learn at the same pace. They operate on the assumption that every brain in the classroom will achieve a firm grasp of the binomial theorem at the same instant and be ready to move on simultaneously to those many cheerful facts about the square of the hypotenuse waiting at the next hitching post.

Readers who met the educators' expectations in mathematics may deduce from the above that my own pace in math was decidedly slow if, as I suspect, you have to master the hypotenuse before proceeding on to the binomial theorem. The truth is that, never understanding either one, I was utterly lost and made a terrible mess of things when I reached the cosine and the secant.

All of this probably resulted because some teacher during the third week of some long-ago September assumed, wrongly, that I understood that 9 times 6 is 54, and rushed on to impress me with the realization that 9 times 8 is 77, or whatever it may be.

Almost all of us have dreadful third weeks of September in our backgrounds somewhere. If psychoanalysts would let up a bit on our libidinal childhood experiences, they might discover a rich new source of adult neurosis here.

The third week of September that mutilated my own life is the reason I am not a brilliant nuclear physicist today. Here let me confess that in youth it was not my intent to become a typewriter pounder hacking out material for Sunday supplements. Hooked on the romance of science, I yearned to take up the torch from Einstein and carry it forward.

Thus I came to physics class. The first week of September was thrilling, as textbooks were issued and the teacher discoursed on Isaac Newton and apples and introduced us to the lab, that frontier of human progress. In the second week, he introduced us to the erg. I was quite happy with the erg, without which blocks of wood could not be made to overcome the villainous friction of inclined ramps and moved upward, triumphantly ascending those ramps.   10

At the end of the week, he introduced the dyne, which seemed excessive. It was not that I couldn't understand the dyne. I could have. What I could not understand was why, since we already had the erg, it was also necessary to have the dyne.

I was still puzzling over this philosophical question the following Monday when the teacher, assuming that everybody now had a firm grip on the dyne, plunged ahead into the centimeter. Perhaps it was only the millimeter. I am hazy here because reality was fading rapidly.

It was disconcerting to have the dyne taken utterly for granted when I still had profound doubts about it and to be asked to cope with the centimeter. The next day was worse. That was the day of the milligram. The following day there was a test.

I was astonished that the rest of the class took it without a roar of protest that it was outrageous to ask us to cope with ergs, dynes, centimeters and milligrams while we were still baffled about the dyne. The rest of the class did not protest. Most passed easily. I failed every question not devoted exclusively to the erg. The rest of that year was a nightmare, and the world still awaits a worthy successor to Einstein.

Lines of Inquiry
"The Cruelest Month"

The organization of this essay seems casual at first, offhand, as if Baker is talking off the top of his head, going from point to point in no particular order. Why do you think Baker tries to create this impression? Study the selection and arrangement of his material from paragraph to paragraph. What would happen if you put these paragraphs in a different order? Do any paragraphs function together as a group? In what respects do you find a design here? In what respects is the piece as casual as it seemed at first?

"The Cruelest Month" is a good example of Baker's unique style of humor. How would you characterize this humor? Is it light or heavy, amusing or slapstick? How is he different from a stand-up comedian? How is he different from Woody Allen? Do you think Baker's purpose is simply to poke fun at himself, to make us laugh—to entertain us—or could there be a serious, darker theme underneath—for example, an attack on American public schools? If so, what aspect(s) of school do you think he is attacking?

Baker says that "almost all of us have a dreadful third week of September in our backgrounds somewhere." Have you ever had a dreadful third week? Have you ever been six months behind after three weeks? Was it in physics and chemistry, or literature and composition? Baker doesn't finally seem too upset about his failures as a student. Are you able to look back on your own failures with the same detachment and equanimity? Why or why not?

A Visit with the Folks

Periodically I go back to a churchyard cemetery on the side of an Appalachian hill in northern Virginia to call on family elders. It slows the juices down something marvelous.

They are all situated right behind an imposing brick church with a tall square brick bell-tower best described as honest but not flossy. Some of the family elders did construction repair work on that church and some of them, the real old timers, may even have helped build it, but I couldn't swear to that because it's been there a long, long time.

The view, especially in early summer, is so pleasing that it's a pity they can't enjoy it. Wild roses blooming on fieldstone fences, fields white with daisies, that soft languorous air turning the mountains pastel blue out toward the West.

The tombstones are not much to look at. Tombstones never are in my book, but they do help in keeping track of the family and, unlike a family, they have the virtue of never chafing at you.

This is not to say they don't talk after a fashion. Every time I pass Uncle Lewis's I can hear it say, "Come around to the barber shop, boy, and I'll cut that hair." Uncle Lewis was a barber. He left up here for a while and went to the city. Baltimore. But he came back after the end. Almost all of them came back finally, those that left, but most stayed right here all along.

Well, not right here in the churchyard, but out there over the fields, two, three, four miles away. Grandmother was born just over that rolling field out there near the woods the year the Civil War ended, lived most of her life about three miles out the other way there near the mountain, and has been right here near this old shade tree for the past 50 years.

We weren't people who went very far. Uncle Harry, her second child, is right beside her. A carpenter. He lived 87 years in these parts without ever complaining about not seeing Paris. To get Uncle Harry to say anything, you have to ask for directions.

"Which way is the schoolhouse?" I ask, though not aloud of course.

"Up the road that way a right good piece," he replies, still the master of indefinite navigation whom I remember from my boyhood.

It's good to call on Uncle Lewis, grandmother and Uncle Harry like this. It improves your perspective to commune with people who are not alarmed about the condition of NATO or whining about the flabbiness of the dollar.

The elders take the long view. Of course, you don't want to indulge too extensively in that long a view, but it's useful to absorb it in

5

short doses. It corrects the blood pressure and puts things in a more sensible light.

After a healthy dose of it, you realize that having your shins kicked in the subway is not the gravest insult to dignity ever suffered by common humanity.   10

Somewhere in the vicinity is my great-grandfather who used to live back there against the mountain and make guns, but I could never find him. He was born out that way in 1817—James Monroe was President then—and I'd like to find him to commune a bit with somebody of blood kin who was around when Andrew Jackson was in his heyday.

After Jackson and Abraham Lincoln and the Civil War, he would probably not be very impressed about much that goes on nowadays, and I would like to get a few resonances off his tombstone, a cool *frisson* of contempt maybe for a great-grandchild who had missed all the really perilous times.

Unfortunately, I am never able to find him, but there is Uncle Irvey, grandmother's oldest boy. An unabashed Hoover Republican. "Eat all those string beans, boy," I hear as I nod at his tombstone.

And here is a surprise: Uncle Edgar. He has been here for years, but I have never bumped into him before. I don't dare disturb him, for he is an important man, the manager of the baseball team, and his two pitchers, my Uncle Harold and my Cousin-in-law Howard, have both been shelled on the mound and Uncle Edgar has to decide whether to ask the shortstop if he knows anything about pitching.

My great-grandfather who made guns is again not to be found, but   15
on the way out I pass the tombstone of another great-grandfather whose distinction was that he left an estate of $3.87. It is the first time I have passed this way since I learned of this, and I smile his way, but something says, "In the long run, boy, we all end up as rich as Rockefeller," and I get into the car and drive out onto the main road, gliding through fields white with daisies, past fences perfumed with roses, and am rather more content with the world.

Lines of Inquiry
"A Visit with the Folks"

Baker uses a good deal of colloquial, folksy language here—"out that way," "blood kin," "nowadays." Yet he also uses words like "resonances" and phrases like "cool *frisson* of contempt." How would you characterize the style of these words and phrases? What kind of personality do they suggest? Often he mixes these two styles, these two ways of talking, in the same paragraph, even the same sentence. How do you react to this mixing? Do you find it inconsistent? What does it suggest about Baker as a person? How does Baker's style compare with that of his relatives? What do you make of the similarities and differences?

"A Visit with the Folks" is in part about a big city man returning to the small country community where he was raised. How does Baker evoke the feel, the sensation, the atmosphere of the country? What does the country represent for him? What do you infer about his attitude toward city life from what he says about this quiet rural place? What do you infer about his attitude toward the country from the fact that all the people he's talking with are dead? What are the implications of this fantasy?

We all have places to escape or return to now and then to get a better perspective on our lives. What places do you return to? What people do you talk to? Do you ever wish you could talk again with a dead family member? Do the dead speak to you in some real ways?

Marriage à la Mode

In our third year of marriage my wife telephoned to ask if I would like to meet her. I did not want to meet her or anyone else. It had been seven years since I had met anybody at all, and though I had recently thought it might do me good to meet somebody—if only to see whether people still looked the way they used to—I did not want to start by meeting my wife.

One of the advantages of electronic living was that you never had to meet your wife. The man who installed my computer and television cables had harped on that. "One of its big advantages," he said, "is that you'll never have to meet your wife."

At the time, of course, I did not intend to marry. I changed my mind only after setting up my tax picture in the computer and discovering that a wife of a certain income profile would cut my tax bill by nearly 2 percent.

It was a simple matter to plug into the central information bank, obtain the names of several thousand single women in the same tax predicament and, for a small fee, have the engagement and marriage arranged by the bank.

The ceremony was performed by a minister of the Ecumenical Computer Church while I was reading the sports news in the electronic newspaper on my video terminal in New York and my bride, who lived in Oregon, was monitoring a Phil Donahue interview with three well-adjusted transsexuals on her cable TV.

At the appropriate moment I punched "I do" and "I will" into my computer, and after she did likewise I switched the computer into "check-account shopping mode" and ordered my bank to authorize an Oregon jeweler to deliver her a wedding ring.

It was exhilarating being married. To celebrate, I put on a video cassette of the Super Bowl game of 1995 and spent half the night watching the Chattanooga Data trounce the Fargo Inputs by a score of 35 to 3.

After that I forgot about being married except at tax time, when it was mighty convenient. Naturally, it was a surprise when she telephoned to propose a meeting.

I should point out that I did not answer the phone myself. I had not answered a telephone for years. I had a machine that not only answered for me, but also made calls for me. My machine, speaking in a voice entirely unlike my own, said, "I am very busy now scanning my display terminal to select a meal to be delivered to my food slot so that I will not have to be interrupted while watching the cricket test match

5

from Pakistan on my cable television during the evening. Please state your message at the sound of the beep and my machine will process your call."

On this evening the machine said, "Your wife has telephoned to ask if you would like to meet her." 10

"Tell her," I told the machine, "I have not met anybody in seven years and do not propose to start now."

While the machine was transmitting the message, a noise at the door indicated that the central restaurant bank was having my dinner delivered at the food slot. Since the restaurant bank had not yet replaced all its delivery people with robots, I waited a safe interval before opening the slot, so as not to risk catching a glimpse of a human being.

This irritated my telephone machine. "You may not want to see a human being," said the machine, "but I'd like to, once in a while."

"Nonsense," I said, "you see me 24 hours a day."

"People ought to see people, ought to talk to people," said the 15 machine.

"If God had meant people to see people, he wouldn't have created electronic living," I said. "If God wanted people to talk to people, he wouldn't have given us the telephone-answering machine."

I went to the slot to collect my dinner. Instead of a steak, I found a small electronic device. "So," I said, "they have finally succeeded in inventing the electronic steak. This ought to teach the beef trust a little humility."

I put my computer in "dining mode." Instantly the TV set activated a 1968 video cassette of "Bowling for Dollars" and presented me with a fork and a steak knife. The small electronic device spoke up. "Do not carve me," it said. "Kiss me. I am your wife and I am dying for love. At the sound of the beep, place your computer in 'osculation mode' and activate my 'input' key by framing your lips in the pursed position."

It was my telephone machine that replied. "Don't waste your time, baby," it said. "That bird has been dead for years." It uttered a highly suggestive "beep." My wife beeped back.

My wife? But I was married to a tax shelter, not to a flirting beeper. 20 Or was I? It had been so long since I had met anybody. I thought of going to the window, raising the blinds, but I didn't. It is better not to know some things.

I sat back to enjoy "Bowling for Dollars." The telephone machine said, "If you'd turn off that tube, machines could have a little privacy around here." I turned it off and sat in the dark. The beeping became intense.

Lines of Inquiry
"Marriage à la Mode"

This piece is obviously ironic and satirical from the very beginning, yet the point of the fantasy isn't immediately clear. When did you figure out the situation? Why do you suppose that Baker develops the story obliquely, indirectly, even somewhat misleadingly at first? After a while, it becomes clear, too, that Baker is simply inventing a possible future world. Is this kind of fictionalizing legitimate in a nonfiction piece?

Baker's concern here is evidently the problematic relationship of humans and machines, particularly computers. But rather than voice his concerns directly, Baker implies them through the imaginary story, told by the imaginary speaker in the piece. What do you suppose is Baker's attitude towards the computer, and how does it differ from the attitude of his imagined speaker? What do you suppose is Baker's attitude towards marriage, and how does it differ from the attitude of his imagined speaker? How do you know that Baker doesn't agree with the speaker on these issues?

Look at Eiseley's "The Bird and the Machine" and compare Baker's thoughts about machines with those of Eiseley. In what respect(s) are they similar? In what respect(s) different? Also consider the different ways in which they voice their concerns. Do you think Baker and Eiseley are just old curmudgeons, blindly resistant to progress? Or do you think they have raised legitimate questions about humanity and high technology?

Completely Different

$\qquad\qquad\qquad\qquad\qquad$ This is all new.

It is completely different.

You have never experienced anything like it.

Now that you are experiencing it you will never be the same again.

You will be all new.   5

You will be completely different.

You will never want to experience the old experiences again.

Everything that is old has been discarded to create a completely different experience.

Long sentences have been.

Discarded.   10

Everything has been completely miniaturized.

Thought. Soap. "King Lear." Liver spots on the backs of hands. Travel time. Sunsets. Spin-dry cycles. Headaches.

All are now reduced to their absolute essentials.

All miniaturized.

This is a revolutionary new concept.   15

It will give you twice as much time as your old unrevolutionary new concept.

You will be twice as dynamic.

You will enjoy endless hours.

You will stay younger twice as fast.

Here is what the critics say: 20

"Since experiencing the revolutionary new concept I have become twice as irresistible to women"—Mr. B. T. of Houma, La.

"—a dynamic new route to newness. . . . I never knew what 'King Lear' could be until I saw it performed without commas or punctuation marks"—Mrs. C. J. of Rochester, N.Y.

You will also smell newer.

Why is this extraordinary advance in newness vital to success?

Because we live in today's world.   25

Today's world is completely different.

Today's world is all new.

Today's world requires people who are completely different.

It requires people who are all new.

We have all seen people who live in yesterday's world.   30

Are those people fun people?

Dynamic people?

When you open their doors do you smell an exciting new fresh-from-the-factory new-people smell?

With a hidden camera we interviewed a typical scrubwoman.

Note that these pictures show her seated before two boxes.   35

She cannot see the labels visible to you.

Note that one box is labeled "New Completely Different Person."

The other is labeled "Old Unchanged Person."

We will now run the tape.

"Mrs. Hummell, you are a weary 67-year-old scrubwoman who   40
spends long nights alone on her knees in this empty building. We ask
you to study these two boxes and tell us which box contains the sort
of person you would prefer to keep you company through the night."

"Easy. That box right there."

"Now, you, Mrs. Hummel, have chosen the box labeled—unbeknownst to you—'New Completely Different Person.' Tell me why
you did not pick this other box labeled 'Old Unchanged Person.' "

"Because it looked too heavy to carry around all night."

"Let's open both boxes and look."

Notice Mrs. Hummel's expression as the "Old Unchanged Person"   45
box is opened and a 135-pound woman emerges and asks her to spend
an hour walking on the beach watching a sunset.

Notice that Mrs. Hummel recoils.

Mrs. Hummel recoils because the woman is not new.

She does not have new-woman smell.

She has not miniaturized the liver spots on the backs of her hands.

She does not propose living dynamically, but instead speaks in the   50
exhausting rhythms of this particular sentence, with its antiquated commas and cumbersomely involuted grammatical structure, thereby making it all too evident that she is incapable of living dynamically by getting
right to the point, a fact which is driven home by her suggestion that
they spend an entire hour watching a sunset, thus consuming precious
time that could be used to have her wrinkles surgically removed and
the dull soap glaze banished from her hair by application of a new,
completely different shampoo.

Note, by contrast, how delighted Mrs. Hummel looks when the
box labeled "New Completely Different Person" is opened.

Yes, the figure emerging is a 10-ounce man.

He has been reduced to the absolute essentials of newness.

Mrs. Hummel can keep him in her apron pocket throughout the
night. She can remove him when she wishes to inhale his exciting new
smell.

He will tell her without commas how to have twice as much time   55
for dynamic living by watching a sunset in 15 seconds.

Mrs. Hummel will never be the same again.

Lines of Inquiry
"Completely Different"

The most striking aspects of this essay's beginning are its short sentences and extremely short paragraphs. How do you react to these features? Are the short sentences easy to read, or hard? How long before you identify the issue, and how do you feel about being forced to solve the puzzle? How does repetition of key words and phrases work to hold this section together?

Despite the compactness and economy of his phrasing, Baker explores a very complex set of interrelated problems here. Try to sort out and define the problems that concern him here. What does Baker mean by "miniaturization"? What things are being reduced, diminished, in contemporary society? Baker has said elsewhere that "the bigger things get, the smaller the results." How does this statement apply to "Completely Different"? How does it apply to that very long sentence that comes near the end of the essay? What do you suppose that Baker is suggesting about language, society, and values through the contrast between that sentence and the others in the piece?

Across these four essays Baker displays a range of different voices and attitudes. Try to define these voices. How do they vary? Yet, how would you know even without the by-line that whatever the style, whatever the tone, each is still a piece by Russell Baker?

James Baldwin
1924–87

It began to seem that one would have to hold in the mind forever two sides which seemed to be in opposition. The first idea was acceptance, the acceptance, totally and without rancor, of life as it is, and men as they are: in the light of this idea, it goes without saying that injustice is a commonplace. But this did not mean that one could be complacent, for the second idea was of equal power: that one must never, in one's own life, accept these injustices as commonplace but must fight them with all one's strength.

In this passage from "Notes of a Native Son," the title piece from his first collection of essays, Baldwin describes his coming to understand what would be his mission as a black writer in white America. Through his writing he waged his war against those commonplace injustices, relentlessly stripping away, often with anger but always with love, the fictions which have clothed race relations in this country. But the "Negro question," as it was called in the days of Baldwin's early writing, was only the point of entry for his cultural criticism, which, while it kept issues of race at its center, always reached beyond them to a critique of Americans' understanding of their history, their national identity, and their place in a shifting global culture.

James Baldwin was born in Harlem in 1924, the child of an unmarried mother who had come north as part of the Great Migration of blacks from the South in the years during and following World War I, making him, as he put it, "but one generation removed from the South." When he was three his mother married David Baldwin, a preacher and laborer who had come to New York from New Orleans, and the couple had eight more children. Baldwin was raised, said one biographer, "under the twin disciplines of poverty and the store-front church." As the eldest child, he took on much of the responsibility for caring for his younger siblings. "As they were born, I took them over with one hand and held a book with the other"; by the time he was thirteen, he claims, he had read nearly all the books in Harlem's two public libraries. Baldwin graduated in 1942 from DeWitt Clinton High School in the Bronx, a mostly white school to which his early writing abilities had won him admittance, but it was his extensive and eclectic reading combined with his firsthand experience of life on the streets and in the hallways and back alleys of Harlem which constituted his real education.

Baldwin's relationship with his stepfather was an intense and complicated one, a confusion of hatred and love. That paradoxical mixture of emotions, combined with his struggle as the stepchild to find his place in a large family of half-brothers and half-sisters, prefigured the lifelong ambivalence of his relationship with his native land and his efforts to claim a place for himself in its culture. When he was fourteen, he experienced a profound religious conversion and, following in his stepfather's footsteps, became a preacher in a store-front pentecostal church in his Harlem neighborhood. Three years later he left the church; some critics have observed, though, that he never really abandoned the role of preacher, continuing to sermonize with the pen rather than from the pulpit.

In 1948, encouraged by novelist Richard Wright, Baldwin left the United States for Paris. There he was able to complete *Go Tell It on the Mountain* (1952), a fictionalized rendering of his own teenage experience of conversion and the call to preach, which received wide critical acclaim. Though he returned many times to the United States, often for lengthy visits to observe, report, speak, write, and teach, he lived abroad, mostly in France, for the remainder of his life. Europe gave him a place distant enough to develop a necessary perspective on the country of his birth and from which to view with penetrating clarity the fabric of American life. He insisted that Europe was not a "haven" for him from the racial strife in the United States and that he was *"not in exile,"* claiming instead that ". . . the world is very small, and it is no longer possible for an American, and certainly not an American black man, and certainly not James Baldwin, to leave America." In Europe Baldwin recognized himself to be "as American as any Texas GI"; it was not possible for him to leave America because wherever he went, he took America with him. Still the distance was necessary for him to work, and while the frequent visits to the United States fueled his writing, it was mostly in Europe that he got the writing done.

In the course of his thirty-five years of professional life, Baldwin published prolifically—novels, plays, short stories, and newspaper articles. It was in the essay form, however, that he achieved his greatest success. Collected in *Notes of a Native Son, Nobody Knows My Name, The Fire Next Time,* and *The Price of the Ticket,* Baldwin's essays moved readers to re-examine what it means to be an American. Calling him "strongest as an essayist," one critic said of his essays that they "probe, deeper than anyone has dared, the psychic history of this nation." When Baldwin died in 1987, the novelist and essayist Norman Mailer praised him by saying, "Nobody has more elegance than Baldwin as an essayist; not one of us hasn't learned something about the art of the essay from him." It was the essay form that could best accommodate the urgency of Baldwin's prophetic voice, the stark realities of his personal narratives, the exhortatory power of his pleas for Americans to rise up and meet the challenge to "end the racial nightmare, and achieve our country, and change the history of the world."

It was at the level of the word that Baldwin worked his changes. "We live in a country in which words are mostly used to cover the sleeper, not to wake him up," he wrote. "For the horrors of the American Negro's life there has been almost no language." Inventing that language in a cadence powerful enough to wake the sleeping country was the charge that he laid himself:

> It is, alas, the truth that to be an American writer today means mounting an unending attack on all that Americans believe themselves to hold sacred. It means fighting an astute and agile guerrilla warfare with that American complacency which so inadequately masks the American panic.

While he was committed to the idea that "one must really do great violence to language, one must somehow disrupt the comforting beat, in order to be heard," the eloquence, rhetoric, and rhythm of his prose arise largely from the traditions of the King James Bible and the great masters of nineteenth-century fiction such as Charles Dickens and Henry James. It was perhaps that precise combination which made Baldwin, of all the black polemicists of his generation, so widely read by whites and blacks alike.

The breadth of his vision never failed; he wrote to and for a whole nation, insisting always that the fate of whites and blacks in America was inextricably bound together. Like Orwell before him, Baldwin stressed that injustice wounds the oppressor as well as the oppressed: "It is a terrible, an inexorable, law that one cannot deny the humanity of another without diminishing one's own: in the face of one's victim, one sees oneself." As an alternative to racial conflict, Baldwin repeatedly offers the haunting vision of black America and white America locked together in the regenerative embrace of love. The future is the awaited fruit of that union, an offspring anticipated with alternating fear and hope:

> For nothing is fixed, forever and forever and forever, it is not fixed; the earth is always shifting, the light is always changing, the sea does not cease to grind down rock. Generations do not cease to be born, and we are responsible to them because we are the only witnesses they have. The sea rises, the light fails, lovers cling to each other, and children cling to us. The moment we cease to hold each other, the moment we break faith with one another, the sea engulfs us and the light goes out.

Like that haunting vision, the trajectory of Baldwin's life was itself remarkable, beginning in the Harlem ghetto and rising to the heights of fame and wealth and achievement. At his death, one eulogist praised him for having possessed to a great degree "that quality of his people that he loved most . . . their ability to turn annihilating hostility into a strength that lifted rather than buried the human spirit." Baldwin once described himself this way: "I am a very tight, tense, lean, abnormally ambitious, abnormally intelligent and hungry black cat. I'm not a nigger. I'm a man." To be a man, he insisted, was to possess a moral vision and the courage to press that vision on the world. "If there is not a moral question, there is no reason to write," he said. "I'm an old-fashioned writer and, despite the odds, I want to change the world. What I hope to convey? Well, joy, love, the passion to feel how our choices affect the world . . . that's all."

Autobiographical Notes

I was born in Harlem thirty-one years ago. I began plotting novels at about the time I learned to read. The story of my childhood is the usual bleak fantasy, and we can dismiss it with the restrained observation that I certainly would not consider living it again. In those days my mother was given to the exasperating and mysterious habit of having babies. As they were born, I took them over with one hand and held a book with the other. The children probably suffered, though they have since been kind enough to deny it, and in this way I read *Uncle Tom's Cabin* and *A Tale of Two Cities* over and over and over again; in this way, in fact, I read just about everything I could get my hands on—except the Bible, probably because it was the only book I was encouraged to read. I must also confess that I wrote—a great deal—and my first professional triumph, in any case, the first effort of mine to be seen in print, occurred at the age of twelve or thereabouts, when a short story I had written about the Spanish revolution won some sort of prize in an extremely short-lived church newspaper. I remember the story was censored by the lady editor, though I don't remember why, and I was outraged.

Also wrote plays, and songs, for one of which I received a letter of congratulations from Mayor La Guardia, and poetry, about which the less said, the better. My mother was delighted by all these goings-on, but my father wasn't; he wanted me to be a preacher. When I was fourteen I became a preacher, and when I was seventeen I stopped. Very shortly thereafter I left home. For God knows how long I struggled with the world of commerce and industry—I guess they would say they struggled with *me*—and when I was about twenty-one I had enough done of a novel to get a Saxton Fellowship. When I was twenty-two the fellowship was over, the novel turned out to be unsalable, and I started waiting on tables in a Village restaurant and writing book reviews—mostly, as it turned out, about the Negro problem, concerning which the color of my skin made me automatically an expert. Did another book, in company with photographer Theodore Pelatowski, about the store-front churches in Harlem. This book met exactly the same fate as my first—fellowship, but no sale. (It was a Rosenwald Fellowship.) By the time I was twenty-four I had decided to stop reviewing books about the Negro problem—which, by this time, was only slightly less horrible in print than it was in life—and I packed my bags and went to France, where I finished, God knows how, *Go Tell It on the Mountain*.

Any writer, I suppose, feels that the world into which he was born is nothing less than a conspiracy against the cultivation of his talent—

which attitude certainly has a great deal to support it. On the other hand, it is only because the world looks on his talent with such a frightening indifference that the artist is compelled to make his talent important. So that any writer, looking back over even so short a span of time as I am here forced to assess, finds that the things which hurt him and the things which helped him cannot be divorced from each other; he could be helped in a certain way only because he was hurt in a certain way; and his help is simply to be enabled to move from one conundrum to the next—one is tempted to say that he moves from one disaster to the next. When one begins looking for influences one finds them by the score. I haven't thought much about my own, not enough anyway; I hazard that the King James Bible, the rhetoric of the store-front church, something ironic and violent and perpetually understated in Negro speech—and something of Dickens' love for bravura—have something to do with me today; but I wouldn't stake my life on it. Likewise, innumerable people have helped me in many ways; but finally, I suppose, the most difficult (and most rewarding) thing in my life has been the fact that I was born a Negro and was forced, therefore, to effect some kind of truce with this reality. (Truce, by the way, is the best one can hope for.)

One of the difficulties about being a Negro writer (and this is not special pleading, since I don't mean to suggest that he has it worse than anybody else) is that the Negro problem is written about so widely. The bookshelves groan under the weight of information, and everyone therefore considers himself informed. And this information, furthermore, operates usually (generally, popularly) to reinforce traditional attitudes. Of traditional attitudes there are only two—For or Against— and I, personally, find it difficult to say which attitude has caused me the most pain. I am speaking as a writer; from a social point of view I am perfectly aware that the change from ill-will to good-will, however motivated, however imperfect, however expressed, is better than no change at all.

But it is part of the business of the writer—as I see it—to examine   5 attitudes, to go beneath the surface, to tap the source. From this point of view the Negro problem is nearly inaccessible. It is not only written about so widely; it is written about so badly. It is quite possible to say that the price a Negro pays for becoming articulate is to find himself, at length, with nothing to be articulate about. ("You taught me language," says Caliban to Prospero, "and my profit on't is I know how to curse.") Consider: the tremendous social activity that this problem generates imposes on whites and Negroes alike the necessity of looking forward, of working to bring about a better day. This is fine, it keeps the waters troubled; it is all, indeed, that has made possible the Negro's progress. Nevertheless, social affairs are not generally speaking the writer's prime concern, whether they ought to be or not; it is absolutely necessary that he establish between himself and these affairs a distance which will allow, at least, for clarity, so that before he can look forward in any meaningful sense, he must first be allowed to take a long look back. In the context of the Negro problem neither whites nor blacks, for excellent reasons of their own, have the faintest desire to look back; but I think that the past is all that makes the present coherent, and further, that the past will remain horrible for exactly as long as we refuse to assess it honestly.

I know, in any case, that the most crucial time in my own development came when I was forced to recognize that I was a kind of bastard of the West; when I followed the line of my past I did not find myself in Europe but in Africa. And this meant that in some subtle way, in a really profound way, I brought to Shakespeare, Bach, Rembrandt, to the stones of Paris, to the cathedral at Chartres, and to the Empire State Building, a special attitude. These were not really my creations, they did not contain my history; I might search in them in vain forever for any reflection of myself. I was an interloper; this was not my heritage. At the same time I had no other heritage which I could possibly hope to use—I had certainly been unfitted for the jungle or the tribe. I would have to appropriate these white centuries, I would have to make them mine—I would have to accept my special attitude, my special place in this scheme—otherwise I would have no place in *any* scheme. What was the most difficult was the fact that I was forced to admit something I had always hidden from myself, which the American Negro has had to hide from himself as the price of his public progress; that I hated and feared white people. This did not mean that I loved black people; on the contrary, I despised them, possibly because they failed to produce Rembrandt. In effect, I hated and feared the world. And this meant, not only that I thus gave the world an altogether murderous power over me, but also that in such a self-destroying limbo I could never hope to write.

One writes out of one thing only—one's own experience. Everything depends on how relentlessly one forces from this experience the last drop, sweet or bitter, it can possibly give. This is the only real concern of the artist, to recreate out of the disorder of life that order which is art. The difficulty then, for me, of being a Negro writer was the fact that I was, in effect, prohibited from examining my own experience too closely by the tremendous demands and the very real dangers of my social situation.

I don't think the dilemma outlined above is uncommon. I do think, since writers work in the disastrously explicit medium of language, that it goes a little way towards explaining why, out of the enormous resources of Negro speech and life, and despite the example of Negro music, prose written by Negroes has been generally speaking so pallid and so harsh. I have not written about being a Negro at such length because I expect that to be my only subject, but only because it was the gate I had to unlock before I could hope to write about anything else. I don't think that the Negro problem in America can be even discussed coherently without bearing in mind its context; its context being the history, traditions, customs, the moral assumptions and preoccupations of the country; in short, the general social fabric. Appearances to the contrary, no one in America escapes its effects and everyone in America bears some responsibility for it. I believe this the more firmly because it is the overwhelming tendency to speak of this problem as though it were a thing apart. But in the work of Faulkner, in the general attitude and certain specific passages in Robert Penn Warren, and, most significantly, in the advent of Ralph Ellison, one sees the beginnings—at least—of a more genuinely penetrating search. Mr. Ellison, by the way, is the first Negro novelist I have ever read to utilize in language, and brilliantly, some of the ambiguity and irony of Negro life.

About my interests: I don't know if I have any, unless the morbid desire to own a sixteen-millimeter camera and make experimental movies can be so classified. Otherwise, I love to eat and drink—it's my melancholy conviction that I've scarcely ever had enough to eat (this is because it's *impossible* to eat enough if you're worried about the next meal)—and I love to argue with people who do not disagree with me too profoundly, and I love to laugh. I do *not* like bohemia, or bohemians, I do not like people whose principal aim is pleasure, and I do not like people who are *earnest* about anything. I don't like people who like me because I'm a Negro; neither do I like people who find in the same accident grounds for contempt. I love America more than any other country in the world, and exactly for this reason, I insist on the right to criticize her perpetually. I think all theories are suspect, that the finest principles may have to be modified, or may even be pulverized by the demands of life, and that one must find, therefore, one's own moral center and move through the world hoping that this center will guide one aright. I consider that I have many responsibilities, but none greater than this: to last, as Hemingway says, and get my work done.

I want to be an honest man and a good writer.   10

Lines of Inquiry
"Autobiographical Notes"

The title of this piece suggests that it might be as casual in its style and as random in its structure as notes or jottings. In what respects does it seem to have the random order that might be expected of someone remembering, free-associating, and thinking to himself about aspects of his past? In what respects does it seem to follow a systematic procedure, as might be expected of someone providing autobiographical information? In what respects does it seem to be guided neither by a desire to remember, nor by a desire to inform, but by an intent to express a personal set of beliefs?

Baldwin makes a striking and paradoxical assertion in the third paragraph when he claims that "any writer . . . finds that the things which hurt him and the things which helped him cannot be divorced from each other." On what basis does he make this seemingly paradoxical assertion? For example, how does he show that being "born a Negro" was "the most difficult (and most rewarding) thing" in his personal life"? In his life as a writer?

How broadly applicable do you consider Baldwin's paradoxical assertion to be? For example, what has been "the most difficult" thing in your life? In what respects, if any, has it also been the "most rewarding"? What has been the most difficult thing for you as a writer? In what respects, if any, has it also been the most rewarding for you as a writer?

Stranger in the Village

From all available evidence no black man had ever set foot in this tiny Swiss village before I came. I was told before arriving that I would probably be a "sight" for the village; I took this to mean that people of my complexion were rarely seen in Switzerland, and also that city people are always something of a "sight" outside of the city. It did not occur to me—possibly because I am an American—that there could be people anywhere who had never seen a Negro.

It is a fact that cannot be explained on the basis of the inaccessibility of the village. The village is very high, but it is only four hours from Milan and three hours from Lausanne. It is true that it is virtually unknown. Few people making plans for a holiday would elect to come here. On the other hand, the villagers are able, presumably, to come and go as they please—which they do: to another town at the foot of the mountain, with a population of approximately five thousand, the nearest place to see a movie or go to the bank. In the village there is no movie house, no bank, no library, no theater; very few radios, one jeep, one station wagon; and, at the moment, one typewriter, mine, an invention which the woman next door to me here had never seen. There are about six hundred people living here, all Catholic—I conclude this from the fact that the Catholic church is open all year round, whereas the Protestant chapel, set off on a hill a little removed from the village, is open only in the summertime when the tourists arrive. There are four or five hotels, all closed now, and four or five *bistros,* of which, however, only two do any business during the winter. These two do not do a great deal, for life in the village seems to end around nine or ten o'clock. There are a few stores, butcher, baker, *épicerie,* a hardware store, and a money-changer—who cannot change travelers' checks, but must send them down to the bank, an operation which takes two or three days. There is something called the *Ballet Haus,* closed in the winter and used for God knows what, certainly not ballet, during the summer. There seems to be only one schoolhouse in the village, and this for the quite young children; I suppose this to mean that their older brothers and sisters at some point descend from these mountains in order to complete their education—possibly, again, to the town just below. The landscape is absolutely forbidding, mountains towering on all four sides, ice and snow as far as the eye can reach. In this white wilderness, men and women and children move all day, carrying washing, wood, buckets of milk or water, sometimes skiing on Sunday afternoons. All week long boys and young men are to be seen shoveling snow off the rooftops, or dragging wood down from the forest in sleds.

The village's only real attraction, which explains the tourist season, is the hot spring water. A disquietingly high proportion of these tourists are cripples, or semi-cripples, who come year after year—from other parts of Switzerland, usually—to take the waters. This lends the village, at the height of the season, a rather terrifying air of sanctity, as though it were a lesser Lourdes. There is often something beautiful, there is always something awful, in the spectacle of a person who has lost one of his faculties, a faculty he never questioned until it was gone, and who struggles to recover it. Yet people remain people, on crutches or indeed on deathbeds; and wherever I passed, the first summer I was here, among the native villagers or among the lame, a wind passed with me—of astonishment, curiosity, amusement, and outrage. That first summer I stayed two weeks and never intended to return. But I did return in the winter, to work; the village offers, obviously, no distractions whatever and has the further advantage of being extremely cheap. Now it is winter again, a year later, and I am here again. Everyone in the village knows my name, though they scarcely ever use it, knows that I come from America—though, this, apparently, they will never really believe: black men come from Africa—and everyone knows that I am the friend of the son of a woman who was born here, and that I am staying in their chalet. But I remain as much a stranger today as I was the first day I arrived, and the children shout *Neger! Neger!* as I walk along the streets.

It must be admitted that in the beginning I was far too shocked to have any real reaction. In so far as I reacted at all, I reacted by trying to be pleasant—it being a great part of the American Negro's education (long before he goes to school) that he must make people "like" him. This smile-and-the-world-smiles-with-you routine worked about as well in this situation as it had in the situation for which it was designed, which is to say that it did not work at all. No one, after all, can be liked whose human weight and complexity cannot be, or has not been, admitted. My smile was simply another unheard-of phenomenon which allowed them to see my teeth—they did not, really, see my smile and I began to think that, should I take to snarling, no one would notice any difference. All of the physical characteristics of the Negro which had caused me, in America, a very different and almost forgotten pain were nothing less than miraculous—or infernal—in the eyes of the village people. Some thought my hair was the color of tar, that it had the texture of wire, or the texture of cotton. It was jocularly suggested that I might let it all grow long and make myself a winter coat. If I sat in the sun for more than five minutes some daring creature was certain to come along and gingerly put his fingers on my hair, as though he were afraid of an electric shock, or put his hand on my hand, astonished that the color did not rub off. In all of this, in which it must be conceded there was the charm of genuine wonder and in which there was certainly no element of intentional unkindness, there was yet no suggestion that I was human: I was simply a living wonder.

I knew that they did not mean to be unkind, and I know it now; it is necessary, nevertheless, for me to repeat this to myself each time that I walk out of the chalet. The children who shout *Neger!* have no way of knowing the echoes this sound raises in me. They are brimming with good humor and the more daring swell with pride when I stop to speak with them. Just the same, there are days when I cannot pause and smile, when I have no heart to play with them; when, indeed, I mutter sourly to myself, exactly as I muttered on the streets of a city these children have never seen, when I was no bigger than these children are now: *Your* mother *was a nigger.* Joyce is right about history being a nightmare—but it may be the nightmare from which no one *can* awaken. People are trapped in history and history is trapped in them.

There is a custom in the village—I am told it is repeated in many   5 villages—of "buying" African natives for the purpose of converting them to Christianity. There stands in the church all year round a small box with a slot for money, decorated with a black figurine, and into this box the villagers drop their francs. During the *carnaval* which precedes Lent, two village children have their faces blackened—out of which bloodless darkness their blue eyes shine like ice—and fantastic horsehair wigs are placed on their blond heads; thus disguised, they solicit among the villagers for money for the missionaries in Africa. Between the box in the church and the blackened children, the village "bought" last year six or eight African natives. This was reported to me with pride by the wife of one of the *bistro* owners and I was careful to express astonishment and pleasure at the solicitude shown by the village for the souls of black folk. The *bistro* owner's wife beamed with a pleasure far more genuine than my own and seemed to feel that I might now breathe more easily concerning the souls of at least six of my kinsmen.

I tried not to think of these so lately baptized kinsmen, of the price paid for them, or the peculiar price they themselves would pay, and said nothing about my father, who having taken his own conversion too literally never, at bottom, forgave the white world (which he described as heathen) for having saddled him with a Christ in whom, to judge at least from their treatment of him, they themselves no longer believed. I thought of white men arriving for the first time in an African village, strangers there, as I am a stranger here, and tried to imagine the astounded populace touching their hair and marveling at the color of their skin. But there is a great difference between being the first white man to be seen by Africans and being the first black man to be seen by whites. The white man takes the astonishment as tribute, for he arrives to conquer and to convert the natives, whose inferiority in relation to himself is not even to be questioned; whereas I, without a thought of conquest, find myself among a people whose culture controls me, has even, in a sense, created me, people who have cost me more in anguish and rage than they will ever know, who yet do not even know of my existence. The astonishment with which I might have greeted them, should they have stumbled into my African village a few hundred years ago, might have rejoiced their hearts. But the astonishment with which they greet me today can only poison mine.

And this is so despite everything I may do to feel differently, despite my friendly conversations with the *bistro* owner's wife, despite their three-year-old son who has at last become my friend, despite the *saluts* and *bonsoirs* which I exchange with people as I walk, despite the fact that I know that no individual can be taken to task for what history is doing, or has done. I say that the culture of these people controls me—but they can scarcely be held responsible for European culture. America comes out of Europe, but these people have never seen America, nor have most of them seen more of Europe than the hamlet at the foot of their mountain. Yet they move with an authority which I shall never have; and they regard me, quite rightly, not only as a stranger in their village but as a suspect latecomer, bearing no credentials, to everything they have—however unconsciously—inherited.

For this village, even were it incomparably more remote and incredibly more primitive, is the West, the West onto which I have been so strangely grafted. These people cannot be, from the point of view of power, strangers anywhere in the world; they have made the modern world, in effect, even if they do not know it. The most illiterate among them is related, in a way that I am not, to Dante, Shakespeare, Michelangelo, Aeschylus, Da Vinci, Rembrandt, and Racine; the cathedral at Chartres says something to them which it cannot say to me, as indeed would New York's Empire State Building, should anyone here ever see it. Out of their hymns and dances come Beethoven and Bach. Go back a few centuries and they are in their full glory—but I am in Africa, watching the conquerors arrive.

The rage of the disesteemed is personally fruitless, but it is also absolutely inevitable; this rage, so generally discounted, so little understood even among the people whose daily bread it is, is one of the things that makes history. Rage can only with difficulty, and never entirely, be brought under the domination of the intelligence and is therefore not susceptible to any arguments whatever. This is a fact which ordinary representatives of the *Herrenvolk,* having never felt this rage and being unable to imagine it, quite fail to understand. Also, rage cannot be hidden, it can only be dissembled. This dissembling deludes the thoughtless, and strengthens rage and adds, to rage, contempt. There are, no doubt, as many ways of coping with the resulting complex of tensions as there are black men in the world, but no black man can hope ever to be entirely liberated from this internal warfare—rage, dissembling, and contempt having inevitably accompanied his first realization of the power of white men. What is crucial here is that, since white men represent in the black man's world so heavy a weight, white men have for black men a reality which is far from being reciprocal; and hence all black men have toward all white men an attitude which is designed, really, either to rob the white man of the jewel of his naïveté, or else to make it cost him dear.

The black man insists, by whatever means he finds at his disposal, that the white man cease to regard him as an exotic rarity and recognize him as a human being. This is a very charged and difficult moment, for there is a great deal of will power involved in the white man's naïveté. Most people are not naturally reflective any more than they are naturally malicious, and the white man prefers to keep the black man at a certain human remove because it is easier for him thus to preserve his simplicity and avoid being called to account for crimes committed by his forefathers, or his neighbors. He is inescapably aware, nevertheless, that he is in a better position in the world than black men are; nor can he quite put to death the suspicion that he is hated by black men therefore. He does not wish to be hated, neither does he wish to change places, and at this point in his uneasiness he can scarcely avoid having recourse to those legends which white men have created about black men, the most usual effect of which is that the white man finds himself enmeshed, so to speak, in his own language which describes hell, as well as the attributes which lead one to hell, as being as black as night.

Every legend, moreover, contains its residuum of truth, and the root function of language is to control the universe by describing it. It is of quite considerable significance that black men remain, in the imagination, and in overwhelming numbers in fact, beyond the disciplines of salvation; and this despite the fact that the West has been "buying" African natives for centuries. There is, I should hazard, an instantaneous necessity to be divorced from this so visibly unsaved stranger, in whose heart, moreover, one cannot guess what dreams of vengeance are being nourished; and, at the same time, there are few things on earth more attractive than the idea of the unspeakable liberty which is allowed the unredeemed. When, beneath the black mask, a human being begins to make himself felt one cannot escape a certain awful wonder as to what kind of human being it is. What one's imagination makes of other people is dictated, of course, by the laws of one's own personality and it is one of the ironies of black-white relations that, by means of what the white man imagines the black man to be, the black man is enabled to know who the white man is.

I have said, for example, that I am as much a stranger in this village today as I was the first summer I arrived, but this is not quite true. The villagers wonder less about the texture of my hair than they did then, and wonder rather more about me. And the fact that their wonder now exists on another level is reflected in their attitudes and in their eyes. There are the children who make those delightful, hilarious, sometimes astonishingly grave overtures of friendship in the unpredictable fashion of children; other children, having been taught that the devil is a black man, scream in genuine anguish as I approach. Some of the older women never pass without a friendly greeting, never pass, indeed, if it seems that they will be able to engage me in conversation; other women look down or look away or rather contemptuously smirk. Some of the men drink with me and suggest that I learn how to ski—partly, I gather, because they cannot imagine what I would look like on skis—and want to know if I am married, and ask questions about my *métier*. But some of the men have accused *le sale nègre*—behind my back—of stealing wood and there is already in the eyes of some of them that peculiar, intent, paranoiac malevolence which one sometimes surprises in the eyes of American white men when, out walking with their Sunday girl, they see a Negro male approach.

There is a dreadful abyss between the streets of this village and the streets of the city in which I was born, between the children who shout *Neger!* today and those who shouted *Nigger!* yesterday—the abyss is experience, the American experience. The syllable hurled behind me today expresses, above all, wonder: I am a stranger here. But I am not a stranger in America and the same syllable riding on the American air expresses the war my presence has occasioned in the American soul.

For this village brings home to me this fact: that there was a day, and not really a very distant day, when Americans were scarcely Americans at all but discontented Europeans, facing a great unconquered continent and strolling, say, into a marketplace and seeing black men for the first time. The shock this spectacle afforded is suggested, surely, by the promptness with which they decided that these black men were not really men but cattle. It is true that the necessity on the part of the settlers of the New World of reconciling their moral assumptions with the fact—and the necessity—of slavery enhanced immensely the charm of this idea, and it is also true that this idea expresses, with a truly American bluntness, the attitude which to varying extents all masters have had toward all slaves.

But between all former slaves and slave-owners and the drama which begins for Americans over three hundred years ago at Jamestown, there are at least two differences to be observed. The American Negro slave could not suppose, for one thing, as slaves in past epochs had supposed and often done, that he would ever be able to wrest the power from his master's hands. This was a supposition which the modern era, which was to bring about such vast changes in the aims and dimensions of power, put to death; it only begins, in unprecedented fashion, and with dreadful implications, to be resurrected today. But even had this supposition persisted with undiminished force, the American Negro slave could not have used it to lend his condition dignity, for the reason that this supposition rests on another: that the slave in exile yet remains related to his past, has some means—if only in memory—of revering and sustaining the forms of his former life, is able, in short, to maintain his identity.

This was not the case with the American Negro slave. He is unique   15
among the black men of the world in that his past was taken from him, almost literally, at one blow. One wonders what on earth the first slave found to say to the first dark child he bore. I am told that there are Haitians able to trace their ancestry back to African kings, but any American Negro wishing to go back so far will find his journey through time abruptly arrested by the signature on the bill of sale which served as the entrance paper for his ancestor. At the time—to say nothing of the circumstances—of the enslavement of the captive black man who was to become the American Negro, there was not the remotest possibility that he would ever take power from his master's hands. There was no reason to suppose that his situation would ever change, nor was there, shortly, anything to indicate that his situation had ever been different. It was his necessity, in the words of E. Franklin Frazier, to find a "motive for living under American culture or die." The identity of the American Negro comes out of this extreme situation, and the evolution of this identity was a source of the most intolerable anxiety in the minds and the lives of his masters.

For the history of the American Negro is unique also in this: that the question of his humanity, and of his rights therefore as a human being, became a burning one for several generations of Americans, so burning a question that it ultimately became one of those used to divide the nation. It is out of this argument that the venom of the epithet *Nigger!* is derived. It is an argument which Europe has never had, and hence Europe quite sincerely fails to understand how or why the argument arose in the first place, why its effects are so frequently disastrous and always so unpredictable, why it refuses until today to be entirely settled. Europe's black possessions remained—and do remain—in Europe's colonies, at which remove they represented no threat whatever to European identity. If they posed any problem at all for the European conscience, it was a problem which remained comfortingly abstract: in effect, the black man, *as a man,* did not exist for Europe. But in America, even as a slave, he was an inescapable part of the general social fabric and no American could escape having an attitude toward him. Americans attempt until today to make an abstraction of the Negro, but the very nature of these abstractions reveals the tremendous effects the presence of the Negro has had on the American character.

When one considers the history of the Negro in America it is of the greatest importance to recognize that the moral beliefs of a person, or a people, are never really as tenuous as life—which is not moral—very often causes them to appear; these create for them a frame of reference and a necessary hope, the hope being that when life has done its worst they will be enabled to rise above themselves and to triumph over life. Life would scarcely be bearable if this hope did not exist. Again, even when the worst has been said, to betray a belief is not by any means to have put oneself beyond its power; the betrayal of a belief is not the same thing as ceasing to believe. If this were not so there would be no moral standards in the world at all. Yet one must also recognize that morality is based on ideas and that all ideas are dangerous—dangerous because ideas can only lead to action and where the action leads no man can say. And dangerous in this respect: that confronted with the impossibility of remaining faithful to one's beliefs, and the equal impossibility of becoming free of them, one can be driven to the most inhuman excesses. The ideas on which American beliefs are based are not, though Americans often seem to think so, ideas which originated in America. They came out of Europe. And the establishment of democracy on the American continent was scarcely as radical a break with the past as was the necessity, which Americans faced, of broadening this concept to include black men.

This was, literally, a hard necessity. It was impossible, for one thing, for Americans to abandon their beliefs, not only because these beliefs alone seemed able to justify the sacrifices they had endured and the blood that they had spilled, but also because these beliefs afforded them their own bulwark against a moral chaos as absolute as the physical chaos of the continent it was their destiny to conquer. But in the situation in which Americans found themselves, these beliefs threatened an idea which, whether or not one likes to think so, is the very warp and woof of the heritage of the West, the idea of white supremacy.

Americans have made themselves notorious by the shrillness and the brutality with which they have insisted on this idea, but they did not invent it; and it has escaped the world's notice that those very excesses of which Americans have been guilty imply a certain, unprecedented uneasiness over the idea's life and power, if not, indeed, the idea's validity. The idea of white supremacy rests simply on the fact that white men are the creators of civilization (the present civilization, which is the only one that matters; all previous civilizations are simply "contributions" to our own) and are therefore civilization's guardians and defenders. Thus it was impossible for Americans to accept the black man as one of themselves, for to do so was to jeopardize their status as white men. But not so to accept him was to deny his human reality, his human weight and complexity, and the strain of denying the overwhelmingly undeniable forced Americans into rationalizations so fantastic that they approached the pathological.

At the root of the American Negro problem is the necessity of the 20 American white man to find a way of living with the Negro in order to be able to live with himself. And the history of this problem can be reduced to the means used by Americans—lynch law and law, segregation and legal acceptance, terrorization and concession—either to come to terms with this necessity, or to find a way around it, or (most usually) to find a way of doing both these things at once. The resulting spectacle, at once foolish and dreadful, led someone to make the quite accurate observation that "the Negro-in-America is a form of insanity which overtakes white men."

In this long battle, a battle by no means finished, the unforeseeable effects of which will be felt by many future generations, the white man's motive was the protection of his identity; the black man was motivated by the need to establish an identity. And despite the terrorization which the Negro in America endured and endures sporadically until today, despite the cruel and totally inescapable ambivalence of his status in his country, the battle for his identity has long ago been won. He is not a visitor to the West, but a citizen there, an American; as American as the Americans who despise him, the Americans who fear him, the Americans who love him—the Americans who became less than themselves, or rose to be greater than themselves by virtue of the fact that the challenge he represented was inescapable. He is perhaps the only black man in the world whose relationship to white men is more terrible, more subtle, and more meaningful than the relationship of bitter possessed to uncertain possessor. His survival depended, and his development depends, on his ability to turn his peculiar status in the Western world to his own advantage and, it may be, to the very great advantage of that world. It remains for him to fashion out of his experience that which will give him sustenance, and a voice.

The cathedral at Chartres, I have said, says something to the people of this village which it cannot say to me; but it is important to understand that this cathedral says something to me which it cannot say to them. Perhaps they are struck by the power of the spires, the glory of the windows; but they have known God, after all, longer than I have known him, and in a different way, and I am terrified by the slippery bottomless well to be found in the crypt, down which heretics were hurled to death, and by the obscene, inescapable gargoyles jutting out of the stone and seeming to say that God and the devil can never be divorced. I doubt that the villagers think of the devil when they face a cathedral because they have never been identified with the devil. But I must accept the status which myth, if nothing else, gives me in the West before I can hope to change the myth.

Yet, if the American Negro has arrived at his identity by virtue of the absoluteness of his estrangement from his past, American white men still nourish the illusion that there is some means of recovering the European innocence, of returning to a state in which black men do not exist. This is one of the greatest errors Americans can make. The identity they fought so hard to protect has, by virtue of that battle, undergone a change: Americans are as unlike any other white people in the world as it is possible to be. I do not think, for example, that it is too much to suggest that the American vision of the world—which allows so little reality, generally speaking, for any of the darker forces in human life, which tends until today to paint moral issues in glaring black and white—owes a great deal to the battle waged by Americans to maintain between themselves and black men a human separation which could not be bridged. It is only now beginning to be borne in on us— very faintly, it must be admitted, very slowly, and very much against our will—that this vision of the world is dangerously inaccurate, and perfectly useless. For it protects our moral high-mindedness at the terrible expense of weakening our grasp of reality. People who shut their eyes to reality simply invite their own destruction, and anyone who insists on remaining in a state of innocence long after that innocence is dead turns himself into a monster.

The time has come to realize that the interracial drama acted out on the American continent has not only created a new black man, it has created a new white man, too. No road whatever will lead Americans back to the simplicity of this European village where white men still have the luxury of looking on me as a stranger. I am not, really, a stranger any longer for any American alive. One of the things that distinguishes Americans from other people is that no other people has ever been so deeply involved in the lives of black men, and vice versa. This fact faced, with all its implications, it can be seen that the history of the American Negro problem is not merely shameful, it is also something of an achievement. For even when the worst has been said, it must also be added that the perpetual challenge posed by this problem was always, somehow, perpetually met. It is precisely this black-white experience which may prove of indispensable value to us in the world we face today. This world is white no longer, and it will never be white again.

Lines of Inquiry
"Stranger in the Village"

Baldwin depicts the Swiss mountain village as being so small, so geographically and culturally isolated, and so thoroughly white as to make it seem completely unrelated to any place in modern America, Europe, or Africa. Why, then, does he devote the first quarter of his piece to describing so strange and atypical a place? How does he manage to keep the village in mind during the last three quarters of the essay when he no longer focuses on his experience there? How does he use his experience in the village to illuminate the "black-white experience" in America? In Europe? In Africa? In the world?

In his final paragraph, Baldwin asserts that "the interracial drama acted out on the American continent has not only created a new black man, it has created a new white man, too." What do you suppose he means by "a new black man" and "a new white man"? How do the "new black man" and the "new white man" differ from their old counterparts? From their counterparts in Europe? In Africa? How does "the interracial drama" of these new persons differ from the interracial drama of their old counterparts?

How does Baldwin's depiction of the black-white experience in Africa compare to Orwell's depiction of that experience at the end of "Marrakech"? How does Baldwin's depiction of the black-white experience in America compare to Walker's depiction of it in "The Black Writer and the Southern Experience"? How does Baldwin's depiction of it compare to your own experience and understanding of it? How do you account for any differences between his perception and yours?

A Fly in Buttermilk

"**Y**ou can take the child out of the country," my elders were fond of saying, "but you can't take the country out of the child." They were speaking of their own antecedents, I supposed; it didn't, anyway, seem possible that they could be warning me; I took myself out of the country and went to Paris. It was there I discovered that the old folks knew what they had been talking about: I found myself, willy-nilly, alchemized into an American the moment I touched French soil.

Now, back again after nearly nine years, it was ironical to reflect that if I had not lived in France for so long I would never have found it necessary—or possible— to visit the American South. The South had always frightened me. How deeply it had frightened me—though I had never seen it—and how soon, was one of the things my dreams revealed to me while I was there. And this made me think of the privacy and mystery of childhood all over again, in a new way. I wondered where children got their strength—the strength, in this case, to walk through mobs to get to school.

"You've got to remember," said an older Negro friend to me in Washington, "that no matter what you see or how it makes you feel, it can't be compared to twenty-five, thirty years ago—you remember those photographs of Negroes hanging from trees?" I looked at him differently. *I* had seen the photographs—but *he* might have been one of them. "I remember," he said, "when conductors on streetcars wore pistols and had police powers." And he remembered a great deal more. He remembered, for example, hearing Booker T. Washington speak, and the day-to-day progress of the Scottsboro case, and the rise and bloody fall of Bessie Smith. These had been books and headlines and music for me but it now developed that they were also a part of my identity.

"You're just one generation away from the South, you know. You'll find," he added, kindly, "that people will be willing to talk to you . . . if they don't feel that you look down on them just because you're from the North."

The first Negro I encountered, an educator, didn't give me any opportunity to look down. He forced me to admit, at once, that I had never been to college; that northern Negroes lived herded together, like pigs in a pen; that the campus on which we met was a tribute to the industry and determination of southern Negroes. "Negroes in the South form a *community*." My humiliation was complete with his discovery that I couldn't even drive a car. I couldn't ask him anything. He made

5

me feel so hopeless an example of the general northern spinelessness that it would have seemed a spiteful counterattack to have asked him to discuss the integration problem which had placed his city in the headlines.

At the same time, I felt that there was nothing which bothered him more; but perhaps he did not really know what he thought about it; or thought too many things at once. His campus risked being very different twenty years from now. Its special function would be gone—and so would his position, arrived at with such pain. The new day a-coming was not for him. I don't think this fact made him bitter but I think it frightened him and made him sad; for the future is like heaven—everyone exalts it but no one wants to go there now. And I imagine that he shared the attitude, which I was to encounter so often later, toward the children who were helping to bring this future about: admiration before the general spectacle and a skepticism before the individual case.

That evening I went to visit G., one of the "integrated" children, a boy of about fifteen. I had already heard something of his first day in school, the peculiar problems his presence caused, and his own extraordinary bearing.

He seemed extraordinary at first mainly by his silence. He was tall for his age and, typically, seemed to be constructed mainly of sharp angles, such as elbows and knees. Dark gingerbread sort of coloring, with ordinary hair, and a face disquietingly impassive, save for his very dark, very large eyes. I got the impression, each time that he raised them, not so much that they spoke but that they registered volumes; each time he dropped them it was as though he had retired into the library.

We sat in the living room, his mother, younger brother and sister, and I, while G. sat on the sofa, doing his homework. The father was at work and the older sister had not yet come home. The boy had looked up once, as I came in, to say, "Good evening, sir," and then left all the rest to his mother.

Mrs. R. was a very strong-willed woman, handsome, quiet-looking, dressed in black. Nothing, she told me, beyond name-calling, had marked G.'s first day at school; but on the second day she received the last of several threatening phone calls. She was told that if she didn't want her son "cut to ribbons" she had better keep him at home. She heeded this warning to the extent of calling the chief of police.

"He told me to go on and send him. He said he'd be there when the cutting started. So I sent him." Even more remarkably, perhaps, G. went.

No one cut him, in fact no one touched him. The students formed a wall between G. and the entrances, saying only enough, apparently, to make their intention clearly understood, watching him, and keeping him outside. (I asked him, "What did you feel when they blocked your way?" G. looked up at me, very briefly, with no expression on his face, and told me, "Nothing, sir.") At last the principal appeared and took him by the hand and they entered the school, while the children shouted behind them, "Nigger-lover!"

G. was alone all day at school.

"But I thought you already knew some of the kids there," I said. I had been told that he had friends among the white students because of their previous competition in a Soapbox Derby.

"Well, none of them are in his classes," his mother told me—a shade 15
too quickly, as though she did not want to dwell on the idea of G.'s daily isolation.

"We don't have the same schedule," G. said. It was as though he were coming to his mother's rescue. Then, unwillingly, with a kind of interior shrug, "Some of the guys had lunch with me but then the other kids called them names." He went back to his homework.

I began to realize that there were not only a great many things G. would not tell me, there was much that he would never tell his mother.

"But nobody bothers you, anyway?'

"No," he said. "They just—call names. I don't let it bother me."

Nevertheless, the principal frequently escorts him through the halls. 20
One day, when G. was alone, a boy tripped him and knocked him down and G. reported this to the principal. The white boy denied it but a few days later, while G. and the principal were together, he came over and said, "I'm sorry I tripped you; I won't do it again," and they shook hands. But it doesn't seem that this boy has as yet developed into a friend. And it is clear that G. will not allow himself to expect this.

I asked Mrs. R. what had prompted her to have her son reassigned to a previously all-white high school. She sighed, paused; then, sharply, "Well, it's not because I'm so anxious to have him around white people." Then she laughed. "I really don't know how I'd feel if I was to carry a white baby around who was calling me Grandma." G. laughed, too, for the first time. "White people say," the mother went on, "that that's all a Negro wants. I don't think they believe that themselves."

Then we switched from the mysterious question of what white folks believe to the relatively solid ground of what she, herself, knows and fears.

"You see that boy? Well, he's always been a straight-A student. He didn't hardly have to work at it. You see the way he's so quiet now on the sofa, with his books? Well, when he was going to——High School, he didn't have no homework or if he did, he could get it done in five minutes. Then, there he was, out in the streets, getting into mischief, and all he did all day in school was just keep clowning to make the

other boys laugh. He wasn't learning nothing and didn't nobody care
if he *never* learned nothing and I could just see what was going to happen to him if he kept on like that."

The boy was very quiet.

"What were you learning in————High?" I asked him. 25

"Nothing!" he exploded, with a very un-boyish laugh. I asked him
to tell me about it.

"Well, the teacher comes in," he said, "and she gives you something to read and she goes out. She leaves some other student in charge
. . . ." ("You can just imagine how much reading gets done," Mrs.
R. interposed.) "At the end of the period," G. continued, "she comes
back and tells you something to read for the next day."

So, having nothing else to do, G. began amusing his classmates and
his mother began to be afraid. G. is just about at the age when boys
begin dropping out of school. Perhaps they get a girl into trouble; she
also drops out; the boy gets work for a time or gets into trouble for a
long time. I was told that forty-five girls had left school for the mater-
nity ward the year before. A week or ten days before I arrived in the
city eighteen boys from G.'s former high school had been sentenced to
the chain gang.

"My boy's a good boy," said Mrs. R., "and I wanted to see him
have a chance."

"Don't the teachers care about the students?" I asked. This brought 30
forth more laughter. How could they care? How much could they do
if they *did* care? There were too many children, from shaky homes and
worn-out parents, in aging, inadequate plants. They could be considered, most of them, as already doomed. Besides, the teachers' jobs
were safe. They were responsible only to the principal, an appointed
official, whose judgment, apparently, was never questioned by his (white)
superiors or confreres.

The principal of G.'s former high school was about seventy-five
when he was finally retired and his idea of discipline was to have two
boys beat each other—"under his supervision"—with leather belts. This
once happened with G., with no other results than that his parents gave
the principal a tongue-lashing. It happened with two boys of G.'s acquaintance with the result that, after school, one boy beat the other so
badly that he had to be sent to the hospital. The teachers have themselves arrived at a dead end, for in a segregated school system they
cannot rise any higher, and the students are aware of this. Both students
and teachers soon cease to struggle.

"If a boy can wash a blackboard," a teacher was heard to say, "I'll
promote him."

I asked Mrs. R. how other Negroes felt about her having had G.
reassigned.

"Well, a lot of them didn't like it," she said—though I gathered that
they did not say so to her. As school time approached, more and more

people asked her, "Are you going to send him?" "Well," she told them, "the man says the door is open and I feel like, yes, I'm going to go on and send him."

Out of a population of some fifty thousand Negroes, there had been only forty-five applications. People had said that they would send their children, had talked about it, had made plans; but, as the time drew near, when the application blanks were actually in their hands, they said, "I don't believe I'll sign this right now. I'll sign it later." Or, "I been thinking about this. I don't believe I'll send him right now."

"Why?" I asked. But to this she couldn't, or wouldn't, give me any answer. 35

I asked if there had been any reprisals taken against herself or her husband, if she was worried while G. was at school all day. She said that, no, there had been no reprisals, though some white people, under the pretext of giving her good advice, had expressed disapproval of her action. But she herself doesn't have a job and so doesn't risk losing one. Nor, she told me, had anyone said anything to her husband, who, however, by her own proud suggestion, is extremely closemouthed. And it developed later that he was not working at his regular trade but at something else.

As to whether she was worried, "No," she told me; in much the same way that G., when asked about the blockade, had said, "Nothing, sir." In her case it was easier to see what she meant: she hoped for the best and would not allow herself, in the meantime, to lose her head. "I don't feel like nothing's going to happen," she said, soberly. "I *hope* not. But I know if anybody tries to harm me or any of my children, I'm going to strike back with all my strength. I'm going to strike them in God's name."

G., in the meantime, on the sofa with his books, was preparing himself for the next school day. His face was as impassive as ever and I found myself wondering—again—how he managed to face what must surely have been the worst moment of his day—the morning, when he opened his eyes and realized that it was all to be gone through again. Insults, and incipient violence, teachers, and—exams.

"One among so many," his mother said, "that's kind of rough."

"Do you think you'll make it?" I asked him. "Would you rather go 40 back to———High?"

"No," he said, "I'll make it. I ain't going back."

"He ain't thinking about going back," said his mother—proudly and sadly. I began to suspect that the boy managed to support the extreme tension of his situation by means of a nearly fanatical concentration on his schoolwork; by holding in the center of his mind the issue on which, when the deal went down, others would be *forced* to judge him. Pride and silence were his weapons. Pride comes naturally, and soon, to a Negro, but even his mother, I felt, was worried about G.'s silence, though she was too wise to break it. For what was all this doing to him really?

"It's hard enough," the boy said later, still in control but with flashing eyes, "to keep quiet and keep walking when they call you nigger. But if anybody ever spits on me, I *know* I'll have to fight."

His mother laughs, laughs to ease them both, then looks at me and says, "I wonder sometimes what makes white folks so mean."

This is a recurring question among Negroes, even among the most 45 "liberated"—which epithet is meant, of course, to describe the writer. The next day, with this question (more elegantly phrased) still beating in my mind, I visited the principal of G.'s new high school. But he didn't look "mean" and he wasn't "mean": he was a thin, young man of about my age, bewildered and in trouble. I asked him how things were working out, what he thought about it, what he thought would happen—in the long run, or the short.

"Well, I've got a job to do," he told me, "and I'm going to do it." He said that there hadn't been any trouble and that he didn't expect any. "Many students, after all, never see G. at all." None of the children have harmed him and the teachers are, apparently, carrying out their rather tall orders, which are to be kind to G. and, at the same time, to treat him like any other student.

I asked him to describe to me the incident, on the second day of school, when G.'s entrance had been blocked by the students. He told me that it was nothing at all—"It was a gesture more than anything else." He had simply walked out and spoken to the students and brought G. inside. "I've seen them do the same thing to other kids when they were kidding," he said. I imagine that he would like to be able to place this incident in the same cheerful if rowdy category, despite the shouts (which he does not mention) of "nigger-lover!"

Which epithet does not, in any case, describe him at all.

"Why," I asked, "is G. the only Negro student here?" According to this city's pupil-assignment plan, a plan designed to allow the least possible integration over the longest period of time, G. was the only Negro student who qualified.

"And, anyway," he said, "I don't think it's right for colored chil- 50 dren to come to white schools just *because* they're white."

"Well," I began, "even if you don't like it . . ."

"Oh," he said quickly, raising his head and looking at me sideways, "I never said I didn't like it."

And then he explained to me, with difficulty, that it was simply contrary to everything he'd ever seen or believed. He'd never dreamed of a mingling of the races; had never lived that way himself and didn't suppose that he ever would; in the same way, he added, perhaps a trifle defensively, that he only associated with a certain stratum of white people. But, "I've never seen a colored person toward whom I had any hatred or ill-will."

His eyes searched mine as he said this and I knew that he was wondering if I believed him.

I certainly did believe him; he impressed me as being a very gentle   55
and honorable man. But I could not avoid wondering if he had ever really *looked* at a Negro and wondered about the life, the aspirations, the universal humanity hidden behind the dark skin. As I wondered, when he told me that race relations in his city were "excellent" and had not been strained by recent developments, how on earth he managed to hold on to this delusion.

I later got back to my interrupted question, which I phrased more tactfully.

"Even though it's very difficult for all concerned—this situation— doesn't it occur to you that the reason colored children wish to come to white schools isn't because they want to be with white people but simply because they want a better education?"

"Oh, I don't know," he replied, "it seems to me that colored schools are just as good as white schools." I wanted to ask him on what evidence he had arrived at this conclusion and also how they could possibly be "as good" in view of the kind of life they came out of, and perpetuated, and the dim prospects faced by all but the most exceptional or ruthless Negro students. But I only suggested that G. and his family, who certainly should have known, so thoroughly disagreed with him that they had been willing to risk G.'s present well-being and his future psychological and mental health in order to bring about a change in his environment. Nor did I mention the lack of enthusiasm evinced by G.'s mother when musing on the prospect of a fair grandchild. There seemed no point in making this man any more a victim of his heritage than he so gallantly was already.

"Still," I said at last, after a rather painful pause, "I should think that the trouble in this situation is that it's very hard for *you* to face a child and treat him unjustly because of something for which he is no more responsible than—than *you* are."

The eyes came to life then, or a veil fell, and I found myself staring   60
at a man in anguish. The eyes were full of pain and bewilderment and he nodded his head. This was the impossibility which he faced every day. And I imagined that his tribe would increase, in sudden leaps and bounds was already increasing.

For segregation has worked brilliantly in the South, and, in fact, in the nation, to this extent: it has allowed white people, with scarcely any pangs of conscience whatever, to *create,* in every generation, only the Negro they wished to see. As the walls come down they will be forced to take another, harder look at the shiftless and the menial and will be forced into a wonder concerning them which cannot fail to be agonizing. It is not an easy thing to be forced to reexamine a way of life and to speculate, in a personal way, on the general injustice.

"What do you think," I asked him, "will happen? What do you think the future holds?"

He gave a strained laugh and said he didn't know. "I don't want to think about it." Then, "I'm a religious man," he said, "and I believe the Creator will always help us find a way to solve our problems. If a man loses that, he's lost everything he had." I agreed, struck by the look in his eyes.

"You're from the North?" he asked me, abruptly.

"Yes," I said.

"Well," he said, "you've got your troubles too."

"Ah, yes, we certainly do," I admitted and shook hands and left him. I did not say what I was thinking, that our troubles were the same trouble and that, unless we were very swift and honest, what is happening in the South today will be happening in the North tomorrow.

65

Lines of Inquiry
"A Fly in Buttermilk"

The spotlight in this piece focuses clearly on G, yet Baldwin's evening with G is not the only incident that he tells about in this piece. Why do you suppose that he precedes G's story by telling about his conversations with an older Negro friend in Washington and a southern Negro educator? Why do you suppose that he follows G's story by giving such a detailed description of his meeting with the principal of G's new school? Imagine how you might have reacted to G's situation if Baldwin had confined himself only to telling about his evening with G and G's mother.

This essay might well be understood as having several important themes: the inexplicable cruelty of racism ("what makes white folks so mean?"); the heroism of lonely black children, such as G, who challenge segregation in the schools; the mixed attitudes of both blacks and whites towards segregation, as well as towards the prospect of integration; the tensions between Northerners and Southerners precipitated by governmental enforcement of integration. Why do you suppose that Baldwin tries to address all of these issues in this piece? How are they interrelated? Which of these themes do you think is Baldwin's primary concern?

Just as this piece deals with the experience of G as the only black student in an all white high school, so "Stranger in the Village" deals with the experience of Baldwin as the only black in an all white community. Have you ever experienced such extreme racial isolation, or observed others experiencing it? Have you ever experienced, or observed others experiencing, extreme isolation on any other account—cultural, religious, or sexual? What similarities, what differences, do you think are at work in these varied forms of extreme human isolation?

If Black English Isn't a Language, Then Tell Me, What Is?

The argument concerning the use, or the status, or the reality, of black English is rooted in American history and has absolutely nothing to do with the question the argument supposes itself to be posing. The argument has nothing to do with language itself but with the role of language. Language, incontestably, reveals the speaker. Language, also, far more dubiously, is meant to define the other—and, in this case, the other is refusing to be defined by a language that has never been able to recognize him.

People evolve a language in order to describe and thus control their circumstances or in order not to be submerged by a situation that they cannot articulate. (And if they cannot articulate it, they are submerged.) A Frenchman living in Paris speaks a subtly and crucially different language from that of the man living in Marseilles; neither sounds very much like a man living in Quebec; and they would all have great difficulty in apprehending what the man from Guadeloupe, or Martinique, is saying, to say nothing of the man from Senegal—although the "common" language of all these areas is French. But each has paid, and is paying, a different price for this "common" language, in which, as it turns out, they are not saying, and cannot be saying, the same things: They each have very different realities to articulate, or control.

What joins all languages, and all men, is the necessity to confront life, in order, not inconceivably, to outwit death: The price for this is the acceptance, and achievement, of one's temporal identity. So that, for example, though it is not taught in the schools (and this has the potential of becoming a political issue) the south of France still clings to its ancient and musical Provençal, which resists being described as a "dialect." And much of the tension in the Basque countries, and in Wales, is due to the Basque and Welsh determination not to allow their languages to be destroyed. This determination also feeds the flames in Ireland for among the many indignities the Irish have been forced to undergo at English hands is the English contempt for their language.

It goes without saying, then, that language is also a political instrument, means, and proof of power. It is the most vivid and crucial key to identity: It reveals the private identity, and connects one with, or divorces one from, the larger, public, or communal identity. There have been, and are, times and places, when to speak a certain language could be dangerous, even fatal. Or, one may speak the same language, but in such a way that one's antecedents are revealed, or (one hopes) hidden. This is true in France, and is absolutely true in England: The range (and reign) of accents on that damp little island make England coherent for the English and totally incomprehensible for everyone else. To open your mouth in England is (if I may use black English) to "put your business in the street." You have confessed your parents, your youth, your school, your salary, your self-esteem, and, alas, your future.

Now, I do not know what white Americans would sound like if   5
there had never been any black people in the United States, but they would not sound the way they sound. *Jazz,* for example, is a very specific sexual term, as in *jazz me, baby,* but white people purified it into the Jazz Age. *Sock it to me,* which means, roughly, the same thing, has been adopted by Nathaniel Hawthorne's descendants with no qualms or hesitations at all, along with *let it all hang out* and *right on! Beat to his socks,* which was once the black's most total and despairing image of poverty, was transformed into a thing called the Beat Generation, which phenomenon was, largely, composed of *uptight,* middle-class white people, imitating poverty, trying to *get down,* to get *with it,* doing their *thing,* doing their despairing best to be *funky,* which we, the blacks, never dreamed of doing—we were funky, baby, like *funk* was going out of style.

Now, no one can eat his cake, and have it, too, and it is late in the day to attempt to penalize black people for having created a language that permits the nation its only glimpse of reality, a language without which the nation would be even more *whipped* than it is.

I say that the present skirmish is rooted in American history, and it is. Black English is the creation of the black diaspora. Blacks came to the United States chained to each other, but from different tribes. Neither could speak the other's language. If two black people, at that bitter hour of the world's history, had been able to speak to each other, the institution of chattel slavery could never have lasted as long as it did. Subsequently, the slave was given, under the eye, and the gun, of his master, Congo Square, and the Bible—or, in other words, and under those conditions, the slave began the formation of the black church, and it is within this unprecedented tabernacle that black English began to be formed. This was not, merely, as in the European example, the adoption of a foreign tongue, but an alchemy that transformed ancient elements into a new language: *A language comes into existence by means of brutal necessity, and the rules of the language are dictated by what the language must convey.*

There was a moment, in time, and in this place, when my brother, or my mother, or my father, or my sister, had to convey to me, for example, the danger in which I was standing from the white man standing just behind me, and to convey this with a speed and in a language, that the white man could not possibly understand, and that, indeed, he cannot understand, until today. He cannot afford to understand it. This understanding would reveal to him too much about himself and smash that mirror before which he has been frozen for so long.

Now, if this passion, this skill, this (to quote Toni Morrison) "sheer intelligence," this incredible music, the mighty achievement of having brought a people utterly unknown to, or despised by "history"—to have brought this people to their present, troubled, troubling, and unassailable and unanswerable place—if this absolutely unprecedented journey does not indicate that black English is a language, I am curious to know what definition of languages is to be trusted.

A people at the center of the western world, and in the midst of so hostile a population, has not endured and transcended by means of what is patronizingly called a "dialect." We, the blacks, are in trouble, certainly, but we are not inarticulate because we are not compelled to defend a morality that we know to be a lie.

The brutal truth is that the bulk of the white people in America never had any interest in educating black people, except as this could serve white purposes. It is not the black child's language that is despised. It is his experience. A child cannot be taught by anyone who despises him, and a child cannot afford to be fooled. A child cannot be taught by anyone whose demand, essentially, is that the child repudiate his experience, and all that gives him sustenance, and enter a limbo in which he will no longer be black, and in which he knows that he can never become white. Black people have lost too many black children that way.

And, after all, finally, in a country with standards so untrustworthy, a country that makes heroes of so many criminal mediocrities, a country unable to face why so many of the nonwhite are in prison, or on the needle, or standing, futureless, in the streets—it may very well be that both the child, and his elder, have concluded that they have nothing whatever to learn from the people of a country that has managed to learn so little.

10

Lines of Inquiry
"If Black English Isn't a Language, Then Tell Me, What Is?"

As his title indicates, Baldwin's purpose in this piece is to argue that black English is a language rather than a dialect. Given this intention, why does he devote his second, third, and fourth paragraphs to discussing languages other than black English? What, in turn, is the point of his showing in paragraph 5 that numerous American words and phrases were originated by black people? What is the point of his concluding comments on the education of black children? In other words, what is the relevance of the material he discusses to the point he is trying to make?

Having considered the relevance of his discussion, you might explore the nature of his assumptions. For example, what assumptions about the nature of language does Baldwin bring to his argument that black English is a language rather than a dialect? Why, for example, does he claim that the issue as a whole is "rooted in American history?" What does he mean by his assertion in the ninth paragraph that "if this absolutely unprecedented journey does not indicate that black English is a language, I am curious to know what definition of language is to be trusted"?

Why do you suppose that Baldwin is so angered over the question of whether black English is referred to as a language or a dialect? What grounds do you think he has for considering language in such a charged social and political context? How do you suppose he might react to the aspects of pronunciation and usage that Wolfe discusses in "Honks and Wonks"? Do you think he would consider honk-talk and wonk-talk to be dialects or languages?

Bruno Bettelheim
1903—

While we are scarcely able to believe any longer that life has a specific goal, but must be satisfied with striving in what seems the right direction, still we must continue to struggle to integrate our personality and master difficult experiences.

A survivor of Nazi concentration camps, an expert in the behavior of emotionally disturbed children, psychoanalyst Bruno Bettelheim has been concerned from the beginning of his long career with the traumatizing effects of what he here calls, in an essay entitled "The Ultimate Limit," the "extreme situations" of modern life. Like his teacher Sigmund Freud, Bettelheim believes that our task as individuals is to "integrate" our personality and achieve "autonomy" in response to life's crucial experiences. But in his view the horrors of the twentieth century—the two world wars, the atomic bomb, and especially the near extermination of European Jews—have made this task even more difficult, breaking down our defenses against the "death anxiety." Over the last forty years, in a distinguished series of books, articles, and essays, Bettelheim has attempted to show us that integration and mastery are still possible even in the absence of "specific goals," but only if we face our traumas rather than deny them, and only if we are willing to accept that some questions are finally not answerable.

Bettelheim was born in Vienna, where he studied under Freud, and before the war had begun working with autistic children. But in 1938, the year he received his PhD in psychology from the University of Vienna, he was arrested by the Nazis and imprisoned in concentration camps at Dachau and Buchenwald, where, along with other prisoners, he was beaten and tortured. He was released a year later, emigrated to the United States, and began in earnest his career as a child psychologist. In 1944 he became professor of psychology at the University of Chicago and director of the Orthogenic School for autistic children, positions he held until his retirement in 1973. Over the years, he has written more than a dozen books, most of them concerning the education and upbringing of children, including *Love Is Not Enough, Truants from Life, The Empty Fortress,* and *A Home for the Heart*—all based on his work with emotionally disturbed children at the Orthogenic School—*The Children of the Dream,* a study of how children are raised on kibbutzes in Israel, and *The Uses of Enchantment,* a study of the psychological value of fairy tales that won him the National Book Award.

But as Bettelheim himself has acknowledged, the central preoccupation of his career, and his underlying motivation as a writer, has been an effort to work out the implications of his experience in the Nazi concentration camps. His first important published article, written immediately after his escape from Germany, was "Individual and Mass Behavior in Extreme Situations," a detailed and lengthy exploration, based on personal experience, of how prisoners in the concentration camps succeeded or failed in maintaining their identity in the face of torture and deprivation, living with "an existential predicament which does not permit of any solution." Though rejected at first by a number of scholarly journals—so resistant was the American public to believing that the camps even existed—the essay was finally published and became extremely influential. "I was so full of the experience that it would not be contained," Bettelheim said. He wanted to "bear witness" to the atrocity of the camps, making it possible for others to "grasp" what happened. But he also wrote the essay for his own benefit, out of a need "to comprehend better what had happened to me while in the camps, so I could gain intellectual mastery over the experience." The rigidly objective style of the essay, he realized even then, its careful abstractions and measured sequence of observations, were part of his "intellectual defense against being overwhelmed" by the memories of "the terrible things done by average people to average persons."

In subsequent essays, the most important of which are collected in *Surviving,* and in a book-length study of the Holocaust, *The Informed Heart: Autonomy in a Mass Age,* Bettelheim continued to develop his argument—that to deal with the death camps and what they represent about human nature we must first admit how horrible they were, not deny their evil. Denial, he says, is "the earliest, most primitive, most inappropriate and ineffective of all psychological defenses used by man" because "it does not permit taking appropriate actions which might safeguard against the real dangers." Only if we face the reality of extreme situations can we then begin the slow, careful, step-by-step process of "adjusting" our personality in "accordance" with our new awareness. There are no simple answers. The task never ends. Somehow, not deluding ourselves about the "death principle" inside of us, we must labor to establish the priority of the "life principle" that also exists in the psyche, saying in effect, "I am trying to make the best of my life, limited as it must be by my shortcomings." As for questions about the ultimate meaning of life, they are "unanswerable," and we must simply do the best we can without a knowable truth.

This model of trauma and reintegration, extremity and response, underlies all of Bettelheim's theories. As his research and writing developed, he says, he began to realize that there was a "parallel" between the personality disintegration caused by the Holocaust and "psychotic collapses" caused by a variety of psychological problems. He began to realize, for example, that the behavior of autistic children can be seen as a struggle for integration in response to extreme situations, though those situations are more often imagined than real. The therapies and routines he developed at the Orthogenic School were designed to give disturbed children exactly the kind of freedom and dignity that prisoners had been denied in the concentration camps. Indeed, Bettelheim came to believe that technology, affluence, and the complexity of modern life are in themselves kinds of extremities that healthy personalities must somehow assimilate—that in a sense all of us are forced to integrate our personalities in response to the traumas of contemporary existence.

With this view of human development as his framework, Bettelheim has gone on to write about a variety of topics. He has argued that elementary and secondary education should teach children how to postpone pleasure for the sake of greater future gains, instilling in them a sense of "the reality principle"; that parents should give children as much freedom as is appropriate for their age level, but also establish limits and demand moral behavior; that urban planners must create environments ensuring privacy without isolating the individual; that the value of art is not its unleashing of the unconscious but the examples it gives of a "disciplined working-over of unconscious material"; that the value of fairy tales is the safe outlet they provide for the violence instinctive in children. All of his writing, Bettelheim says, deals "with what can be done in society, and in persons' life experiences, to promote the achievement of self-respect, integration, and the ability to form meaningful and lasting relations."

Integration characterizes Bettelheim's prose style as well. This passage from "The Ultimate Limit," the full context for our opening epigraph, exemplifies his effort to integrate ideas in balanced clauses and phrases, carefully assimilating a complex set of issues:

> While we are scarcely able to believe any longer that life has a specific goal, but must be satisfied with striving in what seems the right direction, still we must continue to struggle to integrate our personality and master difficult experiences. We can never hope to achieve these elusive goals once and for all. This is true in general, but it is much more pressingly so for the crucial experiences of our lives, especially an extreme experience. Even more unsolvable are extreme experiences that also pose the central problem of our times: the potentially destructive aspects of progress.

In this sequence of assertions, each statement qualified and related to the next, we glimpse something of Bettelheim's desire to "objectify" his experience through academic prose. We see here someone who, as he puts it, has tried to "conform in his writing to the requirements of an acceptable objectivity—the consequences of having lived his life in academe, and of having in large part embraced its values." But at the same time Bettelheim's personal engagement shows through in his deep concern for human values. "The underlying motif" of his writing is "to give words to one man's struggle against the destructive tendency in society and in individual man—which very much includes himself." So, Bettelheim's writing reflects "a very personal effort to extract meaning from life."

Joey: A "Mechanical Boy"

Joey, when we began to work with him, was a mechanical boy. He functioned as if by remote control, run by machines of his own powerfully creative fantasy. Not only did he himself believe that he was a machine but, more remarkably, he created this impression in others. Even while he performed actions that are intrinsically human, they never appeared to be other than machine-started and executed. On the other hand, when the machine was not working we had to concentrate on recollecting his presence, for he seemed not to exist. A human body that functions as if it were a machine and a machine that duplicates human functions are equally fascinating and frightening. Perhaps they are so uncanny because they remind us that the human body can operate without a human spirit, that body can exist without soul. And Joey was a child who had been robbed of his humanity.

Not every child who possesses a fantasy world is possessed by it. Normal children may retreat into realms of imaginary glory or magic powers, but they are easily recalled from these excursions. Disturbed children are not always able to make the return trip; they remain withdrawn, prisoners of the inner world of delusion and fantasy. In many ways Joey presented a classic example of this state of infantile autism.

At the Sonia Shankman Orthogenic School of the University of Chicago it is our function to provide a therapeutic environment in which such children may start life over again. I have previously described in this magazine the rehabilitation of another of our patients ["Schizophrenic Art: A Case Study"; SCIENTIFIC AMERICAN, April, 1952]. This time I shall concentrate upon the illness, rather than the treatment. In any age, when the individual has escaped into a delusional world, he has usually fashioned it from bits and pieces of the world at hand. Joey, in his time and world, chose the machine and froze himself in its image. His story has a general relevance to the understanding of emotional development in a machine age.

Joey's delusion is not uncommon among schizophrenic children today. He wanted to be rid of his unbearable humanity, to become completely automatic. He so nearly succeeded in attaining this goal that he could almost convince others, as well as himself, of his mechanical character. The descriptions of autistic children in the literature take for their point of departure and comparison the normal or abnormal human being. To do justice to Joey I would have to compare him simultaneously to a most inept infant and a highly complex piece of machinery. Often we had to force ourselves by a conscious act of will to realize that Joey was a child. Again and again his acting-out of his delusions froze our own ability to respond as human beings.

During Joey's first weeks with us we would watch absorbedly as   5 this at once fragile-looking and imperious nine-year-old went about his mechanical existence. Entering the dining room, for example, he would string an imaginery wire from his "energy source"—an imaginary electric outlet—to the table. There he "insulated" himself with paper napkins and finally plugged himself in. Only then could Joey eat, for he firmly believed that the "current" ran his ingestive apparatus. So skillful was the pantomime that one had to look twice to be sure there was neither wire nor outlet nor plug. Children and members of our staff spontaneously avoided stepping on the "wires" for fear of interrupting what seemed the source of his very life.

For long periods of time, when his "machinery" was idle, he would sit so quietly that he would disappear from the focus of most conscientious observation. Yet in the next moment he might be "working" and the center of our captivated attention. Many times a day he would turn himself on and shift noisily through a sequence of higher and higher gears until he "exploded," screaming "Crash, crash!" and hurling items from his ever present apparatus—radio tubes, light bulbs, even motors or, lacking these, any handy breakable object. (Joey had an astonishing knack for snatching bulbs and tubes unobserved.) As soon as the object thrown had shattered, he would cease his screaming and wild jumping and retire to mute, motionless nonexistence.

Our maids, inured to difficult children, were exceptionally attentive to Joey; they were apparently moved by his extreme infantile fragility, so strangely coupled with megalomaniacal superiority. Occasionally some of the apparatus he fixed to his bed to "live him" during his sleep would fall down in disarray. This machinery he contrived from masking tape, cardboard, wire and other paraphernalia. Usually the maids would pick up such things and leave them on a table for the children to find, or disregard them entirely. But Joey's machine they carefully restored: "Joey must have the carburetor so he can breathe." Similarly they were on the alert to pick up and preserve the motors that ran him during the day and the exhaust pipes through which he exhaled.

How had Joey become a human machine? From intensive interviews with his parents we learned that the process had begun even before birth. Schizophrenia often results from parental rejection, sometimes combined ambivalently with love. Joey, on the other hand, had been completely ignored.

"I never knew I was pregnant," his mother said, meaning that she had already excluded Joey from her consciousness. His birth, she said, "did not make any difference." Joey's father, a rootless draftee in the wartime civilian army, was equally unready for parenthood. So, of course, are many young couples. Fortunately most such parents lose their indifference upon the baby's birth. But not Joey's parents. "I did not want to see or nurse him," his mother declared. "I had no feeling of actual dislike—I simply didn't want to take care of him." For the first three months of his life Joey "cried most of the time." A colicky baby, he was kept on a rigid four-hour feeding schedule, was not touched unless necessary and was never cuddled or played with. The mother, preoccupied with herself, usually left Joey alone in the crib or playpen during the day. The father discharged his frustration by punishing Joey when the child cried at night.

Soon the father left for overseas duty, and the mother took Joey, now a year and a half old, to live with her at her parents' home. On his arrival the grandparents noticed that ominous changes had occurred in the child. Strong and healthy at birth, he had become frail and irritable; a responsive baby, he had become remote and inaccessible. When he began to master speech, he talked only to himself. At an early date he became preoccupied with machinery, including an old electric fan which he could take apart and put together again with surprising deftness.

Joey's mother impressed us with a fey quality that expressed her insecurity, her detachment from the world and her low physical vitality. We were struck especially by her total indifference as she talked about Joey. This seemed much more remarkable than the actual mistakes she made in handling him. Certainly he was left to cry for hours when hungry, because she fed him on a rigid schedule; he was toilet-trained with great rigidity so that he would give no trouble. These things happen to many children. But Joey's existence never registered with his mother. In her recollections he was fused at one moment with one event or person; at another, with something or somebody else. When she told us about his birth and infancy, it was as if she were talking about some vague acquaintance, and soon her thoughts would wander off to another person or to herself.

When Joey was not yet four, his nursery school suggested that he enter a special school for disturbed children. At the new school his autism was immediately recognized. During his three years there he experienced a slow improvement. Unfortunately a subsequent two years in a parochial school destroyed this progress. He began to develop compulsive defenses, which he called his "preventions." He could not drink, for example, except through elaborate piping systems built of straws. Liquids had to be "pumped" into him, in his fantasy, or he could not suck. Eventually his behavior became so upsetting that he could not be kept in the parochial school. At home things did not improve. Three months before entering the Orthogenic School he made a serious attempt at suicide.

To us Joey's pathological behavior seemed the external expression of an overwhelming effort to remain almost nonexistent as a person.

10

For weeks Joey's only reply when addressed was "Bam." Unless he thus neutralized whatever we said, there would be an explosion, for Joey plainly wished to close off every form of contact not mediated by machinery. Even when he was bathed he rocked back and forth with mute, engine-like regularity, flooding the bathroom. If he stopped rocking, he did this like a machine too; suddenly he went completely rigid. Only once, after months of being lifted from his bath and carried to bed, did a small expression of puzzled pleasure appear on his face as he said very softly: "They even carry you to your bed here."

For a long time after he began to talk he would never refer to anyone by name, but only as "that person" or "the little person" or "the big person." He was unable to designate by its true name anything to which he attached feelings. Nor could he name his anxieties except through neologisms or word contaminations. For a long time he spoke about "master paintings" and "a master painting room" (i.e., masturbating and masturbating room). One of his machines, the "criticizer," prevented him from "saying words which have unpleasant feelings." Yet he gave personal names to the tubes and motors in his collection of machinery. Moreover, these dead things had feelings; the tubes bled when hurt and sometimes got sick. He consistently maintained this reversal between animate and inanimate objects.

In Joey's machine world everything, on pain of instant destruction, obeyed inhibitory laws much more stringent than those of physics. When we came to know him better, it was plain that in his moments of silent withdrawal, with his machine switched off, Joey was absorbed in pondering the compulsive laws of his private universe. His preoccupation with machinery made it difficult to establish even practical contacts with him. If he wanted to do something with a counselor, such as play with a toy that had caught his vague attention, he could not do so: "I'd like this very much, but first I have to turn off the machine." But by the time he had fulfilled all the requirements of his preventions, he had lost interest. When a toy was offered to him, he could not touch it because his motors and his tubes did not leave him a hand free. Even certain colors were dangerous and had to be strictly avoided in toys and clothing, because "some colors turn off the current, and I can't touch them because I can't live without the current."

Joey was convinced that machines were better than people. Once when he bumped into one of the pipes on our jungle gym he kicked it so violently that his teacher had to restrain him to keep him from injuring himself. When she explained that the pipe was much harder than his foot, Joey replied: "That proves it. Machines are better than the body. They don't break; they're much harder and stronger." If he lost or forgot something, it merely proved that his brain ought to be thrown away and replaced by machinery. If he spilled something, his arm should be broken and twisted off because it did not work properly. When his

15

head or arm failed to work as it should, he tried to punish it by hitting it. Even Joey's feelings were mechanical. Much later in his therapy, when he had formed a timid attachment to another child and had been rebuffed, Joey cried: "He broke my feelings."

Gradually, we began to understand what had seemed to be contradictory in Joey's behavior—why he held on to the motors and tubes, then suddenly destroyed them in a fury, then set out immediately and urgently to equip himself with new and larger tubes. Joey had created these machines to run his body and mind because it was too painful to be human. But again and again he became dissatisfied with their failure to meet his need and rebellious at the way they frustrated his will. In a recurrent frenzy he "exploded" his light bulbs and tubes, and for a moment became a human being—for one crowning instant he came alive. But as soon as he had asserted his dominance through the self-created explosion, he felt his life ebbing away. To keep on existing he had immediately to restore his machines and replenish the electricity that supplied his life energy.

What deep-seated fears and needs underlay Joey's delusional system? We were long in finding out, for Joey's preventions effectively concealed the secret of his autistic behavior. In the meantime we dealt with his peripheral problems one by one.

During his first year with us Joey's most trying problem was toilet behavior. This surprised us, for Joey's personality was not "anal" in the Freudian sense; his original personality damage had antedated the period of his toilet-training. Rigid and early toilet-training, however, had certainly contributed to his anxieties. It was our effort to help Joey with this problem that led to his first recognition of us as human beings.

Going to the toilet, like everything else in Joey's life, was surrounded by elaborate preventions. We had to accompany him; he had to take off all his clothes; he could only squat, not sit, on the toilet seat; he had to touch the wall with one hand, in which he also clutched frantically the vacuum tubes that powered his elimination. He was terrified lest his whole body be sucked down.   20

To counteract this fear we gave him a metal wastebasket in lieu of a toilet. Eventually, when eliminating into the wastebasket, he no longer needed to take off all his clothes, nor to hold on to the wall. He still needed the tubes and motors which, he believed, moved his bowels for him. But here again the all-important machinery was itself a source of new terrors. In Joey's world the gadgets had to move their bowels, too. He was terribly concerned that they should, but since they were so much more powerful than men, he was also terrified that if his tubes moved their bowels, their feces would fill all of space and leave him no room to live. He was thus always caught in some fearful contradiction.

Our readiness to accept his toilet habits, which obviously entailed some hardship for his counselors, gave Joey the confidence to express

Elaborate sewage system in Joey's drawing of a house reflects his long preoccupation with excretion. His obsession with sewage reflected intense anxieties produced by his early toilet-training, which was not only rigid but also completely impersonal.

his obsessions in drawings. Drawing these fantasies was a first step toward letting us in, however distantly, to what concerned him most deeply. It was the first step in a yearlong process of externalizing his anal preoccupations. As a result he began seeing feces everywhere; the whole world became to him a mire of excrement. At the same time he began to eliminate wherever he happened to be. But with this release from his infantile imprisonment in compulsive rules, the toilet and the whole process of elimination became less dangerous. Thus far it had been beyond Joey's comprehension that anybody could possibly move his bowels without mechanical aid. Now Joey took a further step forward; defecation became the first physiological process he could perform without the help of vacuum tubes. It must not be thought that he was proud of this ability. Taking pride in an achievement presupposes that one accomplishes it of one's own free will. He still did not feel himself an autonomous person who could do things on his own. To Joey defecation still seemed enslaved to some incomprehensible but utterly binding cosmic law, perhaps the law his parents had imposed on him when he was being toilet-trained.

It was not simply that his parents had subjected him to rigid, early training. Many children are so trained. But in most cases the parents have a deep emotional investment in the child's performance. The child's response in turn makes training an occasion for interaction between them and for the building of genuine relationships. Joey's parents had no emotional investment in him. His obedience gave them no satisfaction and won him no affection or approval. As a toilet-trained child he saved his mother labor, just as household machines saved her labor. As a machine he was not loved for his performance, nor could he love himself.

So it had been with all other aspects of Joey's existence with his parents. Their reactions to his eating or noneating, sleeping or wakening, urinating or defecating, being dressed or undressed, washed or bathed did not flow from any unitary interest in him, deeply embedded in their personalities. By treating him mechanically his parents made him a machine. The various functions of life—even the parts of his body—bore no integrating relationship to one another or to any sense of self that was acknowledged and confirmed by others. Though he had acquired mastery over some functions, such as toilet-training and speech, he had acquired them separately and kept them isolated from each other. Toilet-training had thus not gained him a pleasant feeling of body mastery; speech had not led to communication of thought or feeling. On the contrary, each achievement only steered him away from self-mastery and integration. Toilet-training had enslaved him. Speech left him talking in neologisms that obstructed his and our ability to relate to each other. In Joey's development the normal process of growth had been made to run backward. Whatever he had learned put him not at the end of his infantile development toward integration but, on the contrary, farther behind than he was at its very beginning. Had we understood this sooner, his first years with us would have been less baffling.

It is unlikely that Joey's calamity could befall a child in any time   25
and culture but our own. He suffered no physical deprivation; he starved for human contact. Just to be taken care of is not enough for relating. It is a necessary but not a sufficient condition. At the extreme where utter scarcity reigns, the forming of relationships is certainly hampered. But our society of mechanized plenty often makes for equal difficulties in a child's learning to relate. Where parents can provide the simple creature-comforts for their children only at the cost of significant effort, it is likely that they will feel pleasure in being able to provide for them; it is this, the parents' pleasure, that gives children a sense of personal worth and sets the process of relating in motion. But if comfort is so readily available that the parents feel no particular pleasure in winning it for their children, then the children cannot develop the feeling of being worthwhile around the satisfaction of their basic needs. Of course parents and children can and do develop relationships around other situations. But matters are then no longer so simple and direct. The child must be on the receiving end of care and concern given with pleasure

Growing self-esteem is shown in this sequence of drawings. At left Joey portrays himself as an electrical "papoose," completely enclosed, suspended in empty space and operated by wireless signals. In center drawing his figure is much larger, though still under wireless control. At right he is able to picture the machine which controls him, and he has acquired hands with which he can manipulate his immediate environment.

and without the exaction of return if he is to feel loved and worthy of respect and consideration. This feeling gives him the ability to trust; he can entrust his well-being to persons to whom he is so important. Out of such trust the child learns to form close and stable relationships.

For Joey relationship with his parents was empty of pleasure in comfort giving as in all other situations. His was an extreme instance of a plight that sends many schizophrenic children to our clinics and hospitals. Many months passed before he could relate to us; his despair that anybody could like him made contact impossible.

When Joey could finally trust us enough to let himself become more infantile, he began to play at being a papoose. There was a corresponding change in his fantasies. He drew endless pictures of himself as an electrical papoose. Totally enclosed, suspended in empty space, he is run by unknown, unseen powers through wireless electricity.

As we eventually came to understand, the heart of Joey's delusional system was the artificial, mechanical womb he had created and into which he had locked himself. In his papoose fantasies lay the wish to be entirely reborn in a womb. His new experiences in the school suggested that life, after all, might be worth living. Now he was searching for a way to be reborn in a better way. Since machines were better than men, what was more natural than to try rebirth through them? This was the deeper meaning of his electrical papoose.

As Joey made progress, his pictures of himself became more dominant in his drawings. Though still machine-operated, he has grown in self-importance. *(See illustration above.)* Another great step forward is represented in the picture above. Now he has acquired hands that do

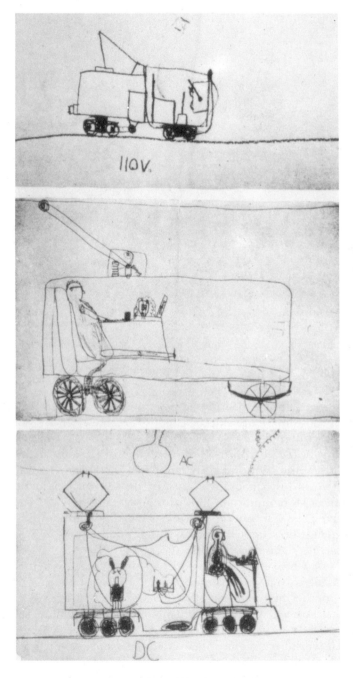

Growing autonomy is shown in Joey's drawings of the imaginary "Carr" (car) family. Top drawing shows a machine which can move but is unoccupied. Machine in center is occupied, but by a passive figure. In bottom drawing figure has gained control of machine.

Gentle landscape painted by Joey after his recovery symbolizes the human emotions he had regained. At 12, having learned to express his feelings, he was no longer a machine.

something, and he has had the courage to make a picture of the machine that runs him. Later still the papoose became a person, rather than a robot encased in glass.

Eventually Joey began to create an imaginary family at the school: the "Carr" family. Why the Carr family? In the car he was enclosed as he had been in his papoose, but at least the car was not stationary; it could move. More important, in a car one was not only driven but also could drive. The Carr family was Joey's way of exploring the possibility of leaving the school, of living with a good family in a safe, protecting car. *(See illustration on page 103.)* 30

Joey at last broke through his prison. In this brief account it has not been possible to trace the painfully slow process of his first true relations with other human beings. Suffice it to say that he ceased to be a mechanical boy and became a human child. This newborn child was, however, nearly 12 years old. To recover the lost time is a tremendous task. That work has occupied Joey and us ever since. Sometimes he sets to it with a will; at other times the difficulty of real life makes him regret that he ever came out of his shell. But he has never wanted to return to his mechanical life.

One last detail and this fragment of Joey's story has been told. When Joey was 12, he made a float for our Memorial Day parade. It carried the slogan: "Feelings are more important than anything under the sun." Feelings, Joey had learned, are what make for humanity; their absence, for a mechanical existence. With this knowledge Joey entered the human condition.

Lines of Inquiry
"Joey: A 'Mechanical Boy' "

Bettelheim tells several stories during the course of his essay: he tells how Joey came to be a "mechanical boy"; how Joey's problems were diagnosed and treated at the Orthogenic School; how Joey's behavior gradually changed from being mechanical to being human. How does Bettelheim organize his material to develop each story clearly? How does Bettelheim organize his material to show the significant relationships among these stories? How do Joey's drawings contribute to Bettelheim's storytelling?

From the beginning to the end of this essay, Bettelheim discusses Joey in terms of his being a mechanical boy. In what senses does this term serve to describe Joey's behavior, to explain the origin of his condition, and to imply an appropriate mode of helping him to deal with his problems? Why is Bettelheim especially interested in telling us about Joey and his mechanical existence? What aspect of Joey's mechanical condition do you find most fascinating? Most disturbing? Most puzzling? Most illuminating?

Though you may not have known anyone so disturbed as Joey, you probably have known someone—a friend or relative—who has gone through a very troubled and difficult period. What do you suppose to have been the nature of this person's problems? What conditions do you think led to the problems? Do you perceive this person to be a unique psychological case? Or do you perceive this person's situation to be in some sense typical of significant problems in his or her culture, much as Bettelheim regards Joey's story as being relevant "to the understanding of emotional development in a machine age"? Can you think of a single adjective, such as mechanical, that would accurately and evocatively explain the condition of this person?

Growing Up Female

In the sixteen years since this essay was first published—it was written a few years earlier—the problems it deals with have become, if anything, more acute. Greater numbers of women are now working. They have made significant strides toward achieving social, economic, and occupational equality with males, and women now more frequently hold positions of considerable importance and prestige. With all this, women have gained much more independence—but they have had to pay a price for it.

An increasing number of marriages now end in divorce, and many more women are having to raise their children without the help of a husband—in general, the number of single parents has jumped significantly in the last decade or so. While women have made great progress towards sexual equality and have achieved considerably greater sexual freedom, this has not necessarily made for greater enjoyment of sex; sexual freedom does not seem to offer deeper and more lasting emotional satisfactions than a good marriage.

The achievements of the women's movement have led to severe identity confusion among many women. The change in social roles women fulfill in society and the home, and changes in their views of themselves and of their relations to males, have led to parallel and equally widespread identity confusion among males regarding their relations to females and their sexual role. All this has made social and sexual relations more problematic for both females and males.

While a traditionally ordered society tightly shackled both females and males to narrowly defined social and sexual roles, society thus provided people with certainty regarding their identities. A few always revolted against being forced to live a life contrary to their desires and suffered, or were made to suffer, for it. But the vast majority had neither the strength nor the opportunity to revolt, and so they more or less accepted and settled into the roles which society decreed. Where there is no doubt, there is also little insecurity. While such tightly regulated social and sexual roles did not permit much freedom or individuality, there was also little need for developing a strong personal identity; identity was settled at the moment of birth.

The historical role for each sex allowed only restricted satisfactions. But as long as nothing better was thought possible, and religion sanctioned these roles, it was easier to make one's peace with the considerable deprivations they imposed, even when there was little satisfaction in sex or the relations to one's partner.

With the breaking down of ancient customs and traditional sex-related traits, and the new freedom to be oneself in whatever way one wishes, comes the difficult task of achieving personal identity, and the related task of gaining autonomy. This is what a technologically advanced society requires of one, if we are not to risk eventually being forced back into rigid patterns of living by a totalitarian system.

The externals of women's lives have changed since this article was written, and so have the externals of male attitudes towards

females. Therefore some of what is said here about external ar-
rangements in women's lives no longer applies to the same degree.
But the internal difficulties of achieving a secure personal and sex-
ual identity have, if anything, become even more of a problem.
Persons who have not achieved a secure identity for themselves
cannot provide each other with those complementary experiences
that make for a happy marital relationship. Although in many
more cases both partners in a marriage now have an independent
life in society, this has not necessarily made it easier for them to be
happier with each other.

The greatest happiness in marriage can come about only when
true independence as socially equal human beings is enriched and
made continually fascinating and satisfying for both partners by
their being sexually completely secure with each other. This secu-
rity is based on a complementary attraction, enriched by the specific
differences in personality and sexual experiences that come from
one partner being female, and the other male.

In the last analysis, it is very difficult to attain one's full iden-
tity as a person all by oneself, as in a vacuum—one must relate to
others. I believe that the essence of a healthy heterosexual identity
requires that it be proven again and again by the depth of satisfac-
tion that a relation which is close emotionally and completely grat-
ifying sexually provides when the particular female qualities bring
out the best in the male; and simultaneously the particular male
qualities bring out the best in the female.

By what models is a mod-
ern girl to measure herself in her growth? Many a psychologist or educator today will find few questions more recurrent or troubling than
this one. On every side one encounters growing girls and educated
women who seem to have followed out the respected modern formulas:
they have "done well" at school, at finding jobs, at finding husbands,
at running homes, at planning activities of all sorts. And yet they remain, as Veblen put it, "touched with a sense of grievance too vivid to
put them at rest." They are frequently baffled by this and so, unhappily, are some of the psychologists they consult. In trying to help
women—to "accept the womanly role," for example—counselors often
seem to aggravate the grievance, rather than cure it.

What I shall try to show in this article is that the grievance is very
real and justified, although it is barely understood. The ways in which
we bring up girls in America, and the goals we set for them, are so
strangely—and often painfully—contradictory that it is only too predictable that their expectations of love and work and marriage should
frequently be confused, and that deep satisfactions should elude them.
Very few human problems have been so transformed by the convulsive
growth and evolution of modern society as those of women; but the

parents and psychologists and educators who guide young women to-day have scarcely begun to inquire into what a modern and satisfying female life might really be.

Many of women's special difficulties spring from the distorted im-ages of females that preoccupy so many men. Freud was probably right in thinking that the male infant's overattachment to his mother projects him into a continuing emotional predicament that is peculiarly difficult for most men to solve, and often warps the demands they make on women. Bound emotionally to the infantile image of his mother as un-assailably pure, a man may seek out a superior woman he can worship. Or, trying to break the infantile bond, he may choose a woman who appears inferior to himself. The different kinds of emotional balm men seek from women are as various as their frustrations when they do not find it. But the female who needs and wants a man—and all normal women do—is often placed in a sadly absurd position: she must shape herself to please a complex male image of what she should be like—but alas, it is often an image having little to do with her own real desires or potentialities; these may well be increasingly stunted or concealed as she grows into womanhood.

Such irrational demands on women are nothing new, as we can learn from the Bible. In the purely psychological sphere, relations be-tween the sexes have always been difficult. But we often forget that until the modern industrial era, the great majority of people had little time or energy to devote to purely emotional "satisfactions" and "re-lationships." Life was still taken up with the basic necessities of food, clothing, and shelter. To secure them, most men and women and their children worked extremely hard—and often worked together—in their homes and shops and fields. If the family was to survive and prosper, the women and girls simply had to do their heavy share, and this earned them a certain respect. It would seem from the available evidence that enough good feeling existed between the sexes to make their emotional difficulties manageable—especially if sex as such was satisfying. What we call "psychological satisfactions" today was frosting on the cake—the cake of economic survival and simple sex.

Now the technological revolution has brought us to precisely the opposite situation. Many women no longer need be bound to men by economic necessity; they rarely share any work with their husbands, and their time is often their own. Women are at last reaching that stage where they can shape their personal relations the way they choose. What choices are they making, and how successful are they?

Most women claim to base their personal relations on what they conceive to be "love"—on "emotional satisfaction." In this, they are clearly the children of modern technology and the easy life it brings. So too is psychoanalysis itself, which aims to make emotional satisfac-tion more possible. But now a savage paradox is slowly—all too slowly—

5

dawning on the psychoanalysts and many of their female patients: it appears that relations entered into chiefly to gain psychological satisfaction more often than not end in psychological despair. "Love," as Saint-Exupéry put it, "does not consist in gazing at each other, but in looking outward in the same direction." For what kind of love, and what kind of life, are we preparing our girls today?

Paul Goodman has suggested that boys today are growing up in ways that he calls "absurd." But how much more absurd are the ways in which we raise our daughters! We tell them early that they are very different from little boys and give them dolls to play with rather than baseballs. But we also provide them, from kindergarten on through college, with exactly the same education given to boys—an education clearly designed to prepare boys for a life of competition and independent responsibility.

Consider the contradictions that are thrust upon the growing girl. For fifteen years or more she is officially encouraged to compete with boys in the schoolroom, to develop her mind and her initiative, to be second to none. She may study the same physics and history as her boy-friends, work part-time at jobs not too different from theirs, share many of the same political and social interests. And then our curious system insists she "fall in love" with a potential husband: she is, in fact, expected to enjoy giving up what she may have loved until then, and suddenly find deep fulfillment in taking care of a child, a home, a mate. Her life is to be filled with what are, to her husband, after-hours occupations, and the training of her youth is seemingly intended to fall away like an afterbirth. After years of apparent equality, it is made clear that males are more equal, and most females resent this, as they should. Our educational system has ostensibly prepared them for a kind of liberated marital and occupational life that in fact rarely exists in our society; at the same time it celebrates the values of an antiquated form of marriage inherited from a time when women were prepared for little else.

If many girls seem to accept these hypocrisies calmly, perhaps it is because they have been made aware, quite early in the game, that their role in society will in fact be very different from that of the boys sitting next to them in the classroom. The boys have no doubt that their schooling is intended to help them succeed in their mature life, to enable them to accomplish something in the outside world. But the girl is made to feel that she must undergo precisely the same training only because she may need it if she is a failure—an unfortunate who somehow cannot gain admission to the haven of marriage and motherhood where she properly belongs.

Actually, the gravest damage is done long before this. The little girl's first storybooks and primers, for example, hardly ever show a woman as working or active outside the home. It makes no difference that many millions of American children under twelve have full-time working mothers. A little girl is expected to shape herself in the image of the maternal housekeeper of these ridiculous primer stories, and never mind what certain unfortunate mothers may be obliged to do. As if to emphasize society's ambivalence, this image of the stay-at-home is usually presented by a female teacher, who may well be a working mother, a contradiction that is not lost on the little girl and tends to teach her that she will have to live a life of contradictions. In these early years, it is rare indeed for girls to hear the slightest suggestion that they might one day do the interesting work of this world quite as well as many men, or even better.

It is little wonder then that as adolescence approaches, many girls are already convinced that what really counts is not any commitment to their studies—although they may be conscientious about them—but their ability to carry on social, emotional, and sexual relations that will make them popular and ultimately attract the right boys. Here matters are made more difficult by the fact that young girls tend to mature faster physically and emotionally than boys, although the boys may do better academically.

The girls soon perceive that they are ahead of the boys in the maturity and sophistication of their desires. The boys seem more childish, less grown up, less certain about their ability to cope with the other sex. What is more, the boys often come from homes where Mother knows best, and they find themselves ruled by female teachers who day after day impress upon them their authority and competence. In this situation it is not easy for a boy to gain confidence in his maleness, to say the least. (Later on, of course, both sexes are exposed to male teachers in high school and college, but by then it is often too late to undo the damage.)[1]

The high school and college girl must face a frequently awful predicament. She—and usually her mother also—feels she must be popular with boys. To get the dates she wants, the girl must try to reassure the boys that they are really superior to her; but deep down she cannot believe in this pretense, and she may well resent the necessity for it. Once she has gained the ultimate objective and is safely married, she will, as likely as not, drop the mask and begin to assert in her home what she is convinced is a superior maturity. By then, however, it may

---

[1]Many boys drop out of school before they meet with many male teachers; in order to protect their own male image, they reject this continuing domination by females. Similarly, the aggressive delinquency which gets boys into trouble is often no more than a desperate attempt to assert their maleness. Since the girls in school are often more mature socially and sexually, the boys find that they can clearly assert male superiority in school only through aggressive and competitive sports. Having learned this, they choose aggressive ways to prove themselves male when outside the school.

no longer exist, for boys typically catch up with girls in this respect during their mid-twenties. And in the meantime the boys are generally given a good deal more freedom to experiment—to "sow their wild oats."

A good many young men, for example, may skirt marriage until they are into their thirties; they are allowed to go their own way, suffering no more than a mild nagging and some teasing from their friends. It is tacitly acknowledged that they need more time to find themselves in their work before they settle down, and they remain popular in both married and unmarried circles. Such men are considered failures only when they cannot support themselves, or make headway in their careers. By contrast, the situation of an unmarried young woman is altogether different, often cruelly so. No matter how gifted she may be in her work—or how brilliantly she has put her education to use—a woman bears a suspicion of failure if she does not marry young.

Indeed, the pressures upon the young girl to marry safely and quickly   15
may seem inexorable just when she is trying to embark on her own path; and these pressures are exerted in ways unfamiliar to boys. During his first years at college, for example, a boy is likely to undergo a "crisis of identity," exposed as he is to conflicting new ideas and ways of acting, and given chances to experiment. As a junior or senior, however, he may start to find himself through serious academic work. A girl may undergo a parallel experience, only to discover that her new dedication to scholarship may rule her out of the marriage market. Fearing that her single-minded absorption will allow her chances to slip by, she stops dead in her tracks; or worse, she cannot make up her mind about what she wants, and she may suffer a college-girl "breakdown."

Nor does this happen only in college. Many a girl emerges from high school with a vague feeling that she can, she should make something of herself. But everyone around her insists that she will find fulfillment through marriage—and her friends are getting married. So she buckles down to a brief course in beauty culture or secretarial work. Later, as the wife of a clerk or skilled worker, she is as restless and bewildered as the college girl who gave up an interest that was becoming "too absorbing," so that she could marry off into the suburbs. Neither girl can quite understand what has gone wrong—she is, after all, an undoubted success in the eyes of others.

And what in fact has gone wrong? What happens when the young bride at last enters the home she has been taught to think of as her true domain? In truth, she may find that the much-touted labors and pleasures of the hearth are among the sad delusions of our times. For if it is hard for male youth nowadays to find meaningful work, as Paul Goodman has argued, the fate of the homebound wife is surely harder.

Of course, modern labor-saving devices have abolished most of the backbreaking housework of the past—and good riddance; but at the same time they are doing away with the real satisfactions this work once yielded. Using her husband's money to buy machine-made clothes for her family involves no unique or essential labors on a woman's part. Much the same can be said about cooking with prepackaged ingredients. What remains, apart from child-rearing, are the most stultifying mechanical tasks—dusting, making beds, washing, and picking up. And beyond these lie chiefly the petty refinements of "homemaking"—what Veblen described as the occupation of ceremonial futility.

The very people who sell women products for the home are shrewdly aware of this futility. A study by the sociologist Florence Kluckhohn has shown that advertising aimed at the housewife often subtly describes the home as a kind of penal colony from which she should escape as quickly and for as long as possible. Typically, an ad for an automatic stove shows a woman putting on her hat, leaving, and coming back hours later to find the dinner all cooked. The advertiser, as Mrs. Kluckhohn points out, does not say where the woman has been; just to get away, it is implied, is a blessing.

Since work around the house is often less than interesting, children   20
are the natural target for the young wife's energies. Here, at least, she feels considerably more sophisticated than her mother. After all, she has had extensive schooling, and has perhaps worked briefly at a demanding job, and motherhood has been depicted to her as another tremendous and enlarging experience—the climax, somehow, to all that has gone before. Yet, in fact, the care of an infant forces a woman to give up most of her old interests, and unless she is fascinated by the minute developments of the baby, she seldom finds that any new and different enrichment has entered her life to replace her relinquished satisfactions.

This impoverishment is particularly acute when a woman has her first child. Later on, the concerns of her older children may enliven her days while she cares for a newcomer. Then, as the time for nurturing babies and taking care of small children passes, many middle-class mothers come to find existence empty without small children to care for. Reluctant to return to the outer world—or lacking confidence in her ability to do so—the housewife must find something to occupy her which seems vital and demanding of her concentration, so she continues to devote herself to her children.

Things change when children become of school age—and change once again when they are in their teens. Schoolchildren certainly need a mother, but they actually need far less of her than she may devote to them. Chauffeuring children around the suburbs, for example, takes time and requires someone who drives a car, but this person need not be a mother. The children themselves would prefer to be free of arranged rides and the tight scheduling this imposes. The same goes for arranging children's social life, which again they would much prefer to do themselves.

Of course the professed concern of many mothers is to watch over their children's educational life, and help them with their problems in growing up. But in these things, too, the children would often rather be on their own, except for those occasional crises when the parents are needed for support. And sadly enough, the modern mother is often in a poor position to give support when her child is doing badly in school or is not very popular or feels defeated. Having invested so much emotionally in her child's achievement, a mother's pride suffers at his failure and as likely as not, she administers a bawling-out when understanding and compassion are needed. Thus she may fail as a mother because her inner needs make her work at it too hard. The children of women who do interesting work of their own during the day often find more sensible and sympathetic mothers to help them with their studies and problems in the evening. On the other hand, the mother who urges her girl on toward intellectual achievement while staying at home herself poses a contradiction that is probably not lost on the girl.

When motherhood does not bring satisfaction, the woman turns to her husband with the demand, spoken or unspoken, that he somehow make up to her for what she is missing in life. She waits for him to come home with word of the outside world and its events. At the same time, she may work hard at being a wife, trying to advance her husband's career, plotting to get him ahead socially. But even if this sort of thing works, he may resent it—it will not be his success, but hers.

Sometimes a wife will spend her husband's money heedlessly and push him to achieve higher earnings and status, blindly demanding things to make up for her empty feelings about her life. Other wives simply nag, or they repress their resentment altogether and accept the prospect of a stultifying life. The husband begins in turn to resent his nagging wife and even his family life; or he may resent his wife for her passive dreariness. In either case both suffer, often without in the least knowing why. Living with such parents, a growing girl may well absorb and keep for life a distorted view of what a man is for, and how he can be used.

No doubt it will be argued that there is more to a modern woman's life than this—that labor-saving devices have so freed housewives from their chores that they can undertake useful and interesting activities of all sorts without actually taking jobs. Such claims seem questionable. Undeniably, a good many housewives do find time for activities outside the home; but all too often the activities themselves are really frivolous or makework, creating futile and unrewarding experiences. Such activities often include gardening—which has replaced the conspicuous embroidery of an earlier age—or the ubiquitous bridge circle and country-club life. There are also activities like the PTA, the League of Women Voters, and charity work which pass as "constructive" and "valuable." Close examination, however, reveals that these pursuits are often used to cover up a lack of really serious and interesting involvement. And according to a recent study, "Volunteer workers are increasingly being

assigned to fund-raising or low level routine, from which little achievement satisfaction is possible."

To quote Veblen again, "Woman is endowed with her share—which
there is reason to believe is more than an even share—of the instinct of
workmanship, to which futility of life or of expenditure is obnoxious."
When this impulse is denied expression, a woman feels that sense of
grievance which runs like a vivid current through the lives of so many
women today.

If the instincts for workmanship are widely frustrated in many modern
women, this is even more true in regard to their sexual instincts. Of
course, sexual difficulties are neither a recent curse of the young, nor
limited to girls. But the way we prepare our children for sexual life has
burdened girls far more than boys.

In Latin countries, as in many other lands, girls are prepared from
early childhood to accept a yielding and passive role, not only in sexual
relations, but in the life of the family, where the man traditionally dominates. But the American girl is raised in contradiction. On the one
hand, she is told that to be feminine means to be yielding and courted,
and that she must respect this norm. She certainly cannot, for example,
ask a boy she likes for a date, nor can she pay the expenses when she
goes out with him (although she may sometimes "go dutch"). She may
feel most reluctant simply to call up a boy to talk with him, or to ask
him to take a walk with her.

Yet at the same time today's young girl has been taught from childhood to think and act for herself; to strive for success, and compete
equally with boys at school. What she has *not* been taught is that men
and women are neither wholly similar, nor wholly opposite, but complementary. She has never been encouraged to quietly consider the ways
in which she and the boys she knows are alike—the talents and aspirations they could build up together and the emotional needs they share—
and the ways in which they are not alike, as in their sexual functions.
As a result, the girl does not know where and when to be "feminine"
and where and when to be "equal."

The adult world has led her to think that the "active woman" is
somehow an unfeminine and sexually inadequate woman—something
patently untrue. Women who strive to "wear the pants" do so for defensive and neurotic reasons, just as the very need to be dominant,
whether in man or woman, is due to feelings of inferiority or to thwarted
desires. But it is quite a different thing for a girl to do purposeful work,
not because of some twisted drive, but because she wants to realize her
own potentials. Unless we distinguish clearly between the two kinds of
striving we stifle the healthy growth of girls by labeling natural ambition as unfeminine.

At the same time, girls are led into an equally dangerous misunderstanding about the sexual act itself. While men and women need not be

30

so different in their personal aspirations as our society now pretends, they are different in the way they experience sex. Here much confusion was created by Wilhelm Reich and his rather too facile following among the intelligentsia; he led both partners to expect that they could and should have a parallel orgastic experience. Too often, a parallel experience is mistakenly thought to mean a similar if not identical experience; the emphasis upon the desirability of orgasm may lead to frustration in both man and woman.

This problem is very different in some societies, where modern technology has not affected the lives of women and their expectations. There it is still sufficient for a woman if her lover or husband enjoys sex with her. Since his enjoyment proves her a good woman, she too can enjoy herself; she does not worry whether she is frigid or torrid, and as likely as not she achieves total release. Since her lover is not obliged by any conscious code to provide her with an orgasm, he can enjoy himself, experience orgasm, and thus help her to feel fully satisfied herself.

In our own society, boys need as much as ever to have their virility attested to by their sexual partners; and girls have a parallel need. But today the boy wants his girl to prove him a man by her so-called orgastic experience, and the girl is even worse off. She not only has to prove him a man by making him experience orgasm; she must also prove her femininity by orgastic release or else fear she is frigid.

She is quite used to performing with males on equal grounds, but she has too little sense of how to complement them. She cannot suddenly learn this in bed. Trying to make sure that the man has an orgastic experience, and also wondering if they can have one themselves, many women become so worried that they truly experience little satisfaction, and end up pretending. Sexual intercourse cannot often bear the burden of *proving* so many things in addition to being enjoyable. It becomes another competition between man and woman: who can make whom have an orgastic experience. And the lovers cannot even enjoy their mutual desire or the forgetting of self in the act.

With both sex and household work often less than satisfying, it is not surprising that so many modern marriages turn sour, and that the phenomenon of homosexuality looms as importantly as it does today.

Many young wives soon realize that their husbands are neither willing nor able to complement them in their motherly tasks in any satisfying way. Resentful, in many cases, of her husband's fuller life, a young wife may nevertheless try to force him to share motherhood with her. But irrespective of whether or not he attempts to do so, and however hard she may try, a woman cannot find compensation in marriage itself for her own thwarted aspirations.

The results are often men who want women, but don't know what to do with them when they get them; and women who get men, but

who are disappointed in them and in themselves when they live together. Mutually disappointed, it is natural that each sex should seek
out its own as company; for only then can they really be themselves on
a truly equal basis, freed of anxiety, disappointment, or inferiority-feel-
ing. Who has not observed the tendency of the sexes to segregate themselves in certain married circles? However, when relations between the
sexes are so plagued, then a kind of homosexuality may also become
rampant. And indeed, psychiatrists have recently been noting an alarming rise in both female and male homosexuality.

Higher statistics concerning "female homosexuality" may reflect an
increasing number of women who are unwilling to pretend they enjoy
having a role forced on them that frustrates their aspirations; and so
they seek the company of a partner who can share them. Sometimes
two such women find it convenient to live together, whether sex is
involved or not, and slowly, as in a good marriage, the partners blend
their lives.

In some cases—but much less often than is sometimes assumed—   40
this leads to a desire for sexual relations. But unlike most male homosexuals, such women can often switch their sexual attention to the other
sex if they can find a male who really wants and needs to "look outward
with them" (and I would add inward) in the same direction. (This, of
course, does not hold true for a hard core of female homosexuals.)

The upbringing of most girls today also fosters something resembling female homosexuality. This is because the old intimacy between
mothers and daughters who actually worked together for the survival
of the family has now practically vanished. As discussed, many women
now feel compelled to prove themselves good mothers by making sure
their daughters are "successes" in life, and so it is difficult for warm
confidence to grow between them. The daughter of such a woman naturally longs for real affection, for the sharing closeness to another woman,
for the tender loving care that she wanted from her mother, and never
got. When they meet with a rewarding response to this need on the
part of a mature woman—which need not, and preferably should not,
be of a gross sexual nature—some young women are enriched by it,
and are then better able to move on to a successful heterosexual relation.

At this point the prospects for the young female hoping for a satisfying marriage may seem fairly bleak. Whether marriage as we know
it is obsolete, I do not know, but frankly I doubt it. Despite its shortcomings, marriage is still the best institution we have developed to
combat loneliness and to provide a structure within which two adults
can find intimate satisfaction and continue to grow; not to mention the
child's need for two parents.

But no institution can provide intimacy or anything else; it can at
best provide a framework. This framework itself cannot ensure that
youthful love will be transmitted into two fulfilled lives, since our chil-

dren need to be prepared for marriage by a kind of upbringing very different from the ones they are getting. People must learn to expect far less of the institution itself and much more of themselves in the way of hard work to help each other live interesting and satisfying lives. They must not marry so early that they peg each other to permanent immaturity, out of anxiety, emptiness, or because they feel unable to make a go of life all by themselves. And they must recognize that a woman's place cannot automatically be confined to the home.

Fortunately, there are more than a few mature marriages to be found. In these, the partners have come to see that the feelings of love—and the affection for idiosyncracies of personality—which lie between them can count for very little by themselves in making their relations work. In the long run, the crucial questions for a married couple concern the kinds of worlds in which they can actively interest themselves as man and woman, and as parents—very much including their connections to their work as well as to each other. If these connections act to bring the members of the family together, then the marriage has a strong chance of survival.

But, of course, this is not so easy. Often the husband's work may 45 split him off from his wife instead of bringing them together. A rather extreme form of this dilemma was presented in a novel called *Command the Morning* by Pearl Buck. She wrote about the wives of scientists working on the secret atomic project at Los Alamos during the war, all of whom were tiresomely caught up in the usual antiquated variety of American marriage. These women had to live lonely lives with secretive husbands who could not share with them the excitement of their work. The only other alternative was to look for some secret excitement of their own, in promiscuous adventure. Only the heroine, a female physicist, is shown to have a complete life, for she shares the creative suspense of the scientists. As she and one of the scientists become involved in work together, they inevitably fall in love. Unfortunately Miss Buck was unable to conceive of any outcome for this affair except a conventional homebound marriage, or no marriage at all. It was apparently beyond her to imagine a marriage where both partners could still love each other and remain part of the same working world. And so, of course, she had the female physicist reject her lover and the prospect of imprisonment in domesticity, so that she didn't have to give up her science.

Obviously I do not think these are the only choices to be made. But I have no doubt that Miss Buck speaks for a great many people who do think so. When such choices do arise, how do we advise young girls to deal with them?

Recently I discussed this problem with some psychoanalytic friends. The majority of these analysts still embraced a nineteenth-century solution to the problem similar to Miss Buck's: a woman belongs in the home, at least for the sake of her children while she is raising them. Her life can be made more bearable if she is helped to gain some meaning from her after-hours community activities, from aesthetic pursuits, and from her sexual life with her husband—or, if need be, from some extramarital sexual adventures.

Such analysts advise a woman to seek meaningful work until the time she gets married or pregnant. Then, she should make an about-face in her way of life, if not also in her emotions. She should then accept the so-called womanly role, stay at home, and raise her children for a decade or longer, during the very years when she is in the prime of life. During this period she must be helped to be not too frustrated a wife, so that when the children are at last in grade or high school, she can make another about-face, recognize the limitations of the PTA life, and return to the more satisfying occupation she pursued before her marriage and children.

What such advice disregards is that having a mother at home who is dissatisfied with her life is no help to the child, even if she does not take it out on the child that his presence prevents her from having a more interesting life. A mother unhappy about the limitations imposed on her life will not be able to make her child happy in his.

Nevertheless the route of working before childbirth, and again after the children have become adolescents, is actually the one that many mothers—voluntarily or involuntarily—have chosen to follow. But one result of such switching back and forth in their major commitments is that many women resentfully feel that they lived a meaningful life only before they got married—a feeling that can have disastrous effects on them, their marriages, and their children. This "switching" solution, in short, leaves the conflict between self-realization and child care unexamined. 50

I am convinced that modern women will have to confront this conflict, and solve it. It might mean adopting the system found in some other societies where women work—i.e., entrusting part of the infant care to the older children, or sharing it with relatives. It might well mean more arrangements whereby young children are entrusted to the care of well-qualified professional people, at least for part of the time.

Some kind of change along these lines is badly needed, but it will not be an easy reform to make, given the resistance which may be expected. In trying to bring such a change about, women unfortunately will not be able to count on much support from their therapists. For, as we have seen, the preconceptions of many a psychologist about the proper feminine role prevent him from really helping a girl to grow up successfully female—that is, generically female in her sexual and emotional relations and in child-rearing, and yet able to develop as fully as a male can in all other respects.

Psychoanalysts' inability to do full justice to this female situation stems from the very nature of psychoanalysis as a method essentially concerned with the exploration of the unconscious recesses of the mind and of infantile fixations. Psychoanalytic therapy is little concerned with how society ought to be organized or even how the patient ought to organize his life in society—its proper task is to help the individual solve some problem which prevents him from being what he wants to be. How the patient arranges his life after this has been achieved is entirely up to him, for enabling the patient to live an independent life is the goal of therapy.

This is why psychoanalysis may help a girl greatly in dealing with problems of sexual repression or preoedipal and oedipal fixations, just as it may help a young student overcome his inability to study—these are problems of personal self-realization. But it cannot help a girl decide what kind of woman she wants to be or what role she wants to play in the community, any more than it can help a student decide what subject to study or what career to choose. These are problems of social self-realization, and to deal with them as personal psychoanalytic problems may muddle and aggravate them.

Since each different female must find her unique solution to the problem of whether or not to combine marriage and motherhood with work, we cannot look to psychoanalysis as such for leadership in solving this issue. But paradoxically enough, hope for a more rational approach to the problems of women can be found in the discoveries of Freud himself.   55

Freud felt rather uneasy in discussing the psychology of women. Basically he remained caught up in his own nineteenth-century middle-class background, with his typical overesteem for his mother and his compensatory feeling that he should dominate his wife. He accepted this view as part of the "natural order of things," and, as we have seen, its shadow still hovers over today's psychoanalysts, and our society generally.

But it is worth noting that Freud himself, while always the courteous gentleman when with his wife, often turned for companionship to intellectually active women who, according to his own view, had chosen the unfeminine role in life. He lived domestically as superior male, but in his work sought the company of women he treated as equals.

Freud thus stood at the threshold of a new era in the relations of man and woman, and was not able to cross it. But he did forge the tools that now might enable us to take the steps impossible for him. He was able to demonstrate that the repressive sex taboos of his time were in fact a counterpart of the Victorian overvaluation of the forbidden woman. By showing us how to uncover these repressions, he opened a way for healthier and more satisfying sexual relations to develop between men and women in the years that followed.

Like most great reforms in man's thinking, this one grew from the most honest and most searching examination possible of the contradictions between what people glibly profess, anxiously evade, and blindly do. We should by now be capable of extending a similar self-examination to the contradictions in our attitudes toward women.

If we do this, I suggest we shall find that although women have been accorded votes and education and jobs over the years, our view of them and their potentials is still far from psychologically mature. Indeed, it is in many ways still biased in the unhappy limitations it imposes on the possibilities for women to make the most of their capacities. A rational and psychologically balanced view would appreciate and enjoy the ways that women are truly different from men, but it would recognize that in most respects women have far more in common with men than our society is now willing to grant.

Above all, such a reform in attitudes must take place among those who have anything whatever to do with bringing up the young. For until parents, teachers, and psychologists honestly perceive the prejudice in their assumptions about the proper roles for women, equal education of the sexes will continue to be a mockery, and we must expect the continuing disintegration of young marriages as emotional distance grows between immature couples. Only a thorough effort by their elders to grow up in their thinking will enable our boys to become adults so secure in their masculinity that they can be truly male in their relations to their female partners, very much including in the sexual relation; and this without any need to assert what used to be viewed as the traditional male role in home or society—because maleness and femaleness reside in how one feels about oneself and the partner, in short in who one is, and not in what one happens to do in the home or society. Only efforts to raise boys and girls to this realization will enable our girls to accept marriage and motherhood as an important part of their future, but a part that will not waste—in desperation, resignation, or boredom—the best of their lives and possibilities.

Lines of Inquiry
"Growing Up Female"

Bettelheim focuses directly on what it is like "growing up female" only in paragraphs 7–16 and 28–34—only one-quarter of his essay. What is the purpose of the material he discusses in the remainder of the piece, particularly in paragraphs 17–27 and 35–61? Make an outline of what Bettelheim discusses in these paragraphs in order to identify exactly how they are related to his concern with growing up female.

One of Bettelheim's major points, which he states in paragraph 7, is that "the ways in which we raise our daughters" are "much more absurd" than the ways in which we raise our sons. For this reason, he has given his essay a title that alludes to Paul Goodman's book, *Growing Up Absurd,* about the absurdities of growing up male. What does Bettelheim mean by absurd? In what respects does he show that growing up female is an absurd process? How does he show it to be more absurd than growing up male?

In his prefatory note, written in 1978, sixteen years after this essay was published, Bettelheim believed that "the problems it deals with have become, if anything, more acute." Given your own experience, observation and reading, how do you think the situation has changed since 1978? In what respects do you think the problems of growing up female have become more absurd? In what respects less absurd? In other words, in what ways and to what degree do you think that Bettelheim's views of female sexuality, male sexuality, and heterosexuality have become dated by events and circumstances of the years since the prefatory note was written?

The Ignored Lesson
of Anne Frank

When the world first learned about the Nazi concentration and death camps, most civilized people felt the horrors committed in them to be so uncanny as to be unbelievable. It came as a severe shock that supposedly civilized nations could stoop to such inhuman acts. The implication that modern man has such inadequate control over his cruel and destructive proclivities was felt as a threat to our views of ourselves and our humanity. Three different psychological mechanisms were most frequently used for dealing with the appalling revelation of what had gone on in the camps:

(1) its applicability to man in general was denied by asserting—contrary to evidence—that the acts of torture and mass murder were committed by a small group of insane or perverted persons;

(2) the truth of the reports was denied by declaring them vastly exaggerated and ascribing them to propaganda (this originated with the German government, which called all reports on terror in the camps "horror propaganda"—*Greuelpropaganda*);

(3) the reports were believed, but the knowledge of the horror repressed as soon as possible.

All three mechanisms could be seen at work after liberation of those   5 prisoners remaining. At first, after the discovery of the camps and their death-dealing, a wave of extreme outrage swept the Allied nations. It was soon followed by a general repression of the discovery in people's minds. Possibly this reaction was due to something more than the blow dealt to modern man's narcissism by the realization that cruelty is still rampant among men. Also present may have been the dim but extremely threatening realization that the modern state now has available the means for changing personality, and for destroying millions it deems undesirable. The ideas that in our day a people's personalities might be changed against their will by the state, and that other populations might be wholly or partially exterminated, are so fearful that one tries to free oneself of them and their impact by defensive denial, or by repression.

The extraordinary world-wide success of the book, play, and movie *The Diary of Anne Frank* suggests the power of the desire to counteract the realization of the personality-destroying and murderous nature of the camps by concentrating all attention on what is experienced as a demonstration that private and intimate life can continue to flourish even under the direct persecution by the most ruthless totalitarian system. And this although Anne Frank's fate demonstrates how efforts at disregarding in private life what goes on around one in society can hasten one's own destruction.

What concerns me here is not what actually happened to the Frank family, how they tried—and failed—to survive their terrible ordeal. It would be very wrong to take apart so humane and moving a story, which aroused so much well-merited compassion for gentle Anne Frank and her tragic fate. What is at issue is the universal and uncritical response to her diary and to the play and movie based on it, and what this reaction tells about our attempts to cope with the feelings her fate—used by us to serve as a symbol of a most human reaction to Nazi terror—arouses in us. I believe that the world-wide acclaim given her story cannot be explained unless we recognize in it our wish to forget the gas chambers, and our effort to do so by glorifying the ability to retreat into an extremely private, gentle, sensitive world, and there to cling as much as possible to what have been one's usual daily attitudes and activities, although surrounded by a maelstrom apt to engulf one at any moment.

The Frank family's attitude that life could be carried on as before may well have been what led to their destruction. By eulogizing how they lived in their hiding place while neglecting to examine first whether it was a reasonable or an effective choice, we are able to ignore the crucial lesson of their story—that such an attitude can be fatal in extreme circumstances.

While the Franks were making their preparations for going passively into hiding, thousands of other Jews in Holland (as elsewhere in Europe) were trying to escape to the free world, in order to survive and/or fight. Others who could not escape went underground—into hiding—each family member with, for example, a different gentile family. We gather from the diary, however, that the chief desire of the Frank family was to continue living as nearly as possible in the same fashion to which they had been accustomed in happier times.

Little Anne, too, wanted only to go on with life as usual, and what 10
else could she have done but fall in with the pattern her parents created for her existence? But hers was not a necessary fate, much less a heroic one; it was a terrible but also a senseless fate. Anne had a good chance to survive, as did many Jewish children in Holland. But she would have had to leave her parents and go to live with a gentile Dutch family, posing as their own child, something her parents would have had to arrange for her.

Everyone who recognized the obvious knew that the hardest way to go underground was to do it as a family; to hide out together made detection by the SS most likely; and when detected, everybody was doomed. By hiding singly, even when one got caught, the others had a chance to survive. The Franks, with their excellent connections among gentile Dutch families, might well have been able to hide out singly, each with a different family. But instead, the main principle of their planning was continuing their beloved family life—an understandable desire, but highly unrealistic in those times. Choosing any other course would have meant not merely giving up living together, but also realizing the full measure of the danger to their lives.

The Franks were unable to accept that going on living as a family as they had done before the Nazi invasion of Holland was no longer a desirable way of life, much as they loved each other; in fact, for them and others like them, it was most dangerous behavior. But even given their wish not to separate, they failed to make appropriate preparations for what was likely to happen.

There is little doubt that the Franks, who were able to provide themselves with so much while arranging for going into hiding, and even while hiding, could have provided themselves with some weapons had they wished. Had they had a gun, Mr. Frank could have shot down at least one or two of the "green police" who came for them. There was no surplus of such police, and the loss of an SS with every Jew arrested would have noticeably hindered the functioning of the police state. Even a butcher knife, which they certainly could have taken with them into hiding, could have been used by them in self-defense. The fate of the Franks wouldn't have been very different, because they all died anyway except for Anne's father. But they could have sold their lives for a high price, instead of walking to their death. Still, although one must assume that Mr. Frank would have fought courageously, as we know he did when a soldier in the first World War, it is not everybody who can plan to kill those who are bent on killing him, although many who would not be ready to contemplate doing so would be willing to kill those who are bent on murdering not only them but also their wives and little daughters.

An entirely different matter would have been planning for escape in case of discovery. The Franks' hiding place had only one entrance; it did not have any other exit. Despite this fact, during their many months of hiding, they did not try to devise one. Nor did they make other plans for escape, such as that one of the family members— as likely as not Mr. Frank—would try to detain the police in the narrow entrance way—maybe even fight them, as suggested above—thus giving other members of the family a chance to escape, either by reaching the roofs of adjacent houses, or down a ladder into the alley behind the house in which they were living.

Any of this would have required recognizing and accepting the desperate straits in which they found themselves, and concentrating on how best to cope with them. This was quite possible to do, even under the terrible conditions in which the Jews found themselves after the Nazi occupation of Holland. It can be seen from many other accounts, for example from the story of Marga Minco, a girl of about Anne Frank's age who lived to tell about it. Her parents had planned that when the police should come for them, the father would try to detain them by arguing and fighting with them, to give the wife and daughter a chance to escape through a rear door. Unfortunately it did not quite work out this way, and both parents got killed. But their short-lived resistance permitted their daughter to make her escape as planned and to reach a Dutch family who saved her.[1]

This is not mentioned as a criticism that the Frank family did not plan or behave along similar lines. A family has every right to arrange their life as they wish or think best, and to take the risks they want to take. My point is not to criticize what the Franks did, but only the universal admiration of their way of coping, or rather of not coping. The story of little Marga who survived, every bit as touching, remains totally neglected by comparison.

Many Jews—unlike the Franks, who through listening to British radio news were better informed than most—had no detailed knowledge of the extermination camps. Thus it was easier for them to make themselves believe that complete compliance with even the most outrageously debilitating and degrading Nazi orders might offer a chance for survival. But neither tremendous anxiety that inhibits clear thinking and with it well-planned and determined action, nor ignorance about what happened to those who responded with passive waiting for being rounded up for their extermination, can explain the reaction of audiences to the play and movie retelling Anne's story, which are all about such waiting that results finally in destruction.

I think it is the fictitious ending that explains the enormous success of this play and movie. At the conclusion we hear Anne's voice from the beyond, saying, "In spite of everything, I still believe that people are really good at heart." This improbable sentiment is supposedly from a girl who had been starved to death, had watched her sister meet the same fate before she did, knew that her mother had been murdered, and had watched untold thousands of adults and children being killed. This statement is not justified by anything Anne actually told her diary.

Going on with intimate family living, no matter how dangerous it might be to survival, was fatal to all too many during the Nazi regime. And if all men are good, then indeed we can all go on with living our lives as we have been accustomed to in times of undisturbed safety and can afford to forget about Auschwitz. But Anne, her sister, her mother, may well have died because her parents could not get themselves to believe in Auschwitz.

While play and movie are ostensibly about Nazi persecution and destruction, in actuality what we watch is the way that, despite this terror, lovable people manage to continue living their satisfying inti-   20

---

[1] Marga Minco, *Bitter Herbs* (New York: Oxford University Press), 1960.

mate lives with each other. The heroine grows from a child into a young adult as normally as any other girl would, despite the most abnormal conditions of all other aspects of her existence, and that of her family. Thus the play reassures us that despite the destructiveness of Nazi racism and tyranny in general, it is possible to disregard it in one's private life much of the time, even if one is Jewish.

True, the ending happens just as the Franks and their friends had feared all along; their hiding place is discovered, and they are carried away to their doom. But the fictitious declaration of faith in the goodness of all men which concludes the play falsely reassures us since it impresses on us that in the combat between Nazi terror and continuance of intimate family living the latter wins out, since Anne has the last word. This is simply contrary to fact, because it was she who got killed. Her seeming survival through her moving statement about the goodness of men releases us effectively of the need to cope with the problems Auschwitz presents. That is why we are so relieved by her statement. It explains why millions loved play and movie, because while it confronts us with the fact that Auschwitz existed, it encourages us at the same time to ignore any of its implications. If all men are good at heart, there never really was an Auschwitz; nor is there any possibility that it may recur.

The desire of Anne Frank's parents not to interrupt their intimate family living, and their inability to plan more effectively for their survival, reflect the failure of all too many others faced with the threat of Nazi terror. It is a failure that deserves close examination because of the inherent warnings it contains for us, the living.

Submission to the threatening power of the Nazi state often led both to the disintegration of what had once seemed well-integrated personalities and to a return to an immature disregard for the dangers of reality. Those Jews who submitted passively to Nazi persecution came to depend on primitive and infantile thought processes: wishful thinking and disregard for the possibility of death. Many persuaded themselves that they, out of all the others, would be spared. Many more simply disbelieved in the possibility of their own death. Not believing in it, they did not take what seemed to them desperate precautions, such as giving up everything to hide out singly; or trying to escape even if it meant risking their lives in doing so; or preparing to fight for their lives when no escape was possible and death had become an immediate possibility. It is true that defending their lives in active combat before they were rounded up to be transported into the camps might have hastened their deaths, and so, up to a point, they were protecting themselves by "rolling with the punches" of the enemy.

But the longer one rolls with the punches dealt not by the normal vagaries of life, but by one's eventual executioner, the more likely it becomes that one will no longer have the strength to resist when death becomes imminent. This is particularly true if yielding to the enemy is accompanied not by a commensurate strengthening of the personality, but by an inner disintegration. We can observe such a process among the Franks, who bickered with each other over trifles, instead of supporting each other's ability to resist the demoralizing impact of their living conditions.

Those who faced up to the announced intentions of the Nazis prepared for the worst as a real and imminent possibility. It meant risking one's life for a self-chosen purpose, but in doing so, creating at least a small chance for saving one's own life or those of others, or both. When Jews in Germany were restricted to their homes, those who did not succumb to inertia took the new restrictions as a warning that it was high time to go underground, join the resistance movement, provide themselves with forged papers, and so on, if they had not done so long ago. Many of them survived. 25

Some distant relatives of mine may furnish an example. Early in the war, a young man living in a small Hungarian town banded together with a number of other Jews to prepare against a German invasion. As soon as the Nazis imposed curfews on the Jews, his group left for Budapest—because the bigger capital city with its greater anonymity offered chances for escaping detection. Similar groups from other towns converged in Budapest and joined forces. From among themselves they selected typically "Aryan"-looking men who equipped themselves with false papers and immediately joined the Hungarian SS. These spies were then able to warn of impending persecution and raids.

Many of these groups survived intact. Furthermore, they had also equipped themselves with small arms, so that if they were detected, they could put up enough of a fight for the majority to escape while a few would die fighting to make the escape possible. A few of the Jews who had joined the SS were discovered and immediately shot, probably a death preferable to one in the gas chambers. But most of even these Jews survived, hiding within the SS until liberation.

Compare these arrangements not just to the Franks' selection of a hiding place that was basically a trap without an outlet but with Mr. Frank's teaching typically academic high-school subjects to his children rather than how to make a getaway: a token of his inability to face the seriousness of the threat of death. Teaching high-school subjects had, of course, its constructive aspects. It relieved the ever-present anxiety about their fate to some degree by concentrating on different matters, and by implication it encouraged hope for a future in which such knowledge would be useful. In this sense such teaching was purposeful, but it was erroneous in that it took the place of much more pertinent teaching and planning: how best to try to escape when detected.

Unfortunately the Franks were by no means the only ones who, out of anxiety, became unable to contemplate their true situation and 30 with it to plan accordingly. Anxiety, and the wish to counteract it by clinging to each other, and to reduce its sting by continuing as much as possible with their usual way of life incapacitated many, particularly when survival plans required changing radically old ways of living that they cherished, and which had become their only source of satisfaction.

My young relative, for example, was unable to persuade other members of his family to go with him when he left the small town where he had lived with them. Three times, at tremendous risk to himself, he returned to plead with his relatives, pointing out first the growing persecution of the Jews, and later the fact that transport to the gas chambers had already begun. He could not convince these Jews to leave their homes and break up their families to go singly into hiding.

As their desperation mounted, they clung more determinedly to their old living arrangements and to each other, became less able to consider giving up the possessions they had accumulated through hard work over a lifetime. The more severely their freedom to act was reduced, and what little they were still permitted to do restricted by insensible and degrading regulations imposed by the Nazis, the more did they become unable to contemplate independent action. Their life energies drained out of them, sapped by their ever-greater anxiety. The less they found strength in themselves, the more they held on to the little that was left of what had given them security in the past—their old surroundings, their customary way of life, their possessions—all these seemed to give their lives some permanency, offer some symbols of security. Only what had once been symbols of security now endangered life, since they were excuses for avoiding change. On each successive visit the young man found his relatives more incapacitated, less willing or able to take his advice, more frozen into inactivity, and with it further along the way to the crematoria where, in fact, they all died.

Levin renders a detailed account of the desperate but fruitless efforts made by small Jewish groups determined to survive to try to save the rest. She tells how messengers were "sent into the provinces to warn Jews that deportation meant death, but their warnings were ignored because most Jews refused to contemplate their own annihilation."[2] I believe the reason for such refusal has to be found in their inability to take action. If we are certain that we are helpless to protect ourselves against the danger of destruction, we cannot contemplate it. We can consider the danger only as long as we believe there are ways to protect ourselves, to fight back, to escape. If we are convinced none of this is possible for us, then there is no point in thinking about the danger; on the contrary, it is best to refuse to do so.

---

[2]Nora Levin, *The Holocaust* (New York: Thomas Y. Crowell, 1968).

As a prisoner in Buchenwald, I talked to hundreds of German Jewish prisoners who were brought there as part of the huge pogrom in the wake of the murder of vom Rath in the fall of 1938. I asked them why they had not left Germany, given the utterly degrading conditions they had been subjected to. Their answer was: How could we leave? It would have meant giving up our homes, our work, our sources of income. Having been deprived by Nazi persecution and degradation of much of their self-respect, they had become unable to give up what still gave them a semblance of it: their earthly belongings. But instead of using possessions, they became captivated by them, and this possession by earthly goods became the fatal mask for their possession by anxiety, fear, and denial.

How the investment of personal property with one's life energy could make people die bit by bit was illustrated throughout the Nazi persecution of the Jews. At the time of the first boycott of Jewish stores, the chief external goal of the Nazis was to acquire the possessions of the Jews. They even let Jews take some things out of the country at that time if they would leave the bulk of their property behind. For a long time the intention of the Nazis, and the goal of their first discriminatory laws, was to force undesirable minorities, including Jews, into emigration.

Although the extermination policy was in line with the inner logic of Nazi racial ideology, one may wonder whether the idea that millions of Jews (and other foreign nationals) could be submitted to extermination did not partially result from seeing the degree of degradation Jews accepted without fighting back. When no violent resistance occurred, persecution of the Jews worsened, slow step by slow step.

Many Jews who on the invasion of Poland were able to survey their situation and draw the right conclusions survived the Second World War. As the Germans approached, they left everything behind and fled to Russia, much as they distrusted and disliked the Soviet system. But there, while badly treated, they could at least survive. Those who stayed on in Poland believing they could go on with life-as-before sealed their fate. Thus in the deepest sense the walk to the gas chamber was only the last consequence of these Jews' inability to comprehend what was in store; it was the final step of surrender to the death instinct, which might also be called the principle of inertia. The first step was taken long before arrival at the death camp.

We can find a dramatic demonstration of how far the surrender to inertia can be carried, and the wish not to know because knowing would create unbearable anxiety, in an experience of Olga Lengyel.[3] She re-

35

---

[3] Olga Lengyel, *Five Chimneys: The Story of Auschwitz* (Chicago: Ziff-Davis, 1947).

ports that although she and her fellow prisoners lived just a few hundred yards from the crematoria and the gas chambers and knew what they were for, most prisoners denied knowledge of them for months. If they had grasped their true situation, it might have helped them save either the lives they themselves were fated to lose, or the lives of others.

When Mrs. Lengyel's fellow prisoners were selected to be sent to the gas chambers, they did not try to break away from the group, as she successfully did. Worse, the first time she tried to escape the gas chambers, some of the other selected prisoners told the supervisors that she was trying to get away. Mrs. Lengyel desperately asks the question: How was it possible that people denied the existence of the gas chambers when all day long they saw the crematoria burning and smelled the odor of burning flesh? Why did they prefer ignoring the exterminations to fighting for their very own lives? She can offer no explanation, only the observation that they resented anyone who tried to save himself from the common fate, because they lacked enough courage to risk action themselves. I believe they did it because they had given up their will to live and permitted their death tendencies to engulf them. As a result, such prisoners were in the thrall of the murdering SS not only physically but also psychologically, while this was not true for those prisoners who still had a grip on life.

Some prisoners even began to serve their executioners, to help speed   40
the death of their own kind. Then things had progressed beyond simple inertia to the death instinct running rampant. Those who tried to serve their executioners in what were once their civilian capacities were merely continuing life as usual and thereby opening the door to their death.

For example, Mrs. Lengyel speaks of Dr. Mengele, SS physician at Auschwitz, as a typical example of the "business as usual" attitude that enabled some prisoners, and certainly the SS, to retain whatever balance they could despite what they were doing. She describes how Dr. Mengele took all correct medical precautions during childbirth, rigorously observing all aseptic principles, cutting the umbilical cord with greatest care, etc. But only half an hour later he sent mother and infant to be burned in the crematorium.

Having made his choice, Dr. Mengele and others like him had to delude themselves to be able to live with themselves and their experience. Only one personal document on the subject has come to my attention, that of Dr. Nyiszli, a prisoner serving as "research physician" at Auschwitz.[4] How Dr. Nyiszli deluded himself can be seen, for example, in the way he repeatedly refers to himself as working in Auschwitz as a physician, although he worked as the assistant of a criminal

---

[4] Miklos Nyiszli, *Auschwitz: A Doctor's Eyewitness Account* (New York: Frederick Fell, 1960).

murderer. He speaks of the Institute for Race, Biological, and Anthropological Investigation as "one of the most qualified medical centers of the Third Reich," although it was devoted to proving falsehoods. That Nyiszli was a doctor didn't alter the fact that he—like any of the prisoner foremen who served the SS better than some SS were willing to serve it—was a participant in the crimes of the SS. How could he do it and live with himself?

The answer is: by taking pride in his professional skills, irrespective of the purpose they served. Dr. Nyiszli and Dr. Mengele were only two among hundreds of other—and far more prominent—physicians who participated in the Nazis' murderous pseudo-scientific human experiments. It was the peculiar pride of these men in their professional skill and knowledge, without regard for moral implications, that made them so dangerous. Although the concentration camps and crematoria are no longer here, this kind of pride still remains with us; it is characteristic of a modern society in which fascination with technical competence has dulled concern for human feelings. Auschwitz is gone, but so long as this attitude persists, we shall not be safe from cruel indifference to life at the core.

I have met many Jews as well as gentile anti-Nazis, similar to the activist group in Hungary described earlier, who survived in Nazi Germany and in the occupied countries. These people realized that when a world goes to pieces and inhumanity reigns supreme, man cannot go on living his private life as he was wont to do, and would like to do; he cannot, as the loving head of a family, keep the family living together peacefully, undisturbed by the surrounding world; nor can he continue to take pride in his profession or possessions, when either will deprive him of his humanity, if not also of his life. In such times, one must radically reevaluate all of what one has done, believed in, and stood for in order to know how to act. In short, one has to take a stand on the new reality—a firm stand, not one of retirement into an even more private world.

If today, Negroes in Africa march against the guns of a police that   45
defends *apartheid*—even if hundreds of dissenters are shot down and tens of thousands rounded up in camps—their fight will sooner or later assure them of a chance for liberty and equality. Millions of the Jews of Europe who did not or could not escape in time or go underground as many thousands did, could at least have died fighting as some did in the Warsaw ghetto at the end, instead of passively waiting to be rounded up for their own extermination.

Lines of Inquiry
"The Ignored Lesson of Anne Frank"

Though Bettelheim focuses on the story of the Frank family, he also refers to stories of other families and persons, some drawn from his own experience and that of his distant Hungarian relative, others from the published accounts of Minco, Levin, Lengyel, and Nyiszli. Why does Bettelheim tell about these other families and persons? How does each of their experiences reflect on the story of the Frank family? Why does he arrange their stories in a sequence beginning with Minco's and ending with Nyiszli's?

As his title indicates, Bettelheim believes that the experience of Anne Frank and her family embodies an important lesson that most people have overlooked. What is "the ignored lesson of Anne Frank"? In what respects is the ignored lesson of her experience at odds with other interpretations of it? What beliefs or values or ways of living are called into question by the ignored lesson? What beliefs or values or ways of living are implicitly affirmed by the ignored lesson? In what respects does Bettelheim consider the ignored lesson to have universal implications?

In this essay, as in "Joey: A 'Mechanical Boy,' " Bettelheim focuses on the experience of a single young person and that person's family, yet he approaches them in completely different ways. What is most distinctive about his analysis of each case? What is most distinctive about his presentation of each case? Despite these important differences, do you see any recurrent beliefs and ideas that Bettelheim conveys in these two pieces?

Some Comments on Privacy

When contemplating the issues raised by an ever more frequent, pervasive, and intrusive invasion of privacy by governmental agencies, private organizations, and the mass media—aggravated by requests from researchers for all kinds of detailed information on one's activities, opinions, and preferences—I am motivated by my considerable personal need and liking for privacy, and my resentment when it is infringed upon. I even dislike intensely what appear to be quite innocuous invasions of my private domain, unless I happen to be momentarily in the mood where it makes no difference to me. For example, there are times when I am quite annoyed if I have to listen to some music in an elevator or airplane, because it may jar with my mood of the moment, stop me from pursuing private thoughts, or interfere with a conversation. While petty, such incidents are indicative of a much larger issue: the usurpation of my right to decide whether, and if so, where I should listen to music, and what kind of music this should be. The fact that it is an anonymous organization which has made these decisions for me only makes it worse; while I am involved as an individual, there is no other individual to whom I can complain about the music, or ask for redress.

What I resent is not the music per se; even as I am disturbed by it, I recognize that it was arranged with the good intention of entertaining me while I am forced to spend time in a dull place. What bothers me is the tacit assumption either that I have no private thoughts I wish to pursue without interruption, or that these thoughts can easily be fitted to the mood of the music, or most offensive of all, that my wish to engage in thoughts of my own need not be respected.

I cite a trivial example because I believe privacy to be an unqualified right. The same principle that one's privacy should be respected and inviolate should apply in minor areas like elevators as well as in major ones such as one's professional life. As a psychoanalyst I am the recipient of highly confidential information about people's most intimate affairs, and not just from patients suffering from severe psychological disturbances. I am frequently subjected to the demand that I divulge this information. Although I reject such requests, to do so is often made very difficult. With all this, I would make a forceful case that privacy must be safeguarded under all circumstances, especially against any infringements by the power of the state. This conviction has been strengthened by my experiences with totalitarian systems.

However, I recognize how much my attitudes were formed in a particular era—the late- and post-Victorian one—and how much things have changed since that time. Reflecting on how things are now, I began to feel not just old, but outright archaic. I have had to accept that privacy is not universally desired, nor an absolute good, as I wished to believe. Instead, its high valuation belongs very much to a particular style of life and historical period, is further characteristic of certain social classes, and thus is culture-bound.

The troublesome nature of this divergence of attitudes began to dawn upon me as I was typing the first draft of these remarks, in solitude, the door of my room closed, in the stillness of the night—the time when I prefer working and when I work best, because no unexpected interruptions interfere with my concentration. As I was typing away, my eyes strayed to a favorite picture hung on the wall over the desk, and I had to laugh at myself. The picture was a copy of a famous painting by Pieter Breughel the Elder, a master I greatly admire. I particularly like this painting of his because it seems to me to be a celebration of life as it really is, not as it pretends to be, as is often rendered in pictures. It shows a world teeming with people, doing all sorts of things. A crowd is depicted who, singly or in groups, are unconcernedly, even happily, going about in public what I, from my very different perspective, would have called their private business. Only for them, such affairs were not at all private—on the contrary. They were fully aware that they transacted their interactions in public; they wanted all to be seen and known by neighbors and strangers; and they did things with more gusto because they did them in the presence of others who reacted to the events being carried on in their presence. I had enjoyed and admired this and other paintings of the Dutch masters, many of which depicted the most "private" aspects of life as being transacted in the public domain, without recognizing that my admiration was incompatible with my feelings about the desirability of privacy. These paintings and many others from later periods indicate how recently our need for privacy has developed; and as I reflected on it, I also realized that this need may already be passing out of our life.

When I studied as a youngster, the door to my room had to be closed; all had to be quiet, and was quiet. Only then could I concentrate on my thoughts and my work, to the exclusion of all other distractions. But my own children—the generation born during and after World War II—studied best with the door open and the record player or the radio going full blast; in this radically different setting they learned as much and as well as I had. Why then do I still need a high degree of privacy and have to work—or at least much prefer to work—only in quiet concentration; and why do they—like the people in the Breughel painting—need to be in continuous close touch with their age-mates, or at

5

least symbolically through a shared musical interest, when they want to concentrate on a mentally demanding task?

Maybe the answer is that we all function best when we feel in communion with what seems to symbolize our highest personal value. I, as a child of the Victorian age, had to create for myself a setting that emphasized privacy, personal uniqueness, and individual development before I could concentrate on a learning task whose ultimate goal—whether or not I was consciously aware of it—was to attain the highest possible degree of individuation. My children, in order to work best, needed to feel that they had not lost touch with their peer group. Nothing and nobody forced them to accept the intrusion of the music into the privacy of their thoughts. If anything, their parents, who were the "authorities" in the home, were most dubious about their studying with the songs of the Beatles distracting them—or at least we thought that this loud music must distract them.

Actually, far from distracting, the music helped my children to concentrate by comforting and reassuring them that they had not lost contact with what they needed most. It gave them the feeling that even when immersed in their studies, they were still somehow in touch with what counted for much in their lives: the connection to their age group. This connection heightened life for them in all of their doings, including the effort to study.

The more lonely they felt, the more these children needed to deny their isolation, to drown it out by the loudness of the music. It expressed for them their angers, their longings, even their loneliness. In doing so, the loud music did for them what they felt unable to do for themselves: to bring their emotions into some semblance of order, put them into a frame which would make them manageable enough to be expressed; emotions which otherwise would be much too chaotic to be coped with in any way. This vicarious expression of their feelings by the music permitted the children—who hardly listened to it but let themselves be enveloped by it—to continue with their studies; otherwise the pressure of these feelings might have prevented them from doing so. The music did this for them because they knew their age-mates who suffered from overpowering parallel emotions listened to the same music. Thus even in their anger, their alienation, their loneliness, it established an invisible—I am tempted to say, an audible—imaginary bond between them and those others with whom, alas, no real bonds existed.

When I came to this country about thirty years ago, among the many customs which struck me as different and thus strange was having the window shades pulled down halfway, more or less all the time. The lowered shade signified a wish for privacy, while leaving half of the window unobstructed expressed that there was no desire, nor any

10

need, to hide from inspection what went on in the room behind the window. This seemed to me to bespeak a strange ambivalence about the wish for privacy. Now the picture window, which exposes so much more of what goes on in the inside to outside scrutiny, while at the same time permitting insiders to observe so much of what is going on in front of the window, has more or less done away with half-pulled-down shades.

In comparison, I remembered how the same problem of seeing and being seen through a window was often dealt with in my native Vienna, and in many other European countries. In the generation of my grandparents, many homes had one window of the living room fitted with an outside mirror that was angled so that a person sitting inside, in a window seat specially fitted for this purpose, could spy on all the comings and goings in the street by watching the mirror without being observed.

I could not help reflecting that a situation where one person would sit hidden in semi-obscurity while observing the behavior of others had its similarities with the psychoanalytic setting, where things go on in utter privacy and confidentiality. If so, the semi-private and semi-public nature of the partly pulled-down shade, and the more public exposure inherent in the picture window, might then be likened to group therapeutic settings or encounter groups, where a mixed group of patients and therapist are equally exposed to each other and things can barely be kept private or confidential. Maybe there were some deeper reasons why a setting that was typically Victorian in its insistence on maintaining total privacy and confidentiality was conducive to the invention of psychoanalysis, and with this to the liberation from Victorian hypocrisy.

How things have changed since Freud explained his reasons for developing the particular psychoanalytic setting! He created it because people, he felt, could not be expected to talk about sexual or other "private" matters while they were aware that somebody was observing their face. But the setting protected the analyst equally: sitting behind the couch where the patient could not observe him was absolutely necessary for the analyst, if he was to be able to concentrate on the patient and what he was saying without worrying about any expressions which might appear on *his* face as he listened to the patient's revelations.

But since Freud's time, and to a considerable degree because of his influence, what used to be eminently private has become quite public—often, I feel defensively, with a vengeance. Feelings and actions a patient could talk about only to the trusted analyst in the carefully guarded privacy of the treatment room are now freely discussed in public, with relative strangers and in the most casual settings. Questions which once a patient broached to his analyst only with great anxiety are now asked in widely and indiscriminately disseminated questionnaires and are readily answered, although they pertain to matters which I still believe ought best to be kept private. What used to be considered most intimate matters are now discussed in great detail in family magazines or shown on the TV or movie screen.

This greater openness, as concerning sexual matters for example, has not altered the fact that today, as in Freud's time, there is much a person will not disclose unless he is absolutely certain that his confidences will be kept secret; but the content of what needs to be kept private has changed. For example, it used to be that the revelation of a person's sexual predilections—ordinary or deviant—had to be protected by complete confidentiality before he dared open up about them. Today many people speak freely about such matters in public. What now is kept secret is often a person's true feelings about behavior which he openly flaunts; feelings which may be the opposite of those he claims to have, for he may secretly be ashamed of what he so openly admits to, or, contrary to his assertions, he may not be able to feel at all.

Thus today, as much as in Freud's time, people insist on confidentiality and on keeping things private, whenever they are ashamed of what they have to reveal. What people may be ashamed of can and does change radically from place to place, and over time. This poses the psychological problem of whether such shame—and with it the demand for confidentiality and privacy—is desirable and beneficial, or rather lessens our well-being as individuals, or that of man in society. Do we benefit more when we are able to hide, keep private and secret, that of which we are ashamed, or is it preferable that this should be made public and openly accepted?

Here the psychoanalyst is caught in his own contradictions, like the rest of us. He tells his patients that there is nothing to be ashamed of in fantasies or feelings, not to mention dreams and daydreams. All these flow of necessity from one's total life history, from the vagaries of experiences and one's reactions to them. Most of all, they reflect early childhood events and reactions, and how one then immaturely interpreted the world; there is no reason for anybody to feel shame about such things. Yet when the same patient behaves in society too openly by acting on the basis of these fantasies, when he thus makes public things he has been told not to shrink from, then as likely as not, the psychoanalyst will consider such openness as acting-out on the part of the patient, viewing it as irresponsible and self-destructive behavior—which indeed it may be.

We all seem caught between our own morality and society's clamor about what should be kept private, and what not. So we all end up functioning by a double standard of morality. But as Freud has shown, keeping a double moral standard—maintaining one for public show and another for private and somehow shameful action—leads only to neurosis and hysteria. Maybe our present dilemma regarding what belongs in the private domain and what in the public, although different from

15

the double standard of Freud's day, is caused by equally severe unresolved inner conflicts about what is right and what wrong.

As a Freudian psychoanalyst I cannot help one further reflection: that the genitals are called a person's private parts, and that the place where one defecates is called a privy. Behind these two "private" designations lies a discomfort with natural functions, a distrust concerning basic parts of oneself, and an uneasiness about how others feel about such things—in short, a deep inner conflict.[1] Maybe these are the emotions behind many demands for privacy.

Lewis Mumford writes: "Today the degradation of the inner life is   20
symbolized by the fact that the only place sacred from intrusion is the private toilet."[2] In this connection it might be mentioned that organizations which wish to de-individualize the individual insist on the use of common toilets, such as in the army, or in summer camps, where the desire is to make everybody feel like "one of the boys." This underlines the relation between individualism and privacy on the one hand, and on the other that between feelings of communality and absence of privacy. (Deliberate deprivation of all privacy can be used not only for purposes of de-individualization, but also of degradation and depersonalization, as happened in the concentration camps.)

Now the degradation Mumford talks of can be interpreted in two ways. One is the thought Mumford had in mind: that unfortunately too little in our lives is as private, as safe from intrusion, as we are while we are on the toilet. But is it not also degrading that functions so natural to our bodies, eliminatory functions we cannot live without, are considered so shameful that they have to be carefully hidden from others, and avoided through lingual circumlocution even with ourselves?

It is precisely the feelings we experience around toilet training, or what is called anality, that often become the greatest source of neurotic anxieties; our inherited shame about elimination sometimes forces us to keep shameful guilty feelings private and hidden from others, causing tremendous unhappiness. At the same time, this very shame is one of the foundations on which our Western civilization rests, although along with it came the discomfort Freud wrote about which bedevils modern man.

Nevertheless in other areas, when and where we crave privacy has undergone great change. My Victorian parents, when they went out to

---

[1] As openly as many people now talk about sexual matters, when it comes to elimination we still talk about "going to the bathroom," or washroom. Elimination is still "dirty." The shame about this finds expression in our circumlocution as we refer not to elimination, but instead to that which will free us from having been engaged in something we consider "dirty"—washing and cleaning ourselves.

[2] Lewis Mumford, *The City in History* (New York: Harcourt, Brace & World, 1961).

dinner, preferred a spacious restaurant with their table set off by an ample distance from the next one. Conversation would then not be overheard, nor their attention imposed on or distracted by too immediate an awareness of others. Nowadays our young people seem to prefer to crowd together in small discotheques, not to speak of the hippies who sleep many to a room. Many of the latter feel so desperately alone and out of contact with others that bodily closeness is sought avidly to bridge the gap. This raises the problem of whether parents have not gone too far in their demand for and in their imposition of privacy.

One need not go as far back as when whole families lived in one room. Nobody had privacy then. One couldn't effectively hide certain skeletons in the closet then because there were no closets. Reconstructions of what life was like in colonial days, even among the affluent, show that parents and children alike lived not only physically close, but with hardly any privacy. A family had to be quite well off to afford separate bedrooms—that is, one for the parents, and one for all the children together. Nowadays the ideal seems to be for each child to have his own room and own bathroom. But the children raised in this spacious isolation are often those who, when they finally come into their own, crowd together into one tiny room.

Our Western society has gone far in seeking privacy and avoiding the pains of closeness; at least as an ideal, although many poor people cannot afford the luxury of privacy, which they desire. On the other hand, many who can afford privacy in consequence suffer from too much distance, from isolation. Maybe what we view as the infringement of privacy today has to do with human efforts at rectifying the balance. 25

Mumford writes that

> the first radical change which was to alter the form of the Medieval house, was the development of a sense of privacy. This means in effect withdrawal at will from the common life and the common interests of one's fellows. Privacy in sleep, privacy in eating, privacy in religious and social rituals, finally privacy in thought. . . . The desire for privacy marked the beginning of that new alignment of classes which was to usher in the merciless class competition and individual self-assertion of a later day. . . . In the castles of the thirteenth century, one notes the existence of a private bedroom for the noble owners; and one also finds, not far from it, perched over the moat, a private toilet. . . . Privacy in bed came first in Italy among the upper classes only, but the desire for it seems to have developed almost as slowly as the means. Michelangelo, for example, on occasion slept with his workmen four to a bed.

From these remarks it seems obvious that an absence of privacy in living conditions did not and need not interfere with creative achievements, which even we moderns regard as the reflection of rarest uniqueness. But it also appears that as long as all the bodily functions, including sex and elimination, were more or less public, no great shame attached to them. Only as they became more and more relegated to a private room which became the privy, did we learn to feel shame about our bodies and bodily functions. The tragedy is that alienation from one's body leads to alienation from oneself and from others. And once we no longer feel comfortable with others, we crave privacy. Maybe what is missing is the right balance between closeness and distance, between public and private.

When we think about privacy we think of the wish for privacy in thought, feeling and experience; these should be exclusively our own. No one should have the right to intrude on these inner processes; they should be open to others only when we wish to give of them. Otherwise they should be and remain our private "business."

The desire for privacy is closely linked to the increased insistence on private property in ever-larger aspects of life. My home ought to be the castle where I am protected from anyone's intruding on my privacy. But my home is my castle only when it is my private possession. Understandably, it was the lord of the castle who first claimed privacy for himself and his doings. Thus from the very beginning, demands for privacy were closely connected with private property. Whoever owned no place of his own, owned no privacy either, and he has very little even today. And private property is virtually inseparable from class structure.

Only in the seventeenth century, for example, did the common din- 30 ner table stop being common to all members of the household, servants and masters alike; no private conversations were held at the dinner table then. In short, the more class-structured a society becomes, the more privacy do its privileged members demand. How understandable, then, that a society which tries to do away with class structure should also try to do away with privacy, and demand that ever larger areas of life should be public.

What comes as harder to realize is that as long as everyone knew everything about everyone else there was no need for informers, for elaborate spy systems, or for bugging in order to know what people did, said, and thought. This brings to mind the absence of crime, delinquency, and other asocial behavior in the Israeli kibbutzim. There are no police there, because there is no need for policing. Everyone lives much more collectively and openly with everyone else than among us, and with this, in essence everybody polices everybody else. There is very little privacy and everyone knows just about everything about everyone else. I personally felt suffocated by the lack of privacy, when I lived there for a time. But I could not blind myself to what to me was an astonishing absence of all asocial behavior in this society, as follows from the absence of privacy—or from having everything in the public domain.

Servan-Schreiber, in comparing Americans to the French, remarks that "France is a country where distrust of one's neighbor still prevails.

This is due to the conviction that men are by nature hostile and ego-tistical. Therefore each protects himself from the other through a complex network of laws, which complexity conforms to the French tendency of carefully limiting and defining all aspects of human existence. The straitjacket which results, quite naturally, prevents all change."[3] And it is true that the demand for privacy implies a distrust of others.

Where does all this leave me? Despite all of my realizations I do not cherish privacy less, and I still resent deeply any intrusion upon it.

I recognize that modern anomy and alienation, even much of modern *tedium vitae,* result from how distantly people live from each other. Most of our social problems, whether distrust by one group in the population of the other—call it racial discrimination, or class hatred—or the prevalence of crime and delinquency, merely reflect this alienation. The best way to do away with them, perhaps the only one, would be to create true communities. But one cannot live in true communality and also keep much of life private to oneself. Many of our laws telling us what to do and what not to do, which even invade our private lives, are intended to make our society more equitable.

If consensus does not arise from communal living, from everyone's sharing the same values and having much the same concerns, then it has to be imposed from the outside. But what suffers then is the individualism my own rearing forces me to cherish so highly. So I am caught in my own contradictions, truly a child of our age of transition. At present I see no way to achieve all these good things together: a true community of living, and an individualism safeguarded by privacy. So let me close with some thoughts on the psychological dimensions of the problem.

Professionally I am confronted daily with the suffering of emotionally disturbed children who were raised in situations where great privacy deteriorated into complete isolation from others, and with it from themselves. As a result they became desperately fearful and ashamed of any relations with others, or any familiarity with their bodies. It remains for the next generation to see if it can design a model of privacy which is not founded on repression—on feelings of shame about one's body, its function in elimination, its desire for various forms of sexual satisfaction. Maybe the solution is in a much better balance between those areas that should remain private and those we are better off assigning to the public domain. What is certainly needed is a privacy which does not dwarf but enhances our capacity for true intimacy with those who ought to be closest to us.

Among the unresolved problems of modern city life today is the prevalence of fear in our streets. I would like to suggest something far removed from reconstructing our cities, or an incredible enlarging of

---

[3]J. J. Servan-Schreiber, *Le Défi américain* (Paris: Denoel, 1967).

the police force and law-enforcing agents within them. What we need, in my opinion, is a return to much smaller, more self-contained communities where a great deal of what is now private can become public; where we would share and know much more about each other, and care about each other, even to the degree of protecting each other's well-being and property. After all, much crime is prevented, and criminals apprehended, when neighbors pay attention and report their observations to the police. In short, what we need is a desire for privacy that is based not on shame or the fear of what others might do to or think of us, but solely on a wish for simple solitude.

Maybe what we must strive for is a way of life where we would wish to share far more with each other because we can trust others more than we presently can, but without the community imposing any rules on how one must think, feel, and shape one's life, as was typical before the anonymity of big city life offered protection against such restraints on the individual's chance to find self-realization in his own ways. What would then be kept private would be kept that way not because it was shameful, but because it was valuable. And if there were less emphasis on private property, as in the kibbutz, there would be less need to protect private property, but only private emotions and experiences. If private property were less valued, it would require less protection and would arouse less desire to grab it away on the part of those who do not own it; and then we might come to value the private experience much more highly. Out of the high value we would then place on our own private experience we would come to respect the privacy of others.

While the millennium is not about to arrive, there is at least reasonable hope that modern technology will make the necessary types of property so readily available that they will no longer need to be anxiously guarded. Certainly our attitudes toward our bodies and what is shameful about them, needing to be hidden, are changing. We are a long way from accepting the body and its functions freely, but there is hope that the time may come when the desire for privacy will no longer be based on the need to hide what is experienced as the shameful functions of the body. The less we feel ashamed of, the less we feel curiosity about the private life of others. After all, it is the Peeping Tom who knows so little about his own body and emotions, is so afraid and confused about his own sexuality that he is sneakily trying to find out about that of others; it is he who is so embarrassed about his own instinctual desires that he tries to gain satisfaction from embarrassing others.

If we all became more secure about our own bodies, more secure economically, socially, and sexually, we would be able to grant others great individual freedom both out of a desire for such freedom for ourselves, and out of a lack of interest in their private lives, because any 40 morbid interest in the other is always the consequence of a felt inadequacy in ourselves. That is why we are dying to know how others manage things. If we all were able to manage our own lives, we would have little reason to try to manage the lives of others.

Neither a medieval absence of privacy, nor a big brother's spying that makes all of our life public, will do. What we must strive for, as so often and in so many other matters, is the right balance between what should be respected and protected as private in our life, and what should be part of our more or less public communal life. Then the home will be just that—neither a castle, nor a public place.

Lines of Inquiry
"Some Comments on Privacy"

In developing and illustrating his ideas, Bettelheim discusses numerous examples of privacy, of intrusions upon privacy, and of communality. Why do you suppose that he uses so many examples? Why doesn't he limit himself instead to just a few closely related ones, such as those dealing with background music, or those dealing with windows and shades, or those dealing with living rooms and bedrooms, or those dealing with bathroom and bodily functions, or those dealing with psychoanalysis, or those dealing with sexuality? How do you account for his selection and arrangement of these varied examples? Why does he begin by talking about background music, then move on to windows and shades, then to psychoanalysis, and so on?

Though Bettelheim begins by complaining about the intrusiveness of background music on his privacy, he ends by envisioning a time "when the desire for privacy will no longer be based on the need to hide what is experienced as the shameful functions of the body." Given these apparently differing attitudes towards privacy, where do you think he really stands on the matter? What kinds of privacy do you think are most important to him? What kinds do you think are least important to him? What aspects of privacy raise the most perplexing and significant problems for him?

Bettelheim wrote this piece in 1966, when communal activities and communal living were prominent aspects of the nationwide counter-cultural movement. Now, twenty-five years later, how far do you think the country has come towards achieving what Bettelheim considers to be "the right balance between what should be respected and protected as private in our life, and what should be part of our more or less public communal life"? How far have you come toward achieving what you consider to be the right balance of privacy and communality in your own life?

Joan Didion
1934—

If I could believe that going to a barricade would affect man's fate in the slightest I would go to that barricade, and quite often I wish that I could, but it would be less than honest to say that I expect to happen upon such a happy ending.

In this frank passage from the *The White Album,* Joan Didion acknowledges that the endings of the stories she tells as novelist and essayist are rarely happy. Relentlessly candid, broodingly perceptive, with a haunting attentiveness to the absurdities in contemporary life, Didion has become a high priestess of postmodern malaise, tracking the dissolution of meaning in the forms of modern culture with the tenacity of a bloodhound and lamenting the loss in essays so beautifully crafted as to earn her a solid reputation as one of the most accomplished prose stylists of her generation.

Didion was born in Sacramento, California, in 1934, a fifth-generation Californian. She grew up in a comfortably well-off family with a strong sense of her pioneer heritage and a passionate attachment to the Sacramento Valley landscape which was her home, running "over the same flat fields that our great-great-grandfather had found virgin and had planted" and swimming in "the same rivers we had swum for a century." That deep sense of generational familiarity, though, was doomed to be short-lived, for before Didion reached adulthood, California experienced the postwar economic boom that transformed it into "the golden land," the last frontier, the final toehold of American culture on the continent, the place where the American Dream, if it was ever to be realized, had to come true. This urgency precipitated change so rapid as to be drastically disorienting, instilling in Didion a presentiment of loss and a nostalgia for what is lost that still infuses her writing. "All that is constant about the California of my childhood is the rate at which it disappears," she wrote in 1965. In that sense, California epitomizes for Didion all "the things we lose and the promises we break as we grow older."

In 1952 Didion entered the University of California at Berkeley and graduated with a degree in English literature in 1956. She describes her undergraduate days this way:

I read Camus and Henry James and I watched a flowering plum come in and out of blossom and at night, most nights, I walked outside and looked up to where the cyclotron and the bevatron glowed on the dark hillside, unspeakable mysteries which engaged me, in the style of my time, only personally.

This passage captures the dilemma which Didion explores in all her work: suspended between the cyclical time of the blossoming plum tree and the fragmenting of time and matter in the accelerators, between the balanced order of James' prose and Camus' exploration of a disintegrating social order, Didion records the sensibilities of the new era, in which cyclotrons rather than stars glow against the night sky, while mourning the loss of the old.

When she was still an undergraduate, Didion won an essay contest sponsored by *Vogue* magazine which secured her a job with the magazine after her graduation. She lived in New York for eight years, moving from copywriter to associate features editor at *Vogue*. During this time she fell "into the habit of writing fiction" and completed a novel, *Run River,* published in 1963. That same year she married John Gregory Dunne, also a writer, and the following year the couple moved to southern California, where they and their daughter still live. Over the years Didion and Dunne have been frequent collaborators on a number of writing projects, from magazine columns to Hollywood screenplays, while continuing to publish individually both fiction and non-fiction. Like her contemporary James Baldwin, Didion set out to be a novelist, and she has written two novels that portray women struggling to survive the painful circumstances of their lives, *Play It As It Lays* (1970) and *A Book of Common Prayer* (1977). But it is her essays that have earned the highest praise of readers and critics.

Didion's first collection of essays, *Slouching Towards Bethlehem,* appeared in 1968 and was an instant success. She took her title from W. B. Yeats' poem "The Second Coming," printing the entire poem as an epigraph to the book and repeatedly evoking the line "Things fall apart; the center cannot hold," as when she describes the experience of writing the title essay, a report on the drug subculture in San Francisco's Haight-Ashbury district, as "the first time I had dealt directly and flatly with the evidence of atomization, the proof that things fall apart." Of herself at the time she wrote the essay she says, "I . . . had been paralyzed by the conviction that writing was an irrelevant act, that the world as I had understood it no longer existed." Didion's mental landscape was, in other words, a mirror of the disintegration she felt herself surrounded by and described so vividly in the essays. She was, as one critic said of her, a "prescient witness" to the character of the time, as was the book itself, which appeared during the same year that Martin Luther King, Jr., and Robert Kennedy were assassinated, violence erupted at the Democratic National Convention in Chicago, and the My Lai massacre brought the blurred backdrop of the Vietnam war into sharp and bitter focus. That same year Didion was named a Los Angeles Times Woman of the Year and suffered a mental breakdown. Later she wrote that "the attack of vertigo and nausea" which first evidenced her breakdown "does not now seem to me an inappropriate response to the summer of 1968."

"I can recall," Didion has said, "always thinking there was more to be had from the dark journey. The dark journey engaged me more." Her preoccupation with that "dark journey" has caused one critic to observe, "One just wishes the woman wasn't in so much pain." But Didion is unapologetic about the refined subjectivity of her work: "I write entirely to find out what I'm thinking, what I'm looking at, what I see and what it means," she says. She has been criticized for being too self-revelatory in her essays—inserting excerpts from her psychiatric evaluation, discussing the possibility of a divorce from her husband, reporting on being diagnosed as having multiple sclerosis (the disease later went into remission). Recording the ways a fragmenting culture has impressed itself on her own consciousness has been her persistent concern; but as one critic has said, "her personality does not self-indulgently intrude itself on her subjects"; it "informs and illuminates them."

Didion's second collection of essays, *The White Album* (1979), is in many ways a return to the earlier terrain—life in California during the chaos of the sixties, replete with senseless mass murders, campus riots, and racial warfare—but it offers a retrospective view and thus in some sense is an awakening from the nightmare of that era. "I remember a time when the dogs barked every night and the moon was always full," she writes, and when the Manson murders occurred, "I also remember this, and wish I did not: *I remember that no one was surprised.*" But it is a memory, and Didion has survived. That is not to say that the essays in *The White Album* are healing or hopeful; Didion persists in detailing the progressive loss of coherence, which she sees as characterizing America in the late twentieth century, pursuing traces of that loss into the realm of language itself. The period from the mid-sixties to the early seventies was for Didion

> a time when I began to doubt the premises of all the stories I had ever told myself, a common condition but one I found troubling. . . . I was supposed to have a script, and had mislaid it. I was supposed to hear cues, and no longer did. I was meant to know the plot, but all I knew was what I saw: flash pictures in variable sequence, images with no "meaning" beyond their temporary arrangement. . . .

This "common condition" of inability "to believe in the narrative and in the narrative's intelligibility" is for her the loss at the heart of the postmodern world.

Her recent non-fiction consists of two book-length essays, *Salvador* (1983) and *Miami* (1987), both of which report the resulting chaos in regions of cultural collapse or confrontation. In *Salvador,* the fragmentation characteristic of the contemporary world extends itself into the very flesh of the inhabitants: "The dead and pieces of the dead turn up in El Salvador everywhere, every day, as taken for granted as in a nightmare, or a horror movie."

In such a world, how is a writer—"a person whose most absorbed and passionate hours are spent arranging words on pieces of paper"— to keep working? For Didion, arranging words and structuring sentences enables her to knit up the ravelling edges of her world:

> To shift the structure of a sentence alters the meaning of that sentence, as definitely and inflexibly as the position of a camera alters the meaning of the object photographed. Many people know about camera angles now but not so many know about sentences. The arrangement of the words matters, and the arrangement you want can be found in the picture in your mind. The picture dictates the arrangement. . . . The picture tells you how to arrange the words and the arrangement of the words tells you, or tells me, what's going on in the picture.

So, in the grammar of her sentences as in the structure of her essays, Didion achieves at least a measure of control in a world she finds largely out of control.

John Wayne: A Love Song

In the summer of 1943 I was eight, and my father and mother and small brother and I were at Peterson Field in Colorado Springs. A hot wind blew through that summer, blew until it seemed that before August broke, all the dust in Kansas would be in Colorado, would have drifted over the tar-paper barracks and the temporary strip and stopped only when it hit Pikes Peak. There was not much to do, a summer like that: there was the day they brought in the first B-29, an event to remember but scarcely a vacation program. There was an Officers' Club, but no swimming pool; all the Officers' Club had of interest was artificial blue rain behind the bar. The rain interested me a good deal, but I could not spend the summer watching it, and so we went, my brother and I, to the movies.

We went three and four afternoons a week, sat on folding chairs in the darkened Quonset hut which served as a theater, and it was there, that summer of 1943 while the hot wind blew outside, that I first saw John Wayne. Saw the walk, heard the voice. Heard him tell the girl in a picture called *War of the Wildcats* that he would build her a house, "at the bend in the river where the cottonwoods grow." As it happened I did not grow up to be the kind of woman who is the heroine in a Western, and although the men I have known have had many virtues and have taken me to live in many places I have come to love, they have never been John Wayne, and they have never taken me to that bend in the river where the cottonwoods grow. Deep in that part of my heart where the artificial rain forever falls, that is still the line I wait to hear.

I tell you this neither in a spirit of self-revelation nor as an exercise in total recall, but simply to demonstrate that when John Wayne rode through my childhood, and perhaps through yours, he determined forever the shape of certain of our dreams. It did not seem possible that such a man could fall ill, could carry within him that most inexplicable and ungovernable of diseases. The rumor struck some obscure anxiety, threw our very childhoods into question. In John Wayne's world, John Wayne was supposed to give the orders. "Let's ride," he said, and "Saddle up." "Forward *ho*," and "A man's gotta do what he's got to do." "Hello, there," he said when he first saw the girl, in a construction camp or on a train or just standing around on the front porch waiting for somebody to ride up through the tall grass. When John Wayne spoke, there was no mistaking his intentions; he had a sexual authority so strong that even a child could perceive it. And in a world we understood early to be characterized by venality and doubt and paralyzing ambiguities, he suggested another world, one which may or may not have existed ever but in any case existed no more: a place where a man could move free, could make his own code and live by it; a world in which, if a man did what he had to do, he could one day take the girl and go riding through the draw and find himself home free, not in a hospital with something going wrong inside, not in a high bed with the flowers and the drugs and the forced smiles, but there at the bend in the bright river, the cottonwoods shimmering in the early morning sun.

"Hello, there." Where did he come from, before the tall grass? Even his history seemed right, for it was no history at all, nothing to intrude upon the dream. Born Marion Morrison in Winterset, Iowa, the son of a druggist. Moved as a child to Lancaster, California, part of the migration to that promised land sometimes called "the west coast of Iowa." Not that Lancaster was the promise fulfilled; Lancaster was a town on the Mojave where the dust blew through. But Lancaster was still California, and it was only a year from there to Glendale, where desolation had a different flavor: antimacassars among the orange groves, a middle-class prelude to Forest Lawn. Imagine Marion Morrison in Glendale. A Boy Scout, then a student at Glendale High. A tackle for U.S.C., a Sigma Chi. Summer vacations, a job moving props on the old Fox lot. There, a meeting with John Ford, one of the several directors who were to sense that into this perfect mold might be poured the inarticulate longings of a nation wondering at just what pass the trail had been lost. "Dammit," said Raoul Walsh later, "the son of a bitch looked like a man." And so after a while the boy from Glendale became a star. He did not become an actor, as he has always been careful to point out to interviewers ("How many times do I gotta tell you, I don't act at all, I *re*-act"), but a star, and the star called John Wayne would spend most of the rest of his life with one or another of those directors, out on some forsaken location, in search of the dream.

> *Out where the skies are a trifle bluer*
> *Out where friendship's a little truer*
> *That's where the West begins.*

Nothing very bad could happen in the dream, nothing a man could not face down. But something did. There it was, the rumor, and after a while the headlines. "I licked the Big C," John Wayne announced, as John Wayne would, reducing those outlaw cells to the level of any other outlaws, but even so we all sensed that this would be the one unpredictable confrontation, the one shoot-out Wayne could lose. I have as much trouble as the next person with illusion and reality, and I did not much want to see John Wayne when he must be (or so I thought) having some trouble with it himself, but I did, and it was down in Mexico when he was making the picture his illness had so long delayed, down in the very country of the dream.

It was John Wayne's 165th picture. It was Henry Hathaway's 84th. It was number 34 for Dean Martin, who was working off an old contract to Hal Wallis, for whom it was independent production number 65. It was called *The Sons of Katie Elder,* and it was a Western, and after the three-month delay they had finally shot the exteriors up in Durango, and now they were in the waning days of interior shooting at Estudio Churubusco outside Mexico City, and the sun was hot and the air was clear and it was lunchtime. Out under the pepper trees the boys from the Mexican crew sat around sucking caramels, and down the road some of the technical men sat around a place which served a stuffed lobster and a glass of tequila for one dollar American, but it was inside the cavernous empty commissary where the talent sat around, the reasons for the exercise, all sitting around the big table picking at *huevos con queso* and Carta Blanca beer. Dean Martin, unshaven. Mack Gray, who goes where Martin goes. Bob Goodfried, who was in charge of Paramount publicity and who had flown down to arrange for a trailer and who had a delicate stomach. "Tea and toast," he warned repeatedly. "That's the ticket. You can't trust the lettuce." And Henry Hathaway, the director, who did not seem to be listening to Goodfried. And John Wayne, who did not seem to be listening to anyone.

"This week's gone slow," Dean Martin said, for the third time.

"How can you say that?" Mack Gray demanded.

"This . . . week's . . . gone . . . slow, that's how I can say it."

"You don't mean you want it to end." 10

"I'll say it right out, Mack, I want it to *end.* Tomorrow night I shave this beard, I head for the airport, I say *adios amigos!* Bye-bye *muchachos!"*

Henry Hathaway lit a cigar and patted Martin's arm fondly. "Not tomorrow, Dino."

"Henry, what are you planning to add? A World War?"

Hathaway patted Martin's arm again and gazed into the middle distance. At the end of the table someone mentioned a man who, some years before, had tried unsuccessfully to blow up an airplane.

"He's still in jail," Hathaway said suddenly. 15

"In jail?" Martin was momentarily distracted from the question whether to send his golf clubs back with Bob Goodfried or consign them to Mack Gray. "What's he in jail for if nobody got killed?"

"Attempted murder, Dino," Hathaway said gently. "A felony."

"You mean some guy just *tried* to kill me he'd end up in jail?"

Hathaway removed the cigar from his mouth and looked across the table. "Some guy just tried to kill *me* he wouldn't end up in jail. How about you, Duke?"

Very slowly, the object of Hathaway's query wiped his mouth,   20
pushed back his chair, and stood up. It was the real thing, the authentic
article, the move which had climaxed a thousand scenes on 165 flick-
ering frontiers and phantasmagoric battlefields before, and it was about
to climax this one, in the commissary at Estudio Churubusco outside
Mexico City. "Right," John Wayne drawled. "I'd kill him."

Almost all the cast of *Katie Elder* had gone home, that last week;
only the principals were left, Wayne, and Martin, and Earl Holliman,
and Michael Anderson, Jr., and Martha Hyer. Martha Hyer was not
around much, but every now and then someone referred to her, usually
as "the girl." They had all been together nine weeks, six of them in
Durango. Mexico City was not quite Durango; wives like to come along
to places like Mexico City, like to shop for handbags, go to parties at
Merle Oberon Pagliai's, like to look at her paintings. But Durango.
The very name hallucinates. Man's country. Out where the West begins. There had been ahuehuete trees in Durango; a waterfall, rattle-
snakes. There had been weather, nights so cold that they had postponed
one or two exteriors until they could shoot inside at Churubusco. "It
was the girl," they explained. "You couldn't keep the girl out in cold
like that." Henry Hathaway had cooked in Durango, *gazpacho* and ribs
and the steaks that Dean Martin had ordered flown down from the
Sands; he had wanted to cook in Mexico City, but the management of
the Hotel Bamer refused to let him set up a brick barbecue in his room.
"You really missed something, *Durango*," they would say, sometimes
joking and sometimes not, until it became a refrain, Eden lost.

But if Mexico City was not Durango, neither was it Beverly Hills.
No one else was using Churubusco that week, and there inside the big
sound stage that said LOS HIJOS DE KATIE ELDER on the door, there with
the pepper trees and the bright sun outside, they could still, for just so
long as the picture lasted, maintain a world peculiar to men who liked
to make Westerns, a world of loyalties and fond raillery, of sentiment
and shared cigars, of interminable desultory recollections; campfire talk,
its only point to keep a human voice raised against the night, the wind,
the rustlings in the brush.

"Stuntman got hit accidentally on a picture of mine once," Hathaway would say between takes of an elaborately choreographed fight
scene. "What was his name, married Estelle Taylor, met her down in
Arizona."

The circle would close around him, the cigars would be fingered.
The delicate art of the staged fight was to be contemplated.

"I only hit one guy in my life," Wayne would say. "Accidentally,   25
I mean. That was Mike Mazurki."

"Some guy. Hey, Duke says he only hit one guy in his life, Mike Mazurki."

"Some choice." Murmurings, assent.

"It wasn't a choice, it was an accident."

"I can believe it."

"You bet." 30

"Oh boy. Mike Mazurki."

And so it would go. There was Web Overlander, Wayne's makeup man for twenty years, hunched in a blue Windbreaker, passing out sticks of Juicy Fruit. *"Insect* spray," he would say. "Don't tell us about insect spray. We saw insect spray in Africa, all right. Remember Africa?" Or, *"Steamer* clams. Don't tell us about steamer clams. We got our fill of steamer clams all right, on the *Hatari!* appearance tour. Remember Bookbinder's?" There was Ralph Volkie, Wayne's trainer for eleven years, wearing a red baseball cap and carrying around a clipping from Hedda Hopper, a tribute to Wayne. "This Hopper's some lady," he would say again and again. "Not like some of these guys, all they write is sick, sick, sick, how can you call that guy *sick,* when he's got pains, coughs, works all day, *never complains.* That guy's got the best hook since Dempsey, not *sick."*

And there was Wayne himself, fighting through number 165. There was Wayne, in his thirty-three-year-old spurs, his dusty neckerchief, his blue shirt. "You don't have too many worries about what to wear in these things," he said. "You can wear a blue shirt, or, if you're down in Monument Valley, you can wear a yellow shirt." There was Wayne, in a relatively new hat, a hat which made him look curiously like William S. Hart. "I had this old cavalry hat I loved, but I lent it to Sammy Davis. I got it back, it was unwearable. I think they all pushed it down on his head and said *O.K., John Wayne*—you know, a joke."

There was Wayne, working too soon, finishing the picture with a bad cold and a racking cough, so tired by late afternoon that he kept an oxygen inhalator on the set. And still nothing mattered but the Code. "That guy," he muttered of a reporter who had incurred his displeasure. "I admit I'm balding. I admit I got a tire around my middle. What man fifty-seven doesn't? Big news. Anyway, that guy."

He paused, about to expose the heart of the matter, the root of the 35 distaste, the fracture of the rules that bothered him more than the alleged misquotations, more than the intimation that he was no longer the Ringo Kid. "He comes down, uninvited, but I ask him over anyway. So we're sitting around drinking mescal out of a water jug."

He paused again and looked meaningfully at Hathaway, readying him for the unthinkable denouement. "He had to be *assisted* to his room."

They argued about the virtues of various prizefighters, they argued about the price of J & B in pesos. They argued about dialogue.

"As rough a guy as he is, Henry, I still don't think he'd raffle off his mother's *Bible.*"

"I like a shocker, Duke."

They exchanged endless training-table jokes. "You know why they call this memory sauce?" Martin asked, holding up a bowl of chili. 40

"Why?"

"Because you *remember it in the morning.*"

"Hear that Duke? Hear why they call this memory sauce?"

They delighted one another by blocking out minute variations in the free-for-all fight which is a set piece in Wayne pictures; motivated or totally gratuitous, the fight sequence has to be in the picture, because they so enjoy making it. "Listen—this'll really be funny. Duke picks up the kid, see, and then it takes both Dino and Earl to throw him out the door—*how's that?*"

They communicated by sharing old jokes; they sealed their cama- 45
raderie by making gentle, old-fashioned fun of wives, those civilizers, those tamers. "So Señora Wayne takes it into her head to stay up and have one brandy. So for the rest of the night it's 'Yes, Pilar, you're right, dear. I'm a bully, Pilar, you're right, I'm impossible.' "

"You hear that? Duke says Pilar threw a table at him."

"Hey, Duke, here's something funny. That finger you hurt today, get the Doc to bandage it up, go home tonight, show it to Pilar, tell her she did it when she threw the table. You know, make her think she was really cutting up."

They treated the oldest among them respectfully; they treated the youngest fondly. "You see that kid?" they said of Michael Anderson, Jr. "What a kid."

"He don't act, it's right from the heart," said Hathaway, patting his heart.

"Hey kid," Martin said. "You're gonna be in my next picture. We'll 50
have the whole thing, no beards. The striped shirts, the girls, the hi-fi, the eye lights."

They ordered Michael Anderson his own chair, with "BIG MIKE" tooled on the back. When it arrived on the set, Hathaway hugged him. "You see that?" Anderson asked Wayne, suddenly too shy to look him in the eye. Wayne gave him the smile, the nod, the final accolade. "I saw it, kid."

On the morning of the day they were to finish *Katie Elder,* Web Overlander showed up not in his Windbreaker but in a blue blazer. "Home, Mama," he said, passing out the last of his Juicy Fruit. "I got on my getaway clothes." But he was subdued. At noon, Henry Hathaway's wife dropped by the commissary to tell him that she might fly over to Acapulco. "Go ahead," he told her. "I get through here, all I'm gonna do is take Seconal to a point just this side of suicide." They were all subdued. After Mrs. Hathaway left, there were desultory attempts at reminiscing, but man's country was receding fast; they were already halfway home, and all they could call up was the 1961 Bel Air fire, during which Henry Hathaway had ordered the Los Angeles Fire Department off his property and saved the place himself by, among other measures, throwing everything flammable into the swimming pool. "Those fire guys might've just given it up," Wayne said. "Just let it burn." In fact this was a good story, and one incorporating several of their favorite themes, but a Bel Air story was still not a Durango story.

In the early afternoon they began the last scene, and although they spent as much time as possible setting it up, the moment finally came when there was nothing to do but shoot it. "Second team out, first team in, *doors closed,*" the assistant director shouted one last time. The stand-ins walked off the set, John Wayne and Martha Hyer walked on. "All right, boys, *silencio,* this is a picture." They took it twice. Twice the girl offered John Wayne the tattered Bible. Twice John Wayne told her that "there's a lot of places I go where that wouldn't fit in." Everyone was very still. And at 2:30 that Friday afternoon Henry Hathaway turned away from the camera, and in the hush that followed he ground out his cigar in a sand bucket. "O.K.," he said. "That's it."

Since that summer of 1943 I had thought of John Wayne in a number of ways. I had thought of him driving cattle up from Texas, and bringing airplanes in on a single engine, thought of him telling the girl at the Alamo that "Republic is a beautiful word." I had never thought of him having dinner with his family and with me and my husband in an expensive restaurant in Chapultepec Park, but time brings odd mutations, and there we were, one night that last week in Mexico. For a while it was only a nice evening, an evening anywhere. We had a lot of drinks and I lost the sense that the face across the table was in certain ways more familiar than my husband's.

And then something happened. Suddenly the room seemed suffused with the dream, and I could not think why. Three men appeared out of nowhere, playing guitars. Pilar Wayne leaned slightly forward, and John Wayne lifted his glass almost imperceptibly toward her. "We'll need some Pouilly-Fuissé for the rest of the table," he said "and some red Bordeaux for the Duke." We all smiled, and drank the Pouilly-Fuissé for the rest of the table and the red Bordeaux for the Duke, and all the while the men with the guitars kept playing, until finally I realized what they were playing, what they had been playing all along: "The Red River Valley" and the theme from *The High and the Mighty.* They did not quite get the beat right, but even now I can hear them, in another country and a long time later, even as I tell you this.

1965

Lines of Inquiry
"John Wayne: A Love Song"

Didion tells three stories in this essay: about the time in her childhood when she first saw John Wayne; about the early life and movie career of John Wayne; and about the final week in the filming of *The Sons of Katie Elder*. Rather than beginning with a story about her own childhood, why doesn't Didion begin with the story of Wayne's early life? What relevance does her story have to the stories about Wayne? Why, in turn, does she devote so little time to the story of Wayne's overall career and so much time to the story of one week in the filming of 1 of his 165 movies? In other words, how do you account for her selection, arrangement, and proportioning of these stories?

In paragraph 3, Didion claims that "when John Wayne rode through my childhood, and perhaps through yours, he determined forever the shape of certain of our dreams." What kinds of dreams is she referring to here? In what sense(s) are those dreams related to the dream (in paragraph 4) that she claims John Wayne was "in search of" for most of his life? How, in turn, are Didion's dreams and Wayne's dream related to the dream that "the room seemed suffused with" in the final paragraph of the essay? What can you infer about Didion's attitudes towards all of the dreams and dreamers that she writes about in her essay? Have you ever had any such dreams yourself?

Didion's essay on Wayne is not her only effort at portraiture, as you can see by looking at her essay on the artist, Georgia O'Keeffe, which also appears in this collection. In what respects does she use similar techniques in portraying these two persons? In what respects does she not? How do you account for the similarities and differences?

Georgia O'Keeffe

"**W**here I was born and where and how I have lived is unimportant," Georgia O'Keeffe told us in the book of paintings and words published in her ninetieth year on earth. She seemed to be advising us to forget the beautiful face in the Stieglitz photographs. She appeared to be dismissing the rather condescending romance that had attached to her by then, the romance of extreme good looks and advanced age and deliberate isolation. "It is what I have done with where I have been that should be of interest." I recall an August afternoon in Chicago in 1973 when I took my daughter, then seven, to see what Georgia O'Keeffe had done with where she had been. One of the vast O'Keeffe "Sky Above Clouds" canvases floated over the back stairs in the Chicago Art Institute that day, dominating what seemed to be several stories of empty light, and my daughter looked at it once, ran to the landing, and kept on looking. "Who drew it," she whispered after a while. I told her. "I need to talk to her," she said finally.

My daughter was making, that day in Chicago, an entirely unconscious but quite basic assumption about people and the work they do. She was assuming that the glory she saw in the work reflected a glory in its maker, that the painting was the painter as the poem is the poet, that every choice one made alone—every word chosen or rejected, every brush stroke laid or not laid down—betrayed one's character. *Style is character.* It seemed to me that afternoon that I had rarely seen so instinctive an application of this familiar principle, and I recall being pleased not only that my daughter responded to style as character but that it was Georgia O'Keeffe's particular style to which she responded: this was a hard woman who had imposed her 192 square feet of clouds on Chicago.

"Hardness" has not been in our century a quality much admired in women, nor in the past twenty years has it even been in official favor for men. When hardness surfaces in the very old we tend to transform it into "crustiness" or eccentricity, some tonic pepperiness to be indulged at a distance. On the evidence of her work and what she has said about it, Georgia O'Keeffe is neither "crusty" nor eccentric. She is simply hard, a straight shooter, a woman clean of received wisdom and open to what she sees. This is a woman who could early on dismiss most of her contemporaries as "dreamy," and would later single out one she liked as "a very poor painter." (And then add, apparently by way of softening the judgment: "I guess he wasn't a painter at all. He had no courage and I believe that to create one's own world in any of the arts takes courage.") This is a woman who in 1939 could advise her admirers that they were missing her point, that their appreciation of her famous flowers was merely sentimental. "When I paint a red hill," she observed coolly in the catalogue for an exhibition that year, "you say it is too bad that I don't always paint flowers. A flower touches almost everyone's heart. A red hill doesn't touch everyone's heart." This is a woman who could describe the genesis of one of her most well-known paintings—the "Cow's Skull: Red, White and Blue" owned by the Metropolitan—as an act of quite deliberate and derisive orneriness. "I thought of the city men I had been seeing in the East," she wrote. "They talked so often of writing the Great American Novel—the Great American Play—the Great American Poetry. . . . So as I was painting my cow's head on blue I thought to myself, 'I'll make it an American painting. They will not think it great with the red stripes down the sides—Red, White and Blue—but they will notice it.' "

The city men. The men. They. The words crop up again and again as this astonishingly aggressive woman tells us what was on her mind when she was making her astonishingly aggressive paintings. It was those city men who stood accused of sentimentalizing her flowers: "I made you take time to look at what I saw and when you took time to really notice my flower you hung all your associations with flowers on my flower and you write about my flower as if I think and see what you think and see—and I don't." *And I don't.* Imagine those words spoken, and the sound you hear is *don't tread on me.* "The men" believed it impossible to paint New York, so Georgia O'Keeffe painted New York. "The men" didn't think much of her bright color, so she made it brighter. The men yearned toward Europe so she went to Texas, and then New Mexico. The men talked about Cézanne, "long involved remarks about the 'plastic quality' of his form and color," and took one another's long involved remarks, in the view of this angelic rattlesnake in their midst, altogether too seriously. "I can paint one of those dismal-colored paintings like the men," the woman who regarded herself always as an outsider remembers thinking one day in 1922, and she did: a painting of a shed "all low-toned and dreary with the tree beside the door." She called this act of rancor "The Shanty" and hung it in her next show. "The men seemed to approve of it," she reported fifty-four years later, her contempt undimmed. "They seemed to think that maybe I was beginning to paint. That was my only low-toned dismal-colored painting."

Some women fight and others do not. Like so many successful   5
guerrillas in the war between the sexes, Georgia O'Keeffe seems to have been equipped early with an immutable sense of who she was and a fairly clear understanding that she would be required to prove it. On the surface her upbringing was conventional. She was a child on the Wisconsin prairie who played with china dolls and painted watercolors

with cloudy skies because sunlight was too hard to paint and, with her brother and sisters, listened every night to her mother read stories of the Wild West, of Texas, of Kit Carson and Billy the Kid. She told adults that she wanted to be an artist and was embarrassed when they asked what kind of artist she wanted to be: she had no idea "what kind." She had no idea what artists did. She had never seen a picture that interested her, other than a pen-and-ink Maid of Athens in one of her mother's books, some Mother Goose illustrations printed on cloth, a tablet cover that showed a little girl with pink roses, and the painting of Arabs on horseback that hung in her grandmother's parlor. At thirteen, in a Dominican convent, she was mortified when the sister corrected her drawing. At Chatham Episcopal Institute in Virginia she painted lilacs and sneaked time alone to walk out to where she could see the line of the Blue Ridge Mountains on the horizon. At the Art Institute in Chicago she was shocked by the presence of live models and wanted to abandon anatomy lessons. At the Art Students League in New York one of her fellow students advised her that, since he would be a great painter and she would end up teaching painting in a girls' school, any work of hers was less important than modeling for him. Another painted over her work to show her how the Impressionists did trees. She had not before heard how the Impressionists did trees and she did not much care.

At twenty-four she left all those opinions behind and went for the first time to live in Texas, where there were no trees to paint and no one to tell her how not to paint them. In Texas there was only the horizon she craved. In Texas she had her sister Claudia with her for a while, and in the late afternoons they would walk away from town and toward the horizon and watch the evening star come out. "That evening star fascinated me," she wrote. "It was in some way very exciting to me. My sister had a gun, and as we walked she would throw bottles into the air and shoot as many as she could before they hit the ground. I had nothing but to walk into nowhere and the wide sunset space with the star. Ten watercolors were made from that star." In a way one's interest is compelled as much by the sister Claudia with the gun as by the painter Georgia with the star, but only the painter left us this shining record. Ten watercolors were made from that star.

1976

Lines of Inquiry
"Georgia O'Keeffe"

Rather than beginning this piece with a statement of her own, Didion opens it with a quotation from O'Keeffe, and at several other points Didion refers to statements by O'Keeffe. What impression of O'Keeffe did you get from these quotations? What purpose do you suppose that Didion had in mind for repeating and echoing bits and pieces of O'Keeffe's remarks as she does in paragraphs 3 and 4?

Given the title of this piece, consider exactly what you learned about O'Keeffe from reading it. What are the most notable things that you learned about O'Keeffe's life? About her personality? About her art? Which of these topics do you think was uppermost in Didion's mind? What do you think is the single most important point about O'Keeffe that Didion is trying to make in this essay?

Now that you know what Didion and some other people have thought and said about O'Keeffe's art, take a look at it yourself to decide what you think of it. You can see one of her works on the cover of this book. Examine the picture carefully to determine what you see in it, what sense you make of it on your own, and how it affects you personally. Once you have thought through your own reactions to the piece, then turn to the back of the title page of this book, where you will find the title of the painting. How do your reactions square with the title of the painting? How typical does this painting seem to be of O'Keeffe's art as it is described in Didion's essay?

On the Mall

They float on the land-
scape like pyramids to the boom years, all those Plazas and Malls and
Esplanades. All those Squares and Fairs. All those Towns and Dales, all
those Villages, all those Forests and Parks and Lands. Stonestown.
Hillsdale. Valley Fair, Mayfair, Northgate, Southgate, Eastgate, West-
gate. Gulfgate. They are toy garden cities in which no one lives but
everyone consumes, profound equalizers, the perfect fusion of the profit
motive and the egalitarian ideal, and to hear their names is to recall
words and phrases no longer quite current. Baby Boom. Consumer
Explosion. Leisure Revolution. Do-It-Yourself Revolution. Backyard
Revolution. Suburbia. "The Shopping Center," the Urban Land Institute could pronounce in 1957, "is today's extraordinary retail business
evolvement. . . . The automobile accounts for suburbia, and suburbia
accounts for the shopping center."

It was a peculiar and visionary time, those years after World War II
to which all the Malls and Towns and Dales stand as climate-controlled
monuments. Even the word "automobile," as in "the automobile accounts for suburbia and suburbia accounts for the shopping center," no
longer carries the particular freight it once did: as a child in the late
Forties in California I recall reading and believing that the "freedom of
movement" afforded by the automobile was "America's fifth freedom."
The trend was up. The solution was in sight. The frontier had been
reinvented, and its shape was the subdivision, that new free land on
which all settlers could recast their lives *tabula rasa*. For one perishable
moment there the American idea seemed about to achieve itself, via
F.H.A. housing and the acquisition of major appliances, and a certain
enigmatic glamour attached to the architects of this newfound land.
They made something of nothing. They gambled and sometimes lost.
They staked the past to seize the future. I have difficulty now imagining
a childhood in which a man named Jere Strizek, the developer of Town
and Country Village outside Sacramento (143,000 square feet gross floor
area, 68 stores, 1000 parking spaces, the Urban Land Institute's "pro-
totype for centers using heavy timber and tile construction for infor-
mality"), could materialize as a role model, but I had such a childhood,
just after World War II, in Sacramento. I never met or even saw Jere
Strizek, but at the age of 12 I imagined him a kind of frontiersman, a
romantic and revolutionary spirit, and in the indigenous grain he was.

I suppose James B. Douglas and David D. Bohannon were too.
I first heard of James B. Douglas and David D. Bohannon not when
I was 12 but a dozen years later, when I was living in New York,

working for *Vogue,* and taking, by correspondence, a University of California Extension course in shopping-center theory. This did not seem to me eccentric at the time. I remember sitting on the cool floor in Irving Penn's studio and reading, in *The Community Builders Handbook,* advice from James B. Douglas on shopping-center financing. I recall staying late in my pale-blue office on the twentieth floor of the Graybar Building to memorize David D. Bohannon's parking ratios. My "real" life was to sit in this office and describe life as it was lived in Djakarta and Caneel Bay and in the great châteaux of the Loire Valley, but my dream life was to put together a Class-A regional shopping center with three full-line department stores as major tenants.

That I was perhaps the only person I knew in New York, let alone 5
on the Condé Nast floors of the Graybar Building, to have memorized the distinctions among "A," "B," and "C" shopping centers did not occur to me (the defining distinction, as long as I have your attention, is that an "A," or "regional," center has as its major tenant a full-time department store which carries major appliances; a "B," or "community," center has as its major tenant a junior department store which does not carry major appliances; and a "C," or "neighborhood," center has as its major tenant only a supermarket): my interest in shopping centers was in no way casual. I did want to build them. I wanted to build them because I had fallen into the habit of writing fiction, and I had it in my head that a couple of good centers might support this habit less taxingly than a pale-blue office at *Vogue.* I had even devised an original scheme by which I planned to gain enough capital and credibility to enter the shopping-center game: I would lease warehouses in, say, Queens, and offer Manhattan delicatessens the opportunity to sell competitively by buying cooperatively, from my trucks. I see a few wrinkles in this scheme now (the words "concrete overcoat" come to mind), but I did not then. In fact I planned to run it out of the pale-blue office.

James B. Douglas and David D. Bohannon. In 1950 James B. Douglas had opened Northgate, in Seattle, the first regional center to combine a pedestrian mall with an underground truck tunnel. In 1954 David D. Bohannon had opened Hillsdale, a forty-acre regional center on the peninsula south of San Francisco. That is the only solid bio I have on James B. Douglas and David D. Bohannon to this day, but many of their opinions are engraved on my memory. David D. Bohannon believed in preserving the integrity of the shopping center by not cutting up the site with any dedicated roads. David D. Bohannon believed that architectural setbacks in a center looked "pretty on paper" but caused "customer resistance." James B. Douglas advised that a small-loan office could prosper in a center only if it were placed away from foot traffic, since people who want small loans do not want to be observed getting them. I do not now recall whether it was James B. Douglas or

David D. Bohannon or someone else altogether who passed along this hint on how to paint the lines around the parking spaces (actually this is called "striping the lot," and the spaces are "stalls"): make each space a foot wider than it need be—ten feet, say, instead of nine—when the center first opens and business is slow. By this single stroke the developer achieves a couple of important objectives, the appearance of a popular center and the illusion of easy parking, and no one will really notice when business picks up and the spaces shrink.

Nor do I recall who first solved what was once a crucial center dilemma: the placement of the major tenant vis-à-vis the parking lot. The dilemma was that the major tenant—the draw, the raison d´être for the financing, the Sears, the Macy's, the May Company—wanted its customer to walk directly from car to store. The smaller tenants, on the other hand, wanted that same customer to *pass their stores* on the way from the car to, say, Macy's. The solution to this conflict of interests was actually very simple: *two major tenants,* one at each end of a mall. This is called "anchoring the mall," and represents seminal work in shopping-center theory. One thing you will note about shopping-center theory is that you could have thought of it yourself, and a course in it will go a long way toward dispelling the notion that business proceeds from mysteries too recondite for you and me.

A few aspects of shopping-center theory do in fact remain impenetrable to me. I have no idea why the Community Builders' Council ranks "Restaurant" as deserving a Number One (or "Hot Spot") location but exiles "Chinese Restaurant" to a Number Three, out there with "Power and Light Office" and "Christian Science Reading Room." Nor do I know why the Council approves of enlivening a mall with "small animals" but specifically, vehemently, and with no further explanation, excludes "monkeys." If I had a center I would have monkeys, and Chinese restaurants, and Mylar kites and bands of small girls playing tambourine.

A few years ago at a party I met a woman from Detroit who told me that the Joyce Carol Oates novel with which she identified most closely was *Wonderland*.

I asked her why.

"Because," she said, "my husband has a branch there."

I did not understand.

"In Wonderland the center," the woman said patiently. "My husband has a branch in Wonderland."

I have never visited Wonderland but imagine it to have bands of small girls playing tambourine.

A few facts about shopping centers.   15

The "biggest" center in the United States is generally agreed to be Woodfield, outside Chicago, a "super" regional or "leviathan" two-million-square-foot center with four major tenants.

The "first" shopping center in the United States is generally agreed to be Country Club Plaza in Kansas City, built in the twenties. There were some other early centers, notably Edward H. Bouton's 1907 Roland Park in Baltimore, Hugh Prather's 1931 Highland Park Shopping Village in Dallas, and Hugh Potter's 1937 River Oaks in Houston, but the developer of Country Club Plaza, the late J. C. Nichols, is referred to with ritual frequency in the literature of shopping centers, usually as "pioneering J. C. Nichols," "trailblazing J. C. Nichols," or "J. C. Nichols, father of the center as we know it."

Those are some facts I know about shopping centers because I still want to be Jere Strizek or James B. Douglas or David D. Bohannon. Here are some facts I know about shopping centers because I never will be Jere Strizek or James B. Douglas or David D. Bohannon: a good center in which to spend the day if you wake feeling low in Honolulu, Hawaii, is Ala Moana, major tenants Liberty House and Sears. A good center in which to spend the day if you wake feeling low in Oxnard, California, is The Esplanade, major tenants the May Company and Sears. A good center in which to spend the day if you wake feeling low in Biloxi, Mississippi, is Edgewater Plaza, major tenant Godchaux's. Ala Moana in Honolulu is larger than The Esplanade in Oxnard, and The Esplanade in Oxnard is larger than Edgewater Plaza in Biloxi. Ala Moana has carp pools. The Esplanade and Edgewater Plaza do not.

These marginal distinctions to one side, Ala Moana, The Esplanade, and Edgewater Plaza are the same place, which is precisely their role not only as equalizers but in the sedation of anxiety. In each of them one moves for a while in an aqueous suspension not only of light but of judgment, not only of judgment but of "personality." One meets no acquaintances at The Esplanade. One gets no telephone calls at Edgewater Plaza. "It's a hard place to run in to for a pair of stockings," a friend complained to me recently of Ala Moana, and I knew that she was not yet ready to surrender her ego to the idea of the center. The last time I went to Ala Moana it was to buy *The New York Times.* Because *The New York Times* was not in, I sat on the mall for a while and ate caramel corn. In the end I bought not *The New York Times* at all but two straw hats at Liberty House, four bottles of nail enamel at Woolworth's, and a toaster, on sale at Sears. In the literature of shopping centers these would be described as impulse purchases, but the impulse here was obscure. I do not wear hats, nor do I like caramel corn. I do not use nail enamel. Yet flying back across the Pacific I regretted only the toaster.

1975

Lines of Inquiry
"On the Mall"

Throughout her essay, Didion conveys quite a bit of information about the history of malls, but not in chronological order. She also conveys quite a bit of information about the story of her own interest in malls, but again not in chronological order. How would you define the organization of the piece? Why do you suppose she divided it into five separate sections? Can you think of clearer, more convincing, or more evocative ways in which she might have arranged these sections and the information they contain?

In the first paragraph of her essay, Didion speaks of malls as "pyramids to the boom years," then as "toy garden cities in which no one lives, but everyone consumes, profound equalizers." What do these metaphors imply about her attitude towards malls? At the end of the essay, she speaks of them as places where "one moves for a while in an aqueous suspension not only of light but of judgment, not only of judgment but of 'personality.' " What does this description imply about her attitude towards malls? What do you infer about her attitude from what she tells about herself and about malls in the rest of the essay? How exactly would you define Didion's attitude toward malls?

Probably, you have grown up near a mall, have spent a good bit of time in malls yourself, and thus have discovered some things on your own about how malls are designed and operated. Just to refresh your thoughts and impressions a bit, spend a few hours examining a mall near where you currently live, keeping your eye open for aspects of the place that strike you as being typical of the way it is designed to attract business and to capitalize on consumer instincts. How does this particular mall fit the portrait of malls that Didion develops in her essay? How typical is your nearby mall of other malls that you have observed in your hometown or elsewhere?

On the Road

*W*here are we heading, they asked in all the television and radio studios. They asked it in New York and Los Angeles and they asked it in Boston and Washington and they asked it in Dallas and Houston and Chicago and San Francisco. Sometimes they made eye contact as they asked it. Sometimes they closed their eyes as they asked it. Quite often they wondered not just where we were heading but where we were heading "as Americans," or "as concerned Americans," or "as American women," or, on one occasion, "as the American guy and the American woman." I never learned the answer, nor did the answer matter, for one of the eerie and liberating aspects of broadcast discourse is that nothing one says will alter in the slightest either the form or the length of the conversation. Our voices in the studios were those of manic actors assigned to do three-minute, four-minute, seven-minute improvs. Our faces on the monitors were those of concerned Americans. On my way to one of those studios in Boston I had seen the magnolias bursting white down Marlborough Street. On my way to another in Dallas I had watched the highway lights blazing and dimming pink against the big dawn sky. Outside one studio in Houston the afternoon heat was sinking into the deep primeval green of the place and outside the next, that night in Chicago, snow fell and glittered in the lights along the lake. Outside all these studios America lay in all its exhilaratingly volatile weather and eccentricity and specificity, but inside the studios we shed the specific and rocketed on to the general, for they were The Interviewers and I was The Author and the single question we seemed able to address together was *where are we heading*.

> *"8:30 A.M. to 9:30 A.M.: LIVE on WFSB TV/THIS MORNING.*
> *"10 A.M. to 10:30 A.M.: LIVE on WINF AM/THE WORLD TODAY.*
> *"10:45 A.M. to 11:45 A.M.: PRESS INTERVIEW with HARTFORD COURANT.*
> *"12 noon to 1:30 P.M.: AUTOGRAPHING at BARNES AND NOBLE.*
> *"2 P.M. to 2:30 P.M.: TAPE at WDRC AM/FM.*
> *"3 P.M. to 3:30 P.M.: PRESS INTERVIEW with THE HILL INK.*
> *"7:30 P.M. to 9 P.M.: TAPE at WHNB TV/WHAT ABOUT WOMEN."*

From 12 noon to 1:30 P.M., that first day in Hartford, I talked to a man who had cut a picture of me from a magazine in 1970 and had come round to Barnes and Noble to see what I looked like in 1977. From 2 P.M. to 2:30 P.M., that first day in Hartford, I listened to the receptionists at WDRC AM/FM talk about the new records and I watched snow drop from the pine boughs in the cemetery across the street. The name of the cemetery was Mt. St. Benedict and my husband's father had been buried there. "Any Steely Dan come in?" the receptionists kept asking. From 8:30 A.M. until 9 P.M., that first day in Hartford, I neglected to mention the name of the book I was supposed to be promoting. It was my fourth book but I had never before done what is called in the trade a book tour. I was not sure what I was doing or why I was doing it. I had left California equipped with two "good" suits, a box of unanswered mail, Elizabeth Hardwick's *Seduction and Betrayal,* Edmund Wilson's *To the Finland Station,* six Judy Blume books and my eleven-year-old daughter. The Judy Blume books were along to divert my daughter. My daughter was along to divert me. Three days into the tour I sent home the box of unanswered mail to make room for a packet of Simon and Schuster press releases describing me in favorable terms. Four days into the tour I sent home *Seduction and Betrayal* and *To the Finland Station* to make room for a thousand-watt hair blower. By the time I reached Boston, ten days into the tour, I knew that I had never before heard and would possibly never again hear America singing at precisely this pitch: ethereal, speedy, an angel choir on Dexamyl.

Where were we heading. The set for this discussion was always the same: a cozy oasis of wicker and ferns in the wilderness of cables and cameras and Styrofoam coffee cups that was the actual studio. On wicker settees across the nation I expressed my conviction that we were heading "into an era" of whatever the clock seemed to demand. In green rooms across the nation I listened to other people talk about where we were heading, and also about their vocations, avocations, and secret interests. I discussed L-dopa and biorhythm with a woman whose father invented prayer breakfasts. I exchanged makeup tips with a former Mouseketeer. I stopped reading newspapers and started relying on bulletins from limo drivers, from Mouseketeers, from the callers-in on call-in shows and from the closed-circuit screens in airports that flashed random stories off the wire ("CARTER URGES BARBITURATE BAN" is one that got my attention at La Guardia) between advertisements for *Shenandoah.* I gravitated to the random. I swung with the non-sequential.

I began to see America as my own, a child's map over which my child and I could skim and light at will. We spoke not of cities but of airports. If rain fell at Logan we could find sun at Dulles. Bags lost at O'Hare could be found at Dallas/Fort Worth. In the first-class cabins of the planes on which we traveled we were often, my child and I, the only female passengers, and I apprehended for the first time those particular illusions of mobility which power American business. Time was money. Motion was progress. Decisions were snap and the ministrations of other people were constant. Room service, for example, assumed paramount importance. We needed, my eleven-year-old and I, instant but erratically timed infusions of consommé, oatmeal, crab salad and asparagus vinaigrette. We needed Perrier water and tea to drink when we were working. We needed bourbon on the rocks and Shirley Temples to drink when we were not. A kind of irritable panic came over us when room service went off, and also when no one answered in the housekeeping department. In short we had fallen into the peculiar hormonal momentum of business travel, and I had begun to understand the habituation many men and a few women have to planes and telephones and schedules. I had begun to regard my own schedule—a sheaf of thick cream-colored pages printed with the words "SIMON & SCHUSTER/A DIVISION OF GULF & WESTERN CORPORATION"—with a reverence approaching the mystical. We wanted 24-hour room service. We wanted direct-dial telephones. We wanted to stay on the road forever.

We saw air as our element. In Houston the air was warm and rich   5
and suggestive of fossil fuel and we pretended we owned a house in River Oaks. In Chicago the air was brilliant and thin and we pretended we owned the 27th floor of the Ritz. In New York the air was charged and crackling and shorting out with opinions, and we pretended we had some. Everyone in New York had opinions. Opinions were demanded in return. The absence of opinion was construed as opinion. Even my daughter was developing opinions. "Had an interesting talk with Carl Bernstein," she noted in the log she had been assigned to keep for her fifth-grade teacher in Malibu, California. Many of these New York opinions seemed intended as tonic revisions, bold corrections to opinions in vogue during the previous week, but since I had just dropped from the sky it was difficult for me to distinguish those opinions which were "bold" and "revisionist" from those which were merely "weary" and "rote." At the time I left New York many people were expressing a bold belief in "joy"—joy in children, joy in wedlock, joy in the dailiness of life—but joy was trickling down fast to show-business personalities. Mike Nichols, for example, was expressing his joy in the pages of *Newsweek,* and also his weariness with "lapidary bleakness." Lapidary bleakness was definitely rote.

We were rethinking the Sixties that week, or Morris Dickstein was.

We were taking another look at the Fifties that week, or Hilton Kramer was.

I agreed passionately. I disagreed passionately. I called room service on one phone and listened attentively on the other to people who seemed convinced that the "texture" of their lives had been agreeably or adversely affected by conversion to the politics of joy, by regression to lapidary bleakness, by the Sixties, by the Fifties, by the recent change in administrations and by the sale of *The Thorn Birds* to paper for one-million-nine.

I lost track of information.

I was blitzed by opinion.   10

I began to see opinions arcing in the air, intersecting flight patterns. The Eastern shuttle was cleared for landing and so was lapidary bleakness. John Leonard and joy were on converging vectors. I began to see the country itself as a projection on air, a kind of hologram, an invisible grid of image and opinion and electronic impulse. There were opinions in the air and there were planes in the air and there were even people in the air: one afternoon in New York my husband saw a man jump from a window and fall to the sidewalk outside the Yale Club. I mentioned this to a *Daily News* photographer who was taking my picture. "You have to catch a jumper in the act to make the paper," he advised me. He had caught two in the act but only the first had made the paper. The second was a better picture but coincided with the crash of a DC-10 at Orly. "They're all over town," the photographer said. "Jumpers. A lot of them aren't even jumpers. They're window washers. Who fall."

What does that say about us as a nation, I was asked the next day when I mentioned the jumpers and window washers on the air. *Where are we headed.* On the 27the floor of the Ritz in Chicago my daughter and I sat frozen at the breakfast table until the window washers glided safely out of sight. At a call-in station in Los Angeles I was told by the guard that there would be a delay because they had a jumper on the line. "I say let him jump," the guard said to me. I imagined a sky dense with jumpers and fallers and DC-10s. I held my daughter's hand at takeoff and landing and watched for antennae on the drive into town. The big antennae with the pulsing red lights had been for a month our landmarks. The big antennae with the pulsing red lights had in fact been for a month our destinations. "Out I-10 to the antenna" was the kind of direction we had come to understand, for we were on the road, on the grid, on the air and also in it. *Where were we heading.* I don't know where you're heading, I said in the studio attached to the last of these antennae, my eyes fixed on still another of the neon FLEETWOOD MAC signs that flickered that spring in radio stations from coast to coast, but I'm heading home.

1977

Lines of Inquiry
"On the Road"

Throughout this piece, Didion relies quite heavily on the repetition or echoing of particular words, phrases, or clauses, as in the opening question, "Where are we headed," which appears several times in various forms later in the piece. What are the effects of these repetitions and echoes? As a way of beginning to answer this question, underline all of the echoes and repetitions you can find in the first paragraph, and then consider their effect in this particular context. How does Didion come across and how does her point come across as a result of these echoes? Then for purposes of comparison, identify and analyze the echoes and repetitions in the final paragraph.

Between the beginning and end of this piece, Didion touches on quite a few subjects, but she keeps veering back to the experience of being "on the road" and to the question of "where are we heading." What does she convey about the experience of her cross-country tour? What does she suggest about where America is headed? What do these two subjects have to do with each other?

More than ten years have passed since Didion made the trip on which this piece is based, so it might be interesting to consider whether or not her experiences and observations are up-to-date. Do you think her piece is consistent with the impressions of America that you get nowadays from reading the newspaper, watching TV, and traveling on your own? Or do you have a significantly different set of perceptions from hers? In what respects do you consider her portrait of America to be up-to-date? In what respects do you consider it out-of-date?

On Keeping a Notebook

" 'That woman Estelle,' " the note reads, " 'is partly the reason why George Sharp and I are separated today.' *Dirty crepe-de-Chine wrapper, hotel bar, Wilmington RR, 9:45 a.m. August Monday morning."*

Since the note is in my notebook, it presumably has some meaning to me. I study it for a long while. At first I have only the most general notion of what I was doing on an August Monday morning in the bar of the hotel across from the Pennsylvania Railroad station in Wilmington, Delaware (waiting for a train? missing one? 1960? 1961? why Wilmington?), but I do remember being there. The woman in the dirty crepe-de-Chine wrapper had come down from her room for a beer, and the bartender had heard before the reason why George Sharp and she were separated today. "Sure," he said, and went on mopping the floor. "You told me." At the other end of the bar is a girl. She is talking, pointedly, not to the man beside her but to a cat lying in the triangle of sunlight cast through the open door. She is wearing a plaid silk dress from Peck & Peck, and the hem is coming down.

Here is what it is: the girl has been on the Eastern Shore, and now she is going back to the city, leaving the man beside her, and all she can see ahead are the viscous summer sidewalks and the 3 a.m. long-distance calls that will make her lie awake and then sleep drugged through all the steaming mornings left in August (1960? 1961?). Because she must go directly from the train to lunch in New York, she wishes that she had a safety pin for the hem of the plaid silk dress, and she also wishes that she could forget about the hem and the lunch and stay in the cool bar that smells of disinfectant and malt and make friends with the woman in the crepe-de-Chine wrapper. She is afflicted by a little self-pity, and she wants to compare Estelles. That is what that was all about.

Why did I write it down? In order to remember, of course, but exactly what was it I wanted to remember? How much of it actually happened? Did any of it? Why do I keep a notebook at all? It is easy to deceive oneself on all those scores. The impulse to write things down is a peculiarly compulsive one, inexplicable to those who do not share it, useful only accidentally, only secondarily, in the way that any compulsion tries to justify itself. I suppose that it begins or does not begin in the cradle. Although I have felt compelled to write things down since I was five years old, I doubt that my daughter ever will, for she is a singularly blessed and accepting child, delighted with life exactly as life presents itself to her, unafraid to go to sleep and unafraid to wake up.

Keepers of private notebooks are a different breed altogether, lonely and resistant rearrangers of things, anxious malcontents, children afflicted apparently at birth with some presentiment of loss.

My first notebook was a Big Five tablet, given to me by my mother   5
with the sensible suggestion that I stop whining and learn to amuse myself by writing down my thoughts., She returned the tablet to me a few years ago; the first entry is an account of a woman who believed herself to be freezing to death in the Arctic night, only to find, when day broke, that she had stumbled onto the Sahara Desert, where she would die of the heat before lunch. I have no idea what turn of a five-year-old's mind could have prompted so insistently "ironic" and exotic a story, but it does reveal a certain predilection for the extreme which has dogged me into adult life; perhaps if I were analytically inclined I would find it a truer story than any I might have told about Donald Johnson's birthday party or the day my cousin Brenda put Kitty Litter in the aquarium.

So the point of my keeping a notebook has never been, nor is it now, to have an accurate factual record of what I have been doing or thinking. That would be a different impulse entirely, an instinct for reality which I sometimes envy but do not possess. At no point have I ever been able successfully to keep a diary; my approach to daily life ranges from the grossly negligent to the merely absent, and on those few occasions when I have tried dutifully to record a day's events, boredom has so overcome me that the results are mysterious at best. What is this business about "shopping, typing piece, dinner with E, depressed"? Shopping for what? Typing what piece? Who is E? Was this "E" depressed, or was I depressed? Who cares?

In fact I have abandoned altogether that kind of pointless entry; instead I tell what some would call lies. "That's simply not true," the members of my family frequently tell me when they come up against my memory of a shared event. "The party was *not* for you, the spider was *not* a black widow, *it wasn't that way at all.*" Very likely they are right, for not only have I always had trouble distinguishing between what happened and what merely might have happened, but I remain unconvinced that the distinction, for my purposes, matters. The cracked crab that I recall having for lunch the day my father came home from Detroit in 1945 must certainly be embroidery, worked into the day's pattern to lend verisimilitude; I was ten years old and would not now remember the cracked crab. The day's events did not turn on cracked crab. And yet it is precisely that fictitious crab that makes me see the afternoon all over again, a home movie run all too often, the father bearing gifts, the child weeping, an exercise in family love and guilt. Or that is what it was to me. Similarly, perhaps it never did snow that

August in Vermont; perhaps there never were flurries in the night wind, and maybe no one else felt the ground hardening and summer already dead even as we pretended to bask in it, but that was how it felt to me, and it might as well have snowed, could have snowed, did snow.

How it felt to me: that is getting closer to the truth about a notebook. I sometimes delude myself about why I keep a notebook, imagine that some thrifty virtue derives from preserving everything observed. See enough and write it down, I tell myself, and then some morning when the world seems drained of wonder, some day when I am only going through the motions of doing what I am supposed to do, which is write—on that bankrupt morning I will simply open my notebook and there it will all be, a forgotten account with accumulated interest, paid passage back to the world out there: dialogue overheard in hotels and elevators and at the hat-check counter in Pavillon (one middle-aged man shows his hat check to another and says, "That's my old football number"); impressions of Bettina Aptheker and Benjamin Sonnenberg and Teddy ("Mr. Acapulco") Stauffer; careful *aperçus* about tennis bums and failed fashion models and Greek shipping heiresses, one of whom taught me a significant lesson (a lesson I could have learned from F. Scott Fitzgerald, but perhaps we all must meet the very rich for ourselves) by asking, when I arrived to interview her in her orchid-filled sitting room on the second day of a paralyzing New York blizzard, whether it was snowing outside.

I imagine, in other words, that the notebook is about other people. But of course it is not. I have no real business with what one stranger said to another at the hat-check counter in Pavillon; in fact I suspect that the line "That's my old football number" touched not my own imagination at all, but merely some memory of something once read, probably "The Eighty-Yard Run." Nor is my concern with a woman in a dirty crepe-de-Chine wrapper in a Wilmington bar. My stake is always, of course, in the unmentioned girl in the plaid silk dress. *Remember what it was to be me:* that is always the point.

It is a difficult point to admit. We are brought up in the ethic that others, any others, all others, are by definition more interesting than ourselves; taught to be diffident, just this side of self-effacing. ("You're the least important person in the room and don't forget it," Jessica Mitford's governess would hiss in her ear on the advent of any social occasion; I copied that into my notebook because it is only recently that I have been able to enter a room without hearing some such phrase in my inner ear.) Only the very young and the very old may recount their dreams at breakfast, dwell upon self, interrupt with memories of beach picnics and favorite Liberty lawn dresses and the rainbow trout in a creek near Colorado Springs. The rest of us are expected, rightly, to affect absorption in other people's favorite dresses, other people's trout.

And so we do. But our notebooks give us away, for however dutifully we record what we see around us, the common denominator of all we see is always, transparently, shamelessly, the implacable "I." We are not talking here about the kind of notebook that is patently for public consumption, a structural conceit for binding together a series of graceful *pensées;* we are talking about something private, about bits of the mind's string too short to use, an indiscriminate and erratic assemblage with meaning only for its maker.

And sometimes even the maker has difficulty with the meaning. There does not seem to be, for example, any point in my knowing for the rest of my life that, during 1964, 720 tons of soot fell on every square mile of New York City, yet there it is in my notebook, labeled "FACT". Nor do I really need to remember that Ambrose Bierce liked to spell Leland Stanford's name "£eland $tanford" or that "smart women almost always wear black in Cuba," a fashion hint without much potential for practical application. And does not the relevance of these notes seem marginal at best?:

> In the basement museum of the Inyo County Courthouse in Independence, California, sign pinned to a mandarin coat: "This MANDARIN COAT was often worn by Mrs. Minnie S. Brooks when giving lectures on her TEAPOT COLLECTION."

> Redhead getting out of car in front of Beverly Wilshire Hotel, chinchilla stole, Vuitton bags with tags reading:

> MRS LOU FOX
> HOTEL SAHARA
> VEGAS

Well, perhaps not entirely marginal. As a matter of fact, Mrs. Minnie S. Brooks and her MANDARIN COAT pull me back into my own childhood, for although I never knew Mrs. Brooks and did not visit Inyo County until I was thirty, I grew up in just such a world, in houses cluttered with Indian relics and bits of gold ore and ambergris and the souvenirs my Aunt Mercy Farnsworth brought back from the Orient. It is a long way from that world to Mrs. Lou Fox's world, where we all live now, and is it not just as well to remember that? Might not Mrs. Minnie S. Brooks help me to remember what I am? Might not Mrs. Lou Fox help me to remember what I am not?

But sometimes the point is harder to discern. What exactly did I have in mind when I noted down that it cost the father of someone I know $650 a month to light the place on the Hudson in which he lived before the Crash? What use was I planning to make of this line by

Jimmy Hoffa: "I may have my faults, but being wrong ain't one of them"? And although I think it interesting to know where the girls who travel with the Syndicate have their hair done when they find themselves on the West Coast, will I ever make suitable use of it? Might I not be better off just passing it on to John O'Hara? What is a recipe for sauerkraut doing in my notebook? What kind of magpie keeps this notebook? *"He was born the night the Titanic went down."* That seems a nice enough line, and I even recall who said it, but is it not really a better line in life than it could ever be in fiction?

But of course that is exactly it: not that I should ever use the line,   15 but that I should remember the woman who said it and the afternoon I heard it. We were on her terrace by the sea, and we were finishing the wine left from lunch, trying to get what sun there was, a California winter sun. The woman whose husband was born the night the *Titanic* went down wanted to rent her house, wanted to go back to her children in Paris. I remember wishing that I could afford the house, which cost $1,000 a month. "Someday you will," she said lazily. "Someday it all comes." There in the sun on her terrace it seemed easy to believe in someday, but later I had a low-grade afternoon hangover and ran over a black snake on the way to the supermarket and was flooded with inexplicable fear when I heard the checkout clerk explaining to the man ahead of me why she was finally divorcing her husband. "He left me no choice," she said over and over as she punched the register. "He has a little seven-month-old baby by her, he left me no choice." I would like to believe that my dread then was for the human condition, but of course it was for me, because I wanted a baby and did not then have one and because I wanted to own the house that cost $1,000 a month to rent and because I had a hangover.

It all comes back. Perhaps it is difficult to see the value in having one's self back in that kind of mood, but I do see it; I think we are well advised to keep on nodding terms with the people we used to be, whether we find them attractive company or not. Otherwise they turn up unannounced and surprise us, come hammering on the mind's door at 4 a.m. of a bad night and demand to know who deserted them, who betrayed them, who is going to make amends. We forget all too soon the things we thought we could never forget. We forget the loves and the betrayals alike, forget what we whispered and what we screamed, forget who we were. I have already lost touch with a couple of people I used to be; one of them, a seventeen-year-old, presents little threat, although it would be of some interest to me to know again what it feels like to sit on a river levee drinking vodka-and-orange-juice and listening to Les Paul and Mary Ford and their echoes sing "How High the Moon" on the car radio. (You see I still have the scenes, but I no longer perceive myself among those present, no longer could even improvise the dialogue.) The other one, a twenty-three-year-old, bothers me more.

She was always a good deal of trouble, and I suspect she will reappear when I least want to see her, skirts too long, shy to the point of aggravation, always the injured party, full of recriminations and little hurts and stories I do not want to hear again, at once saddening me and angering me with her vulnerability and ignorance, an apparition all the more insistent for being so long banished.

It is a good idea, then, to keep in touch, and I suppose that keeping in touch is what notebooks are all about. And we are all on our own when it comes to keeping those lines open to ourselves: your notebook will never help me, nor mine you. *"So what's new in the whiskey business?"* What could that possibly mean to you? To me it means a blonde in a Pucci bathing suit sitting with a couple of fat men by the pool at the Beverly Hills Hotel. Another man approaches, and they all regard one another in silence for a while. "So what's new in the whiskey business?" one of the fat men finally says by way of welcome, and the blonde stands up, arches one foot and dips it in the pool, looking all the while at the cabaña where Baby Pignatari is talking on the telephone. That is all there is to that, except that several years later I saw the blonde coming out of Saks Fifth Avenue in New York with her California complexion and a voluminous mink coat. In the harsh wind that day she looked old and irrevocably tired to me, and even the skins in the mink coat were not worked the way they were doing them that year, not the way she would have wanted them done, and there is the point of the story. For a while after that I did not like to look in the mirror, and my eyes would skim the newspapers and pick out only the deaths, the cancer victims, the premature coronaries, the suicides, and I stopped riding the Lexington Avenue IRT because I noticed for the first time that all the strangers I had seen for years—the man with the seeing-eye dog, the spinster who read the classified pages every day, the fat girl who always got off with me at Grand Central—looked older than they once had.

It all comes back. Even that recipe for sauerkraut: even that brings it back. I was on Fire Island when I first made that sauerkraut, and it was raining, and we drank a lot of bourbon and ate the sauerkraut and went to bed at ten, and I listened to the rain and the Atlantic and felt safe. I made the sauerkraut again last night and it did not make me feel any safer, but that is, as they say, another story.

1966

Lines of Inquiry
"On Keeping a Notebook"

From the beginning to the end of her essay, Didion gives us short, sample excerpts from her notebook, but none of the passages that she cites refers to her own past activities, thoughts, or feelings. What is her purpose in citing these passages? How, exactly, do they fit into her rationale for keeping a notebook? If such passages are meant to keep her in touch with her former selves, why does she tell us that she often has trouble in making sense of these notes?

Near the end of her essay (in paragraph 17), Didion advises us "to keep on nodding terms with the people we used to be." Else, she warns us, "they turn up unannounced and surprise us." What do you think she means by the people we used to be? And how can they possibly turn up unannounced and surprise us? Why does she believe that keeping a notebook is the best way of "keeping those lines open to ourselves"? Why mightn't an album of personal snapshots do just as well?

Near the end of her essay (again in paragraph 17), Didion says that she has "already lost touch with a couple of people I used to be." According to this statement and others like it, she evidently looks upon her self as a changeable person. How changeable—how unchangeable—a person does she seem to be in her essays that appear in this collection? What kind of person does she seem to be in each piece? What aspect of her self does she seem most concerned with in each piece? In what respects does she seem to change—in what respects does she seem to remain the same—from one essay to the next?

Annie Dillard
1945—

I am a frayed and nibbled survivor in a fallen world, and I am getting along. I am aging and eaten and have done my share of eating too. I am not washed and beautiful, in control of a shining world in which everything fits, but instead am wandering awed about on a splintered wreck I've come to care for, whose gnawed trees breathe a delicate air, whose bloodied and scarred creatures are my dearest companions, and whose beauty beats and shines not in its imperfections but overwhelmingly in spite of them, under the wind-rent clouds, upstream and down.

Thus does Annie Dillard characterize herself, the world she inhabits, and her relationship to that world in her best-selling *Pilgrim at Tinker Creek* (1974). That book won Dillard, then only twenty-nine, a Pulitzer Prize and a lasting place in the ranks of contemporary writers of creative nonfiction. Echoing Thoreau's *Walden,* it chronicles a year's sojourn on the banks and in the environs of Tinker Creek in the Roanoke Valley of Virginia by a "wanderer with a background in theology and a penchant for quirky facts," a year of walking, watching, and writing with breath-stopping precision about what she sees—and what she learns to see. Here as in her subsequent works, she sees both sides of the world, dark along with light, and insists on confounding their traditional associations: "If we are blinded by darkness, we are also blinded by light." The effect in her writing is a kind of *chiaroscuro,* light and darkness intensifying each other by juxtaposition with their opposite. And while the world might be "fallen," a "splintered wreck," it is still filled with a "beauty" that "beats and shines," inspiring Dillard to register her response in richly poetic language filled with surprise and delight.

Dillard was born in 1945 in Pittsburgh, the eldest of three daughters in a well-to-do family. She has written of her early years in her most recent book, *An American Childhood* (1987), "I grew up in Pittsburgh in the 1950s, in a house full of comedians, reading books." She attended private girls' schools, spent summers at the lake or the country club pool, took dancing lessons, planned to be an architect, and "began a life of reading books, and drawing, and playing at the sciences." Above all, she read books, "to delirium," and her memoir of childhood is more than anything else the record of an emerging consciousness shaped by reading. Despite the privileged conformity in which she was raised, she thought of herself as fierce, odd, and difficult, and one of her high-school teachers described her this way: "Here, alas, is a child of the twentieth century."

She began writing poetry while she was still in high school, and at Hollins College in Virginia's Blue Ridge Mountains she continued reading and writing, but with more seriousness and discipline. After completing her undergraduate degree in English in 1967, she continued her apprenticeship in the Hollins graduate writing program, earning a master's degree in 1968. Her first book was a collection of poems, *Tickets for a Prayer Wheel* (1973), which appeared while she was still living in the Roanoke Valley. In 1975 she traveled west to teach writing at Western Washington State College on the Puget Sound, and in 1979 she crossed the country again, returning to the east coast to accept a position at Wesleyan College in Connecticut, where she still makes her home.

In her early published prose work, Dillard staked out for herself a distinctive combination of form and content—essays which focus on a personal experience of the natural world and which employ to an elaborate degree the techniques of poetry. Her attention to the sounds and rhythms of language, her evident pleasure in precise and suggestive words, are hallmarks of her style. Readers of her prose have become accustomed to finding sentences or whole passages which are lyric, even rhapsodic, and which, in their use of metaphor, rhyme, and repetition of sound and syntactic structure, would be equally at home in a poem, as would this one: "There are no events but thoughts and the heart's hard turning, the heart's slow learning where to love and whom."

Dillard herself, though, has insisted that "any art, including an art of surface, must do more than dazzle." Her own subject, as she has expressed it, is "the paradoxical nature of all our days, the curious way we bump up against the unexpected everywhere," and that description of her subject applies equally to her style. Beauty is a serious enough motive for writing, to be sure, but other serious impulses are at work in Dillard's writing—in particular the quest for spiritual enlightenment, for knowledge of who made such a world as that in which she finds herself, and why. "What's going on here? Who's in charge?" are the questions which constitute her refrain. She is in bold terms "a seeker, a pilgrim in the religious sense of the word," as one critic puts it, pressing always toward a definition of what it means to be a believer.

Persistently she seeks to know the world in all its minute detail, not to blink at the horror which is the twin of joy, to find in what she sees a key to what it all might mean. Always for Dillard it is language which transforms sight into insight, which opens the door to significance:

> Seeing is of course very much a matter of verbalization. Unless I call my attention to what passes before my eyes, I simply won't see it. It is, as Ruskin says, "not merely unnoticed, but in the full clear sense of the word, unseen." . . . I have to say the words, describe what I'm

seeing. . . . Otherwise, especially in a strange place, I'll never know what's happening.

One critic has said Dillard is "a connoisseur of spirit, who knows that seeing, if intense enough, becomes vision."

Dillard seeks vision, though, in often homely sources: the ways of cats, the wastes of violent weather, a mockingbird's flight, a flash of light from the side of swimming fish, the grotesqueries of the insect world, the profligacy of nature. Far from refusing to acknowledge what is awful about the intricate texture of creation, she confronts it in its most gruesome details—a praying mantis devouring her mate in the act of coition, a giant water bug sucking a frog dry of its liquid life. Yet, even as the emptied frog skin rumples and sinks, it is beauty and grace that Dillard insistently seeks and celebrates:

> As a thinker I keep discovering that beauty itself is as much a fact, and a mystery, as the most gruesome parastic roundworm. I consider nature's facts—its beautiful and grotesque forms and events—in terms of their import to thought and their impetus to the spirit. In nature I find grace tangled in a rapture with violence; I find an intricate landscape whose forms are fringed with death; I find mystery, newness, and a kind of exuberant, spendthrift energy.

The rapturous tangle of grace with violence is for Dillard not an obstacle to faith but the central mystery of being, the paradox which is the doorway to the satisfaction of spiritual longing for contact with a creator who is anything but tame:

> The texture of the world, its filigree and scrollwork, means that there is the possibility for beauty here, a beauty inexhaustible in its complexity, which opens to my knock, which answers in me a call I do not remember calling, and which trains me to the wild and extravagant nature of the spirit I seek.

Her recent essays, collected in *Teaching a Stone to Talk* (1982), continue to press that vision, but in contrast with *Pilgrim at Tinker Creek* their settings are sometimes far-flung and often exotic—an imaginary polar expedition, the Galapagos Islands, the rivers and jungles and villages of South America. "Possibly because Father had loaded his boat one day and gone down the Ohio River, I confused leaving with living, and vowed that when I got my freedom, I would be the one to do both." Always, though, however broad or narrow her setting, the record of the human spirit impressing itself on the world is the central fact of her work. She sees "the mind and the world as inextricably fitted twin puzzles. The mind fits the world and shapes it as a river fits and shapes its own banks." The essay form is particularly well-suited to such a project, and in keeping with her vision Dillard's essays repeatedly confound the distinctions between factual narrative and story, just as in their style they blur the boundaries between poetry and prose:

> What interests me here, and elsewhere, is the possibility for a purified nonfiction narration—a kind of Chekhovian storytelling which might illuminate the actual world with a delicate light—coupled with humor in the American tradition and no comment.

Dillard's preoccupations, finally, are not new ones; she worries in all her work the questions about time, change, mortality, and the presence of evil which have obsessed the race since the dawn of history. Her contributions are to the style and form of the essay, and they have been significant. She has made her mark as a storyteller with a gift for depicting her vision of the world in writing that delights as much as it reveals:

> I intend only to tell some small stories, and to depict precise moments precisely, in the hope that a collection of such moments might give an impression of many sharp points going in different directions—might give a vivid sense of complexity.

The Death of a Moth

Transfiguration in a Candle Flame

I live alone with two cats, who sleep on my legs. There is a yellow one, and a black one whose name is Small. In the morning I joke to the black one, Do you remember last night? Do you remember? I throw them both out before breakfast, so I can eat.

There is a spider, too, in the bathroom, of uncertain lineage, bulbous at the abdomen and drab, whose six-inch mess of web works, works somehow, works miraculously, to keep her alive and me amazed. The web is in a corner behind the toilet, connecting tile wall to tile wall. The house is new, the bathroom immaculate, save for the spider, her web, and the sixteen or so corpses she's tossed to the floor.

The corpses appear to be mostly sow bugs, those little armadillo creatures who live to travel flat out in houses, and die round. In addition to sow-bug husks, hollow and sipped empty of color, there are what seem to be two or three wingless moth bodies, one new flake of earwig, and three spider carcasses crinkled and clenched.

I wonder on what fool's errand an earwig, or a moth, or a sow bug, would visit that clean corner of the house behind the toilet; I have not noticed any blind parades of sow bugs blundering into corners. Yet they do hazard there, at a rate of more than one a week, and the spider thrives. Yesterday she was working on the earwig, mouth on gut; today he's on the floor. It must take a certain genius to throw things away from there, to find a straight line through that sticky tangle to the floor.

Today the earwig shines darkly, and gleams, what there is of him: 5 a dorsal curve of thorax and abdomen, and a smooth pair of pincers by which I knew his name. Next week, if the other bodies are any indication, he'll be shrunk and gray, webbed to the floor with dust. The sow bugs beside him are curled and empty, fragile, a breath away from brittle fluff. The spiders lie on their sides, translucent and ragged, their legs drying in knots. The moths stagger against each other, headless, in a confusion of arcing strips of chitin like peeling varnish, like a jumble of buttresses for cathedral vaults, like nothing resembling moths, so that I would hesitate to call them moths, except that I have had some experience with the figure Moth reduced to a nub.

Two summers ago I was camped alone in the Blue Ridge Mountains of Virginia. I had hauled myself and gear up there to read, among other things, *The Day on Fire,* by James Ullman, a novel about Rimbaud that had made me want to be a writer when I was sixteen; I was hoping it would do it again. So I read every day sitting under a tree by my tent, while warblers sang in the leaves overhead and bristle worms trailed their inches over the twiggy dirt at my feet; and I read every night by candlelight, while barred owls called in the forest and pale moths seeking mates massed round my head in the clearing, where my light made a ring.

Moths kept flying into the candle. They would hiss and recoil, reeling upside down in the shadows among my cooking pans. Or they would singe their wings and fall, and their hot wings, as if melted, would stick to the first thing they touched—a pan, a lid, a spoon—so that the snagged moths could struggle only in tiny arcs, unable to flutter free. These I could release by a quick flip with a stick; in the morning I would find my cooking stuff decorated with torn flecks of moth wings, ghostly triangles of shiny dust here and there on the aluminum. So I read, and boiled water, and replenished candles, and read on.

One night a moth flew into the candle, was caught, burnt dry, and held. I must have been staring at the candle, or maybe I looked up where a shadow crossed my page; at any rate, I saw it all. A golden female moth, a biggish one with a two-inch wingspread, flapped into the fire, dropped abdomen into the wet wax, stuck, flamed, and frazzled in a second. Her moving wings ignited like tissue paper, like angels' wings, enlarging the circle of light in the clearing and creating out of the darkness the sudden blue sleeves of my sweater, the green leaves of jewelweed by my side, the ragged red trunk of a pine; at once the light contracted again and the moth's wings vanished in a fine, foul smoke. At the same time, her six legs clawed, curled, blackened, and ceased, disappearing utterly. And her head jerked in spasms, making a spattering noise; her antennae crisped and burnt away and her heaving mouthparts cracked like pistol fire. When it was all over, her head was, so far as I could determine, gone, gone the long way of her wings and legs. Her head was a hole lost to time. All that was left was the glowing horn shell of her abdomen and thorax—a fraying, partially collapsed gold tube jammed upright in the candle's round pool.

And then this moth-essence, this spectacular skeleton, began to act as a wick. She kept burning. The wax rose in the moth's body from her soaking abdomen to her thorax to the shattered hole where her head should have been, and widened into flame, a saffron-yellow flame that robed her to the ground like an immolating monk. That candle had two wicks, two winding flames of identical light, side by side. The moth's head was fire. She burned for two hours, until I blew her out.

She burned for two hours without changing, without swaying or kneeling—only glowing within, like a building fire glimpsed through silhouetted walls, like a hollow saint, like a flame-faced virgin gone to God, while I read by her light, kindled, while Rimbaud in Paris burnt out his brain in a thousand poems, while night pooled wetly at my feet. 10

So. That is why I think those hollow shreds on the bathroom floor are moths. I believe I know what moths look like, in any state.

I have three candles here on the table which I disentangle from the plants and light when visitors come. The cats avoid them, although Small's tail caught fire once; I rubbed it out before she noticed. I don't mind living alone. I like eating alone and reading. I don't mind sleeping alone. The only time I mind being alone is when something is funny; then, when I am laughing at something funny, I wish someone were around. Sometimes I think it is pretty funny that I sleep alone.

Lines of Inquiry
"The Death of a Moth"

The second section of this piece, in which Dillard vividly describes the striking spectacle of a moth burning to death in a candle flame, could easily stand alone, for like a well-told story it contains a clear-cut beginning, middle, and end. What, then, is the purpose of the first and third sections? Why does Dillard go to so much trouble in the first section to describe all of the insect carcasses littering the corner of her bathroom, and why in the third section does she give so much attention to her feelings about living alone?

Given the fact that she combines details about the moth with details about her own existence, it seems appropriate to consider what they have to do with each other. What does the death of a moth have to do with the life of Dillard? In particular, what does the spectacle of the moth burning for two hours have to do with Dillard's living alone? What does that spectacle have to do with her aspirations as a writer? Why in her subtitle does she refer to that spectacle as a "transfiguration"?

In this piece, as in "Living Like Weasels," Dillard uses the existence or experience of another creature as a metaphor for a way of living that she wishes to emulate. What similarities, what differences, do you see in the way she develops her metaphor in each piece? What similarities, what differences, do you see in the way of living that Dillard is concerned with in each case?

Living Like Weasels

A weasel is wild. Who knows what he thinks? He sleeps in his underground den, his tail draped over his nose. Sometimes he lives in his den for two days without leaving. Outside, he stalks rabbits, mice, muskrats, and birds, killing more bodies than he can eat warm, and often dragging the carcasses home. Obedient to instinct, he bites his prey at the neck, either splitting the jugular vein at the throat or crunching the brain at the base of the skull, and he does not let go. One naturalist refused to kill a weasel who was socketed into his hand deeply as a rattlesnake. The man could in no way pry the tiny weasel off, and he had to walk half a mile to water, the weasel dangling from his palm, and soak him off like a stubborn label.

And once, says Ernest Thompson Seton—once, a man shot an eagle out of the sky. He examined the eagle and found the dry skull of a weasel fixed by the jaws to his throat. The supposition is that the eagle had pounced on the weasel and the weasel swiveled and bit as instinct taught him, tooth to neck, and nearly won. I would like to have seen that eagle from the air a few weeks or months before he was shot: was the whole weasel still attached to his feathered throat, a fur pendant? Or did the eagle eat what he could reach, gutting the living weasel with his talons before his breast, bending his beak, cleaning the beautiful airborne bones?

I have been reading about weasels because I saw one last week. I startled a weasel who startled me, and we exchanged a long glance.

Twenty minutes from my house, through the woods by the quarry and across the highway, is Hollins Pond, a remarkable piece of shallowness, where I like to go at sunset and sit on a tree trunk. Hollins Pond is also called Murray's Pond; it covers two acres of bottomland near Tinker Creek with six inches of water and six thousand lily pads. In winter, brown-and-white steers stand in the middle of it, merely dampening their hooves; from the distant shore they look like miracle itself, complete with miracle's nonchalance. Now, in summer, the steers are gone. The water lilies have blossomed and spread to a green horizontal plane that is terra firma to plodding blackbirds, and tremulous ceiling to black leeches, crayfish, and carp.

This is, mind you, suburbia. It is a five-minute walk in three directions to rows of houses, though none is visible here. There's a 55 mph highway at one end of the pond, and a nesting pair of wood ducks at

5

the other. Under every bush is a muskrat hole or a beer can. The far end is an alternating series of fields and woods, fields and woods, threaded everywhere with motorcycle tracks—in whose bare clay wild turtles lay eggs.

So. I had crossed the highway, stepped over two low barbed-wire fences, and traced the motorcycle path in all gratitude through the wild rose and poison ivy of the pond's shoreline up into high grassy fields. Then I cut down through the woods to the mossy fallen tree where I sit. This tree is excellent. It makes a dry, upholstered bench at the upper, marshy end of the pond, a plush jetty raised from the thorny shore between a shallow blue body of water and a deep blue body of sky.

The sun had just set. I was relaxed on the tree trunk, ensconced in the lap of lichen, watching the lily pads at my feet tremble and part dreamily over the thrusting path of a carp. A yellow bird appeared to my right and flew behind me. It caught my eye; I swiveled around— and the next instant, inexplicably, I was looking down at a weasel, who was looking up at me.

Weasel! I'd never seen one wild before. He was ten inches long, thin as a curve, a muscled ribbon, brown as fruitwood, soft-furred, alert. His face was fierce, small and pointed as a lizard's; he would have made a good arrowhead. There was just a dot of chin, maybe two brown hairs' worth, and then the pure white fur began that spread down his underside. He had two black eyes I didn't see, any more than you see a window.

The weasel was stunned into stillness as he was emerging from beneath an enormous shaggy wild rose bush four feet away. I was stunned into stillness twisted backward on the tree trunk. Our eyes locked, and someone threw away the key.

Our look was as if two lovers, or deadly enemies, met unexpectedly 10 on an overgrown path when each had been thinking of something else: a clearing blow to the gut. It was also a bright blow to the brain, or a sudden beating of brains, with all the charge and intimate grate of rubbed balloons. It emptied our lungs. It felled the forest, moved the fields, and drained the pond; the world dismantled and tumbled into that black hole of eyes. If you and I looked at each other that way, our skulls would split and drop to our shoulders. But we don't. We keep our skulls. So.

He disappeared. This was only last week, and already I don't remember what shattered the enchantment. I think I blinked, I think I retrieved my brain from the weasel's brain, and tried to memorize what I was seeing, and the weasel felt the yank of separation, the careening splashdown into real life and the urgent current of instinct. He vanished under the wild rose. I waited motionless, my mind suddenly full of data and my spirit with pleadings, but he didn't return.

Please do not tell me about "approach-avoidance conflicts." I tell you I've been in that weasel's brain for sixty seconds, and he was in mine. Brains are private places, muttering through unique and secret tapes—but the weasel and I both plugged into another tape simultaneously, for a sweet and shocking time. Can I help it if it was a blank?

What goes on in his brain the rest of the time? What does a weasel think about? He won't say. His journal is tracks in clay, a spray of feathers, mouse blood and bone: uncollected, unconnected, loose-leaf, and blown.

I would like to learn, or remember, how to live. I come to Hollins Pond not so much to learn how to live as, frankly, to forget about it. That is, I don't think I can learn from a wild animal how to live in particular—shall I suck warm blood, hold my tail high, walk with my footprints precisely over the prints of my hands?—but I might learn something of mindlessness, something of the purity of living in the physical senses and the dignity of living without bias or motive. The weasel lives in necessity and we live in choice, hating necessity and dying at the last ignobly in its talons. I would like to live as I should, as the weasel lives as he should. And I suspect that for me the way is like the weasel's: open to time and death painlessly, noticing everything, remembering nothing, choosing the given with a fierce and pointed will.

I missed my chance. I should have gone for the throat. I should have lunged for that streak of white under the weasel's chin and held on, held on through mud and into the wild rose, held on for a dearer life. We could live under the wild rose wild as weasels, mute and uncomprehending. I could very calmly go wild. I could live two days in the den, curled, leaning on mouse fur, sniffing bird bones, blinking, licking, breathing musk, my hair tangled in the roots of grasses. Down is a good place to go, where the mind is single. Down is out, out of your ever-loving mind and back to your careless senses. I remember muteness as a prolonged and giddy fast, where every moment is a feast of utterance received. Time and events are merely poured, unremarked, and ingested directly, like blood pulsed into my gut through a jugular vein. Could two live that way? Could two live under the wild rose, and explore by the pond, so that the smooth mind of each is as everywhere present to the other, and as received and as unchallenged, as falling snow?

We could, you know. We can live any way we want. People take vows of poverty, chastity, and obedience—even of silence—by choice. The thing is to stalk your calling in a certain skilled and supple way, to locate the most tender and live spot and plug into that pulse. This is yielding, not fighting. A weasel doesn't "attack" anything; a weasel

15

lives as he's meant to, yielding at every moment to the perfect freedom of single necessity.

I think it would be well, and proper, and obedient, and pure, to grasp your one necessity and not let it go, to dangle from it limp wherever it takes you. Then even death, where you're going no matter how you live, cannot you part. Seize it and let it seize you up aloft even, till your eyes burn out and drop; let your musky flesh fall off in shreds, and let your very bones unhinge and scatter, loosened over fields, over fields and woods, lightly, thoughtless, from any height at all, from as high as eagles.

Lines of Inquiry
"Living Like Weasels"

From the beginning to the end of this essay, Dillard covers quite a bit of territory. How does she manage to get from her opening description of weasels to her concluding meditation on how to live? How does she organize and develop her essay to show what she perceives to be the relationship between the two? Exactly how does each of the six sections in the piece contribute to Dillard's ideas about "living like weasels"? What would be lost—what gained, perhaps—by omitting most of the second section, except for the first paragraph of it? What would be the effect(s) of omitting the entire fifth section?

Given the importance of weasels in this essay it seems appropriate to consider exactly what information Didion conveys about them. What aspects of weasel life does she report in this piece? What aspects of their behavior are most important to her? Exactly what does Dillard see in their way of living that applies to the lives of human beings? What do you suppose would be some of the consequences—both beneficial and detrimental—of living like weasels?

Think of an animal whose way of living is especially interesting and appealing to you, and do some reading about the animal, much as Dillard read about weasels, to learn about its most distinctive behavior. What aspect of this animal's behavior is most striking and most fraught with implications for the lives of human beings? What would it be like for human beings to live like this animal?

The Deer at Providencia

There were four of us North Americans in the jungle, in the Ecuadorian jungle on the banks of the Napo River in the Amazon watershed. The other three North Americans were metropolitan men. We stayed in tents in one riverside village, and visited others. At the village called Providencia we saw a sight which moved us, and which shocked the men.

The first thing we saw when we climbed the riverbank to the village of Providencia was the deer. It was roped to a tree on the grass clearing near the thatch shelter where we would eat lunch.

The deer was small, about the size of a whitetail fawn, but apparently full-grown. It had a rope around its neck and three feet caught in the rope. Someone said that the dogs had caught it that morning and the villagers were going to cook and eat it that night.

This clearing lay at the edge of the little thatched-hut village. We could see the villagers going about their business, scattering feed corn for hens about their houses, and wandering down paths to the river to bathe. The village headman was our host; he stood beside us as we watched the deer struggle. Several village boys were interested in the deer; they formed part of the circle we made around it in the clearing. So also did four businessmen from Quito who were attempting to guide us around the jungle. Few of the very different people standing in this circle had a common language. We watched the deer, and no one said much.

The deer lay on its side at the rope's very end, so the rope lacked 5 slack to let it rest its head in the dust. It was "pretty," delicate of bone like all deer, and thin-skinned for the tropics. Its skin looked virtually hairless, in fact, and almost translucent, like a membrane. Its neck was no thicker than my wrist; it was rubbed open on the rope, and gashed. Trying to paw itself free of the rope, the deer had scratched its own neck with its hooves. The raw underside of its neck showed red stripes and some bruises bleeding inside the muscles. Now three of its feet were hooked in the rope under its jaw. It could not stand, of course, on one leg, so it could not move to slacken the rope and ease the pull on its throat and enable it to rest its head.

Repeatedly the deer paused, motionless, its eyes veiled, with only its rib cage in motion, and its breaths the only sound. Then, after I would think, "It has given up; now it will die," it would heave. The rope twanged; the tree leaves clattered; the deer's free foot beat the ground. We stepped back and held our breaths. It thrashed, kicking, but only one leg moved; the other three legs tightened inside the rope's loop. Its hip jerked; its spine shook. Its eyes rolled; its tongue, thick with spittle, pushed in and out. Then it would rest again. We watched this for fifteen minutes.

Once three young native boys charged in, released its trapped legs, and jumped back to the circle of people. But instantly the deer scratched up its neck with its hooves and snared its forelegs in the rope again. It was easy to imagine a third and then a fourth leg soon stuck, like Brer Rabbit and the Tar Baby.

We watched the deer from the circle, and then we drifted on to lunch. Our palm-roofed shelter stood on a grassy promontory from which we could see the deer tied to the tree, pigs and hens walking under village houses, and black-and-white cattle standing in the river. There was even a breeze.

Lunch, which was the second and better lunch we had that day, was hot and fried. There was a big fish called *doncella,* a kind of catfish, dipped whole in corn flour and beaten egg, then deep fried. With our fingers we pulled soft fragments of it from its sides to our plates, and ate; it was delicate fish-flesh, fresh and mild. Someone found the roe, and I ate of that too—it was fat and stronger, like egg yolk, naturally enough, and warm.

There was also a stew of meat in shreds with rice and pale brown   10
gravy. I had asked what kind of deer it was tied to the tree; Pepe had answered in Spanish, *"Gama."* Now they told us this was *gama* too, stewed. I suspect the word means merely game or venison. At any rate, I heard that the village dogs had cornered another deer just yesterday, and it was this deer which we were now eating in full sight of the whole article. It was good. I was surprised at its tenderness. But it is a fact that high levels of lactic acid, which builds up in muscle tissues during exertion, tenderizes.

After the fish and meat we ate bananas fried in chunks and served on a tray; they were sweet and full of flavor. I felt terrific. My shirt was wet and cool from swimming; I had had a night's sleep, two decent walks, three meals, and a swim—everything tasted good. From time to time each of us, separately, would look beyond our shaded roof to the sunny spot where the deer was still convulsing in the dust. Our meal completed, we walked around the deer and back to the boats.

That night I learned that while we were watching the deer, the others were watching me.

We four North Americans grew close in the jungle in a way that was not the usual artificial intimacy of travelers. We liked each other. We stayed up all that night talking, murmuring, as though we rocked on hammocks slung above time. The others were from big cities: New York, Washington, Boston. They all said that I had no expression on my face when I was watching the deer—or at any rate, not the expression they expected.

They had looked to see how I, the only woman, and the youngest, was taking the sight of the deer's struggles. I looked detached, apparently, or hard, or calm, or focused, still. I don't know. I was thinking. I remember feeling very old and energetic. I could say like Thoreau that I have traveled widely in Roanoke, Virginia. I have thought a great deal about carnivorousness; I eat meat. These things are not issues; they are mysteries.

Gentlemen of the city, what surprises you? That there is suffering here, or that I know it?   15

We lay in the tent and talked. "If it had been my wife," one man said with special vigor, amazed, "she wouldn't have cared *what* was going on; she would have dropped *everything* right at that moment and gone in the village from here to there to there, she would not have *stopped* until that animal was out of its suffering one way or another. She couldn't *bear* to see a creature in agony like that."

I nodded.

Now I am home. When I wake I comb my hair before the mirror above my dresser. Every morning for the past two years I have seen in that mirror, beside my sleep-softened face, the blackened face of a burnt man. It is a wire-service photograph clipped from a newspaper and taped to my mirror. The caption reads: "Alan McDonald in Miami hospital bed." All you can see in the photograph is a smudged triangle of face from his eyelids to his lower lip; the rest is bandages. You cannot see the expression in his eyes; the bandages shade them.

The story, headed MAN BURNED FOR SECOND TIME, begins:

> "Why does God hate me?" Alan McDonald asked from his hospital bed.
> "When the gunpowder went off, I couldn't believe it," he said. "I just couldn't believe it. I said, 'No, God couldn't do this to me again.'"

He was in a burn ward in Miami, in serious condition. I do not   20
even know if he lived. I wrote him a letter at the time, cringing.

He had been burned before, thirteen years previously, by flaming gasoline. For years he had been having his body restored and his face remade in dozens of operations. He had been a boy, and then a burnt boy. He had already been stunned by what could happen, by how life could veer.

Once I read that people who survive bad burns tend to go crazy; they have a very high suicide rate. Medicine cannot ease their pain;

drugs just leak away, soaking the sheets, because there is no skin to hold them in. The people just lie there and weep. Later they kill themselves. They had not known, before they were burned, that the world included such suffering, that life could permit them personally such pain.

This time a bowl of gunpowder had exploded on McDonald.

> "I didn't realize what had happened at first," he recounted. "And then I heard that sound from 13 years ago. I was burning. I rolled to put the fire out and I thought, 'Oh God, not again.'
>
> "If my friend hadn't been there, I would have jumped into a canal with a rock around my neck."

His wife concludes the piece, "Man, it just isn't fair."

I read the whole clipping again every morning. This is the Big Time here, every minute of it. Will someone please explain to Alan Mc-Donald in his dignity, to the deer at Providencia in his dignity, what is going on? And mail me the carbon.   25

When we walked by the deer at Providencia for the last time, I said to Pepe, with a pitying glance at the deer, *"Pobrecito"*—"poor little thing." But I was trying out Spanish. I knew at the time it was a ridiculous thing to say.

Lines of Inquiry
"The Deer at Providencia"

According to her male traveling companions, Dillard "looked detached, apparently, or hard, or calm" while she was looking at "the deer's struggles." How does she come across when she is describing the deer and its struggles? What does the wording of her description suggest about her attitude? What does her choice of descriptive details suggest about her attitude? What do her remarks in the final paragraph imply about her attitude?

The story of the deer and of people's differing reactions to its struggles, which appears in sections 1–7 and 10, could easily stand on its own. Why, then, do you suppose that Dillard includes the story of Alan McDonald in this piece? What do the deer and Alan McDonald have in common? What sets them apart? How does Dillard's attitude towards McDonald compare with her apparent attitude toward the deer?

In sections 1, 6, and 7, Dillard clearly makes an issue of the difference between her reaction to the deer and the reactions of her male traveling companions, and in sections 6 and 7 she also reports on how the men too made an issue of her reaction, as if to suggest that they perceived it as being atypical of women. In what respects do you think her reaction to the deer is atypical? In what respects, for example, is the supposed reaction of one man's wife, as outlined in section 7, more typical of women? To what extent do you believe that the reaction of women (or of men) can be typified?

Singing with the Fundamentalists

It is early spring. I have a temporary office at a state university on the West Coast. The office is on the third floor. It looks down on the Square, the enormous open courtyard at the center of campus. From my desk I see hundreds of people moving between classes. There is a large circular fountain in the Square's center.

Early one morning, on the first day of spring quarter, I hear singing. A pack of students has gathered at the fountain. They are singing something which, at this distance, and through the heavy window, sounds good.

I know who these singing students are: they are the Fundamentalists. This campus has a lot of them. Mornings they sing on the Square; it is their only perceptible activity. What are they singing? Whatever it is, I want to join them, for I like to sing; whatever it is, I want to take my stand with them, for I am drawn to their very absurdity, their innocent indifference to what people think. My colleagues and students here, and my friends everywhere, dislike and fear Christian fundamentalists. You may never have met such people, but you've heard what they do: they pile up money, vote in blocs, and elect right-wing crazies; they censor books; they carry handguns; they fight fluoride in the drinking water and evolution in the schools; probably they would lynch people if they could get away with it. I'm not sure my friends are correct. I close my pen and join the singers on the Square.

There is a clapping song in progress. I have to concentrate to follow it:

> Come on, rejoice,
> And let your heart sing,
> Come on, rejoice,
> Give power to the king.
> Singing alleluia—
> He is the king of kings;
> Singing alleluia—
> He is the king of kings.

Two song leaders are standing on the broad rim of the fountain; the water is splashing just behind them. The boy is short, hard-faced, with a moustache. He bangs his guitar with the backs of his fingers. The blonde girl, who leads the clapping, is bouncy; she wears a bit of make-up. Both are wearing blue jeans.   5

The students beside me are wearing blue jeans, too—and athletic jerseys, parkas, football jackets, turtlenecks, and hiking shoes or jogging shoes. They all have canvas or nylon book bags. They look like any random batch of seventy or eighty students at this university. They are grubby or scrubbed, mostly scrubbed; they are tall, fair, or redheaded in large proportions. Their parents are white-collar workers, blue-collar workers, farmers, loggers, orchardists, merchants, fishermen; their names are, I'll bet, Olsen, Jensen, Seversen, Hansen, Klokker, Sigurdsen.

Despite the vigor of the clapping song, no one seems to be giving it much effort. And no one looks at anyone else; there are no sentimental glances and smiles, no glances even of recognition. These kids don't seem to know each other. We stand at the fountain's side, out on the broad, bricked Square in front of the science building, and sing the clapping song through three times.

It is quarter to nine in the morning. Hundreds of people are crossing the Square. These passersby—faculty, staff, students—pay very little attention to us; this morning singing has gone on for years. Most of them look at us directly, then ignore us, for there is nothing to see: no animal sacrifices, no lynchings, no collection plate for Jesse Helms, no seizures, snake handling, healing, or glossolalia. There is barely anything to hear. I suspect the people glance at us to learn if we are really singing: how could so many people make so little sound? My fellow singers, who ignore each other, certainly ignore passersby as well. Within a week, most of them will have their eyes closed anyway.

We move directly to another song, a slower one.

> He is my peace
> Who has broken down every wall;
> He is my peace,
> He is my peace.
>
> Cast all your cares on him,
> For he careth for you—oo—oo
> He is my peace,
> He is my peace.

I am paying strict attention to the song leaders, for I am singing at 10
the top of my lungs and I've never heard any of these songs before. They are not the old American low-church Protestant hymns; they are not the old European high-church Protestant hymns. These hymns seem to have been written just yesterday, apparently by the same people who put out lyrical Christian greeting cards and bookmarks.

"Where do these songs come from?" I ask a girl standing next to me. She seems appalled to be addressed at all, and startled by the question. "They're from the praise albums!" she explains, and moves away.

The songs' melodies run dominant, subdominant, dominant, tonic, dominant. The pace is slow, about the pace of "Tell Laura I Love Her," and with that song's quavering, long notes. The lyrics are simple and repetitive; there are very few of them to which a devout Jew or Mohammedan could not give wholehearted assent. These songs are similar to the things Catholics sing in church these days. I don't know if any studies have been done to correlate the introduction of contemporary songs into Catholic churches with those churches' decline in membership, or with the phenomenon of Catholic converts' applying to enter cloistered monasteries directly, without passing through parish churches.

> I'm set free to worship,
> I'm set free to praise him,
> I'm set free to dance before the Lord . . .

At nine o'clock sharp we quit and scatter. I hear a few quiet "see you's." Mostly the students leave quickly, as if they didn't want to be seen. The Square empties.

The next day we show up again, at twenty to nine. The same two leaders stand on the fountain's rim; the fountain is pouring down behind them.

After the first song, the boy with the moustache hollers, "Move on up! Some of you guys aren't paying attention back there! You're talking to each other. I want you to concentrate!" The students laugh, embarrassed for him. He sounds like a teacher. No one moves. The girl breaks into the next song, which we join at once: 10

> In my life, Lord,
> Be glorified, be glorified, be glorified;
> In my life, Lord,
> Be glorified, be glorified, today.

At the end of this singularly monotonous verse, which is straining my tolerance for singing virtually anything, the boy with the moustache startles me by shouting, "Classes!"

At once, without skipping a beat, we sing, "In my classes, Lord, be glorified, be glorified . . ." I give fleet thought to the class I'm teaching this afternoon. We're reading a little "Talk of the Town" piece called "Eggbag," about a cat in a magic store on Eighth Avenue. "Relationships!" the boy calls. The students seem to sing "In my relationships, Lord," more easily than they sang "classes." They seemed embarrassed by "classes." In fact, to my fascination, they seem embarrassed by almost everything. Why are they here? I will sing with the Fundamentalists every weekday morning all spring; I will decide, tentatively, that they come pretty much for the same reasons I do: each has a private relationship with "the Lord" and will put up with a lot of junk for it.

I have taught some Fundamentalist students here, and know a bit of what they think. They are college students above all, worried about their love lives, their grades, and finding jobs. Some support moderate Democrats; some support moderate Republicans. Like their classmates, most support nuclear freeze, ERA, and an end to the draft. I believe they are divided on abortion and busing. They are not particularly political. They read *Christianity Today* and *Campus Life* and *Eternity*—moderate, sensible magazines, I think; they read a lot of C. S. Lewis. (One such student, who seemed perfectly tolerant of me and my shoddy Christianity, introduced me to C. S. Lewis's critical book on Charles Williams.) They read the Bible. I think they all "believe in" organic evolution. The main thing about them is this; there isn't any "them." Their views vary. They don't know each other.

Their common Christianity puts them, if anywhere, to the left of their classmates. I believe they also tend to be more able than their classmates to think well in the abstract, and also to recognize the complexity of moral issues. But I may be wrong.

In 1980, the media were certainly wrong about television evangelists. Printed estimates of Jerry Falwell's television audience ranged from 18 million to 30 million people. In fact, according to Arbitron's actual counts, fewer than 1.5 million people were watching Falwell. And, according to an Emory University study, those who did watch television evangelists didn't necessarily vote with them. Emory University sociologist G. Melton Mobley reports, "When that message turns political, they cut it off." Analysis of the 1982 off-year elections turned up no Fundamentalist bloc voting. The media were wrong, but no one printed retractions. 15

The media were wrong, too, in a tendency to identify all fundamentalist Christians with Falwell and his ilk, and to attribute to them, across the board, conservative views.

Someone has sent me two recent issues of *Eternity: The Evangelical Monthly*. One lead article criticizes a television preacher for saying that the United States had never used military might to take land from another nation. The same article censures Newspeak, saying that government rhetoric would have us believe in a "clean bomb," would have us believe that we "defend" America by invading foreign soil, and would have us believe that the dictatorships we support are "democracies." "When the President of the United States says that one reason to support defense spending is because it creates jobs," this lead article says, "a little bit of *1984* begins to surface." Another article criticizes a "heavy-handed" opinion of Jerry Falwell Ministries—in this case a broadside attack on artificial insemination, surrogate motherhood, and lesbian motherhood. Browsing through *Eternity,* I find a double crosstic. I find an intelligent, analytical, and enthusiastic review of the new London Philharmonic recording of Mahler's second symphony—a review which stresses the "glorious truth" of the Jewish composer's magnificent work, and cites its recent performance in Jerusalem to celebrate the recapture of the Western Wall following the Six Day War. Surely, the evangelical Christians who read this magazine are not book-burners. If by chance they vote with the magazine's editors, then it looks to me as if they vote with the American Civil Liberties Union and Americans for Democratic Action.

Every few years some bold and sincere Christian student at this university disagrees with a professor in class—usually about the professor's out-of-hand dismissal of Christianity. Members of the faculty, outraged, repeat the stories of these rare and uneven encounters for years on end, as if to prove that the crazies are everywhere, and gaining ground. The notion is, apparently, that these kids can't think for themselves. Or they wouldn't disagree.

Now again the moustached leader asks us to move up. There is no harangue, so we move up. (This will be a theme all spring. The leaders want us closer together. Our instinct is to stand alone.) From behind the tall fountain comes a wind; on several gusts we get sprayed. No one seems to notice.

We have time for one more song. The leader, perhaps sensing that   20
no one likes him, blunders on. "I want you to pray this one through," he says. "We have a lot of people here from a lot of different fellowships, but we're all one body. Amen?" They don't like it. He gets a few polite Amens. We sing:

> Bind us together, Lord,
> With a bond that can't be broken;
> Bind us together, Lord,
> With love.

Everyone seems to be in a remarkably foul mood today. We don't like this song. There is no one here under seventeen, and, I think, no one here who believes that love is a bond that can't be broken. We sing the song through three times; then it is time to go.

The leader calls after our retreating backs. "Hey, have a good day! Praise Him all day!" The kids around me roll up their eyes privately. Some groan; all flee.

The next morning is very cold. I am here early. Two girls are talking on the fountain's rim; one is part Indian. She says, "I've got all the

Old Testament, but I can't get the New. I screw up the New." She takes a breath and rattles off a long list, ending with "Jonah, Micah, Nahum, Habakkuk, Zephaniah, Haggai, Zechariah, Malachi." The other girl produces a slow, sarcastic applause. I ask one of the girls to help me with the words to a song. She is agreeable, but says, "I'm sorry, I can't. I just became a Christian this year, so I don't know all the words yet."

The others are coming; we stand and separate. The boy with the moustache is gone, replaced by a big, serious fellow in a green down jacket. The bouncy girl is back with her guitar; she's wearing a skirt and wool knee socks. We begin, without any preamble, by singing a song that has so few words that we actually stretch one syllable over eleven separate notes. Then we sing a song in which the men sing one phrase and the women echo it. Everyone seems to know just what to do. In the context of our vapid songs, the lyrics of this one are extraordinary:

> I was nothing before you found me.
> Heartache! Broken people! Ruined lives
> Is why you died on Calvary.

The last line rises in a regular series of half-notes. Now at last some people are actually singing; they throw some breath into the business. There is a seriousness and urgency to it: "Heartache! Broken people! Ruined lives . . . I was nothing."

We don't look like nothing. We look like a bunch of students of   25
every stripe, ill-shaven or well-shaven, dressed up or down, but dressed warmly against the cold: jeans and parkas, jeans and heavy sweaters, jeans and scarves and blow-dried hair. We look ordinary. But I think, quite on my own, that we are here because we know this business of nothingness, brokenness, and ruination. We sing this song over and over.

Something catches my eye. Behind us, up in the science building, professors are standing alone at opened windows.

The long brick science building has three upper floors of faculty offices, thirty-two windows. At one window stands a bearded man, about forty; his opening his window is what caught my eye. He stands full in the open window, his hands on his hips, his head cocked down toward the fountain. He is drawn to look, as I was drawn to come. Up on the building's top floor, at the far right window, there is another: an Asian-American professor, wearing a white shirt, is sitting with one hip on his desk, looking out and down. In the middle of the row of windows, another one, an old professor in a checked shirt, stands side-ways to the opened window, stands stock-still, his long, old ear to the air. Now another window cranks open, another professor—or maybe a graduate student—leans out, his hands on the sill.

We are all singing, and I am watching these five still men, my colleagues, whose office doors are surely shut—for that is the custom here: five of them alone in their offices at the science building who have opened their windows on this very cold morning, who motionless hear the Fundamentalists sing, utterly unknown to each other.

We sing another four songs, including the clapping song, and one which repeats, "This is the day which the Lord hath made; rejoice and be glad in it." All the professors but one stay still by their opened windows, figures in a frieze. When after ten minutes we break off and scatter, each cranks his windows shut. Maybe they have nine o'clock classes too.

I miss a few sessions. One morning of the following week, I rejoin   30
the Fundamentalists on the Square. The wind is blowing from the north; it is sunny and cold. There are several new developments.

Someone has blown up rubber gloves and floated them in the fountain. I saw them yesterday afternoon from my high office window, and couldn't quite make them out: I seemed to see hands in the fountain waving from side to side, like those hands wagging on springs which people stick in the back windows of their cars. I saw these many years ago in Quito and Guayaquil, where they were a great fad long before they showed up here. The cardboard hands said, on their palms, HOLA GENTE, hello people. Some of them just said HOLA, hello, with a little wave to the universe at large, in case anybody happened to be looking. It is like our sending radio signals to planets in other galaxies: HOLA, if anyone is listening. Jolly folk, these Ecuadorians, I thought.

Now, waiting by the fountain for the singing, I see that these particular hands are long surgical gloves, yellow and white, ten of them, tied off at the cuff. They float upright and they wave, *hola, hola, hola;* they mill around like a crowd, bobbing under the fountain's spray and back again to the pool's rim, *hola.* It is a good prank. It is far too cold for the university's maintenance crew to retrieve them without turning off the fountain and putting on rubber boots.

From all around the Square, people are gathering for the singing. There is no way I can guess which kids, from among the masses crossing the Square, will veer off to the fountain. When they get here, I never recognize anybody except the leaders.

The singing begins without ado as usual, but there is something different about it. The students are growing prayerful, and they show it this morning with a peculiar gesture. I'm glad they weren't like this when I first joined them, or I never would have stayed.

Last night there was an educational television special, part of "Mid-   35
dletown." It was a segment called "Community of Praise," and I watched

it because it was about Fundamentalists. It showed a Jesus-loving family in the Midwest; the treatment was good and complex. This family
attended the prayer meetings, healing sessions, and church services of
an unnamed sect—a very low-church sect, whose doctrine and culture
were much more low-church than those of the kids I sing with. When
the members of this sect prayed, they held their arms over their heads
and raised their palms, as if to feel or receive a blessing or energy from
above.

Now today on the Square there is a new serious mood. The leaders
are singing with their eyes shut. I am impressed that they can bang their
guitars, keep their balance, and not fall into the pool. It is the same
bouncy girl and earnest boy. Their eyeballs are rolled back a bit. I look
around and see that almost everyone in this crowd of eighty or so has
his eyes shut and is apparently praying the words of this song or praying some other prayer.

Now as the chorus rises, as it gets louder and higher and simpler in
melody—

> I exalt thee,
> I exalt thee,
> I exalt thee,
> Thou art the Lord—

then, at this moment, hands start rising. All around me, hands are going
up—that tall girl, that blond boy with his head back, the redheaded boy
up front, the girl with the McDonald's jacket. Their arms rise as if
pulled on strings. Some few of them have raised their arms very high
over their heads and are tilting back their palms. Many, many more of
them, as inconspicuously as possible, have raised their hands to the level
of their chins.

What is going on? Why are these students today raising their palms
in this gesture, when nobody did it last week? Is it because the leaders
have set a prayerful tone this morning? Is it because this gesture always
accompanies this song, just as clapping accompanies other songs? Or is
it, as I suspect, that these kids watched the widely publicized documentary last night just as I did, and are adopting, or trying out, the gesture?

It is a sunny morning, and the sun is rising behind the leaders and
the fountain, so those students have their heads tilted, eyes closed, and
palms upraised toward the sun. I glance up at the science building and
think my own prayer: thank God no one is watching this.

The leaders cannot move around much on the fountain's rim. The
girl has her eyes shut; the boy opens his eyes from time to time, glances
at the neck of the guitar, and closes his eyes again.

When the song is over, the hands go down, and there is some desultory chatting in the crowd, as usual; can I borrow your library card?
And, as usual, nobody looks at anybody.

40

All our songs today are serious. There is a feudal theme to them, or a feudal analogue:

> I will eat from abundance of your household.
> I will dream beside your streams of righteousness.
> You are my king.
> Enter his gates
> with thanksgiving in your heart;
> come before his courts with praise.
> He is the king of kings.
> Thou art the Lord.

All around me, eyes are closed and hands are raised. There is no social pressure to do this, or anything else. I've never known any group to be less cohesive, imposing fewer controls. Since no one looks at anyone, and since passersby no longer look, everyone out here is inconspicuous and free. Perhaps the palm-raising has begun because the kids realize by now that they are not on display; they're praying in their closets, right out here on the Square. Over the course of the next weeks, I will learn that the palm-raising is here to stay.

The sun is rising higher. We are singing our last song. We are praying. We are alone together.

> He is my peace
> Who has broken down every wall . . .

When the song is over, the hands go down. The heads lower, the eyes open and blink. We stay still a second before we break up. We have been standing in a broad current; now we have stepped aside. We have dismantled the radar cups; we have closed the telescope's vault. Students gather their book bags and go. The two leaders step down from the fountain's rim and pack away their guitars. Everyone scatters. I am in no hurry, so I stay after everyone is gone. It is after nine o'clock, and the Square is deserted. The fountain is playing to an empty house. In the pool the cheerful hands are waving over the water, bobbing under the fountain's veil and out again in the current, *hola*. 45

Lines of Inquiry
"Singing with the Fundamentalists"

Though Dillard gives a detailed record of what she observed while singing with the Fundamentalists, she does not ever explicitly define the purpose, or state the point, of this essay. How does she manage to imply the point of this piece? How does she tell about the daily singing sessions to get her point across?

What kinds of details does she repeatedly focus on in her story of the daily singing sessions? How does she establish the significance of these details?

Though Dillard had little if anything to do with Fundamentalists prior to the experience she describes in this piece, she did evidently have some clear-cut opinions of them. What was Dillard's attitude toward Fundamentalists prior to her experience of singing with them? What other attitudes toward Fundamentalists does she discuss during the course of her essay? What does she discover about them during the process of singing with them? How is her attitude affected by her overall experience of singing with them?

What is your attitude toward Christian Fundamentalists? What do you know from firsthand observation and from reading about their beliefs and practices? As a means of checking up on your attitude and understanding of them, as well as on Dillard's, look at some recent issues of the Fundamentalist magazine she refers to in her piece, *Eternity: The Evangelical Monthly*. What impression of them do you get from this material? How does it square with your prior assumptions about them?

Loren Eiseley
1907–77

No utilitarian philosophy explains a snow crystal, no doctrine of use or disuse. Water has merely leapt out of vapor and thin nothingness in the night sky to array itself in form. There is no logical reason for the existence of a snow-flake any more than there is for evolution.

Though Loren Eiseley was a distinguished physical anthropologist, one of several responsible for discovering that early man existed in America thousands of years earlier than previously thought, he came to be most fascinated, as he is in this passage, by the mysteriousness, the illogic, perhaps even the arbitrariness of the physical world and of human evolution. For him, the history of the human species is as beautiful, and as incomprehensible, as the structure of a snowflake: both are "apparition[s] from that mysterious shadow world beyond nature, that final world which contains— if anything contains—the explanation of men and catfish and green leaves." To express his sense of wonder and awe before nature's vastness, and his loneliness, his sense of man's comparative insignificance, Eiseley gradually turned away from the strictures of the scientific article to the literary forms of the personal essay. The "secret" of life, "will not yield to the kind of analysis our science is capable of making."

Eiseley's childhood in Nebraska was full of "terror, anxiety, ostracism, and shame," as he describes it in his autobiography, *All the Strange Hours.* His relationship with his deaf and mentally disturbed mother was particularly troubled, leaving deep scars that afflicted him the rest of his life. So from an early age, he sought refuge in reading and writing. Indeed, as an eighth grader he wrote an essay announcing that "I have selected Nature Writing as my vocation, because at this time it appeals to me more than any other subject." Still, he grew up rootless and unhappy, dropping in and out of college from the mid-1920s to the early 1930s, "bumming about" the West on freight trains, recuperating from tuberculosis in the Mojave desert and the mountains of Colorado—a "child of the early century," "molded of plains' dust and seed of those who came West with the wagons."

Eventually he was able to apply himself to his studies at the University of Nebraska, where he graduated in 1933 with a double major in English and anthropology. His youth and young manhood were marked by these two interests: on the one hand a passion for the history of the earth and the early Plains' people; on the other, a passion for literature and creative writing. As an undergraduate he had not only been part of a paleontological expedition that found artifacts of early man scattered among the bones of extinct bison, but he also served on the staff of the influential creative writing magazine, *The Prairie Schooner,* eventually becoming a contributing editor.

As a graduate student in anthropology at the University of Pennsylvania, he took part in an expedition to the Southwest in search of early man, and quickly proceeded to earn his MA in 1935, his PhD in 1937, as well as to publish his first professional articles. The subject of his dissertation was the usefulness of various scientific measurements of "Quaternary Time," reflecting not only his interests as a scientist but also foreshadowing his obsession in the essays with the vastness and elusiveness of time. From 1937 to 1942, he taught at the University of Kansas in Lawrence. During his first year there, he looked upon himself as "the proverbial Russian fleeing in a sleigh across the steppes before a wolf pack," yet he managed to impress his colleagues and students and to establish a solid reputation for his anthropological research and publications. From Kansas he moved to Oberlin College in Ohio as department chair, then to the University of Pennsylvania, where he succeeded his mentor as chair of the Department of Anthropology, a position he held from 1947 to 1962. He also served at various times as Curator of Early Man at the University of Pennsylvania and, briefly, as University Provost.

In 1942, while still at Kansas, Eiseley began experimenting with forms of writing that would ultimately lead him to develop what he called the "concealed essay." He wanted not only a way of channeling his ambitions and talents as a creative writer but a form of discourse capable of conveying his growing sense of man's insignificance in time. He wanted to humanize his research, both for himself and for his larger audience, writing about the experience of nature and the discoveries of science in a poetic, personal way. As he said of the great Victorian naturalists like Huxley, "even though they were not discoverers in the objective sense, one feels at times that the great nature essayists had more individual perception than their scientific contemporaries." Through the power of their language, they added a new "dimension" to our understanding of nature, "something that lies beyond the careful analysis of professional biology."

Eiseley himself added a new dimension to writing about nature in his first and most widely known imaginative book, *The Immense Journey* (1957), a collection of shorter pieces that had originally appeared in

Scientific American, Prairie Schooner, Harpers, and *The American Scholar,* unified into a coherent sequence of essays that meditate on the evolution of life from Precambrian times to the formation of the human mind. Here he sounds his central themes, his antimaterialism, his opposition to narrow scientific rationalism, his desire to recover the past through the power of the imagination, his fascination with man's physical development and genetic endowments, his awe at the vastness of time and "the enormous interlinked complexity of life." Each piece begins with a concrete, evocative personal experience which then leads to scientific or philosophical meditation—the sight of birds flying from ledges in New York, for example, leads to a meditation on Eiseley's longing for death and on man's separateness from nature. Natural history becomes metaphor for personal history, and vice versa, Eiseley's own personal experience serving as a vehicle for illustrating larger concepts, as well as a strategy for engaging the reader's intense interest. So, Eiseley developed a form that could blend the two facets of his personality, situating himself in the tradition of imaginative naturalists like Thoreau, and preparing the way for scientists turned essayists like Lewis Thomas and Stephen Jay Gould.

A number of books followed, including several more prose meditations—*The Firmament of Time* (1960), *The Unexpected Universe* (1969), and *Night Country* (1971)—several books of poems, and his final work, the disturbing and haunting autobiography, *All the Strange Hours: An Excavation of a Life* (1975), in which ecstasy and wonder give way to sadness, loneliness, even cynicism. He also wrote several more scholarly studies, including an intellectual history clarifying and disputing Darwin's theory of evolution, and an analysis of Francis Bacon's visionary approach to science as an alternative to Darwin's materialism. None of this later writing, to paraphrase *The Immense Journey,* can be regarded as a straightforward "guide," but is, rather, "a somewhat unconventional record of the prowlings of one mind which has sought to explore, to understand, and to enjoy the miracles of this world, both in and out of science."

What characterizes this record, at its best, is a poetic lyricism, as in this meditation on water from *The Immense Journey:*

Once in a lifetime, perhaps, one escapes the actual confines of the flesh. Once in a lifetime, if one is lucky, one so merges with sunlight and air and running water that whole eons, the eons that mountains and deserts know, might pass in a single afternoon without discomfort. The mind has sunk away into its beginning among old roots and the obscure tricklings and movings that stir inanimate things. Like the charmed fairy circle into which a man once stepped, and upon emergence learned that a whole century had passed in a single night, one can never quite define this secret: but it has something to do, I am sure, with common water. Its substance reaches everywhere; it touches the past and prepares the future;

it moves under the poles and wanders thinly in the heights of air. It can assume the forms of exquisite perfection in a snowflake, or strip the living to a single shining bone cast up by the sea.

Here, as elsewhere, Eiseley re-creates what he called a "natural revelation," a temporary merging of man and nature, a brief transcending of time. The language moves through repetition and balanced structure, through metaphor and patterns of sound, to the level of incantation, enabling us to see "in the flow of ordinary events" what Eiseley was always trying to help us see: "the point at which the mundane world gives way to quite another dimension."

How Flowers Changed the World

If it had been possible to observe the Earth from the far side of the solar system over the long course of geological epochs, the watchers might have been able to observe a subtle change in the light emanating from our planet. That world of long ago would, like the red deserts of Mars, have reflected light from vast drifts of stone and gravel, the sands of wandering wastes, the blackness of naked basalt, the yellow dust of endlessly moving storms. Only the ceaseless marching of the clouds and the intermittent flashes from the restless surface of the sea would have told a different story, but still essentially a barren one. Then, as the millennia rolled away and age followed age, a new and greener light would, by degrees, have come to twinkle across those endless miles.

This is the only difference those far watchers, by the use of subtle instruments, might have perceived in the whole history of the planet Earth. Yet that slowly growing green twinkle would have contained the epic march of life from the tidal oozes upward across the raw and unclothed continents. Out of the vast chemical bath of the sea—not from the deeps, but from the element-rich, light-exposed platforms of the continental shelves—wandering fingers of green had crept upward along the meanderings of river systems and fringed the gravels of forgotten lakes.

In those first ages plants clung of necessity to swamps and watercourses. Their productive processes demanded direct access to water. Beyond the primitive ferns and mosses that enclosed the borders of swamps and streams the rocks still lay vast and bare, the winds still swirled the dust of a naked planet. The grass cover that holds our world secure in place was still millions of years in the future. The green marchers had gained a soggy foothold upon the land, but that was all. They did not reproduce by seeds but by microscopic swimming sperm that had to wriggle their way through water to fertilize the female cell. Such plants in their higher forms had clever adaptations for the use of rain water in their sexual phases, and survived with increasing success in a wet land environment. They now seem part of man's normal environment. The truth is, however, that there is nothing very "normal" about nature. Once upon a time there were no flowers at all.

A little while ago—about one hundred million years, as the geologist estimates time in the history of our four-billion-year-old planet—flowers were not to be found anywhere on the five continents.

Wherever one might have looked, from the poles to the equator, one would have seen only the cold dark monotonous green of a world whose plant life possessed no other color. ·

Somewhere, just a short time before the close of the Age of Reptiles, there occurred a soundless, violent explosion. It lasted millions of years, but it was an explosion, nevertheless. It marked the emergence of the angiosperms—the flowering plants. Even the great evolutionist, Charles Darwin, called them "an abominable mystery," because they appeared so suddenly and spread so fast.

Flowers changed the face of the planet. Without them, the world we know—even man himself—would never have existed. Francis Thompson, the English poet, once wrote that one could not pluck a flower without troubling a star. Intuitively he had sensed like a naturalist the enormous interlinked complexity of life. Today we know that the appearance of the flowers contained also the equally mystifying emergence of man.

If we were to go back into the Age of Reptiles, its drowned swamps and birdless forests would reveal to us a warmer but, on the whole, a sleepier world than that of today. Here and there, it is true, the serpent heads of bottom-feeding dinosaurs might be upreared in suspicion of their huge flesh-eating compatriots. Tyrannosaurs, enormous bipedal caricatures of men, would stalk mindlessly across the sites of future cities and go their slow way down into the dark of geologic time.

In all that world of living things nothing saw save with the intense concentration of the hunt, nothing moved except with the grave sleep-walking intentness of the instinct-driven brain. Judged by modern standards, it was a world in slow motion, a cold-blooded world whose occupants were most active at noonday but torpid on chill nights, their brains damped by a slower metabolism than any known to even the most primitive of warm-blooded animals today.

A high metabolic rate and the maintenance of a constant body temperature are supreme achievements in the evolution of life. They enable an animal to escape, within broad limits, from the overheating or the chilling of its immediate surroundings, and at the same time to maintain a peak mental efficiency. Creatures without a high metabolic rate are slaves to weather. Insects in the first frosts of autumn all run down like little clocks. Yet if you pick one up and breathe warmly upon it, it will begin to move about once more.

In a sheltered spot such creatures may sleep away the winter, but they are hopelessly immobilized. Though a few warm-blooded mammals, such as the woodchuck of our day, have evolved a way of reducing their metabolic rate in order to undergo winter hibernation, it is a survival mechanism with drawbacks, for it leaves the animal helplessly exposed if enemies discover him during his period of suspended animation. Thus bear or woodchuck, big animal or small, must seek, in this time of descending sleep, a safe refuge in some hidden den or burrow. Hibernation is, therefore, primarily a winter refuge of small, easily concealed animals rather than of large ones.

A high metabolic rate, however, means a heavy intake of energy in order to sustain body warmth and efficiency. It is for this reason that even some of these later warm-blooded mammals existing in our day have learned to descend into a slower, unconscious rate of living during the winter months when food may be difficult to obtain. On a slightly higher plane they are following the procedure of the cold-blooded frog sleeping in the mud at the bottom of a frozen pond.

The agile brain of the warm-blooded birds and mammals demands a high oxygen consumption and food in concentrated forms, or the creatures cannot long sustain themselves. It was the rise of the flowering plants that provided that energy and changed the nature of the living world. Their appearance parallels in a quite surprising manner the rise of the birds and mammals.

Slowly, toward the dawn of the Age of Reptiles, something over two hundred and fifty million years ago, the little naked sperm cells wriggling their way through dew and raindrops had given way to a kind of pollen carried by the wind. Our present-day pine forests represent plants of a pollen-disseminating variety. Once fertilization was no longer dependent on exterior water, the march over drier regions could be extended. Instead of spores simple primitive seeds carrying some nourishment for the young plant had developed, but true flowers were still scores of millions of years away. After a long period of hesitant evolutionary groping, they exploded upon the world with truly revolutionary violence.

The event occurred in Cretaceous times in the close of the Age of Reptiles. Before the coming of the flowering plants our own ancestral stock, the warm-blooded mammals, consisted of a few mousy little creatures hidden in trees and underbrush. A few lizard-like birds with carnivorous teeth flapped awkwardly on ill-aimed flights among archaic shrubbery. None of these insignificant creatures gave evidence of any remarkable talents. The mammals in particular had been around for some millions of years, but had remained well lost in the shadow of the mighty reptiles. Truth to tell, man was still, like the genie in the bottle, encased in the body of a creature about the size of a rat.

As for the birds, their reptilian cousins the Pterodactyls flew farther 15 and better. There was just one thing about the birds that paralleled the physiology of the mammals. They, too, had evolved warm blood and its accompanying temperature control. Nevertheless, if one had been seen stripped of his feathers, he would still have seemed a slightly uncanny and unsightly lizard.

Neither the birds nor the mammals, however, were quite what they seemed. They were waiting for the Age of Flowers. They were waiting for what flowers, and with them the true encased seed, would bring. Fish-eating, gigantic leather-winged reptiles, twenty-eight feet from wing tip to wing tip, hovered over the coasts that one day would be swarming with gulls.

Inland the monotonous green of the pine and spruce forests with their primitive wooden cone flowers stretched everywhere. No grass hindered the fall of the naked seeds to earth. Great sequoias towered to the skies. The world of that time has a certain appeal but it is a giant's world, a world moving slowly like the reptiles who stalked magnificently among the boles of its trees.

The trees themselves are ancient, slow-growing and immense, like the redwood groves that have survived to our day on the California coast. All is stiff, formal, upright and green, monotonously green. There is no grass as yet; there are no wide plains rolling in the sun, no tiny daisies dotting the meadows underfoot. There is little versatility about this scene; it is, in truth, a giant's world.

A few nights ago it was brought home vividly to me that the world has changed since that far epoch. I was awakened out of sleep by an unknown sound in my living room. Not a small sound—not a creaking timber or a mouse's scurry—but a sharp, rending explosion as though an unwary foot had been put down upon a wine glass. I had come instantly out of sleep and lay tense, unbreathing. I listened for another step. There was none.

Unable to stand the suspense any longer, I turned on the light and   20
passed from room to room glancing uneasily behind chairs and into closets. Nothing seemed disturbed, and I stood puzzled in the corner of the living room floor. Then a small button-shaped object upon the rug caught my eye. It was hard and polished and glistening. Scattered over the length of the room were several more shining up at me like wary little eyes. A pine cone that had been lying in a dish had been blown the length of the coffee table. The dish itself could hardly have been the source of the explosion. Beside it I found two ribbon-like strips of velvety-green. I tried to place the two strips together to make a pod. They twisted resolutely away from each other and would no longer fit.

I relaxed in a chair, then, for I had reached a solution of the midnight disturbance. The twisted strips were wisteria pods that I had brought in a day or two previously and placed in the dish. They had chosen midnight to explode and distribute their multiplying fund of life down the length of the room. A plant, a fixed, rooted thing, immobilized in a single spot, had devised a way of propelling its offspring across open space. Immediately there passed before my eyes the million airy troopers of the milkweed pod and the clutching hooks of the sandburs. Seeds on the coyote's tail, seeds on the hunter's coat, thistledown mounting on the winds—all were somehow triumphing over life's limitations. Yet the ability to do this had not been with them at the beginning. It was the product of endless effort and experiment.

The seeds on my carpet were not going to lie stiffly where they had dropped like their antiquated cousins, the naked seeds on the pine-cone scales. They were travelers. Struck by the thought, I went out next day and collected several other varieties. I line them up now in a row on my desk—so many little capsules of life, winged, hooked or spiked. Every one is an angiosperm, a product of the true flowering plants. Contained in these little boxes is the secret of that far-off Cretaceous explosion of a hundred million years ago that changed the face of the planet. And somewhere in here, I think, as I poke seriously at one particularly resistant seedcase of a wild grass, was once man himself.

When the first simple flower bloomed on some raw upland late in the Dinosaur Age, it was wind pollinated, just like its early pine-cone relatives. It was a very inconspicuous flower because it had not yet evolved the idea of using the surer attraction of birds and insects to achieve the transportation of pollen. It sowed its own pollen and received the pollen of other flowers by the simple vagaries of the wind. Many plants in regions where insect life is scant still follow this principle today. Nevertheless, the true flower—and the seed that it produced—was a profound innovation in the world of life.

In a way, this event parallels, in the plant world, what happened among animals. Consider the relative chance for survival of the exteriorly deposited egg of a fish in contrast with the fertilized egg of a mammal, carefully retained for months in the mother's body until the young animal (or human being) is developed to a point where it may survive. The biological wastage is less—and so it is with the flowering plants. The primitive spore, a single cell fertilized at the beginning by a swimming sperm, did not promote rapid distribution, and the young plant, moreover, had to struggle up from nothing. No one had left it any food except what it could get by its own unaided efforts.

By contrast, the true flowering plants (angiosperm itself means "encased seed") grew a seed in the heart of a flower, a seed whose development was initiated by a fertilizing pollen grain independent of outside moisture. But the seed, unlike the developing spore, is already a fully equipped *embryonic plant* packed in a little enclosed box stuffed full of nutritious food. Moreover, by featherdown attachments, as in dandelion or milkweed seed, it can be wafted upward on gusts and ride the wind for miles; or with hooks it can cling to a bear's or a rabbit's hide; or like some of the berries, it can be covered with a juicy, attractive fruit to lure birds, pass undigested through their intestinal tracts and be voided miles away.

The ramifications of this biological invention were endless. Plants traveled as they had never traveled before. They got into strange environments heretofore never entered by the old spore plants or stiff pine-cone-seed plants. The well-fed, carefully cherished little embryos raised their heads everywhere. Many of the older plants with more primitive reproductive mechanisms began to fade away under this unequal contest. They contracted their range into secluded environments. Some, like the giant redwoods, lingered on as relics; many vanished entirely.

The world of the giants was a dying world. These fantastic little seeds skipping and hopping and flying about the woods and valleys brought with them an amazing adaptability. If our whole lives had not been spent in the midst of it, it would astound us. The old, stiff, sky-reaching wooden world had changed into something that glowed here and there with strange colors, put out queer, unheard-of fruits and little intricately carved seed cases, and, most important of all, produced concentrated foods in a way that the land had never seen before, or dreamed of back in the fish-eating, leaf-crunching days of the dinosaurs.

That food came from three sources, all produced by the reproductive system of the flowering plants. There were the tantalizing nectars and pollens intended to draw insects for pollenizing purposes, and which are responsible also for that wonderful jeweled creation, the hummingbird. There were the juicy and enticing fruits to attract larger animals, and in which tough-coated seeds were concealed, as in the tomato, for example. Then, as if this were not enough, there was the food in the actual seed itself, the food intended to nourish the embryo. All over the world, like hot corn in a popper, these incredible elaborations of the flowering plants kept exploding. In a movement that was almost instantaneous, geologically speaking, the angiosperms had taken over the world. Grass was beginning to cover the bare earth until, today, there are over six thousand species. All kinds of vines and bushes squirmed and writhed under new trees with flying seeds.

The explosion was having its effect on animal life also. Specialized groups of insects were arising to feed on the new sources of food and, incidentally and unknowingly, to pollinate the plant. The flowers bloomed and bloomed in ever larger and more spectacular varieties. Some were pale unearthly night flowers intended to lure moths in the evening twilight, some among the orchids even took the shape of female spiders in order to attract wandering males, some flamed redly in the light of noon or twinkled modestly in the meadow grasses. Intricate mechanisms splashed pollen on the breasts of hummingbirds, or stamped it on the bellies of black, grumbling bees droning assiduously from blossom to blossom. Honey ran, insects multiplied, and even the descendants of that toothed and ancient lizard-bird had become strangely altered. Equipped with prodding beaks instead of biting teeth they pecked the seeds and gobbled the insects that were really converted nectar.

Across the planet grasslands were now spreading. A slow continental upthrust which had been a part of the early Age of Flowers had cooled the world's climates. The stalking reptiles and the leather-winged black imps of the seashore cliffs had vanished. Only birds roamed the air now, hot-blooded and high-speed metabolic machines.

30

The mammals, too, had survived and were venturing into new domains, staring about perhaps a bit bewildered at their sudden eminence now that the thunder lizards were gone. Many of them, beginning as small browsers upon leaves in the forest, began to venture out upon this new sunlit world of the grass. Grass has a high silica content and demands a new type of very tough and resistant tooth enamel, but the seeds taken incidentally in the cropping of the grass are highly nutritious. A new world had opened out for the warm-blooded mammals. Great herbivores like the mammoths, horses and bisons appeared. Skulking about them had arisen savage flesh-feeding carnivores like the now extinct dire wolves and the saber-toothed tiger.

Flesh eaters though these creatures were, they were being sustained on nutritious grasses one step removed. Their fierce energy was being maintained on a high, effective level, through hot days and frosty nights, by the concentrated energy of the angiosperms. That energy, thirty per cent or more of the weight of the entire plant among some of the cereal grasses, was being accumulated and concentrated in the rich proteins and fats of the enormous game herds of the grasslands.

On the edge of the forest, a strange, old-fashioned animal still hesitated. His body was the body of a tree dweller, and though tough and knotty by human standards, he was, in terms of that world into which he gazed, a weakling. His teeth, though strong for chewing on the tough fruits of the forest, or for crunching an occasional unwary bird caught with his prehensile hands, were not the tearing sabers of the great cats. He had a passion for lifting himself up to see about, in his restless, roving curiosity. He would run a little stiffly and uncertainly, perhaps, on his hind legs, but only in those rare moments when he ventured out upon the ground. All this was the legacy of his climbing days; he had a hand with flexible fingers and no fine specialized hoofs upon which to gallop like the wind.

If he had any idea of competing in that new world, he had better forget it; teeth or hooves, he was much too late for either. He was a ne'er-do-well, and in-betweener. Nature had not done well by him. It was as if she had hesitated and never quite made up her mind. Perhaps as a consequence he had a malicious gleam in his eye, the gleam of an outcast who has been left nothing and knows he is going to have to take what he gets. One day a little band of these odd apes—for apes they were—shambled out upon the grass; the human story had begun.

Apes were to become men, in the inscrutable wisdom of nature, 35 because flowers had produced seeds and fruits in such tremendous quantities that a new and totally different store of energy had become available in concentrated form. Impressive as the slow-moving, dim-brained dinosaurs had been, it is doubtful if their age had supported anything like the diversity of life that now rioted across the planet or flashed in and out among the trees. Down on the grass by a streamside, one of those apes with inquisitive fingers turned over a stone and hefted it vaguely. The group clucked together in a throaty tongue and moved off through the tall grass foraging for seeds and insects. The one still held, sniffed, and hefted the stone he had found. He liked the feel of it in his fingers. The attack on the animal world was about to begin.

If one could run the story of that first human group like a speeded-up motion picture through a million years of time, one might see the stone in the hand change to the flint ax and the torch. All that swarming grassland world with its giant bison and trumpeting mammoths would go down in ruin to feed the insatiable and growing numbers of a carnivore who, like the great cats before him, was taking his energy indirectly from the grass. Later he found fire and it altered the tough meats and drained their energy even faster into a stomach ill adapted for the ferocious turn man's habits had taken.

His limbs grew longer, he strode more purposefully over the grass. The stolen energy that would take man across the continents would fail him at last. The great Ice Age herds were destined to vanish. When they did so, another hand like the hand that grasped the stone by the river long ago would pluck a handful of grass seed and hold it contemplatively.

In that moment, the golden towers of man, his swarming millions, his turning wheels, the vast learning of his packed libraries, would glimmer dimly there in the ancestor of wheat, a few seeds held in a muddy hand. Without the gift of flowers and the infinite diversity of their fruits, man and bird, if they had continued to exist at all, would be today unrecognizable. Archaeopteryx, the lizard-bird, might still be a nocturnal insectivore gnawing a roach in the dark. The weight of a petal has changed the face of the world and made it ours.

Lines of Inquiry
"How Flowers Changed the World"

Although this essay is explicitly concerned with explaining "how flowers changed the world," Eiseley doesn't actually get into this explanation in detail until the second half of his piece. What is the purpose of the material that he discusses in the first half of his piece? What topics does he discuss, what things does he describe, what stories does he tell in the first half, and exactly how does each bit of material pertain to the cause and effect process that he is trying to explain in this piece?

Given the title of this piece, it seems appropriate to consider exactly how the world was changed by the appearance of flowers. What specific changes, according to Eiseley, did flowers actually bring about in the world? How did flowers cause each of those changes? In particular, how did "the appearance of flowers [contain] also the equally mystifying emergence of man"? How did the appearance of flowers, in turn, lead to man's domination of the world, as Eiseley claims in the final sentence of his essay?

In what respects do you think it would be accurate to say that Eiseley's essay is essentially an anthropocentric piece of natural history? In other words, do you think it implies that man is the central being, final aim, or ultimate creature in the universe? In what respects do you think it would be inaccurate to define his views as anthropocentric? What do you consider to be the strengths and weaknesses of viewing the world anthropocentrically? For another point of view on this issue, look at Twain's essay, "Was the World Made for Man?"

The Bird and the Machine

I suppose their little bones have years ago been lost among the stones and winds of those high glacial pastures. I suppose their feathers blew eventually into the piles of tumbleweed beneath the straggling cattle fences and rotted there in the mountain snows, along with dead steers and all the other things that drift to an end in the corners of the wire. I do not quite know why I should be thinking of birds over the *New York Times* at breakfast, particularly the birds of my youth half a continent away. It is a funny thing what the brain will do with memories and how it will treasure them and finally bring them into odd juxtapositions with other things, as though it wanted to make a design, or get some meaning out of them, whether you want it or not, or even see it.

It used to seem marvelous to me, but I read now that there are machines that can do these things in a small way, machines that can crawl about like animals, and that it may not be long now until they do more things—maybe even make themselves—I saw that piece in the *Times* just now. And then they will, maybe—well, who knows—but you read about it more and more with no one making any protest, and already they can add better than we and reach up and hear things through the dark and finger the guns over the night sky.

This is the new world that I read about at breakfast. This is the world that confronts me in my biological books and journals, until there are times when I sit quietly in my chair and try to hear the little purr of the cogs in my head and the tubes flaring and dying as the messages go through them and the circuits snap shut or open. This is the great age, make no mistake about it; the robot has been born somewhat appropriately along with the atom bomb, and the brain they say now is just another type of more complicated feedback system. The engineers have its basic principles worked out; it's mechanical, you know; nothing to get superstitious about; and man can always improve on nature once he gets the idea. Well, he's got it all right and that's why, I guess, that I sit here in my chair, with the article crunched in my hand, remembering those two birds and that blue mountain sunlight. There is another magazine article on my desk that reads "Machines Are Getting Smarter Every Day." I don't deny it, but I'll still stick with the birds. It's life I believe in, not machines.

Maybe you don't believe there is any difference. A skeleton is all joints and pulleys, I'll admit. And when man was in his simpler stages of machine building in the eighteenth century, he quickly saw the resemblances. "What," wrote Hobbes, "is the heart but a spring, and the nerves but so many strings, and the joints but so many wheels, giving motion to the whole body?" Tinkering about in their shops it was inevitable in the end that men would see the world as a huge machine "subdivided into an infinite number of lesser machines."

The idea took on with a vengeance. Little automatons toured the country—dolls controlled by clockwork. Clocks described as little worlds were taken on tours by their designers. They were made up of moving figures, shifting scenes, and other remarkable devices. The life of the cell was unknown. Man, whether he was conceived as possessing a soul or not, moved and jerked about like these tiny puppets. A human being thought of himself in terms of his own tools and implements. He had been fashioned like the puppets he produced and was only a more clever model made by a greater designer.

Then in the nineteenth century, the cell was discovered, and the 5 single machine in its turn was found to be the product of millions of infinitesimal machines—the cells. Now, finally, the cell itself dissolved away into an abstract chemical machine, and that into some intangible, inexpressible flow of energy. The secret seems to lurk all about, the wheels get smaller and smaller, and they turn more rapidly, but when you try to seize it the life is gone—and so, by popular definition, some would say that life was never there in the first place. The wheels and the cogs are the secret and we can make them better in time—machines that will run faster and more accurately than real mice to real cheese.

I have no doubt it can be done, though a mouse harvesting seeds on an autumn thistle is to me a fine sight and more complicated, I think, in his multiform activity than a machine "mouse" running a maze. Also, I like to think of the possible shape of the future brooding in mice, just as it brooded once in a rather mousy insectivore who became a man. It leaves a nice fine indeterminate sense of wonder that even an electronic brain hasn't got, because you know perfectly well that if the electronic brain changes, it will be because of something man has done to it. But what man will do to himself he doesn't really know. A certain scale of time and a ghostly intangible thing called change are ticking in him. Powers and potentialities like the oak in the seed, or a red and awful ruin. Either way, it's impressive; and the mouse has it, too. Or those birds, I'll never forget those birds—yet before I measured their significance, I learned the lesson of time first of all. I was young then and left alone in a great desert—part of an expedition that had scattered its men over several hundred miles in order to carry on research more effectively. I learned there that time is a series of planes existing superficially in the same universe. The tempo is a human illusion, a subjective clock ticking in our own kind of protoplasm.

As the long months passed, I began to live on the slower planes and to observe more readily what passed for life there. I sauntered, I passed more and more slowly up and down the canyons in the dry baking heat of midsummer. I slumbered for long hours in the shade of huge brown boulders that had gathered in tilted companies out on the flats. I had forgotten the world of men and the world had forgotten me. Now and then I found a skull in the canyons, and these justified my remaining there. I took a serene cold interest in these discoveries. I had come, like many a naturalist before me, to view life with a wary and subdued attention. I had grown to take pleasure in the divested bone.

I sat once on a high ridge that fell away before me into a waste of sand dunes. I sat through hours of a long afternoon. Finally, as I glanced beside my boot an indistinct configuration caught my eye. It was a coiled rattlesnake, a big one. How long he had sat with me I do not know. I had not frightened him. We were both clocked in the sleep-walking tempo of the earlier world, baking in the same high air and sunshine. Perhaps he had been there when I came. He slept on as I left, his coils, so ill-discerned by me, dissolving once more among the stones and gravel from which I had barely made him out.

Another time I got on a higher ridge, among some tough little wind-warped pines half covered over with sand in a basinlike depression that caught everything carried by the air up to those heights. There were a few thin bones of birds, some cracked shells of indeterminable age, and the knotty fingers of pine roots bulged out of shape from their long and agonizing grasp upon the crevices of the rock. I lay under the pines in the sparse shade and went to sleep once more.

It grew cold finally, for autumn was in the air by then, and the few   10
things that lived thereabouts were sinking down into an even chillier scale of time. In the moments between sleeping and waking I saw the roots about me and slowly, slowly, a foot in what seemed many centuries, I moved my sleep-stiffened hands over the scaling bark and lifted my numbed face after the vanishing sun. I was a great awkward thing of knots and aching limbs, trapped up there in some long, patient endurance that involved the necessity of putting living fingers into rocks and by slow, aching expansion bursting those rocks asunder. I suppose, so thin and slow was the time of my pulse by then, that I might have stayed on to drift still deeper into the lower cadences of the frost, or the crystalline life that glistens pebbles, or shines in a snowflake, or dreams in the meteoric iron between the worlds.

It was a dim descent, but time was present in it. Somewhere far down in that scale the notion struck me that one might come the other way. Not many months thereafter I joined some colleagues heading higher into a remote windy tableland where huge bones were reputed to protrude like boulders from the turf. I had drowsed with reptiles and moved with the century-long pulse of trees; now, lethargically, I was climbing back up some invisible ladder of quickening hours. There had been talk of birds in connection with my duties. Birds are intense, fast-living creatures—reptiles, I suppose one might say, that have escaped out of the heavy sleep of time, transformed fairy creatures dancing over sunlit meadows. It is a youthful fancy, no doubt, but because of something that happened up there among the escarpments of that range, it remains with me a lifelong impression. I can never bear to see a bird imprisoned.

We came into that valley through the trailing mists of a spring night. It was a place that looked as though it might never have known the foot of man, but our scouts had been ahead of us and we knew all about the abandoned cabin of stone that lay far up on one hillside. It had been built in the land rush of the last century and then lost to the cattlemen again as the marginal soils failed to take to the plow.

There were spots like this all over that country. Lost graves marked by unlettered stones and old corroding rim-fire cartridge cases lying where somebody had made a stand among the boulders that rimmed the valley. They are all that remain of the range wars; the men are under the stones now. I could see our cavalcade winding in and out through the mist below us: torches, the reflection of the truck lights on our collecting tins, and the far-off bumping of a loose dinosaur thigh bone in the bottom of a trailer. I stood on a rock a moment looking down and thinking what it cost in money and equipment to capture the past.

We had, in addition, instructions to lay hands on the present. The word had come through to get them alive—birds, reptiles, anything. A zoo somewhere abroad needed restocking. It was one of those reciprocal matters in which science involves itself. Maybe our museum needed a stray ostrich egg and this was the payoff. Anyhow, my job was to help capture some birds and that was why I was there before the trucks.

The cabin had not been occupied for years. We intended to clean it out and live in it, but there were holes in the roof and the birds had come in and were roosting in the rafters. You could depend on it in a place like this where everything blew away, and even a bird needed some place out of the weather and away from coyotes. A cabin going back to nature in a wild place draws them till they come in, listening at the eaves, I imagine, pecking softly among the shingles till they find a hole, and then suddenly the place is theirs and man is forgotten.

Sometimes of late years I find myself thinking the most beautiful sight in the world might be the birds taking over New York after the last man has run away to the hills. I will never live to see it, of course, but I know just how it will sound because I've lived up high and I know the sort of watch birds keep on us. I've listened to sparrows tapping tentatively on the outside of air conditioners when they thought no one was listening, and I know how other birds test the vibrations that come up to them through the television aerials.

15

"Is he gone?" they ask, and the vibrations come up from below, "Not yet, not yet."

Well, to come back, I got the door open softly and I had the spot-light all ready to turn on and blind whatever birds there were so they couldn't see to get out through the roof. I had a short piece of ladder to put against the far wall where there was a shelf on which I expected to make the biggest haul. I had all the information I needed, just like any skilled assassin. I pushed the door open, the hinges squeaking only a little. A bird or two stirred—I could hear them—but nothing flew and there was a faint starlight through the holes in the roof.

I padded across the floor, got the ladder up and the light ready, and slithered up the ladder till my head and arms were over the shelf. Everything was dark as pitch except for the starlight at the little place back of the shelf near the eaves. With the light to blind them, they'd never make it. I had them. I reached my arm carefully over in order to be ready to seize whatever was there and I put the flash on the edge of the shelf where it would stand by itself when I turned it on. That way I'd be able to use both hands.

Everything worked perfectly except for one detail—I didn't know   20
what kind of birds were there. I never thought about it at all, and it wouldn't have mattered if I had. My orders were to get something interesting. I snapped on the flash and sure enough there was a great beating and feathers flying, but instead of my having them, they, or rather he, had me. He had my hand, that is, and for a small hawk not much bigger than my fist he was doing all right. I heard him give one short metallic cry when the light went on and my hand descended on the bird beside him; after that he was busy with his claws and his beak was sunk in my thumb. In the struggle I knocked the lamp over on the shelf, and his mate got her sight back and whisked neatly through the hole in the roof and off among the stars outside. It all happened in fifteen seconds and you might think I would have fallen down the lad-der, but no, I had a professional assassin's reputation to keep up, and the bird, of course, made the mistake of thinking the hand was the enemy and not the eyes behind it. He chewed my thumb up pretty effectively and lacerated my hand with his claws, but in the end I got him, having two hands to work with.

He was a sparrow hawk and a fine young male in the prime of life. I was sorry not to catch the pair of them, but as I dripped blood and folded his wings carefully, holding him by the back so that he couldn't strike again, I had to admit the two of them might have been more than I could have handled under the circumstances. The little fellow had saved his mate by diverting me, and that was that. He was born to it and made no outcry now, resting in my hand hopelessly but peering toward me in the shadows behind the lamp with a fierce, almost indifferent glance. He neither gave nor expected mercy and something out of the high air passed from him to me, stirring a faint embarrassment.

I quit looking into that eye and managed to get my huge carcass with its fist full of prey back down the ladder. I put the bird in a box too small to allow him to injure himself by struggle and walked out to welcome the arriving trucks. It had been a long day, and camp still to make in the darkness. In the morning that bird would be just another episode. He would go back with the bones in the truck to a small cage in a city where he would spend the rest of his life. And a good thing, too. I sucked my aching thumb and spat out some blood. An assassin has to get used to these things. I had a professional reputation to keep up.

In the morning, with the change that comes on suddenly in that high country, the mist that had hovered below us in the valley was gone. The sky was a deep blue, and one could see for miles over the high outcroppings of stone. I was up early and brought the box in which the little hawk was imprisoned out onto the grass where I was building a cage. A wind as cool as a mountain spring ran over the grass and stirred my hair. It was a fine day to be alive. I looked up and all around and at the hole in the cabin roof out of which the other little hawk had fled. There was no sign of her anywhere that I could see.

"Probably in the next county by now," I thought cynically, but before beginning work I decided I'd have a look at my last night's capture.

Secretively, I looked again all around the camp and up and down and opened the box. I got him right out in my hand with his wings folded properly and I was careful not to startle him. He lay limp in my grasp and I could feel his heart pound under the feathers but he only looked beyond me and up.

I saw him look that last look away beyond me into a sky so full of light that I could not follow his gaze. The little breeze flowed over me again, and nearby a mountain aspen shook all its tiny leaves. I suppose I must have had an idea then of what I was going to do, but I never let it come up into consciousness. I just reached over and laid the hawk on the grass.

He lay there a long minute without hope, unmoving, his eyes still fixed on that blue vault above him. It must have been that he was already so far away in heart that he never felt the release from my hand. He never even stood. He just lay with his breast against the grass.

In the next second after that long minute he was gone. Like a flicker of light, he had vanished with my eyes full on him but without actually seeing even a premonitory wing beat. He was gone straight into that towering emptiness of light and crystal that my eyes could scarcely bear

25

to penetrate. For another long moment there was silence. I could not see him. The light was too intense. Then from far up somewhere a cry came ringing down.

I was young then and had seen little of the world, but when I heard that cry my heart turned over. It was not the cry of the hawk I had captured; for, by shifting my position against the sun, I was now seeing farther up. Straight out of the sun's eye, where she must have been soaring restlessly above us for untold hours, hurtled his mate. And from far up, ringing from peak to peak of the summits over us, came a cry of such unutterable and ecstatic joy that it sounds down across the years and tingles among the cups of my quiet breakfast table.

I saw them both now. He was rising fast to meet her. They met in   30 a great soaring gyre that turned to a whirling circle and a dance of wings. Once more, just once, their two voices, joined in a harsh wild medley of question and response, struck and echoed against the pinnacles of the valley. Then they were gone forever somewhere into those upper regions beyond the eyes of men.

I am older now, and sleep less, and have seen most of what there is to see and am not very much impressed any more, I suppose, by anything. "What Next in the Attributes of Machines?" my morning headline runs. "It Might Be the Power to Reproduce Themselves."

I lay the paper down and across my mind a phrase floats insinuatingly: "It does not seem that there is anything in the construction, constituents, or behavior of the human being which it is essentially impossible for science to duplicate and synthesize. On the other hand . . ."

All over the city the cogs in the hard, bright mechanisms have begun to turn. Figures move through computers, names are spelled out, a thoughtful machine selects the fingerprints of a wanted criminal from an array of thousands. In the laboratory an electronic mouse runs swiftly through a maze toward the cheese it can neither taste nor enjoy. On the second run it does better than a living mouse.

"On the other hand . . ." Ah, my mind takes up, on the other hand the machine does not bleed, ache, hang for hours in the empty sky in a torment of hope to learn the fate of another machine, nor does it cry out with joy nor dance in the air with the fierce passion of a bird. Far off, over a distance greater than space, that remote cry from the heart of heaven makes a faint buzzing among my breakfast dishes and passes on and away.

Lines of Inquiry
"The Bird and the Machine"

Although the bird is one of the title characters in this piece, Eiseley doesn't begin telling the story of the birds until the middle of his essay. Why do you suppose he withholds the story until that point? Why doesn't he tell it right off, rather than preceding it with the story of his time up in the canyons with the snake? How does the story of his time in the canyons reflect upon his story of the birds? How is your reaction to the story of the bird—and your understanding of the story—shaped by everything that precedes it? What about the machine? What story, if any, does he tell about that?

At the end of the first paragraph, Eiseley is moved by the strange process of his own thoughts to reflect on "how it is a funny thing what the brain will do with memories," how it will "bring them into odd juxtapositions with other things, as though it wanted to make a design, or get some meaning out of them." Trace the process of Eiseley's musings through the first eight paragraphs and try to account for the memories, the images, and the ideas that are mingled in each paragraph. What does this associative or meditative form have to do with the point of the piece, with the things that are uppermost in Eiseley's mind?

In another memory piece, "Once More to the Lake," White also is moved to reflect upon how the mind works, how "you remember one thing, and that suddenly reminds you of another thing." In what respects do Eiseley and White have similar ideas about the workings of the mind? In what respects different? In what respects do they depict their minds as working in similar ways? In what respects do they depict them as working differently?

The Long Loneliness

There is nothing more alone in the universe than man. He is alone because he has the intellectual capacity to know that he is separated by a vast gulf of social memory and experiment from the lives of his animal associates. He has entered into the strange world of history, of social and intellectual change, while his brothers of the field and forest remain subject to the invisible laws of biological evolution. Animals are molded by natural forces they do not comprehend. To their minds there is no past and no future. There is only the everlasting present of a single generation—its trails in the forest, its hidden pathways of the air and in the sea.

Man, by contrast, is alone with the knowledge of his history until the day of his death. When we were children we wanted to talk to animals and struggled to understand why this was impossible. Slowly we gave up the attempt as we grew into the solitary world of human adulthood; the rabbit was left on the lawn, the dog was relegated to his kennel. Only in acts of inarticulate compassion, in rare and hidden moments of communion with nature, does man briefly escape his solitary destiny. Frequently in science fiction he dreams of worlds with creatures whose communicative power is the equivalent of his own.

It is with a feeling of startlement, therefore, and eager interest touching the lost child in every one of us, that the public has received the recent accounts of naval research upon the intelligence of one of our brother mammals—the sea-dwelling bottle-nosed porpoise or dolphin.

These small whales who left the land millions of years ago to return to the great mother element of life, the sea, are now being regarded by researchers as perhaps the most intelligent form of life on our planet next to man. Dr. John Lilly of the Communications Research Institute in the Virgin Islands reports that the brain of the porpoise is 40 per cent larger than man's and is just as complex in its functional units. Amazed by the rapidity with which captive porpoises solved problems that even monkeys found difficult, Dr. Lilly is quoted as expressing the view that "man's position at the top of the hierarchy [of intelligence] begins to be questioned."

Dr. Lilly found that his captives communicated in a series of underwater whistles and that, in addition, they showed an amazing "verbalizing" ability in copying certain sounds heard in the laboratory. The experimental animal obviously hoped to elicit by this means a reproduction of the pleasurable sensations he had been made to experience under laboratory conditions. It is reported that in spite of living in a medium different from the one that man inhabits, and therefore having

5

quite a different throat structure, one of the porpoises even uttered in a Donald-Duckish voice a short number series it had heard spoken by one of the laboratory investigators.

The import of these discoveries is tremendous and may not be adequately known for a long time. An animal from a little-explored medium, which places great barriers in the way of the psychologist, has been found to have not only a strong social organization but to show a degree of initiative in experimental communicative activity unmatched by man's closest relatives, the great apes. The porpoises reveal, moreover, a touching altruism and friendliness in their attempts to aid injured companions. Can it be, one inevitably wonders, that man is so locked in his own type of intelligence—an intelligence that is linked to a prehensile, grasping hand giving him power over his environment—that he is unable to comprehend the intellectual life of a highly endowed creature from another domain such as the sea?

Perhaps the water barrier has shut us away from a potentially communicative and jolly companion. Perhaps we have some things still to learn from the natural world around us before we turn to the far shores of space and whatever creatures may await us there. After all, the porpoise is a mammal. He shares with us an ancient way of birth and affectionate motherhood. His blood is warm, he breathes air as we do. We both bear in our bodies the remnants of a common skeleton torn asunder for divergent purposes far back in the dim dawn of mammalian life. The porpoise has been superficially streamlined like a fish.

His are not, however, the cold-blooded ways of the true fishes. Far higher on the tree of life than fishes, the dolphin's paddles are made-over paws, rather than fins. He is an ever-constant reminder of the versatility of life and its willingness to pass through strange dimensions of experience. There are environmental worlds on earth every bit as weird as what we may imagine to revolve by far-off suns. It is our superficial familiarity with this planet that inhibits our appreciation of the unknown until a porpoise, rearing from a tank to say Three-Two-Three, re-creates for us the utter wonder of childhood.

Unless we are specialists in the study of communication and its relation to intelligence, however, we are apt to oversimplify or define poorly what intelligence is, what communication and language are, and thus confuse and mystify both ourselves and others. The mysteries surrounding the behavior of the bottle-nosed porpoise, and even of man himself, are not things to be probed simply by the dissector's scalpel. They lie deeper. They involve the whole nature of the mind and its role in the universe.

We are forced to ask ourselves whether native intelligence in another form than man's might be as high as or even higher than his own, yet be marked by no such material monuments as man has placed upon the earth. At first glance we are alien to this idea, because man is

10

particularly a creature who has turned the tables on his environment so that he is now engrossed in shaping it, rather than being shaped by it. Man expresses himself upon his environment through the use of tools. We therefore tend to equate the use of tools in a one-to-one relationship with intelligence.

The question we must now ask ourselves, however, is whether this involves an unconsciously man-centered way of looking at intelligence. Let us try for a moment to enter the dolphin's kingdom and the dolphin's body, retaining, at the same time, our human intelligence. In this imaginative act, it may be possible to divest ourselves of certain human preconceptions about our kind of intelligence and at the same time to see more clearly why mind, even advanced mind, may have manifestations other than the tools and railroad tracks and laboratories that we regard as evidence of intellect. If we are particularly adept in escaping from our own bodies, we may even learn to discount a little the kind of world of rockets and death that our type of busy human curiosity, linked to a hand noted for its ability to open assorted Pandora's boxes, has succeeded in foisting upon the world as a symbol of universal intelligence.

We have now sacrificed, in our imagination, our hands for flippers and our familiar land environment for the ocean. We will go down into the deep waters as naked of possessions as when we entered life itself. We will take with us one thing alone that exists among porpoises as among men: an ingrained biological gregariousness—a sociality that in our new world will permit us to run in schools, just as early man ran in the packs that were his ancient anthropoid heritage. We will assume in the light of Dr. Lilly's researches that our native intelligence, as distinguished from our culturally transmitted habits, is very high. The waters have closed finally over us, our paws have been sacrificed for the necessary flippers with which to navigate.

The result is immediately evident and quite clear: No matter how well we communicate with our fellows through the water medium we will never build drowned empires in the coral; we will never inscribe on palace walls the victorious boasts of porpoise kings. We will know only water and the wastes of water beyond the power of man to describe. We will be secret visitors in hidden canyons beneath the mouths of torrential rivers. We will survey in innocent astonishment the flotsam that pours from the veins of continents—dead men, great serpents, giant trees—or perhaps the little toy boat of a child loosed far upstream will come floating past. Bottles with winking green lights will plunge by us into the all-embracing ooze. Meaningless appearances and disappearances will comprise our philosophies. We will hear the earth's heart ticking in its thin granitic shell. Volcanic fires will growl ominously in steam-filled crevices. Vapor, bird cries, and sea wrack will compose our memories. We will see death in many forms and, on occasion, the slow majestic fall of battleships through the green light that comes from beyond our domain.

Over all that region of wondrous beauty we will exercise no more control than the simplest mollusk. Even the octopus with flexible arms will build little shelters that we cannot imitate. Without hands we will have only the freedom to follow the untrammeled sea winds across the planet.

Perhaps if those whistling sounds that porpoises make are truly symbolic and capable of manipulation in our brains, we will wonder about the world in which we find ourselves—but it will be a world not susceptible to experiment. At best we may nuzzle in curiosity a passing shipbottom and be harpooned for our pains. Our thoughts, in other words, will be as limited as those of the first men who roved in little bands in the times before fire and the writing that was to open to man the great doorway of his past.

Man without writing cannot long retain his history in his head. His intelligence permits him to grasp some kind of succession of generations; but without writing, the tale of the past rapidly degenerates into fumbling myth and fable. Man's greatest epic, his four long battles with the advancing ice of the great continental glaciers, has vanished from human memory without a trace. Our illiterate fathers disappeared and with them, in a few scant generations, died one of the great stories of all time. This episode has nothing to do with the biological quality of a brain as between then and now. It has to do instead with a device, an invention made possible by the hand. That invention came too late in time to record eyewitness accounts of the years of the Giant Frost.

Primitives of our own species, even today, are historically shallow in their knowledge of the past. Only the poet who writes speaks his message across the millennia to other hearts. Only in writing can the cry from the great cross on Golgotha still be heard in the minds of men. The thinker of perceptive insight, even if we allow him for the moment to be a porpoise rather than a man, has only his individual glimpse of the universe until such time as he can impose that insight upon unnumbered generations. In centuries of pondering, man has come upon but one answer to this problem: speech translated into writing that passes beyond human mortality.

Writing, and later printing, is the product of our adaptable many-purposed hands. It is thus, through writing, with no increase in genetic, inborn capacity since the last ice advance, that modern man carries in his mind the intellectual triumphs of all his predecessors who were able to inscribe their thoughts for posterity.

All animals which man has reason to believe are more than usually intelligent—our relatives the great apes, the elephant, the raccoon, the wolverine, among others—are problem solvers, and in at least a small way manipulators of their environment. Save for the instinctive calls of their species, however, they cannot communicate except by direct imitation. They cannot invent words for new situations nor get their fellows to use such words. No matter how high the individual intelligence, its private world remains a private possession locked forever within a single, perishable brain. It is this fact that finally balks our hunger to communicate even with the sensitive dog who shares our fireside.

Dr. Lilly insists, however, that the porpoises communicate in high-pitched, underwater whistles that seem to transmit their wishes and problems. The question then becomes one of ascertaining whether these sounds represent true language—in the sense of symbolic meanings, additive, learned elements—or whether they are simply the instinctive signals of a pack animal. To this there is as yet no clear answer, but the eagerness with which laboratory sounds and voices were copied by captive porpoises suggests a vocalizing ability extending perhaps to or beyond the threshold of speech.

Most of the intelligent land animals have prehensile, grasping organs for exploring their environment—hands in man and his anthropoid relatives, the sensitive inquiring trunk in the elephant. One of the surprising things about the porpoise is that his superior brain is unaccompanied by any type of manipulative organ. He has, however, a remarkable range-finding ability involving some sort of echo-sounding. Perhaps this acute sense—far more accurate than any man has been able to devise artificially—brings him greater knowledge of his watery surroundings than might at first seem possible. Human beings think of intelligence as geared to things. The hand and the tool are to us the unconscious symbols of our intellectual achievement. It is difficult for us to visualize another kind of lonely, almost disembodied intelligence floating in the wavering green fairyland of the sea—an intelligence possibly near or comparable to our own but without hands to build, to transmit knowledge by writing, or to alter by one hairsbreadth the planet's surface. Yet at the same time there are indications that this is a warm, friendly and eager intelligence quite capable of coming to the assistance of injured companions and striving to rescue them from drowning. Porpoises left the land when mammalian brains were still small and primitive. Without the stimulus provided by agile exploring fingers, these great sea mammals have yet taken a divergent road toward intelligence of a high order. Hidden in their sleek bodies is an impressively elaborated instrument, the reason for whose appearance is a complete enigma. It is as though both man and porpoise were each part of some great eye which yearned to look both outward on eternity and inward to the sea's heart—that fertile entity so like the mind in its swarming and grotesque life.

Perhaps man has something to learn after all from fellow creatures without the ability to drive harpoons through living flesh, or poison with strontium the planetary winds. One is reminded of those watery blue vaults in which, as in some idyllic eternity, Herman Melville once saw the sperm whales nurse their young. And as Melville wrote of the sperm whale, so we might now paraphrase his words in speaking of the porpoise. "Genius in the porpoise? Has the porpoise ever written a book, spoken a speech? No, his great genius is declared in his doing nothing particular to prove it. It is declared in his pyramidical silence." If man had sacrificed his hands for flukes, the moral might run, he would still be a philosopher, but there would have been taken from him the devastating power to wreak his thought upon the body of the world. Instead he would have lived and wandered, like the porpoise, homeless across currents and winds and oceans, intelligent, but forever the lonely and curious observer of unknown wreckage falling through the blue light of eternity. This role would now be a deserved penitence for man. Perhaps such a transformation would bring him once more into that mood of childhood innocence in which he talked successfully to all things living but had no power and no urge to harm. It is worth at least a wistful thought that someday the porpoise may talk to us and we to him. It would break, perhaps, the long loneliness that has made man a frequent terror and abomination even to himself.

Lines of Inquiry
"The Long Loneliness"

In paragraph 11, Eiseley decides to enter imaginatively into the point of view of the porpoise, and in paragraphs 12–15 he follows through on this decision. What did you discover from this imaginative excursion? What purpose(s) does this excursion serve in the later development of the essay, particularly in the final paragraph? Why do you suppose that Eiseley didn't continue the excursion beyond paragraph 15? In what respect(s), if any, does the excursion seem to be biased by "a man-centered way of looking" at things?

In paragraphs 16–19, Eiseley makes a special claim for writing as endowing human beings with unique powers. What special powers and achievements does Eiseley attribute to writing? In what respects does he regard these powers and achievements as also being the cause of man's "long loneliness"? Exactly what does Eiseley mean by the long loneliness? Why might it not be argued that every creature suffers from a long loneliness?

In this essay, as in his other pieces in this collection, the relationship of human beings to other creatures in the world concerns Eiseley. Based on a reading of these four pieces, what do you consider to be the most important elements in Eiseley's view of that relationship?

The Hidden Teacher

*Sometimes the best teacher teaches only once to a single child or to
a grownup past hope.*

—*Anonymous*

I

The putting of formidable
riddles did not arise with today's philosophers. In fact, there is a sense
in which the experimental method of science might be said merely to
have widened the area of man's homelessness. Over two thousand years
ago, a man named Job, crouching in the Judean desert, was moved to
challenge what he felt to be the injustice of his God. The voice in the
whirlwind, in turn, volleyed pitiless questions upon the supplicant—
questions that have, in truth, precisely the ring of modern science. For
the Lord asked of Job by whose wisdom the hawk soars, and who had
fathered the rain, or entered the storehouses of the snow.

A youth standing by, one Elihu, also played a role in this drama,
for he ventured diffidently to his protesting elder that it was not true
that God failed to manifest Himself. He may speak in one way or another, though men do not perceive it. In consequence of this remark
perhaps it would be well, whatever our individual beliefs, to consider
what may be called the hidden teacher, lest we become too much concerned with the formalities of only one aspect of the education by which
we learn.

We think we learn from teachers, and we sometimes do. But the
teachers are not always to be found in school or in great laboratories.
Sometimes what we learn depends upon our own powers of insight.
Moreover, our teachers may be hidden, even the greatest teacher. And
it was the young man Elihu who observed that if the old are not always
wise, neither can the teacher's way be ordered by the young whom he
would teach.

For example, I once received an unexpected lesson from a spider.

It happened far away on a rainy morning in the West. I had come   5
up a long gulch looking for fossils, and there, just at eye level, lurked
a huge yellow-and-black orb spider, whose web was moored to the tall
spears of buffalo grass at the edge of the arroyo. It was her universe,
and her senses did not extend beyond the lines and spokes of the great
wheel she inhabited. Her extended claws could feel every vibration
throughout that delicate structure. She knew the tug of wind, the fall
of a raindrop, the flutter of a trapped moth's wing. Down one spoke
of the web ran a stout ribbon of gossamer on which she could hurry
out to investigate her prey.

Curious, I took a pencil from my pocket and touched a strand of the web. Immediately there was a response. The web, plucked by its menacing occupant, began to vibrate until it was a blur. Anything that had brushed claw or wing against that amazing snare would be thoroughly entrapped. As the vibrations slowed, I could see the owner fingering her guidelines for signs of struggle. A pencil point was an intrusion into this universe for which no precedent existed. Spider was circumscribed by spider ideas; its universe was spider universe. All outside was irrational, extraneous, at best raw material for spider. As I proceeded on my way along the gully, like a vast impossible shadow, I realized that in the world of spider I did not exist.

Moreover, I considered, as I tramped along, that to the phagocytes, the white blood cells, clambering even now with some kind of elementary intelligence amid the thin pipes and tubing of my body—creatures without whose ministrations I could not exist—the conscious "I" of which I was aware had no significance to these amoeboid beings. I was, instead, a kind of chemical web that brought meaningful messages to them, a natural environment seemingly immortal if they could have thought about it, since generations of them had lived and perished, and would continue to so live and die, in that odd fabric which contained my intelligence—a misty light that was beginning to seem floating and tenuous even to me.

I began to see that, among the many universes in which the world of living creatures existed, some were large, some small, but that all, including man's, were in some way limited or finite. We were creatures of many different dimensions passing through each other's lives like ghosts through doors.

In the years since, my mind has many times returned to that far moment of my encounter with the orb spider. A message has arisen only now from the misty shreds of that webbed universe. What was it that had so troubled me about the incident? Was it that spidery indifference to the human triumph?

If so, that triumph was very real and could not be denied. I saw, 10 had many times seen, both mentally and in the seams of exposed strata, the long backward stretch of time whose recovery is one of the great feats of modern science. I saw the drifting cells of the early seas from which all life, including our own, has arisen. The salt of those ancient seas is in our blood, its lime is in our bones. Every time we walk along a beach some ancient urge disturbs us so that we find ourselves shedding shoes and garments or scavenging among seaweed and whitened timbers like the homesick refugees of a long war.

And war it has been indeed—the long war of life against its inhospitable environment, a war that has lasted for perhaps three billion years. It began with strange chemicals seething under a sky lacking in oxygen; it was waged through long ages until the first green plants learned to harness the light of the nearest star, our sun. The human brain, so frail, so perishable, so full of inexhaustible dreams and hungers, burns by the power of the leaf.

The hurrying blood cells charged with oxygen carry more of that element to the human brain than to any other part of the body. A few moments' loss of vital air and the phenomenon we know as consciousness goes down into the black night of inorganic things. The human body is a magical vessel, but its life is linked with an element it cannot produce. Only the green plant knows the secret of transforming the light that comes to us across the far reaches of space. There is no better illustration of the intricacy of man's relationship with other living things.

The student of fossil life would be forced to tell us that if we take the past into consideration the vast majority of earth's creatures—perhaps over 90 percent—have vanished. Forms that flourished for a far longer time than man has existed upon earth have become either extinct or so transformed that their descendants are scarcely recognizable. The specialized perish with the environment that created them, the tooth of the tiger fails at last, the lances of men strike down the last mammoth.

In three billion years of slow change and groping effort only one living creature has succeeded in escaping the trap of specialization that has led in time to so much death and wasted endeavor. It is man, but the word should be uttered softly, for his story is not yet done.

With the rise of the human brain, with the appearance of a creature 15
whose upright body enabled two limbs to be freed for the exploration and manipulation of his environment, there had at last emerged a creature with a specialization—the brain—that, paradoxically, offered escape from specialization. Many animals driven into the nooks and crannies of nature have achieved momentary survival only at the cost of later extinction.

Was it this that troubled me and brought my mind back to a tiny universe among the grass blades, a spider's universe concerned with spider thought?

Perhaps.

The mind that once visualized animals on a cave wall is now engaged in a vast ramification of itself through time and space. Man has broken through the boundaries that control all other life. I saw, at last, the reason for my recollection of that great spider on the arroyo's rim, fingering its universe against the sky.

The spider was a symbol of man in miniature. The wheel of the web brought the analogy home clearly. Man, too, lies at the heart of a web, a web extending through the starry reaches of sidereal space, as well as backward into the dark realm of prehistory. His great eye upon Mount Palomar looks into a distance of millions of light-years, his radio ear hears the whisper of even more remote galaxies, he peers through the electron microscope upon the minute particles of his own being. It is a web no creature of earth has ever spun before. Like the orb spider, man lies at the heart of it, listening. Knowledge has given him the memory of earth's history beyond the time of his emergence. Like the spider's claw, a part of him touches a world he will never enter in the flesh. Even now, one can see him reaching forward into time with new machines, computing, analyzing, until elements of the shadowy future will also compose part of the invisible web he fingers.

Yet still my spider lingers in memory against the sunset sky. Spider thoughts in a spider universe—sensitive to raindrop and moth flutter, nothing beyond, nothing allowed for the unexpected, the inserted pencil from the world outside.   20

Is man at heart any different from the spider, I wonder: man thoughts, as limited as spider thoughts, contemplating now the nearest star with the threat of bringing with him the fungus rot from earth, wars, violence, the burden of a population he refuses to control, cherishing again his dream of the Adamic Eden he had pursued and lost in the green forests of America. Now it beckons again like a mirage from beyond the moon. Let man spin his web, I thought further; it is his nature. But I considered also the work of the phagocytes swarming in the rivers of my body, the unresting cells in their mortal universe. What is it we are a part of that we do not see, as the spider was not gifted to discern my face, or my little probe into her world?

We are too content with our sensory extensions, with the fulfillment of that Ice Age mind that began its journey amidst the cold of vast tundras and that pauses only briefly before its leap into space. It is no longer enough to see as a man sees—even to the ends of the universe. It is not enough to hold nuclear energy in one's hand like a spear, as a man would hold it, or to see the lightning, or times past, or time to come, as a man would see it. If we continue to do this, the great brain—the human brain—will be only a new version of the old trap, and nature is full of traps for the beast that cannot learn.

It is not sufficient any longer to listen at the end of a wire to the rustlings of galaxies; it is not enough even to examine the great coil of DNA in which is coded the very alphabet of life. These are our extended perceptions. But beyond lies the great darkness of the ultimate Dreamer, who dreamed the light and the galaxies. Before act was, or substance existed, imagination grew in the dark. Man partakes of that ultimate wonder and creativeness. As we turn from the galaxies to the swarming cells of our own being, which toil for something, some entity beyond their grasp, let us remember man, the self-fabricator who came across an ice age to look into the mirrors and the magic of science. Surely he did not come to see himself or his wild visage only. He came because he is at heart a listener and a searcher for some transcendent realm beyond himself. This he has worshiped by many names, even in the dismal caves of his beginning. Man, the self-fabricator, is so by reason of gifts he had no part in devising—and so he searches as the single living cell in the beginning must have sought the ghostly creature it was to serve.

II

The young man Elihu, Job's counselor and critic, spoke simply of the "Teacher," and it is of this teacher I speak when I refer to gifts man had no part in devising. Perhaps—though it is purely a matter of emotional reactions to words—it is easier for us today to speak of this teacher as "nature," that omnipresent all which contained both the spider and my invisible intrusion into her carefully planned universe. But nature does not simply represent reality. In the shapes of life, it prepares the future; it offers alternatives. Nature teaches, though what it teaches is often hidden and obscure, just as the voice from the spinning dust cloud belittled Job's thought but gave back no answers to its own formidable interrogation.

A few months ago I encountered an amazing little creature on a windy corner of my local shopping center. It seemed, at first glance, some long-limbed, feathery spider teetering rapidly down the edge of a store front. Then it swung into the air and, as hesitantly as a spider on a thread, blew away into the parking lot. It returned in a moment on a gust of wind and ran toward me once more on its spindly legs with amazing rapidity.

With great difficulty I discovered the creature was actually a filamentous seed, seeking a hiding place and scurrying about with the uncanny surety of a conscious animal. In fact, it *did* escape me before I could secure it. Its flexible limbs were stiffer than milkweed down, and, propelled by the wind, it ran rapidly and evasively over the pavement. It was like a gnome scampering somewhere with a hidden packet—for all that I could tell, a totally new one: one of the jumbled alphabets of life.

A new one? So stable seem the years and all green leaves, a botanist might smile at my imaginings. Yet bear with me a moment. I would like to tell a tale, a genuine tale of childhood. Moreover, I was just old enough to know the average of my kind and to marvel at what I saw. And what I saw was straight from the hidden Teacher, whatever be his name.

It is told in the Orient of the Hindu god Krishna that his mother, wiping his mouth when he was a child, inadvertently peered in and beheld the universe, though the sight was mercifully and immediately veiled from her. In a sense, this is what happened to me. One day there arrived at our school a newcomer, who entered the grade above me. After some days this lad, whose look of sleepy-eyed arrogance is still

25

before me as I write, was led into my mathematics classroom by the principal. Our class was informed severely that we should learn to work harder.

With this preliminary exhortation, great rows of figures were chalked upon the blackboard, such difficult mathematical problems as could be devised by adults. The class watched in helpless wonder. When the preparations had been completed, the young pupil sauntered forward and, with a glance of infinite boredom that swept from us to his fawning teachers, wrote the answers, as instantaneously as a modern computer, in their proper place upon the board. Then he strolled out with a carelessly exaggerated yawn.

Like some heavy-browed child at the wood's edge, clutching the last stone hand ax, I was witnessing the birth of a new type of humanity—one so beyond its teachers that it was being used for mean purposes while the intangible web of the universe in all its shimmering mathematical perfection glistened untaught in the mind of a chance little boy. The boy, by then grown self-centered and contemptuous, was being dragged from room to room to encourage us, the paleanthropes, to duplicate what, in reality, our teachers could not duplicate. He was too precious an object to be released upon the playground among us, and with reason. In a few months his parents took him away.

Long after, looking back from maturity, I realized that I had been exposed on that occasion, not to human teaching, but to the Teacher, toying with some sixteen billion nerve cells interlocked in ways past understanding. Or, if we do not like the anthropomorphism implied in the word teacher, then nature, the old voice from the whirlwind fumbling for the light. At all events, I had been the fortunate witness to life's unbounded creativity—a creativity seemingly still as unbalanced and chance-filled as in that far era when a black-scaled creature had broken from an egg and the age of the giant reptiles, the creatures of the prime, had tentatively begun.

Because form cannot be long sustained in the living, we collapse inward with age. We die. Our bodies, which were the product of a kind of hidden teaching by an alphabet we are only beginning dimly to discern, are dismissed into their elements. What is carried onward, assuming we have descendants, is the little capsule of instructions such as I encountered hastening by me in the shape of a running seed. We have learned the first biological lesson: that in each generation life passes through the eye of a needle. It exists for a time molecularly and in no recognizable semblance to its adult condition. It *instructs* its way again into man or reptile. As the ages pass, so do variants of the code. Occasionally, a species vanishes on a wind as unreturning as that which took the pterodactyls.

Or the code changes by subtle degrees through the statistical altering of individuals; until I, as the fading Neanderthals must once have

30

done, have looked with still-living eyes upon the creature whose genotype was quite possibly to replace me. The genetic alphabets, like genuine languages, ramify and evolve along unreturning pathways.

If nature's instructions are carried through the eye of a needle, through the molecular darkness of a minute world below the field of human vision and of time's decay, the same, it might be said, is true of those monumental structures known as civilizations. They are transmitted from one generation to another in invisible puffs of air known as words— words that can also be symbolically incised on clay. As the delicate printing on the mud at the water's edge retraces a visit of autumn birds long since departed, so the little scrabbled tablets in perished cities carry the seeds of human thought across the deserts of millennia. In this instance the teacher is the social brain, but it, too, must be compressed into minute hieroglyphs, and the minds that wrought the miracle efface themselves amidst the jostling torrent of messages, which, like the genetic code, are shuffled and reshuffled as they hurry through eternity. Like a mutation, an idea may be recorded in the wrong time, to lie latent like a recessive gene and spring once more to life in an auspicious era.

Occasionally, in the moments when an archaeologist lifts the slab 35 over a tomb that houses a great secret, a few men gain a unique glimpse through that dark portal out of which all men living have emerged, and through which messages again must pass. Here the Mexican archaeologist Ruz Lhuillier speaks of his first penetration of the great tomb hidden beneath dripping stalactites at the pyramid of Palenque: "Out of the dark shadows, rose a fairy-tale vision, a weird ethereal spectacle from another world. It was like a magician's cave carved out of ice, with walls glittering and sparkling like snow crystals." After shining his torch over hieroglyphs and sculptured figures, the explorer remarked wonderingly: "We were the first people for more than a thousand years to look at it."

Or again, one may read the tale of an unknown pharaoh who had secretly arranged that a beloved woman of his household should be buried in the tomb of the god-king—an act of compassion carrying a personal message across the milennia in defiance of all precedent.

Up to this point we have been talking of the single hidden teacher, the taunting voice out of that old Biblical whirlwind which symbolizes nature. We have seen incredible organic remembrance passed through the needle's eye of a microcosmic world hidden completely beneath the observational powers of creatures preoccupied and ensorcelled by dissolution and decay. We have seen the human mind unconsciously seize upon the principles of that very code to pass its own societal memory forward into time. The individual, the momentary living cell of the society, vanishes, but the institutional structures stand, or if they change, do so in an invisible flux not too dissimilar from that persisting in the stream of genetic continuity.

Upon this world, life is still young, not truly old as stars are measured. Therefore it comes about that we minimize the role of the synapsid reptiles, our remote forerunners, and correspondingly exalt our own intellectual achievements. We refuse to consider that in the old eye of the hurricane we may be, and doubtless are, in aggregate, a slightly more diffuse and dangerous dragon of the primal morning that still enfolds us.

Note that I say "in aggregate." For it is just here, among men, that the role of messages, and, therefore, the role of the individual teacher—or, I should say now, the hidden teachers—begin to be more plainly apparent and their instructions become more diverse. The dead pharaoh, though unintentionally, by a revealing act, had succeeded in conveying an impression of human tenderness that has outlasted the trappings of a vanished religion.

Like most modern educators I have listened to student demands to   40
grade their teachers. I have heard the words repeated until they have become a slogan, that no man over thirty can teach the young of this generation. How would one grade a dead pharaoh, millennia gone, I wonder, one who did not intend to teach, but who, to a few perceptive minds, succeeded by the simple nobility of an act.

Many years ago, a student who was destined to become an internationally known anthropologist sat in a course in linguistics and heard his instructor, a man of no inconsiderable wisdom, describe some linguistic peculiarities of Hebrew words. At the time, the young student, at the urging of his family, was contemplating a career in theology. As the teacher warmed to his subject, the student, in the back row, ventured excitedly, "I believe I can understand that, sir. It is very similar to what exists in Mohegan."

The linguist paused and adjusted his glasses. "Young man," he said, "Mohegan is a dead language. Nothing has been recorded of it since the eighteenth century. Don't bluff."

"But sir," the young student countered hopefully, "It can't be dead so long as an old woman I know still speaks it. She is Pequot-Mohegan. I learned a bit of vocabulary from her and could speak with her myself. She took care of me when I was a child."

"Young man," said the austere, old-fashioned scholar, "be at my house for dinner at six this evening. You and I are going to look into this matter."

A few months later, under careful guidance, the young student pub-   45
lished a paper upon Mohegan linguistics, the first of a long series of studies upon the forgotten languages and ethnology of the Indians of the northeastern forests. He had changed his vocation and turned to anthropology because of the attraction of a hidden teacher. But just who was the teacher? The young man himself, his instructor, or that solitary speaker of a dying tongue who had so yearned to hear her people's voice that she had softly babbled it to a child?

Later, this man was to become one of my professors. I absorbed much from him, though I hasten to make the reluctant confession that he was considerably beyond thirty. Most of what I learned was gathered over cups of coffee in a dingy campus restaurant. What we talked about were things some centuries older than either of us. Our common interest lay in snakes, scapulimancy, and other forgotten rites of benighted forest hunters.

I have always regarded this man as an extraordinary individual, in fact, a hidden teacher. But alas, it is all now so old-fashioned. We never protested the impracticality of his quaint subjects. We were all too ready to participate in them. He was an excellent canoeman, but he took me to places where I fully expected to drown before securing my degree. To this day, fragments of his unused wisdom remain stuffed in some back attic of my mind. Much of it I have never found the opportunity to employ, yet it has somehow colored my whole adult existence. I belong to that elderly professor in somewhat the same way that he, in turn, had become the wood child of a hidden forest mother.

There are, however, other teachers. For example, among the hunting peoples there were the animal counselors who appeared in prophetic dreams. Or, among the Greeks, the daemonic supernaturals who stood at the headboard while a man lay stark and listened—sometimes to dreadful things. "You are asleep," the messengers proclaimed over and over again, as though the man lay in a spell to hear his doom pronounced. "You, Achilles, you, son of Atreus. You are asleep, asleep," the hidden ones pronounced and vanished.

We of this modern time know other things of dreams, but we know also that they can be interior teachers and healers as well as the anticipators of disaster. It has been said that great art is the night thought of man. It may emerge without warning from the soundless depths of the unconscious, just as supernovas may blaze up suddenly in the farther reaches of void space. The critics, like astronomers, can afterward triangulate such worlds but not account for them.

A writer friend of mine with bitter memories of his youth, and estranged from his family, who, in the interim, had died, gave me this account of the matter in his middle years. He had been working, with an unusual degree of reluctance, upon a novel that contained certain autobiographical episodes. One night he dreamed; it was a very vivid and stunning dream in its detailed reality.

He found himself hurrying over creaking snow through the blackness of a winter night. He was ascending a familiar path through a long-vanished orchard. The path led to his childhood home. The house, as he drew near, appeared dark and uninhabited, but, impelled by the power of the dream, he stepped upon the porch and tried to peer through a dark window into his own old room.

50

"Suddenly," he told me, "I was drawn by a strange mixture of repulsion and desire to press my face against the glass. I knew intuitively they were all there waiting for me within, if I could but see them. My mother and my father. Those I had loved and those I hated. But the window was black to my gaze. I hesitated a moment and struck a match. For an instant in that freezing silence I saw my father's face glimmer wan and remote behind the glass. My mother's face was there, with the hard, distorted lines that marked her later years.

"A surge of fury overcame my cowardice. I cupped the match before me and stepped closer, closer toward that dreadful confrontation. As the match guttered down, my face was pressed almost to the glass. In some quick transformation, such as only a dream can effect, I saw that it was my own face into which I stared, just as it was reflected in the black glass. My father's haunted face was but my own. The hard lines upon my mother's aging countenance were slowly reshaping themselves upon my living face. The light burned out. I awoke sweating from the terrible psychological tension of that nightmare. I was in a far port in a distant land. It was dawn. I could hear the waves breaking on the reef."

"And how do you interpret the dream?" I asked, concealing a sympathetic shudder and sinking deeper into my chair.

"It taught me something," he said slowly, and with equal slowness 55 a kind of beautiful transfiguration passed over his features. All the tired lines I had known so well seemed faintly to be subsiding.

"Did you ever dream it again?" I asked out of a comparable experience of my own.

"No, never," he said, and hesitated. "You see, I had learned it was just I, but more, much more, I had learned that I was they. It makes a difference. And at the last, late—much too late—it was all right. I understood. My line was dying, but I understood. I hope they understood, too." His voice trailed into silence.

"It is a thing to learn," I said. "You were seeking something and it came." He nodded, wordless. "Out of a tomb," he added after a silent moment, "my kind of tomb—the mind."

On the dark street, walking homeward, I considered my friend's experience. Man, I concluded, may have come to the end of that wild being who had mastered the fire and the lightning. He can create the web but not hold it together, not save himself except by transcending his own image. For at last, before the ultimate mystery, it is himself he shapes. Perhaps it is for this that the listening web lies open: that by knowledge we may grow beyond our past, our follies, and ever closer to what the Dreamer in the dark intended before the dust arose and walked. In the pages of an old book it has been written that we are in the hands of a Teacher, nor does it yet appear what man shall be.

Lines of Inquiry
"The Hidden Teacher"

In paragraphs 4, 5, and 6, Eiseley tells about "an unexpected lesson" that he learned "from a spider," and he refers to or alludes to the spider throughout the remainder of the essay. Make a note of all the explicit and implicit references to the spider. How are these references connected to each other, constituting something like a web of related images and ideas in the essay? How are the spider images related, in turn, to the other images and stories that Eiseley tells about in the piece? Why do you suppose that he chooses to make the spider the predominant metaphor in the essay?

Taking into account all of the hidden teachers that Eiseley refers to in his essay, what characteristics exactly distinguish "the hidden teacher"? How is a hidden teacher different from the teachers "to be found in school or in great laboratories"? In what respects does the knowledge that comes from hidden teachers differ from the knowledge conveyed by school teachers? In what respects do these different kinds of knowledge also imply different beliefs and values? What are the hidden beliefs and values that Eiseley attributes to the hidden teachers?

To what extent do you consider this essay to be a critique of traditional education? To what extent do you consider it a critique of the scientific method? To what extent do you consider it a critique of materialistic values? In thinking about these questions, you might find it useful to compare and contrast Eiseley's essay with Thomas' "The Art of Teaching Science," or Gould's "On Heroes and Fools in Science," or Thoreau's "Where I Lived, and What I Lived For."

E. M. Forster
1879–1970

Body and spirit, reason and emotion, work and play, architecture and scenery, laughter and seriousness, life and art—these pairs which are elsewhere contrasted were there fused into one.

In this description of the world that he found as a student at Cambridge University, E. M. Forster could just as well have been outlining his vision of utopia, for throughout his career as a novelist, short-story writer, and essayist, he repeatedly expressed his belief in the need to bring harmony between the disparate and often conflicting aspects of human nature and experience. He was especially concerned to awaken his fellow Englishmen, whom he thought of as being too "practical" and "afraid to feel," to the life of the emotions and the imagination. So one of the dominant themes of his writing is the synthesis envisioned by the heroine of his novel *Howard's End* (1910)—"Only connect! That was the whole of her sermon. Only connect the prose and the passion and both will be exalted, and human love will be seen at its height."

Born in London, Edward Morgan Forster was an only child, raised by his mother and paternal aunts after the death of his father when he was still a baby. His aesthetic interests came from his mother's side of the family, his moral seriousness from his father's side. A happy childhood in the rolling English countryside was followed by the regimented life of an English private school, "with its boarding houses, its compulsory games, its system of prefects and fagging, its insistence on good form and *esprit de corps.*" There, as at other such schools that he was later to criticize, he saw his fellow schoolmates acquire "well-developed bodies, fairly developed minds, and undeveloped hearts." By contrast, his life at King's College, Cambridge from 1897 to 1901 was obviously a very liberating and satisfying experience.

At Cambridge, Forster developed his broadly humanistic belief in the value of "body and spirit, reason and emotion," intellect and intuition—in the value of the fully developed individual. There as a student of classics and history, he developed his abiding interest in literature and culture. There as a member of two notable discussion societies, he developed his love of ideas and of personal relationships. There he discovered the homosexual side of his nature. And there at the suggestion of his teachers and friends, he began writing essays for the undergraduate literary magazine. After graduation, he spent a year traveling with his mother in Italy and Austria, and the following year he spent some time traveling alone in Greece.

His experiences at Cambridge together with his foreign travels clearly must have awakened in him an acute sense of deficiency in English middle-class life and an equally strong desire to delineate its problems through the art of fiction. In fact, between 1905 and 1911, he came out with four novels and one short story collection—all concerned with challenging what he perceived to be the stuffy rules, the hypocrisies, the emotional evasions, the repressions, and the trivial values of English middle-class life. In his first novel, *Where Angels Fear to Tread* (1905), he made his point through a dramatic contrast between the artificial world of English suburban society and the spontaneous, instinctual world of Italian village life. In his fourth novel *Howard's End* (1910), which established him as a major writer, he focused on the contrasting values of two markedly different English families, one that cares about art, literature, and social reform, the other about business and proper behavior.

During this period of intense creative activity, Forster came into contact with the Bloomsbury group, a circle of remarkably gifted artists, writers, and intellectuals that grew out of the Cambridge discussion groups with which he had been affiliated. This "aristocracy of the sensitive, the considerate, and the plucky," which included such well-known figures as the art critic, Roger Fry; the economist, John Maynard Keynes; the biographer, Lytton Strachey; and the novelist, Virginia Woolf, clearly worked its critically inquiring influence on Forster's outlook and writing. But even more decisive an influence was produced by a six-month trip that he made to India in 1912–13.

Out of his experiences in India came most of the material for his greatest novel, *A Passage to India* (1924). Though he did not complete the novel until he had made a second visit to India in 1921, it was his first trip that made him intensely conscious of the striking differences and conflicts between English and Indian cultures—and thus of the mysterious and paradoxical dualities of life—that he dramatizes in the book. Forster's trips to India together with his three years of service with the Red Cross in Alexandria during World War I ultimately served to produce the very spacious cultural and political awareness that is reflected in most of his subsequent writing.

After *A Passage to India*, Forster did not write any other novels during the more than fifty-five remaining years of his life, though a novel of homosexual experience, *Maurice,* that he had drafted during 1913 and

1914 was published after his death. The social climate and the censorship laws of his era did not give him the freedom to write and publish the kind of fiction that had come to interest him. So during the remainder of his life he dedicated himself wholly to nonfictional writing. His nonfiction books cover a wide range of subjects: two devoted to the culture and history of Alexandria, *Alexandria* (1922) and *Pharos and Pharillon* (1923); one to the nature of fiction, *Aspects of the Novel* (1927); one to his most influential teacher at Cambridge, *Goldsworthy Lowes Dickinson* (1934); one to India and his personal recollections of it, *The Hill of Devi* (1953); and one to his paternal aunt who left him a substantial legacy that gave him the independence to be a writer, *Marianne Thornton: A Domestic Biography* (1956).

An even greater range of subject matter is reflected in his two volumes of articles, essays, and radio broadcasts, *Abinger Harvest* (1936) and *Two Cheers for Democracy* (1951). The volumes include aesthetic, cultural, literary, social, and political commentary, along with biographical, historical, and personal pieces. So, too, the form of his pieces ranges from notes and anecdotes to statements of belief. "Temperamentally," as he said, "I am an individualist," so the tone of his individual essays is often unpredictable, mixing "reason and emotion," as well as "laughter and seriousness." Though they vary in subject, form, and tone, his essays are always informed by his humane and liberal-minded outlook, by the "tolerance, good temper and sympathy" that he considered imperative "if the human race is not to collapse."

The Game of Life

O Life, what art thou? Life
seldom answers this question. But her silence is of little consequence,
for schoolmasters and other men of good will are well qualified to answer for her. She is, they inform us, a game. Which game? Bagatelle?
No, Life is serious, so not bagatelle, but any game that . . . er . . . is
not a game of mere chance; not Baccarat, but Chess; or, in moderation,
Bridge; yes, or better still, Football with its goals and healthy open-air
atmosphere and its *esprit de corps;* Fate is the umpire and Hope is the
ball: hie to the football ground all, all, all.—Thus far and even further
the men of good will. Once started on the subject of Life they lose all
diffidence, because to them it is ethical. They love discussing what we
ought to be instead of what we have to face—reams about conduct and
nothing about those agitating apparitions that rise from the ground or
fall from the sky. When they say that Life is a game they only mean
that some games develop certain qualities, such as heartiness, which
they appreciate.

Still, they may have used the right phrase. There are some curious
features about games, moments of piercing reality when an unknown
process is suddenly reflected like a star. Upon the simple little universes
that have been created by the device of rules and by the convention of
a beginning and an end, there sometimes descends an endorsement, as
it were, from the actual universe. Similar endorsements descend upon
works of art. But there their effect upon us is different. They gratify.
They make us feel we could be artists too. Whereas the game, when it
becomes real, becomes disquieting. A win always seems shallow: it is
the loss that is so profound and suggests nasty infinities. Games of mere
chance must, it is true, be excluded from this charge. They have abandoned any pretence of Free Will, and consequently their irony is too
mechanical to be endorsed by Life's: Life may also be mere chance, but
she has evolved the imposing doctrine of effort and reward to obscure
her purposelessness, and any game that mirrors her must do the same.
Let us therefore turn to games of skill, and in the first place to Chess.

I play the Evans.

The invention of a naval officer, the Evans Gambit is noted for its
liquidity. A heavy current rapidly sets in from the southwest and laps
against the foundations of Black's King's Bishop's Pawn. The whole
surface of the board breaks into whirlpools. But sooner or later out of
this marine display there rises a familiar corpse. It is mine. Oh, what
have I been doing, what have I been doing? The usual thing. Premature
attack, followed by timidity. Oh, why didn't I move out my Rook's

Pawn? Because as always I was misled by superficial emotions. No, not as always. It must be that the Evans doesn't suit my style. Henceforward I play Old Stodge.

I do so. There is nothing liquid about Old Stodge. He smacks of the soil. On either side runs a dreary ridge of Knights and Bishops. Between them is a plain (whence the term of Giuoco Piano) where the pawns butt one another like rams. The powers of earth move slowly to the shock, then topple over with alternate and uninspiring thuds. It's supposed to be an exchange. But when the lines of the new landscape emerge from the dust, what familiar corpse is disclosed? Mine. Oh, what have I been doing? The usual thing. My character has come out. If I go down to the depths of the sea, it is there; if I seek the heart of the hills it is there also. Chess, which severely eliminates accident, is a forcing house where the fruits of character can ripen more fully than in Life. In Life we can always blame the unknowable for our failures, wave the hand to some horizon, shake the fist at some star. But surely when we make the same mistakes in the Evans, Old Stodge, the choice of a tie, a row in the office and a love affair, the same defect must be to blame—character; for which, the men of goodwill hasten to remind us, we are entirely and eternally responsible.

Since there are these two elements in life, the uncontrollable and that which we are supposed to control; and since games of chance exaggerate the former and Chess the latter—what game reflects their actual proportion? 5

Piquet.

Those who reply Bridge or Football introduce the incalculable element of partners and sides. One complexity cannot interpret another, and though Life may be Bridge, it is so only to the eye of faith: the resemblance cannot be grasped by an intellectual effort. But think for a moment about Piquet. It is in the first place obviously and overwhelmingly unfair. Fate is dealt, despite skill in discarding, and neither in the rules of play nor in the marking is there the least attempt to redress misfortune or to give the sufferer a fresh chance. The bias is all the other way. Disaster is an additional reason for disaster—culminating in the crowning butchery of Rubicon, where the very bones of the victim are gathered up by the conqueror and flung like sticks upon his bonfire. Yet this savage pastime admits the element of Free Will. It is possible to retard or accelerate Fate. Play, subtle and vigorous play, goes on all the time, though the player is being swept to disaster or victory by causes beyond his control, and it is in the play, rather than the result, that the real interest of the game resides. Another affair, in which all the living and possibly all the dead are engaged, runs on similar lines. Failure or success seem to have been allotted to men by their stars. But they retain the power of wriggling, of fighting with their star or against it, and in the whole universe the only really interesting movement is this wriggle. O Life, thou art Piquet, in fact. A grim relaxation. Still, she might have been Golf.

1919

Lines of Inquiry
"The Game of Life"

This essay works somewhat like a set of variations on a theme—in this case the theme that life is a game. What are the major variations that Forster plays on this theme? How does he manage to make his way from one variation to another? How would you characterize his tone of voice in each variation? Why do you suppose that he uses the structure of theme and variations? Why doesn't he just give a straightforward explanation of his view of life?

Though Forster begins his essay by mocking "schoolmasters and other men of good will" who compare life to a game, he then comes to think that "they may have used the right phrase". What do you think accounts for his change of mind? In what sense(s) does he think the comparison is right? What aspects of life is Forster most concerned with and how are these reflected in games, particularly the game of piquet? How serious do you take him to be in comparing life to piquet?

What relationship do you see between the nature of games and the nature of life? What relationship do you think exists between games and life in contemporary American society? What game that you know of comes closest to your view of life? In what sense(s) is life not like a game? What do you think it is like?

My Wood

A few years ago I wrote a book which dealt in part with the difficulties of the English in India. Feeling that they would have had no difficulties in India themselves, the Americans read the book freely. The more they read it the better it made them feel, and a cheque to the author was the result. I bought a wood with the cheque. It is not a large wood—it contains scarcely any trees, and it is intersected, blast it, by a public footpath. Still, it is the first property that I have owned, so it is right that other people should participate in my shame, and should ask themselves, in accents that will vary in horror, this very important question: What is the effect of property upon the character? Don't let's touch economics; the effect of private ownership upon the community as a whole is another question—a more important question, perhaps, but another one. Let's keep to psychology. If you own things, what's their effect on you? What's the effect on me of my wood?

In the first place, it makes me feel heavy. Property does have this effect. Property produces men of weight, and it was a man of weight who failed to get into the Kingdom of Heaven. He was not wicked, that unfortunate millionaire in the parable, he was only stout; he stuck out in front, not to mention behind, and as he wedged himself this way and that in the crystalline entrance and bruised his well-fed flanks, he saw beneath him a comparatively slim camel passing through the eye of a needle and being woven into the robe of God. The Gospels all through couple stoutness and slowness. They point out what is perfectly obvious, yet seldom realized: that if you have a lot of things you cannot move about a lot, that furniture requires dusting, dusters require servants, servants require insurance stamps, and the whole tangle of them makes you think twice before you accept an invitation to dinner or go for a bathe in the Jordan. Sometimes the Gospels proceed further and say with Tolstoy that property is sinful; they approach the difficult ground of asceticism here, where I cannot follow them. But as to the immediate effects of property on people, they just show straightforward logic. It produces men of weight. Men of weight cannot, by definition, move like the lightning from the East unto the West, and the ascent of a fourteen-stone bishop into a pulpit is thus the exact antithesis of the coming of the Son of Man. My wood makes me feel heavy.

In the second place, it makes me feel it ought to be larger.

The other day I heard a twig snap in it. I was annoyed at first, for I thought that someone was blackberrying, and depreciating the value of the undergrowth. On coming nearer, I saw it was not a man who had trodden on the twig and snapped it, but a bird, and I felt pleased. My bird. The bird was not equally pleased. Ignoring the relation between us, it took fright as soon as it saw the shape of my face, and flew straight over the boundary hedge into a field, the property of Mrs. Henessy, where it sat down with a loud squawk. It had become Mrs. Henessy's bird. Something seemed grossly amiss here, something that would not have occurred had the wood been larger. I could not afford to buy Mrs. Henessy out, I dared not murder her, and limitations of this sort beset me on every side. Ahab did not want that vineyard—he only needed it to round off his property, preparatory to plotting a new curve—and all the land around my wood has become necessary to me in order to round off the wood. A boundary protects. But—poor little thing—the boundary ought in its turn to be protected. Noises on the edge of it. Children throw stones. A little more, and then a little more, until we reach the sea. Happy Canute! Happier Alexander! And after all, why should even the world be the limit of possession? A rocket containing a Union Jack, will, it is hoped, be shortly fired at the moon. Mars. Sirius. Beyond which . . . But these immensities ended by saddening me. I could not suppose that my wood was the destined nucleus of universal dominion—it is so very small and contains no mineral wealth beyond the blackberries. Nor was I comforted when Mrs. Henessy's bird took alarm for the second time and flew clean away from us all, under the belief that it belonged to itself.

In the third place, property makes its owner feel that he ought to do something to it. Yet he isn't sure what. A restlessness comes over him, a vague sense that he has a personality to express—the same sense which, without any vagueness, leads the artist to an act of creation. Sometimes I think I will cut down such trees as remain in the wood, at other times I want to fill up the gaps between them with new trees. Both impulses are pretentious and empty. They are not honest movements towards money-making or beauty. They spring from a foolish desire to express myself and from an inability to enjoy what I have got. Creation, property, enjoyment form a sinister trinity in the human mind. Creation and enjoyment are both very, very good, yet they are often unattainable without a material basis, and at such moments property pushes itself in as a substitute, saying, "Accept me instead—I'm good enough for all three." It is not enough. It is, as Shakespeare said of lust, "The expense of spirit in a waste of shame": it is "Before, a joy proposed; behind, a dream." Yet we don't know how to shun it. It is forced on us by our economic system as the alternative to starvation. It is also forced on us by an internal defect in the soul, by the feeling that in property may lie the germs of self-development and of exquisite or heroic deeds. Our life on earth is, and ought to be, material and carnal. But we have not yet learned to manage our materialism and carnality properly; they are still entangled with the desire for ownership, where (in the words of Dante) "Possession is one with loss."

5

And this brings us to our fourth and final point: the blackberries.

Blackberries are not plentiful in this meagre grove, but they are easily seen from the public footpath which traverses it, and all too easily gathered. Foxgloves, too—people will pull up the foxgloves, and ladies of an educational tendency even grub for toadstools to show them on the Monday in class. Other ladies, less educated, roll down the bracken in the arms of their gentlemen friends. There is paper, there are tins. Pray, does my wood belong to me or doesn't it? And, if it does, should I not own it best by allowing no one else to walk there? There is a wood near Lyme Regis, also cursed by a public footpath, where the owner has not hesitated on this point. He had built high stone walls each side of the path, and has spanned it by bridges, so that the public circulate like termites while he gorges on the blackberries unseen. He really does own his wood, this able chap. Dives in Hell did pretty well, but the gulf dividing him from Lazarus could be traversed by vision, and nothing traverses it here. And perhaps I shall come to this in time. I shall wall in and fence out until I really taste the sweets of property. Enormously stout, endlessly avaricious, pseudo-creative, intensely selfish, I shall weave upon my forehead the quadruple crown of possession until those nasty Bolshies come and take it off again and thrust me aside into the outer darkness.

Lines of Inquiry
"My Wood"

Forster organizes his essay in terms of four clearly enumerated points. What do you suppose accounts for his arrangement of these points from first to last? Do they appear in an order of increasing importance? Do they build on each other logically? Or do they come in a random order? Consider arranging the points in a couple of different ways. What are the effects of your rearrangements?

Early on in his piece, Forster claims to be concerned with examining the "effect of property upon character," in particular, the psychological effect on him of his wood. How closely does he stick to this purpose? What other effects of property does he touch on in this piece? What point do you think Forster is actually trying to make about property by describing how he has been affected by his wood? Or do you think he is simply interested in reporting how he has been affected by his wood?

Forster is not the only author in this collection to write about the effect of property upon character, as you can see by looking at Thoreau's "Where I Lived and What I Lived For." Read the first thirteen paragraphs of Thoreau's piece, then consider how his ideas are similar to Forster's and how they differ. Given the uneasiness of both authors about owning property, imagine what the world would be like if people did not own property but held it in common.

What I Believe

I do not believe in Belief. But this is an age of faith, and there are so many militant creeds that, in self-defence, one has to formulate a creed of one's own. Tolerance, good temper and sympathy are no longer enough in a world which is rent by religious and racial persecution, in a world where ignorance rules, and science, who ought to have ruled, plays the subservient pimp. Tolerance, good temper and sympathy—they are what matter really, and if the human race is not to collapse they must come to the front before long. But for the moment they are not enough, their action is no stronger than a flower, battered beneath a military jack-boot. They want stiffening, even if the process coarsens them. Faith, to my mind, is a stiffening process, a sort of mental starch, which ought to be applied as sparingly as possible. I dislike the stuff. I do not believe in it, for its own sake, at all. Herein I probably differ from most people, who believe in Belief, and are only sorry they cannot swallow even more than they do. My law-givers are Erasmus and Montaigne, not Moses and St. Paul. My temple stands not upon Mount Moriah but in that Elysian Field where even the immortal are admitted. My motto is "Lord, I disbelieve—help thou my unbelief."

I have, however, to live in an Age of Faith—the sort of epoch I used to hear praised when I was a boy. It is extremely unpleasant really. It is bloody in every sense of the word. And I have to keep my end up in it. Where do I start?

With personal relationships. Here is something comparatively solid in a world full of violence and cruelty. Not absolutely solid, for psychology has split and shattered the idea of a "Person," and has shown that there is something incalculable in each of us, which may at any moment rise to the surface and destroy our normal balance. We don't know what we are like. We can't know what other people are like. How, then, can we put any trust in personal relationships, or cling to them in the gathering political storm? In theory we cannot. But in practice we can and do. Though A is not unchangeably A or B unchangeably B, there can still be love and loyalty between the two. For the purpose of living one has to assume that the personality is solid, and the "self" is an entity, and to ignore all contrary evidence. And since to ignore evidence is one of the characteristics of faith, I certainly can proclaim that I believe in personal relationships.

Starting from them, I get a little order into the contemporary chaos. One must be fond of people and trust them if one is not to make a mess of life, and it is therefore essential that they should not let one down. They often do. The moral of which is that I must, myself, be as reliable as possible, and this I try to be. But reliability is not a matter of contract—that is the main difference between the world of personal relationships and the world of business relationships. It is a matter for the heart, which signs no documents. In other words, reliability is impossible unless there is a natural warmth. Most men possess this warmth, though they often have bad luck and get chilled. Most of them, even when they are politicians, *want* to keep faith. And one can, at all events, show one's own little light here, one's own poor little trembling flame, with the knowledge that it is not the only light that is shining in the darkness, and not the only one which the darkness does not comprehend. Personal relations are despised today. They are regarded as bourgeois luxuries, as products of a time of fair weather which is now past, and we are urged to get rid of them, and to dedicate ourselves to some movement or cause instead. I hate the idea of causes, and if I had to choose between betraying my country and betraying my friend, I hope I should have the guts to betray my country. Such a choice may scandalize the modern reader, and he may stretch out his patriotic hand to the telephone at once and ring up the police. It would not have shocked Dante, though. Dante places Brutus and Cassius in the lowest circle of Hell because they had chosen to betray their friend Julius Caesar rather than their country Rome. Probably one will not be asked to make such an agonising choice. Still, there lies at the back of every creed something terrible and hard for which the worshipper may one day be required to suffer, and there is even a terror and a hardness in this creed of personal relationships, urbane and mild though it sounds. Love and loyalty to an individual can run counter to the claims of the State. When they do—down with the State, say I, which means that the State would down me.

This brings me along to Democracy, "even Love, the Beloved Republic, which feeds upon Freedom and lives." Democracy is not a Beloved Republic really, and never will be. But it is less hateful than other contemporary forms of government, and to that extent it deserves our support. It does start from the assumption that the individual is important, and that all types are needed to make a civilisation. It does not divide its citizens into the bossers and the bossed—as an efficiency-regime tends to do. The people I admire most are those who are sensitive and want to create something or discover something, and do not see life in terms of power, and such people get more of a chance under a democracy than elsewhere. They found religions, great or small, or they produce literature and art, or they do disinterested scientific research, or they may be what is called "ordinary people," who are creative in their private lives, bring up their children decently, for instance, or help their neighbours. All these people need to express themselves;

they cannot do so unless society allows them to do so, and the society which allows them most liberty is a democracy.

Democracy has another merit. It allows criticism, and if there is not public criticism there are bound to be hushed-up scandals. That is why I believe in the Press, despite all its lies and vulgarity, and why I believe in Parliament. Parliament is often sneered at because it is a Talking Shop. I believe in it *because* it is a talking shop. I believe in the Private Member who makes himself a nuisance. He gets snubbed and is told that he is cranky or ill-informed, but he does expose abuses which would otherwise never have been mentioned, and very often an abuse gets put right just by being mentioned. Occasionally, too, a well-meaning public official starts losing his head in the cause of efficiency, and thinks himself God Almighty. Such officials are particularly frequent in the Home Office. Well, there will be questions about them in Parliament sooner or later, and then they will have to mind their steps. Whether Parliament is either a representative body or an efficient one is questionable, but I value it because it criticises and talks, and because its chatter gets widely reported.

So Two Cheers for Democracy: one because it admits variety and two because it permits criticism. Two cheers are quite enough: there is no occasion to give three. Only Love the Beloved Republic deserves that.

What about Force, though? While we are trying to be sensitive and advanced and affectionate and tolerant, an unpleasant question pops up: does not all society rest upon force? If a government cannot count upon the police and the army, how can it hope to rule? And if an individual gets knocked on the head or sent to a labour camp, of what significance are his opinions?

This dilemma does not worry me as much as it does some. I realise that all society rests upon force. But all the great creative actions, all the decent human relations, occur during the intervals when force has not managed to come to the front. These intervals are what matter. I want them to be as frequent and as lengthy as possible, and I call them "civilisation." Some people idealise force and pull it into the foreground and worship it, instead of keeping it in the background as long as possible. I think they make a mistake, and I think that their opposites, the mystics, err even more when they declare that force does not exist. I believe that it exists, and that one of our jobs is to prevent it from getting out of its box. It gets out sooner or later, and then it destroys us and all the lovely things which we have made. But it is not out all the time, for the fortunate reason that the strong are so stupid. Consider their conduct for a moment in the Niebelung's Ring.[1] The

---

[1] A cycle of four musical dramas by Richard Wagner which were based on the Germanic epic *Nibelungenlied*.

giants there have the guns, or in other words the gold; but they do nothing with it, they do not realise that they are all-powerful with the result that the catastrophe is delayed and the castle of Walhalla, insecure but glorious, fronts the storms. Fafnir, coiled round his hoard, grumbles and grunts; we can hear him under Europe today; the leaves of the wood already tremble, and the Bird calls its warnings uselessly. Fafnir will destroy us, but by a blessed dispensation he is stupid and slow, and creation goes on just outside the poisonous blast of his breath. The Nietzschean would hurry the monster up, the mystic would say he did not exist, but Wotan, wiser than either, hastens to create warriors before doom declares itself. The Valkyries are symbols not only of courage but of intelligence; they represent the human spirit snatching its opportunity while the going is good, and one of them even finds time to love. Brünnhilde's last song hymns the recurrence of love, and since it is the privilege of art to exaggerate, she goes even further, and proclaims the love which is eternally triumphant and feeds upon freedom, and lives.

So that is what I feel about force and violence. It is, alas! the ultimate reality on this earth, but it does not always get to the front. Some people call its absences "decadence"; I call them "civilisation" and find in such interludes the chief justification for the human experiment. I look the other way until fate strikes me. Whether this is due to courage or to cowardice in my own case I cannot be sure. But I know that if men had not looked the other way in the past, nothing of any value would survive. The people I respect most behave as if they were immortal and as if society was eternal. Both assumptions are false: both of them must be accepted as true if we are to go on eating and working and loving, and are to keep open a few breathing holes for the human spirit. No millennium seems likely to descend upon humanity; no better and stronger League of Nations will be instituted; no form of Christianity and no alternative to Christianity will bring peace to the world or integrity to the individual; no "change of heart" will occur. And yet we need not despair, indeed, we cannot despair; the evidence of history shows us that men have always insisted on behaving creatively under the shadow of the sword; that they have done their artistic and scientific and domestic stuff for the sake of doing it, and that we had better follow their example under the shadow of the aeroplanes. Others, with more vision or courage than myself, see the salvation of humanity ahead, and will dismiss my conception of civilisation as paltry, a sort of tip-and-run game. Certainly it is presumptuous to say that we *cannot* improve, and that Man, who has only been in power for a few thousand years, will never learn to make use of his power. All I mean is that, if people continue to kill one another as they do, the world cannot get better than it is, and that since there are more people than formerly, and their means for destroying one another superior, the world may well get worse. What is good in people—and consequently in the world— is their insistence on creation, their belief in friendship and loyalty for their own sakes; and though Violence remains and is, indeed, the major partner in this muddled establishment, I believe that creativeness remains too, and will always assume direction when violence sleeps. So, though I am not an optimist, I cannot agree with Sophocles that it were better never to have been born. And although, like Horace, I see no evidence that each batch of births is superior to the last, I leave the field open for the more complacent view. This is such a difficult moment to live in, one cannot help getting gloomy and also a bit rattled, and perhaps short-sighted.

In search of a refuge, we may perhaps turn to hero-worship. But here we shall get no help, in my opinion. Hero-worship is a dangerous vice, and one of the minor merits of a democracy is that it does not encourage it, or produce that unmanageable type of citizen known as the Great Man. It produces instead different kinds of small men—a much finer achievement. But people who cannot get interested in the variety of life, and cannot make up their own minds, get discontented over this, and they long for a hero to bow down before and to follow blindly. It is significant that a hero is an integral part of the authoritarian stock-in-trade today. An efficiency-regime cannot be run without a few heroes stuck about it to carry off the dullness—much as plums have to be put into a bad pudding to make it palatable. One hero at the top and a smaller one each side of him is a favourite arrangement, and the timid and the bored are comforted by the trinity, and, bowing down, feel exalted and strengthened.

No, I distrust Great Men. They produce a desert of uniformity around them and often a pool of blood too, and I always feel a little man's pleasure when they come a cropper. Every now and then one reads in the newspapers some such statement as: "The coup d'etat appears to have failed, and Admiral Toma's whereabouts is at present unknown." Admiral Toma had probably every qualification for being a Great Man— an iron will, personal magnetism, dash, flair, sexlessness—but fate was against him, so he retires to unknown whereabouts instead of parading history with his peers. He fails with a completeness which no artist and no lover can experience, because with them the process of creation is itself an achievement, whereas with him the only possible achievement is success.

I believe in aristocracy, though—if that is the right word, and if a democrat may use it. Not an aristocracy of power, based upon rank and influence, but an aristocracy of the sensitive, the considerate and the plucky. Its members are to be found in all nations and classes, and all through the ages, and there is a secret understanding between them when they meet. They represent the true human tradition, the one permanent victory of our queer race over cruelty and chaos. Thousands of them perish in obscurity, a few are great names. They are sensitive for others as well as for themselves, they are considerate without being fussy, their pluck is not swankiness but the power to endure, and they can take a joke. I give no examples—it is risky to do that—but the reader may as well consider whether this is the type of person he would like to meet and to be, and whether (going farther with me) he would prefer that this type should *not* be an ascetic one. I am against asceticism myself. I am with the old Scotsman who wanted less chastity and more delicacy. I do not feel that my aristocrats are a real aristocracy if they thwart their bodies, since bodies are the instruments through which we register and enjoy the world. Still, I do not insist. This is not a major point. It is clearly possible to be sensitive, considerate and plucky and yet be an ascetic too; if anyone possesses the first three qualities, I will let him in! On they go—an invincible army, yet not a victorious one. The aristocrats, the elect, the chosen, the Best People—all the words that describe them are false, and all attempts to organise them fail. Again and again Authority, seeing their value, has tried to net them and to utilise them as the Egyptian Priesthood or the Christian Church or the Chinese Civil Service or the Group movement, or some other worthy stunt. But they slip through the net and are gone; when the door is shut, they are no longer in the room; their temple, as one of them remarked, is the Holiness of the Heart's Affection, and their kingdom, though they never possess it, is the wide-open world.

With this type of person knocking about, and constantly crossing one's path if one has eyes to see or hands to feel, the experiment of earthly life cannot be dismissed as a failure. But it may well be hailed as a tragedy, the tragedy being that no device has been found by which these private decencies can be transmitted to public affairs. As soon as the people have power they go crooked and sometimes dotty as well, because the possession of power lifts them into a region where normal honesty never pays. For instance, the man who is selling newspapers outside the Houses of Parliament can safely leave his papers to go for a drink and his cap beside them: anyone who takes a paper is sure to drop a copper into the cap. But the men who are inside the Houses of Parliament—they cannot trust one another like that, still less can the Government they compose trust other governments. No caps upon the pavement here, but suspicion, treachery and armaments. The more highly public life is organised the lower does its morality sink; the nations of today behave to each other worse than they ever did in the past, they cheat, rob, bully and bluff, make war without notice, and kill as many women and children as possible; whereas primitive tribes were at all events restrained by taboos. It is a humiliating outlook—though the greater the darkness, the brighter shine the little lights, reassuring one another, signaling: "Well, at all events, I'm still here. I don't like it very much, but how are you?" Unquenchable lights of my aristocracy!

Signals of the invincible army! "Come along—anyway, let's have a good time while we can." I think they signal that too.

The Saviour of the future—if ever he comes—will not preach a new   15
Gospel. He will merely utilise my aristocracy, he will make effective the good will and the good temper which are already existing. In other words, he will introduce a new technique. In economics, we are told that if there was a new technique of distribution, there need be no poverty, and people would not starve in one place while crops were being ploughed under in another. A similar change is needed in the sphere of morals and politics. The desire for it is by no means new; it was expressed, for example, in theological terms by Jacopone da Todi[2] over six hundred years ago. *"Ordina questo amore, O tu che m'ami,"* he said; "O thou who lovest me—set this love in order." His prayer was not granted, and I do not myself believe that it ever will be, but here, and not through a change of heart, is our probable route. Not by becoming better, but by ordering and distributing his native goodness, will Man shut up Force into its box, and so gain time to explore the universe and to set his mark upon it worthily. At present he only explores it at odd moments, when Force is looking the other way, and his divine creativeness appears as a trivial by-product, to be scrapped as soon as the drums beat and the bombers hum.

Such a change, claim the orthodox, can only be made by Christianity, and will be made by it in God's good time: man always has failed and always will fail to organise his own goodness, and it is presumptuous of him to try. This claim—solemn as it is—leaves me cold. I cannot believe that Christianity will ever cope with the present worldwide mess, and I think that such influence as it retains in modern society is due to the money behind it, rather than to its spiritual appeal. It was a spiritual force once, but the indwelling spirit will have to be restated if it is to calm the waters again, and probably restated in a nonChristian form. Naturally a lot of people, and people who are not only good but able and intelligent, will disagree here; they will vehemently deny that Christianity has failed, or they will argue that its failure proceeds from the wickedness of men, and really proves its ultimate success. They have Faith, with a large F. My faith has a very small one, and I only intrude it because these are strenuous and serious days, and one likes to say what one thinks while speech is comparatively free: it may not be free much longer.

The above are the reflections of an individualist and a liberal who has found liberalism crumbling beneath him and at first felt ashamed. Then, looking around, he decided there was no special reason for shame, since other people, whatever they felt, were equally insecure. And as

---

[2] An Italian religious poet.

for individualism—there seems no way of getting off this, even if one wanted to. The dictator-hero can grind down his citizens till they are all alike, but he cannot melt them into a single man. That is beyond his power. He can order them to merge, he can incite them to mass-antics, but they are obliged to be born separately, and to die separately, and, owing to these unavoidable termini, will always be running off the totalitarian rails. The memory of birth and the expectation of death always lurk within the human being, making him separate from his fellows and consequently capable of intercourse with them. Naked I came into the world, naked I shall go out of it! And a very good thing too, for it reminds me that I am naked under my shirt, whatever its colour.

1939

Lines of Inquiry
"What I Believe"

Given his assertion in the opening paragraph that "Tolerance, good temper, and sympathy . . . are what really matter," it seems appropriate to consider how tolerant, good tempered, and sympathetic Forster appears to be in this essay. How would you describe his tone of voice, or the way his personality comes across, as he moves from one topic to the next—for example, from personal relationships to democracy to force?

In the course of this essay, Forster stands up for or speaks out against a number of things. Make a list of the main things that he defends and the main things that he attacks. What kinship do you do you see among the things he defends? Among the things he attacks? What relationship do you see between the things he defends and the things he attacks? Based on this examination of his ideas, what do you think is the essence of Forster's beliefs?

Forster also voices his beliefs in "The Game of Life" and "My Wood." What kinship do you see among the values he espouses in these three pieces? What differences do you see in the focus of each piece? Consider how the emphasis of each piece might have been affected by political, social, or economic circumstances that prevailed at the time when it was written: "The Game of Life" (1919), "My Wood" (1926), and "What I Believe" (1939).

Anonymity: An Enquiry

Do you like to know who a book's by?

The question is more profound than may appear. A poem for example: do we gain more or less pleasure from it when we know the name of the poet? The *Ballad of Sir Patrick Spens,* for example. No one knows who wrote *Sir Patrick Spens.* It comes to us out of the northern void like a breath of ice. Set beside it another ballad whose author is known—*The Rime of the Ancient Mariner.* That, too, contains a tragic voyage and the breath of ice, but it is signed Samuel Taylor Coleridge, and we know a certain amount about this Coleridge. Coleridge signed other poems and knew other poets; he ran away from Cambridge, he enlisted as a Dragoon under the name of Trooper Comberbacke, but fell so constantly from his horse that it had to be withdrawn from beneath him permanently; he was employed instead upon matters relating to sanitation; he married Southey's sister, and gave lectures; he became stout, pious and dishonest, took opium and died. With such information in our heads, we speak of the *Ancient Mariner* as "a poem by Coleridge," but of *Sir Patrick Spens* as "a poem." What difference, if any, does this difference between them make upon our minds? And in the case of novels and plays—does ignorance or knowledge of their authorship signify? And newspaper articles—do they impress more when they are signed or unsigned? Thus—rather vaguely—let us begin our quest.

Books are composed of words, and words have two functions to perform: they give information or they create an atmosphere. Often they do both, for the two functions are not incompatible, but our enquiry shall keep them distinct. Let us turn for our next example to Public Notices. There is a word that is sometimes hung up at the edge of a tramline: the word "Stop." Written on a metal label by the side of the line, it means that a tram should stop here presently. It is an example of pure information. It creates no atmosphere—at least, not in my mind. I stand close to the label and wait and wait for the tram. If the tram comes, the information is correct; if it doesn't come, the information is incorrect; but in either case it remains information, and the notice is an excellent instance of one of the uses of words.

Compare it with another public notice which is sometimes exhibited in the darker cities of England: "Beware of pick-pockets, male and female." Here, again, there is information. A pickpocket may come along presently, just like a tram, and we take our measures accordingly.

But there is something else besides. Atmosphere is created. Who can see those words without a slight sinking feeling at the heart? All the people around look so honest and nice, but they are not, some of them are pickpockets, male or female. They hustle old gentlemen, the old gentleman glances down, his watch is gone. They steal up behind an old lady and cut out the back breadth of her beautiful sealskin jacket with sharp and noiseless pairs of scissors. Observe that happy little child running to buy sweets. Why does he suddenly burst into tears? A pick-pocket, male or female, has jerked his halfpenny out of his hand. All this, and perhaps much more, occurs to us when we read the notice in question. We suspect our fellows of dishonesty, we observe them suspecting us. We have been reminded of several disquieting truths, of the general insecurity of life, human frailty, the violence of the poor, and the fatuous trustfulness of the rich, who always expect to be popular without having done anything to deserve it. It is a sort of *memento mori,* set up in the midst of Vanity Fair. By taking the form of a warning it has made us afraid, although nothing is gained by fear; all we need to do is to protect our precious purses, and fear will not help us to do this. Besides conveying information it has created an atmosphere, and to that extent is literature. "Beware of pickpockets, male and female," is not good literature, and it is unconscious. But the words are performing two functions, whereas the word "Stop" only performed one, and this is an important difference, and the first step in our journey.

Next step. Let us now collect together all the printed matter of the world into a single heap; poetry books, exercise books, plays, newspapers, advertisements, street notices, everything. Let us arrange the contents of the heap into a line, with the works that convey pure information at one end, and the works that create pure atmosphere at the other end, and the works that do both in their intermediate positions, the whole line being graded so that we pass from one attitude to another. We shall find that at the end of the pure information stands the tramway notice "Stop," and that at the extreme other end is lyric poetry. Lyric poetry is absolutely no use. It is the exact antithesis of a street notice, for it conveys no information of any kind. What's the use of "A slumber did my spirit steal" or "Whether on Ida's snowy brow" or "So we'll go no more a roving" or "Far in a western brookland"? They do not tell us where the tram will stop or even whether it exists. And, passing from lyric poetry to ballad, we are still deprived of information. It is true that the *Ancient Mariner* describes an antarctic expedition, but in such a muddled way that it is no real help to the explorer, the accounts of the polar currents and winds being hopelessly inaccurate. It is true that the *Ballad of Sir Patrick Spens* refers to the bringing home of the Maid of Norway in the year 1285, but the reference is so vague and confused that the historians turn from it in despair. Lyric poetry is absolutely no use, and poetry generally is almost no use.

5

But when, proceeding down the line, we leave poetry behind and arrive at the drama, and particularly at those plays that purport to contain normal human beings, we find a change. Uselessness still predominates, but we begin to get information as well. *Julius Caesar* contains some reliable information about Rome. And when we pass from the drama to the novel, the change is still more marked. Information abounds. What a lot we learn from *Tom Jones* about the west countryside! And from *Northanger Abbey* about the same countryside fifty years later! In psychology too the novelist teaches us much. How carefully has Henry James explored certain selected recesses of the human mind! What an analysis of a country rectory in *The Way of All Flesh!* The instincts of Emily Brontë—they illuminate passion. And Proust—how amazingly does Proust describe not only French Society, not only the working of his characters, but the personal equipment of the reader, so that one keeps stopping with a gasp to say "Oh! how how did he find that out about me? I didn't even know it myself until he informed me, but it is so!" The novel, whatever else it may be, is partly a notice-board. And that is why many men who do not care for poetry or even for the drama enjoy novels and are well qualified to criticise them.

Beyond the novel we come to works whose avowed aim is information, works of learning, history, sociology, philosophy, psychology, science, etc. Uselessness is now subsidiary, though it still may persist as it does in the *Decline and Fall* or the *Stones of Venice.* And next come those works that give, or profess to give, us information about contemporary events: the newspapers. (Newspapers are so important and so peculiar that I shall return to them later, but mention them here in their place in the procession of printed matter.) And then come advertisements, time tables, the price list inside a taxi, and public notices: the notice warning us against pickpockets, which incidentally produced an atmosphere, though its aim was information, and the pure information contained in the announcement "Stop." It is a long journey from lyric poetry to a placard beside a tramline, but it is a journey in which there are no breaks. Words are all of one family, and do not become different because some are printed in a book and others on a metal disc. It is their functions that differentiate them. They have two functions, and the combination of those functions is infinite. If there is on earth a house with many mansions, it is the house of words.

Looking at this line of printed matter, let us again ask ourselves: Do I want to know who wrote that? Ought it to be signed or not? The question is becoming more interesting. Clearly, in so far as words convey information, they ought to be signed. Information is supposed to be true. That is its only reason for existing, and the man who gives it ought to sign his name, so that he may be called to account if he has told a lie. When I have waited for several hours beneath the notice "Stop," I have the right to suggest that it be taken down, and I cannot do this unless I know who put it up. Make your statement, sign your name. That's common sense. But as we approach the other function of words—the creation of atmosphere—the question of signature surely loses its importance. It does not matter who wrote "A slumber did my spirit steal" because the poem itself does not matter. Ascribe it to Ella Wheeler Wilcox and the trams will run as usual. It does not matter much who wrote *Julius Caesar* and *Tom Jones.* They contain descriptions of ancient Rome and eighteenth-century England, and to that extent we wish them signed, for we can judge from the author's name whether the description is likely to be reliable; but beyond that, the guarantee of Shakespeare or Fielding might just as well be Charles Garvice's. So we come to the conclusion, firstly, that what is information ought to be signed; and secondly, that what is not information need not be signed.

The question can now be carried a step further.

What is this element in words that is not information? I have called it "atmosphere," but it requires stricter definition than that. It resides not in any particular word, but in the order in which words are arranged—that is to say, in style. It is the power that words have to raise our emotions or quicken our blood. It is also something else, and to define that other thing would be to explain the secret of the universe. This "something else" in words is undefinable. It is their power to create not only atmosphere, but a world, which, while it lasts, seems more real and solid than this daily existence of pickpockets and trams. Before we begin to read the *Ancient Mariner* we know that the Polar Seas are not inhabited by spirits, and that if a man shoots an albatross he is not a criminal but a sportsman, and that if he stuffs the albatross afterwards he becomes a naturalist also. All this is common knowledge. But when we are reading the *Ancient Mariner,* or remembering it intensely, common knowledge disappears and uncommon knowledge takes its place. We have entered a universe that only answers to its own laws, supports itself, internally coheres, and has a new standard of truth. Information is true if it is accurate. A poem is true if it hangs together. Information points to something else. A poem points to nothing but itself. Information is relative. A poem is absolute. The world created by words exists neither in space nor time though it has semblances of both, it is eternal and indestructible, and yet its action is no stronger than a flower: it is adamant, yet it is also what one of its practitioners thought it to be, namely, the shadow of a shadow. We can best define it by negations. It is not this world, its laws are not the laws of science or logic, its conclusions not those of common sense. And it causes us to suspend our ordinary judgments.

Now comes the crucial point. While we are reading the *Ancient Mariner* we forget our astronomy and geography and daily ethics. Do we not also forget the author? Does not Samuel Taylor Coleridge, lecturer, opium eater, and dragoon, disappear with the rest of the world of information? We remember him before we begin the poem and after we finish it, but during the poem nothing exists but the poem. Consequently while we read the *Ancient Mariner* a change takes place in it. It becomes anonymous, like the *Ballad of Sir Patrick Spens*. And here is the point I would support: that all literature tends towards a condition of anonymity, and that, so far as words are creative, a signature merely distracts us from their true significance. I do not say literature "ought" not to be signed, because literature is alive, and consequently "ought" is the wrong word to use. It wants not to be signed. That puts my point. It is always tugging in that direction and saying in effect: "I, not my author, exist really." So do the trees, flowers and human beings say "I really exist, not God," and continue to say so despite the admonitions to the contrary addressed to them by clergymen and scientists. To forget its Creator is one of the functions of a Creation. To remember him is to forget the days of one's youth. Literature does not want to remember. It is alive—not in a vague complementary sense—but alive tenaciously, and it is always covering up the tracks that connect it with the laboratory.

It may here be objected that literature expresses personality, that it is the result of the author's individual outlook, that we are right in asking for his name. It is his property—he ought to have the credit.

An important objection; also a modern one, for in the past neither writers nor readers attached the high importance to personality that they do today. It did not trouble Homer or the various people who were Homer. It did not trouble the writers in the Greek Anthology, who would write and re-write the same poem in almost identical language, their notion being that the poem, not the poet, is the important thing, and that by continuous rehandling the perfect expression natural to the poem may be attained. It did not trouble the mediaeval balladists, who, like the Cathedral builders, left their works unsigned. It troubled neither the composers nor the translators of the Bible. The Book of Genesis today contains at least three different elements—Jahvist, Elohist and Priestly—which were combined into a single account by a committee who lived under King Josiah at Jerusalem and translated into English by another committee who lived under King James I at London. And yet the Book of Genesis is literature. These earlier writers and readers knew that the words a man writes express him, but they did not make a cult of expression as we do today. Surely they were right, and modern critics go too far in their insistence on personality.

They go too far because they do not reflect what personality is. Just as words have two functions—information and creation—so each human mind has two personalities, one on the surface, one deeper down. The upper personality has a name. It is called S. T. Coleridge, or William Shakespeare, or Mrs. Humphry Ward. It is conscious and alert, it does things like dining out, answering letters, etc., and it differs vividly and amusingly from other personalities. The lower personality is a very queer affair. In many ways it is a perfect fool, but without it there is no literature, because unless a man dips a bucket down into it occasionally he cannot produce first-class work. There is something general about it. Although it is inside S. T. Coleridge, it cannot be labelled with his name. It has something in common with all other deeper personalities, and the mystic will assert that the common quality is God, and that here, in the obscure recesses of our being, we near the gates of the Divine. It is in any case the force that makes for anonymity. As it came from the depths, so it soars to the heights, out of local questionings; as it is general to all men, so the works it inspires have something general about them, namely beauty. The poet wrote the poem, no doubt, but he forgot himself while he wrote it, and we forget him while we read. What is so wonderful about great literature is that it transforms the man who reads it towards the condition of the man who wrote, and brings to birth in us also the creative impulse. Lost in the beauty where he was lost, we find more than we ever threw away, we reach what seems to be our spiritual home, and remember that it was not the speaker who was in the beginning but the Word.

If we glance at one or two writers who are not first class this point will be illustrated. Charles Lamb and R. L. Stevenson will serve. Here are two gifted, sensitive, fanciful, tolerant, humorous fellows, but they always write with their surface-personalities and never let down buckets into their underworld. Lamb did not try: bbbbuckets, he would have said, are bbeyond me, and he is the pleasanter writer in consequence. Stevenson was always trying oh ever so hard, but the bucket either stuck or else came up again full of the R.L.S. who let it down, full of the mannerisms, the self-consciousness, the sentimentality, the quaintness which he was hoping to avoid. He and Lamb append their names in full to every sentence they write. They pursue us page after page, always to the exclusion of higher joy. They are letter writers, not creative artists, and it is no coincidence that each of them did write charming letters. A letter comes off the surface: it deals with the events of the day or with plans: it is naturally signed. Literature tries to be unsigned. And the proof is that, whereas we are always exclaiming "How like Lamb!" or "How typical of Stevenson!" we never say "How like Shakespeare!" or "How typical of Dante!" We are conscious only of the world they have created, and we are in a sense co-partners in it. Coleridge, in his smaller domain, makes us co-partners too. We forget for ten minutes his name and our own, and I contend that this temporary forgetfulness, this momentary and mutual anonymity, is sure evidence of good stuff. The demand that literature should express personality is far too insistent in these days, and I look back with longing to the earlier modes of criticism where a poem was not an expression but a discovery, and was sometimes supposed to have been shown to the poet by God.

The personality of a writer does become important after we have read his book and begin to study it. When the glamour of creation ceases, when the leaves of the divine tree are silent, when the co-partnership is over, then a book changes its nature, and we can ask ourselves questions about it such as "What is the author's name?" "Where did he live?" "Was he married?" and "Which was his favourite flower?" Then we are no longer reading the book, we are studying it and making it subserve our desire for information. "Study" has a very solemn sound. "I am studying Dante" sounds much more solemn than "I am reading Dante." It is really much less. Study is only a serious form of gossip. It teaches us everything about the book except the central thing, and between that and us it raises a circular barrier which only the wings of the spirit can cross. The study of science, history, etc., is necessary and proper, for they are subjects that belong to the domain of information, but a creative subject like literature—to study that is excessively dangerous, and should never be attempted by the immature. Modern education promotes the unmitigated study of literature and concentrates our attention on the relation between a writer's life—his surface life—and his work. That is one reason why it is such a curse. There are no questions to be asked about literature while we read it because "la paix succède à la pensée,"[1] in the words of Paul Claudel. An examination paper could not be set on the *Ancient Mariner* as it speaks to the heart of the reader, and it was to speak to the heart that it was written, and otherwise it would not have been written. Questions only occur when we cease to realise what it was about and become inquisitive and methodical.

A word in conclusion on the newspapers—for they raise an interesting contributory issue. We have already defined a newspaper as something which conveys, or is supposed to convey, information about passing events. It is true, not to itself like a poem, but to the facts it purports to relate—like the tram notice. When the morning paper arrives it lies upon the breakfast table simply steaming with truth in regard to something else. Truth, truth, and nothing but the truth. Unsated by the banquet, we sally forth in the afternoon to buy an evening paper, which is published at midday as the name implies, and feast anew. At the end of the week we buy a weekly, or a Sunday paper, which as the name implies has been written on the Saturday, and at the end of the month we buy a monthly. Thus do we keep in touch with the world of events as practical men should.

---

[1] Peace follows thought.

And who is keeping us in touch? Who gives us this information upon which our judgments depend, and which must ultimately influence our characters? Curious to relate, we seldom know. Newspapers are for the most part anonymous. Statements are made and no signature appended. Suppose we read in a paper that the Emperor of Guatemala is dead. Our first feeling is one of mild consternation; out of snobbery we regret what has happened, although the Emperor didn't play much part in our lives, and if ladies we say to one another "I feel so sorry for the poor Empress." But presently we learn that the Emperor cannot have died, because Guatemala is a Republic, and the Empress cannot be a widow, because she does not exist. If the statement is signed, and we know the name of the goose who made it, we shall discount anything he tells us in the future. If—which is more probable—it is unsigned or signed "Our Special Correspondent"—we remain defenceless against future misstatements. The Guatemala lad may be turned on to write about the Fall of the Franc and mislead us over that.

It seems paradoxical that an article should impress us more if it is unsigned than if it is signed. But it does, owing to the weakness of our psychology. Anonymous statements have, as we have seen, a universal air about them. Absolute truth, the collected wisdom of the universe, seems to be speaking, not the feeble voice of a man. The modern newspaper has taken advantage of this. It is a pernicious caricature of literature. It has usurped that divine tendency towards anonymity. It has claimed for information what only belongs to creation. And it will claim it as long as we allow it to claim it, and to exploit the defects of our psychology. "The High Mission of the Press." Poor Press! as if it were in a position to have a mission! It is we who have a mission to it. To cure a man through the newspapers or through propaganda of any sort is impossible: you merely alter the symptoms of his disease. We shall only be cured by purging our minds of confusion. The papers trick us not so much by their lies as by their exploitation of our weakness. They are always confusing the two functions of words and insinuating that "The Emperor of Guatemala is dead" and "A slumber did my spirit seal" belong to the same category. They are always usurping the privileges that only uselessness may claim, and they will do this as long as we allow them to do it.

This ends our enquiry. The question "Ought things to be signed?" seemed, if not an easy question, at all events an isolated one, but we could not answer it without considering what words are, and disentangling the two functions they perform. We decided pretty easily that information ought to be signed: common sense leads to this conclusion, and newspapers which are largely unsigned have gained by that device their undesirable influence over civilisation. Creation—that we found a more difficult matter. "Literature wants not to be signed," I suggested.

Creation comes from the depths—the mystic will say from God. The signature, the name, belongs to the surface-personality, and pertains to the world of information, it is a ticket, not the spirit of life. While the author wrote he forgot his name; while we read him we forget both his name and our own. When we have finished reading we begin to ask questions, and to study the book and the author, we drag them into the realm of information. Now we learn a thousand things, but we have lost the pearl of great price, and in the chatter of question and answer, in the torrents of gossip and examination papers we forget the purpose for which creation was performed. I am not asking for reverence. Reverence is fatal to literature. My plea is for something more vital: imagination. Imagination is as the immortal God which should assume flesh for the redemption of mortal passion (Shelley). Imagination is our only guide into the world created by words. Whether those words are signed or unsigned becomes, as soon as the imagination redeems us, a matter of no importance, because we have approximated to the state in which they were written, and there are no names down there, no personality as we understand personality, no marrying or giving in marriage. What there is down there—ah, that is another enquiry, and may the clergymen and the scientists pursue it more successfully in the future than they have in the past.

Lines of Inquiry
"Anonymity: An Enquiry"

Though Forster refers to his piece as an enquiry (enquiry is the English spelling), it might well be called an argument, since it seeks to make a persuasive case for a new set of rules pertaining to the identification of authors. How does Forster attempt to build a strong case for his proposition? How does he attempt to attack the prevailing rules? What kinds of issues, evidence, logic, and other appeals does he rely on most heavily? What do you consider to be the strongest and weakest points in his argument?

In paragraphs 5–7, Forster defines and illustrates a method for classifying "all the printed matter in the world," in terms of a spectrum of possibilities ranging from the purely informational and practical to the purely atmospheric, literary, and useless. But he does not indicate where he would locate the essay in this spectrum of writing. Where do you think it belongs? For example where would you locate each of Forster's essays or some of the others you have read in this collection? What problems, if any, do you have in applying Forster's system of classification to individual essays?

In paragraphs 12–16, Forster outlines a theory of personality and its relationship to writing and reading. How does this theory square with the ideas that Hoagland discusses in "What I Think, What I Am," or that White discusses in "The Essayist and the Essay," or that Woolf discusses in "The Modern Essay"? How does this theory square with your own experience in reading and writing?

Ellen Goodman
1941—

I never wanted to be a package-tour sort of columnist who covered thirteen countries in twenty-seven days. Nor do I want to write at arm's length about the Major Issues of Our Times. I think it's more important for all of us to be able to make links between our personal lives and public issues.

Linking the public and private realms has consistently been Ellen Goodman's special contribution to the editorial pages of newspapers across America. As one journalist has said, Goodman's "trademark is a disarming personal approach to weighty subjects." So, while she writes on topics "as diverse as quiche, summer vacations, and collecting coffee cups," she is best known for her incisive commentary on social turmoil, especially the shifting sex roles in contemporary society. From sober analysis of rape to humorous yet serious reflection on advertising's depiction of women, Goodman's perspective manages to blend a sharp feminist edge with a steady devotion to the values which have traditionally given meaning to women's lives—mothering, hometending, gardening, and a strong sense of community. As a result, her widely syndicated columns have managed to engage the interest of a very diverse readership.

A third-generation Bostonian, Goodman grew up in so nurturing and secure a family that as a child she "wanted everything to stay the same." Her mother was a patient woman who "would listen to your problems until you were sick of them." Her father was a politically active lawyer who "discouraged mushy thinking" and encouraged his daughters to express and defend their opinions. He also encouraged his daughters to take part in his two unsuccessful campaigns for Congress. So, by the time she was only ten, Goodman had "learned the voting patterns of wards and precincts the way other kids learned the batting averages of the Red Sox and the battles of World War II." So, too, she learned to be "very comfortable speaking up."

Her prep school graduation yearbook predicted she would be the first woman president, but instead of entering politics she married shortly after graduating from Radcliffe College in 1963, and went to work as a researcher for *Newsweek,* where, she says, "All of the researchers were women and all of the reporters were men. We didn't like it but that's the way it was." In 1965, she moved with her husband to Detroit and began writing for the Detroit *Free Press*. In 1967, after returning with her husband to Boston, she went to work for the Boston *Globe* as a columnist and feature writer for the women's section. But the political and social upheavals of the late sixties and early seventies worked their influence on Goodman, as they did on the lives and views of countless others, leading her to take a strong interest in the issues addressed by the feminist movement, as well as in the "great ambivalence between tradition and non-tradition" that was then an overwhelming cultural concern.

In 1971 Goodman's marriage ended in divorce. That same year, her columns broke the traditional newspaper divisions of the "male" editorial page and the "female" features section and moved to the *Globe*'s editorial page. By 1976 her column was syndicated—it now appears in nearly four hundred newspapers throughout the country. In 1980 she received the Pulitzer Prize for distinguished commentary. She has published three collections of her columns: *Close to Home* (1979), *At Large* (1981), and *Keeping in Touch* (1985).

Characteristically still "close to home" and "in touch" with her roots, Goodman lives in a Boston suburb, near her relatives and her birthplace, in a renovated townhouse and in what she calls a "renovated" family that includes her second husband, also a writer for the *Globe*, her daughter, and her two stepchildren.

Though Goodman's work appears on the editorial page, she has never been willing to give up writing about her day-to-day experience. So she has persistently and quite self-consciously sought to juxtapose the personal and the political, in the hopes of illuminating both:

> They used to tell me a columnist can't write about politics one day and housework the next. So I made it a point to do just that. It was a conscious decision. I wanted to add something to the newspaper profession. . . . My definition of the political is broader. It is a political issue if Americans feel anxious about their family life, feel anxious about the future of their children.

Goodman's point of view is that of a woman who has struggled with "the greatest social change of our time—the evolving roles of men and women." Her preoccupation with that evolution led her in 1974 to spend a year as a Nieman fellow at Harvard studying the dynamics of personal and social change in American society. The fruit of her study was *Turning Points* (1979), which she calls "a storybook of change." Based on interviews with men and women throughout the country, the book proved Goodman's seriousness as a social analyst and critic, and it also helped her to understand and accept her own ambivalence about change. "People want all the safety that comes from sameness and all the excitement that comes from change," she has said; "In short, we want it all." She admits, of course, that we can never have it all, but believes "that with some help, we can have a very rich sampling."

With characteristic humor, Goodman has reflected on the pressure of newspaper deadlines and the constraints of a 750-word column space: "I only write two columns a week. So I only have to have two opinions a week. So I only have to think twice a week." More seriously, she says that "it is a full-time job to make sense of a society that is changing like ours." Being restricted to the space of a column has led Goodman to produce pieces that are pithy rather than dense, but she manages just the same to achieve a familiar, neighborly manner that has moved one observer to describe her as "a back-fence moralist." So, while her pieces appear in a journalistic context they ultimately transcend the limits of conventional journalism by virtue of her steady insistence on the personal perspective together with her witty and wise approach to experience:

> I don't want to present myself as a disembodied voice of authority but as a woman, mother, vegetable gardener, failed jogger and expert on only one subject, the ambivalence of life.

Anxiety Is the Class Uniform

The college senior came up to the front of the room, wearing her anxiety like a hair shirt. The woman wasn't surprised to see it. She had been on enough campuses lately to know that anxiety is the class uniform. The students scratch their way to Commencement.

But this senior had been home for the weekend. Her parents had not understood what she was worried about. You have all these choices, they said, with pale-green edges to their voices. You are lucky, they said. The senior in anxiety had broken out in hives and she slammed the door between them. Now she stood in front of the woman, scratching.

You see, she said, if she didn't get into graduate school she didn't know what she would do. It would be, quite simply, The End. She wanted the woman to hand her some kind of prescription, a solution, some calamine lotion of experience.

Well, the woman had heard so much of this lately. There was the senior who was "desperate" for a job in television and the senior who "had" to go to medical school, and the senior whose life depended on getting a job in publishing, or architecture, or government.

The hair shirts were woven, she was told, out of the threads of the tight professional-school market and no-job market. Five years ago, seniors had difficulty deciding just what, if anything, they wanted to do. Now they simply competed for the available slots. They wanted to Get In—as if life were a final club and they had only once chance. It seemed to the woman that in their effort to be realistic, to be inalterably pragmatic, to be the certified public accountants of studentry, they had become incredibly unrealistic.

They believed, among other things, in one-track careers. The senior in front of her *had* to be accepted for a Ph.D. The Ph.D ahead of her *had* to be assistant professor. The assistant professor wanted only to get tenure. Meanwhile, somewhere, another tenured professor had acquired sideburns, a graduate student and a rash that woke him up in the middle of the night wondering what he had missed, and why he now had the fifty-year-old itch.

Recently, the woman had talked and mused with Matina Horner, the president of Radcliffe College, as humane and down-to-earth a person as sits in a president's chair. They had come around to the confusing subject of "contract careers." Dr. Horner had said: "I just don't think people are going to have one-track careers anymore. Society can't

absorb it. There's going to be much more career shifting, second careers, third careers.''

So, it seems that just when students needed to be open to change,
even serendipity, there they were, in their hair shirts, seeking the salves
of a false security.

There was a certain bookkeeping attitude among students, and that
was understandable. If you paid $20,000 for college, one male student
had told her, then surely you should be guaranteed $5,000 more a year
than someone who had not gone to college. He launched an anxiety
attack against his college—because it wasn't a successful trade school.
Relevancy wasn't a matter of social action. It was, he said, what looked
good on a résumé. Scratch, scratch.

The woman knew that colleges were open to that kind of attack. 10
But she hoped that they would not become so practically impractical.

What, after all, do college students need to know if they are going
to have three careers? What is the best preparation for five decades? My
answer: Just what college was supposed to teach people from the beginning. How to think. About themselves and their lives and whatever
work they plunge into, sidle into, or fall into.

The woman wanted to tell the senior something like that. But she
couldn't reach her through the hair shirt.

The senior was totally convinced that her life was a problem to be
solved. She believed she absolutely *had* to solve it by the day after
Commencement. And, wherever she went, she wore this uncomfortable conviction like a second skin.

March 1978

Lines of Inquiry
"Anxiety Is the Class Uniform"

In Goodman's opening description of the senior, she portrays her as "wearing her anxiety like a hair shirt." What are the implications of this unusual
figure of speech? What are the implications of Goodman's reference to her in
paragraph 2 as "the senior in anxiety," who "had broken out in hives"? How
does Goodman develop these descriptive expressions and images in the remainder of her piece? Exactly how does the portrayal of the senior that results from
these images serve to make Goodman's point in this essay?

Goodman's title makes clear her concern for anxiety-ridden students. But
exactly where does she place the blame for this state of affairs? On the students?
Their teachers? Career planning? Professionally oriented education? What do
you think is Goodman's primary point in this piece? To what extent do you
think that student attitudes and collegiate situations have changed since Goodman wrote this piece in 1978? To what extent are her concerns still relevant?

Based on this piece, what do you think is Goodman's idea of the central
purpose of education? How does her idea of education compare with Bacon's
in "Of Studies"? Or with Thomas' in "The Art of Teaching Science"? Or with
your own?

Protection from the Prying Camera

Maybe it was the year-end picture roundup that finally did it. Maybe it was the double exposure to the same vivid photographs. Or perhaps it was the memory of three amateur photographers carefully standing in the cold last fall, calculating their *f* stops and exposures with light meters, trying to find the best angle, pointing their cameras at a drunk in a doorway. Or maybe it was simply my nine-year-old cousin playing Candid Camera at the family gathering.

But whatever the reason, it has finally hit me. We have become a nation of Kodachrome, Nikon, Instamatic addicts. But we haven't yet developed a clear idea of the ethics of picture-taking. We haven't yet determined the parameters of privacy in a world of flash cubes and telescopic lenses.

We "take" pictures. As psychologist Stanley Milgram puts it, "A photographer takes a picture, he does not create it or borrow it." But who has given us the right to "take" those pictures and under what circumstances?

Since the camera first became portable, we have easily and repeatedly aimed it at public people. It has always been open shooting season on them. With new technology, however, those intrusions have intensified. This year, someone with a camera committed the gross indecency of shooting an unaware Greta Garbo in the nude—and *People* printed it.

This year, again, Ron Galella "took" the image of Jacqueline Onassis and sold it as if it belonged to him. This year, we have pictures of a crumpled Wayne Hays, an indiscreet Nelson Rockefeller and two presidential candidates in every imaginable pose from the absurd to the embarrassing. 5

We have accepted the idea that public people are always free targets for the camera—without even a statute of limitations for Jackie or Garbo. We have also accepted the idea that a private person becomes public by being involved in a public event. The earthquake victims of Guatemala, the lynched leftists of Thailand, the terror-stricken of Ireland—their emotions and their bodies become frozen images.

The right of the public to know, to see and to be affected is considered more important than the right of the individual to mourn, or even die, in privacy.

What happens now, however, when cameras proliferate until they are as common as television sets? What happens when the image being "taken" is that of a butcher, a baker or a derelict, rather than a public figure? Do we all lose our right to privacy simply by stepping into view?

Should we be allowed to point cameras at each other? To regard each other as objects of art? Does the photographer or the photographed own the image?

Several years ago, *Time* photographer Steve Northup, who had   10 covered Vietnam, and Watergate, took a group of students around Cambridge shooting pictures. He quietly insisted that they ask every pizza-maker, truck driver and beautician for permission. His attitude toward private citizens was one of careful respect for the power of "exposure." In contrast to this, the average camera bug—like the average tourist—too often goes about snapping "quaint" people, along with "quaint" scenes: See the natives smile, see the natives carrying baskets of fruit, see the native children begging, see the drunk in the doorway. As Milgram wrote, "I find it hard to understand wherein the photographer has derived the right to keep for his own purposes the image of the peasant's face."

Where do we get the right to bring other people home in a canister? Where did we lose the right to control our image?

In a study that Milgram conducted last year, a full 65 percent of the people to whom his students talked in midtown Manhattan refused to have their pictures taken, refused to be photographed. I don't think they were camera shy, in the sense of being vain. Rather, they were reluctant to have their pictures "taken."

The Navahos long believed that the photographer took a piece of them away in his film. Like them, we are coming to understand the power of these frozen images. Photographs can help us to hold onto the truth of our past, to make our history and identity more real. Or they can rip something away from us as precious as the privacy which once clothed Greta Garbo.

January 1977

Lines of Inquiry
"Protection from the Prying Camera"

Notice how Goodman repeatedly plays upon the familiar expression, "picture-taking," as a means of provoking readers to sympathize with her position. What does she imply with her variations on this phrase? Notice how she plays upon other familiar expressions, such as "pointing cameras" and "shooting pictures." What are the implications of her variations on these expressions? What other verbal plays does Goodman use here in her attempt to make a persuasive case?

Given the title of this piece, it would seem that Goodman considers the camera to be an essentially intrusive and offensive device. What reasons does she have for being upset with picture-taking? What limits do you think she would like to impose on photographers? What kinds of rules do you think she would propose?

Probably, you've had your picture taken quite a few times, and you've probably also taken some pictures of others, so you're familiar with the pervasiveness of the camera in contemporary life. Have you ever felt a camera to be prying so much upon you or upon others that you wanted to do something about it? What benefits—what problems—do you think would arise from developing an "ethics of picture-taking"?

Sinking the Relationship

There was this kid in my grammar school, the kind of kid who only got valentines from those of us whose mothers made us send them to everyone. Even then, he would only get the ones that were 25 cards for 25 cents.

I mean, it was sad. But to tell you the truth, Willie was a real wonk.

Last week I ran into Willie the Wonk at the five and ten. It turns out that since we'd last met, Willie had gotten a Ph.D. and married, and then settled down and gotten divorced. Now, he was, and I quote, "relating to a woman in Providence." Together they were "really into exploring intimate relationships."

Now let me tell you, I covered my mouth lest anything untoward spill out. At that moment I regretted sending him even the crummy valentine that had come out on the perforated cardboard saying, "Gee, you're swell."

But, as they say, everything has its sunny side. Meeting Willie finally pushed me into making public my radical Valentine's Day proposal for 1977. Which is, ladies and gentlemen, boys and girls, sons and lovers, to renounce "relationships." In word, though not in deed.

I hereby propose striking out meaningful relationships (gag), intimate relationships (bleh), and working relationships (ugh).

Once upon a time, the only Relation Ship was a boat that carried the family over from the old country. Those were the days when only New Yorkers and battered wives got divorced. The rich may have had relationships, but they called them affairs. The only affairs Willie's forebears attended were the kind where they fought over who would take the centerpiece home.

Now, as I recall, somewhere along in the sixties, international relations became too grim and we all turned to our personal lives. Which we instantly turned equally grim. At that moment, the word "relationship" was born.

A relationship, unlike a love affair, is something which is carefully negotiated to be "self-actualizing" and "growth-oriented" and "nonbinding." It is written along the lines of the model approved by the National Mental Health Association. It is then signed by two consenting adults who are too embarrassed to tell their friends that they've fallen in love.

In truth, one never falls into a relationship. One is too mature, healthy, sensible and dreary for that. Rather, one enters a relationship as if it were a law firm.

"Relationship" is a cool, McLuhan-ish word. After all, one can relate to almost anything—a food processor, a book, even Willie. The word has always sounded more mathematical than poetic. Try as they might, few poets could ever work with: "How do I relate to thee, let me count the ways," or "Come live with me and be my relationship."

It is even harder to write a relationship song: "Relationship is a many-splendored thing." "I relate to you a bushel and a peck."

It just won't sell. The term is too measured, calibrated, passionless. It is hard to send flowers to a relationship.

As for Working Relationships, well, that has always reminded me of a mom-and-pop store of the feelings. Meaningful Relationships make me think of the English professor who had us read *Hamlet* and count the water images. And Intimate Relationship sounds like something you'd only have with a bathing-suit saleslady.

It is time that we bid farewell and jump this particular ship. I hereby take the pledge. Up with love, down with relationships. Even Willie the Wonk deserves better than that.

15

February 1977

Lines of Inquiry
"Sinking the Relationship"

Notice the following passages from the first two paragraphs of this piece: "There was this kid in my grammar school"; "I mean, it was sad"; "Willie was a real wonk". How could you describe the style of these passages? How would you characterize the tone of voice that Goodman projects in these passages? How typical are these passages of her style and tone in the rest of the piece? In her other pieces? What reason(s) do you suppose she might have in this piece for using such a style and tone?

In paragraphs 7–15, Goodman makes fun of the word "relationship." But why exactly do you think she is so strongly opposed to it? Do you think she opposes it completely, or do you think she is only opposed to it in certain contexts and situations? What advantages or disadvantages do you think would result from her proposal "to renounce 'relationships' "?

Can you think of any other words like relationship that might be equally as objectionable to Goodman? What objectionable qualities do these words have in common with "relationship"? What objectionable qualities do these words and "relationship" have in common with the words and expressions that Orwell objects to in "Politics and the English Language"?

In the Male Direction

BOSTON—There was a time in my life, I confess, when I thought that the only inherent differences between men and women were the obvious ones.

In my callous youth, I scoffed at the mental gymnastics of sociobiologists who leaped to conclusions about men and women from long years spent studying bugs. I suspected the motives of brain researchers who split the world of the sexes into left and right hemispheres.

But now, in my midlife, I can no longer deny the evidence of my senses or experiences.

Like virtually every woman in America who has spent time beside a man behind a wheel, like every woman in America who has ever been a lost passenger outward bound with a male driver, I know that there is one way in which the male sex is innately different from the female: Men are by their very nature congenitally unable to ask directions.

The historical record of their unwillingness was always clear. Con- 5
sider, for example, the valiant 600 cavalrymen who plunged into the Valley of Death . . . because they refused to ask if there wasn't some other way around the cannons.

Consider the entire wagon train that drove into the Donner Pass . . . because the wagon master wouldn't stop at the station marked Last Gas before the Disaster.

Consider even my own childhood. My father—a man with a great sense of humor and no sense of direction—constantly led us on what he referred to as "scenic routes."

But for centuries we assumed that this refusal was a weird idiosyncrasy. We never dreamed that it came with the testosterone.

In recent years, I have from time to time found myself sitting beside men who would not admit they were lost until I lit matches under their fingertips in an attempt to read maps in a box canyon.

One particular soul would consult an astronomical chart for his 10
whereabouts before he would consult a police officer. Another would use a divining rod or a compass before he would use a gas station attendant.

In the 1970s, people believed in roles instead of genes, and I assumed that this behavior came from growing up male in America. I figured that males were taught that being lost was a challenge and seeking help was a cop-out. I assumed that the lost highwayman thought of himself as the Daniel Boone of Route 66.

Finally, however, the new breed of scientists are offering us new insights, not into upbringing but into biology and brains.

The male brain, according to researchers, is organized differently than the female. Men have better spatial abilities; women have better verbal abilities. Thus, we see the problem: Men read maps and women read people. The average man uses instruments. The average woman uses the voice.

Due to this fact, the husband who is able to adequately drive into a toll booth and roll down the car window is handicapped with the inability to then ask the question: "Where is Route Twenty?" A man who can stick-shift and double-clutch, using his right hemisphere, is handicapped by his left hemisphere when it comes to asking, "Do we take a right here?"

It isn't his fault, you understand. It has to do with our Darwinian   15
roots (what doesn't these days?). The primeval hunter couldn't ask a highway patrolman which way the antelopes were running. He had to shut up and follow the tracks. A good berry picker, on the other hand, could follow advice.

These primitive differences have all the value of the appendix. They are likely to rupture in modern life. In my own life, the differences between the sexes has led to all sorts of misunderstandings and midnight hysterics. In other cases, they have led to deserted roadways, and divorce instead of doorsteps.

It is time for the female who finds herself in the passenger seat on a scenic tour to take the wheel or to be more understanding. After all, anatomy may not be destiny—but it has a lot to do with destination.

September 1981

Lines of Inquiry
"In the Male Direction"

Goodman devotes quite a bit of space in this essay to discussing and illustrating her conviction that "men are by their very nature congenitally unable to ask directions." Yet, many of her remarks on this point are clearly meant to be humorous, as in her obviously fictitious statement that "the wagon master wouldn't stop at the station marked Last Gas before the Disaster." How serious is she, then, in commenting on the inability of men "to ask directions"? What is the purpose of all her humorous remarks along the way?

In paragraph 12, Goodman reports that "the new breed of scientists are offering us new insights, not into upbringing but into biology and brains." What are some of the insights to which Goodman refers? To what extent do you think Goodman agrees with the scientists' claims about biology and brains? Exactly what point(s) do you think she is making about men and women in her final paragraph?

For other views about the origin and causes of human behavior, look at Bettelheim's "Growing Up Female" or Mead's "Warfare: An Invention—Not a Biological Necessity." To what extent do they seem to be in agreement, to what extent do they seem to be at odds, about the causes of human behavior?

Stephen Jay Gould
1941—

Evolution is one of the half-dozen shattering ideas that science has developed to overturn past hopes and assumptions, and to enlighten our current thoughts. Evolution is also more personal than the quantum, or the relative motion of earth and sun; it speaks directly to the questions of genealogy that so fascinate us—how and when did we arise, what are our biological relationships with other creatures? And evolution has built all those creatures in stunning variety—an endless source of delight (though not the reason for their existence!), not to mention of essays.

For the past fifteen years, Harvard paleontologist Stephen Jay Gould has been explaining and defending the "shattering idea" of Darwin's theory of evolution, as he puts it here in this passage from the preface to *The Flamingo's Smile*. With example after example, fact after fact, he tries to demonstrate how the inescapable logic of evolutionary theory "overturns past hopes and assumptions," challenging our most basic cultural prejudices. But evolution ought to "fascinate" and "delight" us as well, Gould thinks. It tells the story of who we are and where we came from. It helps us appreciate "the stunning variety" of life on earth. And properly understood, without fear or prejudice, it leads us to the realization that we, not nature, are finally responsible for our behavior and the values of our culture.

Though he writes about natural history, Gould grew up in New York and loves the life of the city. "I resonate when I walk across the Brooklyn Bridge and look at lower Manhattan," he said in an interview, and he is an avid baseball fan. As a child he was taken by his father, a court stenographer, to the American Museum of Natural History, where the sight of a Tyrannosaurus Rex convinced him that he wanted to become a paleontologist. "I was just so fascinated by it, because there wasn't any information about it. There were just these skeletons, these awesome skeletons." As an undergraduate at Antioch College, Gould integrated courses in geology, history, and philosophy, then did graduate work at Columbia University, writing a doctoral dissertation on the Bahamian land snail. Now a professor of geology at Harvard, he established himself in scientific circles when he collaborated in developing the controversial theory that evolution moves in abrupt fits and starts, rather than gradually and progressively over time.

In 1974 Gould was invited to write a column for *Natural History,* the monthly magazine of the American Museum, and though he at first regarded the essay form as "ephemeral," he soon established a reputation for the readable exposition of difficult ideas, becoming, like Loren Eiseley and Lewis Thomas, one of our most important bridges between science and the rest of the culture. His essays have been collected in *Ever Since Darwin* (1977); *The Panda's Thumb* (1980), winner of the National Book Award; *Hen's Teeth and Horses' Toes* (1983); and *The Flamingo's Smile* (1985). In 1981, his book-length study of the scientific measurement of intelligence, *The Mismeasure of Man,* won the National Book Critics Award.

Evolutionary theory has from the beginning been Gould's dominant concern. As he puts it in a retrospective essay in *The Flamingo's Smile,* "I have a wonderful advantage among essayists because no other theme so beautifully encompasses both the particulars that fascinate and the generalities that instruct." Evolution, he argues over and over again, has no purpose. It just happens as "individuals struggle to increase the representation of their genes in future generations" and "that is all." So, he believes that harmony or order arises only as an "incidental result" of randomness. So, too, he argues that "Homo sapiens is not the foreordained product of a ladder that was reaching toward our exalted estate from the start. We are merely the surviving branch of a once luxuriant bush."

In other words, nature, according to Gould, is not exquisitely designed, nor is it proof of an exquisite designer. The bone structure of a horse, for example, is rickety and unsound, surviving only by accident, not at all the best way to design a running animal. The panda's thumb is not a perfect adaptation for the eating of bamboo but simply an enlarged wristbone resulting from a biological accident which the panda has clumsily adapted for its own purposes. Thus Gould finds it difficult to read nature as moral in any way. How can we derive a pleasing lesson from the spectacle of the offspring of cecidomyian gall midgets devouring their mothers in order to grow? The process is neither moral nor immoral but rather an adaptation that serves to the need of the animal to reproduce quickly.

But Gould's belief that "evolution is purposeless, nonprogressive, and materialistic" doesn't lead him to cynicism or despair. "Yes, the world has been different ever since Darwin," he says. "But no less exciting, instructing, or uplifting; for if we cannot find purpose in nature, we will have to define it for ourselves." Gould's real project is to get us to accept our responsibility for what we are rather than "fobbing it off" on nature; to help us recognize our arrogance in assuming that we are "the loftiest product of a preordained process" with the right to destroy the environment for our own purposes.

Throughout his work, Gould takes pleasure in exploring the facts of nature, turning each shell or fossil over and over in his mind like a delighted child, often with the intent of making a specific moral point. In many essays, in fact, he takes his argument into an attack on scientists and others who use the supposed design and purposefulness of nature—or their own biased interpretation of this design—as a way of defending unjust social policies. In *The Mismeasure of Man,* he exposes in intricate detail the work of scientists who have claimed to measure human intelligence objectively, revealing that they consistently, if inadvertently, distorted their data to support their prior prejudices about the inferiority of certain races. So, Gould shows us that "science is no inexorable march to truth," and that scientists are "ordinary human beings" who "unconsciously reflect in their theories the social and political constraints of their times."

Given his no-nonsense views of evolution and of scientific investigation, Gould is rarely inclined to be lyrical or mystical like Loren Eiseley and Lewis Thomas, the two other notable scientist-essayists with whom he is most often compared. Though his style is often witty and eloquent, marked by balanced and ringing phrases, he relies most of all on the strategies of detailed explanation, sustained analysis, and painstakingly logical argumentation. So, each of his essays is invariably grounded on a hard fact, a piece of evidence, a natural oddity, such as the structure of hen's teeth, the configuration of Siamese twins, the evolution of Mickey Mouse's features, or the disappearance of the .400 hitter. As Gould says, he "treats generality only as it emerges from little things that arrest us and open our eyes with an 'aha.'" To show us the emergence of the generality, to open our eyes, he takes us step by step through a logical exposition of the problem. Though he wants to be clear, even entertaining, he insists that he "will not simplify concepts." In his essays as in his specialized research, Gould's commitment is to "science and rationality in its proper sphere," because without science and rationality, "there can be no solution to the problems that engulf us."

A Biological Homage to Mickey Mouse

Age often turns fire to placidity. Lytton Strachey, in his incisive portrait of Florence Nightingale, writes of her declining years:

> Destiny, having waited very patiently, played a queer trick on Miss Nightingale. The benevolence and public spirit of that long life had only been equalled by its acerbity. Her virtue had dwelt in hardness. . . . And now the sarcastic years brought the proud woman her punishment. She was not to die as she had lived. The sting was to be taken out of her; she was to be made soft; she was to be reduced to compliance and complacency.

I was therefore not surprised—although the analogy may strike some people as sacrilegious—to discover that the creature who gave his name as a synonym for insipidity had a gutsier youth. Mickey Mouse turned a respectable fifty last year. To mark the occasion, many theaters replayed his debut performance in *Steamboat Willie* (1928). The original Mickey was a rambunctious, even slightly sadistic fellow. In a remarkable sequence, exploiting the exciting new development of sound, Mickey and Minnie pummel, squeeze, and twist the animals on board to produce a rousing chorus of "Turkey in the Straw." They honk a duck with a tight embrace, crank a goat's tail, tweak a pig's nipples, bang a cow's teeth as a stand-in xylophone, and play bagpipe on her udder.

Christopher Finch, in his semiofficial pictorial history of Disney's work, comments: "The Mickey Mouse who hit the movie houses in the late twenties was not quite the well-behaved character most of us are familiar with today. He was mischievous, to say the least, and even displayed a streak of cruelty." But Mickey soon cleaned up his act, leaving to gossip and speculation only his unresolved relationship with Minnie and the status of Morty and Ferdie. Finch continues: "Mickey . . . had become virtually a national symbol, and as such he was expected to behave properly at all times. If he occasionally stepped out of line, any number of letters would arrive at the Studio from citizens and organizations who felt that the nation's moral well-being was in their hands. . . . Eventually he would be pressured into the role of straight man."

As Mickey's personality softened, his appearance changed. Many Disney fans are aware of this transformation through time, but few (I suspect) have recognized the coordinating theme behind all the alterations—in fact, I am not sure that the Disney artists themselves explicitly

Mickey's evolution during 50 years (left to right). As Mickey became increasingly well behaved over the years, his appearance became more youthful. Measurements of three stages in his development revealed a larger relative head size, larger eyes, and an enlarged cranium—all traits of juvenility. © Walt Disney Productions

realized what they were doing, since the changes appeared in such a halting and piecemeal fashion. In short, the blander and inoffensive Mickey became progressively more juvenile in appearance. (Since Mickey's chronological age never altered—like most cartoon characters he stands impervious to the ravages of time—this change in appearance at a constant age is a true evolutionary transformation. Progressive juvenilization as an evolutionary phenomenon is called neoteny. More on this later.)

The characteristic changes of form during human growth have inspired a substantial biological literature. Since the head-end of an embryo differentiates first and grows more rapidly in utero than the foot-end (an antero-posterior gradient, in technical language), a newborn child possesses a relatively large head attached to a medium-sized body with diminutive legs and feet. This gradient is reversed through growth as legs and feet overtake the front end. Heads continue to grow but so much more slowly than the rest of the body that relative head size decreases.

In addition, a suite of changes pervades the head itself during human growth. The brain grows very slowly after age three, and the bulbous cranium of a young child gives way to the more slanted, lowerbrowed configuration of adulthood. The eyes scarcely grow at all and relative eye size declines precipitously. But the jaw gets bigger and bigger. Children, compared with adults, have larger heads and eyes, smaller jaws, a more prominent, bulging cranium, and smaller, pudgier legs and feet. Adult heads are altogether more apish, I'm sorry to say.

Mickey, however, has traveled this ontogenetic pathway in reverse during his fifty years among us. He has assumed an ever more childlike appearance as the ratty character of *Steamboat Willie* became the cute and inoffensive host to a magic kingdom. By 1940, the former tweaker of pig's nipples gets a kick in the ass for insubordination (as the *Sorcerer's Apprentice* in *Fantasia*). By 1953, his last cartoon, he has gone fishing and cannot even subdue a squirting clam.

The Disney artists transformed Mickey in clever silence, often using suggestive devices that mimic nature's own changes by different routes. To give him the shorter and pudgier legs of youth, they lowered his pants line and covered his spindly legs with a baggy outfit. (His arms and legs also thickened substantially—and acquired joints for a floppier appearance.) His head grew relatively larger and its features more youthful. The length of Mickey's snout has not altered, but decreasing protrusion is more subtly suggested by a pronounced thickening. Mickey's eye has grown in two modes: first, by a major, discontinuous evolutionary shift as the entire eye of ancestral Mickey became the pupil of his descendants, and second, by gradual increase thereafter.

Mickey's improvement in cranial bulging followed an interesting path since his evolution has always been constrained by the unaltered convention of representing his head as a circle with appended ears and an oblong snout. The circle's form could not be altered to provide a bulging cranium directly. Instead, Mickey's ears moved back, increasing the distance between nose and ears, and giving him a rounded, rather than a sloping, forehead.

To give these observations the cachet of quantitative science, I applied my best pair of dial calipers to three stages of the official phylogeny—the thin-nosed, ears-forward figure of the early 1930s (stage 1), the latter-day Jack of Mickey and the Beanstalk (1947, stage 2), and the modern mouse (stage 3). I measured three signs of Mickey's creeping juvenility: increasing eye size (maximum height) as a percentage of head length (base of the nose to top of rear ear); increasing head length as a percentage of body length; and increasing cranial vault size measured by rearward displacement of the front ear (base of the nose to top of front ear as a percentage of base of the nose to top of rear ear).

All three percentages increased steadily—eye size from 27 to 42 percent of head length; head length from 42.7 to 48.1 percent of body length; and nose to front ear from 71.7 to a whopping 95.6 percent of

10

The "Evolution" of Mickey Mouse

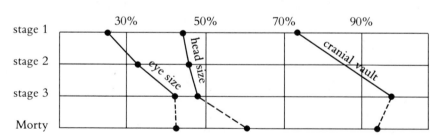

At an early stage in his evolution, Mickey had a smaller head, cranial vault, and eyes. He evolved toward the characteristics of his young nephew Morty (connected to Mickey by a dotted line).

nose to rear ear. For comparison, I measured Mickey's young "nephew" Morty Mouse. In each case, Mickey has clearly been evolving toward youthful stages of his stock, although he still has a way to go for head length.

You may, indeed, now ask what an at least marginally respectable scientist has been doing with a mouse like that. In part, fiddling around and having fun, of course. (I still prefer *Pinocchio* to *Citizen Kane*.) But I do have a serious point—two, in fact—to make. We must first ask why Disney chose to change his most famous character so gradually and persistently in the same direction? National symbols are not altered capriciously and market researchers (for the doll industry in particular) have spent a good deal of time and practical effort learning what features appeal to people as cute and friendly. Biologists also have spent a great deal of time studying a similar subject in a wide range of animals.

In one of his most famous articles, Konrad Lorenz argues that humans use the characteristic differences in form between babies and adults as important behavioral cues. He believes that features of juvenility trigger "innate releasing mechanisms" for affection and nurturing in adult humans. When we see a living creature with babyish features, we feel an automatic surge of disarming tenderness. The adaptive value of this response can scarcely be questioned, for we must nurture our babies. Lorenz, by the way, lists among his releasers the very features of babyhood that Disney affixed progressively to Mickey: "a relatively large head, predominance of the brain capsule, large and low-lying eyes, bulging cheek region, short and thick extremities, a springly elastic consistency, and clumsy movements." (I propose to leave aside for this article the contentious issue of whether or not our affectionate response to babyish features is truly innate and inherited directly from ancestral primates—as Lorenz argues—or whether it is simply learned from our immediate experience with babies and grafted upon an evolutionary predisposition for attaching ties of affection to certain learned signals. My argument works equally well in either case for I only claim that babyish features tend to elicit strong feelings of affection in adult humans, whether the biological basis be direct programming or the capacity to learn and fix upon signals. I also treat as collateral to my point the major thesis of Lorenz's article—that we respond not to the totality or *Gestalt,* but to a set of specific features acting as releasers. This argument is important to Lorenz because he wants to argue for evolutionary identity in modes of behavior between other vertebrates and humans, and we know that many birds, for example, often respond to abstract features rather than *Gestalten.* Lorenz' article, published in 1950, bears the title *Ganzheit und Teil in der tierischen und menschlichen Gemein-schaft*—"Entirety and part in animal and human society." Disney's piecemeal change of Mickey's appearance does make sense in this context—he operated in sequential fashion upon Lorenz's primary releasers.)

Lorenz emphasizes the power that juvenile features hold over us, and the abstract quality of their influence, by pointing out that we judge other animals by the same criteria—although the judgment may be utterly inappropriate in an evolutionary context. We are, in short, fooled by an evolved response to our own babies, and we transfer our reaction to the same set of features in other animals.

Many animals, for reasons having nothing to do with the inspira- 15 tion of affection in humans, possess some features also shared by human babies but not by human adults—large eyes and a bulging forehead with retreating chin, in particular. We are drawn to them, we cultivate them as pets, we stop and admire them in the wild—while we reject their small-eyed, long-snouted relatives who might make more affectionate companions or objects of admiration. Lorenz points out that the German names of many animals with features mimicking human babies end in the diminutive suffix *chen,* even though the animals are often larger than close relatives without such features—*Rotkehlchen* (robin), *Eichhörnchen* (squirrel), and *Kaninchen* (rabbit), for example.

Humans feel affection for animals with juvenile features: large eyes, bulging craniums, retreating chins (left column). Small-eyed, long-snouted animals (right column) do not elicit the same response. From Studies in Animal and Human Behavior, *vol. II, by Konrad Lorenz, 1971. Methuen & Co. Ltd.*

In a fascinating section, Lorenz then enlarges upon our capacity for biologically inappropriate response to other animals, or even to inanimate objects that mimic human features. "The most amazing objects can acquire remarkable, highly specific emotional values by 'experiential attachment' of human properties. . . . Steeply rising, somewhat overhanging cliff faces or dark storm-clouds piling up have the same, immediate display value as a human being who is standing at full height and leaning slightly forwards"—that is, threatening.

We cannot help regarding a camel as aloof and unfriendly because it mimics, quite unwittingly and for other reasons, the "gesture of haughty rejection" common to so many human cultures. In this gesture, we raise our heads, placing our nose above our eyes. We then half-close our eyes and blow out through our nose—the "harumph" of the stereotyped upperclass Englishman or his well-trained servant. "All this," Lorenz argues quite cogently, "symbolizes resistance against all sensory modalities emanating from the disdained counterpart." But the poor camel cannot help carrying its nose above its elongate eyes, with mouth drawn down. As Lorenz reminds us, if you wish to know whether a camel will eat out of your hand or spit, look at its ears, not the rest of its face.

In his important book *Expression of the Emotions in Man and Animals,* published in 1872, Charles Darwin traced the evolutionary basis of many common gestures to originally adaptive actions in animals later internalized as symbols in humans. Thus, he argued for evolutionary continuity of emotion, not only of form. We snarl and raise our upper lip in fierce anger—to expose our nonexistent fighting canine tooth. Our gesture of disgust repeats the facial actions associated with the highly adaptive act of vomiting in necessary circumstances. Darwin concluded, much to the distress of many Victorian contemporaries: "With mankind some expressions, such as the bristling of the hair under the influence of extreme terror, or the uncovering of the teeth under that of furious rage, can hardly be understood, except on the belief that man once existed in a much lower and animal-like condition."

In any case, the abstract features of human childhood elicit powerful emotional responses in us, even when they occur in other animals. I submit that Mickey Mouse's evolutionary road down the course of his own growth in reverse reflects the unconscious discovery of this biological principle by Disney and his artists. In fact, the emotional status of most Disney characters rests on the same set of distinctions. To this extent, the magic kingdom trades on a biological illusion—our ability to abstract and our propensity to transfer inappropriately to other animals the fitting responses we make to changing form in the growth of our own bodies.

Donald Duck also adopts more juvenile features through time. His
elongated beak recedes and his eyes enlarge; he converges on Huey, Louie, and Dewey as surely as Mickey approaches Morty. But Donald, 20

Dandified, disreputable Mortimer (here stealing Minnie's affections) has strikingly more adult features than Mickey. His head is smaller in proportion to body length; his nose is a full 80 percent of head length. © *Walt Disney Productions*

having inherited the mantle of Mickey's original misbehavior, remains more adult in form with his projecting beak and more sloping forehead.

Mouse villains or sharpies, contrasted with Mickey, are always more adult in appearance, although they often share Mickey's chronological age. In 1936, for example, Disney made a short entitled *Mickey's Rival.* Mortimer, a dandy in a yellow sports car, intrudes upon Mickey and Minnie's quiet country picnic. The thoroughly disreputable Mortimer has a head only 29 percent of body length, to Mickey's 45, and a snout 80 percent of head length, compared with Mickey's 49. (Nonetheless, and was it ever different, Minnie transfers her affection until an obliging bull from a neighboring field dispatches Mickey's rival.) Consider also the exaggerated adult features of other Disney characters—the swaggering bully Peg-leg Pete or the simple, if lovable, dolt Goofy.

As a second, serious biological comment on Mickey's odyssey in form, I note that his path to eternal youth repeats, in epitome, our own evolutionary story. For humans are neotenic. We have evolved by retaining to adulthood the originally juvenile features of our ancestors. Our australopithecine forebears, like Mickey in *Steamboat Willie,* had projecting jaws and low vaulted craniums.

Our embryonic skulls scarcely differ from those of chimpanzees. And we follow the same path of changing form through growth: relative decrease of the cranial vault since brains grow so much more slowly than bodies after birth, and continuous relative increase of the jaw. But

Cartoon villains are not the only Disney characters with exaggerated adult features. Goofy, like Mortimer, has a small head relative to body length and a prominent snout. © *Walt Disney Productions*

while chimps accentuate these changes, producing an adult strikingly different in form from a baby, we proceed much more slowly down the same path and never get nearly so far. Thus, as adults, we retain juvenile features. To be sure, we change enough to produce a notable difference between baby and adult, but our alteration is far smaller than that experienced by chimps and other primates.

A marked slowdown of developmental rates has triggered our neoteny. Primates are slow developers among mammals, but we have accentuated the trend to a degree matched by no other mammal. We have very long periods of gestation, markedly extended childhoods, and the longest life span of any mammal. The morphological features of eternal youth have served us well. Our enlarged brain is, at least in part, a result of extending rapid prenatal growth rates to later ages. (In all mammals, the brain grows rapidly in utero but often very little after birth. We have extended this fetal phase into postnatal life.)

But the changes in timing themselves have been just as important. We are preeminently learning animals, and our extended childhood permits the transference of culture by education. Many animals display flexibility and play in childhood but follow rigidly programmed patterns as adults. Lorenz writes, in the same article cited above: "The   25 characteristic which is so vital for the human peculiarity of the true man—that of always remaining in a state of development—is quite certainly a gift which we owe to the neotenous nature of mankind."

In short, we, like Mickey, never grow up although we, alas, do grow old. Best wishes to you, Mickey, for your next half-century. May we stay as young as you, but grow a bit wiser.

Lines of Inquiry
"A Biological Homage to Mickey Mouse"

In paragraph 12, Gould says that in discussing Mickey Mouse he is "in part, fiddling around and having fun . . . but I do have a serious point—two, in fact—to make." What aspects of his organization, evidence, analysis, and style suggest that he is having fun; what aspects suggest that he is serious? What issues does he treat lightly; what issues does he treat seriously? In what respects are the playful and serious sides of this essay related?

As his title suggests, Gould's approach in this piece is to examine a cartoon character scientifically, to look at a fictitious animal as if it were a biological creature. What purpose(s) does he have for doing so? To what extent do you think Gould is concerned with the evolution of Mickey Mouse? To what extent do you think he is concerned with shedding light on the psychology of cartooning? To what extent do you think he is concerned with shedding light on the evolving pattern of human features? What other points is he concerned with in this piece?

Examine another cartoon character who has existed for a long time to see if this character has evolved (rather than aged) over time. Use Gould's analytic methods to take note of any significant changes in the character's facial or body features. Take note of any other significant changes that seem to have occurred in the character's physical behavior, gestures, style of dressing, and way of talking. How do you account for the change(s) or lack of change that you've noticed in this character?

Women's Brains

In the prelude to *Middle-march*, George Eliot lamented the unfulfilled lives of talented women:

> Some have felt that these blundering lives are due to the inconvenient indefiniteness with which the Supreme Power has fashioned the natures of women: if there were one level of feminine incompetence as strict as the ability to count three and no more, the social lot of women might be treated with scientific certitude.

Eliot goes on to discount the idea of innate limitation, but while she wrote in 1872, the leaders of European anthropometry were trying to measure "with scientific certitude" the inferiority of women. Anthropometry, or measurement of the human body, is not so fashionable a field these days, but it dominated the human sciences for much of the nineteenth century and remained popular until intelligence testing replaced skull measurement as a favored device for making invidious comparisons among races, classes, and sexes. Craniometry, or measurement of the skull, commanded the most attention and respect. Its unquestioned leader, Paul Broca (1824–80), professor of clinical surgery at the Faculty of Medicine in Paris, gathered a school of disciples and imitators around himself. Their work, so meticulous and apparently irrefutable, exerted great influence and won high esteem as a jewel of nineteenth-century science.

Broca's work seemed particularly invulnerable to refutation. Had he not measured with the most scrupulous care and accuracy? (Indeed, he had. I have the greatest respect for Broca's meticulous procedure. His numbers are sound. But science is an inferential exercise, not a catalog of facts. Numbers, by themselves, specify nothing. All depends upon what you do with them.) Broca depicted himself as an apostle of objectivity, a man who bowed before facts and cast aside superstition and sentimentality. He declared that "there is no faith, however respectable, no interest, however legitimate, which must not accommodate itself to the progress of human knowledge and bend before truth." Women, like it or not, had smaller brains than men and, therefore, could not equal them in intelligence. This fact, Broca argued, may reinforce a common prejudice in male society, but it is also a scientific truth. L. Manouvrier, a black sheep in Broca's fold, rejected the inferiority of women and wrote with feeling about the burden imposed upon them by Broca's numbers:

Women displayed their talents and their diplomas. They also invoked philosophical authorities. But they were opposed by *numbers* unknown to Condorcet or to John Stuart Mill. These numbers fell upon poor women like a sledge hammer, and they were accompanied by commentaries and sarcasms more ferocious than the most misogynist imprecations of certain church fathers. The theologians had asked if women had a soul. Several centuries later, some scientists were ready to refuse them a human intelligence.

Broca's argument rested upon two sets of data: the larger brains of men in modern societies, and a supposed increase in male superiority through time. His most extensive data came from autopsies performed personally in four Parisian hospitals. For 292 male brains, he calculated an average weight of 1,325 grams; 140 female brains averaged 1,144 grams for a difference of 181 grams, or 14 percent of the male weight. Broca understood, of course, that part of this difference could be attributed to the greater height of males. Yet he made no attempt to measure the effect of size alone and actually stated that it cannot account for the entire difference because we know, a priori, that women are not as intelligent as men (a premise that the data were supposed to test, not rest upon):

> We might ask if the small size of the female brain depends exclusively upon the small size of her body. Tiedemann has proposed this explanation. But we must not forget that women are, on the average, a little less intelligent than men, a difference which we should not exaggerate but which is, nonetheless, real. We are therefore permitted to suppose that the relatively small size of the female brain depends in part upon her physical inferiority and in part upon her intellectual inferiority.

In 1873, the year after Eliot published *Middlemarch,* Broca measured   5
the cranial capacities of prehistoric skulls from L'Homme Mort cave. Here he found a difference of only 99.5 cubic centimeters between males and females, while modern populations range from 129.5 to 220.7. Topinard, Broca's chief disciple, explained the increasing discrepancy through time as a result of differing evolutionary pressures upon dominant men and passive women:

> The man who fights for two or more in the struggle for existence, who has all the responsibility and the cares of tomorrow, who is constantly active in combating the environment and human rivals, needs more brain than the woman whom he must protect and nourish, the sedentary woman, lacking any interior occupations, whose role is to raise children, love, and be passive.

In 1879, Gustave Le Bon, chief misogynist of Broca's school, used these data to publish what must be the most vicious attack upon women in modern scientific literature (no one can top Aristotle). I do not claim his views were representative of Broca's school, but they were published in France's most respected anthropological journal. Le Bon concluded:

> In the most intelligent races, as among the Parisians, there are a large number of women whose brains are closer in size to those of gorillas than to the most developed male brains. This inferiority is so obvious that no one can contest it for a moment; only its degree is worth discussion. All psychologists who have studied the intelligence of women, as well as poets and novelists, recognize today that they represent the most inferior forms of human evolution and that they are closer to children and savages than to an adult, civilized man. They excel in fickleness, inconstancy, absence of thought and logic, and incapacity to reason. Without doubt there exist some distinguished women, very superior to the average man, but they are as exceptional as the birth of any monstrosity, as, for example, of a gorilla with two heads; consequently, we may neglect them entirely.

Nor did Le Bon shrink from the social implications of his views. He was horrified by the proposal of some American reformers to grant women higher education on the same basis as men:

> A desire to give them the same education, and, as a consequence, to propose the same goals for them, is a dangerous chimera. . . . The day when, misunderstanding the inferior occupations which nature has given her, women leave the home and take part in our battles; on this day a social revolution will begin, and everything that maintains the sacred ties of the family will disappear.

Sound familiar?[1]

I have reexamined Broca's data, the basis for all this derivative pronouncement, and I find his numbers sound but his interpretation illfounded, to say the least. The data supporting his claim for increased difference through time can be easily dismissed. Broca based his contention on the samples from L'Homme Mort alone—only seven male and six female skulls in all. Never have so little data yielded such far ranging conclusions.

In 1888, Topinard published Broca's more extensive data on the Parisian hospitals. Since Broca recorded height and age as well as brain size, we may use modern statistics to remove their effect. Brain weight decreases with age, and Broca's women were, on average, considerably older than his men. Brain weight increases with height, and his average

---

[1] When I wrote this essay, I assumed that Le Bon was a marginal, if colorful, figure. I have since learned that he was a leading scientist, one of the founders of social psychology, and best known for a seminal study on crowd behavior, still cited today (*La psychologie des foules*, 1895), and for his work on unconscious motivation.

man was almost half a foot taller than his average woman. I used multiple regression, a technique that allowed me to assess simultaneously the influence of height and age upon brain size. In an analysis of the data for women, I found that, at average male height and age, a woman's brain would weigh 1,212 grams. Correction for height and age reduces Broca's measured difference of 181 grams by more than a third, to 113 grams.

I don't know what to make of this remaining difference because I cannot assess other factors known to influence brain size in a major way. Cause of death has an important effect: degenerative disease often entails a substantial diminution of brain size. (This effect is separate from the decrease attributed to age alone.) Eugene Schreider, also working with Broca's data, found that men killed in accidents had brains weighing, on average, 60 grams more than men dying of infectious diseases. The best modern data I can find (from American hospitals) records a full 100-gram difference between death by degenerative arteriosclerosis and by violence or accident. Since so many of Broca's subjects were elderly women, we may assume that lengthy degenerative disease was more common among them than among the men.

More importantly, modern students of brain size still have not agreed on a proper measure for eliminating the powerful effect of body size. Height is partly adequate, but men and women of the same height do not share the same body build. Weight is even worse than height, because most of its variation reflects nutrition rather than intrinsic size— fat versus skinny exerts little influence upon the brain. Manouvrier took up this subject in the 1880s and argued that muscular mass and force should be used. He tried to measure this elusive property in various ways and found a marked difference in favor of men, even in men and women of the same height. When he corrected for what he called "sexual mass," women actually came out slightly ahead in brain size.

Thus, the corrected 113-gram difference is surely too large; the true figure is probably close to zero and may as well favor women as men. And 113 grams, by the way, is exactly the average difference between a 5 foot 4 inch and a 6 foot 4 inch male in Broca's data. We would not (especially us short folks) want to ascribe greater intelligence to tall men. In short, who knows what to do with Broca's data? They certainly don't permit any confident claim that men have bigger brains than women.

To appreciate the social role of Broca and his school, we must recognize that his statements about the brains of women do not reflect an isolated prejudice toward a single disadvantaged group. They must be weighed in the context of a general theory that supported contemporary social distinctions as biologically ordained. Women, blacks, and poor people suffered the same disparagement, but women bore the brunt of Broca's argument because he had easier access to data on women's

10

brains. Women were singularly denigrated but they also stood as surrogates for other disenfranchised groups. As one of Broca's disciples wrote in 1881: "Men of the black races have a brain scarcely heavier than that of white woman." This juxtaposition extended into many other realms of anthropological argument, particularly to claims that, anatomically and emotionally, both women and blacks were like white children—and that white children, by the theory of recapitulation, represented an ancestral (primitive) adult stage of human evolution. I do not regard as empty rhetoric the claim that women's battles are for all of us.

Maria Montessori did not confine her activities to educational reform for young children. She lectured on anthropology for several years at the University of Rome, and wrote an influential book entitled *Pedagogical Anthropology* (English edition, 1913). Montessori was no egalitarian. She supported most of Broca's work and the theory of innate criminality proposed by her compatriot Cesare Lombroso. She measured the circumference of children's heads in her schools and inferred that the best prospects had bigger brains. But she had no use for Broca's conclusions about women. She discussed Manouvrier's work at length and made much of his tentative claim that women, after proper correction of the data, had slightly larger brains than men. Women, she concluded, were intellectually superior, but men had prevailed heretofore by dint of physical force. Since technology has abolished force as an instrument of power, the era of women may soon be upon us: "In such an epoch there will really be superior human beings, there will really be men strong in morality and in sentiment. Perhaps in this way the reign of women is approaching, when the enigma of her anthropological superiority will be deciphered. Woman was always the custodian of human sentiment, morality and honor."

This represents one possible antidote to "scientific" claims for the constitutional inferiority of certain groups. One may affirm the validity of biological distinctions but argue that the data have been misinterpreted by prejudiced men with a stake in the outcome, and that disadvantaged groups are truly superior. In recent years, Elaine Morgan has followed this strategy in her *Descent of Woman,* a speculative reconstruction of human prehistory from the woman's point of view—and as farcical as more famous tall tales by and for men.

I prefer another strategy. Montessori and Morgan followed Broca's philosophy to reach a more congenial conclusion. I would rather label the whole enterprise of setting a biological value upon groups for what it is: irrelevant and highly injurious. George Eliot well appreciated the special tragedy that biological labeling imposed upon members of disadvantaged groups. She expressed it for people like herself—women of extraordinary talent. I would apply it more widely—not only to those whose dreams are flouted but also to those who never realize that they

15

may dream—but I cannot match her prose. In conclusion, then, the rest of Eliot's prelude to *Middlemarch:*

> The limits of variation are really much wider than anyone would imagine from the sameness of women's coiffure and the favorite love stories in prose and verse. Here and there a cygnet is reared uneasily among the ducklings in the brown pond, and never finds the living stream in fellowship with its own oary-footed kind. Here and there is born a Saint Theresa, foundress of nothing, whose loving heartbeats and sobs after an unattained goodness tremble off and are dispersed among hindrances instead of centering in some long-recognizable deed.

Lines of Inquiry
"Women's Brains"

In paragraph 3, Gould asserts that "science is an inferential exercise, not a catalog of facts. Numbers, by themselves, specify nothing. All depends upon what you do with them." What does Gould do with numbers? Exactly how does it differ from what Broca and his followers did with numbers? Specifically, what distinguishes Gould's and Broca's methods of calculating and interpreting the facts about women's brains?

It might also be said that quotations, by themselves, specify nothing. All depends upon what you do with them. What does Gould do with quotations in this essay? Why does he begin and end his piece with passages by George Eliot? Why does he quote so extensively from Broca and his followers, particularly from Le Bon? Why does he quote from Montessori? What purpose do all of these quotations serve in connection with the points that Gould is trying to make about women's brains and "biological labeling"?

Gould is not the only essayist in this collection to write about the denigration of women, as you can see by reading Bettelheim's "Growing Up Female." In what respects are they concerned with similar problems? In what respects with different problems? In what respects do they attack the problems in similar ways? In what respects do they attack them differently?

On Heroes and Fools
in Science

As a romantic teen-ager, I believed that my future life as a scientist would be justified if I could discover a single new fact and add a brick to the bright temple of human knowledge. The conviction was noble enough; the metaphor was simply silly. Yet that metaphor still governs the attitude of many scientists toward their subject.

In the conventional model of scientific "progress," we begin in superstitious ignorance and move toward final truth by the successive accumulation of facts. In this smug perspective, the history of science contains little more than anecdotal interest—for it can only chronicle past errors and credit the bricklayers for discerning glimpses of final truth. It is as transparent as an old-fashioned melodrama: truth (as we perceive it today) is the only arbiter and the world of past scientists is divided into good guys who were right and bad guys who were wrong.

Historians of science have utterly discredited this model during the past decade. Science is not a heartless pursuit of objective information. It is a creative human activity, its geniuses acting more as artists than as information processors. Changes in theory are not simply the derivative results of new discoveries but the work of creative imagination influenced by contemporary social and political forces. We should not judge the past through anachronistic spectacles of our own convictions—designating as heroes the scientists whom we judge to be right by criteria that had nothing to do with their own concerns. We are simply foolish if we call Anaximander (sixth century B.C.) an evolutionist because, in advocating a primary role for water among the four elements, he held that life first inhabited the sea; yet most textbooks so credit him.

In this essay, I will take the most notorious of textbook baddies and try to display their theory as both reasonable in its time and enlightening in our own. Our villains are the eighteenth century "preformationists," adherents to an outmoded embryology. According to the textbooks, preformationists believed that a perfect miniature homunculus inhabited the human egg (or sperm), and that embryological development involved nothing more than its increase in size. The absurdity of this claim, the texts continue, is enhanced by its necessary corollary of *emboîtement* or encasement—for if Eve's ovum contained a homunculus, then the ovum of that homunculus contained a tinier homunculus, and so on into the inconceivable—a fully formed human smaller than an electron. The preformationists must have been blind, antiempirical dogmatists supporting an a *priori* doctrine of immutability against clear evidence of the senses—for one only has to open a chicken's egg in order to watch an embryo develop from simplicity to complexity. Indeed, their leading spokesman, Charles Bonnet, had proclaimed that "preformationism is the greatest triumph of reason over the senses." The heroes of our textbooks, on the other hand, were the "epigeneticists"; they spent their time looking at eggs rather than inventing fantasies. They proved by observation that the complexity of adult form developed gradually in the embryo. By the mid-nineteenth century, they had triumphed. One more victory for unsullied observation over prejudice and dogma.

In reality, the story is not so simple. The preformationists were as   5
careful and accurate in their empirical observations as the epigeneticist. Moreover, if heroes we must have, that honor might as well fall to the preformationists who upheld, against the epigeneticists, a view of science quite congenial with our own.

The imagination of a few peripheral figures must not be taken as the belief of an entire school. The great preformationists—Malpighi, Bonnet, and von Haller—all knew perfectly well that the chick embryo seemed to begin as a simple tube and become more and more complex as organs differentiated within the egg. They had studied and drawn the embryology of the chick in a series of astute observations that matched anything achieved by contemporary epigeneticists.

Preformationists and epigeneticists did not disagree about their observations; but, whereas epigeneticists were prepared to take those observations literally, the preformationists insisted on probing "behind appearance." They claimed that the visual manifestations of development were deceptive. The early embryo is so tiny, so gelatinous, and so transparent that the preformed structures could not be discerned by the crude microscopes then available. Bonnet wrote in 1762: "Do not mark the time when organized beings begin to exist by the time when they begin to become visible; and do not constrain nature by the strict limits of our senses and instruments." Moreover, the preformationists never believed that preformed structures were organized into a perfect miniature homunculus in the egg itself. The rudiments existed in the egg to be sure, but in relative positions and proportions bearing little relationship to adult morphology. Again, Bonnet in 1762: "While the chick is still a germ, all its parts have forms, proportions and positions which differ greatly from those that they will attain during development. If we were able to see the germ enlarged, as it is when small, it would be impossible for us to recognize it as a chick. All the parts of the germ do not develop at the same time and uniformly."

But how did the preformationists explain the *reductio ad absurdum* of encasement—the encapsulation of our entire history in the ovaries of

Eve? Very simply—this concept was not absurd in an eighteenth-century context.

First of all, scientists believed that the world had existed—and would endure—for only a few thousand years. One had, therefore, to encapsulate only a limited number of generations, not the potential products of several million years on a twentieth-century geological time chart.

Secondly, the eighteenth century had no cell theory to set a lower boundary to organic size. It now seems absurd to postulate a fully formed homunculus smaller than the minimum size of a single cell. But an eighteenth-century scientist had no reason to postulate a lower limit to size. In fact, it was widely believed that Leeuwenhoek's animalcules, the single-celled microscopic creatures that had so aroused the imagination of Europe, had complete sets of miniature organs. Thus Bonnet, supporting the corpuscular theory (that light is made of discrete particles), rhapsodized about the inconceivable tininess of the several million globules of light that penetrate all at once into the supposed eyes of animalcules. "Nature works as small as it wishes. We know not at all the lower boundary of the division of matter, but we see that it has been prodigiously divided. From the elephant to the mite, from the whale to the animalcule 27 million times smaller than the mite, from the globe of the sun to the globule of light, what an inconceivable multitude of intermediate degrees!"

Why did the preformationists feel such a need to penetrate behind appearances? Why would they not accept the direct evidence of their senses? Consider the alternatives. Either the parts are present from the first or the fertilized egg is utterly formless. If the egg is formless, then some external force must unerringly impose a design upon matter only potentially capable of producing it. But what kind of a force could this be? And must there be a different force for each species of animal? How can we learn about it, test it, perceive it, touch it, or understand it? How could it represent any more than an insubstantial appeal to a mysterious and mystical vitalism?

Preformationism represented the best of Newtonian science. It was designed to save a general attitude, which we would recognize today as "scientific," from a vitalism that the evidence of raw sensation implied. If the egg were truly unorganized, homogeneous material without preformed parts, then how could it yield such wondrous complexity without a mysterious directing force? It does so, and can do so, only because the structure (not merely the raw material) needed to build this complexity already resides in the egg. In this light, Bonnet's statement about the triumph of reason over the senses seems itself more reasonable.

Finally, who can say that our current understanding of embryology marks the triumph of epigenesis? Most great debates are resolved at Aristotle's golden mean, and this is no exception. From our perspective today, the epigeneticists were right; organs differentiate sequentially from simpler rudiments during embryological development; there are no pre-formed parts. But the preformationists were also right in insisting that complexity cannot arise from formless raw material—that there must be something within the egg to regulate its development. All we can say (as if it mattered) is that they incorrectly identified this "something" as preformed parts, where we now understand it as encoded instructions built of DNA. But what else could we expect from eighteenth-century scientists, who knew nothing of the player piano, not to mention the computer program? The idea of a coded program was not part of their intellectual equipment.

And, come to think of it, what could be more fantastic than the claim that an egg contains thousands of instructions, written on molecules that tell the cell to turn on and off the production of certain substances that regulate the speed of chemical processes? The notion of preformed parts sounds far less contrived to me. The only thing going for coded instructions is that they seem to be there.

Lines of Inquiry
"On Heroes and Fools in Science"

Gould begins his essay by noting that "as a romantic teen-ager," he believed his "life as a scientist would be justified if [he] could discover a single new fact and add a brick to the bright temple of human knowledge." Why does he then go on to say that "the conviction was noble enough; the metaphor simply silly"? What is so silly about the metaphor? What do you think would be a more appropriate metaphor for his teenage conviction?

In his second paragraph, Gould disparages an approach to science that regards "truth (as we perceive it today)" as "the only arbiter." What grounds does he have for questioning the authority of truth? Why does he quarrel with the tendency of historians to divide the world of past scientists "into good guys who were right and bad guys who were wrong"? Why does he consider this kind of division to be "as transparent as an old-fashioned melodrama"? How does his story of the preformationists and the epigeneticists serve to challenge that melodramatic view of past scientists?

Where does Gould stand in connection with "right" and "wrong," "truth" and "falsehood" in the world of science? What would be an appropriate metaphor for the idea of science and scientific knowledge that he develops in this piece and that he displays in "A Biological Homage to Mickey Mouse" and "Women's Brains"? How do Gould's ideas of scientific knowledge and truth compare with the ideas that Thomas sets forth in "The Tucson Zoo," "The Corner of the Eye," and "The Art of Teaching Science"?

Darwin's Dilemma: The Odyssey of Evolution

The exegesis of evolution as a concept has occupied the lifetimes of a thousand scientists. In this essay, I present something almost laughably narrow in comparison—an exegesis of the word itself. I shall trace how organic change came to be called *evolution*. The tale is complex and fascinating as a purely anti-quarian exercise in etymological detection. But more is at stake, for a past usage of this word has contributed to the most common, current misunderstanding among laymen of what scientists mean by evolution.

To begin with a paradox: Darwin, Lamarck, and Haeckel—the greatest nineteenth-century evolutionists of England, France, and Germany, respectively—did not use the word evolution in the original editions of their great works. Darwin spoke of "descent with modification," Lamarck of "transformisme." Haeckel preferred "Transmutations-Theorie" or "Descendenz-Theorie." Why did they not use "evolution" and how did their story of organic change acquire its present name?

Darwin shunned evolution as a description of his theory for two reasons. In his day, first of all, evolution already had a technical meaning in biology. In fact, it described a theory of embryology that could not be reconciled with Darwin's views of organic development.

In 1744, the German biologist Albrecht von Haller had coined the term *evolution* to describe the theory that embryos grew from pre-formed homunculi enclosed in the egg or sperm (and that, fantastic as it may seem today, all future generations had been created in the ovaries of Eve or testes of Adam, enclosed like Russian dolls, one within the next—a homunculus in each of Eve's ova, a tinier homunculus in each ovum of the homunculus, and so on). This theory of evolution (or preformation) was opposed by the epigeneticists who believed that the complexity of adult shape arose from an originally formless egg. Haller chose his term carefully, for the Latin *evolvere* means "to unroll"; indeed, the tiny homunculus unfolded from its originally cramped quarters and simply increased in size during its embryonic development.

Yet Haller's embryological evolution seemed to preclude Darwin's 5
descent with modification. If the entire history of the human race were prepackaged into Eve's ovaries, how could natural selection (or any other force for that matter) alter the preordained course of our sojourn on earth?

Our mystery seems only to deepen. How could Haller's term be transformed into a nearly opposite meaning? This became possible only because Haller's theory was in its death throes by 1859; with its demise, the term that Haller had used became available for other purposes.

"Evolution" as a description of Darwin's "descent with modification" was not borrowed from a previous technical meaning; it was, rather, expropriated from the vernacular. Evolution, in Darwin's day, had become a common English word with a meaning quite different from Haller's technical sense. The *Oxford English Dictionary* traces it to a 1647 poem of H. More: "Evolution of outward forms spread in the world's vast spright [spirit]." But this was "unrolling" in a sense very different from Haller's. It implied "the appearance in orderly succession of a long train of events," and more important, it embodied a *concept of progressive development*—an orderly unfolding from simple to complex. The *O.E.D.* continues, "The process of developing from a rudimentary to a mature or complete state." This evolution, in the vernacular, was firmly tied to a concept of progress.

Darwin did use evolve in this vernacular sense—in fact it is the very last word of his book.

> There is grandeur in this view of life, with its several powers, having been originally breathed into a few forms or into one; and that, whilst this planet has gone cycling on according to the fixed law of gravity, from so simple a beginning endless forms most beautiful and most wonderful have been, and are being evolved.

Darwin chose it for this passage because he wanted to contrast the flux of organic development with the fixity of such physical laws as gravitation. But it was a word he used very rarely indeed, for Darwin explicitly rejected the common equation of what we now call evolution with any notion of progress.

In a famous epigram, Darwin reminded himself never to say "higher" or "lower" in describing the structure of organisms—for if an amoeba is as well adapted to its environment as we are to ours, who is to say that we are higher creatures? Thus Darwin shunned evolution as a description for his descent with modification, both because its technical meaning contrasted with his beliefs and because he was uncomfortable with the notion of inevitable progress inherent in its vernacular meaning.

Evolution entered the English language as a synonym for "descent with modification" through the propaganda of Herbert Spencer, that indefatigable Victorian pundit of nearly everything. Evolution, to Spencer, was the overarching law of all development. And, to a smug Victorian, what principle other than progress could rule the developmental processes of the universe? Thus, Spencer defined the universal law in his *First Principles* of 1862: "Evolution is an integration of matter and concomitant dissipation of motion; during which the matter passes from an indefinite, incoherent homogeneity to a definite coherent heterogeneity."

Two other aspects of Spencer's work contributed to the establishment of evolution in its present meaning: First, in writing his very popular *Principles of Biology* (1864–67), Spencer constantly used "evolution" as a description of organic change. Second, he did not view progress as an intrinsic capacity of matter, but as a result of "cooperation" between internal and external (environmental) forces. This view fit nicely with most nineteenth-century concepts of organic evolution, for Victorian scientists easily equated organic change with organic progress. Thus evolution was available when many scientists felt a need for a term more succinct than Darwin's descent with modification. And since most evolutionists saw organic change as a process directed toward increasing complexity (that is, to us), their appropriation of Spencer's general term did no violence to his definition.

Ironically, however, the father of evolutionary theory stood almost alone in insisting that organic change led only to increasing adaptation between organisms and their own environment and not to an abstract ideal of progress defined by structural complexity of increasing heterogeneity—never say higher or lower. Had we heeded Darwin's warning, we would have been spared much of the confusion and misunderstanding that exists between scientists and laymen today. For Darwin's view has triumphed among scientists who long ago abandoned the concept of necessary links between evolution and progress as the worst kind of anthropocentric bias. Yet most laymen still equate evolution with progress and define human evolution not simply as change, but as increasing intelligence, increasing height, or some other measure of assumed improvement.

In what may well be the most widespread antievolutionary document of modern times, the Jehovah's Witnesses' pamphlet "Did Man Get Here by Evolution or by Creation" proclaims: "Evolution, in very simple terms, means that life progressed from one-celled organisms to its highest state, the human being, by means of a series of biological changes taking place over millions of years. . . . Mere change within a basic type of living thing is not to be regarded as evolution."

This fallacious equation of organic evolution with progress continues to have unfortunate consequences. Historically, it engendered the abuses of Social Darwinism (which Darwin himself held in such suspicion). This discredited theory ranked human groups and cultures according to their assumed level of evolutionary attainment, with (not surprisingly) white Europeans at the top and people dwelling in their conquered colonies at the bottom. Today, it remains a primary component of our global arrogance, our belief in dominion over, rather than fellowship with, more than a million other species that inhabit our planet. The moving finger has written, of course, and nothing can be done; yet I am rather sorry that scientists contributed to a fundamental misunderstanding by selecting a vernacular word meaning progress as a name for Darwin's less euphonious but more accurate "descent with modification."

Lines of Inquiry
"Darwin's Dilemma: The Odyssey of Evolution"

In the opening paragraph, immediately after promising to "trace how organic change came to be called *evolution*," Gould refers to his promised explanation as a "tale," which he considers to be "complex and fascinating as a purely antiquarian exercise in etymological detection." In what sense(s) is his study a tale? In what sense(s) is it an exercise? In what sense(s) does it involve detection?

Though Gould admittedly has a "purely antiquarian" interest in the word evolution, he also has some other reasons for being fascinated with the origin and derivation of the word. What is the significance of Gould's investigation for an understanding of the concept of evolution? Why does Gould believe that the use of this particular term has led to so much misunderstanding that he would prefer the "less euphonious but more accurate 'descent with modification' "?

Think about your own understanding of evolution. What did you consider to be the meaning of the word before your reading of this essay? In what respect(s), if any, has your understanding of the term changed? To expand your understanding of the term, consult the *Oxford English Dictionary,* and note the derivation of the word as well as all the numbered definitions. In what respects are the origins of the word preserved in its principal definitions? How has your understanding of the word changed as a result of this investigation? How do the results of your inquiry compare to the meanings outlined by Gould?

Ernest Hemingway
1899–1961

Without an instant's hesitation the bull charged Chicuelo. The kid stood his ground, simply swung back on his heels and floated his cape like a ballet dancer's skirt into the bull's face as he passed.

From the time he first witnessed a bullfight, which he describes in this passage, to the end of his life, Ernest Hemingway was fascinated by the image of the bull charging and the matador standing his ground, performing his moves like a ballet dancer. That image epitomized for Hemingway the "moment of truth" in the drama of death that he considered to be the essence of bullfighting. So the matador's courage and skill and poise at that perilous moment exemplified for Hemingway the quality of "grace under pressure"—the essence of his "definition of guts." Hemingway turned that quality into the hallmark of his fictional heroes. Indeed, that idea of heroism preoccupied him throughout his career not only as a short story writer and novelist, but also as a journalist, big game hunter, and adventurous public figure.

Born in the Chicago suburb of Oak Park, Illinois, he was the second of six children of a wealthy physician and his musically gifted wife. Throughout his school years, he was more talented in English than in any other subject, and more interested in athletics than anything else. Most of all, he prized his summers in northern Michigan, where his father taught him to fish and hunt and handle weapons and cook wild game and cherish the direct physical sensation of things that figures in all of his writing. After graduating from high school in 1917, he rejected the idea of going to college. Instead, he went to work as a cub reporter at the Kansas City *Star,* which gave him his first no-nonsense experience in how to write clearly and tersely.

In the spring of 1918, he signed on as an ambulance driver with the American Red Cross, and after only a few months of duty on the Italian front, he was badly wounded, decorated for heroism, hospitalized in Milan, and cured of his illusions about the glories of war. Like Frederic Henry, the hero of *A Farewell to Arms* (1929), whom he based on his

World War I experiences, Hemingway had come to believe that "Abstract words such as glory, honor, courage, or hallow were obscene beside the concrete names of villages, the numbers of roads, the names of rivers, the numbers of regiments and the dates." After going home in 1919, he took a job with the Toronto *Star,* married his first of four wives, decided to return to Europe as a foreign correspondent, and in 1921 settled down with his wife in a cramped fourth-floor apartment in Paris.

In Paris Hemingway met Ezra Pound, Gertrude Stein, and other American avant-garde writers, who encouraged him in his effort to develop a highly economical form of storytelling—"to put down what really happened in action" and to put it down in "short sentences" without any "scrollwork or ornament." And he did so in a critically well-received collection of sketches and short stories called *In Our Time* (1925). Then in his first—and possibly his finest—novel, *The Sun Also Rises* (1926), he used his taut narrative style to evoke the aimless existence of "a lost generation," the disillusioned generation of his own post-war contemporaries, wandering back and forth between the bistros of Paris and the bullfights of Spain. And in the character of Jake Barnes, who stoically accepts his bleak situation, Hemingway created his prototypical hero, the model of "grace under pressure."

During the next fifteen years, Hemingway explored and expounded that code of conduct in a broad range of writing, including not only such well-known novels and short stories as *A Farewell to Arms* (1929), *For Whom the Bell Tolls* (1940), "The Short Happy Life of Francis Macomber" (1936), and "The Snows of Kilimanjaro" (1936), but also in two substantial documentary books, *Death in the Afternoon* (1932), a detailed study of bullfighting in Spain, and *Green Hills of Africa* (1935), a narrative account of big game hunting in the Serengeti Plain. During the mid-thirties, he also did pieces about big game fishing and hunting and bullfighting for *Esquire,* then a newly founded magazine; and during the late thirties, he also wrote dispatches about the Spanish Civil War for the North American Newspaper Alliance, a cable news service of the period, as well as anti-fascist pieces for *Ken,* a political magazine of the period.

By the end of the thirties, his hunting and fishing and war-reporting adventures, as well as his marital escapades, had made him a well-known public figure, a machismo-like character in his own right. During the last twenty years of his life, he seemed less concerned with his writing than with his wide-ranging adventures and his public image. At the opening of World War II, for example, not content simply to be a war correspondent, he ran an anti-espionage and anti-submarine patrol off of his deep sea fishing boat in the Caribbean. Later in the war, he organized an underground guerilla group in Europe. After the war—though he settled down in his country house outside of Havana, Cuba, with the intention of seriously writing once again—he continued to travel widely on fishing and hunting expeditions, and continued to be good copy for magazine and newspaper reporters. Indeed, the only publishing success of his last twenty years was *The Old Man and The Sea* (1952), which was instrumental in his winning the Nobel Prize for Literature in 1954. In 1959, he moved to Ketchum, Idaho, a small town near the fishing, hunting, and skiing resort of Sun Valley, and there when his health declined and his memory failed him and he found himself unable to write, he took a double-barreled shotgun and put an end to his life.

Following his death, a few of his manuscripts were posthumously published, most notably *A Movable Feast* (1964), an autobiographical work which consists of sketches about his life in Paris in the twenties. Here, as elsewhere, Hemingway occasionally wrote about the "good and severe discipline" of writing, of trying to put things down as clearly and simply and briefly as possible. As he made clear in *Death in the Afternoon,* his concern with brevity was not an end in itself but a means of stripping away irrelevant material, of getting at "actual things," at a "sequence of motion and fact" that "would be as valid in a year or in ten years or, with luck and if you stated it purely enough, always. . . ." Ultimately, his concern with brevity also turns out to have been a means of writing with grace under pressure.

> If a writer of prose knows enough about what he is writing about he may omit things that he knows and the reader, if the writer is writing truly enough, will have a feeling of those things as strongly as though the writer had stated them. The dignity of movement of an iceberg is due to only one-eighth of it being above water.

The Three Acts
of a Bullfight

There are three acts to the fighting of each bull and they are called in Spanish los tres tercios de la lidia, or the three thirds of the combat. The first act, where the bull charges the picadors, is the suerte de varas, or the trial of the lances. Suerte is an important word in Spanish. It means, according to the dictionary: Suerte, f., chance, hazard, lots, fortune, luck, good luck, haphazard; state, condition, fate, doom, destiny, kind, sort; species, manner, mode, way, skillful manoeuvre; trick, feat, juggle, and piece of ground separated by landmark. So the translation of trial or man-oeuvre is quite arbitrary, as any translation must be from the Spanish.

The action of the picadors in the ring and the work of the matadors who are charged with protecting them with their capes when they are dismounted make up the first act of the bullfight. When the president signals for the end of this act and the bugle blows the picadors leave the ring and the second act begins. There are no horses in the ring after the first act except the dead horses which are covered with canvas. Act one is the act of the capes, the pics and the horses. In it the bull has the greatest opportunity to display his bravery or cowardice.

Act two is that of the banderillas. These are pairs of sticks about a yard long, seventy centimetres to be exact, with a harpoon–shaped steel point four centimetres long at one end. They are supposed to be placed, two at a time, in the humped muscle at the top of the bull's neck as he charges the man who holds them. They are designed to complete the work of slowing up the bull and regulating the carriage of his head which has been begun by the picadors: so that his attack will be slower, but surer and better directed. Four pair of banderillas are usually put in. If they are placed by the banderilleros or peones they must be placed, above all other considerations, quickly and in the proper position. If the matador himself places them he may indulge in a preparation which is usually accompanied by music. This is the most picturesque part of the bullfight and the part most spectators care for the most when first seeing fights. The mission of the banderilleros is not only to force the bull by hooking to tire his neck muscles and carry his head lower but also, by placing them at one side or another, to correct a tendency to hook to that side. The entire act of the banderillas should not take more than five minutes. If it is prolonged the bull becomes discomposed and the fight loses the tempo it must keep, and if the bull is an uncertain and dangerous one he has too many opportunities to see and charge men unarmed with any lure, and so develops a tendency to search for the man, the bundle, as the Spanish call him, behind the cloth when the matador comes out for the last act with the sword and muleta.

The president changes the act after three or at most four pairs of banderillas have been placed and the third and final division is the death. It is made up of three parts. First the brindis or salutation of the president and dedication or toasting of the death of the bull, either to him or to some other person by the matador, followed by the work of the matador with the muleta. This is a scarlet serge cloth which is folded over a stick which has a sharp spike at one end and a handle at the other. The spike goes through the cloth which is fastened to the other end of the handle with a thumb screw so that it hangs in folds along the length of the stick. Muleta means literally crutch, but in bullfighting it refers to the scarlet-serge-draped stick with which the matador is supposed to master the bull, prepare him for killing and finally hold in his left hand to lower the bull's head and keep it lowered while he kills the animal by a sword thrust high up between his shoulder blades.

These are the three acts in the tragedy of the bullfight, and it is the 5 first one, the horse part, which indicates what the others will be and, in fact, makes the rest possible. It is in the first act that the bull comes out in full possession of all of his faculties, confident, fast, vicious and conquering. All his victories are in the first act. At the end of the first act he has apparently won. He has cleared the ring of mounted men and is alone. In the second act he is baffled completely by an unarmed man and very cruelly punished by the banderillas so that his confidence and his blind general rage goes and he concentrates his hatred on an individual object. In the third act he is faced by only one man who must, alone, dominate him by a piece of cloth placed over a stick, and kill him from in front, going in over the bull's right horn to kill him with a sword thrust between the arch of his shoulder blades.

When I first saw bullfights the only part that I did not like was the banderillas. They seemed to make such a great and cruel change in the bull. He became an altogether different animal when the banderillas were in and I resented the loss of the free, wild quality he brought with him into the ring; that quality that reaches its greatest expression when he faces the picadors. When the banderillas are in he is done for. They are the sentencing. The first act is the trial, the second act is the sentencing and the third the execution. But afterwards when I learned how much more dangerous the bull becomes as he goes on the defensive, how, after the banderillas have sobered him and his speed of foot has been cut he aims every horn stroke, as a hunter aims at an individual bird in a covey rather than shooting at them all and missing, and finally, when I learned the things that can be done with him as an artistic property when he is properly slowed and still has kept his bravery and his strength I kept my admiration for him always, but felt no more sympathy for him than for a canvas or the marble a sculptor cuts or the dry powder snow your skis cut through.

Lines of Inquiry
"The Three Acts of a Bullfight"

During the first four paragraphs of this piece, Hemingway carefully explains the three-part structure of a bullfight. Then in the last two paragraphs, he goes over that structure two more times. Why do you suppose that he keeps going over the structure again and again? What, if anything, did you discover from each additional overview of the structure that you had not previously perceived?

Though Spaniards speak of a bullfight as being divided into "thirds," Hemingway speaks of it as being divided into "acts," as if to suggest that the structure and process of a bullfight are comparable to the structure and process of a play. What aspects and elements of bullfighting does he emphasize by using this comparison in his piece? In what ways is a bullfight like a play? In what respects is it not like a play at all?

Think of some other sport or public activity with which you are familiar that might also be thought of as being divided into acts, as if it, too, were like a play. How many acts does it contain? What takes place in each act? In what respects is it not like a play, but like some other kind of performing art?

A New Kind of War

MADRID.—The window of
the hotel is open and, as you lie in bed, you hear the firing in the front
line seventeen blocks away. There is a rifle fire all night long. The rifles
go tacrong, capong, craang, tacrong, and then a machine gun opens
up. It has a bigger calibre and is much louder, rong, cararong, rong,
rong. Then there is the incoming boom of a trench mortar shell and a
burst of machine gun fire. You lie and listen to it and it is a great thing
to be in bed with your feet stretched out gradually warming the cold
foot of the bed and not out there in University City or Carabanchel. A
man is singing hard-voiced in the street below and three drunks are
arguing when you fall asleep.

In the morning, before your call comes from the desk, the roaring
burst of a high explosive shell wakes you and you go to the window
and look out to see a man, his head down, his coat collar up, sprinting
desperately across the paved square. There is the acrid smell of high
explosive you hoped you'd never smell again, and, in a bathrobe and
bedroom slippers, you hurry down the marble stairs and almost into a
middle-aged woman, wounded in the abdomen, who is being helped
into the hotel entrance by two men in blue workmen's smocks. She has
her two hands crossed below her big, old-style Spanish bosom and from
between her fingers the blood is spurting in a thin stream. On the corner, twenty yards away, is a heap of rubble, smashed cement and thrown
up dirt, a single dead man, his torn clothes dusty, and a great hole in
the sidewalk from which the gas from a broken main is rising, looking
like a heat mirage in the cold morning air.

"How many dead?" you ask a policeman.

"Only one," he says. "It went through the sidewalk and burst below. If it would have burst on the solid stone of the road there might
have been fifty."

A policeman covers the top of the trunk, from which the head is   5
missing; they send for someone to repair the gas main and you go in
to breakfast. A charwoman, her eyes red, is scrubbing the blood off the
marble floor of the corridor. The dead man wasn't you nor anyone you
know and everyone is very hungry in the morning after a cold night
and a long day the day before up at the Guadalajara front.

"Did you see him?" asked someone else at breakfast.

"Sure," you say.

"That's where we pass a dozen times a day. Right on that corner."
Someone makes a joke about missing teeth and someone else says not

to make that joke. And everyone has the feeling that characterizes war. It wasn't me, see? It wasn't me.

The Italian dead up on the Guadalajara front weren't you, although Italian dead, because of where you had spent your boyhood, always seemed, still, like our dead. No. You went to the front early in the morning in a miserable little car with a more miserable little chauffeur who suffered visibly the closer he came to the fighting. But at night, sometimes late, without lights, with the big trucks roaring past, you came on back to sleep in a bed with sheets in a good hotel, paying a dollar a day for the best rooms on the front. The smaller rooms in the back, on the side away from the shelling, were considerably more expensive. After the shell that lit on the sidewalk in front of the hotel you got a beautiful double corner room on that side, twice the size of the one you had had, for less than a dollar. It wasn't me they killed. See? No. Not me. It wasn't me anymore.

Then, in a hospital given by the American Friends of Spanish Democracy, located out behind the Morata front along the road to Valencia, they said, "Raven[1] wants to see you."

"Do I know him?"

"I don't think so," they said, "but he wants to see you."

"Where is he?"

"Upstairs."

In the room upstairs they are giving a blood transfusion to a man with a very gray face who lay on a cot with his arm out, looking away from the gurgling bottle and moaning in a very impersonal way. He moaned mechanically and at regular intervals and it did not seem to be him that made the sound. His lips did not move.

"Where's Raven?" I asked.

"I'm here," said Raven.

The voice came from a high mound covered by a shoddy gray blanket. There were two arms crossed on the top of the mound and at one end there was something that had been a face, but now was a yellow scabby area with a wide bandage cross where the eyes had been.

"Who is it?" asked Raven. He didn't have lips, but he talked pretty well without them and with a pleasant voice.

"Hemingway," I said. "I came up to see how you were doing."

"My face was pretty bad," he said. "It got sort of burned from the grenade, but it's peeled a couple of times and it's doing better."

"It looks swell," I said. "It's doing fine."

I wasn't looking at it when I spoke.

"How are things in America?" he asked. "What do they think of us over there?"

---

[1] J. Robert Raven

"Sentiment's changed a lot," I said. "They're beginning to realize   25
the government is going to win this war."

"Do you think so?"

"Sure," I said.

"I'm awfully glad," he said. "You know, I wouldn't mind any of
this if I could just watch what was going on. I don't mind the pain,
you know. It never seemed important really. But I was always awfully
interested in things and I really wouldn't mind the pain at all if I could
just sort of follow things intelligently. I could even be some use. You
know, I didn't mind the war at all. I did all right in the war. I got hit
once before and I was back and rejoined the battalion in two weeks. I
couldn't stand to be away. Then I got this."

He had put his hand in mine. It was not a worker's hand. There
were no callouses and the nails on the long, spatulate fingers were smooth
and rounded.

"How did you get it?" I asked.   30

"Well, there were some troops that were routed and we went over
to sort of reform them and we did and then we had quite a fight with
the fascists and we beat them. It was quite a bad fight, you know, but
we beat them and then someone threw this grenade at me."

Holding his hand and hearing him tell it, I did not believe a word
of it. What was left of him did not sound like the wreckage of a soldier
somehow. I did not know how he had been wounded, but the story
did not sound right. It was the sort of way everyone would like to have
been wounded. But I wanted him to think I believed it.

"Where did you come from?" I asked.

"From Pittsburgh. I went to the University there."

"What did you do before you joined up here?"   35

"I was a social worker," he said. Then I knew it couldn't be true
and I wondered how he had really been so frightfully wounded and I
didn't care. In the war that I had known, men often lied about the
manner of their wounding. Not at first; but later. I'd lied a little myself
in my time. Especially late in the evening. But I was glad he thought I
believed it, and we talked about books, he wanted to be a writer, and
I told him about what happened north of Guadalajara and promised to
bring some things from Madrid next time we got out that way. I hoped
maybe I could get a radio.

"They tell me Dos Passos and Sinclair Lewis are coming over, too,"
he said.

"Yes," I said. "And when they come I'll bring them up to see you."

"Gee, that will be great," he said. "You don't know what that will
mean to me."

"I'll bring them," I said.   40

"Will they be here pretty soon?"

"Just as soon as they come I'll bring them."

"Good boy, Ernest," he said. "You don't mind if I call you Ernest, do you?"

The voice came very clear and gentle from that face that looked like some hill that had been fought over in muddy weather and then baked in the sun.

"Hell, no," I said. "Please. Listen, old-timer, you're going to be fine. You'll be a lot of good, you know. You can talk on the radio." 45

"Maybe," he said. "You'll be back?"

"Sure," I said. "Absolutely."

"Goodbye, Ernest," he said.

"Goodbye," I told him.

Downstairs they told me he'd lost both eyes as well as his face and was also badly wounded all through the legs and in the feet. 50

"He's lost some toes, too," the doctor said, "but he doesn't know that."

"I wonder if he'll ever know it."

"Oh, sure he will," the doctor said. "He's going to get well."

And it still isn't you that gets hit but it is your countryman now. Your countryman from Pennsylvania, where once we fought at Gettysburg.

Then, walking along the road, with his left arm in an airplane splint, 55 walking with the gamecock walk of the professional British soldier that neither ten years of militant party work nor the projecting metal wings of the splint could destroy, I met Raven's commanding officer, Jock Cunningham, who had three fresh rifle wounds through his upper left arm (I looked at them, one was septic) and another rifle bullet under his shoulder blade that had entered his left chest, passed through, and lodged there. He told me, in military terms, the history of the attempt to rally retiring troops on his battalion's right flank, of his bombing raid down a trench which was held at one end by the fascists and at the other end by the government troops, of the taking of this trench and, with six men and a Lewis gun, cutting off a group of some eighty fascists from their own lines, and of the final desperate defense of their impossible position his six men put up until the government troops came up and, attacking, straightened out the line again. He told it clearly, completely convincingly, and with a strong Glasgow accent. He had deep, piercing eyes sheltered like an eagle's, and, hearing him talk, you could tell the sort of soldier he was. For what he had done he would have had a V.C. in the last war. In this war there are no decorations. Wounds are the only decorations and they do not award wound stripes.

"Raven was in the same show," he said. "I didn't know he'd been hit. Ay, he's a good mon. He got his after I got mine. The fascists we'd cut off were very good troops. They never fired a useless shot when we were in that bad spot. They waited in the dark there until they had us located and then opened with volley fire. That's how I got four in the same place."

We talked for a while and he told me many things. They were all important, but nothing was as important as what Jay Raven, the social worker from Pittsburgh with no military training, had told me was true. This is a strange new kind of war where you learn just as much as you are able to believe.

April 14, 1937

Lines of Inquiry
"A New Kind of War"

After the opening hotel scenes and street scenes, which are primarily descriptive, Hemingway relies very heavily on dialogue, particularly in the hospital scene with Jay Raven. Why do you suppose that he devotes so much space to the dialogue with Raven? What does that dialogue convey about Raven, about Hemingway, and about their attitude towards each other and towards war? How does the last bit of dialogue with Jock Cunningham reflect on the earlier dialogue with Raven?

What impressions of the Spanish Civil War did you get from each of the scenes in this piece—the hotel scene, the street scene, the hospital scene, and the concluding road scene? Why does Hemingway consider it a "new kind of war"? Why do you suppose that Hemingway "did not believe a word of" Raven's war story when he first heard it? Why did he later come to speak of Raven's story as being so "important"?

This essay is not the only one in which Hemingway relies heavily on dialogue, as you can see by looking at "Monologue to the Maestro: A High Seas Letter." In both of these pieces, Hemingway figures quite prominently as one of the participants in the dialogue. What kind of a person does he appear to be in each dialogue? How does the personality that he displays in each dialogue affect your reaction to the ideas and attitudes he is trying to convey in each piece?

The Clark's Fork Valley,
Wyoming

At the end of the summer, the big trout would be out in the centre of the stream; they were leaving the pools along the upper part of the river and dropping down to spend the winter in the deep water of the canyon. It was wonderful fly-fishing then in the first weeks of September. The native trout were sleek, shining, and heavy, and nearly all of them leaped when they took the fly. If you fished two flies, you would often have two big trout on and the need to handle them very delicately in that heavy current.

The nights were cold, and, if you woke in the night, you would hear the coyotes. But you did not want to get out on the stream too early in the day because the nights were so cold they chilled the water, and the sun had to be on the river until almost noon before the trout would start to feed.

You could ride in the morning, or sit in front of the cabin, lazy in the sun, and look across the valley where the hay was cut so the meadows were cropped brown and smooth to the line of quaking aspens along the river, now turning yellow in the fall. And on the hills rising beyond, the sage was silvery grey.

Up the river were the two peaks of Pilot and Index, where we would hunt mountain-sheep later in the month, and you sat in the sun and marvelled at the formal, clean-lined shape mountains can have at a distance, so that you remember them in the shapes they show from far away, and not as the broken rock-slides you crossed, the jagged edges you pulled up by, and the narrow shelves you sweated along, afraid to look down, to round that peak that looked so smooth and geometrical. You climbed around it to come out on a clear space to look down to where an old ram and three young rams were feeding in the juniper bushes in a high, grassy pocket cupped against the broken rock of the peak.

The old ram was purple-grey, his rump was white, and when he   5
raised his head you saw the great heavy curl of his horns. It was the white of his rump that had betrayed him to you in the green of the junipers when you had lain in the lee of a rock, out of the wind, three miles away, looking carefully at every yard of the high country through a pair of good Zeiss glasses.

Now as you sat in front of the cabin, you remembered that down-hill shot and the young rams standing, their heads turned, staring at him, waiting for him to get up. They could not see you on that high ledge, nor wind you, and the shot made no more impression on them than a boulder falling.

You remembered the year we had built a cabin at the head of Timber Creek, and the big grizzly that tore it open every time we were away. The snow came late that year, and this bear would not hibernate, but spent his autumn tearing open cabins and ruining a trap-line. But he was so smart you never saw him in the day. Then you remembered coming on the three grizzlies in the high country at the head of Crandall Creek. You heard a crash of timber and thought it was a cow elk bolting, and then there they were, in the broken shadow, running with an easy, lurching smoothness, the afternoon sun making their coats a soft, bristling silver.

You remembered elk bugling in the fall, the bull so close you could see his chest muscles swell as he lifted his head, and still not see his head in the thick timber; but hear that deep, high mounting whistle and the answer from across another valley. You thought of all the heads you had turned down and refused to shoot, and you were pleased about every one of them.

You remembered the children learning to ride; how they did with different horses; and how they loved the country. You remembered how this country had looked when you first came into it, and the year you had to stay four months after you had brought the first car ever to come in for the swamp roads to freeze solid enough to get the car out. You could remember all the hunting and all the fishing and the riding in the summer sun and the dust of the pack-train, the silent riding in the hills in the sharp cold of fall going up after the cattle on the high range, finding them wild as deer and as quiet, only bawling noisily when they were all herded together being forced along down into the lower country.

Then there was the winter; the trees bare now, the snow blowing   10
so you could not see, the saddle wet, then frozen as you came downhill, breaking a trail through the snow, trying to keep your legs moving, and the sharp, warming taste of whiskey when you hit the ranch and changed your clothes in front of the big open fireplace. It's a good country.

February 1939

Lines of Inquiry
"The Clark's Fork Valley, Wyoming"

As you probably noticed, Hemingway narrates this piece from an unusual and striking point of view, namely the second person—"you." What effects are produced by this orientation of the piece? Consider the possible effects of a different point of view by rewriting the first three or four paragraphs in the first person singular—"I"—and then in the first person plural—"we." What effects are produced by Hemingway's repeated use of the statement "you remembered" in the last five paragraphs of the piece? Why do you suppose that he does not use this expression in the first five paragraphs?

Judging from the details that he emphasizes in his essay, Hemingway clearly considers the Clark's Fork Valley to be "good country." What aspects of the landscape, of its natural inhabitants, and of his experiences there appeal most to him? In celebrating the place, what values is he implicitly affirming?

Hemingway is not the only essayist in this collection to write about a piece of "good country," as you can see by looking at Thoreau's "Where I Lived and What I Lived For," E. M. Forster's "My Wood," E. B. White's "Once More to the Lake," or Russell Baker's "A Visit with the Folks." After reading or rereading one or two of these pieces, consider what values these authors share in their celebration of these special places. What values set them apart?

Monologue to the Maestro: A High Seas Letter

About a year and a half ago a young man came to the front door of the house in Key West and said that he had hitch-hiked down from upper Minnesota to ask your correspondent a few questions about writing. Arrived that day from Cuba, having to see some good friends off on the train in an hour, and to write some letters in the meantime, your correspondent, both flattered and appalled at the prospect of the questioning, told the young man to come around the next afternoon. He was a tall, very serious young man with very big feet and hands and a porcupine hair-cut.

It seemed that all his life he had wanted to be a writer. Brought up on a farm he had gone through high school and the University of Minnesota, had worked as a newspaper man, a rough carpenter, a harvest hand, a day laborer, and had bummed his way across America twice. He wanted to be a writer and he had good stories to write. He told them very badly but you could see that there was something there if he could get it out. He was so entirely serious about writing that it seemed that seriousness would overcome all obstacles. He had lived by himself for a year in a cabin he had built in North Dakota and written all that year. He did not show me anything that he had written then. It was all bad, he said.

I thought, perhaps, that this was modesty until he showed me a piece he had published in one of the Minneapolis papers. It was abominably written. Still, I thought, many other people write badly at the start and this boy is so extremely serious that he must have something; real seriousness in regard to writing being one of the two absolute necessities. The other, unfortunately, is talent.

Besides writing this young man had one other obsession. He had always wanted to go to sea. So, to shorten this account, we gave him a job as night watchman on the boat which furnished him a place to sleep and work and gave him two or three hours work each day at cleaning up and a half of each day free to do his writing. To fulfill his desire to go to sea, we promised to take him to Cuba when we went across.

He was an excellent night watchman and worked hard on the boat and at his writing but at sea he was a calamity; slow where he should be agile, seeming sometimes to have four feet instead of two feet and two hands, nervous under excitement, and with an incurable tendency

5

toward sea-sickness and a peasant reluctance to take orders. Yet he was always willing and hard working if given plenty of time to work in.

We called him the Maestro because he played the violin, this name was eventually shortened to the Mice, and a big breeze would so effectually slow up his co-ordination that your correspondent once remarked to him, "Mice, you certainly must be going to be a hell of a good writer because you certainly aren't worth a damn at anything else."

On the other hand his writing improved steadily. He may yet be a writer. But your correspondent, who sometimes has an evil temper, is never going to ship another hand who is an aspirant writer; nor go through another summer off the Cuban or any other coast accompanied by questions and answers on the practice of letters. If any more aspirant writers come on board the Pilar let them be females, let them be very beautiful, and let them bring champagne.

Your correspondent takes the practice of letters, as distinct from the writing of these monthly letters, very seriously; but dislikes intensely talking about it with almost anyone alive. Having had to mouth about many aspects of it during a period of one hundred and ten days with the good old Maestro, during much of which time your correspondent had to conquer an urge to throw a bottle at the Mice whenever he would open his mouth and pronounce the word writing, he hereby presents some of these mouthings written down.

If they can deter anyone from writing he should be deterred. If they can be of use to anyone your correspondent is pleased. If they bore you there are plenty of pictures in the magazine that you may turn to.

Your correspondent's excuse for presenting them is that some of the information contained would have been worth fifty cents to him when he was twenty-one.   10

Mice: What do you mean by good writing as opposed to bad writing?

Your correspondent: Good writing is true writing. If a man is making a story up it will be true in proportion to the amount of knowledge of life that he has and how conscientious he is; so that when he makes something up it is as it would truly be. If he doesn't know how many people work in their minds and actions his luck may save him for a while, or he may write fantasy. But if he continues to write about what he does not know about he will find himself faking. After he fakes a few times he cannot write honestly any more.

Mice: Then what about imagination?

Y.C.: Nobody knows a damned thing about it except that it is what we get for nothing. It may be racial experience. I think that is quite possible. It is the one thing beside honesty that a good writer must have. The more he learns from experience the more truly he can imagine. If he gets so he can imagine truly enough people will think that the things he relates all really happened and that he is just reporting.

Mice: Where will it differ from reporting? 15

Y.C.: If it was reporting they would not remember it. When you describe something that has happened that day the timeliness makes people see it in their own imaginations. A month later that element of time is gone and your account would be flat and they would not see it in their minds nor remember it. But if you make it up instead of describe it you can make it round and whole and solid and give it life. You create it, for good or bad. It is made; not described. It is just as true as the extent of your ability to make it and the knowledge you put into it. Do you follow me?

Mice: Not always.

Y.C. (crabbily): Well for chrisake let's talk about something else then.

Mice (undeterred): Tell me some more about the mechanics of writing.

Y.C.: What do you mean? Like pencil or typewriter? For chrisake. 20

Mice: Yes.

Y.C.: Listen. When you start to write you get all the kick and the reader gets none. So you might as well use a typewriter because it is that much easier and you enjoy it that much more. After you learn to write your whole object is to convey everything, every sensation, sight, feeling, place and emotion to the reader. To do this you have to work over what you write. If you write with a pencil you get three different sights at it to see if the reader is getting what you want him to. First when you read it over; then when it is typed you get another chance to improve it, and again in the proof. Writing it first in pencil gives you one-third more chance to improve it. That is .333 which is a damned good average for a hitter. It also keeps it fluid longer so that you can better it easier.

Mice: How much should you write a day?

Y.C.: The best way is always to stop when you are going good and when you know what will happen next. If you do that every day when you are writing a novel you will never be stuck. That is the most valuable thing I can tell you so try to remember it.

Mice: All right. 25

Y.C.: Always stop while you are going good and don't think about it or worry about it until you start to write the next day. That way your subconscious will work on it all the time. But if you think about it consciously or worry about it you will kill it and your brain will be tired before you start. Once you are into the novel it is as cowardly to worry about whether you can go on the next day as to worry about having to go into inevitable action. You *have* to go on. So there is no sense to worry. You have to learn that to write a novel. The hard part about a novel is to finish it.

Mice: How can you learn not to worry?

Y.C.: By not thinking about it. As soon as you start to think about it stop it. Think about something else. You have to learn that.

Mice: How much do you read over every day before you start to write?

Y.C.: The best way is to read it all every day from the start, cor-   30
recting as you go along, then go on from where you stopped the day before. When it gets so long that you can't do this every day read back two or three chapters each day; then each week read it all from the start. That's how you make it all of one piece. And remember to stop while you are still going good. That keeps it moving instead of having it die whenever you go on and write yourself out. When you do that you find that the next day you are pooped and can't go on.

Mice: Do you do the same on a story?

Y.C.: Yes, only sometimes you can write a story in a day.

Mice: Do you know what is going to happen when you write a story?

Y.C.: Almost never. I start to make it up and have happen what would have to happen as it goes along.

Mice: That isn't the way they teach you to write in college.   35

Y.C.: I don't know about that. I never went to college. If any son-ofabitch could write he wouldn't have to teach writing in college.

Mice: You're teaching me.

Y.C.: I'm crazy. Besides this is a boat, not a college.

Mice: What books should a writer have to read?

Y.C.: He should have read everything so he knows what he has to   40
beat.

Mice: He can't have read everything.

Y.C.: I don't say what he can. I say what he should. Of course he can't.

Mice: Well what books are necessary?

Y.C.: He should have read *War and Peace* and *Anna Karenina* by Tolstoi, *Midshipman Easy, Frank Mildmay* and *Peter Simple* by Captain Marryat, *Madame Bovary* and *L'Education Sentimentale* by Flaubert, *Buddenbrooks* by Thomas Mann, Joyce's *Dubliners, Portrait of the Artist* and *Ulysses, Tom Jones* and *Joseph Andrews* by Fielding, *Le Rouge et le Noir* and *La Chartreuse de Parme* by Stendhal, *The Brothers Karamazov* and any two other Dostoevskis, *Huckleberry Finn* by Mark Twain, *The Open Boat* and *The Blue Hotel* by Stephen Crane, *Hail and Farewell* by George Moore, Yeats's *Autobiographies,* all the good De Maupassant, all the good Kipling, all of Turgenev, *Far Away and Long Ago* by W. H. Hudson, Henry James's short stories, especially *Madame de Mauves,* and *The Turn of the Screw, The Portrait of a Lady, The American—*

Mice: I can't write them down that fast. How many more are there?   45

Y.C.: I'll give you the rest another day. There are about three times that many.

Mice: Should a writer have read all of those?

Y.C.: All of those and plenty more. Otherwise he doesn't know what he has to beat.

Mice: What do you mean "has to beat"?

Y.C.: Listen. There is no use writing anything that has been written 50 before unless you can beat it. What a writer in our time has to do is write what hasn't been written before or beat dead men at what they have done. The only way he can tell how he is going is to compete with dead men. Most live writers do not exist. Their fame is created by critics who always need a genius of the season, someone they understand completely and feel safe in praising, but when these fabricated genuises are dead they will not exist. The only people for a serious writer to compete with are the dead that he knows are good. It is like a miler running against the clock rather than simply trying to beat whoever is in the race with him. Unless he runs against time he will never know what he is capable of attaining.

Mice: But reading all the good writers might discourage you.

Y.C.: Then you ought to be discouraged.

Mice: What is the best early training for a writer?

Y.C.: An unhappy childhood.

Mice: Do you think Thomas Mann is a great writer? 55

Y.C.: He would be a great writer if he had never written another thing than *Buddenbrooks*.

Mice: How can a writer train himself?

Y.C.: Watch what happens today. If we get into a fish see exactly what it is that everyone does. If you get a kick out of it while he is jumping remember back until you see exactly what the action was that gave you the emotion. Whether it was the rising of the line from the water and the way it tightened like a fiddle string until drops started from it, or the way he smashed and threw water when he jumped. Remember what the noises were and what was said. Find what gave you the emotion; what the action was that gave you the excitement. Then write it down making it clear so the reader will see it too and have the same feeling that you had. That's a five finger exercise.

Mice: All right.

Y.C.: Then get in somebody else's head for a change. If I bawl you 60 out try to figure what I'm thinking about as well as how you feel about it. If Carlos curses Juan think what both their sides of it are. Don't just think who is right. As a man things are as they should or shouldn't be. As a man you know who is right and who is wrong. You have to make decisions and enforce them. As a writer you should not judge. You should understand.

Mice: All right.

Y.C.: Listen *now*. When people talk listen completely. Don't be thinking what you're going to say. Most people never listen. Nor do they observe. You should be able to go into a room and when you come out know everything that you saw there and not only that. If that room gave you any feeling you should know exactly what it was that gave you that feeling. Try that for practice. When you're in town stand outside the theatre and see how the people differ in the way they get out of taxis or motor cars. There are a thousand ways to practice. And always think of other people.

Mice: Do you think I will be a writer?

Y.C.: How the hell should I know? Maybe you have no talent. Maybe you can't feel for other people. You've got some good stories if you can write them.

Mice: How can I tell?   65

Y.C.: Write. If you work at it five years and you find you're no good you can just as well shoot yourself then as now.

Mice: I wouldn't shoot myself.

Y.C.: Come around then and I'll shoot you.

Mice: Thanks.

Y.C.: Perfectly welcome, Mice. Now should we talk about something else?

Mice: What else?

Y.C.: Anything else, Mice, old timer, anything else at all.

Mice: All right. But—

Y.C.: No but. Finish. Talk about writing finish. No more. All gone for today. Store all close up. Boss he go home.

Mice: All right then. But tomorrow I've got some things to ask you.

Y.C.: I'll bet you'll have fun writing after you know just how it's done.

Mice: What do you mean?

Y.C.: You know. Fun. Good times. Jolly. Dashing off an old masterpiece.

Mice: Tell me—

Y.C.: Stop it.

Mice: All right. But tomorrow—

Y.C.: Yes. All right. Sure. But tomorrow.

October 1935

Lines of Inquiry
"Monologue to the Maestro: A High Seas Letter"

As the form of this piece makes clear, Hemingway clearly prefers to give his advice to young writers by means of a conversation between himself and Mice, rather than in a straightforward explanatory essay. Why do you suppose that he uses the form of a dialogue? Why does he call it a "monologue" rather than a dialogue? Given the fact that he includes only a small portion of what must have been said during "a period of one hundred and ten days with the good old Maestro," how do you account for the selection and organization of the "mouthings" he has "written down"? How "true" does the conversation sound to you?

Throughout the conversation, Hemingway is especially concerned with the nature of truth in writing. What do you think Hemingway means by a "true" story? How do you account for his statement that "true writing" depends not only on a writer's "knowledge of life" but also on his "imagination"? Why do you suppose he believes that "if you make it up instead of describe it you can make it round and whole and solid and give it life," but that you cannot do so if you are "just reporting"? Given this belief, why does he advise Mice to "train himself" to "see exactly what it is that everyone does" and to "listen completely" to what everyone says?

Think of a memorable and long-running conversation that you have had with a friend, relative, teacher, or employer. What was the primary topic of conversation? Were you on the giving or the receiving end of the conversation? Or was it a matter of give and take on both sides of the discussion? What did you learn from that conversation that you could not have learned quite so well from a comparable amount of reading? Why was the conversation a more effective form of learning for you?

Edward Hoagland
1937—

Pain, love, boredom, and glee, and anticipation or anxiety—these
are the pilings we build our lives from. In love we beget more love
and in pain we beget more pain. Since we must like it or lump it,
we like it. And why not, indeed?

Edward Hoagland builds
his essays from the "pilings" of both pain and love, boredom and glee,
as he puts it in this excerpt from his essay exploring "The Threshold
and the Jolt of Pain"—formed out of both the darkness and the light of
his own nature. Whether he writes about the city or the country, the
behavior of people or of animals, Hoagland is fascinated with the actual
experience of living in the world, in all its complexity. He is ecstatic
and admittedly "kinky" by turns, sometimes celebrating the beauties of
the natural landscape, sometimes delving into his own sadistic impulses. Whatever he uncovers in his own sensibility, whatever he observes in the behavior of others moves him in the end to "like it" rather
than "lump it." For him even pain can be "converted to serve as a
purpose," since it jolts us for a moment into a new vitality.

Hoagland grew up in a rural suburb of New York, where he experienced the joys of both the country and the city, both of which are
centers of interest in his writing. "The out-of-doors was everything to
me. I spent the summer mornings . . . vaulting the brooks, climbing
the pines, creeping along the rabbit paths." Yet he also grew up a "city
rat," walking the streets of New York "delightedly," an expert in the
"innumerable street nooks and faces which epitomized New York." All
his life, to paraphrase the title of one of his more famous essays, "home
has been two places." A more problematic relationship in Hoagland's
background is the tension between his upper-middle-class upbringing
and his desire for a wider range of experiences. The son of affluent
parents, Hoagland went to Deerfield Academy and then "sumptuous"
Harvard, rubbing elbows with Kennedys, Rockefellers, and Du Ponts.
But partly as a "clumsy penance" for his life of privilege, partly out of
a hunger for new sensations, Hoagland has also spent much of his time

living with winos on Skid Row, sleeping in flophouses, tramping across the country, fighting forest fires, or working in a circus. "To live is to see," he says in one of his later travel essays, "and traveling sometimes speeds up the process."

As a young man Hoagland felt himself to be an "oddball," a "little askew," and worried about a streak of cruelty and even masochism he discovered in himself: "I was a bunch of nerves." What most set him apart was a severe stammer—something he still struggles with today— an inability to talk under pressure that earlier in his life made social situations unbearable, driving Hoagland deeper into himself. The effects of this stammer are evident in his writing, particularly in his fascination with animals and his detachment as an observer. "Words are spoken at considerable cost to me," he says, "so a great value is placed on each one. That has had some effect on me as a writer. As a child, since I couldn't talk to people, I became close to animals. I became an observer, and in all my books, even the novels, witnessing things is what counts." In fact, Hoagland has even suggested that "being in these vocal handcuffs has made me a desperate, devoted writer" in the first place, the written word allowing him to express what he could not say out loud.

His first novel, *Cat Man* (1956), a depiction of life in a traveling circus, was published soon after his graduation from Harvard, and he has since produced two other novels, *The Circle Home* (1960) and *The Peacock's Tail* (1965). But in the late 1960s, after writing the first of his many essays and reviews, Hoagland began to realize that "what I wanted to do most was to tell my own story" and "that the easiest way to do so was by writing directly to the reader without filtering myself through the artifices of fiction." At first these nonfiction pieces had seemed like quick and easy work, a nice break from the "main-force adventure" of writing novels. "But then I realized that since the essays themselves were breaking ground for me, perhaps they were just as directly to the point." They were a "relief," a more generous, open-ended way of expressing the feelings "bottled up" inside of him. But more than that, as he refined and perfected his technique, Hoagland saw that the essay is an art form in itself, capable of embodying experience and ideas not expressible in other ways, as he has explained in his essay on the essay, "What I Think, What I Am." Over the last twenty years, devoting himself exclusively to the essay, he has produced four essay collections— *The Courage of Turtles* (1971), *Walking the Dead Diamond River* (1973), *Red Wolves and Black Bears* (1976), and *The Tugman's Passage* (1982)— and two travel books—*Notes from the Century Before: A Journal of British Columbia* (1969) and *African Calliope: a Journey to the Sudan* (1979).

Hoagland divides his time now between a Greenwich Village apartment and an isolated cabin in Vermont, writing essays on a wide variety of subjects, from boxing and taxidermy to marriage and success. Like E. B. White, though with an entirely different tone and outlook, he alternates between writing about life in the country, where "the peepers sing in a ringing, monotonous, fitfully exhilarating call" and "the wood frogs congregate in the woodside pools," and life in the city, where commuters dodge muggers and choke on the smoggy air. "The problem everywhere nowadays turns on how we shall decide to live." Hoagland keeps a foot in both the country and the city, balancing the values of each without retreating from the challenges of contemporary life. Another of his central preoccupations is the idea of skill and performance, in tugboat captains, animal trainers, athletes, rodeo performers, and other writers. As he says of boxing, "I go to admire a trial of skills." He also remains fascinated with animals, especially turtles and bears, but also with any animal that is hunted or tamed. What compels him is the physicality and power of animals as they resist human attempts to subdue them, and also their strangeness, their otherness.

Hoagland is also compelled by his own strange, dark impulses, and he is arrestingly frank and precise in describing such feelings. "There is a monster in me that I keep at bay," he says, "a secret hunchback residing inside of me." In writing of an early lover, for example, he admits that "I was not an ogre to her, but I did by stages develop the habit of beating her briefly with my belt or hairbrush before we made love, a practice which I have foregone ever since." In other essays he describes with a kind of steady, almost scientific relish his secret satisfaction in seeing people and animals trapped or hurt, his own enjoyment at being restrained or abused, even his desire to beat his infant daughter.

Hoagland explores such feelings not for the sake of sensationalism but rather out of a belief in the importance of honesty, and more than that, for the purpose in the end of making a moral point. "What is kinky in me worries me less than the dead spots," he says. "Kinkiness, like a reversible coat, can be turned inside out." So, Hoagland values most the ability to be aware, fully human, not deadened by the routines and pressures of daily life. Admitting to kinkiness can be one step to recognizing the other side of human nature, the human capacity for joy, which is equally Hoagland's subject. "I'm an optimist in the same way that I'm right-handed, and will always be. It's simpler to be an optimist and it's a sensible defense against the uncertainties and abysses which otherwise confront us prematurely."

Thus when he isn't divulging some intimacy of his inner life, Hoagland describes as accurately as he can the splendor of the circus, the thrill of the city, the serenity of the morning forest, or the courage of turtles. Given the extraordinary range of his interests and the vigor of his impulses, Hoagland's essays are often rambling, full of tangents and false cues, intricate digressions, fractures. Yet the vividness of his metaphors, the strength of his verbs, and the drive of his sentences also enable him to achieve "a combination of personality and originality and energetic loose ends" that for him characterizes the essay.

A Run of Bad Luck

Bad ions in the air, bad stars, or bad luck: call it what you will—a run of bad luck, in fact. I was driving down the Thruway in Vermont to consult a doctor in New York, and hit a deer. Didn't see the deer till the impact, sharing its surprise. Deer, unlike domestic animals, are afraid of cars and leap as you pass, either into you or away. It lay in the deep grass, heaving like a creature stranded on the beach.

Sure enough, as befitted the omen, in New York City the doctor's news was bad. Then within a day or two, Pier 50, a huge ramshackle structure across the street from where I live, caught fire and burned hectically for seven hours, although surrounded by fireboats, as only an abandoned pier can. The neighborhood was layered in smoke for a couple of days—for me, acrid testimony to what the doctor had said. There were also a few of the usual New York hang-up phone calls, and then, as if to push me into a sump of depression, somebody—a vandal aroused by the fire, or someone who thought I had parked in his parking space— poured sugar into the gas tank of my car, not enough to destroy the engine but enough so that I returned to Vermont in relief.

In the meantime, my mother, in another city, had gone into the hospital for surgery, and one evening that week my daughter and I were out walking along a wooded road (I was carrying her on my shoulders), when a car passing another car bore down on us at high speed, its roar not easy to distinguish from that of the slower one; I barely heard it in time. This, in the context of the other incidents, particularly shook me because it seemed to bear a hint of malevolence; I felt very small. Then, within days, my next-door neighbor there, an old man as close as a relative to us, died of a stroke. Another good friend and country mentor went into the hospital after a heart attack. News came from New York as well that a friend in the city had killed herself. I marshaled a motley assortment of tranquilizers and sleeping pills left over from the past—divorce, career crisis, other bad occasions. I had that feeling of luck running out, that I must be *very careful,* although, on the contrary, I was becoming deadened, not alert. At such a time, the opposite of invulnerable, one must take care to move in a gingerly fashion and not get so rattled that an accident happens. I had considered myself a sort of a Sunday's child much of my life, but suddenly intimations of death and calamity were all about.

I remembered talking to a woman who had survived a snowslide by swimming along on the surface while whooshing downhill for a hundred yards—as people caught in an undertow or even in quicksand save themselves by flattening out and floating if they can. Just so, I should ride the current until it turned. The best advice I have heard on bearing pain is to fix one's mind upon the idea that the pain is in one place—the other side of the room—and that you are in another; then, where you are, play cards or whatever. Cooking, fooling with my daughter, I realized more distinctly than at any time in years that although in fact my life was not at stake right now, I believed in some form of reincarnation or immortality—this a conviction, not a wish. I pray in airplanes during takeoff, but it is with a sense of praying *pro forma,* as if the location of my belief weren't really there, but were more generalized, in a bigger God. There are ideas central to society which we seldom question in order that society will hold together—as, for instance, the notion basic to medical care that everybody has a contribution to make, or "a right to life." But there are other conceptions, such as the idea of God, which we disparage and scarcely consider, until later, smiling sheepishly in our mind's eye as if we had disputed the fact that the moon moves in the sky, we admit to having been wrong, and to having known all along that we were wrong.

Once, highborn ladies would flee to a convent if some unnerving sequence of events overtook them, not necessarily taking orders, but resting, collecting their wits. And when they strolled in the cloister around a bubbling fountain, the walkway itself possessed a soothing, perpetual quality, with each right-angle turn leading straight to another. Walking for many hours, they looked at the lindenwood saints, the robust faces—at the Virgin's implacable verve, or else at a dolor portrayed with an equally saving exaggeration. Coincidentally, I went to New York's own Cloisters, and because the reality of each bad event had been dulled by the others, it was for me one of those queer times when people recognize how much they can adjust to—how quickly, for example, they could settle into the routine of life in a prison camp.

Of course I had my daughter to entertain, and in the country I walked in the woods, watching the aspens quake (said by legend to occur because Christ's cross was of aspen). I have an old army siren, hand-cranked, that I climbed with up on the mountain at twilight, to persuade a family of coyotes nearby to answer. I was relieved that the random incidents seemed to have ended. I thought of two friends in the city who had recently suffered crises—heart attacks at forty. One fellow, as the pain surged through him, found himself muttering stubbornly, "No groveling, Death!" When he was out of danger he wrote seventy-some letters to friends from his hospital bed, each with a numbered series of thoughts directed to the recipient. The other man is that rare case where one can put one's finger exactly on the characteristics of which one is so fond. He married the same woman twice. Although it didn't work out either time, she was well worth marrying twice, and to my way of thinking this showed that he was at once a man of fervent, rash, abiding love, and yet a man of flexibility, ready to admit an error and to act to correct it.

Both my mother and country mentor were now on the mend, and my own doctor reported good news. Prospects began looking up. What I'd gained from the period, besides a flood of relief, was the memory of how certain I'd been that the intricacy and brilliance of life cannot simply fold up with one's death—that, as in the metaphor of a fountain, or the great paradigm of rain and the ocean, it sinks down but comes up, blooms up and sinks down again.

Lines of Inquiry
"A Run of Bad Luck"

In the preface to his first collection of essays, Hoagland says that writing essays is "the next thing to writing letters." What aspects of style, detailing, and organization make "A Run of Bad Luck" seem like a letter? How would you respond to it, if you actually received this as a letter? On the other hand, how does this piece differ from a letter? What aspects of style, organization, and content make this an essay?

Though Hoagland devotes much of this essay to describing "a run of bad luck," he ends by saying that what he gained from the experience "was the memory of how certain I'd been that the intricacy and brilliance of life cannot simply fold up with one's death." How does he manage to arrive at this affirmative conclusion? How exactly does he get from the terrible things in the beginning to the optimism at the end? What does his belief in "some form of reincarnation or immortality" have to do with this movement from dread to joy? How does this conviction also relate to the dread and fear he felt during his run of bad luck?

Think about a run of bad luck that you—or someone close to you—have lived through. How did it begin? What happened over the course of it? How did it end? Did you feel any of the dread that Hoagland describes, or the superstition? What did you think about it all when the run of bad luck was over?

Dogs, and the Tug of Life

It used to be that you could tell just about how poor a family was by how many dogs they had. If they had one, they were probably doing all right. It was only American to keep a dog to represent the family's interests in the intrigues of the back alley; not to have a dog at all would be like not acknowledging one's poor relations. Two dogs meant that the couple were dog lovers, with growing children, but still might be members of the middle class. But if a citizen kept three, you could begin to suspect he didn't own much else. Four or five irrefutably marked the household as poor folk, whose yard was also full of broken cars cannibalized for parts. The father worked not much, fancied himself a hunter; the mother's teeth were black. And an old bachelor living in a shack might possibly have even more, but you knew that if one of them, chasing a moth, didn't upset his oil lamp some night and burn him up, he'd fetch up in the poorhouse soon, with the dogs shot. Nobody got poor feeding a bunch of dogs, needless to say, because the more dogs a man had, the less he fed them. Foraging as a pack, they led an existence of their own, but served as evidence that life was awfully lonesome for him and getting out of hand. If a dog really becomes a man's best friend his situation is desperate.

That dogs, low-comedy confederates of small children and ragged bachelors, should have turned into an emblem of having made it to the middle class—like the hibachi, like golf clubs and a second car—seems at the very least incongruous. Puppies which in the country you would have to carry in a box to the church fair to give away are bringing seventy-five dollars apiece in some of the pet stores, although in fact dogs are in such oversupply that one hundred and fifty thousand are running wild in New York City alone.

There is another line of tradition about dogs, however. Show dogs, toy dogs, foxhounds for formal hunts, Doberman guard dogs, bulldogs as ugly as a queen's dwarf. An aristocratic Spanish lady once informed me that when she visits her Andalusian estate each fall the mastiffs rush out and fawn about her but would tear to pieces any of the servants who have accompanied her from Madrid. In Mississippi it was illegal for a slave owner to permit his slaves to have a dog, just as it was to teach them how to read. A "negro dog" was a hound trained by a bounty hunter to ignore the possums, raccoons, hogs and deer in the woods that other dogs were supposed to chase, and trail and tree a runaway. The planters themselves, for whom hunting was a principal recreation, whooped it up when a man unexpectedly became their quarry.

They caught each other's slaves and would often sit back and let the dogs do the punishing. Bennet H. Barrow of West Feliciana Parish in Louisiana, a rather moderate and representative plantation owner, recounted in his diary of the 1840s, among several similar incidents, this for November 11, 1845: In "5 minutes had him up & a going, And never in my life did I ever see as excited beings as R & myself, ran ½ miles & caught him dogs soon tore him naked, took him Home Before the other negro(es) at dark & made the dogs give him another over hauling." Only recently in Louisiana I heard what happened to two Negroes who happened to be fishing in a bayou off the Blind River, where four white men with a shotgun felt like fishing alone. One was forced to pretend to be a scampering coon and shinny up a telephone pole and hang there till he fell, while the other impersonated a baying, bounding hound.

Such memories are not easy to shed, particularly since childhood, the time when people can best acquire a comradeship with animals, is also when they are likely to pick up their parents' fears. A friend of mine hunts quail by jeep in Texas with a millionaire who brings along forty bird dogs, which he deploys in eight platoons that spell each other off. Another friend, though, will grow apprehensive at a dinner party if the host lets a dog loose in the room. The toothy, mysterious creature lies dreaming on the carpet, its paws pulsing, its eyelids open, the nictitating membranes twitching; how can he be certain it won't suddenly jump up and attack his legs under the table? Among Eastern European Jews, possession of a dog was associated with the hard-drinking *goyishe* peasantry, traditional antagonists, or else with the gentry, and many carried this dislike to the New World. An immigrant fleeing a potato famine or the hunger of Calabria might be no more equipped with the familiar British-German partiality to dogs—a failing which a few rugged decades in a great city's slums would not necessarily mend. The city had urbanized plenty of native farmers' sons as well, and so it came about that what to rural America had been the humblest, most natural amenity—friendship with a dog—has been transmogrified into a piece of the jigsaw of moving to the suburbs: there to cook outdoors, another bit of absurdity to the old countryman, whose toilet was outdoors but who was pleased to be able to cook and eat his meals inside the house.

There are an estimated forty million dogs in the United States (nearly two for every cat). Thirty-seven thousand of them are being destroyed in humane institutions every day, a figure which indicates that many more are in trouble. Dogs are hierarchal beasts, with several million years of submission to the structure of a wolf pack in their breeding. This explains why the Spanish lady's mastiffs can distinguish immediately between the mistress and her retainers, and why it is about as likely that one of the other guests at the dinner party will attack my

5

friend's legs under the table as that the host's dog will, once it has accepted his presence in the room as proper. Dogs need leadership, however; they seek it, and when it's not forthcoming quickly fall into difficulties in a world where they can no longer provide their own.

"Dog" is "God" spelled backwards—one might say, way backwards. There's "a dog's life," "dog days," "dog-sick," "dog-tired," "dog-cheap," "dog-eared," "doghouse," and "dogs" meaning villains or feet. Whereas a wolf's stamina was measured in part by how long he could go without water, a dog's is becoming a matter of how long he can *hold* his water. He retrieves a rubber ball instead of coursing deer, chases a broom instead of hunting marmots. His is the lowest form of citizenship: that tug of life at the end of the leash is like the tug at the end of a fishing pole, and then one doesn't have to kill it. On stubby, amputated-looking feet he leads his life, which if we glance at it attentively is a kind of cutout of our own, all the more so for being riskier and shorter. Bam! A member of the family is dead on the highway, as we expected he would be, and we just cart him to the dump and look for a new pup.

Simply the notion that he lives on four legs instead of two has come to seem astonishing—like a goat or cow wearing horns on its head. And of course to keep a dog is a way of attempting to bring nature back. The primitive hunter's intimacy, telepathy, with the animals he sought, surprising them at their meals and in their beds, then stripping them of their warm coats to expose a frame so like our own, is all but lost. Sport hunters, especially the older ones, retain a little of it still; and naturalists who have made up their minds not to kill wild animals nevertheless appear to empathize primarily with the predators at first, as a look at the tigers, bears, wolves, mountain lions on the project list of an organization such as the World Wildlife Fund will show. This is as it should be, these creatures having suffered from our brotherly envy before. But in order to really enjoy a dog, one doesn't merely try to train him to be semihuman. The point of it is to open oneself to the possibility of becoming partly a dog (after all, there are plenty of sub- or semi-human beings around whom we don't wish to adopt). One wants to rediscover the commonality of animal and man—to see an animal eat and sleep that hasn't forgotten how to enjoy doing such things—and the directness of its loyalty.

The trouble with the current emphasis on preserving "endangered species" is that, however beneficial to wildlife the campaign works out to be, it makes all animals seem like museum pieces, worth saving for sentimental considerations and as figures of speech (to "shoot a sitting duck"), but as a practical matter already dead and gone. On the contrary, some animals are flourishing. In 1910 half a million deer lived in the United States, in 1960 seven million, in 1970 sixteen million. What has happened is that now that we don't eat them we have lost that close interest.

Wolf behavior prepared dogs remarkably for life with human beings. So complete and complicated was the potential that it was only a logical next step for them to quit their packs in favor of the heady, hopeless task of trying to keep pace with our own community development. The contortions of fawning and obeisance which render group adjustment possible among such otherwise forceful fighters—sometimes humping the inferior members into the shape of hyenas—are what squeezes them past our tantrums, too. Though battling within the pack is mostly accomplished with the body checks that do no damage, a subordinate wolf bitch is likely to remain so in awe of the leader that she will cringe and sit on her tail in response to his amorous advances, until his female co-equal has had a chance to notice and dash over and re-direct his attention. Altogether, he is kept so busy asserting his dominance that this top-ranked female may not be bred by him, finally, but by the male which occupies the second rung. Being breadwinners, dominant wolves feed first and best, just as we do, so that to eat our scraps and leavings strikes a dog as normal procedure. Nevertheless a wolf puppy up to eight months old is favored at a kill, and when smaller can extract a meal from any pack member—uncles and aunts as well as parents—by nosing the lips of the adult until it regurgitates a share of what it's had. The care of the litter is so much a communal endeavor that the benign sort of role we expect dogs to play within our own families toward children not biologically theirs comes naturally to them.

For dogs and wolves the tail serves as a semaphore of mood and social code, but dogs carry their tails higher than wolves do, as a rule, which is appropriate, since the excess spirits that used to go into lengthy hunts now have no other outlet than backyard negotiating. In addition to an epistolary anal gland, whose message-carrying function has not yet been defined, the anus itself, or stool when sniffed, conveys how well the animal has been eating—in effect, its income bracket—although most dog foods are sorrily monotonous compared to the hundreds of tastes a wolf encounters, perhaps dozens within the carcass of a single moose. We can speculate on a dog's powers of taste because its olfactory area is proportionately fourteen times larger than a man's, its sense of smell at least a hundred times as keen.

The way in which a dog presents his anus and genitals for inspection indicates the hierarchal position that he aspires to, and other dogs who sniff his genitals are apprised of his sexual condition. From his urine they can undoubtedly distinguish age, build, state of sexual activity and general health, even hours after he's passed by. Male dogs dislike running out of urine, as though an element of potency were involved, and try to save a little; they prefer not to use a scent post again until

10

another dog has urinated there, the first delight and duty of the ritual being to stake out a territory, so that when they are walked hurriedly in the city it is a disappointment to them. The search is also sexual, because bitches in heat post notices about. In the woods a dog will mark his drinking places, and watermark a rabbit's trail after chasing it, as if to notify the next predator that happens by exactly who it was that put such a whiff of fear into the rabbit's scent. Similarly, he squirts the tracks of bobcats and of skunks with an aloof air unlike his brisk and cheery manner of branding another dog's or fox's trail, and if he is in a position to do so, will defecate excitedly on a bear run, leaving behind his best effort, which no doubt he hopes will strike the bear as a bombshell.

The chief complaint people lodge against dogs is their extraordinary stress upon lifting the leg and moving the bowels. Scatology did take up some of the slack for them when they left behind the entertainments of the forest. The forms of territoriality replaced the substance. But apart from that, a special zest for life is characteristic of dogs and wolves—in hunting, eating, relieving themselves, in punctiliously maintaining a home territory, a pecking order and a love life, and educating the resulting pups. They grin and grimace and scrawl graffiti with their piss. A lot of inherent strategy goes into these activities: the way wolves spell each other off, both when hunting and in their governess duties around the den, and often "consult" as a pack with noses together and tails wagging before flying in to make a kill. (Tigers, leopards, house cats base their social relations instead upon what ethologists call "mutual avoidance.") The nose is a dog's main instrument of discovery, corresponding to our eyes, and so it is that he is seldom offended by organic smells, such as putrefaction, and sniffs intently for the details of illness, gum bleeding and diet in his master and his fellows, and for the story told by scats, not closing off the avenue for any reason—just as we rarely shut our eyes against new information, even the tragic or unpleasant kind.

Though dogs don't see as sharply as they smell, trainers usually rely on hand signals to instruct them, and most firsthand communication in a wolf pack also seems to be visual—by the expressions of the face, by body english and the cant of the tail. A dominant wolf squares his mouth, stares at and "rides up" on an inferior, standing with his front legs on its back, or will pretend to stalk it, creeping along, taking its muzzle in his mouth, and performing nearly all of the other discriminatory pranks and practices familiar to anybody who has a dog. In fact, what's funny is to watch a homely mutt as tiny as a shoebox spin through the rigmarole which a whole series of observers in the wilderness have gone to great pains to document for wolves.

Dogs proffer their rear ends to each other in an intimidating fashion, but when they examine the region of the head it is a friendlier gesture, a snuffling between pals. One of them may come across a tell-tale bone fragment caught in the other's fur, together with a bit of mud to give away the location of bigger bones. On the same impulse, wolves and free-running dogs will sniff a wanderer's toes to find out where he has been roaming. They fondle and propitiate with their mouths also, and lovers groom each other's fur with tongues and teeth adept as hands. A bitch wolf's period in heat includes a week of preliminary behavior and maybe two weeks of receptivity—among animals, exceptionally long. Each actual copulative tie lasts twenty minutes or a half an hour, which again may help to instill affection. Wolves sometimes begin choosing a mate as early as the age of one, almost a year before they are ready to breed. Dogs mature sexually a good deal earlier, and arrive in heat twice a year instead of once—at any season instead of only in mid-winter, like a wolf, whose pups' arrival must be scheduled unfailingly for spring. Dogs have not retained much responsibility for raising their young, and the summertime is just as perilous as winter for them because, apart from the whimsy of their owners, who put so many of them to sleep, their nemesis is the automobile. Like scatology, sex helps fill the gulf of what is gone.

The scientist David Mech has pointed out how like the posture of a   15
wolf with a nosehold on a moose (as other wolves attack its hams) are the antics of a puppy playing tug-of-war at the end of a towel. Anybody watching a dog's exuberance as it samples bites of long grass beside a brook, or pounds into a meadow bristling with the odors of woodchucks, snowshoe rabbits, grouse, a doe and buck, field mice up on the seedheads of the weeds, kangaroo mice jumping, chipmunks whistling, weasels and shrews on the hunt, a plunging fox, a porcupine couched in a tree, perhaps can begin to imagine the variety of excitements under the sky that his ancestors relinquished in order to move indoors with us. He'll lie down with a lamb to please us, but as he sniffs its haunches, surely he must remember atavistically that this is where he'd start to munch.

There is poignancy in the predicament of a great many animals: as in the simple observation which students of the California condor have made that this huge, most endangered bird prefers the carrion meat of its old standby, the deer, to all the dead cows, sheep, horses and other substitutes it sees from above, sprawled about. Animals are stylized characters in a kind of old saga—stylized because even the most acute of them have little leeway as they play out their parts. (*Rabbits,* for example, I find terribly affecting, imprisoned in their hop.) And as we drift away from any cognizance of them, we sacrifice some of the intricacy and grandeur of life. Having already lost so much, we are hardly aware of what remains, but to a primitive snatched forward from an earlier existence it might seem as if we had surrendered a richness comparable to all the tapestries of childhood. Since this is a matter of the imagination as well as of animal demographics, no Noah projects, no bionomic discoveries on the few sanctuaries that have been established are going to reverse the swing. The very specialists in the forefront of finding out how animals behave, when one meets them, appear to be no more intrigued than any ordinary Indian was.

But we continue to need—as aborigines did, as children do—a parade of morality tales which are more concise than those that politics, for instance, later provides. So we've had Aesop's and medieval and modern fables about the grasshopper and the ant, the tiger and Little Black Sambo, the wolf and the three pigs, Br'er Rabbit and Br'er Bear, Goldilocks and her three bears, Pooh Bear, Babar and the rhinos, Walt Disney's animals, and assorted humbler scary bats, fat hippos, funny frogs and eager beavers. Children have a passion for clean, universal definitions, and so it is that animals have gone with children's literature as Latin has with religion. Through them they first encountered death, birth, their own maternal feelings, the gap between beauty and cleverness, or speed and good intentions. The animal kingdom boasted the powerful lion, the mothering goose, the watchful owl, the tardy tortoise, Chicken Little, real-life dogs that treasure bones, and mink that grow posh pelts from eating crawfish and mussels.

In the cartoons of two or three decades ago, Mouse doesn't get along with Cat because Cat must catch Mouse or miss his supper. Dog, on the other hand, detests Cat for no such rational reason, only the capricious fact that dogs don't dote on cats. Animal stories are bounded, yet enhanced, by each creature's familiar lineaments, just as a parable about a prince and peasant, a duchess and a milkmaid, a blacksmith and a fisherman, would be. Typecasting, like the roll of a metered ode, adds resonance and dignity, summoning up all of the walruses and hedgehogs that went before: the shrewd image of Br'er Rabbit to assist his suburban relative Bugs Bunny behind the scenes. But now, in order to present a tale about the contest between two thieving crows and a scarecrow, the storyteller would need to start by explaining that once upon a time crows used to eat a farmer's corn if he didn't defend it with a mock man pinned together from old clothes. Crows are having a hard go of it and may soon receive game-bird protection.

One way childhood is changing, therefore, is that the nonhuman figures—"Wild Things" or puppet monsters—constructed by the best of the new artificers, like Maurice Sendak or the *Sesame Street* writers, are distinctly humanoid, ballooned out of faces, torsos met on the subway. The televised character Big Bird does not resemble a bird the way Bugs Bunny remained a rabbit—though already he was less so than Br'er or Peter Rabbit. Big Bird's personality, her confusion, haven't the faintest connection to an ostrich's. Lest she be confused with an ostrich, her voice has been slotted unmistakably toward the prosaic. Dr. Seuss did transitional composites of worldwide fauna, but these new shapes—a beanbag like the *Sesame Street* Grouch or Cookie Monster or Herry Monster, and the floral creations in books—have been conceived practically from scratch by the artist ("in the night kitchen," to use a Sendak phrase), and not transferred from the existing caricatures of nature. In their conversational conflicts they offer him a fresh start, which may be a valuable commodity, whereas if he were dealing with an alligator, it would, while giving him an old-fashioned boost in the traditional manner, at the same time box him in. A chap called Alligator, with that fat snout and tail, cannot squirm free of the solidity of actual alligators. Either it must stay a heavy weight or else play on the sternness of reality by swinging over to impersonate a cream puff and a Ferdinand.

Though animal programs on television are popular, what with the   20 wave of nostalgia and "ecology" in the country, we can generally say about the animal kingdom, "The King is dead, long live the King." Certainly the talent has moved elsewhere. Those bulbous Wild Things and slant-mouthed beanbag puppets derived from the denizens of Broadway—an argumentative night news vendor, a lady on a traffic island—have grasped their own destinies, as characters on the make are likely to. It was inevitable they would. There may be a shakedown to remove the elements that would be too bookish for children's literature in other hands, and another shakedown because these first innovators have been more city-oriented than suburban. New authors will shift the character sources away from Broadway and the subway and the ghetto, but the basic switch has already been accomplished—from the ancient juxtaposition of people, animals, and dreams blending the two, to people and monsters that grow solely out of people by way of dreams.

Which leaves us in the suburbs, with dogs as a last link. Cats are too independent to care, but dogs are in an unenviable position, they hang so much upon our good opinion. We are coming to *have* no opinion; we don't pay enough attention to form an opinion. Though they admire us, are thrilled by us, heroize us, we regard them as a hobby or a status symbol, like a tennis racquet, and substitute leash laws for leadership—expect them not simply to learn English but to grow hands, because their beastly paws seem stranger to us every year. If they try to fondle us with their handyjack mouths, we read it as a bite; and like used cars, they are disposed of when the family relocates, changes its "bag," or in the scurry of divorce. The first reason people kept a dog was to acquire an ally on the hunt, a friend at night. Then it was to maintain an avenue to animality, as our own nearness began to recede. But as we lose our awareness of all animals, dogs are becoming a bridge to nowhere. We can only pity their fate.

Lines of Inquiry
"Dogs, and the Tug of Life"

Hoagland is known for his striking and often startling imagery and metaphor. Make a record of the images and metaphors that stand out most prominently here in his description of dogs. What do these figures of speech suggest about the nature of dogs? What do they suggest about the differences between the behavior of dogs and humans? What do they suggest about Hoagland's attitude toward dogs?

Hoagland seems to see our treatment of dogs as an index to the state of our culture. How has our treatment of dogs changed over the centuries according to Hoagland? Why does he deplore our current attitude toward dogs? What contemporary problems does it represent in his view? Why does he consider the appearance of television characters such as Big Bird and the Cookie Monster to be instances—perhaps even causes—of the problem?

Virginia Woolf's "On a Faithful Friend" is also about human beings and dogs. To what extent do Woolf and Hoagland have similar views about dogs and the treatment they receive from their owners? In what respects, if any, do you think that Woolf's story of her pet dog illustrates the essential nature of dogs as described by Hoagland? In what respects do you think Woolf's story illustrates the disturbing problems that Hoagland raises concerning the relationship of human beings and dogs?

The Problem of the
Golden Rule

Like a good many New Yorkers, I've often wondered whether I was going to be mugged. I've lived in a number of neighborhoods, and being a night walker, have many times changed my course or speeded my stride, eying a formidable-looking figure as he approached. But it's never happened, and I imagine that if it finally does there may actually be a kind of relief, even a species of exhilaration, as I pick myself up—assuming that I am not badly hurt—because a danger anticipated for a long time may come to seem worse than the reality. People who come home and encounter a robber in their apartment who flees are likely to be less shaken up than the householder is who simply steps into a shambles of ransacked bureaus and upended beds: they've seen the fellow; they know he's human. A friend of mine wrestled a burglar for several minutes around the floor of his living room, both of them using the trips and hip throws that they remembered from their teens, until by the time my friend won and phoned the police they were old acquaintances.

I know, too, that to describe the few incidents of violence I've met with in the past makes them sound more grisly than they were in fact. In the army, my platoon was put in the charge of a peculiar sergeant who, mostly for reasons of his own, had us do squat jumps one noontime until we could no longer walk or stand up. Then he strolled among us kicking us to make sure that we weren't faking. It was a hot drill field strewn with packs and stacked rifles and other movie props, and yet the experience was not nearly as bad as one would anticipate if he were told at breakfast what to expect that day. We just followed orders until we couldn't get up and then we lay where we were on the ground until the sergeant was satisfied that we had done what was humanly possible. Even in a true atrocity situation that's all that is ever done: what is humanly possible. Afterwards one becomes unresponsive and fatalistic; terror is no longer a factor.

Next day the sergeant wanted to have it both ways, so he set us into formation and told us what he was going to make us do, and thereupon went off to the latrine to give us a chance to stand at attention and think and stew. Another sergeant promptly walked up and dismissed us, however. We hobbled away in every direction as fast as possible, while the two sergeants met to discuss the issue in the barracks door. They met person-to-person, and we had been punished person-to-person, and the facelessness of the mugger whom one anticipates meeting on Little West 12th Street was never a part of it. This, like our doing whatever was humanly possible, made the experience supportable.

I visualize Armageddon not as a steel-muzzled affair of push-button silos under the earth but as a rusty freighter, flying the Liberian flag, perhaps, which sails inconspicuously up the Hudson past my apartment and goes off. Beyond that I don't see any details—though, as a non sequitur, I expect the tunnels and bridges would fill up with hikers leaving the city before it was too late. A woman I know says she sees Armageddon as getting under the bed. What we do with the insupportable is to turn it to terms we can file and forget. Unfortunately we are able to deal almost as handily with the nuclear bombs that have already gone off as we are with the ones that haven't. If as individual fighting men we had razed Hiroshima, then the horror of its destruction would persist as a legend to our great-grandchildren because it would have been witnessed and done on the spot—also because of the somber old notion that residing in every man is a spark of divinity, whether the man is an enemy or a friend. This putative spark is central to most religious belief; and right at the root of Western ethics is what is called, under one of its names, the Golden Rule. But spark or no spark, since in practice we cannot react to others with unabashed fellow-feeling, we usually reduce the Golden Rule to a sort of silver rule, doing to them just about what we think they would do to us if they had the opportunity. And this works—has been working—though the new impersonalized technology is challenging its workability, along with another behemoth among changes, which is that today there are too many people. Where there are too many people, we get tired of following even the silver rule, tired of paying that much attention, of noticing whom we are with and who is who. For the agnostic as well, basing his reverence for life on its variety and on a Jeffersonian fascination with the glimmerings of talent in every man, the glut is discouraging. Although we don't ridicule these old ideas, the sentiments that people have for one another in a traffic jam are becoming our sentiments more and more. A groan goes up in any suburb when it's announced that a new complex of housing for two thousand souls is going to be built on Lone Tree Hill. And the vast sigh of impatience which greeted Pope Paul's traditionalist statement of faith in the sanctity of the seed germs of life points to the tone to come. *Life for the living,* people will say: body-counts in war and baby-counts in peace. We grant each union man his $10,500 a year, and then the hell with him. He, for his part, doesn't care if our garbage cans fester with rats when the union goes after $10,900.

Never have people dealt so briskly with strangers as now. Many of us have ceased to see strangers at all; our eyes simply don't register them except as verticals on the sidewalk, and when we must parley with them we find out quickly what they are asking from us, do it— maybe—and that's that. When I was a child I remember how my aston-

ishment evolved as I realized that people often would not do the smallest thing to convenience another person or make him feel easier for the
moment. Of course I'd known that *kids* wouldn't, but I had thought
that was because they were kids. It was my first comprehension of the
deadness of life. Everyone has discovered at some particular point life's
deadness, but the galloping sense of deadness which alarms so many
people lately, and especially the young, goes way beyond such individual discoveries to dimensions and contexts that have brought revolution
to the U.S. Even in the arts the ancient austerities have been deemed
insufficient, and we have actors who jump into the audience and do
their acting there. When acting seems to fail, they improvise, and finally improvisation isn't enough either, and instead of having an actor
play the drug addict, the addict himself must appear onstage and play
himself—like the toothpaste tube blown up and hanging on the museum wall: "Look, if nothing else, I'm real." This is the era when students are so busy trying to teach their teachers that they are hard to
teach, and when the chip on the shoulder of the man in the street is his
"personality"—personality is quarrelsomeness. The revolution, in any
case, is overdue, but maybe our best hope is that we remain at least
idiosyncratic creatures, absorbed close to home. Dog owners, when they
walk their dogs, show nearly as exact an interest in their pets' defeca-
tions as they would in their own. The same communing silence steals
over their faces, the look of musing solemnity, that usually only the
bathroom mirror gets a glimpse of.

The worst public tragedy I've witnessed was in Boston, when from
a distance I saw a brick wall fall on a company of firemen. Some, with
a great shout, got away, but even the leap that they made while the
rest crumpled is blurred as a memory compared to the images of two
old men whom I knew slightly at the time. Mr. Kate wrote cookbooks
in the winter and hired out as a cook on a private yacht during the
warm months. His other love, besides cooking, was opera, and he lived
in a room shaped like a shoebox that cost him eight dollars a week. He
served himself candlelit meals on a folding table and concocted all of
his recipes on a hotplate set in the sink. By contrast, Mr. Hurth, although a somewhat less cultivated man, was an alumnus of Brown
University and lived in a large ground-floor room in the same house.
He had ruined himself in a scandal in St. Louis, where he had been a
businessman, but that was all I learned. What he'd done next was to
come to Boston and throw himself on the old-fashioned, private or
"Christian" charity, as it used to be called, of a roommate from college,
though thirty years had passed. He was a pleasant subdued man ordinarily, swinging from sweet to vaguely hangdog, but he was a drinker,
and so this benefactor no longer asked him to Newton Centre for
Thanksgiving because he was likely to break the furniture. When he
did, he'd leave his glasses behind by mistake so that he'd have to go

back out again for a whole second festival of apologies. Through charitable intercession, Mr. Hurth was on the payroll of the John Hancock Insurance Company, being listed on the books as a claims investigator, though actually (charity compounding charity) his single duty was to work for the United Fund once a year on a loan basis. The campaign was a brief one, but he was a bitter, floundering functionary, faced with his fate if his drinking should snap off his last sticks of presence and respectability.

As I say, next to the memory of two nodding acquaintances the death of some distant firemen is small potatoes. I was reminded of that catastrophe the other night for the first time in years while watching a fire on Third Avenue. Here in the bigger city one is witness to such a cataract of appalling happenings that they pass remembering. I saw a man who had just been burned out of his apartment turned away from a hotel in the neighborhood because he had a little blacking on him, although the shock and fear stood in his eyes. "Sure, there was a fire there, all right," the manager told me with a laugh. "I never take them in, those victims. They're dirty and they're scared to death. They're not worth the nuisance."

He was a modern, casual villain, however, impartial, just the kind who is not memorable. I came upon a much less gratuitous drama a few days afterwards. A child of two or three had been stuck inside one of those all-glass phone booths with a spring door which cannot be opened except by a grown person because of where the handle is placed. The world was passing—this was on the open street—but he was feeling his way around the glass in gathering panic, trying to find an escape route, reaching up and reaching down. Every few seconds he let out a thin, fluting scream so pure in pitch that it was hardly human; it was *pre*-human. You could see him thinking, learning, recording discoveries. He reached for the phone, but that was too high up; he thumped each pane of glass, searching for the door, and pounded on the metal frame, and screamed to find whether screaming would work. He was boxed into his terror, and you could see him grow older by leaps and bounds. I'm just this month a new father, so I was as transfixed as if he were my child. His governess or baby-sitter, baby-walker, or whatever she was, a short shadowy woman such as you might see manning a subway change booth, was standing right next to the glass, apparently feasting her eyes. Whether it was supposed to be a "punishment" or merely a pleasure fest, the child was too frightened by now to notice her.

Maybe our cruelty will save us. At least the cruel do pay attention, and the woman would probably have let him out before the crowd got around to hearing him. She had moved to the door, looking down at him intently as he pushed on the glass. I was seething, partly because I found that some of the woman's sexual excitement had communicated itself to me, which was intolerable, and partly because my cowardice in not interfering was equally outrageous. We've all become reluctant to stop and stick our noses in—a man is run over by a Breakstone cream-cheese truck and we pass quickly by. But cowardice was what it was in this particular event, since even under happy circumstances I stutter and it requires an enormous gearing up of nerve for me to step into a public fracas on the street. I strangle; I can't speak at all and must either use my hands on the stranger or gag and quaver, unable to put two words together. The seams of human nature frighten me in this regard, and the whole confrontation ethic of the sixties, much as I have entered into it on occasion, gives me nightmare visions because I have no conventional means of battling. I see myself as unable to protest in words to the person whose behavior has angered me and so using my hands on him; then just as unable to explain myself to the crowd that gathers, but only shuddering and stuttering; and then in court again enforcedly silent, dependent on the empathy or telepathic capacities of the people who are there to convey my side of the controversy.

Weaving like a nauseous moose, I was working my way toward her, when the woman, with a glance at me, pushed the door of the booth open, reached inside, and pulled the boy to her and walked away. In effect, I was let off, because only an exceptional well-doer would have tracked the woman down from that point on and questioned her about her psyche.

However, there are times one isn't let off, when one's very humanity hangs at issue and perhaps my specific problems with my stutter are an epitome of what each of us meets. Once in northern New England when I was snowshoeing, a hunter started shooting at me, really only to scare me, pinging with his .22 in my immediate vicinity. I was on an open hillside which I'd already realized was too slippery to climb, but as long as I kept scrabbling there in silence on the ice, like an animal in trouble, he was going to keep on pinging. Because a stutterer's every impulse is to stutter softly, unobtrusively, it's twice as hard to shout one's way through a stutter as to wedge through in quiet tones; but from the sheer imperatives of survival I shouted, "I CAN SEE YOU!" I shouted it several times again, although I couldn't see him; he was in the woods. I was insisting and reiterating that I was a human being: if I could get that message across to him he would stop shooting at me. It was even worse than my conception of a courtroom trial because this was one of those rare emergencies when we can't trust to all our faculties to operate together for us—the movements of our hands, our youth or age, our manner and expression—some compensating for the inadequacies of the others. I had to go to bat with my speaking abilities and nothing else. So I shouted to him that I could see him, by which I meant I was a man, and he stopped shooting.

More recently, I was on a tiny Danish island off the coast of Sweden, wandering around some seventeenth-century fortifications and the walled town, now a huddled fishing village. I had sat on the sea wall to watch the cloud action but was distracted by the spectacle below me of a boy mistreating a wild duck. Oddly enough, many times an incident where a person, rather than an animal, is being mauled and manhandled is easier to shrug off. The fact that he's a person complicates the case. As an onlooker you can see, for example, that he has gotten himself drunk and let his guard down, lost his dignity, talked out of turn. But the duck, with its wings clipped, presumably, was only trying to run away. The boy would catch it, pummel it and grip it tightly, trundling it about. Finally I got off my bench and went over and told him falteringly to cut that out. Many Danes speak English, but he was twelve or so and he may not have understood me. Like a mirror of myself, he stared at me without trying to say a word. Then he squeezed the duck again hard in both hands. My bugaboo about trying to explain myself to strangers rose in me, along with my indignation. Instead of looking for a local fellow to translate and take over, I lifted the duck from his arms, and with the sense of right and doom that I have dreaded in foreseeing a confrontation on the street, carried it down the stairs of the sea wall and released it on the beach. The boy ran for help; the duck paddled into the waves; I climbed to the promenade and started walking as deliberately as I could toward the small boat which had brought me to the island.

Uncannily soon, before I'd gone a dozen yards, practically the whole male populace was on the scene. "Hey! Turn around!" they yelled. I took another couple of steps away and then did so. They told me very plainly in English that they were going to throw me over the sea wall. They said the duck had been rescued by the boys of the island—their sons—after it had swum through an oil slick and almost drowned. Now, because of what I'd done, it really *was* about to drown, and when it went under, they would toss me over. This was not spoken in joking tones, and I could see the duck getting heavier in the water; its feathers, though as tidy to the eye as a healthy duck's feathers, had no buoyancy. Meanwhile, I'd fallen into something like what a prizefighter would call a clinch by refusing to acknowledge by any sign that I understood what was being said to me. It is a psychological necessity that when you punish somebody he understand the reason why. Even if he doesn't accept the guilty finding, you must explain to him why you are punishing him or you can't do it. So while they could scarcely contain their frustration, my face displayed bewilderment; I kept pretending to grope to understand. I was doing this instinctively, of course, and as their first impetus to violence passed, I found myself acting out with vehemence how I had seen the boy mistreat the duck. The men, who wanted at the least to take a poke at me, watched doubtfully, but there was a Coast Guardsman, an off-islander, who seemed to be arguing in Danish on my behalf. Another man went down to where the duck was swimming and reached out; the duck perceiving itself to be sinking, had moved cautiously closer to shore. And when the duck was saved I was saved; I only had the island's boys waiting for me in the embrasures of the wall.

Yet this quite comic misadventure, when every dread came real—I couldn't say a single word to save my life—was just as numbing as those ninety-five squat jumps at Fort Dix—only later was it terrifying. And in a way it makes up for the memories I have as a teenager of watching flocks of bats murdered with brooms and frogs tormented— moments when I didn't interfere, but giggled ruefully to keep my popularity and stifle my outcries.

Sociology progresses; the infant mortality rate among Negroes goes down. Nevertheless we know that if the announcement were made that there was going to be a public hanging in Central Park, Sheep Meadow would be crowded with spectators, like Tyburn mall. Sometimes at night my standing lamp shapes itself into an observant phantom figure which takes a position next to my bed. It doesn't threaten me directly, and I stretch out to clutch its throat with careful anger. My final grab bumps the lamp over. This electric phantom is a holdover from my vivid night demons when I was eight or ten. I never saw them outright, thank the Lord, but for years I fell asleep facing the wall to avoid beholding my destruction. I'd "whisper," as I called it, when I went to bed, telling myself an installment of a round-robin story, and when the installment was over I'd wait for the demons, until I fell asleep. Later, just as invariably, I faced the outer room so I could see them come and have warning to fight. Such archaisms in our minds are not an unmixed evil, however, because they link us to humanity and to our history as human beings. My wife says every man she's been familiar with would smell his socks at night before he went to bed: just a whiff—each sock, not only one. I do this too, although the smell has been of no intrinsic interest to me for twenty years. The smell of each sock checks precisely with the other one and smells as vital as pigs do. Maybe it reassures us that we're among the living still. We need to know. In the fifties I also liked the smell of air pollution. I didn't think of it as air pollution then— nobody did—but as the smell of industry and the highways I hitchhiked on, the big-shouldered America I loved.

In 1943 George Orwell said the problem of the times was the decay in the belief in personal immortality. Several French novelists had turned existentialist and several English novelists Catholic (possibly the same reaction), while he himself, like many of the more likable writers, had adopted a hardy humanist's masculine skepticism. Twenty-odd years later, the problem appears only to have grown more piercing, though it is not put into the same terms. You can't have as many people walking around as there are now and still simply see them as chips off the divine lodestone. Nor is the future *1984:* that's too succinct. At first the new nuclear bullying, the new technocracy, made mere survival more the point, because we wanted to be sure of surviving here on earth before we worried about heaven. Lately, instead the talk has been about overpopulation, and city people have started venturing to the outback, buying acreage with all the premonitory fervor of Noah sawing logs. Everyone wants space to breathe; the character of city life has drastically deteriorated, and there's no questioning the statistics, just as there used to be no questioning the odds that eventually a nuclear war was going to penetrate our precautions through that old fontanel of existence: human mix-up.

When we say that enough is enough, that we have enough people on hand now for any good purpose, we mean that the divine spark has become something of a conflagration, besides an embarrassment of riches. We're trying to make a start at sorting the riches, buying Edwardian clothes but also Volkswagens, and settling down to the process of zoning the little land there is. As we also begin to cogitate on how the quality of life can be improved, we may be in for a religious revival, too. It's a natural beginning, and faddism will probably swing that way, and after all, we *are* extraordinary—we're so extraordinary we're everywhere. Next to the new mysticisms, old-fashioned, run-of-the-mill religion is not so hard to swallow. The difficulty will be how we regard individual people, a question which involves not only whether we think we're immortal but whether we think they are. The crowded impatience of suburb-city living doesn't often evoke intimations of other people's immortality, and neither do the hodge-podge leveling procedures of a modern democracy. So much of the vigor of the Victorian church, for instance, grew out of the contrast between its members and the raw, destitute brown masses who covered the rest of the globe. Among an elite, self-congratulatory minority even the greatest of attributes—immortality—seemed plausible.

But maybe I'm being overly sour. We have wiped tigers off the earth and yet our children hear as much about the symbolism of tigers as children did in the old days. And next to the subway station I use there is a newsdealer who was blinded in Orwell's war, the Spanish War, in the mountains behind Motril. He wears the aura of a revolutionary volunteer. He dresses bulkily, as if for weather at the front, and rigs canvas around his hut as neatly as a soldier's tent. Not one of your meek blind men, he's on his feet most of the day, especially in tough weather, pacing, marching, standing tall. He's gray and grim, hard and spare, and doubtless lives surrounded by the companions that he had in the Sierra Nevada. But he's too bluff and energetic to be a museum piece. If you help him cross the street you get the rough edge of his tongue. He searches for the lamppost with his cane like a tennis player swinging backhand, and if he loses his bearings and bumps against something, he jerks abruptly back like a cavalier insulted, looking gaunt and fierce. I pity him, but I take note of him; he counts himself among the living. I buy a paper and go home to my newborn baby, who is as intense and focused (to my eye) as a flight of angels dancing on a pinhead.

I don't believe in a god you can pray to, but I do find I believe in God—I do more than I don't. I believe in glee and in the exuberance I feel with friends and animals and in the fields, and in other emotions besides that. Anyway, as we know, it really isn't necessary to see sparks of a grand divinity in someone else to feel with the old immediacy that he is kin; we can evolve a more sophisticated Golden Rule than that. We will be trying to refine and revivify the qualities of life, and the chief stumbling block is that we must somehow reduce the density of people in our own comings and goings without doing it as we do now, which is by simply not seeing them, by registering them as shadows to dodge by on the street. Without degenerating into callousness, we must develop our ability to switch on and off—something analogous to what we do already with body temperature in a harsh world. Generally we'd button up if we were out walking, but when the Breakstone cream-cheese truck ran over an old man, this would be a time when our ancient instinct for cherishing a stranger would spring to being.

I live in a high-rise apartment and keep a pair of field glasses next to the window to use whenever somebody emerges on one of the rooftops nearby. There are ten or fifteen regulars—old people hanging wash, high school kids who have come up into the open to talk where they can be alone. All of them are neighbors to me now, though on the street I probably would turn away from them—even the bathing beauties would not be beauties there. Admittedly I am a bit of a voyeur, as who isn't, but the population density on the rooftops seems about right. In fact, I roused myself not long ago to drive some robbers off a roof across the street by gesticulating sternly. They waved back as they went down the stairs like people who've escaped a fall.

20

Lines of Inquiry
"The Problem of the Golden Rule"

Hoagland reveals a number of surprising things about himself in this essay, including some that you might regard as unattractive or shocking. Why do you suppose that he makes these revelations? What kind of person do they make him seem to be? How did you react to these revelations? What bearing do you think they have upon his topic in this piece, namely "the problem of the golden rule"?

Hoagland says that the Golden Rule has disintegrated into the "silver rule" and then into no rule at all. What factors have caused this process according to Hoagland? Why is this disintegration less of a problem in Vermont than in New York? If such a moral decline is really taking place, how can Hoagland conclude this essay by talking about his "glee" and "exuberance"? What has he done to deal with the dehumanization he describes in the beginning?

Hoagland describes his astonishment when he realized "that people often would not do the smallest things to convenience another person or to make him feel easier for the moment." In the community where you live, are people indifferent to others, or are they more cooperative and humane? Why do you suppose they behave one way or another—what factors in the environment of your community encourage or discourage humane behavior? How would you rate your own behavior over the past few months—golden, silver, or worse? What factors have been influencing you on this score?

What I Think, What I Am

Our loneliness makes us avid column readers these days. The personalities in the San Francisco *Chronicle,* Chicago *Daily News,* New York *Post* constitute our neighbors now, some of them local characters but also the opinionated national stars. And movie reviewers thrive on our yearning for somebody emotional who is willing to pay attention to us and return week after week, year after year, through all the to-and-fro of other friends, to flatter us by pouring out his/her heart. They are essayists of a type, as Elizabeth Hardwick is, James Baldwin was.

We sometimes hear that essays are an old-fashioned form, that so-and-so is the "last essayist," but the facts of the marketplace argue quite otherwise. Essays of nearly any kind are so much easier than short stories for a writer to sell, so many more see print, it's strange that though two fine anthologies remain that publish the year's best stories, no comparable collection exists for essays. Such changes in the reading public's taste aren't always to the good, needless to say. The art of telling stories predated even cave painting, surely; and if we ever find ourselves living in caves again, it (with painting and drumming) will be the only art left, after movies, novels, photography, essays, biography, and all the rest have gone down the drain—the art to build from.

One has the sense with the short story as a form that while everything may have been done, nothing has been overdone; it has a permanence. Essays, if a comparison is to be made, although they go back four hundred years to Montaigne, seem a mercurial, newfangled, sometimes hokey affair that has lent itself to many of the excesses of the age, from spurious autobiography to spurious hallucination, as well as to the shabby careerism of traditional journalism. It's a greased pig. Essays are associated with the way young writers fashion a name—on plain, crowded newsprint in hybrid vehicles like the *Village Voice, Rolling Stone,* the *New York Review of Books,* instead of the thick paper stock and thin readership of *Partisan Review.*

Essays, however, hang somewhere on a line between two sturdy poles: this is what I think, and this is what I am. Autobiographies which aren't novels are generally extended essays, indeed. A personal essay is like the human voice talking, its order the mind's natural flow, instead of a systematized outline of ideas. Though more wayward or informal than an article or treatise, somewhere it contains a point which is its real center, even if the point couldn't be uttered in fewer words than the essayist has used. Essays don't usually boil down to a summary, as articles do, and the style of the writer has a "nap" to it, a combination of personality and originality and energetic loose ends that stand up like the nap on a piece of wool and can't be brushed flat. Essays belong to the animal kingdom, with a surface that generates sparks, like a coat of fur, compared with the flat, conventional cotton of the magazine article writer, who works in the vegetable kingdom, instead. But essays, on the other hand, may have fewer "levels" than fiction, because we are not supposed to argue much about their meaning. In the old distinction between teaching and storytelling, the essayist, however cleverly he camouflages his intentions, is a bit of a teacher or reformer, and an essay is intended to convey the same point to each of us.

This emphasis upon mind speaking to mind is what makes essays   5 less universal in their appeal than stories. They are addressed to an educated, perhaps a middle-class, reader, with certain presuppositions, a frame of reference, even a commitment to civility that is shared—not the grand and golden empathy inherent in every man or woman that a storyteller has a chance to tap.

Nevertheless, the artful "I" of an essay can be as chameleon as any narrator in fiction; and essays do tell a story quite as often as a short story stakes a claim to a particular viewpoint. Mark Twain's piece called "Corn-pone Opinions," for example, which is about public opinion, begins with a vignette as vivid as any in *Huckleberry Finn*. Twain says that when he was a boy of fifteen, he used to hang out a back window and listen to the sermons preached by a neighbor's slave standing on top of a woodpile: "He imitated the pulpit style of the several clergymen of the village, and did it well and with fine passion and energy. To me he was a wonder. I believed he was the greatest orator in the United States and would some day be heard from. But it did not happen; in the distribution of rewards he was overlooked. . . . He interrupted his preaching now and then to saw a stick of wood, but the sawing was a pretense—he did it with his mouth, exactly imitating the sound the bucksaw makes in shrieking its way through the wood. But it served its purpose, it kept his master from coming out to see how the work was getting along."

A novel would go on and tell us what happened next in the life of the slave—and we miss that. But the extraordinary flexibility of essays is what has enabled them to ride out rough weather and hybridize into forms that suit the times. And just as one of the first things a fiction writer learns is that he needn't actually be writing fiction to write a short story—that he can tell his own history or anybody else's as exactly as he remembers it and it will be "fiction" if it remains primarily a story—an essayist soon discovers that he doesn't have to tell the whole truth and nothing but the truth; he can shape or shave his memories, as long as the purpose is served of elucidating a truthful point. A personal essay frequently is not autobiographical at all, but what it does keep in common with autobiography is that, through its tone and tumbling progression, it conveys the quality of the author's mind. Nothing gets in the way. Because essays are directly concerned with the mind and the mind's idiosyncrasy, the very freedom the mind possesses is bestowed on this branch of literature that does honor to it, and the fascination of the mind is the fascination of the essay.

1976

Lines of Inquiry
"What I Think, What I Am"

Given Hoagland's attempt to define the essay in this piece, how well does he conform to his own definition? Does this essay about the the essay fit Hoagland's definition of the essay? Does it seem to be organized according to "the mind's natural flow," or is it "systematized" instead like an "outline of ideas"? Does it have "a combination of personality and originality and energetic loose ends that stand up like the nap on a piece of wool" or is it instead more nearly like "the flat conventional cotton of the magazine writer"?

Throughout this piece, Hoagland examines the essay in relation to the short story and the article. According to Hoagland, what qualities does the essay have in common with each of these kinds of writing? In what important respects does it differ from both fiction and the article? Why do you suppose that he puts so much emphasis on the character of the "I" in relating the essay to the article and the story? How is the "I" of the essay similar to and different from that of the story?

For another American essayist's view of the essay, look at E. B. White's "The Essayist and the Essay." In what respects do they seem to agree, in what respects do they seem to disagree, about the nature of the essay? About the purpose of the essay? About the form of the essay? About the role of the essayist? About the place of personality in the essay? Whose ideas seem most applicable to the essays you've recently been reading and writing?

Martin Luther King, Jr.
1929–68

In a world facing the revolt of ragged and hungry masses of God's children; in a world torn between the tensions of East and West, white and colored, individualists and collectivists; in a world whose cultural and spiritual power lags so far behind her technological capabilities that we live each day on the verge of nuclear co-annihilation; in this world, nonviolence is no longer an option for intellectual analysis, it is an imperative for action.

Martin Luther King's impassioned call for action in the form of nonviolent resistance to racial injustice was heard throughout America from the mid-fifties to his death in 1968. And it was heeded. Under his leadership, civil rights protesters marched, boycotted, staged sit-ins, faced police dogs and fire hoses, and won strategic victories in the struggle to achieve equal opportunity for black Americans. King always couched his urgent pleas for change in the framework of moral argument, and he stressed the interdependence of citizens throughout the world as well as the nation to explain the need for "helping to make this nation and this world a better place to live in—for *all* men, black and white alike."

King was born and raised in Atlanta, Georgia, where his father had raised himself out of poverty to become pastor of Ebenezer Baptist Church and one of the most respected leaders of Atlanta's middle-class black community. His mother was a gentle and genteel woman, the daughter of an influential Atlanta preacher who had been born a slave and had founded Ebenezer Baptist Church. So, King grew up in a comfortable and deeply religious home in which the church's presence always was felt. A precocious child who from an early age exhibited a love of books and language, according to one biographer he possessed "a remarkable vocabulary that dazzled teachers and peers alike" and "sailed through school, skipping grades as he went." King later said that his "greatest talent, strongest tradition, and most constant interest was the eloquent statement of ideas." He gave evidence of his eloquence and his budding social concerns in high school by winning an oratorical contest with a speech on "The Negro and the Constitution."

King entered Morehouse College in Atlanta in 1944, when he was only fifteen, and graduated four years later with a degree in sociology. At Morehouse he came under the influence of black intellectuals who introduced him to a world of new ideas that freed him, as he later said, of "the shackles of fundamentalism," showing him that the insights of sociology and religion were not at odds, but instead could cooperate to shape a commitment to social and spiritual activism for the improvement of his race. Inspired by this vision, he decided to enter the ministry, was ordained at seventeen, and became assistant pastor to his father at Ebenezer Baptist Church.

After graduating from Morehouse, King entered Crozer Seminary in Pennsylvania to study for a B.A. in divinity. Though he was a model student, earning As in all his courses, the conventional Crozer curriculum did not satisfy his quest for a definition of what the church's role might be as a force for social protest. So, he began to read widely in history and political philosophy, and thus encountered the thinking of Mahatma Ghandi, the Indian leader who had used nonviolent resistance and "soul force" to free his country from British colonialism. King was profoundly influenced by Ghandi as well as by Thoreau's "On Civil Disobedience," and from their ideas and examples he began to synthesize the commitment to "militant nonviolent resistance" that would become his major contribution to the civil rights movement.

From Crozer he went to Boston University to earn a PhD in philosophical theology. In Boston he met Coretta Scott, a fellow Southerner who was studying music at the Boston Conservatory, and they were married in 1953. As a doctoral student King continued to excel, and his passionate love for the intellectual life led him to decide on a career as a teacher and writer in the academic world. But he felt that he first needed to serve for a few years as an active minister. So in May 1954 he accepted the pastorate of the Dexter Avenue Baptist Church in Montgomery, Alabama, the "cradle of the Confederacy." It was a historic juncture, for within months of King's arrival in Montgomery, Rosa Parks was arrested for refusing to give up her seat on a city bus to a white man, and King found himself spearheading what proved to be a successful boycott of the city bus system to protest racist seating policies. Thus he was suddenly thrust into the forefront as a national leader in the civil rights movement.

In 1960, in order to devote more of his time to the movement, he resigned his pastorate in Montgomery and moved his family back to Atlanta, where he once again served as associate pastor at his father's church. Leading a social reform movement allowed King to exercise his extraordinary intelligence, his moral and personal force, and his charismatic powers of oratory. Yet in other ways King was an unlikely public figure, attracted as he was to the retiring life of the scholar and author. Indeed, he once called himself an "ambivert," a "cross between an extrovert and an introvert." Throughout his life, in fact, he somehow managed to balance his public commitments to preaching and social reforming with his personal interests in reading and writing about religion, philosophy, and social issues. Thus before his early death, he managed to produce two collections of his sermons, rewritten for publication, *The Strength to Love* (1963) and *The Trumpet.of Conscience* (1967), as well as three other books, *Stride Toward Freedom* (1958), *Why We Can't Wait* (1964), and *Where Do We Go From Here: Chaos or Community?* (1967), and a host of articles and essays that bear witness to the depth and breadth of King's social concerns. Indeed, they clearly reveal how his social concerns expanded from a desire for racial equality to a concern for the plight of the poor and disadvantaged of every color and beyond that to a concern for harmony and community throughout the world.

King is probably most well remembered, of course, for "I Have a Dream," his stirring speech which climaxed the massive civil rights march on Washington in March 1963. For in that speech, he gave powerful voice to the idea of America as being "essentially a dream, a dream as yet unfulfilled." His criticism, though, was inspired by a powerful faith in America's future, a profound optimism that the dream could and would become reality. So, when he received the Nobel Peace Prize in 1964, he declared that "I accept this award today with an abiding faith in America and an audacious faith in the future of mankind." By the late sixties, however, a new generation of black leaders was restless and impatient with King's moderate pacifist approach to social change. They called for "Black Power," for active resistance, and thus opposed King for being a "militant conservative." Though wearied by attacks from both white defenders of the status quo and black power advocates, King doggedly stood by his commitment to peaceful nonviolent resistance, insisting with even greater determination that violence would lead only to greater violence, that the only appropriate weapon is "fabricated of love."

The violence which had been repeatedly directed at King since the earliest days of his protest activities reached its peak when he was assassinated in April 1968, in Memphis, where he had gone to march in support of a strike by the city's sanitation workers. In 1977, he was posthumously awarded the Presidential Medal of Freedom for having "made our nation stronger because he made it better." In 1983, his birthday, January 15, was declared a national holiday, in honor of his tireless commitment to justice and peace. But perhaps the greatest tributes to King have come from the generation of younger blacks and other minorities who have been inspired by his example to act on their civil rights. As Alice Walker has written, "at the moment I saw his resistance I knew I would never be able to live in this country without resisting everything that sought to disinherit me."

An Experiment in Love: Nonviolent Resistance

From the beginning a basic philosophy guided the movement. This guiding principle has since been referred to variously as nonviolent resistance, noncooperation, and passive resistance. But in the first days of the protest none of these expressions was mentioned; the phrase most often heard was "Christian love." It was the Sermon on the Mount, rather than a doctrine of passive resistance, that initially inspired the Negroes of Montgomery to dignified social action. It was Jesus of Nazareth that stirred the Negroes to protest with the creative weapon of love.

As the days unfolded, however, the inspiration of Mahatma Gandhi began to exert its influence. I had come to see early that the Christian doctrine of love operating through the Gandhian method of nonviolence was one of the most potent weapons available to the Negro in his struggle for freedom. About a week after the protest started, a white woman who understood and sympathized with the Negroes' efforts wrote a letter to the editor of the *Montgomery Advertiser* comparing the bus protest with the Gandhian movement in India. Miss Juliette Morgan, sensitive and frail, did not long survive the rejection and condemnation of the white community, but long after she died in the summer of 1957 the name of Mahatma Gandhi was well known in Montgomery. People who had never heard of the little brown saint of India were now saying his name with an air of familiarity. Nonviolent resistance had emerged as the technique of the movement, while love stood as the regulating ideal. In other words, Christ furnished the spirit and motivation, while Gandhi furnished the method.

One of the glories of the Montgomery movement was that Baptists, Methodists, Lutherans, Presbyterians, Episcopalians, and others all came together with a willingness to transcend denominational lines. Although no Catholic priests were actively involved in the protest, many of their parishioners took part. All joined hands in the bond of Christian love. Thus the mass meetings accomplished on Monday and Thursday nights what the Christian Church had failed to accomplish on Sunday mornings.

In my weekly remarks as president of the resistance committee, I stressed that the use of violence in our struggle would be both impractical and immoral. To meet hate with retaliatory hate would do nothing but intensify the existence of evil in the universe. Hate begets hate; violence begets violence; toughness begets a greater toughness. We must meet the forces of hate with the power of love; we must meet physical force with soul force. Our aim must never be to defeat or humiliate the white man, but to win his friendship and understanding.

In a real sense, Montgomery's Negroes showed themselves willing to grapple with a new approach to the crisis in race relations. It is probably true that most of them did not believe in nonviolence as a philosophy of life, but because of their confidence in their leaders and because nonviolence was presented to them as a simple expression of Christianity in action, they were willing to use it as a technique. Admittedly, nonviolence in the truest sense is not a strategy that one uses simply because it is expedient at the moment; nonviolence is ultimately a way of life that men live by because of the sheer morality of its claim. But even granting this, the willingness to use nonviolence as a technique is a step forward. For he who goes this far is more likely to adopt nonviolence later as a way of life.

It must be emphasized that nonviolent resistance is not a method for cowards; it does resist. If one uses this method because he is afraid or merely because he lacks the instruments of violence, he is not truly nonviolent. This is why Gandhi often said that if cowardice is the only alternative to violence, it is better to fight. He made this statement conscious of the fact that there is always another alternative: no individual or group need submit to any wrong, nor need they use violence to right that wrong; there is the way of nonviolent resistance. This is ultimately the way of the strong man. It is not a method of stagnant passivity. The phrase "passive resistance" often gives the false impression that this is a sort of "do-nothing method" in which the resister quietly and passively accepts evil. But nothing is further from the truth. For while the nonviolent resister is passive in the sense that he is not physically aggressive toward his opponent, his mind and emotions are always active, constantly seeking to persuade his opponent that he is wrong. The method is passive physically but strongly active spiritually. It is not passive non-resistance to evil, it is active nonviolent resistance to evil.

A second basic fact that characterizes nonviolence is that it does not seek to defeat or humiliate the opponent, but to win his friendship and understanding. The nonviolent resister must often express his protest through noncooperation or boycotts, but he realizes that these are not ends in themselves; they are merely means to awaken a sense of moral shame in the opponent. The end is redemption and reconciliation. The aftermath of nonviolence is the creation of the beloved community, while the aftermath of violence is tragic bitterness.

A third characteristic of this method is that the attack is directed against forces of evil rather than against persons who happen to be doing the evil. It is evil that the nonviolent resister seeks to defeat, not the persons victimized by evil. If he is opposing racial injustice, the nonviolent resister has the vision to see that the basic tension is not between

5

races. As I like to say to the people in Montgomery: "The tension in this city is not between white people and Negro people. The tension is, at bottom, between justice and injustice, between the forces of light and the forces of darkness. And if there is a victory, it will be a victory not merely for fifty thousand Negroes, but a victory for justice and the forces of light. We are out to defeat injustice and not white persons who may be unjust."

A fourth point that characterizes nonviolent resistance is a willingness to accept suffering without retaliation, to accept blows from the opponent without striking back. "Rivers of blood may have to flow before we gain our freedom, but it must be our blood," Gandhi said to his countrymen. The nonviolent resister is willing to accept violence if necessary, but never to inflict it. He does not seek to dodge jail. If going to jail is necessary, he enters it "as a bridegroom enters the bride's chamber."

One may well ask: "What is the nonviolent resister's justification   10
for this ordeal to which he invites men, for this mass political application of the ancient doctrine of turning the other cheek?" The answer is found in the realization that unearned suffering is redemptive. Suffering, the nonviolent resister realizes, has tremendous educational and transforming possibilities. "Things of fundamental importance to people are not secured by reason alone, but have to be purchased with their suffering," said Gandhi. He continues: "Suffering is infinitely more powerful than the law of the jungle for converting the opponent and opening his ears which are otherwise shut to the voice of reason."

A fifth point concerning nonviolent resistance is that it avoids not only external physical violence but also internal violence of spirit. The nonviolent resister not only refuses to shoot his opponent but he also refuses to hate him. At the center of nonviolence stands the principle of love. The nonviolent resister would contend that in the struggle for human dignity, the oppressed people of the world must not succumb to the temptation of becoming bitter or indulging in hate campaigns. To retaliate in kind would do nothing but intensify the existence of hate in the universe. Along the way of life, someone must have sense enough and morality enough to cut off the chain of hate. This can only be done by projecting the ethic of love to the center of our lives.

In speaking of love at this point, we are not referring to some sentimental or affectionate emotion. It would be nonsense to urge men to love their oppressors in an affectionate sense. Love in this connection means understanding, redemptive good will. When we speak of loving those who oppose us, we refer to neither *eros* nor *philia;* we speak of a love which is expressed in the Greek word *agape. Agape* means understanding, redeeming good will for all men. It is an overflowing love which is purely spontaneous, unmotivated, groundless, and creative. It is not set in motion by any quality or function of its object. It is the love of God operating in the human heart.

Agape is disinterested love. It is a love in which the individual seeks not his own good, but the good of his neighbor (1 Cor. 10:24). *Agape* does not begin by discriminating between worthy and unworthy people, or any qualities people possess. It begins by loving others *for their sakes.* It is an entirely "neighbor-regarding concern for others," which discovers the neighbor in every man it meets. Therefore, *agape* makes no distinction between friends and enemy; it is directed toward both. If one loves an individual merely on account of his friendliness, he loves him for the sake of the benefits to be gained from the friendship, rather than for the friend's own sake. Consequently, the best way to assure oneself that love is disinterested is to have love for the enemy-neighbor from whom you can expect no good in return, but only hostility and persecution.

Another basic point about *agape* is that it springs from the *need* of the other person—his need for belonging to the best in the human family. The Samaritan who helped the Jew on the Jericho Road was "good" because he responded to the human need that he was presented with. God's love is eternal and fails not because man needs his love. Saint Paul assures us that the loving act of redemption was done "while we were yet sinners"—that is, at the point of our greatest need for love. Since the white man's personality is greatly distorted by segregation, and his soul is greatly scarred, he needs the love of the Negro. The Negro must love the white man, because the white man needs his love to remove his tensions, insecurities, and fears.

Agape is not a weak, passive love. It is love in action. *Agape* is love   15
seeking to preserve and create community. It is insistence on community even when one seeks to break it. *Agape* is a willingness to go to any length to restore community. It doesn't stop at the first mile, but it goes the second mile to restore community. It is a willingness to forgive, not seven times, but seventy times seven to restore community. The cross is the eternal expression of the length to which God will go in order to restore broken community. The resurrection is a symbol of God's triumph over all the forces that seek to block community. The Holy Spirit is the continuing community creating reality that moves through history. He who works against community is working against the whole of creation. Therefore, if I respond to hate with a reciprocal hate I do nothing but intensify the cleavage in broken community. I can only close the gap in broken community by meeting hate with love. If I meet hate with hate, I become depersonalized, because creation is so designed that my personality can only be fulfilled in the context of community. Booker T. Washington was right: "Let no man pull you so low as to make you hate him." When he pulls you that low he brings you to the point of defying creation, and thereby becoming depersonalized.

In the final analysis, *agape* means a recognition of the fact that all life is interrelated. All humanity is involved in a single process, and all men are brothers. To the degree that I harm my brother, no matter what he is doing to me, to that extent I am harming myself. For example, white men often refuse federal aid to education in order to avoid giving the Negro his rights; but because all men are brothers they cannot deny Negro children without harming their own. They end, all efforts to the contrary, by hurting themselves. Why is this? Because men are brothers. If you harm me, you harm yourself.

A sixth basic fact about nonviolent resistance is that it is based on the conviction that the universe is on the side of justice. Consequently, the believer in nonviolence has deep faith in the future. This faith is another reason why the nonviolent resister can accept suffering without retaliation. For he knows that in his struggle for justice he has cosmic companionship. It is true that there are devout believers in nonviolence who find it difficult to believe in a personal God. But even these persons believe in the existence of some creative force that works for universal wholeness. Whether we call it an unconscious process, an impersonal Brahman, or a Personal Being of matchless power and infinite love, there is a creative force in this universe that works to bring the disconnected aspects of reality into a harmonious whole.

Lines of Inquiry
"An Experiment in Love: Nonviolent Resistance"

In this piece, King is evidently concerned with both defining and justifying the practice of nonviolent resistance. Given this dual purpose, how do you account for the selection and organization of material that he discusses here? For example, why does he begin by telling how nonviolent resistance "emerged as the technique of the movement"? Why does he then take up his six points about nonviolent resistance in exactly the order that he follows? What would be the effect of rearranging, or even reversing, the order of the points? Why does he place his discussion of *agape* between his fifth and sixth points? Why doesn't he discuss this concept much earlier or later in the piece?

In his opening paragraph, King notes that the "guiding principle" of the civil rights movement has "been referred to variously as nonviolent resistance, noncooperation, and passive resistance," but subsequently he only refers to it as "nonviolent resistance"? Why does he evidently prefer to call it nonviolent resistance? Why does he not use the three terms interchangeably? Why does he define the concept of nonviolent resistance by reference not only to the Christian idea of love but also to the Greek idea of love known as *agape?*

In what respects does King's idea of nonviolent resistance change, in what respects does it remain the same, in his other civil rights pieces that appear in this collection? In what respects is King's idea of nonviolent resistance comparable to the idea of resistance that Bettelheim defends in "The Ignored Lesson of Anne Frank"? In what respects do their ideas differ?

Letter from
Birmingham Jail

April 16, 1963

My Dear Fellow Clergymen:

While confined here in the Birmingham city jail, I came across your recent statement calling my present activities "unwise and untimely." Seldom do I pause to answer criticism of my work and ideas. If I sought to answer all the criticisms that cross my desk, my secretaries would have little time for anything other than such correspondence in the course of the day, and I would have no time for constructive work. But since I feel that you are men of genuine good will and that your criticisms are sincerely set forth, I want to try to answer your statement in what I hope will be patient and reasonable terms.

I think I should indicate why I am here in Birmingham, since you have been influenced by the view which argues against "outsiders coming in." I have the honor of serving as president of the Southern Christian Leadership Conference, an organization operating in every southern state, with headquarters in Atlanta, Georgia. We have some eighty-five affiliated organizations across the South, and one of them is the Alabama Christian Movement for Human Rights. Frequently we share staff, educational and financial resources with our affiliates. Several months ago the affiliate here in Birmingham asked us to be on call to engage in a nonviolent direct-action program if such were deemed necessary. We readily consented, and when the hour came we lived up to our promise. So I, along with several members of my staff, am here because I was invited here. I am here because I have organizational ties here.

But more basically, I am in Birmingham because injustice is here. Just as the prophets of the eighth century B.C. left their villages and

---

AUTHOR'S NOTE: This response to a published statement by eight fellow clergymen from Alabama (Bishop C. C. J. Carpenter, Bishop Joseph A. Durick, Rabbi Hilton L. Grafman, Bishop Paul Hardin, Bishop Holan B. Harmon, the Reverend George M. Murray, the Reverend Edward V. Ramage and the Reverend Earl Stallings) was composed under somewhat constricting circumstances. Begun on the margins of the newspaper in which the statement appeared while I was in jail, the letter was continued on scraps of writing paper supplied by a friendly Negro trusty, and concluded on a pad my attorneys were eventually permitted to leave me. Although the text remains in substance unaltered, I have indulged in the author's prerogative of polishing it for publication.

carried their "thus saith the Lord" far beyond the boundaries of their home towns, and just as the Apostle Paul left his village of Tarsus and carried the gospel of Jesus Christ to the far corners of the Greco-Roman world, so am I compelled to carry the gospel of freedom beyond my own home town. Like Paul, I must constantly respond to the Macedonian call for aid.

Moreover, I am cognizant of the interrelatedness of all communities and states. I cannot sit idly by in Atlanta and not be concerned about what happens in Birmingham. Injustice anywhere is a threat to justice everywhere. We are caught in an inescapable network of mutuality, tied in a single garment of destiny. Whatever affects one directly, affects all indirectly. Never again can we afford to live with the narrow, provincial "outside agitator" idea. Anyone who lives inside the United States can never be considered an outsider anywhere within its bounds.

You deplore the demonstrations taking place in Birmingham. But your statement, I am sorry to say, fails to express a similar concern for the conditions that brought about the demonstrations. I am sure that none of you would want to rest content with the superficial kind of social analysis that deals merely with effects and does not grapple with underlying causes. It is unfortunate that demonstrations are taking place in Birmingham, but it is even more unfortunate that the city's white power structure left the Negro community with no alternative.

In any nonviolent campaign there are four basic steps: collection of the facts to determine whether injustices exist; negotiation; self-purification; and direct action. We have gone through all these steps in Birmingham. There can be no gainsaying the fact that racial injustice engulfs this community. Birmingham is probably the most thoroughly segregated city in the United States. Its ugly record of brutality is widely known. Negroes have experienced grossly unjust treatment in the courts. There have been more unsolved bombings of Negro homes and churches in Birmingham than in any other city in the nation. These are the hard brutal facts of the case. On the basis of these conditions, Negro leaders sought to negotiate with the city fathers. But the latter consistently refused to engage in good-faith negotiation.

Then, last September, came the opportunity to talk with leaders of Birmingham's economic community. In the course of the negotiations, certain promises were made by the merchants—for example, to remove the stores' humiliating racial signs. On the basis of these promises, the Reverend Fred Shuttlesworth and the leaders of the Alabama Christian Movement for Human Rights agreed to a moratorium on all demonstrations. As the weeks and months went by, we realized that we were the victims of a broken promise. A few signs, briefly removed, returned; the others remained.

As in so many past experiences, our hopes had been blasted, and the shadow of deep disappointment settled upon us. We had no alternative except to prepare for direct action, whereby we would present our very bodies as a means of laying our case before the conscience of the local and the national community. Mindful of the difficulties involved, we decided to undertake a process of self-purification. We began a series of workshops on nonviolence, and we repeatedly asked ourselves: "Are you able to accept blows without retaliating?" "Are you able to endure the ordeal of jail?" We decided to schedule our direct-action program for the Easter season, realizing that except for Christmas, this is the main shopping period of the year. Knowing that a strong economic-withdrawal program would be the by-product of direct action, we felt that this would be the best time to bring pressure to bear on the merchants for the needed change.

Then it occurred to us that Birmingham's mayoralty election was coming up in March, and we speedily decided to postpone action until after election day. When we discovered that the Commissioner of Public Safety, Eugene "Bull" Connor, had piled up enough votes to be in the run-off, we decided again to postpone action until the day after the run-off so that the demonstrations could not be used to cloud the issues. Like many others, we waited to see Mr. Connor defeated, and to this end we endured postponement after postponement. Having aided in this community need, we felt that our direct-action program could be delayed no longer.

You may well ask: "Why direct action? Why sit-ins, marches and   10
so forth? Isn't negotiation a better path?" You are quite right in calling for negotiation. Indeed, this is the very purpose of direct action. Nonviolent direct action seeks to create such a crisis and foster such a tension that a community which has constantly refused to negotiate is forced to confront the issue. It seeks so to dramatize the issue that it can no longer be ignored. My citing the creation of tension as part of the work of the nonviolent-resister may sound rather shocking. But I must confess that I am not afraid of the word "tension." I have earnestly opposed violent tension, but there is a type of constructive nonviolent tension which is necesssary for growth. Just as Socrates felt that it was necessary to create a tension in the mind so that individuals could rise from the bondage of myths and half-truths to the unfettered realm of creative analysis and objective appraisal, so must we see the need for nonviolent gadflies to create the kind of tension in society that will help men rise from the dark depths of prejudice and racism to the majestic heights of understanding and brotherhood.

The purpose of our direct-action program is to create a situation so crisis-packed that it will inevitably open the door to negotiation. I therefore concur with you in your call for negotiation. Too long has our beloved Southland been bogged down in a tragic effort to live in monologue rather than dialogue.

One of the basic points in your statement is that the action that I and my associates have taken in Birmingham is untimely. Some have asked: "Why didn't you give the new city administration time to act?"

The only answer that I can give to this query is that the new Birmingham administration must be prodded about as much as the outgoing one, before it will act. We are sadly mistaken if we feel that the election of Albert Boutwell as mayor will bring the millennium to Birmingham. While Mr. Boutwell is a much more gentle person than Mr. Connor, they are both segregationists, dedicated to maintenance of the status quo. I have hope that Mr. Boutwell will be reasonable enough to see the futility of massive resistance to desegregation. But he will not see this without pressure from devotees of civil rights. My friends, I must say to you that we have not made a single gain in civil rights without determined legal and nonviolent pressure. Lamentably, it is an historical fact that privileged groups seldom give up their privileges voluntarily. Individuals may see the moral light and voluntarily give up their unjust posture; but, as Reinhold Niebuhr has reminded us, groups tend to be more immoral than individuals.

We know through painful experience that freedom is never voluntarily given by the oppressor; it must be demanded by the oppressed. Frankly, I have yet to engage in a direct-action campaign that was "well timed" in the view of those who have not suffered unduly from the disease of segregation. For years now I have heard the word "Wait!" It rings in the ear of every Negro with piercing familiarity. This "Wait" has almost always meant "Never." We must come to see, with one of our distinguished jurists, that "justice too long delayed is justice denied."

We have waited for more than 340 years for our constitutional and Godgiven rights. The nations of Asia and Africa are moving with jet-like speed toward gaining political independence, but we still creep at horse-and-buggy pace toward gaining a cup of coffee at a lunch counter. Perhaps it is easy for those who have never felt the stinging darts of segregation to say, "Wait." But when you have seen vicious mobs lynch your mothers and fathers at will and drown your sisters and brothers at whim; when you have seen hate-filled policemen curse, kick and even kill your black brothers and sisters; when you see the vast majority of your twenty million Negro brothers smothering in an airtight cage of poverty in the midst of an affluent society; when you suddenly find your tongue twisted and your speech stammering as you seek to explain to your six-year-old daughter why she can't go to the public amusement park that has just been advertised on television, and see tears welling up in her eyes when she is told that Funtown is closed to colored children, and see ominous clouds of inferiority beginning to form in her little mental sky, and see her beginning to distort her personality by developing an unconscious bitterness toward white people; when you have to concoct an answer for a five-year-old son who is asking: "Daddy, why do white people treat colored people so mean?"; when you take a cross-country drive and find it necessary to sleep night after night in the uncomfortable corners of your automobile because no motel will accept you; when you are humiliated day in and day out by nagging signs reading "white" and "colored"; when your first name becomes "nigger," your middle name becomes "boy" (however old you are) and your last name becomes "John," and your wife and mother are never given the respected title "Mrs."; when you are harried by day and haunted by night by the fact that you are a Negro, living constantly at tiptoe stance, never quite knowing what to expect next, and are plagued with inner fears and outer resentments; when you are forever fighting a degenerating sense of "nobodiness"—then you will understand why we find it difficult to wait. There comes a time when the cup of endurance runs over, and men are no longer willing to be plunged into the abyss of despair. I hope, sirs, you can understand our legitimate and unavoidable impatience.

You express a great deal of anxiety over our willingness to break laws. This is certainly a legitimate concern. Since we so diligently urge people to obey the Supreme Court's decision of 1954 outlawing segregation in the public schools, at first glance it may seem rather paradoxical for us consciously to break laws. One may well ask: "How can you advocate breaking some laws and obeying others?" The answer lies in the fact that there are two types of laws: just and unjust. I would be the first to advocate obeying just laws. One has not only a legal but a moral responsibility to obey just laws. Conversely, one has a moral responsibility to disobey unjust laws. I would agree with St. Augustine that "an unjust law is no law at all."

Now, what is the difference between the two? How does one determine whether a law is just or unjust? A just law is a man-made code that squares with the moral law or the law of God. An unjust law is a code that is out of harmony with the moral law. To put it in the terms of St. Thomas Aquinas: An unjust law is a human law that is not rooted in eternal law and natural law. Any law that uplifts human personality is just. Any law that degrades human personality is unjust. All segregation statutes are unjust because segregation distorts the soul and damages the personality. It gives the segregator a false sense of superiority and the segregated a false sense of inferiority. Segregation, to use the terminology of the Jewish philosopher Martin Buber, substitutes an "I-it" relationship for an "I-thou" relationship and ends up relegating persons to the status of things. Hence segregation is not only politically, economically and sociologically unsound, it is morally wrong and sinful. Paul Tillich has said that sin is separation. Is not segregation an existential expression of man's tragic separation, his awful estrangement, his terrible sinfulness? Thus it is that I can urge men to obey the 1954 decision of the Supreme Court, for it is morally right; and I can urge them to disobey segregation ordinances, for they are morally wrong.

Let us consider a more concrete example of just and unjust laws. An unjust law is a code that a numerical or power majority group compels a minority group to obey but does not make binding on itself. This is *difference* made legal. By the same token, a just law is a code that a majority compels a minority to follow and that it is willing to follow itself. This is *sameness* made legal.

Let me give another explanation. A law is unjust if it is inflicted on a minority that, as a result of being denied the right to vote, had no part in enacting or devising the law. Who can say that the legislature of Alabama which set up that state's segregation laws was democratically elected? Throughout Alabama all sorts of devious methods are used to prevent Negroes from becoming registered voters, and there are some counties in which even though Negroes constitute a majority of the population, not a single Negro is registered. Can any law enacted under such circumstances be considered democratically structured?

Sometimes a law is just on its face and unjust in its application. For instance, I have been arrested on a charge of parading without a permit. Now, there is nothing wrong in having an ordinance which requires a permit for a parade. But such an ordinance becomes unjust when it is used to maintain segregation and to deny citizens the First-Amendment privilege of peaceful assembly and protest.

I hope you are able to see the distinction I am trying to point out. 20
In no sense do I advocate evading or defying the law, as would the rabid segregationist. That would lead to anarchy. One who breaks an unjust law must do so openly, lovingly, and with a willingness to accept the penalty. I submit that an individual who breaks a law that conscience tells him is unjust, and who willingly accepts the penalty of imprisonment in order to arouse the conscience of the community over its injustice, is in reality expressing the highest respect for law.

Of course, there is nothing new about this kind of civil disobedience. It was evidenced sublimely in the refusal of Shadrach, Meshach and Abednego to obey the laws of Nebuchadnezzar, on the ground that a higher moral law was at stake. It was practiced superbly by the early Christians, who were willing to face hungry lions and the excruciating pain of chopping blocks rather than submit to certain unjust laws of the Roman Empire. To a degree, academic freedom is a reality today because Socrates practiced civil disobedience. In our own nation, the Boston Tea Party represented a massive act of civil disobedience.

We should never forget that everything Adolf Hitler did in Germany was "legal" and everything the Hungarian freedom fighters did in Hungary was "illegal." It was "illegal" to aid and comfort a Jew in Hitler's Germany. Even so, I am sure that, had I lived in Germany at the time, I would have aided and comforted my Jewish brothers. If today I lived in a Communist country where certain principles dear to the Christian faith are suppressed, I would openly advocate disobeying that country's anti-religious laws.

I must make two honest confessions to you, my Christian and Jewish brothers. First, I must confess that over the past few years I have been gravely disappointed with the white moderate. I have almost reached the regrettable conclusion that the Negro's great stumbling block in his stride toward freedom is not the White Citizen's Counciler or the Ku Klux Klanner, but the white moderate, who is more devoted to "order" than to justice; who prefers a negative peace which is the absence of tension to a positive peace which is the presence of justice; who constantly says: "I agree with you in the goal you seek, but I cannot agree with your methods of direct action"; who paternalistically believes he can set the timetable for another man's freedom; who lives by a mythical concept of time and who constantly advises the Negro to wait for a "more convenient season." Shallow understanding from people of good will is more frustrating than absolute misunderstanding from people of ill will. Lukewarm acceptance is much more bewildering than outright rejection.

I had hoped that the white moderate would understand that law and order exist for the purpose of establishing justice and that when they fail in this purpose they become the dangerously structured dams that block the flow of social progress. I had hoped that the white moderate would understand that the present tension in the South is a necessary phase of the transition from an obnoxious negative peace, in which the Negro passively accepted his unjust plight, to a substantive and positive peace, in which all men will respect the dignity and worth of human personality. Actually, we who engage in nonviolent direct action are not the creators of tension. We merely bring to the surface the hidden tension that is already alive. We bring it out in the open, where it can be seen and dealt with. Like a boil that can never be cured so long as it is covered up but must be opened with all its ugliness to the natural medicines of air and light, injustice must be exposed, with all the tension its exposure creates, to the light of human conscience and the air of national opinion before it can be cured.

In your statement you assert that our actions, even though peaceful, must be condemned because they precipitate violence. But is this a logical assertion? Isn't this like condemning a robbed man because his possession of money precipitated the evil act of robbery? Isn't this like condemning Socrates because his unswerving commitment to truth and his philosophical inquiries precipitated the act by the misguided populace in which they made him drink hemlock? Isn't this like condemning Jesus because his unique God-consciousness and never-ceasing devotion to God's will precipitated the evil act of crucifixion? We must come to see that, as the federal courts have consistently affirmed, it is wrong to urge an individual to cease his efforts to gain his basic constitutional rights because the quest may precipitate violence. Society must protect the robbed and punish the robber.

I had also hoped that the white moderate would reject the myth concerning time in relation to the struggle for freedom. I have just received a letter from a white brother in Texas. He writes: "All Christians know that the colored people will receive equal rights eventually, but it is possible that you are in too great a religious hurry. It has taken Christianity almost two thousand years to accomplish what it has. The teachings of Christ take time to come to earth." Such an attitude stems from a tragic misconception of time, from the strangely irrational notion that there is something in the very flow of time that will inevitably cure all ills. Actually, time itself is neutral; it can be used either destructively or constructively. More and more I feel that the people of ill will have used time much more effectively than have the people of good will. We will have to repent in this generation not merely for the hateful words and actions of the bad people but for the appalling silence of the good people. Human progress never rolls in on wheels of inevitability; it comes through the tireless efforts of men willing to be co-workers with God, and without this hard work, time itself becomes an ally of the forces of social stagnation. We must use time creatively, in the knowledge that the time is always ripe to do right. Now is the time to make real the promise of democracy and transform our pending national elegy into a creative psalm of brotherhood. Now is the time to lift our national policy from the quicksand of racial injustice to the solid rock of human dignity.

You speak of our activity in Birmingham as extreme. At first I was rather disappointed that fellow clergymen would see my nonviolent efforts as those of an extremist. I began thinking about the fact that I stand in the middle of two opposing forces in the Negro community. One is a force of complacency, made up in part of Negroes who, as a result of long years of oppression, are so drained of self-respect and a sense of "somebodiness" that they have adjusted to segregation; and in part of a few middle-class Negroes who, because of a degree of academic and economic security and because in some ways they profit by segregation, have become insensitive to the problems of the masses. The other force is one of bitterness and hatred, and it comes perilously close to advocating violence. It is expressed in the various black nationalist groups that are springing up across the nation, the largest and best-known being Elijah Muhammad's Muslim movement. Nourished by the Negro's frustration over the continued existence of racial discrimination, this movement is made up of people who have lost faith in America, who have absolutely repudiated Christianity, and who have concluded that the white man is an incorrigible "devil."

I have tried to stand between these two forces, saying that we need emulate neither the "do-nothingism" of the complacent nor the hatred and despair of the black nationalist. For there is the more excellent way of love and nonviolent protest. I am grateful to God that, through the influence of the Negro church, the way of nonviolence became an integral part of our struggle.

If this philosophy had not emerged, by now many streets of the South would, I am convinced, be flowing with blood. And I am further convinced that if our white brothers dismiss as "rabble-rousers" and "outside agitators" those of us who employ nonviolent direct action, and if they refuse to support our non-violent efforts, millions of Negroes will, out of frustration and despair, seek solace and security in black-nationalist ideologies—a development that would inevitably lead to a frightening racial nightmare.

Oppressed people cannot remain oppressed forever. The yearning for freedom eventually manifests itself, and that is what has happened to the American Negro. Something within has reminded him of his birthright of freedom, and something without has reminded him that it can be gained. Consciously or unconsciously, he has been caught up by the *Zeitgeist,* and with his black brothers of Africa and his brown and yellow brothers of Asia, South America and the Caribbean, the United States Negro is moving with a sense of great urgency toward the promised land of racial justice. If one recognizes this vital urge that has engulfed the Negro community, one should readily understand why public demonstrations are taking place. The Negro has many pent-up resentments and latent frustrations, and he must release them. So let him march; let him make prayer pilgrimages to the city hall; let him go on freedom rides—and try to understand why he must do so. If his repressed emotions are not released in nonviolent ways, they will seek expression through violence; this is not a threat but a fact of history. So I have not said to my people: "Get rid of your discontent." Rather, I have tried to say that this normal and healthy discontent can be channeled into the creative outlet of nonviolent direct action. And now this approach is being termed extremist.

But though I was initially disappointed at being categorized as an extremist, as I continued to think about the matter I gradually gained a measure of satisfaction from the label. Was not Jesus an extremist for love: "Love your enemies, bless them that curse you, do good to them that hate you, and pray for them which despitefully use you, and persecute you." Was not Amos an extremist for justice: "Let justice roll down like waters and righteousness like an ever-flowing stream." Was not Paul an extremist for the Christian gospel: "I bear in my body the marks of the Lord Jesus." Was not Martin Luther an extremist: "Here I stand; I cannot do otherwise, so help me God." And John Bunyan: "I will stay in jail to the end of my days before I make a butchery of my conscience." And Abraham Lincoln: "This nation cannot survive half slave and half free." And Thomas Jefferson: "We hold these truths to be self-evident, that all men are created equal. . . ." So the question is not whether we will be extremists, but what kind of extremists we will be. Will we be extremists for hate or for love? Will we be extremists for the preservation of injustice or for the extension of justice? In that dramatic scene on Calvary's hill three men were crucified. We must never forget that all three were crucified for the same crime—the crime of extremism. Two were extremists for immorality, and thus fell below their environment. The other, Jesus Christ, was an extremist for love, truth and goodness, and thereby rose above his environment. Perhaps the South, the nation and the world are in dire need of creative extremists.

I had hoped that the white moderate would see this need. Perhaps I was too optimistic; perhaps I expected too much. I suppose I should have realized that few members of the oppressor race can understand the deep groans and passionate yearnings of the oppressed race, and still fewer have the vision to see that injustice must be rooted out by strong, persistent and determined action. I am thankful, however, that some of our white brothers in the South have grasped the meaning of this social revolution and committed themselves to it. They are still all too few in quantity, but they are big in quality. Some—such as Ralph McGill, Lillian Smith, Harry Golden, James McBride Dabbs, Ann Braden and Sarah Patton Boyle—have written about our struggle in eloquent and prophetic terms. Others have marched with us down nameless streets of the South. They have languished in filthy, roach-infested jails, suffering the abuse and brutality of policemen who view them as "dirty nigger-lovers." Unlike so many of their moderate brothers and sisters, they have recognized the urgency of the moment and sensed the need for powerful "action" antidotes to combat the disease of segregation.

Let me take note of my other major disappointment. I have been so greatly disappointed with the white church and its leadership. Of course, there are some notable exceptions. I am not unmindful of the fact that each of you has taken some significant stands on this issue. I commend you, Reverend Stallings, for your Christian stand on this past Sunday, in welcoming Negroes to your worship service on a nonsegregated basis. I commend the Catholic leaders of this state for integrating Spring Hill College several years ago.

But despite these notable exceptions, I must honestly reiterate that I have been disappointed with the church. I do not say this as one of those negative critics who can always find something wrong with the church. I say this as a minister of the gospel, who loves the church; who was nurtured in its bosom; who has been sustained by its spiritual blessings and who will remain true to it as long as the cord of life shall lengthen.

When I was suddenly catapulted into the leadership of the bus protest in Montgomery, Alabama, a few years ago, I felt we would be supported by the white church. I felt that the white ministers, priests and rabbis of the South would be among our strongest allies. Instead, some have been outright opponents, refusing to understand the freedom movement and misrepresenting its leaders; all too many others have been more cautious than courageous and have remained silent behind the anesthetizing security of stained-glass windows.

In spite of my shattered dreams, I came to Birmingham with the hope that the white religious leadership of this community would see the justice of our cause and, with deep moral concern, would serve as the channel through which our just grievances could reach the power structure. I had hoped that each of you would understand. But again I have been disappointed.

I have heard numerous southern religious leaders admonish their worshipers to comply with a desegregation decision because it is the law, but I have longed to hear white ministers declare: "Follow this decree because integration is morally right and because the Negro is your brother." In the midst of blatant injustices inflicted upon the Negro, I have watched white churchmen stand on the sideline and mouth pious irrelevancies and sanctimonious trivialities. In the midst of a mighty struggle to rid our nation of racial and economic injustice, I have heard many ministers say: "Those are social issues, with which the gospel has no real concern." And I have watched many churches commit themselves to a completely other-worldly religion which makes a strange, un-Biblical distinction between body and soul, between the sacred and the secular.

I have traveled the length and breadth of Alabama, Mississippi and all the other southern states. On sweltering summer days and crisp autumn mornings I have looked at the South's beautiful churches with their lofty spires pointing heavenward. I have beheld the impressive outlines of her massive religious-education buildings. Over and over I have found myself asking: "What kind of people worship here? Who is their God? Where were their voices when the lips of Governor Barnett dripped with words of interposition and nullification? Where were they when Governor Wallace gave a clarion call for defiance and hatred? Where were their voices of support when bruised and weary Negro men and women decided to rise from the dark dungeons of complacency to the bright hills of creative protest?"

Yes, these questions are still in my mind. In deep disappointment I have wept over the laxity of the church. But be assured that my tears have been tears of love. There can be no deep disappointment where there is not deep love. Yes, I love the church. How could I do otherwise? I am in the rather unique position of being the son, the grandson and the great-grandson of preachers. Yes, I see the church as the body of Christ. But, oh! How we have blemished and scarred that body through social neglect and through fear of being nonconformists.

There was a time when the church was very powerful—in the time 40 when the early Christians rejoiced at being deemed worthy to suffer for what they believed. In those days the church was not merely a thermometer that recorded the ideas and principles of popular opinion; it was a thermostat that transformed the mores of society. Whenever the early Christians entered a town, the people in power became disturbed and immediately sought to convict the Christians for being "disturbers of the peace" and "outside agitators." But the Christians pressed on, in the conviction that they were "a colony of heaven," called to obey God rather than man. Small in number, they were big in commitment. They were too God-intoxicated to be "astronomically intimidated." By their effort and example they brought an end to such ancient evils as infanticide and gladiatorial contests.

Things are different now. So often the contemporary church is a weak, ineffectual voice with an uncertain sound. So often it is an arch-defender of the status quo. Far from being disturbed by the presence of the church, the power structure of the average community is consoled by the church's silent—and often even vocal—sanction of things as they are.

But the judgment of God is upon the church as never before. If today's church does not recapture the sacrificial spirit of the early church, it will lose its authenticity, forfeit the loyalty of millions, and be dismissed as an irrelevant social club with no meaning for the twentieth century. Every day I meet young people whose disappointment with the church has turned into outright disgust.

Perhaps I have once again been too optimistic. Is organized religion too inextricably bound to the status quo to save our nation and the world? Perhaps I must turn my faith to the inner spiritual church, the church within the church, as the true *ekklesia* and the hope of the world. But again I am thankful to God that some noble souls from the ranks of organized religion have broken loose from the paralyzing chains of conformity and joined us as active partners in the struggle for freedom. They have left their secure congregations and walked the streets of Albany, Georgia, with us. They have gone down the highways of the South on tortuous rides for freedom. Yes, they have gone to jail with us. Some have been dismissed from their churches, have lost the support of their bishops and fellow ministers. But they have acted in the faith that right defeated is stronger than evil triumphant. Their witness has been the spiritual salt that has preserved the true meaning of the gospel in these troubled times. They have carved a tunnel of hope through the dark mountain of disappointment.

I hope the church as a whole will meet the challenge of this decisive hour. But even if the church does not come to the aid of justice, I have no despair about the future. I have no fear about the outcome of our struggle in Birmingham, even if our motives are at present misunderstood. We will reach the goal of freedom in Birmingham and all over the nation, because the goal of America is freedom. Abused and scorned though we may be, our destiny is tied up with America's destiny. Before the pilgrims landed at Plymouth, we were here. Before the pen of

Jefferson etched the majestic words of the Declaration of Independence across the pages of history, we were here. For more than two centuries our forebears labored in this country without wages; they made cotton king; they built the homes of their masters while suffering gross injustice and shameful humiliation—and yet out of a bottomless vitality they continued to thrive and develop. If the inexpressible cruelties of slavery could not stop us, the opposition we now face will surely fail. We will win our freedom because the sacred heritage of our nation and the eternal will of God are embodied in our echoing demands.

Before closing I feel impelled to mention one other point in your statement that has troubled me profoundly. You warmly commended the Birmingham police force for keeping "order" and "preventing violence." I doubt that you would have so warmly commended the police force if you had seen its dogs sinking their teeth into unarmed, nonviolent Negroes. I doubt that you would so quickly commend the policemen if you were to observe their ugly and inhumane treatment of Negroes here in the city jail; if you were to watch them push and curse old Negro women and young Negro girls; if you were to see them slap and kick old Negro men and young boys; if you were to observe them as they did on two occasions, refuse to give us food because we wanted to sing our grace together. I cannot join you in your praise of the Birmingham police department.

It is true that the police have exercised a degree of discipline in handling the demonstrators. In this sense they have conducted themselves rather "nonviolently" in public. But for what purpose? To preserve the evil system of segregation. Over the past few years I have consistently preached that nonviolence demands that the means we use must be as pure as the ends we seek. I have tried to make clear that it is wrong to use immoral means to attain moral ends. But now I must affirm that it is just as wrong, or perhaps even more so, to use moral means to preserve immoral ends. Perhaps Mr. Connor and his policemen have been rather nonviolent in public, as was Chief Pritchett in Albany, Georgia, but they have used the moral means of nonviolence to maintain the immoral end of racial injustice. As T. S. Eliot has said: "The last temptation is the greatest treason: To do the right deed for the wrong reason."

I wish you had commended the Negro sit-inners and demonstrators of Birmingham for their sublime courage, their willingness to suffer and their amazing discipline in the midst of great provocation. One day the South will recognize its real heroes. They will be the James Merediths, with the noble sense of purpose that enables them to face jeering and hostile mobs, and with the agonizing loneliness that characterizes the life of the pioneer. They will be old, oppressed, battered Negro women, symbolized in a seventy-two-year-old woman in Montgomery, Alabama, who rose up with a sense of dignity and with her people decided not to ride segregated buses, and who responded with ungrammatical profundity to one who inquired about her weariness: "My feet is tired, but my soul is at rest." They will be the young high school and college students, the young ministers of the gospel and a host of their elders, courageously and nonviolently sitting in at lunch counters and willingly going to jail for conscience's sake. One day the South will know that when these disinherited children of God sat down at lunch counters, they were in reality standing up for what is best in the American dream and for the most sacred values in our Judaeo-Christian heritage, thereby bringing our nation back to those great wells of democracy which were dug by the founding fathers in their formulation of the Constitution and the Declaration of Independence.

Never before have I written so long a letter. I'm afraid it is much too long to take your precious time. I can assure you that it would have been much shorter if I had been writing from a comfortable desk, but what else can one do when he is alone in a narrow jail cell, other than write long letters, think long thoughts and pray long prayers?

If I have said anything in this letter that overstates the truth and indicates an unreasonable impatience, I beg you to forgive me. If I have said anything that understates the truth and indicates my having a patience that allows me to settle for anything less than brotherhood, I beg God to forgive me.

I hope this letter finds you strong in the faith. I also hope that circumstances will soon make it possible for me to meet each of you, not as an integrationist or a civil-rights leader but as a fellow clergyman and a Christian brother. Let us all hope that the dark clouds of racial prejudice will soon pass away and the deep fog of misunderstanding will be lifted from our fear-drenched communities, and in some not too distant tomorrow the radiant stars of love and brotherhood will shine over our great nation with all their scintillating beauty.

50

Yours for the cause of Peace and Brotherhood,
Martin Luther King, Jr.

Lines of Inquiry
"Letter from Birmingham Jail"

As King indicates in his Author's Note on the first page, this letter was written in "response to a published statement by eight fellow clergymen from Alabama" who had objected to the civil rights protest that King was then leading in Birmingham, Alabama. Identify the various kinds of arguments, evidence, appeals, and assumptions that he uses to answer each of their objections. In what respects do you suppose his varied supporting material was meant to appeal to the eight clergyman? In what respects does it seem to be intended for the worldwide audience that was then closely following King's activities? In what respect does it seem to be occasioned by the substance of each controversial issue?

How do you account for the order in which King takes up the clergymen's objections? Why does he begin by answering their arguments against "outsiders coming in," then move on to their arguments against public demonstrations, then to their arguments against the timing of the protests, then to their arguments against the legality of the protests, then to their arguments against the extremity of the protests? Why does he then devote most of the remainder of his letter to an extended attack on "the white church and its leadership"? What do you consider to be the major source—the essence—of his "disappointment" with the white church?

In "Civil Disobedience," Thoreau offers a lengthy defense of the protest he made against the racial prejudice of his own time. What common issues do King and Thoreau address in their self-defense? What similar arguments do they offer in their defense? In what respects are their arguments most notably different, and how do you account for the differences?

I Have a Dream

I am happy to join with you today in what will go down in history as the greatest demonstration for freedom in the history of our nation.

Five score years ago, a great American, in whose symbolic shadow we stand today, signed the Emancipation Proclamation. This momentous decree came as a great beacon light of hope to millions of Negro slaves who had been seared in the flames of withering injustice. It came as a joyous daybreak to end the long night of their captivity.

But one hundred years later, the Negro still is not free; one hundred years later, the life of the Negro is still sadly crippled by the manacles of segregation and the chains of discrimination; one hundred years later, the Negro lives on a lonely island of poverty in the midst of a vast ocean of material prosperity; one hundred years later, the Negro is still languished in the corners of American society and finds himself in exile in his own land.

So we've come here today to dramatize a shameful condition. In a sense we've come to our nation's capital to cash a check. When the architects of our republic wrote the magnificent words of the Constitution and the Declaration of Independence, they were signing a promissory note to which every American was to fall heir. This note was the promise that all men, yes, black men as well as white men, would be guaranteed the unalienable rights of life, liberty, and the pursuit of happiness.

It is obvious today that America has defaulted on this promissory note in so far as her citizens of color are concerned. Instead of honoring this sacred obligation, America has given the Negro people a bad check, a check which has come back marked "insufficient funds." But we refuse to believe that the bank of justice is bankrupt. We refuse to believe that there are insufficient funds in the great vaults of opportunity of this nation. And so we've come to cash this check, a check that will give us upon demand the riches of freedom and the security of justice.

We have also come to this hallowed spot to remind America of the fierce urgency of now. This is no time to engage in the luxury of cooling off or to take the tranquilizing drug of gradualism. Now is the time to make real the promises of democracy; now is the time to rise from the dark and desolate valley of segregation to the sunlit path of racial justice; now is the time to lift our nation from the quicksands of racial injustice to the solid rock of brotherhood; now is the time to make justice a reality for all of God's children. It would be fatal for the nation to overlook the urgency of the moment. This sweltering summer of the Negro's legitimate discontent will not pass until there is an invigo-rating autumn of freedom and equality.

Nineteen sixty-three is not an end, but a beginning. And those who hope that the Negro needed to blow off steam and will now be content, will have a rude awakening if the nation returns to business as usual. There will be neither rest nor tranquility in America until the Negro is granted his citizenship rights. The whirlwinds of revolt will continue to shake the foundations of our nation until the bright day of jus-tice emerges.

But there is something that I must say to my people, who stand on the worn threshold which leads into the palace of justice. In the process of gaining our rightful place, we must not be guilty of wrongful deeds. Let us not seek to satisfy our thirst for freedom by drinking from the cup of bitterness and hatred. We must forever conduct our struggle on the high plain of dignity and discipline. We must not allow our creative protests to degenerate into physical violence. Again and again we must rise to the majestic heights of meeting physical force with soul force. The marvelous new militancy, which has engulfed the Negro commu-nity, must not lead us to a distrust of all white people. For many of our white brothers, as evidenced by their presence here today, have come to realize that their destiny is tied up with our destiny. And they have come to realize that their freedom is inextricably bound to our freedom. We cannot walk alone. And as we walk, we must make the pledge that we shall always march ahead. We cannot turn back.

There are those who are asking the devotees of Civil Rights, "When will you be satisfied?" We can never be satisfied as long as the Negro is the victim of the unspeakable horrors of police brutality; we can never be satisfied as long as our bodies, heavy with the fatigue of travel, can-not gain lodging in the motels of the highways and the hotels of the cities; we cannot be satisfied as long as the Negro's basic mobility is from a smaller ghetto to a larger one; we can never be satisfied as long as our children are stripped of their selfhood and robbed of their dignity by signs stating "For Whites Only"; we cannot be satisfied as long as the Negro in Mississippi cannot vote and a Negro in New York be-lieves he has nothing for which to vote. No! No, we are not satisfied, and we will not be satisfied until "justice rolls down like waters and righteousness like a mighty stream."

I am not unmindful that some of you have come here out of great   10 trials and tribulations. Some of you have come fresh from narrow jail cells. Some of you have come from areas where your quest for freedom left you battered by the storms of persecution and staggered by the winds of police brutality. You have been the veterans of creative suf-fering. Continue to work with the faith that unearned suffering is re-demptive. Go back to Mississippi. Go back to Alabama. Go back to South Carolina. Go back to Georgia. Go back to Louisiana. Go back to the slums and ghettos of our Northern cities, knowing that somehow this situation can and will be changed. Let us not wallow in the valley of despair.

I say to you today, my friends, so even though we face the difficulties of today and tomorrow, I still have a dream. It is a dream deeply rooted in the American dream. I have a dream that one day this nation will rise up and live out the true meaning of its creed, "We hold these truths to be self-evident, that all men are created equal." I have a dream that one day on the red hills of Georgia, sons of former slaves and the sons of former slave owners will be able to sit down together at the table of brotherhood. I have a dream that one day even the state of Mississippi, a state sweltering with the heat of injustice, sweltering with the heat of oppression, will be transformed into an oasis of freedom and justice. I have a dream that my four little children will one day live in a nation where they will not be judged by the color of their skin, but by the content of their character.

I HAVE A DREAM TODAY!

I have a dream that one day down in Alabama—with its vicious racists, with its Governor having his lips dripping with the words of interposition and nullification—one day right there in Alabama, little black boys and black girls will be able to join hands with little white boys and white girls as sisters and brothers.

I HAVE A DREAM TODAY!

I have a dream that one day every valley shall be exalted, and every hill and mountain shall be made low. The rough places will be plain and the crooked places will be made straight, "and the glory of the Lord shall be revealed, and all flesh shall see it together."

15

This is our hope. This is the faith that I go back to the South with. With this faith we will be able to hew out of the mountain of despair a stone of hope. With this faith we will be able to transform the jangling discords of our nation into a beautiful symphony of brotherhood. With this faith we will be able to work together, to pray together, to struggle together, to go to jail together, to stand up for freedom together, knowing that we will be free one day. And this will be the day. This will be the day when all of God's children will be able to sing with new meaning, "My country 'tis of thee, sweet land of liberty, of thee I sing. Land where my father died, land of the pilgrim's pride, from every mountainside, let freedom ring." And if America is to be a great nation, this must become true.

So let freedom ring from the prodigious hilltops of New Hampshire; let freedom ring from the mighty mountains of New York; let freedom ring from the heightening Alleghenies of Pennsylvania; let freedom ring from the snow-capped Rockies of Colorado; let freedom ring from the curvaceous slopes of California. But not only that. Let freedom ring from Stone Mountain of Georgia; let freedom ring from

Lookout Mountain of Tennessee; let freedom ring from every hill and mole hill of Mississippi. "From every mountainside, let freedom ring."

And when this happens, and when we allow freedom to ring, when we let it ring from every village and every hamlet, from every state and every city, we will be able to speed up that day when all of God's children, black men and white men, Jews and Gentiles, Protestants and Catholics, will be able to join hands and sing in the words of the old Negro spiritual: "Free at last. Free at last. Thank God Almighty, we are free at last."

Lines of Inquiry
"I Have a Dream"

King relies heavily in this piece on a stylistic device known as *anaphora,* which involves the repetition of a word or group of words at the beginning of two or more successive clauses or sentences. Make a note of all the words that he chooses to repeat in this way. What do you suppose accounts for each such instance of anaphora? What do you suppose accounts for the relative length of each case of anaphora? Be sure to read the piece aloud to get an understanding of how it would have sounded to a listening audience and how the sound of it would have been determined by King's use of anaphora.

King also relies heavily on analogies, metaphors, and other figures of speech, as when he compares the Constitution and Declaration of Independence to "a promissory note to which every American was to fall heir." Make a note of all the figures of speech that you can find in this piece. Why does King rely so heavily on these figures? Why does he develop some of these figures at length, such as the "promissory note" and the "bad check" metaphors, whereas others, such as "to rise from the dark and desolate valley of segregation to the sunlit path of racial justice," are mentioned only once?

What is the essence of King's dream as he defines it in this piece? Judging from King's "Black Power" essay (1967), how far did he think he had come at that point in achieving his dream? Judging from Walker's "The Civil Rights Movement" (1967), how far did she think he had come at that point in achieving his dream? Judging from the current state of affairs in the United States, how close is the nation to achieving King's dream?

Black Power

"**J**ames Meredith has been shot!"

It was about three o'clock in the afternoon on a Monday in June, 1966, and I was presiding over the regular staff meeting of the Southern Christian Leadership Conference in our Atlanta headquarters. When we heard that Meredith had been shot in the back only a day after he had begun his Freedom March through Mississippi, there was a momentary hush of anger and dismay throughout the room. Our horror was compounded by the fact that the early reports announced that Meredith was dead. Soon the silence was broken, and from every corner of the room came expressions of outrage. The business of the meeting was forgotten in the shock of this latest evidence that a Negro's life is still worthless in many parts of his own country.

When order was finally restored, our executive staff immediately agreed that the march must continue. After all, we reasoned, Meredith had begun his lonely journey as a pilgrimage against fear. Wouldn't failure to continue only intensify the fears of the oppressed and deprived Negroes of Mississippi? Would this not be a setback for the whole civil rights movement and a blow to nonviolent discipline?

After several calls between Atlanta and Memphis, we learned that the earlier reports of Meredith's death were false and that he would recover. This news brought relief, but it did not alter our feeling that the civil rights movement had a moral obligation to continue along the path that Meredith had begun.

The next morning I was off to Memphis along with several members of my staff. Floyd McKissick, national director of CORE, flew in from New York and joined us on the flight from Atlanta to Memphis. After landing we went directly to the Municipal Hospital to visit Meredith. We were happy to find him resting well. After expressing our sympathy and gratitude for his courageous witness, Floyd and I shared our conviction with him that the march should continue in order to demonstrate to the nation and the world that Negroes would never again be intimidated by the terror of the extremist white violence. Realizing that Meredith was often a loner and that he probably wanted to continue the march without a large group, we felt that it would take a great deal of persuasion to convince him that the issue involved the whole civil rights movement. Fortunately, he soon saw this and agreed that we should continue without him. We spent some time discussing the character and logistics of the march, and agreed that we would consult with him daily on every decision.

5

As we prepared to leave, the nurse came to the door and said, "Mr. Meredith, there is a Mr. Carmichael in the lobby who would like to see you and Dr. King. Should I give him permission to come in?" Meredith consented. Stokely Carmichael entered with his associate, Cleveland Sellers, and immediately reached out for Meredith's hand. He expressed his concern and admiration and brought messages of sympathy from his colleagues in the Student Nonviolent Coordinating Committee. After a brief conversation we all agreed that James should get some rest and that we should not burden him with any additional talk. We left the room assuring him that we would conduct the march in his spirit and would seek as never before to expose the ugly racism that pervaded Mississippi and to arouse a new sense of dignity and manhood in every Negro who inhabited that bastion of man's inhumanity to man.

In a brief conference Floyd, Stokely and I agreed that the march would be jointly sponsored by CORE, SNCC and SCLC, with the understanding that all other civil rights organizations would be invited to join. It was also agreed that we would issue a national call for support and participation.

One hour later, after making staff assignments and setting up headquarters at the Rev. James Lawson's church in Memphis, a group of us packed into four automobiles and made our way to that desolate spot on Highway 51 where James Meredith had been shot the day before. So began the second stage of the Meredith Mississippi Freedom March.

As we walked down the meandering highway in the sweltering heat, there was much talk and many questions were raised.

"I'm not for that nonviolence stuff any more," shouted one of the younger activists. 10

"If one of these damn white Mississippi crackers touches me, I'm gonna knock the hell out of him," shouted another.

Later on a discussion of the composition of the march came up.

"This should be an all-black march," said one marcher. "We don't need any more white phonies and liberals invading our movement. This is our march."

Once during the afternoon we stopped to sing "We Shall Overcome." The voices rang out with all the traditional fervor, the glad thunder and gentle strength that had always characterized the singing of this noble song. But when we came to the stanza which speaks of "black and white together," the voices of a few of the marchers were muted. I asked them later why they refused to sing that verse. The retort was:

"This is a new day, we don't sing those words any more. In fact, 15 the whole song should be discarded. Not 'We Shall Overcome,' but 'We Shall Overrun.' "

As I listened to all these comments, the words fell on my ears like strange music from a foreign land. My hearing was not attuned to the sound of such bitterness. I guess I should not have been surprised. I should have known that in an atmosphere where false promises are daily realities, where deferred dreams are nightly facts, where acts of unpunished violence toward Negroes are a way of life, nonviolence would eventually be seriously questioned. I should have been reminded that disappointment produces despair and despair produces bitterness, and that the one thing certain about bitterness is its blindness. Bitterness has not the capacity to make the distinction between some and *all*. When some members of the dominant group, particularly those in power, are racist in attitude and practice, bitterness accuses the whole group.

At the end of the march that first day we all went back to Memphis and spent the night in a Negro motel, since we had not yet secured the tents that would serve as shelter each of the following nights on our journey. The discussion continued at the motel. I decided that I would plead patiently with my brothers to remain true to the time-honored principles of our movement. I began with a plea for nonviolence. This immediately aroused some of our friends from the Deacons for Defense, who contended that self-defense was essential and that therefore nonviolence should not be a prerequisite for participation in the march. They were joined in this view by some of the activists from CORE and SNCC.

I tried to make it clear that besides opposing violence on principle, I could imagine nothing more impractical and disastrous than for any of us, through misguided judgment, to precipitate a violent confrontation in Mississippi. We had neither the resources nor the techniques to win. Furthermore, I asserted, many Mississippi whites, from the government on down, would enjoy nothing more than for us to turn to violence in order to use this as an excuse to wipe out scores of Negroes in and out of the march. Finally, I contended that the debate over the question of self-defense was unnecessary since few people suggested that Negroes should not defend themselves as individuals when attacked. The question was not whether one should use his gun when his home was attacked, but whether it was tactically wise to use a gun while participating in an organized demonstration. If they lowered the banner of nonviolence, I said, Mississippi injustice would not be exposed and the moral issues would be obscured.

Next the question of the participation of whites was raised. Stokely Carmichael contended that the inclusion of whites in the march should be de-emphasized and that the dominant appeal should be for black participation. Others in the room agreed. As I listened to Stokely, I thought about the years that we had worked together in communities all across the South, and how joyously we had then welcomed and accepted our white allies in the movement. What accounted for this reversal in Stokely's philosophy?

I surmised that much of the change had its psychological roots in 20
the experience of SNCC in Mississippi during the summer of 1964,
when a large number of northern white students had come down to
help in that racially torn state. What the SNCC workers saw was the
most articulate, powerful and self-assured young white people coming
to work with the poorest of the Negro people—and simply overwhelming them. That summer Stokely and others in SNCC had probably unconsciously concluded that this was no good for Negroes, for it
simply increased their sense of their own inadequacies. Of course, the
answer to this dilemma was not to give up, not to conclude that blacks
must work with blacks in order for Negroes to gain a sense of their
own meaning. The answer was only to be found in persistent trying,
perpetual experimentation, persevering togetherness.

Like life, racial understanding is not something that we find but
something that we must create. What we find when we enter these
mortal plains is existence; but existence is the raw material out of which
all life must be created. A productive and happy life is not something
that you find; it is something that you make. And so the ability of
Negroes and whites to work together, to understand each other, will
not be found ready made; it must be created by the fact of contact.

Along these lines, I implored everyone in the room to see the morality of making the march completely interracial. Consciences must be
enlisted in our movement, I said, not merely racial groups. I reminded
them of the dedicated whites who had suffered, bled and died in the
cause of racial justice, and suggested that to reject white participation now would be a shameful repudiation of all for which they
had sacrificed.

Finally, I said that the formidable foe we now faced demanded more
unity than ever before and that I would stretch every point to maintain
this unity, but that I could not in good conscience agree to continue
my personal involvement and that of SCLC in the march if it were not
publicly affirmed that it was based on nonviolence and the participation
of both black and white. After a few more minutes of discussion Floyd
and Stokely agreed that we could unite around these principles as far
as the march was concerned. The next morning we had a joint press
conference affirming that the march was nonviolent and that whites
were welcomed.

As the days progressed, debates and discussions continued, but they
were usually pushed to the background by the onrush of enthusiasm
engendered by the large crowds that turned out to greet us in every
town. We had been marching for about ten days when we passed through
Grenada on the way to Greenwood. Stokely did not conceal his growing eagerness to reach Greenwood. This was SNCC territory, in the
sense that the organization had worked courageously there during that
turbulent summer of 1964.

As we approached the city, large crowds of old friends and new   25
turned out to welcome us. At a huge mass meeting that night, which
was held in a city park, Stokely mounted the platform and after arousing the audience with a powerful attack on Mississippi justice, he proclaimed: "What we need is black power." Willie Ricks, the fiery orator
of SNCC, leaped to the platform and shouted, "What do you want?"
The crowd roared, "Black Power." Again and again Ricks cried, "What
do you want?" and the response "Black Power" grew louder and louder,
until it had reached fever pitch.

So Greenwood turned out to be the arena for the birth of the Black
Power slogan in the civil rights movement. The phrase had been used
long before by Richard Wright and others, but never until that night
had it been used as a slogan in the civil rights movement. For people
who had been crushed so long by white power and who had been taught
that black was degrading, it had a ready appeal.

Immediately, however, I had reservations about its use. I had the
deep feeling that it was an unfortunate choice of words for a slogan.
Moreover, I saw it bringing about division within the ranks of the
marchers. For a day or two there was fierce competition between those
who were wedded to the Black Power slogan and those wedded to
Freedom Now. Speakers on each side sought desperately to get the
crowds to chant their slogan the loudest.

Sensing this widening split in our ranks, I asked Stokely and Floyd
to join me in a frank discussion of the problem. We met the next morning, along with members of each of our staffs, in a small Catholic parish house in Yazoo City. For five long hours I pleaded with the group
to abandon the Black Power slogan. It was my contention that a leader
has to be concerned about the problem of semantics. Each word, I said,
has a denotative meaning—its explicit and recognized sense—and a con-
notative meaning—its suggestive sense. While the concept of legitimate
Black Power might be denotatively sound, the slogan "Black Power"
carried the wrong connotations. I mentioned the implication of violence
that the press had already attached to the phrase. And I went on to say
that some of the rash statements on the part of a few marchers only
reinforced this impression.

Stokely replied by saying that the question of violence versus nonviolence was irrelevant. The real question was the need for black people
to consolidate their political and economic resources to achieve power.
"Power," he said, "is the only thing respected in this world, and we
must get it at any cost." Then he looked me squarely in the eye and
said, "Martin, you know as well as I do that practically every other
ethnic group in America has done just this. The Jews, the Irish and the
Italians did it, why can't we?"

"That is just the point," I answered. "No one has ever heard the   30
Jews publicly chant a slogan of Jewish power, but they have power.

Through group unity, determination and creative endeavor, they have gained it. The same thing is true of the Irish and Italians. Neither group has used a slogan of Irish or Italian power, but they have worked hard to achieve it. This is exactly what we must do," I said. "We must use every constructive means to amass economic and political power. This is the kind of legitimate power we need. We must work to build racial pride and refute the notion that black is evil and ugly. But this must come through a program, not merely through a slogan."

Stokely and Floyd insisted that the slogan itself was important. "How can you arouse people to unite around a program without a slogan as a rallying cry? Didn't the labor movement have slogans? Haven't we had slogans all along in the freedom movement? What we need is a new slogan with 'black' in it."

I conceded the fact that we must have slogans. But why have one that would confuse our allies, isolate the Negro community and give many prejudiced whites, who might otherwise be ashamed of their anti-Negro feeling, a ready excuse for self-justification?

"Why not use the slogan 'black consciousness' or 'black equality'?" I suggested. "These phrases would be less vulnerable and would more accurately describe what we are about. The words 'black' and 'power' together give the impression that we are talking about black domination rather than black equality."

Stokely responded that neither would have the ready appeal and persuasive force of Black Power. Throughout the lengthy discussion, Stokely and Floyd remained adamant, and Stokely concluded by saying, with candor, "Martin, I deliberately decided to raise this issue on the march in order to give it a national forum, and force you to take a stand for Black Power."

I laughed. "I have been used before," I said to Stokely. "One more time won't hurt." 35

The meeting ended with the SCLC staff members still agreeing with me that the slogan was unfortunate and would only divert attention for the evils of Mississippi, while most CORE and SNCC staff members joined Stokely and Floyd in insisting that it should be projected nationally. In a final attempt to maintain unity I suggested that we compromise by not chanting either "Black Power" or "Freedom Now" for the rest of the march. In this way neither the people nor the press would be confused by the apparent conflict, and staff members would not appear to be at loggerheads. They all agreed with this compromise.

But while the chant died out, the press kept the debate going. News stories now centered, not on the injustices of Mississippi, but on the apparent ideological division in the civil rights movement. Every revolutionary movement has its peaks of united activity and its valleys of debate and internal confusion. This debate might well have been little more than a healthy internal difference of opinion, but the press loves the sensational and it could not allow the issue to remain within the private domain of the movement. In every drama there has to be an antagonist and a protagonist, and if the antagonist is not there the press will find and build one.

II

So Black Power is now a part of the nomenclature of the national community. To some it is abhorrent, to others dynamic; to some it is repugnant, to others exhilarating; to some it is destructive; to others it is useful. Since Black Power means different things to different people and indeed, being essentially an emotional concept, can mean different things to the same person on differing occasions, it is impossible to attribute its ultimate meaning to any single individual or organization. One must look beyond personal styles, verbal flourishes and the hysteria of the mass media to assess its values, its assets and liabilities honestly.

First, it is necessary to understand that Black Power is a cry of disappointment. The Black Power slogan did not spring full grown from the head of some philosophical Zeus. It was born from the wounds of despair and disappointment. It is a cry of daily hurt and persistent pain. For centuries the Negro has been caught in the tentacles of white power. Many Negroes have given up faith in the white majority because "white power" with total control has left them empty-handed. So in reality the call for Black Power is a reaction to the failure of white power.

It is no accident that the birth of this slogan in the civil rights movement took place in Mississippi—the state symbolizing the most blatant abuse of white power. In Mississippi the murder of civil rights workers is still a popular pastime. In that state more than forty Negroes and whites have either been lynched or murdered over the last three years, and not a single man has been punished for these crimes. More than fifty Negro churches have been burned or bombed in Mississippi in the last two years, yet the bombers still walk the streets surrounded by the halo of adoration.[1] This is white power in its most brutal, cold-blooded and vicious form.

Many of the young people proclaiming Black Power today were but yesterday the devotees of black-white cooperation and nonviolent direct action. With great sacrifice and dedication and a radiant faith in the future they labored courageously in the rural areas of the South; with idealism they accepted blows without retaliating; with dignity they allowed themselves to be plunged into filthy, stinking jail cells; with a majestic scorn for risk and danger they nonviolently confronted the Jim

[1] Southern Regional Council, 1966.

Clarks and the Bull Connors of the South, and exposed the disease of racism in the body politic. If they are America's angry children today, this anger is not congenital. It is a response to the feeling that a real solution is hopelessly distant because of the inconsistencies, resistance and faintheartedness of those in power. If Stokely Carmichael now says that nonviolence is irrelevant, it is because he, as a dedicated veteran of many battles, has seen with his own eyes the most brutal white violence against Negroes and white civil rights workers, and he has seen it go unpunished.

Their frustration is further fed by the fact that even when blacks and whites die together in the cause of justice, the death of the white person gets more attention and concern than the death of the black person. Stokely and his colleagues from SNCC were with us in Alabama when Jimmy Lee Jackson, a brave young Negro man, was killed and when James Reeb, a committed Unitarian white minister, was fatally clubbed to the ground. They remembered how President Johnson sent flowers to the gallant Mrs. Reeb, and in his eloquent "We Shall Overcome" speech paused to mention that one person, James Reeb, had already died in the struggle. Somehow the president forgot to mention Jimmy, who died first. The parents and sister of Jimmy received no flowers from the president. The students felt this keenly. Not that they felt that the death of James Reeb was less than tragic, but because they felt that the failure to mention Jimmy Jackson only reinforced the impression that to white America the life of a Negro is insignificant and meaningless.

There is also great disappointment with the federal government and its timidity in implementing the civil rights laws on its statute books. The gap between promise and fulfillment is distressingly wide. Millions of Negroes are frustrated and angered because extravagant promises made little more than a year ago are a mockery today. When the 1965 Voting Rights Law was signed, it was proclaimed as the dawn of freedom and the open door to opportunity. What was minimally required under the law was the appointment of hundreds of registrars and thousands of federal marshals to inhibit southern terror. Instead, fewer than sixty registrars were appointed and not a single federal law officer capable of making arrests was sent into the South. As a consequence the old way of life—economic coercion, terrorism, murder and inhuman contempt—has continued unabated. This gulf between the laws and their enforcement is one of the basic reasons why Black Power advocates express contempt for the legislative process.

The disappointment mounts as they turn their eyes to the North. In the northern ghettos, unemployment, housing discrimination and slum schools mock the Negro who tries to hope. There have been accomplishments and some material gain, but these beginnings have revealed how far we have yet to go. The economic plight of the masses of

Negroes has worsened. The gap between the wages of the Negro worker and those of the white worker has widened. Slums are worse and Negroes attend more thoroughly segregated schools today than in 1954.

The Black Power advocates are disenchanted with the inconsistencies in the militaristic posture of our government. Over the last decade they have seen America applauding nonviolence whenever the Negroes have practiced it. They have watched it being praised in the sit-in movements of 1960, in the freedom rides of 1961, in the Albany movement of 1962, in the Birmingham movement of 1963 and in the Selma movement of 1965. But then these same black young men and women have watched as America sends black young men to burn Vietnamese with napalm, to slaughter men, women and children; and they wonder what kind of nation it is that applauds nonviolence whenever Negroes face white people in the streets of the United States but then applauds violence and burning and death when these same Negroes are sent to the fields of Vietnam.

All of this represents disappointment lifted to astronomical proportions. It is disappointment with timid white moderates who feel that they can set the timetable for the Negro's freedom. It is disappointment with a federal administration that seems to be more concerned about winning an ill-considered war in Vietnam than about winning the war against poverty here at home. It is disappointment with white legislators who pass laws in behalf of Negro rights that they never intended to implement. It is disappointment with the Christian church that appears to be more white than Christian, and with many white clergymen who prefer to remain silent behind the security of stained-glass windows. It is disappointment with some Negro clergymen who are more concerned about the size of the wheel base on their automobiles than about the quality of their service to the Negro community. It is disappointment with the Negro middle class that has sailed or struggled out of the muddy ponds into the relatively fresh-flowing waters of the mainstream, and in the process has forgotten the stench of the back-waters where their brothers are still drowning.

Second, Black Power, in its broad and positive meaning, is a call to black people to amass the political and economic strength to achieve their legitimate goals. No one can deny that the Negro is in dire need of this kind of legitimate power. Indeed, one of the great problems that the Negro confronts is his lack of power. From the old plantations of the South to the newer ghettos of the North, the Negro has been confined to a life of voicelessness and powerlessness. Stripped of the right to make decisions concerning his life and destiny, he has been subject to the authoritarian and sometimes whimsical decisions of the white power structure. The plantation and the ghetto were created by those who had power both to confine those who had no power and to perpetuate their powerlessness. The problem of transforming the ghetto is, therefore, a problem of power—a confrontation between the forces of power demanding change and the forces of power dedicated to preserving the status quo.

Power, properly understood, is the ability to achieve purpose. It is the strength required to bring about social, political or economic changes. In this sense power is not only desirable but necessary in order to implement the demands of love and justice. One of the greatest problems of history is that the concepts of love and power are usually contrasted as polar opposites. Love is identified with a resignation of power and power with a denial of love. It was this misinterpretation that caused Nietzsche, the philosopher of the "will to power," to reject the Christian concept of love. It was this same misinterpretation which induced Christian theologians to reject Nietzsche's philosophy of the "will to power" in the name of the Christian idea of love. What is needed is a realization that power without love is reckless and abusive and that love without power is sentimental and anemic. Power at its best is love implementing the demands of justice. Justice at its best is love correcting everything that stands against love.

There is nothing essentially wrong with power. The problem is that in America power is unequally distributed. This has led Negro Americans in the past to seek their goals through love and moral suasion devoid of power and white Americans to seek their goals through power devoid of love and conscience. It is leading a few extremists today to advocate for Negroes the same destructive and conscienceless power that they have justly abhorred in whites. It is precisely this collision of immoral power with powerless morality which constitutes the major crisis of our times.

In his struggle for racial justice, the Negro must seek to transform his condition of powerlessness into creative and positive power. One of the most obvious sources of this power is political. In *Why We Can't Wait*[2] I wrote at length of the need for Negroes to unite for political action in order to compel the majority to listen. I urged the development of political awareness and strength in the Negro community, the election of blacks to key positions, and the use of the bloc vote to liberalize the political climate and achieve our just aspirations for freedom and human dignity. To the extent that Black Power advocates these goals, it is a positive and legitimate call to action that we in the civil rights movement have sought to follow all along and which we must intensify in the future.

Black Power is also a call for the pooling of black financial resources to achieve economic security. While the ultimate answer to the

[2]Harper, 1964, pp. 162ff.

Negroes' economic dilemma will be found in a massive federal program for all the poor along the lines of A. Philip Randolph's Freedom Budget, a kind of Marshall Plan for the disadvantaged, there is something that the Negro himself can do to throw off the shackles of poverty. Although the Negro is still at the bottom of the economic ladder, his collective annual income is upwards of $30 billion. This gives him a considerable buying power that can make the difference between profit and loss in many businesses.

Through the pooling of such resources and the development of habits of thrift and techniques of wise investment, the Negro will be doing his share to grapple with his problem of economic deprivation. If Black Power means the development of this kind of strength within the Negro community, then it is a quest for basic, necessary, legitimate power.

Finally, Black Power is a psychological call to manhood. For years the Negro has been taught that he is nobody, that his color is a sign of his biological depravity, that his being has been stamped with an indelible imprint of inferiority, that his whole history has been soiled with the filth of worthlessness. All too few people realize how slavery and racial segregation have scarred the soul and wounded the spirit of the black man. The whole dirty business of slavery was based on the premise that the Negro was a thing to be used, not a person to be respected.

The historian Kenneth Stampp, in his remarkable book *The Peculiar Institution*[3], has a fascinating section on the psychological indoctrination that was necessary from the master's viewpoint to make a good slave. He gathered the material for this section primarily from the manuals and other documents which were produced by slaveowners on the subject of training slaves. Stampp notes five recurring aspects of this training.

First, those who managed the slaves had to maintain strict discipline. One master said, "Unconditional submission is the only footing upon which slavery should be placed." Another said, "The slave must know that his master is to govern absolutely and he is to obey implicitly, that he is never, for a moment, to exercise either his will or judgment in opposition to a positive order." Second, the masters felt that they had to implant in the bondsman a consciousness of personal inferiority. This sense of inferiority was deliberately extended to his past. The slaveowners were convinced that in order to control the Negroes, the slaves "had to feel that African ancestry tainted them, that their color was a badge of degradation." The third step in the training process was to awe the slaves with a sense of the masters' enormous power. It was necessary, various owners said, "to make them stand in fear."   55

---

[3] Knopf, 1956.

The fourth aspect was the attempt to "persuade the bondsman to take an interest in the master's enterprise and to accept his standards of good conduct." Thus the master's criteria of what was good and true and beautiful were to be accepted unquestioningly by the slaves. The final step, according to Stampp's documents, was "to impress Negroes with their helplessness: to create in them a habit of perfect dependence upon their masters."

Here, then, was the way to produce a perfect slave. Accustom him to rigid discipline, demand from him unconditional submission, impress upon him a sense of his innate inferiority, develop in him a paralyzing fear of white men, train him to adopt the master's code of good behavior, and instill in him a sense of complete dependence.

Out of the soil of slavery came the psychological roots of the Black Power cry. Anyone familiar with the Black Power movement recognizes that defiance of white authority and white power is a constant theme; the defiance almost becomes a kind of taunt. Underneath it, however, there is a legitimate concern that the Negro break away from "unconditional submission" and thereby assert his own selfhood.

Another obvious reaction of Black Power to the American system of slavery is the determination to glory in blackness and to resurrect joyously the African past. In response to the emphasis on their masters' "enormous power," Black Power advocates contend that the Negro must develop his own sense of strength. No longer are "fear, awe and obedience" to rule. This accounts for, though it does not justify, some Black Power advocates who encourage contempt and even uncivil disobedience as alternatives to the old patterns of slavery. Black Power assumes that Negroes will be slaves unless there is a new power to counter the force of the men who are still determined to be masters rather than brothers.

It is in the context of the slave tradition that some of the ideologues of the Black Power movement call for the need to develop new and indigenous codes of justice for the ghettos, so that blacks may move entirely away from their former masters' "standards of good conduct." Those in the Black Power movement who contend that blacks should cut themselves off from every level of dependence upon whites for advice, money or other help are obviously reacting against the slave pattern of "perfect dependence" upon the masters.

Black Power is a psychological reaction to the psychological indoctrination that led to the creation of the perfect slave. While this reaction has often led to negative and unrealistic responses and has frequently brought about intemperate words and actions, one must not overlook the positive value in calling the Negro to a new sense of manhood, to a deep feeling of racial pride and to an audacious appreciation of his heritage. The Negro must be grasped by a new realization of his dignity and worth. He must stand up amid a system that still oppresses him and develop an unassailable and majestic sense of his own value. He must no longer be ashamed of being black.

The job of arousing manhood within a people that have been taught for so many centuries that they are nobody is not easy. Even semantics have conspired to make that which is black seem ugly and degrading. In Roget's Thesaurus there are some 120 synonyms for "blackness" and at least sixty of them are offensive—such words as "blot," "soot," "grime," "devil," and "foul." There are 134 synonyms for "whiteness," and all are favorable, expressed in such words as "purity," "cleanliness," "chastity," and "innocence." A white lie is better than a black lie. The most degenerate member of a family is the "black sheep," not the "white sheep." Ossie Davis has suggested that maybe the English language should be "reconstructed" so that teachers will not be forced to teach the Negro child sixty ways to despise himself and thereby perpetuate his false sense of inferiority and the white child 134 ways to adore himself and thereby perpetuate his false sense of superiority.

The history books, which have almost completely ignored the contribution of the Negro in American history, have only served to intensify the Negroes' sense of worthlessness and to augment the anachronistic doctrine of white supremacy. All too many Negroes and whites are unaware of the fact that the first American to shed blood in the revolution which freed this country from British oppression was a black seaman named Crispus Attucks. Negroes and whites are almost totally oblivious of the fact that it was a Negro physician, Dr. Daniel Hale Williams, who performed the first successful operation on the heart in America, and that another Negro physician, Dr. Charles Drew, was largely responsible for developing the method of separating blood plasma and storing it on a large scale, a process that saved thousands of lives in World War II and has made possible many of the important advances in postwar medicine. History books have virtually overlooked the many Negro scientists and inventors who have encircled American life. Although a few refer to George Washington Carver, whose research in agricultural products helped to revive the economy of the South when the throne of King Cotton began to totter, they ignore the contribution of Norbert Rillieux, whose invention of an evaporating pan revolutionized the process of sugar refining. How many people know that the multimillion-dollar United Shoe Machinery Company developed from the shoe-lasting machine invented in the last century by a Negro from Dutch Guiana, Jan Matzeliger; or that Granville T. Woods, an expert in electric motors, whose many patents speeded the growth and improvement of the railroads at the beginning of this century, was a Negro?

Even the Negroes' contribution to the music of America is sometimes overlooked in astonishing ways. Two years ago my oldest son and daughter entered an integrated school in Atlanta. A few months later my wife and I were invited to attend a program entitled "music that has made America great." As the evening unfolded, we listened to the folk songs and melodies of the various immigrant groups. We were certain that the program would end with the most original of all American music, the Negro spiritual. But we were mistaken. Instead, all the students, including our children, ended the program by singing "Dixie."

As we rose to leave the hall, my wife and I looked at each other with a combination of indignation and amazement. All the students, black and white, all the parents present that night, and all the faculty members had been victimized by just another expression of America's penchant for ignoring the Negro, making him invisible and making his contributions insignificant. I wept within that night. I wept for my children and all black children who have been denied a knowledge of their heritage; I wept for all white children, who, through daily miseducation, are taught that the Negro is an irrelevant entity in American society; I wept for all the white parents and teachers who are forced to overlook the fact that the wealth of cultural and technological progress in America is a result of the commonwealth of inpouring contributions.

The tendency to ignore the Negro's contribution to American life 65 and strip him of his personhood is as old as the earliest history books and as contemporary as the morning's newspaper. To offset this cultural homicide, the Negro must rise up with an affirmation of his own Olympian manhood. Any movement for the Negro's freedom that overlooks this necessity is only waiting to be buried. As long as the mind is enslaved the body can never be free. Psychological freedom, a firm sense of self-esteem, is the most powerful weapon against the long night of physical slavery. No Lincolnian emancipation proclamation or Kennedyan or Johnsonian civil rights bill can totally bring this kind of freedom. The Negro will only be truly free when he reaches down to the inner depths of his own being and signs with the pen and ink of assertive selfhood his own emancipation proclamation. With a spirit straining toward true self-esteem, the Negro must boldly throw off the manacles of self-abnegation and say to himself and the world: "I am somebody. I am a person. I am a man with dignity and honor. I have a rich and noble history, however painful and exploited that history has been. I am black *and* comely." This self-affirmation is the black man's need made compelling by the white man's crimes against him. This is positive and necessary power for black people.

III

Nevertheless, in spite of the positive aspects of Black Power, which are compatible with what we have sought to do in the civil rights movement all along without the slogan, its negative values, I believe, prevent it from having the substance and program to become the basic strategy for the civil rights movement in the days ahead.

Beneath all the satisfaction of a gratifying slogan, Black Power is a nihilistic philosophy born out of the conviction that the Negro can't win. It is, at bottom, the view that American society is so hopelessly corrupt and enmeshed in evil that there is no possibility of salvation from within. Although this thinking is understandable as a response to a white power structure that never completely committed itself to true equality for the Negro, and a die-hard mentality that sought to shut all windows and doors against the winds of change, it nonetheless carries the seeds of its own doom.

Before this century, virtually all revolutions had been based on hope and hate. The hope was expressed in the rising expectation of freedom and justice. The hate was an expression of bitterness toward the perpetrators of the old order. It was the hate that made revolutions bloody and violent. What was new about Mahatma Gandhi's movement in India was that he mounted a revolution on hope and love, hope and nonviolence. This same new emphasis characterized the civil rights movement in our country dating from the Montgomery bus boycott of 1956 to the Selma movement of 1965. We maintained the hope while transforming the hate of traditional revolutions into positive nonviolent power. As long as the hope was fulfilled there was little questioning of nonviolence. But when the hopes were blasted, when people came to see that in spite of progress their conditions were still insufferable, when they looked out and saw more poverty, more school segregation and more slums, despair began to set in.

Unfortunately, when hope diminishes, the hate is often turned most bitterly toward those who originally built up the hope. In all the speaking that I have done in the United States before varied audiences, including some hostile whites, the only time that I have been booed was one night in a Chicago mass meeting by some young members of the Black Power movement. I went home that night with an ugly feeling. Selfishly I thought of my sufferings and sacrifices over the last twelve years. Why would they boo one so close to them? But as I lay awake thinking, I finally came to myself, and I could not for the life of me have less than patience and understanding for those young people. For twelve years I, and others like me, had held out radiant promises of progress. I had preached to them about my dream. I had lectured to them about the not too distant day when they would have freedom, "all, here and now." I had urged them to have faith in America and in white society. Their hopes had soared. They were now booing because they felt that we were unable to deliver on our promises. They were booing because we had urged them to have faith in people who had too often proved to be unfaithful. They were now hostile because they were watching the dream that they had so readily accepted turn into a frustrating nightmare.

But revolution, though born of despair, cannot long be sustained by despair. This is the ultimate contradiction of the Black Power move- 70 ment. It claims to be the most revolutionary wing of the social revolution taking place in the United States. Yet it rejects the one thing that keeps the fire of revolutions burning: the ever-present flame of hope. When hope dies, a revolution degenerates into an undiscriminating catchall for evanescent and futile gestures. The Negro cannot entrust his destiny to a philosophy nourished solely on despair, to a slogan that cannot be implemented into a program.

The Negro's disappointment is real and a part of the daily menu of our lives. One of the most agonizing problems of human experience is how to deal with disappointment. In our individual lives we all too often distill our frustrations into an essence of bitterness, or drown ourselves in the deep waters of self-pity, or adopt a fatalistic philosophy that whatever happens must happen and all events are determined by necessity. These reactions poison the soul and scar the personality, always harming the person who harbors them more than anyone else. The only healthy answer lies in one's honest recognition of disappointment even as he still clings to hope, one's acceptance of finite disappointment even while clinging to infinite hope.

We Negroes, who have dreamed for so long of freedom, are still confined in a prison of segregation and discrimination. Must we respond with bitterness and cynicism? Certainly not, for this can lead to black anger so desperate that it ends in black suicide. Must we turn inward in self-pity? Of course not, for this can lead to a self-defeating black paranoia. Must we conclude that we cannot win? Certainly not, for this can lead to black nihilism that seeks disruption for disruption's sake. Must we, by fatalistically concluding that segregation is a foreordained pattern of the universe, resign ourselves to oppression? Of course not, for passively to cooperate with an unjust system makes the oppressed as evil as the oppressors. Our most fruitful course is to stand firm, move forward nonviolently, accept disappointments and cling to hope. Our determined refusal not to be stopped will eventually open the door to fulfillment. By recognizing the necessity of suffering in a righteous cause, we may achieve our humanity's full stature. To guard ourselves from bitterness, we need the vision to see in this generation's ordeals the opportunity to transfigure both ourselves and American society.

In 1956 I flew from New York to London in the propeller-type aircraft that required nine and a half hours for a flight now made in six hours by jet. Returning from London to the United States, the stewardess announced that the flying time would be twelve and a half hours. The distance was the same. Why an additional three hours? When the pilot entered the cabin to greet the passengers, I asked him to explain.

"You must understand about the winds," he said. "When we leave New York, a strong tail wind is in our favor, but when we return, a strong head wind is against us." Then he added, "Don't worry. These four engines are capable of battling the winds."

In any social revolution there are times when the tail winds of triumph and fulfillment favor us, and other times when strong head winds of disappointment and setbacks beat against us relentlessly. We must not permit adverse winds to overwhelm us as we journey across life's mighty Atlantic; we must be sustained by our engines of courage in spite of the winds. This refusal to be stopped, this "courage to be," this determination to go on "in spite of" is the hallmark of any great movement.

The Black Power movement of today, like the Garvey "Back to Africa" movement of the 1920s, represents a dashing of hope, a conviction of the inability of the Negro to win and a belief in the infinitude of the ghetto. While there is much grounding in past experience for all these feelings, a revolution cannot succumb to any of them. Today's despair is a poor chisel to carve out tomorrow's justice.

Black Power is an implicit and often explicit belief in black separatism. Notice that I do not call it black racism. It is inaccurate to refer to Black Power as racism in reverse, as some have recently done. Racism is a doctrine of the congenital inferiority and worthlessness of a people. While a few angry proponents of Black Power have, in moments of bitterness, made wild statements that come close to this kind of racism, the major proponents of Black Power have never contended that the white man is innately worthless.

Yet behind Black Power's legitimate and necessary concern for group unity and black identity lies the belief that there can be a separate black road to power and fulfillment. Few ideas are more unrealistic. There is no salvation for the Negro through isolation.

One of the chief affirmations of Black Power is the call for the mobilization of political strength for black people. But we do not have to look far to see that effective political power for Negroes cannot come through separatism. Granted that there are cities and counties in the country where the Negro is in a majority, there are so few that concentration on them alone would still leave the vast majority of Negroes outside the mainstream of American political life.

Out of the eighty-odd counties in Alabama, the state where SNCC sought to develop an all-black party, only nine have a majority of Negroes. Even if blacks could control each of these counties, they would have little influence in overall state politics and could do little to improve conditions in the major Negro population centers of Birmingham, Mobile and Montgomery. There are still relatively few congressional districts in the South that have such large black majorities that Negro candidates could be elected without the aid of whites. Is it a sounder program to concentrate on the election of two or three Negro congressmen from predominantly Negro districts or to concentrate on the election of fifteen or twenty Negro congressmen from southern districts where a coalition of Negro and white moderate voters is possible?

Moreover, any program that elects all black candidates simply because they are black and rejects all white candidates simply because they are white is politically unsound and morally unjustifiable. It is true that in many areas of the South Negroes still must elect Negroes in order to be effectively represented. SNCC staff members are eminently correct when they point out that in Lowndes County, Alabama, there are no white liberals or moderates and no possibility for cooperation between the races at the present time. But the Lowndes County experience cannot be made a measuring rod for the whole of America. The basic thing in determining the best candidate is not his color but his integrity.

Black Power alone is no more insurance against social injustice than white power. Negro politicians can be as opportunistic as their white counterparts if there is not an informed and determined constituency demanding social reform. What is most needed is a coalition of Negroes and liberal whites that will work to make both major parties truly responsive to the needs of the poor. Black Power does not envision or desire such a program.

Just as the Negro cannot achieve political power in isolation, neither can he gain economic power through separatism. While there must be a continued emphasis on the need for blacks to pool their economic resources and withdraw consumer support from discriminating firms, we must not be oblivious to the fact that the larger economic problems confronting the Negro community will only be solved by federal programs involving billions of dollars. One unfortunate thing about Black Power is that it gives priority to race precisely at a time when the impact of automation and other forces have made the economic question fundamental for blacks and whites alike. In this context a slogan "Power for Poor People" would be much more appropriate than the slogan "Black Power."

However much we pool our resources and "buy black," this cannot create the multiplicity of new jobs and provide the number of low-cost houses that will lift the Negro out of the economic depression caused by centuries of deprivation. Neither can our resources supply quality integrated education. All of this requires billions of dollars which only an alliance of liberal-labor-civil-rights forces can stimulate. In short, the Negroes' problem cannot be solved unless the whole of American society takes a new turn toward greater economic justice.

In a multiracial society no group can make it alone. It is a myth to 85 believe that the Irish, the Italians and the Jews—the ethnic groups that Black Power advocates cite as justification for their views—rose to power through separatism. It is true that they stuck together. But their group unity was always enlarged by joining in alliances with other groups such as political machines and trade unions. To succeed in a pluralistic society, and an often hostile one at that, the Negro obviously needs organized strength, but that strength will only be effective when it is consolidated through constructive alliances with the majority group.

Those proponents of Black Power who have urged Negroes to shun alliances with whites argue that whites as a group cannot have a genuine concern for Negro progress. Therefore, they claim, the white man's main interest in collaborative effort is to diminish Negro militancy and deflect it from constructive goals.

Undeniably there are white elements that cannot be trusted, and no militant movement can afford to relax its vigilance against halfhearted associates or conscious betrayers. Every alliance must be considered on its own merits. Negroes may embrace some and walk out on others where their interests are imperiled. Occasional betrayals, however, do not justify the rejection of the principle of Negro–white alliance.

The oppression of Negroes by whites has left an understandable residue of suspicion. Some of this suspicion is a healthy and appropriate safeguard. An excess of skepticism, however, becomes a fetter. It denies that there can be reliable white allies, even though some whites have died heroically at the side of Negroes in our struggle and others have risked economic and political peril to support our cause.

The history of the movement reveals that Negro–white alliances have played a powerfully constructive role, especially in recent years. While Negro initiative, courage and imagination precipitated the Birmingham and Selma confrontations and revealed the harrowing injustice of segregated life, the organized strength of Negroes alone would have been insufficient to move Congress and the administration without the weight of the aroused conscience of white America. In the period ahead Negroes will continue to need this support. Ten percent of the population cannot by tensions alone induce ninety percent to change a way of life.

Within the white majority there exists a substantial group who cherish democratic principles above privilege and who have demonstrated a will to fight side by side with the Negro against injustice. Another and more substantial group is composed of those having common needs with the Negro and who will benefit equally with him in the achievement of social progress. There are, in fact, more poor white Americans than there are Negro. Their need for a war on poverty is no less desperate than the Negro's. In the South they have been deluded by race prejudice and largely remained aloof from common action. Ironically, with this posture they were fighting not only the Negro but themselves. Yet there are already signs of change. Without formal alliances, Negroes and whites have supported the same candidates in many *de facto* electoral coalitions in the South because each sufficiently served his own needs.

The ability of Negroes to enter alliances is a mark of our growing 90 strength, not of our weakness. In entering an alliance, the Negro is not relying on white leadership or ideology; he is taking his place as an equal partner in a common endeavor. His organized strength and his new independence pave the way for alliances. Far from losing independence in an alliance, he is using it for constructive and multiplied gains.

Negroes must shun the very narrow-mindedness that in others has so long been the source of our own afflictions. We have reached the stage of organized strength and independence to work securely in alliances. History has demonstrated with major victories the effectiveness, wisdom and moral soundness of Negro-white alliance. The cooperation of Negro and white based on the solid ground of honest conscience and proper self-interest can continue to grow in scope and influence. It can attain the strength to alter basic institutions by democratic means. Negro isolation can never approach this goal.

In the final analysis the weakness of Black Power is its failure to see that the black man needs the white man and the white man needs the black man. However much we may try to romanticize the slogan, there is no separate black path to power and fulfillment that does not intersect white paths, and there is no separate white path to power and fulfillment, short of social disaster, that does not share that power with black aspirations for freedom and human dignity. We are bound together in a single garment of destiny. The language, the cultural patterns, the music, the material prosperity and even the food of America are an amalgam of black and white.

James Baldwin once related how he returned home from school and his mother asked him whether his teacher was colored or white. After a pause he answered: "She is a little bit colored and a little bit white."[4] This is the dilemma of being a Negro in America. In physical as well as cultural terms every Negro is a little bit colored and a little bit white. In our search for identity we must recognize this dilemma.

Every man must ultimately confront the question "Who am I?" and seek to answer it honestly. One of the first principles of personal adjustment is the principle of self-acceptance. The Negro's greatest dilemma is that in order to be healthy he must accept his ambivalence. The Negro is the child of two cultures—Africa and America. The problem is that in the search for wholeness all too many Negroes seek to embrace only one side of their natures. Some, seeking to reject their heritage, are ashamed of their color, ashamed of black art and music, and determine what is beautiful and good by the standards of white society. They end up frustrated and without cultural roots. Others seek to reject everything American and to identify totally with Africa, even to the point of wearing African clothes. But this approach leads also to frustration because the American Negro is not an African. The old Hegelian synthesis still offers the best answer to many of life's dilemmas.

---

[4]In *The Negro Protest,* Kenneth B. Clark (ed.), Beacon, 1963.

The American Negro is neither totally African nor totally Western. He is Afro-American, a true hybrid, a combination of two cultures.

Who are we? We are the descendants of slaves. We are the offspring   95
of noble men and women who were kidnapped from their native land and chained in ships like beasts. We are the heirs of a great and exploited continent known as Africa. We are the heirs of a past of rope, fire and murder. I for one am not ashamed of this past. My shame is for those who became so inhuman that they could inflict this torture upon us.

But we are also Americans. Abused and scorned though we may be, our destiny is tied up with the destiny of America. In spite of the psychological appeals of identification with Africa, the Negro must face the fact that America is now his home, a home that he helped to build through "blood, sweat and tears." Since we are Americans the solution to our problem will not come through seeking to build a separate black nation within a nation, but by finding that creative minority of the concerned from the ofttimes apathetic majority, and together moving toward that colorless power that we all need for security and justice.

In the first century B.C., Cicero said: "Freedom is participation in power." Negroes should never want all power because they would deprive others of their freedom. By the same token, Negroes can never be content without participation in power. America must be a nation in which its multiracial people are partners in power. This is the essence of democracy toward which all Negro struggles have been directed since the distant past when he was transplanted here in chains.

Probably the most destructive feature of Black Power is its unconscious and often conscious call for retaliatory violence. Many well-meaning persons within the movement rationalize that Black Power does not really mean black violence, that those who shout the slogan don't really mean it that way, that the violent connotations are solely the distortions of a vicious press. That the press has fueled the fire is true. But as one who has worked and talked intimately with devotees of Black Power, I must admit that the slogan is mainly used by persons who have lost faith in the method and philosophy of nonviolence. I must make it clear that no guilt by association is intended. Both Floyd McKissick and Stokely Carmichael have declared themselves opponents of aggressive violence. This clarification is welcome and useful, despite the persistence of some of their followers in examining the uses of violence.

Over cups of coffee in my home in Atlanta and my apartment in Chicago, I have often talked late at night and over into the small hours of the morning with the proponents of Black Power who argued passionately about the validity of violence and riots. They don't quote Gandhi or Tolstoy. Their bible is Frantz Fanon's *The Wretched of the*

Earth.[5] This black psychiatrist from Martinique, who went to Algeria to work with the National Liberation Front in its fight against the French, argues in his book—a well-written book, incidentally, with many penetrating insights—that violence is a psychologically healthy and tactically sound method for the oppressed. And so, realizing that they are a part of that vast company of the "wretched of the earth," these young American Negroes, who are predominantly involved in the Black Power movement, often quote Fanon's belief that violence is the only thing that will bring about liberation. As they say, "Sing us no songs of nonviolence, sing us no songs of progress, for nonviolence and progress belong to middle-class Negroes and whites and we are not interested in you."

As we have seen, the first public expression of disenchantment with nonviolence arose around the question of "self-defense." In a sense this is a false issue, for the right to defend one's home and one's person when attacked has been guaranteed through the ages by common law. In a nonviolent demonstration, however, self-defense must be approached from another perspective.

The cause of a demonstration is the existence of some form of exploitation or oppression that has made it necessary for men of courage and good will to protest the evil. For example, a demonstration against *de facto* school segregation is based on the awareness that a child's mind is crippled by inadequate educational opportunities. The demonstrator agrees that it is better to suffer publicly for a short time to end the crippling evil of school segregation than to have generation after generation of children suffer in ignorance. In such a demonstration the point is made that the schools are inadequate. This is the evil one seeks to dramatize; anything else distracts from that point and interferes with the confrontation of the primary evil. Of course no one wants to suffer and be hurt. But it is more important to get at the cause than to be safe. It is better to shed a little blood from a blow on the head or a rock thrown by an angry mob than to have children by the thousands finishing high school who can only read at a sixth-grade level.

Furthermore, it is dangerous to organize a movement around self-defense. The line of demarcation between defensive violence and aggressive violence is very thin. The minute a program of violence is enunciated, even for self-defense, the atmosphere is filled with talk of violence, and the words falling on unsophisticated ears may be interpreted as an invitation to aggression.

One of the main questions that the Negro must confront in his pursuit of freedom is that of effectiveness. What is the most effective way to achieve the desired goal? If a method is not effective, no matter

100

---

[5] Evergreen, 1966.

how much steam it releases, it is an expression of weakness, not of strength. Now the plain, inexorable fact is that any attempt of the American Negro to overthrow his oppressor with violence will not work. We do not need President Johnson to tell us this by reminding Negro rioters that they are outnumbered ten to one. The courageous efforts of our own insurrectionist brothers, such as Denmark Vesey and Nat Turner, should be eternal reminders to us that violent rebellion is doomed from the start. In violent warfare one must be prepared to face the fact that there will be casualties by the thousands. Anyone leading a violent rebellion must be willing to make an honest assessment regarding the possible casualties to a minority population confronting a well-armed, wealthy majority with a fanatical right wing that would delight in exterminating thousands of black men, women and children.

Arguments that the American Negro is a part of a world which is two-thirds colored and that there will come a day when the oppressed people of color will violently rise together to throw off the yoke of white oppression are beyond the realm of serious discussion. There is no colored nation, including China, that now shows even the potential of leading a violent revolution of color in any international proportions. Ghana, Zambia, Tanganyika and Nigeria are so busy fighting their own battles against poverty, illiteracy and the subversive influence of neocolonialism that they offer little hope to Angola, Southern Rhodesia and South Africa, much less to the American Negro. The hard cold facts today indicate that the hope of the people of color in the world may well rest on the American Negro and his ability to reform the structure of racist imperialism from within and thereby turn the technology and wealth of the West to the task of liberating the world from want.

The futility of violence in the struggle for racial justice has been 105 tragically etched in all the recent Negro riots. There is something painfully sad about a riot. One sees screaming youngsters and angry adults fighting hopelessly and aimlessly against impossible odds. Deep down within them you perceive a desire for self-destruction, a suicidal longing. Occasionally Negroes contend that the 1965 Watts riot and other riots in various cities represented effective civil rights action. But those who express this view always end up with stumbling words when asked what concrete gains have been won as a result. At best the riots have produced a little additional antipoverty money, allotted by frightened government officials, and a few water sprinklers to cool the children of the ghettos. It is something like improving the food in a prison while the people remain securely incarcerated behind bars. Nowhere have the riots won any concrete improvement such as have the organized protest demonstrations.

It is not overlooking the limitations of nonviolence and the distance we have yet to go to point out the remarkable record of achievements that have already come through nonviolent action. The 1960 sit-ins desegregated lunch counters in more than 150 cities within a year. The 1961 freedom rides put an end to segregation in interstate travel. The 1956 bus boycott in Montgomery, Alabama, ended segregation on the buses not only of that city but in practically every city of the South. The 1963 Birmingham movement and the climactic March on Washington won passage of the most powerful civil rights law in a century. The 1965 Selma movement brought enactment of the Voting Rights Law. Our nonviolent marches in Chicago last summer brought about a housing agreement which, if implemented, will be the strongest step toward open housing taken in any city in the nation. Most significant is the fact that this progress occurred with minimum human sacrifice and loss of life. Fewer people have been killed in ten years of nonviolent demonstrations across the South than were killed in one night of rioting in Watts.

When one tries to pin down advocates of violence as to what acts would be effective, the answers are blatantly illogical. Sometimes they talk of overthrowing racist state and local governments. They fail to see that no internal revolution has ever succeeded in overthrowing a government by violence unless the government has already lost the allegiance and effective control of its armed forces. Anyone in his right mind knows that this will not happen in the United States. In a violent racial situation, the power structure has the local police, the state troopers, the national guard and finally the army to call on, all of which are predominantly white.

Furthermore, few if any violent revolutions have been successful unless the violent minority had the sympathy and support of the nonresisting majority. Castro may have had only a few Cubans actually fighting with him, but he would never have overthrown the Batista regime unless he had had the sympathy of the vast majority of the Cuban people. It is perfectly clear that a violent revolution on the part of American blacks would find no sympathy and support from the white population and very little from the majority of the Negroes themselves.

This is no time for romantic illusions and empty philosophical debates about freedom. This is a time for action. What is needed is a strategy for change, a tactical program that will bring the Negro into the mainstream of American life as quickly as possible. So far, this has only been offered by the nonviolent movement. Without recognizing this we will end up with solutions that don't solve, answers that don't answer and explanations that don't explain.

Beyond the pragmatic invalidity of violence is its inability to appeal to conscience. Some Black Power advocates consider an appeal to conscience irrelevant. A Black Power exponent said to me not long ago: "To hell with conscience and morality. We want power." But power and morality must go together, implementing, fulfilling and ennobling each other. In the quest for power I cannot bypass the concern for morality. I refuse to be driven to a Machiavellian cynicism with respect to power. Power at its best is the right use of strength. The words of Alfred the Great are still true: "Power is never good unless he who has it is good."

Nonviolence is power, but it is the right and good use of power.   110
Constructively it can save the white man as well as the Negro. Racial segregation is buttressed by such irrational fears as loss of preferred economic privilege, altered social status, intermarriage and adjustment to new situations. Through sleepless nights and haggard days numerous white people struggle pitifully to combat these fears. By following the path of escape, some seek to ignore the questions of race relations and to close their minds to the issues involved. Others, placing their faith in legal maneuvers, counsel massive resistance. Still others hope to drown their fears by engaging in acts of meanness and violence toward their Negro brethren. But how futile are all these remedies! Instead of eliminating fear, they instill deeper and more pathological fears. The white man, through his own efforts, through education and goodwill, through searching his conscience and through confronting the fact of integration, must do a great deal to free himself of these paralyzing fears. But to master fear he must also depend on the spirit the Negro generates toward him. Only through our adherence to nonviolence—which also means love in its strong and commanding sense—will the fear in the white community be mitigated.

A guilt-ridden white minority fears that if the Negro attains power, he will without restraint or pity act to revenge the accumulated injustices and brutality of the years. The Negro must show that the white man has nothing to fear, for the Negro is willing to forgive. A mass movement exercising nonviolence and demonstrating power under discipline should convince the white community that as such a movement attained strength, its power would be used creatively and not for revenge.

In a moving letter to his nephew on the one hundredth anniversary of emancipation, James Baldwin wrote concerning white people:

> The really terrible thing, old buddy, is that *you* must accept *them*. And I mean that very seriously. You must accept them and accept them with love. For these innocent people have no other hope. They are, in effect, still trapped in a history which they do not understand; and until they understand it, they cannot be released from it. They have had to believe for many years, and for innumerable reasons, that black men are inferior to white men. Many of them, indeed, know better, but, as you will discover, people find it very difficult to act on what they know. To act is to be committed, and to be committed is to be in danger. In this case, the danger, in the minds of most white Americans, is the loss of their identity. . . . But these men are your brothers—your lost, younger brothers. And if the word *integration* means anything, this is what is means:

that we, with love, shall force our brothers to see themselves as they are, to cease fleeing from reality and begin to change it. . . .[6]

The problem with hatred and violence is that they intensify the fears of the white majority, and leave them less ashamed of their prejudices toward Negroes. In the guilt and confusion confronting our society, violence only adds to the chaos. It deepens the brutality of the oppressor and increases the bitterness of the oppressed. Violence is the antithesis of creativity and wholeness. It destroys community and makes brotherhood impossible.

My friend John Killens recently wrote in the *Negro Digest:* "Integration comes after liberation. A slave cannot integrate with his master. In the whole history of revolts and revolutions, integration has never been the main slogan of the revolution. The oppressed fights to free himself from his oppressor, not to integrate with him. Integration is the step after freedom when the freedman makes up his mind as to whether he wishes to integrate with his former master."[7]

At first glance this sounds very good. But after reflection one has to face some inescapable facts about the Negro and American life. This is a multiracial nation where all groups are dependent on each other, whether they want to recognize it or not. In this vast interdependent nation no racial group can retreat to an island entire of itself. The phenomena of integration and liberation cannot be as neatly divided as Killens would have it.

There is no theoretical or sociological divorce between liberation and integration. In our kind of society liberation cannot come without integration and integration cannot come without liberation. I speak here of integration in both the ethical and the political senses. On the one hand, integration is true intergroup, interpersonal living. On the other hand, it is the mutual sharing of power. I cannot see how the Negro will be totally liberated from the crushing weight of poor education, squalid housing and economic strangulation until he is integrated, with power, into every level of American life.

Mr. Killens's assertion might have some validity in a struggle for independence against a foreign invader. But the Negro's struggle in America is quite different from and more difficult than the struggle for independence. The American Negro will be living tomorrow with the very people against whom he is struggling today. The American Negro is not in a Congo where the Belgians will go back to Belgium after the battle is over, or in an India where the British will go back to England after independence is won. In the struggle for national independence one can talk about liberation now and integration later, but in the

---

[6] *The Fire Next Time,* Dial, 1963, pp. 22–23.
[7] November 1966.

struggle for racial justice in a multiracial society where the oppressor and the oppressed are both "at home," liberation must come through integration.

Are we seeking power for power's sake? Or are we seeking to make the world and our nation better places to live? If we seek the latter, violence can never provide the answer. The ultimate weakness of violence is that it is a descending spiral, begetting the very thing it seeks to destroy. Instead of diminishing evil, it multiplies it. Through violence you may murder the liar, but you cannot murder the lie, nor establish the truth. Through violence you may murder the hater, but you do not murder hate. In fact, violence merely increases hate. So it goes. Returning violence for violence multiplies violence, adding deeper darkness to a night already devoid of stars. Darkness cannot drive out darkness: only light can do that. Hate cannot drive out hate: only love can do that.

The beauty of nonviolence is that in its own way and in its own time it seeks to break the chain reaction of evil. With a majestic sense of spiritual power, it seeks to elevate truth, beauty and goodness to the throne. Therefore I will continue to follow this method because I think it is the most practically sound and morally excellent way for the Negro to achieve freedom.

Lines of Inquiry
"Black Power"

King has clearly divided this piece into distinctly separate sections, each of which builds carefully on the one preceding it. What is the form and purpose of the first section? How does it differ from the form and purpose of the next two sections? How is it related to the next two sections? What is the form and purpose of the next two sections? How are they related to each other?

Given his strong opposition to the black power movement, why do you suppose that King goes to such lengths to explain and defend it as he does in much of this piece? Among King's objections to the movement is his claim that "probably the most destructive feature of Black Power is its unconscious and often conscious call for retaliatory violence." What do you think he means by an unconscious call? And how do you suppose the call could be both unconscious and conscious? Why does King devote more attention to discussing this objection than to any of the others that he raises?

Based on your personal experience, firsthand observation, and reading, what do you think has come of the black power movement in America? In what ways does it seem to have affected black culture in America? In what ways does it seem to have affected white culture in America? In what ways does it seem to have affected racial relations in America?

Margaret Mead
1901–78

I have spent most of my life studying the lives of other peoples,
faraway peoples, so that Americans might better understand
themselves.

In this passage from her
autobiography, *Blackberry Winter* (1972), Margaret Mead does not really
do justice to the far-reaching scope of her efforts and influence. True
enough, she did devote herself to "studying the lives of other peoples,"
particularly primitive peoples of the South Pacific, and she did use her
studies of these other cultures to help Americans "better understand
themselves" and their changing cultural situation. But her progressive
and reformist instincts were not limited only to American self-under-
standing. Indeed, as a cultural anthropologist, she addressed virtually
all the circumstances that impinge on the condition of human beings
throughout the world—the family, the community, the environment,
education, nutrition, religion, sex, race, technology, and war. She worked
her good influence not only as a worldwide researcher and teacher, but
also as a member of national and international commissions, as an officer of national and international organizations, and as an author and
editor of forty-five books and several hundred articles. So it is hardly
surprising that in 1969, *Time* magazine named her "Mother of the
World."

Born in Philadelphia, she was the oldest of five children of an exceptionally well-educated family. Her father, a professor of economics
who had "an enormous respect for facts," gave her a vivid "sense of
the way theory and practice must be related." Her mother, who earned
a doctorate for her research on Italian immigrant families, gave her an
intense "concern for other people and the state of the world." But her
paternal grandmother, a former schoolteacher and principal, who lived
with the family, was "the most decisive influence" in her life. During
most of her childhood years, Mead did not attend school, but was educated at home by her grandmother, who taught her early on "to observe the world around [her] and to note what [she] saw." From her

resourceful and strong-willed grandmother, she ultimately gained a special respect not only for the capacities of women, but also for the importance of grandparents in the life of the family, especially in the development of children and adolescents.

After graduating from high school in 1918, she spent an unhappy freshman year at DePauw University, "confronted by the snobbery and cruelty of the sorority system at its worst." So, she transferred to Barnard, the women's college of Columbia University, and found there an intellectually stimulating group of friends. She found also that though not quite talented enough to succeed as a creative writer, she could "make a true contribution" in one of the social sciences. Her eventual choice of anthropology was sparked by an elective course in her senior year with Franz Boas, one of the leading figures in the early development of the field, and by a friendship that she developed with Ruth Benedict, the gifted disciple and teaching assistant of Boas. From Boas and Benedict, she discovered the unique value of studying primitive cultures not only in and of themselves, but also in relation to other cultures, and in connection with a variety of questions concerning the influence of culture on human development.

As a graduate student at Columbia, she developed so strong an interest in Polynesian culture that she convinced Boas to support her in doing fieldwork there, despite his fear of the risks she would run living and working in a primitive tropical village—"in a world that had not been constructed for a woman to work in." So in the late summer of 1925, after a brief vacation with her husband of two years' standing, she went off on her own to a tiny village in Samoa, to examine the influence of that primitive culture on the development of its young people, especially adolescent girls. The results of her nine-month study, which she wrote up in her first published book, *Coming of Age in Samoa* (1928), earned her a doctorate in 1929. It also brought her immediate nationwide attention for her vividly clear description of the culture and for her striking insights into the problems of American adolescents, whose situation she illuminated by detailing "the ways in which Samoan education, in its broadest sense, differs from our own."

Knowing as she did that "the last primitive peoples . . . would soon become changed beyond recovery," Mead devoted much of the next ten years to fieldwork in other primitive South Pacific cultures. During that time, she was twice divorced and twice remarried, both times to anthropologists whom she had met in the South Pacific. In the course of her pre-World War II research, she broadened the perspective of anthropology by taking into account the knowledge to be gained from other social sciences. She also developed important new methods for observing, recording, and analyzing specific aspects of primitive culture, which she described in several books, most notably *Growing Up in New Guinea* (1930) and *Sex and Temperament in Three Primitive*

Societies (1935). In these and other studies, she persistently used her insights into primitive culture to raise bold questions about aspects of modern American culture, particularly about the traditional roles of men and women, which she explored at greater length in *Male and Female: A Study of the Sexes in a Changing World* (1949).

During World War II, when firsthand cultural observation was virtually impossible, Mead, in collaboration with other social scientists, spearheaded the development of a new methodology for "the study of culture at a distance." Using this method to define the underlying character of various national groups, she and her colleagues provided strategically useful wartime and postwar information about the culture and behavior of Germany, Japan, and Russia. After the war, she returned to Manus, the New Guinea village that she had first studied in 1928, and in *New Lives for Old* (1956) she recorded the dramatic cultural changes that had taken place there during the wartime presence of Americans. During the sixties, she became increasingly concerned with the worldwide cultural changes that she perceived to be taking place as a result of young people having "grown up in a world their elders never knew," and she systematically examined those changes in *Culture and Commitment: A Study of the Generation Gap* (1970).

During most of her professional life, she not only served as a curator at the American Museum of Natural History in New York City, but she also taught at Columbia University as well as at more than forty other schools throughout the country. On top of everything else, she kept up a monthly column in *Redbook* magazine during the last seventeen years of her life. In her columns, as in her other writing, she spoke out on a broad range of issues, in a vividly clear, detailed, and humane style. Given her persistent desire to help others "better understand themselves," she knew that "what one says must be intelligible and bearable for those about whom one writes and, at the same time, for the members of one's own culture and for the people of all the other cultures in the world who may read what one has written."

A Day in Samoa

The life of the day begins at dawn, or if the moon has shown until daylight, the shouts of the young men may be heard before dawn from the hillside. Uneasy in the night, populous with ghosts, they shout lustily to one another as they hasten with their work. As the dawn begins to fall among the soft brown roofs and the slender palm trees stand out against a colourless, gleaming sea, lovers slip home from trysts beneath the palm trees or in the shadow of beached canoes, that the light may find each sleeper in his appointed place. Cocks crow, negligently, and a shrill-voiced bird cries from the breadfruit trees. The insistent roar of the reef seems muted to an undertone for the sounds of a waking village. Babies cry, a few short wails before sleepy mothers give them the breast. Restless little children roll out of their sheets and wander drowsily down to the beach to freshen their faces in the sea. Boys, bent upon an early fishing, start collecting their tackle and go to rouse their more laggard companions. Fires are lit, here and there, the white smoke hardly visible against the paleness of the dawn. The whole village, sheeted and frowsy, stirs, rubs its eyes, and stumbles towards the beach. "Talofa!" "Talofa!" "Will the journey start to-day?" "Is it bonito fishing your lordship is going?" Girls stop to giggle over some young ne'er-do-well who escaped during the night from an angry father's pursuit and to venture a shrewd guess that the daughter knew more about his presence than she told. The boy who is taunted by another, who has succeeded him in his sweetheart's favour, grapples with his rival, his foot slipping in the wet sand. From the other end of the village comes a long drawn-out, piercing wail. A messenger has just brought word of the death of some relative in another village. Half-clad, unhurried women, with babies at their breasts, or astride their hips, pause in their tale of Losa's outraged departure from her father's house to the greater kindness in the home of her uncle, to wonder who is dead. Poor relatives whisper their requests to rich relatives, men make plans to set a fish trap together, a woman begs a bit of yellow dye from a kinswoman, and through the village sounds the rhythmic tattoo which calls the young men together. They gather from all parts of the village, digging sticks in hand, ready to start inland to the plantation. The older men set off upon their more lonely occupations, and each household, reassembled under its peaked roof, settles down to the routine of the morning. Little children, too hungry to wait for the late breakfast, beg lumps of cold taro which they munch greedily. Women carry piles of washing to the sea or to the spring at the far end of the village, or set off inland after weaving materials. The older girls go fishing on the reef, or perhaps set themselves to weaving a new set of Venetian blinds.

In the houses, where the pebbly floors have been swept bare with a stiff long-handled broom, the women great with child and the nursing mothers sit and gossip with one another. Old men sit apart, unceasingly twisting palm husk on their bare thighs and muttering old tales under their breath. The carpenters begin work on the new house, while the owner bustles about trying to keep them in a good humour. Families who will cook today are hard at work; the taro, yams and bananas have already been brought from inland; the children are scuttling back and forth, fetching sea water, or leaves to stuff the pig. As the sun rises higher in the sky, the shadows deepen under the thatched roofs, the sand is burning to the touch, the hibiscus flowers wilt on the hedges, and little children bid the smaller ones, "Come out of the sun." Those whose excursions have been short return to the village, the women with strings of crimson jelly fish, or baskets of shell fish, the men with cocoanuts, carried in baskets slung on a shoulder pole. The women and children eat their breakfasts, just hot from the oven, if this is cook day, and the young men work swiftly in the mid-day heat, preparing the noon feast for their elders.

It is high noon. The sand burns the feet of the little children, who leave their palm leaf balls and their pin-wheels of frangipani blossoms to wither in the sun, as they creep into the shade of the houses. The women who must go abroad carry great banana leaves as sun-shades or wind wet cloths about their heads. Lowering a few blinds against the slanting sun, all who are left in the village wrap their heads in sheets and go to sleep. Only a few adventurous children may slip away for a swim in the shadow of a high rock, some industrious woman continues with her weaving, or a close little group of women bend anxiously over a woman in labour. The village is dazzling and dead; any sound seems oddly loud and out of place. Words have to cut through the solid heat slowly. And then the sun gradually sinks over the sea.

A second time, the sleeping people stir, roused perhaps by the cry of "a boat," resounding through the village. The fishermen beach their canoes, weary and spent from the heat, in spite of the slaked lime on their heads, with which they have sought to cool their brains and redden their hair. The brightly coloured fishes are spread out on the floor, or piled in front of the houses until the women pour water over them to free them from taboo. Regretfully, the young fishermen separate out the "Taboo fish," which must be sent to the chief, or proudly they pack the little palm leaf baskets with offerings of fish to take to their sweethearts. Men come home from the bush, grimy and heavy laden, shouting as they come, greeted in a sonorous rising cadence by those who have remained at home. They gather in the guest house for their evening kava drinking. The soft clapping of hands, the high-pitched intoning of the talking chief who serves the kava echoes through the village. Girls gather flowers to weave into necklaces; children, lusty from their naps and bound to no particular task, play circular games in the half shade of the late afternoon. Finally the sun sets, in a flame which stretches from the mountain behind to the horizon on the sea, the last bather comes up from the beach, children straggle home, dark little figures etched against the sky; lights shine in the houses, and each household gathers for its evening meal. The suitor humbly presents his offering, the children have been summoned from their noisy play, perhaps there is an honoured guest who must be served first, after the soft, barbaric singing of Christian hymns and the brief and graceful evening prayer. In front of a house at the end of the village, a father cries out the birth of a son. In some family circles a face is missing, in others little runaways have found a haven! Again quiet settles upon the village, as first the head of the household, then the women and children, and last of all the patient boys, eat their supper.

After supper the old people and the little children are bundled off 5 to bed. If the young people have guests the front of the house is yielded to them. For day is the time for the councils of old men and the labours of youth, and night is the time for lighter things. Two kinsmen, or a chief and his councillor, sit and gossip over the day's events or make plans for the morrow. Outside a crier goes through the village announcing that the communal breadfruit pit will be opened in the morning, or that the village will make a great fish trap. If it is moonlight, groups of young men, women by twos and threes, wander through the village, and crowds of children hunt for land crabs or chase each other among the breadfruit trees. Half the village may go fishing by torchlight and the curving reef will gleam with wavering lights and echo with shouts of triumph or disappointment, teasing words or smothered cries of outraged modesty. Or a group of youths may dance for the pleasure of some visiting maiden. Many of those who have retired to sleep, drawn by the merry music, will wrap their sheets about them and set out to find the dancing. A white-clad, ghostly throng will gather in a circle about the gaily lit house, a circle from which every now and then a few will detach themselves and wander away among the trees. Sometimes sleep will not descend upon the village until long past midnight; then at last there is only the mellow thunder of the reef and the whisper of lovers, as the village rests until dawn.

Lines of Inquiry
"A Day in Samoa"

In keeping with her title, Mead describes the events that take place during a typical day in Samoa. What kinds of details does Mead emphasize in her description to help you *feel* what it might be like to live through a day in Samoa? How does she try to keep her description from turning into a mechanical summary of information? How does she describe a typical day so that it seems lively and interesting from beginning to end? How, in turn, does she organize her material overall, and in each of her five paragraphs, so as to provide an orderly description of the day?

As a cultural anthropologist, Mead tells about "a day in Samoa," because she aims to reveal the typical incidents and patterns of life in this tropical island culture. What incidents and patterns of life seem to stand out as being most distinctive and important in Samoan culture? What incidents and patterns of life did you find most surprising and unusual? In what respects does a day in Samoa seem most different from a day in your own culture? In what respects, if any, does a day there seem like a day in your own culture?

Imagine that a cultural anthropologist were to observe a typical day on your campus, or in your hometown. What incidents and patterns of life do you think such an observer would consider to be most distinctive and important in providing an accurate description of a typical day in your culture? What incidents or patterns of life do you suppose would strike an anthropologist as most surprising and unusual?

Warfare: An Invention—
Not a Biological Necessity

Is war a biological neces-
sity, a sociological inevitability or just a bad invention? Those who argue for the first view endow man with such pugnacious instincts that
some outlet in aggressive behavior is necessary if man is to reach full
human stature. It was this point of view which lay back of William
James's famous essay, "The Moral Equivalent of War," in which he
tried to retain the warlike virtues and channel them in new directions.
A similar point of view has lain back of the Soviet Union's attempt to
make competition between groups rather than between individuals. A
basic, competitive, aggressive, warring human nature is assumed, and
those who wish to outlaw war or outlaw competitiveness merely try to
find new and less socially destructive ways in which these biologically
given aspects of man's nature can find expression. Then there are those
who take the second view: warfare is the inevitable concomitant of the
development of the state, the struggle for land and natural resources of
class societies springing, not from the nature of man, but from the nature of history. War is nevertheless inevitable unless we change our
social system and outlaw classes, the struggle for power, and possessions; and in the event of our success warfare would disappear, as a
symptom vanishes when the disease is cured.

One may hold a compromise position between these two extremes;
one may claim that all aggression springs from the frustration of man's
biologically determined drives and that, since all forms of culture are
frustrating, it is certain each new generation will be aggressive and the
aggression will find its natural and inevitable expression in race war,
class war, nationalistic war, and so on.

All three positions are very popular today among those who think
seriously about the problems of war and its possible prevention, but I
wish to urge another point of view, less defeatist perhaps than the first
and third, and more accurate than the second: that is, that warfare, by
which I mean organized conflict between two groups *as groups,* in which
each group puts an army (even if the army is only fifteen Pygmies) into
the field to fight and kill, if possible, some of the members of the army
of the other group—that warfare of this sort is an invention like any
other of the inventions in terms of which we order our lives, such as
writing, marriage, cooking our food instead of eating it raw, trial by
jury, or burial of the dead, and so on. Some of this list any one will
grant are inventions: trial by jury is confined to very limited portions

of the globe; we know that there are tribes that do not bury their dead but instead expose or cremate them; and we know that only part of the human race has had a knowledge of writing as its cultural inheritance. But, whenever a way of doing things is found universally, such as the use of fire or the practice of some form of marriage, we tend to think at once that it is not an invention at all but an attribute of humanity itself. And yet even such universals as marriage and the use of fire are inventions like the rest, very basic ones, inventions which were perhaps necessary if human history was to take the turn it has taken, but nevertheless inventions. At some point in his social development man was undoubtedly without the institution of marriage or the knowledge of the use of fire.

The case for warfare is much clearer because there are peoples even today who have no warfare. Of these the Eskimo are perhaps the most conspicuous example, but the Lepchas of Sikkim are an equally good one. Neither of these peoples understands war, not even defensive warfare. The idea of warfare is lacking, and this idea is as essential to carrying on war as an alphabet or a syllabary is to writing. But whereas the Lepchas are a gentle, unquarrelsome people, and the advocates of other points of view might argue that they are not full human beings or that they had never been frustrated and so had no aggression to expend in warfare, the Eskimo case gives no such possibility of interpretation. The Eskimo are not a mild and meek people; many of them are turbulent and troublesome. Fights, theft of wives, murder, cannibalism occur among them—all outbursts of passionate men goaded by desire or intolerable circumstance. Here are men faced with hunger, men faced with loss of their wives, men faced with the threat of extermination by other men, and here are orphan children, growing up miserably with no one to care for them, mocked and neglected by those about them. The personality necessary for war, the circumstances necessary to goad men to desperation are present, but there is no war. When a traveling Eskimo entered a settlement he might have to fight the strongest man in the settlement to establish his position among them, but this was a test of strength and bravery, not war. The idea of warfare, of one *group* organizing against another *group* to maim and wound and kill them, was absent. And without that idea passions might rage but there was no war.

But, it may be argued, isn't this because the Eskimo have such a low and undeveloped form of social organization? They own no land, they move from place to place, camping, it is true, season after season on the same site, but this is not something to fight for as the modern nations of the world fight for land and raw materials. They have no permanent possessions that can be looted, no towns that can be burned. They have no social classes to produce stress and strains within the society which might force it to go to war outside. Doesn't the absence

5

of war among the Eskimo, while disproving the biological necessity of war, just go to confirm the point that it is the state of development of the society which accounts for war, and nothing else?

We find the answer among the Pygmy peoples of the Andaman Islands in the Bay of Bengal. The Andamans also represent an exceedingly low level of society: they are a hunting and food-gathering people; they live in tiny hordes without any class stratification; their houses are simpler than the snow houses of the Eskimo. But they knew about warfare. The army might contain only fifteen determined pygmies marching in a straight line, but it was the real thing none the less. Tiny army met tiny army in open battle, blows were exchanged, casualties suffered, and the state of warfare could only be concluded by a peace-making ceremony.

Similarly, among the Australian aborigines, who built no permanent dwellings but wandered from water hole to water hole over their almost desert country, warfare—and rules of "international law"—were highly developed. The student of social evolution will seek in vain for his obvious causes of war, struggle for lands, struggle for power of one group over another, expansion of population, need to divert the minds of a populace restive under tyranny, or even the ambition of a successful leader to enhance his own prestige. All are absent, but warfare as a practice remained, and men engaged in it and killed one another in the course of a war because killing is what is done in wars.

From instances like these it becomes apparent that an inquiry into the causes of war misses the fundamental point as completely as does an insistence upon the biological necessity of war. If a people have an idea of going to war and the idea that war is the way in which certain situations, defined within their society, are to be handled, they will sometimes go to war. If they are a mild and unaggressive people, like the Pueblo Indians, they may limit themselves to defensive warfare; but they will be forced to think in terms of war because there are peoples near them who have warfare as a pattern, and offensive, raiding, pillaging warfare at that. When the pattern of warfare is known, people like the Pueblo Indians will defend themselves, taking advantage of their natural defenses, the *mesa* village site, and people like the Lepchas, having no natural defenses and no idea of warfare, will merely submit to the invader. But the essential point remains the same. There is a way of behaving which is known to a given people and labeled as an appropriate form of behavior. A bold and warlike people like the Sioux or the Maori may label warfare as desirable as well as possible; a mild people like the Pueblo Indians may label warfare as undesirable; but to the minds of both peoples the possibility of warfare is present. Their thoughts, their hopes, their plans are oriented about this idea, that warfare may be selected as the way to meet some situation.

So simple peoples and civilized peoples, mild peoples and violent, assertive peoples, will all go to war if they have the invention, just as those peoples who have the custom of dueling will have duels and peoples who have the pattern of vendetta will indulge in vendetta. And, conversely, peoples who do not know of dueling will not fight duels, even though their wives are seduced and their daughters ravished; they may on occasion commit murder but they will not fight duels. Cultures which lack the idea of the vendetta will not meet every quarrel in this way. A people can use only the forms it has. So the Balinese have their special way of dealing with a quarrel between two individuals; if the two feel that the causes of quarrel are heavy they may go and register their quarrel in the temple before the gods, and, making offerings, they may swear never to have anything to do with each other again. Under the Dutch government they registered such mutual "not-speaking" with the Dutch government officials. But in other societies, although individuals might feel as full of animosity and as unwilling to have any further contact as do the Balinese, they cannot register their quarrel with the gods and go on quietly about their business because registering quarrels with the gods is not an invention of which they know.

Yet, if it be granted that warfare is after all an invention, it may nevertheless be an invention that lends itself to certain types of personality, to the exigent needs of autocrats, to the expansionist desires of crowded peoples, to the desire for plunder and rape and loot which is engendered by a dull and frustrating life. What, then, can we say of this congruence between warfare and its uses? If it is a form which fits so well, is not this congruence the essential point? But even here the primitive material causes us to wonder, because there are tribes who go to war merely for glory, having no quarrel with the enemy, suffering from no tyrant within their boundaries, anxious neither for land nor loot nor women, but merely anxious to win prestige which within that tribe has been declared obtainable only by war and without which no young man can hope to win his sweetheart's smile of approval. But if, as was the case with the Bush Negroes of Dutch Guiana, it is artistic ability which is necessary to win a girl's approval, the same young man would have to be carving rather than going out on a war party.

In many parts of the world, war is a game in which the individual can win counters—counters which bring him prestige in the eyes of his own sex or of the opposite sex; he plays for these counters as he might, in our society, strive for a tennis championship. Warfare is a frame for such prestige-seeking merely because it calls for the display of certain skills and certain virtues; all of these skills—riding straight, shooting straight, dodging the missiles of the enemy and sending one's own straight to the mark—can be equally well exercised in some other framework and, equally, the virtues—endurance, bravery, loyalty, steadfastness—can be displayed in other contexts. The tie-up between proving oneself a man and proving this by a success in organized killing is due to a definition which many societies have made of manliness. And often, even in those societies which counted success in warfare a

10

proof of human worth, strange turns were given to the idea, as when the Plains Indians gave their highest awards to the man who touched a live enemy rather than to the man who brought in a scalp—from a dead enemy—because killing a man was less risky. Warfare is just an invention known to the majority of human societies by which they permit their young men either to accumulate prestige or avenge their honor or acquire loot or wives or slaves or sago lands or cattle or appease the blood lust of their gods or the restless souls of the recently dead. It is just an invention, older and more widespread than the jury system, but none the less an invention.

But, once we have said this, have we said anything at all? Despite a few instances, dear to the hearts of controversialists, of the loss of the useful arts, once an invention is made which proves congruent with human needs or social forms, it tends to persist. Grant that war is an invention, that it is not a biological necessity nor the outcome of certain special types of social forms, still, once the invention is made, what are we to do about it? The Indian who had been subsisting on the buffalo for generations because with his primitive weapons he could slaughter only a limited number of buffalo did not return to his primitive weapons when he saw that the white man's more efficient weapons were exterminating the buffalo. A desire for the white man's cloth may mortgage the South Sea Islander to the white man's plantation, but he does not return to making bark cloth, which would have left him free. Once an invention is known and accepted, men do not easily relinquish it. The skilled workers may smash the first steam looms which they feel are to be their undoing, but they accept them in the end, and no movement which has insisted upon the mere abandonment of usable inventions has ever had much success. Warfare is here, as part of our thought; the deeds of warriors are immortalized in the words of our poets; the toys of our children are modeled upon the weapons of the soldier; the frame of reference within which our statesmen and our diplomats work always contains war. If we know that it is not inevitable, that it is due to historical accident that warfare is one of the ways in which we think of behaving, are we given any hope by that? What hope is there of persuading nations to abandon war, nations so thoroughly imbued with the idea that resort to war is, if not actually desirable and noble, at least inevitable whenever certain defined circumstances arise?

In answer to this question I think we might turn to the history of other social inventions, inventions which must once have seemed as firmly entrenched as warfare. Take the methods of trial which preceded the jury system: ordeal and trial by combat. Unfair, capricious, alien as they are to our feeling today, they were once the only methods open to individuals accused of some offense. The invention of trial by jury gradually replaced these methods until only witches, and finally not even witches, had to resort to the ordeal. And for a long time the jury system seemed the one best and finest method of settling legal disputes, but today new inventions, trial before judges only or before commissions, are replacing the jury system. In each case the old method was replaced by a new social invention; the ordeal did not go out because people thought it unjust or wrong, it went out because a method more congruent with the institutions and feelings of the period was invented. And, if we despair over the way in which war seems such an ingrained habit of most of the human race, we can take comfort from the fact that a poor invention will usually give place to a better invention.

For this, two conditions at least are necessary. The people must recognize the defects of the old invention, and some one must make a new one. Propaganda against warfare, documentation of its terrible cost in human suffering and social waste, these prepare the ground by teaching people to feel that warfare is a defective social institution. There is further needed a belief that social invention is possible and the invention of new methods which will render warfare as out-of-date as the tractor is making the plow, or the motor car the horse and buggy. A form of behavior becomes out-of-date only when something else takes its place, and in order to invent forms of behavior which will make war obsolete, it is a first requirement to believe that an invention is possible.

Lines of Inquiry
"Warfare: An Invention—Not a Biological Necessity"

Mead argues in this essay that warfare is "an invention—not a biological necessity" or an inevitable outgrowth of social development. In what respects is warfare "an invention"? Have you ever heard it referred to in that way? What evidence and logic does she use to support her claim that warfare is an invention? What kind of evidence and logic does she use to challenge the views of her opponents? In what respects do you find her arguments most convincing? In what respects do you find them least convincing?

Given her claim that warfare is an invention, she also believes that a better invention can replace it, "which will make war obsolete." What kind of invention do you think she has in mind as being sufficient to put an end to war? What kinds of inventions do you know of that have been tried as alternatives to war? Why do you suppose they failed to make war obsolete?

Other essays in this collection are concerned with the origin, nature, and significance of war, such as Thoreau's "War of the Ants" or Hemingway's "A New Kind of War." What view of war seems uppermost in each of these three pieces? What strategy does each author use to present his or her idea of war? How do you account for the strikingly different modes of presentation that each author uses in his or her piece about war?

Adolescents

At adolescence children begin to move toward an unknown future. The translucent walls of childhood no longer close them in, for suddenly they discover the wide gateways and the gates ready to swing open at a touch of the hand. The way is open for them to move away from the family, away from the familiar gardens and ponds and woods where they came to know the natural world, away from the fireside stories told them by their grandmothers, away from the brothers and sisters who will always be older and younger than they, and away from the playmates who shared their earliest games.

Up to adolescence the child lived in a circumscribed world. However individual and gifted, lively and intelligent he seemed to his parents, he was still a child for whom others had to plan, who had to be admonished, hedged about with protective rules, and kept within bounds. But with adolescence the old rules lose their meaning, and children begin to look beyond the old boundaries with new farseeing eyes. The adolescent boy gives up the dream of competition with his father in which he sometimes triumphed and sometimes despaired of ever accomplishing as much as his father had. Instead, he now looks forward to what he actually may become. The adolescent girl who once held her doll as her mother held her baby now looks forward in earnest, picturing the woman she will become and the living child she may rock in her arms. At adolescence, children stand at the gates, vividly seeing— and yet not seeing—the pathways of their own lives. For better or worse, each family has accomplished the task of caring for its sons and daughters, and they have learned, well or badly, the essential lessons their parents could teach them.

For the adolescent the paths leading out from the swinging gates are both entrancing and frightening. Even for the youth who has been an intrepid child traveler, the first journeys away from home may seem too difficult to accomplish. Girls who ranged the streams and mountains beside their brothers become shy and timid, their hands hot and cold, their smiles precarious. One day they want to dress as children, the next as women of the world. Each adolescent in his own way hesitates at the threshold. One sallies out and then, frightened by his own temerity, hurries back; but safely inside he looks out longingly, ready to be off again. Another hangs back, willing and unwilling, until at some sign known only to himself he moves ahead boldly, once and for all.

Everywhere in the world people mark the moment when a girl passes from childhood to physical maturity and the time when the boy's voice cracks and deepens and his beard, slight as it may be for some racial stocks, begins to grow. For the elders these changes signal the end of one kind of responsibility and the beginning of another more onerous one. Little children must be ceaselessly guarded and cared for, but adolescents, who still are in need of protection, are creatures whom it is almost impossible to protect. Their safety now depends on their earlier learning in childhood and on the way the other adolescents around them are growing toward adulthood.

In a society in which boys go out on dangerous raids, a mother   5 may make magic to protect her adolescent son's life, but any attempt to keep him at home when others go out will also endanger him. Where adolescent girls have a special house to which boys come with flutes to court them, a father may tremble for his daughter's safety and fear that the wooing may go wrong, but by interfering he will only create new difficulties. In every society adolescents take over the world's ways and parents must yield their assent.

Sometimes parents are permitted to lock up their daughters, and girls can only whisper to their lovers through barred windows. Sometimes boys are shut up in schools where older boys teach and harry them and men wearing the masks of frightening authority give them a last set of admonitions about manliness. Sometimes, at the beginning of adolescence, boys are sent as war scouts on dangerous missions and on long night errands through the enemy-infested bush. And sometimes each boy must go out alone and wait, fasting and vigilant, in the hope of winning the protection of a guardian spirit. Whatever the customary ways are for children to emerge into youth, these indicate the kinds of paths adolescents must take. Individual families can neither shield their children nor safely direct them along different paths. Individual parents who set themselves against custom become involved in a much greater struggle than those who watch with bated breath as their children set out on their first adventures.

The world over, adolescence is the period of greatest differentiation between boys and girls, not only in the anxieties felt by their parents but also in the dreams that animate them. Yet the boy and the girl, each in a different way, are equally preoccupied by the task of becoming, physically, a man and a woman—no longer someone's child, but potentially the parent of a child. Within their own bodies changes are taking place that they cannot ignore, and in the world outside they are confronted by alterations in treatment that match their visible growth and approaching maturity.

In some societies adolescents are left to realize change at their own pace. No one records their age. No one complains about the slow pace of this boy or the fast pace of that girl in growing up. Children are safe in their childhood as long as they are unready; and each chooses when to begin courtship and the first tentative search for a mate. One by one, the boys drift away from the boys' gang, take on the stance of young

men, and move toward the girls who also, one by one, grow into readiness to receive them. No one will hurry them.

But in most societies adults express old fears and new fears, old
hopes and new hopes as they urge on and hold back adolescent boys
and girls, guard them and leave them to fend for themselves. All the
girls may be betrothed early in childhood and sent to their prospective
husbands' homes before they reach puberty. In this the girls have no
choice. They must accept their new families as unquestioningly as they
accepted the families into which they were born. And the boys, given
their wives, have as little choice and yet are expected to be grateful to
those who have made this provision for their future.

At the other extreme are the adolescents who are trapped in the   10
neglect and poverty of great cities. Growing up in families whose kinship ties are disrupted and whose links to a more stable past are broken,
they can expect no help from parents who do not understand their new
urban life. Unschooled, unprotected, and unguided, each adolescent is
left to follow the initiative of other adolescents. In a society that makes
no coherent plan for them and coming from families who do not know
what plans to make, they turn to radio and television, mass magazines
and comic strips in search of guidance. Children of the mass media,
they learn from headlines how other adolescents, equally at sea, dress
and talk, think and act. In a simpler society, adolescents share the channeled dreams of all young people, and their parents, whose adolescence
differed hardly at all from their own, can set up guideposts that will
lead a new generation safely into adulthood. In contrast, modern adolescents are exposed to the fads and extreme actions of hundreds of
thousands of young people who drift on a chartless course between a
narrower, traditional world and a world whose dimensions are still un-
clear. All they have to follow are the published statistics of how many
of them are now—this year, this month, this week—turning in questing
masses first in one direction and then in another. For these adolescents,
as in no other generation, the end of the journey in adulthood is unknown.

An unbridgeable gulf seems to separate the life of the five boys who
are growing up in a shepherd hamlet, each of whom will choose a wife
from among the six girls in that hamlet or the twenty girls living in
nearby villages, from the life of young people who crowd, ten thousand strong, to welcome a television star at an airport. Yet the tasks
confronting the shepherd boy are no different from those facing the
teen-age city boy who moves so lightly to the rhythm set last week by
a new hit record. For now, at adolescence, both boys must give up the
dependence of childhood and move toward the autonomy and interdependence of adulthood.

Wherever a boy grows up, he must learn to leave home without
fear, leaving behind him the old battles of childhood, and learn to re-

turn home from school or work or an assignment in a far city or over-seas ready to treat his parents differently. Where he is permitted choice, he must be prepared to make a choice. Where no choice is open to him, the decision to go another way means that he must be prepared to blaze a new and lonely path. If he succeeds, he may open that path to others. If he fails, others coming after him may have a harder time.

For the young boy who rebels against the choices that have been made for him—refuses the wife who has been chosen in his name, de-serts the craft to which he has been apprenticed, leaves the school or college to which he has been sent—the battle is a lonely one. At the moment of rebellion the battle is joined not with his whole society— for if it is, he becomes a criminal—but with his own parents whose demands he cannot meet. Such a battle generates an almost unbearable tension, as his old childish love and dependence must be opposed both to a desire for independence which his parents approve and to a course which they disapprove. In some societies, it is not only the rebel who suffers, but also the boy struggling to meet the demands made on him— to show bravery in battle, seek a vision on a mountainside, endure a period of poverty and self-discipline in a monastery, work as an ill-fed and much-abused apprentice, last out the hard grind before he can enter a profession, practice every day the difficult skills that will make him an athlete, a mountain guide, or a pilot. If he fails, or even thinks he has failed, he has been taught to feel he will betray his parents, and he may be tempted to revenge himself on them by killing the child they failed to rear in their image of what their child should be. In still other societies grandfathers stand behind the springing young boys, guarding their inexperience. But elsewhere there are no such safeguards. Fathers relinquish their authority early, and boys of thirteen or fourteen, long before they can break away in rebellion, are pushed into man-hood and have the cares and responsibilities of manhood thrust on their shoulders.

The problems girls face, the world over, are not those that confront their brothers, but very different ones. For the adolescent girl may still feel like a child or she may still long to roam the hills with her brothers as she did when she was a child, but now, unlike a child, she can con-ceive. And long before she has the discretion or the judgment to choose among suitors or to weigh the temptation of the moment against her hopes for the future, her body, outstripping her imagination, or her imagination, outstripping her physical readiness, may involve her in an irrevocable act. The boy who breaks his bow string, turns tail in battle, hesitates before an order, or fails in school can still retrieve his losses by stringing the bow better, returning to school, learning to obey and to command. But for the girl herself and for society, the change is irreversible. It does not matter whether the child she has conceived is lost immediately after conception, whether it is born in wedlock or out of wedlock, whether it lives or dies. The event cannot be set aside. One more child, if it lives, will have started life in one way and not in another, and the girl herself can go on, but she cannot begin afresh.

Because parenthood for the girl and parenthood for the boy are fundamentally different, it has taken a very long time to develop contexts in which girls can be allowed to become persons before they become mothers. And because, in the end, the education of boys depends partly on the mothers who rear them, and the sisters with whom they play and compete or whom they cherish and protect, it also took a long time before boys were permitted to become full persons. Throughout human history, most peoples have been intent, most of the time, on turning most young boys and girls into parents whose primary task it has been to rear children who, in their turn, would become parents also. With rare exceptions, girls have always been reared to become parents, and persons only incidentally, and boys, too, have been reared to become parents, and persons only if they have belonged to some specially privileged elite. 15

But very slowly the burden has been lifting. Each small savage society had to lay on every able member the responsibility of reproduction first and then for continual, unremitting daily concern for food and for protection against cold and danger. The burden was lifted first from the sons of those of high rank and, occasionally, the youth of high promise, and later from a few daughters who shared, almost accidentally, in their brothers' privileges. Gradually it has been lifted also from larger and larger numbers of young people in those countries that have conquered the relentless problems of hunger and cold. In the past, most boys, as soon as they left childhood, had no choice but to hunt, herd sheep, fish, toil in the fields, or work at a craft, or, in more recent times, work as unskilled laborers who never earned more than was enough to buy tomorrow's food and pay next week's rent. But in modern societies, it has been possible to keep an ever larger number of adolescents in school and to give them an opportunity to think further than their fathers thought, explore the life of other periods and other cultures, and to become both civilized men, inheritors of the past, and modern men, ready to make a different future. And as our capacity to free more adolescents has increased, our willingness also has grown to permit them to become what they have the potentiality to be as persons.

This change has coincided with a tremendous increase in the world's population. In the past, men struggled desperately to preserve the small tribes or nations to which they owed their sense of identity. Today we are engaged in a common enterprise in the attempt to preserve mankind, as all men are endangered by the weapons of destruction they have now—and will always have—the knowledge to build. In the past people counted the children who were born, wept for the many who died, and wondered whether the living were enough to do the work, guard the group from danger, and reproduce the group in the next generation. Now we know we must stem the uncontrolled growth of the earth's population. When almost all children live, fewer children need be born. When almost no mothers die, fewer women need bear children. When as many children grow up in small families as once survived only in very large families, so many of whose children died, men and women need not marry so early or devote so large a part of their lives to parenthood. Now, when our task is to balance the world's population at a level at which every child who is born anywhere, in the most remote valley and on the highest plateau, will have an opportunity to become a person, we do not need to organize the world in such a way that the relentless, unremitting needs of parenthood and poverty weigh down adolescents as soon as they leave childhood behind, making them old before their time. Our new command of nature, which makes it possible for the first time in human history to organize a world without war, save the children who are born, and feed and clothe every child, also allows us to offer to all adolescents, not only the chosen and privileged few, a chance to grow further.

Man's history has been one of longer and longer periods of growth. In the very distant past, before men as we know them had evolved, the period of growth must have been even shorter and boys must have been ready for the tasks of procreation and parenthood very young. Later, when members of our own species were living under extremely primitive conditions, boys had learned all they needed to know in order to survive by the time they were six or seven years of age, but they matured more slowly. At adolescence they were ready to assume the responsibilities of manhood, and so it has remained for primitive men, for peasants, and for the poor in industrial cities. The demands made on them permitted them to grow no more. Even when the years of education lengthened a little in the more fortunate modern countries, the idea survived that growth stopped somewhere in mid-adolescence. There was, as there still is, a general expectation that most young people would give up learning and growing when they left school. Set in a mold, they were ready to work day in and day out, because otherwise they and their children would not eat. They stepped from childhood to adolescence and from early adolescence immediately into maturity, and then aged early.

But in the last ten thousand years—and possibly for a longer time—some societies began to benefit from the accumulated knowledge that made it possible for men to plan ahead—to raise more food than they immediately needed, to store food, and to feed a larger number of people—so that some men were freed to study, to think, and to build a larger tradition. In time, in some societies, men watched the stars and measured the phases of the sun and the moon, designed great buildings, carved, painted, created systems of notation, built cities and organized nations, and dreamed of including all men, not merely the members of their own tribe, their own city, or their own race, within one system of values, cherishing common goals.

With leisure and the freedom given to some young men to pursue 20
the new arts and sciences of civilization, a new human capacity was discovered: the idealism of adolescence. Among a primitive people, as each new generation lives much the same life the parent generation also lived, adolescents do not reveal their capacity to dream soaring dreams, make mighty plans, leap in thought to new formulations of the relations of mind and matter, and visualize the place of man on earth, in the solar system, in the galaxy, in an expanding universe. Until men lived in the kinds of societies in which leisure was a possibility, and a few adolescents had time to grow further away from childhood, youth was untouched by idealism. Indeed, in many societies, young people were more cowed, more submissive, and less rebellious than their aging and less responsible elders.

With the development of civilization, as knowledge accumulated and systems of writing made it possible to preserve and communicate to others, as yet unborn, what was known, new processes of development were also revealed in adolescents. Moving away from childhood, boys and young men were no longer exposed only to the drudgery and the small excitements of the daily round. Some of them, at least, heard and saw and read about the things earlier great men had dreamed of and sung of, written about, and built. The spacious vision of the exceptional man did not die with him, but became the property of young men who came after him. In each generation there were young men, and occasionally young women, who could match the unsatisfactory present against the prophecies of a better future or the dream of a golden past, and these young people, in their turn, were led to prophesy, strike out in bold adventure, break the bonds of tradition, discover new fields, and plunge forward into some new understanding of the universe and man.

In any growing civilization, some young men have been allowed to live out and prolong their adolescence, free from the pressure to marry and from the necessity of working for their bread. This leisure not only has given them time to grow, but also time for friendship before parenthood. It is essentially in the continuation of companionship outside the family, in relationships other than those concerned with courtship, marriage, and parenthood, that adolescents can seek and find the strength and the vision to carry one step farther the civilization into which they were born and of which they are the heirs. The urgent desire, everywhere in the world, to give children more schooling and more time to learn has at its base a very profound need. The rationale of educational plans in the contemporary world is the necessity of having a more literate population, able to do the work of a more literate and complicated society. But the underlying need goes far beyond this. Giving children time to prolong their growing is intrinsic to the very creation of that literate and complicated society. Without vision the people perish, and the power of seeing visions must be fostered in adolescents if we are to have the visionaries the world needs.

For many centuries civilizations have struggled with the problem of how to give men—and sometimes women—the freedom in which inspiration, knowledge, and art can flower. One solution has been to create a dichotomy in which the life of sex and parenthood has been set apart from a life of celibacy, asceticism, and thought or prayer. In a society that accepted this solution, the parent was never so specialized or developed a person as were those who carried on the spiritual, intellectual, and artistic work of the world. Moreover, every child was presented with two conflicting life paths, as he had to choose between the pursuit of knowledge, on the one hand, and the life of the family, on the other. Only in the next generation, if he chose to have children, might a son realize his other dreams and, turning away from parenthood, devote himself entirely to religion, the arts, scholarship, or science. In other societies, all boys have lived for a period apart from the secular world, as a way of giving them access to traditional knowledge and insight into the spiritual resources of a great religion, as one aspect of their on-going lives. In still other societies, childhood and old age were equated in the sense that the intensive learning of childhood, practiced throughout life, came to flower only when men retired from everyday responsibilities and could devote themselves wholly to thought, poetry, painting, and music. But all these have been essentially conservative solutions, the solutions worked out by societies among whom only a few were the chosen carriers of a great tradition, and only a few had the freedom to become creative individuals.

In most modern societies this selection and segregation of the few from the many is breaking down. Those who dedicate themselves wholly to important work now live in the world. Even though they may not marry, they do not live a life apart. However, where once the population was divided into the many who bore and reared children and the few who had time all their lives to think and to grow, there is now developing in many parts of the modern world a new dichotomy based on sex. For increasingly, adolescent boys are being educated, while girls, like the vast majority of men and women in medieval Europe who chose parenthood, are asked to set aside their dreams of what they might become in favor of immediate marriage and parenthood.

In creating this new dichotomy we resemble the primitive peoples 25 who did not understand paternity. For we do not take into account fatherhood or realize that in establishing a kind of society in which girls must become mothers as adolescents, before they have had time to become individuals, we also are forcing boys to become fathers before they have become individuals. In our civilization we are the beneficiaries of poor societies in which only a few had leisure, but we are not yet fully conscious of the power our new affluence gives us to make all men the beneficiaries of that past and to open the way for every adolescent to grow slowly through a long youth into mature individuality.

All around the world, youth is stirring. Often that stirring is the blind movement of disorganized mobs. There is a restlessness that is widely expressed in demands for privilege, for power, for change, for marriage as a right rather than as a responsibility, and for parenthood as a pleasure rather than as a vocation. That blind movement and those demands express the deep contradictions characteristic of our time—a time of transition.

Perhaps even more important than the revolution in the lives of peoples who for centuries have been subjected to tyranny and alien authority is the surging revolution of young people who are seeking a new place in a new kind of world. The more rapidly the world changes, the greater is the contrast between older people, who have had to learn so many new things during their lifetime, and younger people, who take the same things for granted. Young people who all their lives have been familiar with cars and how they are driven, who know how a jet plane is operated and how a computer is built, have an appearance of startling precocity as they move among adults for whom this knowledge and these skills are still new and strange. How can parents feel that their adolescent children are, in fact, adolescents, when these children know so much that they, the parents, learned only yesterday and with great difficulty? The authority in adult voices flickers, hesitates, grows shrill, and young people, sensing adult uncertainty and weakness, press harder against the barriers that hold them back from full participation in life. From their viewpoint they are asking for full citizenship and the right to be men and women at once, because they are already more skilled and knowledgeable than their parents. But the fulfillment of their demands would have the effect of putting the clock back, rather than moving it forward, and of reinstating a kind of world in which all young people were set to work at sober, confining tasks as soon as they were able to undertake them. At the threshold of a new age, it is as if a generation was turning in blind flight from its vast possibilities.

For all over the world a new age is struggling to be born, an age in which all children can grow up in families and all adolescents can have time to become individuals who are able to meet the demands of a fully adult life. In this new age, in which adolescents need not be forced to become mothers and fathers and grow old before their time, we can set a new value on adolescence of the mind and the spirit. In a society in which no one will be forced into premature adulthood, many people will remain adolescents all their lives, following a vision that is not yet clear, puzzling over a theory that is not yet fully formulated, attempting to create in sound or in color, in meditation or in prayer, in the laboratory or in the library, in the halls of government or in the councils of the nations something as yet unknown.

For long ages the prospect opening out from childhood closed in almost at once. Only a few were free long enough to glimpse a wider horizon, a visionary gleam. With the knowledge gained through their labor and their imagination, still more could be set free. When childhood stretched only a few years ahead, early man was set free to learn a little; when adolescence was prolonged, the men of earlier civilizations were able to leap ahead. In the future we may hope to meet the magnificent responsibilities of our knowledge through the visions of boys and girls who will remain all their lives, not only as adolescents but as adults, open to the widest prospects, "moving about in worlds not realized."

Lines of Inquiry
"Adolescents"

Mead opens this essay with a very specific image that depicts adolescents suddenly discovering "the wide gateways and the gates ready to swing open at a touch of the hand." What does this opening image imply about Mead's idea of adolescence? How does she develop this image in the remainder of the opening paragraph and in the next two paragraphs? What additional implications does the image carry as Mead elaborates on it over the course of these paragraphs? In what ways does the image relate to Mead's subsequent discussion of adolescence? How does it relate to her concluding discussion of the topic?

Notice that Mead titles her essay "Adolescents" rather than "Adolescence." What do you make of this title? What do you infer about her idea of adolescence from the fact that her examples of adolescent experience reflect so many different cultures and periods of history? Near the end of her essay, Mead hopefully envisions "a new age," in which "many people will remain adolescents all their lives." What does this vision imply about Mead's idea of adolescence?

How does Mead's idea of adolescence compare with the behavior of the adolescents whom Wolfe portrays in "The Pump House Gang"? How does her idea of adolescence compare with your own experience of it? What do you think is the essence of adolescence? What distinguishes adolescents from children and adults?

New Superstitions for Old

Once in a while there is a day when everything seems to run smoothly and even the riskiest venture comes out exactly right. You exclaim, "This is my lucky day!" Then as an afterthought you say, "Knock on wood!" Of course, you do not really believe that knocking on wood will ward off danger. Still, boasting about your own good luck gives you a slightly uneasy feeling—and you carry out the little protective ritual. If someone challenged you at that moment, you would probably say, "Oh, that's nothing. Just an old superstition."

But when you come to think about it, what is a superstition?

In the contemporary world most people treat old folk beliefs as superstitions—the belief, for instance, that there are lucky and unlucky days or numbers, that future events can be read from omens, that there are protective charms or that what happens can be influenced by casting spells. We have excluded magic from our current world view, for we know that natural events have natural causes.

In a religious context, where truths cannot be demonstrated, we accept them as a matter of faith. Superstitions, however, belong to the category of beliefs, practices and ways of thinking that have been discarded because they are inconsistent with scientific knowledge. It is easy to say that other people are superstitious because they believe what we regard to be untrue. "Superstition" used in that sense is a derogatory term for the beliefs of other people that we do not share. But there is more to it than that. For superstitions lead a kind of half life in a twilight world where, sometimes, we partly suspend our disbelief and act as if magic worked.

Actually, almost every day, even in the most sophisticated home, something is likely to happen that evokes the memory of some old folk belief. The salt spills. A knife falls to the floor. Your nose tickles. Then perhaps, with a slightly embarrassed smile, the person who spilled the salt tosses a pinch over his left shoulder. Or someone recites the old rhyme, "Knife falls, gentleman calls." Or as you rub your nose you think, That means a letter. I wonder who's writing? No one takes these small responses very seriously or gives them more than a passing thought. Sometimes people will preface one of these ritual acts—walking around instead of under a ladder or hastily closing an umbrella that has been opened inside a house—with such a remark as "I remember my great-aunt used to . . ." or "Germans used to say you ought not . . ." And then, having placed the belief at some distance away in time or space, they carry out the ritual.

Everyone also remembers a few of the observances of childhood—wishing on the first star; looking at the new moon over the right shoulder; avoiding the cracks in the sidewalk on the way to school while chanting, "Step on a crack, break your mother's back"; wishing on white horses, on loads of hay, on covered bridges, on red cars; saying quickly, "Bread-and-butter" when a post or a tree separated you from the friend you were walking with. The adult may not actually recite the formula "Star light, star bright . . ." and may not quite turn to look at the new moon, but his mood is tempered by a little of the old thrill that came when the observance was still freighted with magic.

Superstition can also be used with another meaning. When I discuss the religious beliefs of other peoples, especially primitive peoples, I am often asked, "Do they really have a religion, or is it all just superstition?" The point of contrast here is not between a scientific and a magical view of the world but between the clear, theologically defensible religious beliefs of members of civilized societies and what we regard as the false and childish views of the heathen who "bow down to wood and stone." Within the civilized religions, however, where membership includes believers who are educated and urbane and others who are ignorant and simple, one always finds traditions and practices that the more sophisticated will dismiss offhand as "just superstition" but that guide the steps of those who live by older ways. Mostly these are very ancient beliefs, some handed on from one religion to another and carried from country to country around the world.

Very commonly, people associate superstition with the past, with very old ways of thinking that have been supplanted by modern knowledge. But new superstitions are continually coming into being and flourishing in our society. Listening to mothers in the park in the 1930's, one heard them say, "Now, don't you run out into the sun, or Polio will get you." In the 1940's elderly people explained to one another in tones of resignation, "It was the Virus that got him down." And every year the cosmetics industry offers us new magic—cures for baldness, lotions that will give every woman radiant skin, hair coloring that will restore to the middle-aged the charm and romance of youth—results that are promised if we will just follow the simple directions. Families and individuals also have their cherished, private superstitions. You must leave by the back door when you are going on a journey, or you must wear a green dress when you are taking an examination. It is a kind of joke, of course, but it makes you feel safe.

These old half-beliefs and new half-beliefs reflect the keenness of our wish to have something come true or to prevent something bad from happening. We do not always recognize new superstitions for what they are, and we still follow the old ones because someone's faith long ago matches our contemporary hopes and fears. In the past people "knew" that a black cat crossing one's path was a bad omen, and they turned back home. Today we are fearful of taking a journey and would give anything to turn back—and then we notice a black cat running across the road in front of us.

Child psychologists recognize the value of the toy a child holds in   10
his hand at bedtime. It is different from his thumb, with which he can close himself in from the rest of the world, and it is different from the real world, to which he is learning to relate himself. Psychologists call these toys—these furry animals and old, cozy baby blankets—"transitional objects"; that is, objects that help the child move back and forth between the exactions of everyday life and the world of wish and dream.

Superstitions have some of the qualities of these transitional objects. They help people pass between the areas of life where what happens has to be accepted without proof and the areas where sequences of events are explicable in terms of cause and effect, based on knowledge. Bacteria and viruses that cause sickness have been identified; the cause of symptoms can be diagnosed and a rational course of treatment prescribed. Magical charms no longer are needed to treat the sick; modern medicine has brought the whole sequence of events into the secular world. But people often act as if this change had not taken place. Laymen still treat germs as if they were invisible, malign spirits, and physicians sometimes prescribe antibiotics as if they were magic substances.

Over time, more and more of life has become subject to the controls of knowledge. However, this is never a one-way process. Scientific investigation is continually increasing our knowledge. But if we are to make good use of this knowledge, we must not only rid our minds of old, superseded beliefs and fragments of magical practice, but also recognize new superstitions for what they are. Both are generated by our wishes, our fears and our feeling of helplessness in difficult situations.

Civilized peoples are not alone in having grasped the idea of superstitions—beliefs and practices that are superseded but that still may evoke compliance. The idea is one that is familiar to every people, however primitive, that I have ever known. Every society has a core of transcendent beliefs—beliefs about the nature of the universe, the world and man—that no one doubts or questions. Every society also has a fund of knowledge related to practical life—about the succession of day and night and of the seasons; about correct ways of planting seeds so that they will germinate and grow; about the processes involved in making dyes or the steps necessary to remove the deadly poison from manioc roots so they become edible. Island peoples know how the winds shift and they know the star toward which they must point the prow of the canoe exactly so that as the sun rises they will see the first fringing palms on the shore toward which they are sailing.

This knowledge, based on repeated observations of reliable sequences, leads to ideas and hypotheses of the kind that underlie scientific thinking. And gradually as scientific knowledge, once developed without conscious plan, has become a great self-corrective system and the foundation for rational planning and action, old magical beliefs and observances have had to be discarded.

But it takes time for new ways of thinking to take hold, and often 15 the transition is only partial. Older, more direct beliefs live on in the hearts and minds of elderly people. And they are learned by children who, generation after generation, start out life as hopefully and fearfully as their forebears did. Taking their first steps away from home, children use the old rituals and invent new ones to protect themselves against the strangeness of the world into which they are venturing.

So whatever has been rejected as no longer true, as limited, provincial and idolatrous, still leads a half life. People may say, "It's just a superstition," but they continue to invoke the ritual's protection or potency. In this transitional, twilight state such beliefs come to resemble dreaming. In the dream world a thing can be either good or bad; a cause can be an effect and an effect can be a cause. Do warts come from touching toads, or does touching a toad cure the wart? Is sneezing a good omen or a bad omen? You can have it either way—or both ways at once. In the same sense, the half-acceptance and half-denial accorded superstitions give us the best of both worlds.

Superstitions are sometimes smiled at and sometimes frowned upon as observances characteristic of the old-fashioned, the unenlightened, children, peasants, servants, immigrants, foreigners or backwoods people. Nevertheless, they give all of us ways of moving back and forth among the different worlds in which we live—the sacred, the secular and the scientific. They allow us to keep a private world also, where, smiling a little, we can banish danger with a gesture and summon luck with a rhyme, make the sun shine in spite of storm clouds, force the stranger to do our bidding, keep an enemy at bay and straighten the paths of those we love.

Lines of Inquiry
"New Superstitions for Old"

Throughout this essay, Mead relies heavily on specific details to define, illustrate, and explain the nature of superstition. What areas of experience does she draw on as a primary source for these details? What do these details imply about the nature of superstition? Mead also defines and explains superstition by contrasting it with religious belief and scientific knowledge. How does this mode of definition reinforce, modify, or complicate the idea of superstition that she develops by means of specific examples? What does the title of Mead's essay imply about the nature of superstition?

Mead not only defines superstition, but she also seeks to make sense of its place in human experience. What does she believe to be the value of superstition? What dangers does she implicitly attribute to it? What exactly is Mead's attitude towards superstition, and why does she consider it to be so prominent an aspect of human culture? Does she appear to be superstitious or to have been writing about it as if she were largely free of superstitions?

What evidence or signs of superstition do you see in contemporary American culture? In your family? In yourself? What areas of contemporary life, of your family's life, of your own life seem most prone to superstition? What areas seem least prone to it? What do you believe to be the benefits and dangers of superstition in each case?

George Orwell
(Eric Arthur Blair)
1903–50

This is a political age. War, Fascism, concentration camps, rubber truncheons, atomic bombs, etc., are what we daily think about, and therefore to a great extent what we write about, even when we do not name them openly. We cannot help this. When you are on a sinking ship, your thoughts will be about sinking ships.

Eric Blair (who took the pen name of George Orwell in 1933) stands out as one of the most politically conscious writers in an age of political writing. As he makes clear in this passage, written in 1948, his intensely political concern was aroused not by trivial issues, but by the globally disastrous conditions of his age—"War, Fascism, concentration camps, rubber truncheons, atomic bombs . . . ." During his brief career as a journalist, novelist, satirist, and essayist, he devoted himself almost wholly to writing with a "political purpose," but " 'political' in the widest sense of the word"—with a "desire to push the world in a certain direction, to alter other people's idea of the kind of society they should strive after." Driven by that desire, he managed—despite the affliction of tuberculosis—to produce three documentary books, six novels, a book-length collection of essays, and more than seven hundred journalistic articles and reviews.

Born in Bengal, then a province of British India, Orwell was the second of three children of a minor colonial officer in the Indian Civil Service. In keeping with the social ambitions of his family, he was raised and educated in England, at a convent school in Henley-on-Thames, then at St. Cyprians, a prep school on the south coast, and finally at Eton. At St. Cyprians he first encountered the "snobbish" world "of the English upper and upper-middle classes," a world in which "a glittering car, a title, or a horde of servants was mixed up in people's minds with the idea of actual moral virtue." At Eton he was for a time "both a snob and a revolutionary." After failing to win a university scholarship, he entered the Indian Imperial Police in 1922 and served as a police officer at various posts throughout Burma until he resigned in 1927, "partly because the climate had ruined my health, partly because I already had vague ideas of writing books, but mainly because I could not go on any longer serving an imperialism I had come to regard as very largely a racket."

Orwell moved to Paris in 1928 and worked unsuccessfully at his writing until he ran out of money and was forced to support himself as a dishwasher, an experience that made him realize how little he knew "about working class conditions," about unemployment, and about poverty. So when he returned to England at the end of 1929, he deliberately chose to immerse himself in the world of "social outcasts: tramps, beggars, criminals, prostitutes." His experiences "among the oppressed" provided the material for his first documentary book, *Down and Out in Paris and London* (1933). His experiences in Burma provided the material for his first novel, *Burmese Days* (1934), which expressed the disgust with British imperialism that he was to convey once again in "Shooting an Elephant" (1936). Early in 1936, he accepted the invitation of a socialist group to observe the plight of unemployed coal miners in the north of England and to write about their impoverished situation, as he did in *The Road to Wigan Pier* (1937), a documentary work that also includes several autobiographical chapters about the political and social transformation he underwent between his time in the Imperial Indian Police and his subsequent work as a chronicler of the oppressed. In June 1936 he was married, and in late 1936 he went to observe and take part in the Spanish Civil War.

Though he stayed in Spain only for six months, fighting on the Republican side until he was shot in the throat by a Fascist sniper, his experiences there "turned the scale" for him. From then on "every line of serious work" that he produced was "written, directly or indirectly, *against* totalitarianism and *for* democratic socialism." Fighting and living in the Spanish countryside and then in revolutionary Barcelona, Orwell had glimpsed, however briefly, what appeared to be the ideal of a classless socialist society, only to see it undermined by the devious "efforts of the Russian Government to prevent revolution in Spain." His account of the war in *Homage to Catalonia* (1938) reveals that the political situation was far more complex than he had originally supposed. The difficulty of understanding that situation, as he makes clear in "Looking Back on the Spanish Civil War" (1943), was compounded by the widespread distortion of truth, both in outright political propaganda and in "newspaper reports which did not bear any relation to the facts." From that disturbing experience he developed the passionate commitment to clear and honest writing that he later expressed in "Politics and the English Language" (1946).

During the last ten years of his life, Orwell produced his two most well-known political novels, the beast fable of *Animal Farm* (1945) and the nightmarish political vision of *1984* (1949), which together convey what he perceived to be the special horrors of totalitarianism—the brutality, the lies, the corruption of language, the thought control, the overwhelming tyranny of the state. During the same period, though increasingly weakened by his tubercular condition, he also gave voice to his political concerns in articles, book reviews, columns, letters, and essays for a broad range of magazines and newspapers. In virtually all of this work, "directly or indirectly" he sought "to push the world" in the direction of decency, honesty, liberty, and human well-being. Given his intense concern with the dangers of propaganda, of party lines, he never let himself become too closely aligned with any political position, not even with socialism. Indeed, he was at last too individualistic, too intellectually curious, too devoted to getting at the truth of things ever to let himself be strictly hemmed in by any political position.

Orwell's concern for clear and truthful writing is reflected in the very direct style of his own prose—in the familiar words, the straightforward sentences, the vividly detailed images, scenes and events through which he expresses his thoughts. He is equally straightforward whether he is writing about the beauty of toads or the horror of capital punishment:

> I mention the spawning of toads because it is one of the phenomena of spring that most deeply appeal to me, and because the toad, unlike the skylark and the primose, has never had much of a boost from the poets.

> When I saw the prisoner step aside to avoid the puddle, I saw the mystery, the unspeakable wrongness, of cutting a life short when it is in full tide.

Here as elsewhere, his style is forceful because he follows his own advice of "using the fewest and shortest words that will cover one's meaning." Ultimately his prose is forceful because he is always true to his commitment "to see things as they are," and to present things as he sees them, no matter how painful the vision might be:

> I thought of a rather cruel trick I once played on a wasp. He was sucking jam on my plate, and I cut him in half. He paid no attention, merely went on with his meal, while a tiny stream of jam trickled out of his severed oesophagus. Only when he tried to fly away did he grasp the dreadful thing that had happened to him. It is the same with modern man. The thing that has been cut away is his soul, and there was a period—twenty years, perhaps—during which he did not notice it.

A Hanging

It was in Burma, a sodden morning of the rains. A sickly light, like yellow tinfoil, was slanting over the high walls into the jail yard. We were waiting outside the condemned cells, a row of sheds fronted with double bars, like small animal cages. Each cell measured about ten feet by ten and was quite bare within except for a plank bed and a pot for drinking water. In some of them brown, silent men were squatting at the inner bars, with their blankets draped round them. These were the condemned men, due to be hanged within the next week or two.

One prisoner had been brought out of his cell. He was a Hindu, a puny wisp of a man, with a shaven head and vague liquid eyes. He had a thick, sprouting moustache, absurdly too big for his body, rather like the moustache of a comic man on the films. Six tall Indian warders were guarding him and getting him ready for the gallows. Two of them stood by with rifles and fixed bayonets, while the others handcuffed him, passed a chain through his handcuffs and fixed it to their belts, and lashed his arms tight to his sides. They crowded very close about him, with their hands always on him in a careful, caressing grip, as though all the while feeling him to make sure he was there. It was like men handling a fish which is still alive and may jump back into the water. But he stood quite unresisting, yielding his arms limply to the ropes, as though he hardly noticed what was happening.

Eight o'clock struck and a bugle call, desolately thin in the wet air, floated from the distant barracks. The superintendent of the jail, who was standing apart from the rest of us, moodily prodding the gravel with his stick, raised his head at the sound. He was an army doctor, with a grey toothbrush moustache and a gruff voice. "For God's sake hurry up, Francis," he said irritably. "The man ought to have been dead by this time. Aren't you ready yet?"

Francis, the head jailer, a fat Dravidian in a white drill suit and gold spectacles, waved his black hand. "Yes sir, yes sir," he bubbled. "All iss satisfactorily prepared. The hangman iss waiting. We shall proceed."

"Well, quick march, then. The prisoners can't get their breakfast till this job's over." 5

We set out for the gallows. Two warders marched on either side of the prisoner, with their rifles at the slope; two others marched close against him, gripping him by arm and shoulder, as though at once pushing and supporting him. The rest of us, magistrates and the like, followed behind. Suddenly, when we had gone ten yards, the procession stopped short without any order or warning. A dreadful thing had happened—a dog, come goodness knows whence, had appeared in the yard. It came bounding among us with a loud volley of barks and leapt round us wagging its whole body, wild with glee at finding so many human beings together. It was a large woolly dog, half Airedale, half pariah. For a moment it pranced round us, and then, before anyone could stop it, it had made a dash for the prisoner, and jumping up tried to lick his face. Everybody stood aghast, too taken aback even to grab the dog.

"Who let that bloody brute in here?" said the superintendent angrily. "Catch it, someone!"

A warder detached from the escort, charged clumsily after the dog, but it danced and gambolled just out of his reach, taking everything as part of the game. A young Eurasian jailer picked up a handful of gravel and tried to stone the dog away, but it dodged the stones and came after us again. Its yaps echoed from the jail walls. The prisoner, in the grasp of the two warders, looked on incuriously, as though this was another formality of the hanging. It was several minutes before someone managed to catch the dog. Then we put my handkerchief through its collar and moved off once more, with the dog still straining and whimpering.

It was about forty yards to the gallows. I watched the bare brown back of the prisoner marching in front of me. He walked clumsily with his bound arms, but quite steadily, with that bobbing gait of the Indian who never straightens his knees. At each step his muscles slid neatly into place, the lock of hair on his scalp danced up and down, his feet printed themselves on the wet gravel. And once, in spite of the men who gripped him by each shoulder, he stepped slightly aside to avoid a puddle on the path.

It is curious, but till that moment I had never realized what it means 10 to destroy a healthy, conscious man. When I saw the prisoner step aside to avoid the puddle I saw the mystery, the unspeakable wrongness, of cutting a life short when it is in full tide. This man was not dying, he was alive just as we are alive. All the organs of his body were working—bowels digesting food, skin renewing itself, nails growing, tissues forming—all toiling away in solemn foolery. His nails would still be growing when he stood on the drop, when he was falling through the air with a tenth-of-a-second to live. His eyes saw the yellow gravel and the grey walls, and his brain still remembered, foresaw, reasoned—even about puddles. He and we were a party of men walking together, seeing, hearing, feeling, understanding the same world; and in two minutes, with a sudden snap, one of us would be gone—one mind less, one world less.

The gallows stood in a small yard, separate from the main grounds of the prison, and overgrown with tall prickly weeds. It was a brick erection like three sides of a shed, with planking on top, and above that two beams and a crossbar with the rope dangling. The hangman, a grey-haired convict in the white uniform of the prison, was waiting beside his machine. He greeted us with a servile crouch as we entered. At a word from Francis the two warders, gripping the prisoner more closely than ever, half led, half pushed him to the gallows and helped him clumsily up the ladder. Then the hangman climbed up and fixed the rope round the prisoner's neck.

We stood waiting, five yards away. The warders had formed in a rough circle round the gallows. And then, when the noose was fixed, the prisoner began crying out to his god. It was a high, reiterated cry of "Ram! Ram! Ram! Ram!" not urgent and fearful like a prayer or cry for help, but steady, rhythmical, almost like the tolling of a bell. The dog answered the sound with a whine. The hangman, still standing on the gallows, produced a small cotton bag like a flour bag and drew it down over the prisoner's face. But the sound, muffled by the cloth, still persisted, over and over again: "Ram! Ram! Ram! Ram! Ram!"

The hangman climbed down and stood ready, holding the lever. Minutes seemed to pass. The steady, muffled crying from the prisoner went on and on, "Ram! Ram! Ram!" never faltering for an instant. The superintendent, his head on his chest, was slowly poking the ground with his stick; perhaps he was counting the cries, allowing the prisoner a fixed number—fifty, perhaps, or a hundred. Everyone had changed colour. The Indians had gone grey like bad coffee, and one or two of the bayonets were wavering. We looked at the lashed, hooded man on the drop, and listened to his cries—each cry another second of life; the same thought was in all our minds: oh, kill him quickly, get it over, stop that abominable noise!

Suddenly the superintendent made up his mind. Throwing up his head he made a swift motion with his stick. "Chalo!" he shouted almost fiercely.

There was a clanking noise, and then dead silence. The prisoner had   **15** vanished, and the rope was twisting on itself. I let go of the dog, and it galloped immediately to the back of the gallows; but when it got there it stopped short, barked, and then retreated into a corner of the yard, where it stood among the weeds, looking timorously out at us. We went round the gallows to inspect the prisoner's body. He was dangling with his toes pointed straight downwards, very slowly revolving, as dead as a stone.

The superintendent reached out with his stick and poked the bare brown body; it oscillated slightly. "*He's* all right," said the superintendent. He backed out from under the gallows, and blew out a deep breath. The moody look had gone out of his face quite suddenly. He glanced at his wrist-watch. "Eight minutes past eight. Well, that's all for this morning, thank God."

The warders unfixed bayonets and marched away. The dog, sobered and conscious of having misbehaved itself, slipped after them. We walked out of the gallows yard, past the condemned cells with their waiting prisoners, into the big central yard of the prison. The convicts, under the command of warders armed with lathis, were already receiving their breakfast. They squatted in long rows, each man holding a tin pannikin, while two warders with buckets marched round ladling out rice; it seemed quite a homely, jolly scene, after the hanging. An enormous relief had come upon us now that the job was done. One felt an impulse to sing, to break into a run, to snigger. All at once everyone began chattering gaily.

The Eurasian boy walking beside me nodded towards the way we had come, with a knowing smile: "Do you know, sir, our friend (he meant the dead man), when he heard his appeal had been dismissed, he pissed on the floor of his cell. From fright. Kindly take one of my cigarettes, sir. Do you not admire my new silver case, sir? From the boxwallah, two rupees eight annas. Classy European style."

Several people laughed—at what, nobody seemed certain.

Francis was walking by the superintendent, talking garrulously: "Well, sir, all hass passed off with the utmost satisfactoriness. It was all finished—flick! like that. It iss not always so—oah, no! I have known cases where the doctor wass obliged to go beneath the gallows and pull the prissoner's legs to ensure decease. Most disagreeable!"

"Wriggling about, eh? That's bad," said the superintendent.

"Ach, sir, it iss worse when they become refractory! One man, I recall, clung to the bars of hiss cage when we went to take him out. You will scarcely credit, sir, that it took six warders to dislodge him, three pulling at each leg. We reasoned with him. 'My dear fellow,' we said, 'think of all the pain and trouble you are causing to us!' But no, he would not listen! Ach, he wass very troublesome!"

I found that I was laughing quite loudly. Everyone was laughing. Even the superintendent grinned in a tolerant way. "You'd better all come out and have a drink," he said quite genially. "I've got a bottle of whisky in the car. We could do with it."

We went through the big double gates of the prison into the road. "Pulling at his legs!" exclaimed a Burmese magistrate suddenly, and burst into a loud chuckling. We all began laughing again. At that moment Francis' anecdote seemed extraordinarily funny. We all had a drink together, native and European alike, quite amicably. The dead man was a hundred yards away.

1931

Lines of Inquiry
"A Hanging"

In a pointed story such as Orwell's, every character presumably contributes something to the meaning of the essay. Given this premise, what particular significance do you attribute to the dog and to the reactions of the other characters to its behavior? Why do you suppose that Orwell devotes so much attention to describing the dog's behavior? At one point, the dog is referred to as "having misbehaved itself." In what sense has it misbehaved? How do the dog's reactions to the prisoner and to the hanging compare to the reactions of the other witnesses?

Midway through this essay, Orwell expresses what many people have taken to be the point of his story about the hanging, namely "the unspeakable wrongness of cutting a life short when it is in full tide." If this statement against capital punishment is the point of the story, why doesn't Orwell end the story and his essay at this point? What is the purpose of all the material that follows this statement? What other issues does the essay deal with that are developed in the remainder of the story?

In this essay, as in "Shooting an Elephant," Orwell presents himself in a distinctly unpleasant light by showing how he went along with a deed that went against his own moral judgment. Why do you suppose that he depicts himself in each piece in so unfavorable a way? How did his personal moral compromise affect your reaction to him and to the ideas that he is trying to convey in each piece?

Shooting an Elephant

In Moulmein, in lower Burma, I was hated by large numbers of people—the only time in my life that I have been important enough for this to happen to me. I was sub-divisional police officer of the town, and in an aimless, petty kind of way anti-European feeling was very bitter. No one had the guts to raise a riot, but if a European woman went through the bazaars alone somebody would probably spit betel juice over her dress. As a police officer I was an obvious target and was baited whenever it seemed safe to do so. When a nimble Burman tripped me up on the football field and the referee (another Burman) looked the other way, the crowd yelled with hideous laughter. This happened more than once. In the end the sneering yellow faces of young men that met me everywhere, the insults hooted after me when I was at a safe distance, got badly on my nerves. The young Buddhist priests were the worst of all. There were several thousands of them in the town and none of them seemed to have anything to do except stand on street corners and jeer at Europeans.

All this was perplexing and upsetting. For at that time I had already made up my mind that imperialism was an evil thing and the sooner I chucked up my job and got out of it the better. Theoretically—and secretly, of course—I was all for the Burmese and all against their oppressors, the British. As for the job I was doing, I hated it more bitterly than I can perhaps make clear. In a job like that you see the dirty work of Empire at close quarters. The wretched prisoners huddling in the stinking cages of the lock-ups, the gray, cowed faces of the long-term convicts, the scarred buttocks of the men who had been flogged with bamboos—all these oppressed me with an intolerable sense of guilt. But I could get nothing into perspective. I was young and ill educated and I had had to think out my problems in the utter silence that is imposed on every Englishman in the East. I did not even know that the British Empire is dying, still less did I know that it is a great deal better than the younger empires that are going to supplant it. All I knew was that I was stuck between my hatred of the empire I served and my rage against the evil-spirited little beasts who tried to make my job impossible. With one part of my mind I thought of the British Raj as an unbreakable tyranny, as something clamped down, in *saecula saeculorum,* upon the will of prostrate peoples; with another part I thought that the greatest joy in the world would be to drive a bayonet into a Buddhist priest's guts. Feelings like these are the normal by-products of imperialism; ask any Anglo-Indian official, if you can catch him off duty.

One day something happened which in a roundabout way was enlightening. It was a tiny incident in itself; but it gave me a better glimpse than I had had before of the real nature of imperialism—the real motives for which despotic governments act. Early one morning the sub-inspector at a police station the other end of the town rang me up on the 'phone and said that an elephant was ravaging the bazaar. Would I please come and do something about it? I did not know what I could do, but I wanted to see what was happening and I got on to a pony and started out. I took my rifle, an old .44 Winchester and much too small to kill an elephant, but I thought the noise might be useful *in terrorem*. Various Burmans stopped me on the way and told me about the elephant's doings. It was not, of course, a wild elephant, but a tame one which had gone "must." It had been chained up, as tame elephants always are when their attack of "must" is due, but on the previous night it had broken its chain and escaped. Its mahout, the only person who could manage it when it was in that state, had set out in pursuit, but had taken the wrong direction and was now twelve hours' journey away, and in the morning the elephant had suddenly reappeared in the town. The Burmese population had no weapons and were quite helpless against it. It had already destroyed somebody's bamboo hut, killed a cow and raided some fruit-stalls and devoured the stock; also it had met the municipal rubbish van and, when the driver jumped out and took to his heels, had turned the van over and inflicted violences upon it.

The Burmese sub-inspector and some Indian constables were waiting for me in the quarter where the elephant had been seen. It was a very poor quarter, a labyrinth of squalid bamboo huts, thatched with palm-leaf, winding all over a steep hillside. I remember that it was a cloudy, stuffy morning at the beginning of the rains. We began questioning the people as to where the elephant had gone and, as usual, failed to get any definite information. That is invariably the case in the East; a story always sounds clear enough at a distance, but the nearer you get to the scene of events the vaguer it becomes. Some of the people said that the elephant had gone in one direction, some said that he had gone in another, some professed not even to have heard of any elephant. I had almost made up my mind that the whole story was a pack of lies, when we heard yells a little distance away. There was a loud, scandalized cry of "Go away, child! Go away this instant!" and an old woman with a switch in her hand came round the corner of a hut, violently shooing away a crowd of naked children. Some more women followed, clicking their tongues and exclaiming; evidently there was something that the children ought not to have seen. I rounded the hut and saw a man's dead body sprawling in the mud. He was an Indian, a black Dravidian coolie, almost naked, and he could not have been dead many minutes. The people said that the elephant had come suddenly upon him round the corner of the hut, caught him with its trunk, put its foot on his back and ground him into the earth. This was the rainy season and the ground was soft, and his face had scored a trench a foot deep and a couple of yards long. He was lying on his belly with arms crucified and head sharply twisted to one side. His face was coated with mud, the eyes wide open, the teeth bared and grinning with an expression of unendurable agony. (Never tell me, by the way, that the dead look peaceful. Most of the corpses I have seen looked devilish.) The friction of the great beast's foot had stripped the skin from his back as neatly as one skins a rabbit. As soon as I saw the dead man I sent an orderly to a friend's house nearby to borrow an elephant rifle. I had already sent back the pony, not wanting it to go mad with fright and throw me if it smelt the elephant.

The orderly came back in a few minutes with a rifle and five car- 5 tridges, and meanwhile some Burmans had arrived and told us that the elephant was in the paddy fields below, only a few hundred yards away. As I started forward practically the whole population of the quarter flocked out of the houses and followed me. They had seen the rifle and were all shouting excitedly that I was going to shoot the elephant. They had not shown much interest in the elephant when he was merely ravaging their homes, but it was different now that he was going to be shot. It was a bit of fun to them, as it would be to an English crowd; besides they wanted the meat. It made me vaguely uneasy. I had no intention of shooting the elephant—I had merely sent for the rifle to defend myself if necessary—and it is always unnerving to have a crowd following you. I marched down the hill, looking and feeling a fool, with the rifle over my shoulder and an ever-growing army of people jostling at my heels. At the bottom, when you got away from the huts, there was a metalled road and beyond that a miry waste of paddy fields a thousand yards across, not yet ploughed but soggy from the first rains and dotted with coarse grass. The elephant was standing eight yards from the road, his left side toward us. He took not the slightest notice of the crowd's approach. He was tearing up bunches of grass, beating them against his knees to clean them, and stuffing them into his mouth.

I had halted on the road. As soon as I saw the elephant I knew with perfect certainty that I ought not to shoot him. It is a serious matter to shoot a working elephant—it is comparable to destroying a huge and costly piece of machinery—and obviously one ought not to do it if it can possibly be avoided. And at that distance, peacefully eating, the elephant looked no more dangerous than a cow. I thought then and I think now that his attack of "must" was already passing off; in which case he would merely wander harmlessly about until the mahout came back and caught him. Moreover, I did not in the least want to shoot him. I decided that I would watch him for a little while to make sure that he did not turn savage again, and then go home.

But at that moment I glanced round at the crowd that had followed me. It was an immense crowd, two thousand at the least and growing every minute. It blocked the road for a long distance on either side. I looked at the sea of yellow faces above the garish clothes—faces all happy and excited over this bit of fun, all certain that the elephant was going to be shot. They were watching me as they would watch a conjurer about to perform a trick. They did not like me, but with the magical rifle in my hands I was momentarily worth watching. And suddenly I realized that I should have to shoot the elephant after all. The people expected it of me and I had got to do it; I could feel their two thousand wills pressing me forward, irresistibly. And it was at this moment, as I stood there with the rifle in my hands, that I first grasped the hollowness, the futility of the white man's dominion in the East. Here was I, the white man with his gun, standing in front of the unarmed native crowd—seemingly the leading actor of the piece; but in reality I was only an absurd puppet pushed to and fro by the will of those yellow faces behind. I perceived in this moment that when the white man turns tyrant it is his own freedom that he destroys. He becomes a sort of hollow, posing dummy, the conventionalized figure of a sahib. For it is the condition of his rule that he shall spend his life in trying to impress the "natives," and so in every crisis he has got to do what the "natives" expect of him. He wears a mask, and his face grows to fit it. I had got to shoot the elephant. I had committed myself to doing it when I sent for the rifle. A sahib has got to act like a sahib; he has got to appear resolute, to know his own mind and do definite things. To come all that way, rifle in hand, with two thousand people marching at my heels, and then to trail feebly away, having done nothing— no, that was impossible. The crowd would laugh at me. And my whole life, every white man's life in the East, was one long struggle not to be laughed at.

But I did not want to shoot the elephant. I watched him beating his bunch of grass against his knees with that preoccupied grandmotherly air that elephants have. It seemed to me that it would be murder to shoot him. At that age I was not squeamish about killing animals, but I had never shot an elephant and never wanted to. (Somehow it always seems worse to kill a *large* animal.) Besides, there was the beast's owner to be considered. Alive, the elephant was worth at least a hundred pounds; dead, he would only be worth the value of his tusks, five pounds, possibly. But I had got to act quickly. I turned to some experienced-looking Burmans who had been there when we arrived, and asked them how the elephant had been behaving. They all said the same thing: he took no notice of you if you left him alone, but he might charge if you went too close to him.

It was perfectly clear to me what I ought to do. I ought to walk up to within, say, twenty-five yards of the elephant and test his behavior.

If he charged, I could shoot; if he took no notice of me, it would be safe to leave him until the mahout came back. But also I knew that I was going to do no such thing. I was a poor shot with a rifle and the ground was soft mud into which one would sink at every step. If the elephant charged and I missed him, I should have about as much chance as a toad under a steam-roller. But even then I was not thinking particularly of my own skin, only of the watchful yellow faces behind. For at that moment, with the crowd watching me, I was not afraid in the ordinary sense, as I would have been if I had been alone. A white man mustn't be frightened in front of "natives"; and so, in general, he isn't frightened. The sole thought in my mind was that if anything went wrong those two thousand Burmans would see me pursued, caught, trampled on, and reduced to a grinning corpse like that Indian up the hill. And if that happened it was quite probable that some of them would laugh. That would never do. There was only one alternative. I shoved the cartridges into the magazine and lay down on the road to get a better aim.

The crowd grew very still, and a deep, low, happy sigh, as of people who see the theater curtain go up at last, breathed from innumerable throats. They were going to have their bit of fun after all. The rifle was a beautiful German thing with crosshair sights. I did not then know that in shooting an elephant one would shoot to cut an imaginary bar running from ear-hole to ear-hole. I ought, therefore, as the elephant was sideways on, to have aimed straight at his ear-hole; actually I aimed several inches in front of this, thinking the brain would be further forward.

When I pulled the trigger I did not hear the bang or feel the kick—one never does when a shot goes home—but I heard the devilish roar of glee that went up from the crowd. In that instant, in too short a time, one would have thought, even for the bullet to get there, a mysterious terrible change had come over the elephant. He neither stirred, nor fell, but every line of his body had altered. He looked suddenly stricken, shrunken, immensely old, as though the frightful impact of the bullet had paralyzed him without knocking him down. At last, after what seemed a long time—it might have been five seconds, I dare say—he sagged flabbily to his knees. His mouth slobbered. An enormous senility seemed to have settled upon him. One could have imagined him thousands of years old. I fired again into the same spot. At the second shot he did not collapse but climbed with desperate slowness to his feet and stood weakly upright, with legs sagging and head drooping. I fired a third time. That was the shot that did for him. You could see the agony of it jolt his whole body and knock the last remnant of strength from his legs. But in falling he seemed for a moment to rise, for as his hind legs collapsed beneath him he seemed to tower upward like a huge rock toppling, his trunk reaching skyward like a tree. He

10

trumpeted, for the first and only time. And then down he came, his belly toward me, with a crash that seemed to shake the ground even where I lay.

I got up. The Burmans were already racing past me across the mud. It was obvious that the elephant would never rise again, but he was not dead. He was breathing very rhythmically with long rattling gasps, his great mound of a side painfully rising and falling. His mouth was wide open—I could see far down into caverns of pale pink throat. I waited a long time for him to die, but his breathing did not weaken. Finally I fired my two remaining shots into the spot where I thought his heart must be. The thick blood welled out of him like red velvet, but still he did not die. His body did not even jerk when the shots hit him, the tortured breathing continued without a pause. He was dying, very slowly and in great agony, but in some world remote from me where not even a bullet could damage him further. I felt that I had got to put an end to that dreadful noise. It seemed dreadful to see the great beast lying there, powerless to move and yet powerless to die, and not even to be able to finish him. I sent back for my small rifle and poured shot after shot into his heart and down his throat. They seemed to make no impression. The tortured gasps continued as steadily as the ticking of a clock.

In the end I could not stand it any longer and went away. I heard later that it took him half an hour to die. Burmans were bringing dahs and baskets even before I left, and I was told they had stripped his body almost to the bones by the afternoon.

Afterward, of course, there were endless discussions about the shooting of the elephant. The owner was furious, but he was only an Indian and could do nothing. Besides, legally I had done the right thing, for a mad elephant has to be killed, like a mad dog, if its owner fails to control it. Among the Europeans opinion was divided. The older men said I was right, the younger men said it was a damn shame to shoot an elephant for killing a coolie, because an elephant was worth more than any damn Coringhee coolie. And afterward I was very glad that the coolie had been killed; it put me legally in the right and it gave me a sufficient pretext for shooting the elephant. I often wondered whether any of the others grasped that I had done it solely to avoid looking a fool.

1936

Lines of Inquiry
"Shooting an Elephant"

Throughout this essay, Orwell is remarkably frank not only in telling about his actions and experiences, but also in revealing his personal thoughts and feelings. What did you discover about Orwell as a result of his frankness? Did you ever find yourself being offended either by his frankly confessional manner or by what he revealed about himself? Why do you suppose that he chose to be so frank about himself?

Orwell refers to his experience of shooting the elephant as an "enlightening . . . incident" that gave him a "better glimpse" than he "had had before of the real nature of imperialism." What in particular did Orwell discover about imperialism from the experience of shooting the elephant, and at what point during the experience did he make his discoveries? What did you discover about imperialism from reading the essay, and at what point(s) in the essay did you make your discoveries?

Think about a time in your life when an unpleasant incident that you were involved in, or that you witnessed, helped you to discover something important about "the real nature" of social or political tyranny. What did you discover? When did you make your discovery—during the incident or sometime later? Did you find yourself, like Orwell, to be divided in your loyalties and confused about what to think or do? Or did you have a clear-cut view of the situation from beginning to end? How has your discovery affected your subsequent political or social outlook?

Marrakech

As the corpse went past the flies left the restaurant table in a cloud and rushed after it, but they came back a few minutes later.

The little crowd of mourners—all men and boys, no women— threaded their way across the market-place between the piles of pome- granates and the taxis and the camels, wailing a short chant over and over again. What really appeals to the flies is that the corpses here are never put into coffins, they are merely wrapped in a piece of rag and carried on a rough wooden bier on the shoulders of four friends. When the friends get to the burying-ground they hack an oblong hole a foot or two deep, dump the body in it and fling over it a little of the dried- up, lumpy earth, which is like broken brick. No gravestone, no name, no identifying mark of any kind. The burying-ground is merely a huge waste of hummocky earth, like a derelict building-lot. After a month or two no one can even be certain where his own relatives are buried.

When you walk through a town like this—two hundred thousand inhabitants, of whom at least twenty thousand own literally nothing except the rags they stand up in—when you see how the people live, and still more how easily they die, it is always difficult to believe that you are walking among human beings. All colonial empires are in real- ity founded upon that fact. The people have brown faces—besides, there are so many of them! Are they really the same flesh as yourself? Do they even have names? Or are they merely a kind of undifferentiated brown stuff, about as individual as bees or coral insects? They rise out of the earth, they sweat and starve for a few years, and then they sink back into the nameless mounds of the graveyard and nobody notices that they are gone. And even the graves themselves soon fade back into the soil. Sometimes, out for a walk, as you break your way through the prickly pear, you notice that it is rather bumpy underfoot, and only a certain regularity in the bumps tells you that you are walking over skeletons.

I was feeding one of the gazelles in the public gardens.

Gazelles are almost the only animals that look good to eat when 5 they are still alive, in fact, one can hardly look at their hindquarters without thinking of mint sauce. The gazelle I was feeding seemed to know that this thought was in my mind, for though it took the piece of bread I was holding out it obviously did not like me. It nibbled rapidly at the bread, then lowered its head and tried to butt me, then took another nibble and then butted again. Probably its idea was that if it could drive me away the bread would somehow remain hanging in mid-air.

An Arab navvy working on the path nearby lowered his heavy hoe and sidled towards us. He looked from the gazelle to the bread and from the bread to the gazelle, with a sort of quiet amazement, as though he had never seen anything quite like this before. Finally he said shyly in French:

"I could eat some of that bread."

I tore off a piece and he stowed it gratefully in some secret place under his rags. This man is an employee of the Municipality.

When you go through the Jewish quarters you gather some idea of what the medieval ghettoes were probably like. Under their Moorish rulers the Jews were only allowed to own land in certain restricted areas, and after centuries of this kind of treatment they have ceased to bother about overcrowding. Many of the streets are a good deal less than six feet wide, the houses are completely windowless, and sore-eyed children cluster everywhere in unbelievable numbers, like clouds of flies. Down the centre of the street there is generally running a little river of urine.

In the bazaar huge families of Jews, all dressed in the long black 10 robe and little black skull-cap, are working in dark fly-infested booths that look like caves. A carpenter sits cross-legged at a prehistoric lathe, turning chair-legs at lightning speed. He works the lathe with a bow in his right hand and guides the chisel with his left foot, and thanks to a lifetime of sitting in this position his left leg is warped out of shape. At his side his grandson, aged six, is already starting on the simpler parts of the job.

I was just passing the coppersmiths' booths when somebody noticed that I was lighting a cigarette. Instantly, from the dark holes all round, there was a frenzied rush of Jews, many of them old grandfathers with flowing grey beards, all clamouring for a cigarette. Even a blind man somewhere at the back of one of the booths heard a rumour of cigarettes and came crawling out, groping in the air with his hand. In about a minute I had used up the whole packet. None of these people, I suppose, works less than twelve hours a day, and every one of them looks on a cigarette as a more or less impossible luxury.

As the Jews live in self-contained communities they follow the same trades as the Arabs, except for agriculture. Fruit-sellers, potters, silversmiths, blacksmiths, butchers, leather-workers, tailors, water-carriers, beggars, porters—whichever way you look you see nothing but Jews. As a matter of fact there are thirteen thousand of them, all living in the space of a few acres. A good job Hitler isn't here. Perhaps he is on his way, however. You hear the usual dark rumours about the Jews, not only from the Arabs but from the poorer Europeans.

"Yes, *mon vieux,* they took my job away from me and gave it to a Jew. The Jew.! They're the real rulers of this country, you know. They've got all the money. They control the banks, finance—everything."

"But," I said, "isn't it a fact that the average Jew is a labourer working for about a penny an hour?"

"Ah, that's only for show! They're all moneylenders really. They're cunning, the Jews."   15

In just the same way, a couple of hundred years ago, poor old women used to be burned for witchcraft when they could not even work enough magic to get themselves a square meal.

All people who work with their hands are partly invisible, and the more important the work they do, the less visible they are. Still, a white skin is always fairly conspicuous. In northern Europe, when you see a labourer ploughing a field, you probably give him a second glance. In a hot country, anywhere south of Gibraltar or east of Suez, the chances are that you don't even see him. I have noticed this again and again. In a tropical landscape one's eye takes in everything except the human beings. It takes in the dried-up soil, the prickly pear, the palm-tree and the distant mountain, but it always misses the peasant hoeing at his patch. He is the same colour as the earth, and a great deal less interesting to look at.

It is only because of this that the starved countries of Asia and Africa are accepted as tourist resorts. No one would think of running cheap trips to the Distressed Areas. But where the human beings have brown skins their poverty is simply not noticed. What does Morocco mean to a Frenchman? An orange-grove or a job in government service. Or to an Englishman? Camels, castles, palm-trees, Foreign Legionnaires, brass trays and bandits. One could probably live here for years without noticing that for nine-tenths of the people the reality of life is an endless, back-breaking struggle to wring a little food out of an eroded soil.

Most of Morocco is so desolate that no wild animal bigger than a hare can live on it. Huge areas which were once covered with forest have turned into a treeless waste where the soil is exactly like broken-up brick. Nevertheless a good deal of it is cultivated, with frightful labour. Everything is done by hand. Long lines of women, bent double like inverted capital Ls, work their way slowly across the field, tearing up the prickly weeds with their hands, and the peasant gathering lucerne for fodder pulls it up stalk by stalk instead of reaping it, thus saving an inch or two on each stalk. The plough is a wretched wooden thing, so frail that one can easily carry it on one's shoulder, and fitted underneath with a rough iron spike which stirs the soil to a depth of about four inches. This is as much as the strength of the animals is equal to. It is usual to plough with a cow and a donkey yoked together. Two donkeys would not be quite strong enough, but on the other hand two cows would cost a little more to feed. The peasants possess no harrows, they merely plough the soil several times over in different directions, finally leaving it in rough furrows, after which the whole field has to be shaped with hoes into small oblong patches, to conserve water. Except for a day or two after the rare rainstorms there is never enough water. Along the edges of the fields channels are hacked out to a depth of thirty or forty feet to get at the tiny trickles which run through the subsoil.

Every afternoon a file of very old women passes down the road 20 outside my house, each carrying a load of firewood. All of them are mummified with age and the sun, and all of them are tiny. It seems to be generally the case in primitive communities that the women, when they get beyond a certain age, shrink to the size of children. One day a poor old creature who could not have been more than four feet tall crept past me under a vast load of wood. I stopped her and put a five-sou piece (a little more than a farthing) into her hand. She answered with a shrill wail, almost a scream, which was partly gratitude but mainly surprise. I suppose that from her point of view, by taking any notice of her, I seemed almost to be violating a law of nature. She accepted her status as an old woman, that is to say as a beast of burden. When a family is travelling it is quite usual to see a father and a grown-up son riding ahead on donkeys, and an old woman following on foot, carrying the baggage.

But what is strange about these people is their invisibility. For several weeks, always at about the same time of day, the file of old women had hobbled past the house with their firewood, and though they had registered themselves on my eyeballs I cannot truly say that I had seen them. Firewood was passing—that was how I saw it. It was only that one day I happened to be walking behind them, and the curious up-and-down motion of a load of wood drew my attention to the human being underneath it. Then for the first time I noticed the poor old earth-coloured bodies, bodies reduced to bones and leathery skin, bent double under the crushing weight. Yet I suppose I had not been five minutes on Moroccan soil before I noticed the overloading of the donkeys and was infuriated by it. There is no question that the donkeys are damnably treated. The Moroccan donkey is hardly bigger than a St Bernard dog, it carries a load which in the British army would be considered too much for a fifteen-hands mule, and very often its pack-saddle is not taken off its back for weeks together. But what is peculiarly pitiful is that it is the most willing creature on earth, it follows its master like a dog and does not need either bridle or halter. After a dozen years of devoted work it suddenly drops dead, whereupon its master tips it into the ditch and the village dogs have torn its guts out before it is cold.

This kind of thing makes one's blood boil, whereas—on the whole—the plight of the human beings does not. I am not commenting, merely pointing to a fact. People with brown skins are next door to invisible.

Anyone can be sorry for the donkey with its galled back, but it is generally owing to some kind of accident if one even notices the old woman under her load of sticks.

As the storks flew northward the Negroes were marching southward—a long, dusty column, infantry, screw-gun batteries and then more infantry, four or five thousand men in all, winding up the road with a clumping of boots and a clatter of iron wheels.

They were Senegalese, the blackest Negroes in Africa, so black that sometimes it is difficult to see whereabouts on their necks the hair begins. Their splendid bodies were hidden in reach-me-down khaki uniforms, their feet squashed into boots that looked like blocks of wood, and every tin hat seemed to be a couple of sizes too small. It was very hot and the men had marched a long way. They slumped under the weight of their packs and the curiously sensitive black faces were glistening with sweat.

As they went past a tall, very young Negro turned and caught my 25 eye. But the look he gave me was not in the least the kind of look you might expect. Not hostile, not contemptuous, not sullen, not even inquisitive. It was the shy, wide-eyed Negro look, which actually is a look of profound respect. I saw how it was. This wretched boy, who is a French citizen and has therefore been dragged from the forest to scrub floors and catch syphilis in garrison towns, actually has feelings of reverence before a white skin. He has been taught that the white race are his masters, and he still believes it.

But there is one thought which every white man (and in this connection it doesn't matter twopence if he calls himself a Socialist) thinks when he sees a black army marching past. "How much longer can we go on kidding these people? How long before they turn their guns in the other direction?"

It was curious, really. Every white man there has this thought stowed somewhere or other in his mind. I had it, so had the other onlookers, so had the officers on their sweating chargers and the white NCOs marching in the ranks. It was a kind of secret which we all knew and were too clever to tell; only the Negroes didn't know it. And really it was almost like watching a flock of cattle to see the long column, a mile or two miles of armed men, flowing peacefully up the road, while the great white birds drifted over them in the opposite direction, glittering like scraps of paper.

1939

Lines of Inquiry
"Marrakech"

Orwell's essay consists of five distinctly separate sections. How do you account for Orwell's organization of the five sections? For example, what is the effect of his beginning with the funeral procession, then moving to the incident with the gazelle and the navvy in the public garden, then depicting the scene in the Jewish ghetto, and so on. Try some different ways of arranging the five sections. How does each of your rearrangements affect the pacing, the buildup, the climax, and the overall significance of the piece?

Each of the five sections offers a vividly detailed picture, somewhat like a snapshot, of a particular scene or happening in Marrakech. What kinds of details, images, and scenes does Orwell emphasize in these snapshots? What do you suppose is his primary purpose in focusing on such scenes? What do you suppose is his main purpose in writing about Marrakech?

The title of this piece suggests that it will provide an informative description of Marrakech. What did you discover about the place from reading Orwell's piece about it? About its size, its geography, its commerce, its history, its social makeup, its inhabitants? What more would you like to have known about Marrakech that Orwell does not consider in his essay? Do some research in the library to find out what Marrakech is like today. In what ways has Marrakech (and the world that it symbolizes) changed since Orwell wrote his essay? In what respects has it remained the same?

Some Thoughts on the Common Toad

Before the swallow, before the daffodil, and not much later than the snowdrop, the common toad salutes the coming of spring after his own fashion, which is to emerge from a hole in the ground, where he has lain buried since the previous autumn, and crawl as rapidly as possible towards the nearest suitable patch of water. Something—some kind of shudder in the earth, or perhaps merely a rise of a few degrees in the temperature—has told him that it is time to wake up: though a few toads appear to sleep the clock round and miss out a year from time to time—at any rate, I have more than once dug them up, alive and apparently well, in the middle of the summer.

At this period, after his long fast, the toad has a very spiritual look, like a strict Anglo-Catholic toward the end of Lent. His movements are languid but purposeful, his body is shrunken, and by contrast his eyes look abnormally large. This allows one to notice, what one might not at another time, that a toad has about the most beautiful eye of any living creature. It is like gold, or more exactly it is like the golden-colored semi-precious stone which one sometimes sees in signet rings, and which I think is called a chrysoberyl.

For a few days after getting into the water the toad concentrates on building up his strength by eating small insects. Presently he has swollen to his normal size again, and then he goes through a phase of intense sexiness. All he knows, at least if he is a male toad, is that he wants to get his arms round something, and if you offer him a stick, or even your finger, he will cling to it with surprising strength and take a long time to discover that it is not a female toad. Frequently one comes upon shapeless masses of ten or twenty toads rolling over and over in the water, one clinging to another without distinction of sex. By degrees, however, they sort themselves out into couples, with the male duly sitting on the female's back. You can now distinguish males from females, because the male is smaller, darker and sits on top, with his arms tightly clasped round the female's neck. After a day or two the spawn is laid in long strings which wind themselves in and out of the reeds and soon become invisible. A few more weeks, and the water is alive with masses of tiny tadpoles which rapidly grow larger, sprout hind legs, then forelegs, then shed their tails: and finally, about the middle of the summer, the new generation of toads, smaller than one's thumb-nail but perfect in every particular, crawl out of the water to begin the game anew.

I mention the spawning of the toads because it is one of the phenomena of spring which most deeply appeal to me, and because the toad, unlike the skylark and the primrose, has never had much of a boost from the poets. But I am aware that many people do not like reptiles or amphibians, and I am not suggesting that in order to enjoy the spring you have to take an interest in toads. There are also the crocus, the missel thrush, the cuckoo, the blackthorn, etc. The point is that the pleasures of spring are available to everybody, and cost nothing. Even in the most sordid street the coming of spring will register itself by some sign or other, if it is only a brighter blue between the chimney pots or the vivid green of an elder sprouting on a blitzed site. Indeed it is remarkable how Nature goes on existing unofficially, as it were, in the very heart of London. I have seen a kestrel flying over the Deptford gasworks, and I have heard a first-rate performance by a black bird in the Euston Road. There must be some hundreds of thousands, if not millions, of birds living inside the four-mile radius, and it is rather a pleasing thought that none of them pays a half-penny of rent.

As for spring, not even the narrow and gloomy streets round the Bank of England are quite able to exclude it. It comes seeping in everywhere, like one of those new poison gases which pass through all filters. The spring is commonly referred to as "a miracle," and during the past five or six years this worn-out figure of speech has taken on a new lease of life. After the sort of winters we have had to endure recently, the spring does seem miraculous, because it has become gradually harder and harder to believe that it is actually going to happen. Every February since 1940 I have found myself thinking that this time winter is going to be permanent. But Persephone, like the toads, always rises from the dead at about the same moment. Suddenly, toward the end of March, the miracle happens and the decaying slum in which I live is transfigured. Down in the square the sooty privets have turned bright green, the leaves are thickening on the chestnut trees, the daffodils are out, the wallflowers are budding, the policeman's tunic looks positively a pleasant shade of blue, the fish-monger greets his customers with a smile, and even the sparrows are quite a different color, having felt the balminess of the air and nerved themselves to take a bath, their first since last September.

Is it wicked to take a pleasure in spring, and other seasonal changes? To put it more precisely, is it politically reprehensible, while we are all groaning, under the shackles of the capitalist system, to point out that life is frequently more worth living because of a blackbird's song, a

5

yellow elm tree in October, or some other natural phenomenon which does not cost money and does not have what the editors of the left-wing newspapers call a class angle? There is no doubt that many people think so. I know by experience that a favorable reference to "Nature" in one of my articles is liable to bring me abusive letters, and though the keyword in these letters is usually "sentimental," two ideas seem to be mixed up in them. One is that any pleasure in the actual process of life encourages a sort of political quietism. People, so the thought runs, ought to be discontented, and it is our job to multiply our wants and not simply to increase our enjoyment of the things we have already. The other idea is that this is the age of machines and that to dislike the machine, or even to want to limit its domination, is backward-looking, reactionary, and slightly ridiculous. This is often backed up by the statement that a love of Nature is a foible of urbanized people who have no notion what Nature is really like. Those who really have to deal with the soil, so it is argued, do not love the soil, and do not take the faintest interest in birds or flowers, except from a strictly utilitarian point of view. To love the country one must live in the town, merely taking an occasional week-end ramble at the warmer times of year.

This last idea is demonstrably false. Medieval literature, for instance, including the popular ballads, is full of an almost Georgian enthusiasm for Nature, and the art of agricultural peoples such as the Chinese and Japanese centers always round trees, birds, flowers, rivers, mountains. The other idea seems to me to be wrong in a subtler way. Certainly we ought to be discontented, we ought not simply to find out ways of making the best of a bad job, and yet if we kill all pleasure in the actual process of life, what sort of future are we preparing for ourselves? If a man cannot enjoy the return of spring, why should he be happy in a labor-saving Utopia? What will he do with the leisure that the machine will give him? I have always suspected that if our economic and political problems are ever really solved, life will become simpler instead of more complex, and that the sort of pleasure one gets from finding the first primrose will loom larger than the sort of pleasure one gets from eating an ice to the tune of a Wurlitzer. I think that by retaining one's childhood love of such things as trees, fishes, butterflies, and—to return to my first instance—toads, one makes a peaceful and decent future a little more probable, and that by preaching the doctrine that nothing is to be admired except steel and concrete, one merely makes it a little surer that human beings will have no outlet for their surplus energy except in hatred and leader-worship.

At any rate, spring is here, even in London, N.1, and they can't stop you enjoying it. This is a satisfying reflection. How many a time have I stood watching the toads mating, or a pair of hares having a boxing match in the young corn, and thought of all the important persons who would stop me enjoying this if they could. But luckily they can't. So long as you are not actually ill, hungry, frightened, or immured in a prison or a holiday camp, spring is still spring. The atom bombs are piling up in the factories, the police are prowling through the cities, the lies are streaming from the loudspeakers, but the earth is still going round the sun, and neither the dictators nor the bureaucrats, deeply as they disapprove of the process, are able to prevent it.

1946

Lines of Inquiry
"Some Thoughts on the Common Toad"

Though the title of this essay might lead one to expect that it is primarily, even exclusively, concerned with "the common toad," Orwell focuses on the toad only in the opening section of his essay. In the remaining two sections, he does not discuss toads any longer, but merely alludes to them four or five times. Why do you suppose he features "the common toad" in his title? In what sense does the toad figure in the piece even when Orwell is not discussing it explicitly? In what sense does the significance of the toad remain constant from one section to the next? In what senses, if any, does it change?

Given Orwell's commitment to writing with a political purpose, how do you account for his decision to write an essay such as this one, which seems far more interested in the spawning of toads, the coming of spring, and the pleasures of nature than it is in any specific political issue? Or, might it be argued that despite all of his talk about toads and spring and nature (indeed, by means of focusing on such things), Orwell is actually exploring some serious political issues, such as the nature of the good life, the implications of a machine-age culture, and the perils of thought control? If so, which of these concerns do you think is uppermost in his mind?

Other essayists in this collection have also used natural creatures as a focus for meditations about some aspect of experience, as you can see by looking at Dillard's "Living Like Weasels," Eiseley's "The Bird and the Machine," or Woolf's "The Death of the Moth." After reading or rereading one of these pieces, think about how it compares to Orwell's essay in its descriptive and meditative techniques.

Politics and
the English Language

Most people who bother with the matter at all would admit that the English language is in a bad way, but it is generally assumed that we cannot by conscious action do anything about it. Our civilization is decadent and our language—so the argument runs—must inevitably share in the general collapse. It follows that any struggle against the abuse of language is a sentimental archaism, like preferring candles to electric light or hansom cabs to aeroplanes. Underneath this lies the half-conscious belief that language is a natural growth and not an instrument which we shape for our own purposes.

Now, it is clear that the decline of a language must ultimately have political and economic causes: it is not due simply to the bad influence of this or that individual writer. But an effect can become a cause, reinforcing the original cause and producing the same effect in an intensified form, and so on indefinitely. A man may take to drink because he feels himself to be a failure, and then fail all the more completely because he drinks. It is rather the same thing that is happening to the English language. It becomes ugly and inaccurate because our thoughts are foolish, but the slovenliness of our language makes it easier for us to have foolish thoughts. The point is that the process is reversible. Modern English, especially written English, is full of bad habits which spread by imitation and which can be avoided if one is willing to take the necessary trouble. If one gets rid of these habits one can think more clearly, and to think clearly is a necessary first step toward political regeneration: so that the fight against bad English is not frivolous and is not the exclusive concern of professional writers. I will come back to this presently, and I hope that by that time the meaning of what I have said here will have become clearer. Meanwhile, here are five specimens of the English language as it is now habitually written.

These five passages have not been picked out because they are especially bad—I could have quoted far worse if I had chosen—but because they illustrate various of the mental vices from which we now suffer. They are a little below the average, but are fairly representative samples. I number them so that I can refer back to them when necessary:

> (1) I am not, indeed, sure whether it is not true to say that the Milton who once seemed not unlike a seventeenth-century Shelley had not become, out of an experience ever more bitter in each year, more alien [*sic*]

to the founder of that Jesuit sect which nothing could induce him to tolerate.

Professor Harold Laski
(Essay in Freedom of Expression)

(2) Above all, we cannot play ducks and drakes with a native battery of idioms which prescribes such egregious collocations of vocables as the basic *put up with* for *tolerate* or *put at a loss* for *bewilder*.

Professor Lancelot Hogben (Interglossa)

(3) On the one side we have the free personality: by definition it is not neurotic, for it has neither conflict nor dream. Its desires, such as they are, are transparent, for they are just what institutional approval keeps in the forefront of consciousness; another institutional pattern would alter their number and intensity; there is little in them that is natural, irreducible, or culturally dangerous. But *on the other side,* the social bond itself is nothing but the mutual reflection of these self-secure integrities. Recall the definition of love. Is not this the very picture of a small academic? Where is there a place in this hall of mirrors for either personality or fraternity?

Essay on psychology in Politics (New York)

(4) All the "best people" from the gentlemen's clubs, and all the frantic fascist captains, united in common hatred of Socialism and bestial horror of the rising tide of the mass revolutionary movement, have turned to acts of provocation, to foul incendiarism, to medieval legends of poisoned wells, to legalize their own destruction of proletarian organizations, and rouse the agitated petty-bourgeoisie to chauvinistic fervor on behalf of the fight against the revolutionary way out of the crisis.

Communist pamphlet

(5) If a new spirit *is* to be infused into this old country, there is one thorny and contentious reform which must be tackled, and that is the humanization and galvanization of the B.B.C. Timidity here will bespeak canker and atrophy of the soul. The heart of Britain may be sound and of strong beat, for instance, but the British lion's roar at present is like that of Bottom in Shakespeare's *Midsummer Night's Dream*—as gentle as any sucking dove. A virile new Britain cannot continue indefinitely to be traduced in the eyes, or rather ears, of the world by the effete languors of Langham Place, brazenly masquerading as "standard English." When the Voice of Britain is heard at nine o'clock, better far and infinitely less ludicrous to hear aitches honestly dropped than the present priggish, inflated, inhibited, school-ma'amish arch braying of blameless bashful mewing maidens!

Letter in Tribune

Each of these passages has faults of its own, but, quite apart from avoidable ugliness, two qualities are common to all of them. The first is staleness of imagery; the other is lack of precision. The writer either has a meaning and cannot express it, or he inadvertently says something else, or he is almost indifferent as to whether his words mean anything or not. This mixture of vagueness and sheer incompetence is the most marked characteristic of modern English prose, and especially of any kind of political writing. As soon as certain topics are raised, the concrete melts into the abstract and no one seems able to think of turns of speech that are not hackneyed: prose consists less and less of *words* chosen for the sake of their meaning, and more and more of *phrases* tacked together like the sections of a prefabricated henhouse. I list below, with notes and examples, various of the tricks by means of which the work of prose-construction is habitually dodged:

Dying metaphors. A newly invented metaphor assists thought by 5 evoking a visual image, while on the other hand a metaphor which is technically "dead" (e.g. *iron resolution*) has in effect reverted to being an ordinary word and can generally be used without loss of vividness. But in between these two classes there is a huge dump of worn-out metaphors which have lost all evocative power and are merely used because they save people the trouble of inventing phrases for themselves. Examples are: *Ring the changes on, take up the cudgels for, toe the line, ride roughshod over, stand shoulder to shoulder with, play into the hands of, no axe to grind, grist to the mill, fishing in troubled waters, on the order of the day, Achilles' heel, swan song, hotbed*. Many of these are used without knowledge of their meaning (what is a "rift," for instance?), and incompatible metaphors are frequently mixed, a sure sign that the writer is not interested in what he is saying. Some metaphors now current have been twisted out of their original meaning without those who use them ever being aware of the fact. For example, *toe the line* is sometimes written *tow the line*. Another example is *the hammer and the anvil*, now always used with the implication that the anvil gets the worst of it. In real life it is always the anvil that breaks the hammer, never the other way about: a writer who stopped to think what he was saying would be aware of this, and would avoid perverting the original phrase.

Operators or *verbal false limbs*. These save the trouble of picking out appropriate verbs and nouns, and at the same time pad each sentence with extra syllables which give it an appearance of symmetry. Characteristic phrases are *render inoperative, militate against, make contact with, be subjected to, give rise to, give grounds for, have the effect of, play a leading part (role) in, make itself felt, take effect, exhibit a tendency to, serve the purpose of*, etc., etc. The key-note is the elimination of simple verbs. Instead of being a single word, such as *break, stop, spoil, mend, kill*, a verb becomes a *phrase*, made up of a noun or adjective tacked on to some general-purpose verb such as *prove, serve, form, play, render*. In addition, the passive voice is wherever possible used in preference to the active, and noun constructions are used instead of gerunds (*by examination of* instead of *by examining*). The range of verbs is further cut down by means of the *-ize* and *de-* formations, and the banal statements are given an appearance of profundity by means of the *not un-* formation. Simple conjunctions and prepositions are replaced by such phrases as *with respect to, having regard to, the fact that, by dint of, in view of, in the interests of, on the hypothesis that;* and the ends of sentences are saved from anticlimax by such resounding commonplaces as *greatly to be desired, cannot be left out of account, a development to be expected in the near future, deserving of serious consideration, brought to a satisfactory conclusion,* and so on and so forth.

Pretentious diction. Words like *phenomenon, element, individual* (as noun), *objective, categorical, effective, virtual, basic, primary, promote, constitute, exhibit, exploit, utilize, eliminate, liquidate,* are used to dress up simple statements and give an air of scientific impartiality to biased judgments. Adjectives like *epoch-making, epic, historic, unforgettable, triumphant, age-old, inevitable, inexorable, veritable,* are used to dignify the sordid process of international politics, while writing that aims at glorifying war usually takes on an archaic color, its characteristic words being: *realm, throne, chariot, mailed fist, trident, sword, shield, buckler, banner, jackboot, clarion.* Foreign words and expressions such as *cul de sac, ancien régime, deus ex machina, mutatis mutandis, status quo, gleichschaltung, weltanschauung,* are used to give an air of culture and elegance. Except for the useful abbreviations *i.e., e.g.,* and *etc.,* there is no real need for any of the hundreds of foreign phrases now current in English. Bad writers, and especially scientific, political, and sociological writers, are nearly always haunted by the notion that Latin or Greek words are grander than Saxon ones, and unnecessary words like *expedite, ameliorate, predict, extraneous, deracinated, clandestine, subaqueous,* and hundreds of others constantly gain ground from their Anglo-Saxon opposite numbers.[1] The jargon peculiar to Marxist writing (*hyena, hangman, cannibal, petty bourgeois, these gentry, lackey, flunkey, mad dog, White Guard,* etc.) consists largely of words and phrases translated from Russian, German, or French; but the normal way of coining a new word is to use a Latin or Greek root with the appropriate affix and, where necessary, the -ize formation. It is often easier to make up words of this kind (*deregionalize, impermissible, extramarital, nonfragmentary* and so forth) than to think up the English words that will cover one's meaning. The result, in general, is an increase in slovenliness and vagueness.

---

[1] An interesting illustration of this is the way in which the English flower names which were in use till very recently are being ousted by Greek ones, *snapdragon* becoming *antirrhinum, forget-me-not* becoming *myosotis,* etc. It is hard to see any practical reason for this change of fashion: it is probably due to an instinctive turning away from the more homely word and a vague feeling that the Greek word is scientific.

Meaningless words. In certain kinds of writing, particularly in art criticism and literary criticism, it is normal to come across long passages which are almost completely lacking in meaning.[2] Words like *romantic, plastic, values, human, dead, sentimental, natural, vitality,* as used in art criticism, are strictly meaningless, in the sense that they not only do not point to any discoverable object, but are hardly ever expected to do so by the reader. When one critic writes, "The outstanding feature of Mr. X's work is its living quality," while another writes, "The immediately striking thing about Mr. X's work is its peculiar deadness," the reader accepts this as a simple difference of opinion. If words like *black* and *white* were involved, instead of the jargon words *dead* and *living,* he would see at once that language was being used in an improper way. Many political words are similarly abused. The word *Fascism* has now no meaning except in so far as it signifies "something not desirable." The words *democracy, socialism, freedom, patriotic, realistic, justice,* have each of them several different meanings which cannot be reconciled with one another. In the case of a word like *democracy,* not only is there no agreed definition, but the attempt to make one is resisted from all sides. It is almost universally felt that when we call a country democratic we are praising it: consequently the defenders of every kind of régime claim that it is a democracy, and fear that they might have to stop using the word if it were tied down to any one meaning. Words of this kind are often used in a consciously dishonest way. That is, the person who uses them has his own private definition, but allows his hearer to think he means something quite different. Statements like *Marshal Pétain was a true patriot, The Soviet press is the freest in the world, The Catholic Church is opposed to persecution,* are almost always made with intent to deceive. Other words used in variable meanings, in most cases more or less dishonestly, are: *class, totalitarian, science, progressive, reactionary, bourgeois, equality.*

Now that I have made this catalogue of swindles and perversions, let me give another example of the kind of writing that they lead to. This time it must of its nature be an imaginary one. I am going to translate a passage of good English into modern English of the worst sort. Here is a well-known verse from *Ecclesiastes:*

> I returned and saw under the sun, that the race is not to the swift, nor the battle to the strong, neither yet bread to the wise, nor yet riches

[2]Example: "Comfort's catholicity of perception and image, strangely Whitmanesque in range, almost the exact opposite in aesthetic compulsion, continues to evoke that trembling atmospheric accumulative hinting at a cruel, an inexorably serene timelessness. . . . Wrey Gardiner scores by aiming at simple bull's-eyes with precision. Only they are not so simple, and through this contented sadness runs more than the surface bittersweet of resignation." (*Poetry Quarterly.*)

to men of understanding, nor yet favor to men of skill; but time and chance happeneth to them all.

Here it is in modern English: 10

> Objective consideration of contemporary phenomena compels the conclusion that success or failure in competitive activities exhibits no tendency to be commensurate with innate capacity, but that a considerable element of the unpredictable must invariably be taken into account.

This is a parody, but not a very gross one. Exhibit (3), above, for instance, contains several patches of the same kind of English. It will be seen that I have not made a full translation. The beginning and ending of the sentence follow the original meaning fairly closely, but in the middle the concrete illustration—race, battle, bread—dissolve into the vague phrase "success or failure in competitive activities." This had to be so, because no modern writer of the kind I am discussing—no one capable of using phrases like "objective consideration of contemporary phenomena"—would ever tabulate his thoughts in that precise and detailed way. The whole tendency of modern prose is away from concreteness. Now analyze these two sentences a little more closely. The first contains forty-nine words but only sixty syllables, and all its words are those of everyday life. The second contains thirty-eight words of ninety syllables: eighteen of its words are from Latin roots and one from Greek. The first sentence contains six vivid images, and only one phrase ("time and chance") that could be called vague. The second contains not a single fresh, arresting phrase, and in spite of its ninety syllables it gives only a shortened version of the meaning contained in the first. Yet without a doubt it is the second kind of sentence that is gaining ground in modern English. I do not want to exaggerate. This kind of writing is not yet universal, and outcrops of simplicity will occur here and there in the worst-written page. Still, if you or I were told to write a few lines on the uncertainty of human fortunes, we should probably come much nearer to my imaginary sentence than to the one from *Ecclesiastes*.

As I have tried to show, modern writing at its worst does not consist in picking out words for the sake of their meaning and inventing images in order to make the meaning clearer. It consists in gumming together long strips of words which have already been set in order by someone else, and making the results presentable by sheer humbug. The attraction of this way of writing is that it is easy. It is easier—even quicker, once you have the habit—to say *In my opinion it is not an unjustifiable assumption that* than to say *I think*. If you use ready-made phrases, you not only don't have to hunt about for words; you also don't have to bother with the rhythms of your sentences, since these phrases are generally so arranged as to be more or less euphonious. When you are composing in a hurry—when you are dictating to a stenographer, for instance, or making a public speech—it is natural to fall into a pretentious, Latinized style. Tags like *a consideration which we should do well to bear in mind* or *a conclusion to which all of us would readily assent* will save many a sentence from coming down with a bump. By using stale metaphors, similes, and idioms, you save much mental effort, at the cost of leaving your meaning vague, not only for your reader but for yourself. This is the significance of mixed metaphors. The sole aim of a metaphor is to call up a visual image. When these images clash—as in *The Fascist octopus has sung its swan song, the jackboot is thrown into the melting pot*—it can be taken as certain that the writer is not seeing a mental image of the objects he is naming; in other words he is not really thinking. Look again at the examples I gave at the beginning of this essay. Professor Laski (1) uses five negatives in fifty-three words. One of these is superfluous, making nonsense of the whole passage, and in addition there is the slip—*alien* for akin—making further nonsense, and several avoidable pieces of clumsiness which increase the general vagueness. Professor Hogben (2) plays ducks and drakes with a battery which is able to write prescriptions, and, while disapproving of the everyday phrase *put up with,* is unwilling to look *egregious* up in the dictionary and see what it means; (3), if one takes an uncharitable attitude towards it, is simply meaningless: probably one could work out its intended meaning by reading the whole of the article in which it occurs. In (4), the writer knows more or less what he wants to say, but an accumulation of stale phrases chokes him like tea leaves blocking a sink. In (5), words and meaning have almost parted company. People who write in this manner usually have a general emotional meaning—they dislike one thing and want to express solidarity with another—but they are not interested in the detail of what they are saying. A scrupulous writer, in every sentence that he writes, will ask himself at least four questions, thus: What am I trying to say? What words will express it? What image or idiom will make it clearer? Is this image fresh enough to have an effect? And he will probably ask himself two more: Could I put it more shortly? Have I said anything that is avoidably ugly? But you are not obliged to go to all this trouble. You can shirk it by simply throwing your mind open and letting the ready-made phrases come crowding in. They will construct your sentences for you—even think your thoughts for you, to a certain extent—and at need they will perform the important service of partially concealing your meaning even from yourself. It is at this point that the special connection between politics and the debasement of language becomes clear.

In our time it is broadly true that political writing is bad writing. Where it is not true, it will generally be found that the writer is some kind of rebel, expressing his private opinions and not a "party line."

Orthodoxy, of whatever color, seems to demand a lifeless, imitative style. The political dialects to be found in pamphlets, leading articles, manifestoes, White Papers and the speeches of undersecretaries do, of course, vary from party to party, but they are all alike in that one almost never finds in them a fresh, vivid, home-made turn of speech. When one watches some tired hack on the platform mechanically repeating the familiar phrases—*bestial atrocities, iron heel, bloodstained tyranny, free peoples of the world, stand shoulder to shoulder*—one often has a curious feeling that one is not watching a live human being but some kind of dummy: a feeling which suddenly becomes stronger at moments when the light catches the speaker's spectacles and turns them into blank discs which seem to have no eyes behind them. And this is not altogether fanciful. A speaker who uses that kind of phraseology has gone some distance towards turning himself into a machine. The appropriate noises are coming out of his larynx, but his brain is not involved as it would be if he were choosing his words for himself. If the speech he is making is one that he is accustomed to make over and over again, he may be almost unconscious of what he is saying, as one is when one utters the responses in church. And this reduced state of consciousness, if not indispensable, is at any rate favorable to political conformity.

In our time, political speech and writing are largely the defense of the indefensible. Things like the continuance of British rule in India, the Russian purges and deportations, the dropping of the atom bombs on Japan, can indeed be defended, but only by arguments which are too brutal for most people to face, and which do not square with the professed aims of political parties. Thus political language has to consist largely of euphemism, question-begging and sheer cloudy vagueness. Defenseless villages are bombarded from the air, the inhabitants driven out into the countryside, the cattle machine-gunned, the huts set on fire with incendiary bullets: this is called *pacification*. Millions of peasants are robbed of their farms and sent trudging along the roads with no more than they can carry: this is called *transfer of population* or *rectification of frontiers*. People are imprisoned for years without trial, or shot in the back of the neck or sent to die of scurvy in Arctic lumber camps: this is called *elimination of unreliable elements*. Such phraseology is needed if one wants to name things without calling up mental pictures of them. Consider for instance some comfortable English professor defending Russian totalitarianism. He cannot say outright, "I believe in killing off your opponents when you can get good results by doing so." Probably, therefore, he will say something like this:

"While freely conceding that the Soviet régime exhibits certain features which the humanitarian may be inclined to deplore, we must, I think, agree that a certain curtailment of the right to political opposition is an unavoidable concomitant of transitional periods, and that the

15

rigors which the Russian people have been called upon to undergo have been amply justified in the sphere of concrete achievement."

The inflated style is itself a kind of euphemism. A mass of Latin words falls upon the facts like soft snow, blurring the outlines and covering up all the details. The great enemy of clear language is insincerity. When there is a gap between one's real and one's declared aims, one turns as it were instinctively to long words and exhausted idioms, like a cuttlefish squirting out ink. In our age there is no such thing as "keeping out of politics." All issues are political issues, and politics itself is a mass of lies, evasions, folly, hatred and schizophrenia. When the general atmosphere is bad, language must suffer. I should expect to find— this is a guess which I have not sufficient knowledge to verify—that the German, Russian, and Italian languages have all deteriorated in the last ten or fifteen years, as a result of dictatorship.

But if thought corrupts language, language can also corrupt thought. A bad usage can spread by tradition and imitation, even among people who should and do know better. The debased language that I have been discussing is in some ways very convenient. Phrases like *a not unjustifiable assumption, leaves much to be desired, would serve no good purpose, a consideration which we should do well to bear in mind,* are a continuous temptation, a packet of aspirins always at one's elbow. Look back through this essay, and for certain you will find that I have again and again committed the very faults I am protesting against. By this morning's post I have received a pamphlet dealing with conditions in Germany. The author tells me that he "felt impelled" to write it. I open it at random, and here is almost the first sentence that I see: "[The Allies] have an opportunity not only of achieving a radical transformation of Germany's social and political structure in such a way as to avoid a nationalistic reaction in Germany itself, but at the same time of laying the foundations of a co-operative and unified Europe." You see, he "feels impelled" to write—feels, presumably, that he has something new to say—and yet his words, like cavalry horses answering the bugle, group themselves automatically into the familiar dreary pattern. This invasion of one's mind by ready-made phrases (*lay the foundations, achieve a radical transformation*) can only be prevented if one is constantly on guard against them, and every such phrase anaesthetizes a portion of one's brain.

I said earlier that the decadence of our language is probably curable. Those who deny this would argue, if they produced an argument at all, that language merely reflects existing social conditions, and that we cannot influence its development by any direct tinkering with words and constructions. So far as the general tone or spirit of a language goes, this may be true, but it is not true in detail. Silly words and expressions have often disappeared, not through any evolutionary process but owing to the conscious action of a minority. Two recent examples were *explore every avenue* and *leave no stone unturned,* which were killed by the jeers of a few journalists. There is a long list of flyblown metaphors which could similarly be got rid of if enough people would interest themselves in the job; and it should also be possible to laugh the *not un-* formation out of existence,[3] to reduce the amount of Latin and Greek in the average sentence, to drive out foreign phrases and strayed scientific words, and, in general, to make pretentiousness unfashionable. But all these are minor points. The defense of the English language implies more than this, and perhaps it is best to start by saying what it does *not* imply.

To begin with it has nothing to do with archaism, with the salvaging of obsolete words and turns of speech, or with the setting up of a "standard English" which must never be departed from. On the contrary, it is especially concerned with the scrapping of every word or idiom which has outworn its usefulness. It has nothing to do with correct grammar and syntax, which are of no importance so long as one makes one's meaning clear, or with the avoidance of Americanisms, or with having what is called a "good prose style." On the other hand it is not concerned with fake simplicity and the attempt to make written English colloquial. Nor does it even imply in every case preferring the Saxon word to the Latin one, though it does imply using the fewest and shortest words that will cover one's meaning. What is above all needed is to let the meaning choose the word, and not the other way about. In prose, the worst thing one can do with words is to surrender to them. When you think of a concrete object, you think wordlessly, and then, if you want to describe the thing you have been visualizing you probably hunt about till you find the exact words that seem to fit it. When you think of something abstract you are more inclined to use words from the start, and unless you make a conscious effort to prevent it, the existing dialect will come rushing in and do the job for you, at the expense of blurring or even changing your meaning. Probably it is better to put off using words as long as possible and get one's meaning as clear as one can through pictures or sensations. Afterward one can choose—not simply *accept*—the phrases that will best cover the meaning, and then switch round and decide what impression one's words are likely to make on another person. This last effort of the mind cuts out all stale or mixed images, all prefabricated phrases, needless repetitions, and humbug and vagueness generally. But one can often be in doubt about the effect of a word or a phrase, and one needs rules that one can rely on when instinct fails. I think the following rules will cover most cases:

---

[3] One can cure oneself of the *not un-* formation by memorizing this sentence: *A not unblack dog was chasing a not unsmall rabbit across a not ungreen field.*

   (i) Never use a metaphor, simile, or other figure of speech which you are used to seeing in print.
   (ii) Never use a long word where a short one will do.
  (iii) If it is possible to cut a word out, always cut it out.
  (iv) Never use the passive where you can use the active.
   (v) Never use a foreign phrase, a scientific word, or a jargon word if you can think of an everyday English equivalent.
  (vi) Break any of these rules sooner than say anything outright barbarous.

These rules sound elementary, and so they are, but they demand a deep change of attitude in anyone who has grown used to writing in the style now fashionable. One could keep all of them and still write bad English, but one could not write the kind of stuff that I quoted in those five specimens at the beginning of this article.

I have not here been considering the literary use of language, but merely language as an instrument for expressing and not for concealing or preventing thought. Stuart Chase and others have come near to claiming that all abstract words are meaningless, and have used this as a pretext for advocating a kind of political quietism. Since you don't know what Fascism is, how can you struggle against Fascism? One need not swallow such absurdities at this, but one ought to recognize that the present political chaos is connected with the decay of language, and that one can probably bring about some improvement by starting at the verbal end. If you simplify your English, you are freed from the worst follies of orthodoxy. You cannot speak any of the necessary dialects, and when you make a stupid remark its stupidity will be obvious, even to yourself. Political language—and with variations this is true of all political parties, from Conservatives to Anarchists—is designed to make lies sound truthful and murder respectable, and to give an appearance of solidity to pure wind. One cannot change this all in a moment, but one can at least change one's own habits, and from time to time one can even, if one jeers loudly enough, send some worn-out and useless phrase—some *jackboot, Achilles' heel, hotbed, melting pot, acid test, veritable inferno,* or other lump of verbal refuse—into the dustbin where it belongs.

1946

Lines of Inquiry
"Politics and the English Language"

Given his attack on "inflated" writing, Orwell presumably must have taken considerable pains to avoid any "kind of euphemism" in his own prose, so that this essay itself would be a model of politically responsible English. How effective is Orwell in fulfilling his own standards? In his diction? In his sentence structure? In his analogies and metaphors?

At the beginning of paragraph 16, Orwell says that "the inflated style is itself a kind of euphemism." What does Orwell mean by "the inflated style"? Why does he consider it to be "a kind of euphemism"? In paragraphs 5–8, Orwell identifies and illustrates four different kinds of stylistic "tricks by means of which the work of prose-construction is habitually dodged." In what sense is each of these tricks "a kind of euphemism"? In what sense might the euphemistic impulse be considered the root of all the problems that Orwell discusses in his essay? In what senses might it not?

More than forty years have passed since Orwell made his "catalogue of swindles and perversions," so an updating of his work is certainly in order. Find four or five passages from current American writing that you consider to be representative of what is worst about the way people are writing today. In what respects do these passages exhibit the same basic problems that Orwell was attacking? In what respects do they reflect what you consider to be new problems? How would you categorize, define, and account for these new problems?

Why I Write

From a very early age, perhaps the age of five or six, I knew that when I grew up I should be a writer. Between the ages of about seventeen and twenty-four I tried to abandon this idea, but I did so with the consciousness that I was outraging my true nature and that sooner or later I should have to settle down and write books.

I was the middle child of three, but there was a gap of five years on either side, and I barely saw my father before I was eight. For this and other reasons I was somewhat lonely, and I soon developed disagreeable mannerisms which made me unpopular throughout my schooldays. I had the lonely child's habit of making up stories and holding conversations with imaginary persons, and I think from the very start my literary ambitions were mixed up with the feeling of being isolated and undervalued. I knew that I had a facility with words and a power of facing unpleasant facts, and I felt that this created a sort of private world in which I could get my own back for my failure in everyday life. Nevertheless the volume of serious—i.e., seriously intended—writing which I produced all through my childhood and boyhood would not amount to half a dozen pages. I wrote my first poem at the age of four or five, my mother taking it down to dictation. I cannot remember anything about it except that it was about a tiger and the tiger had "chair-like teeth"—a good enough phrase, but I fancy the poem was a plagiarism of Blake's "Tiger, Tiger." At eleven, when the war of 1914–18 broke out, I wrote a patriotic poem which was printed in the local newspaper, as was another, two years later, on the death of Kitchener. From time to time, when I was a bit older, I wrote bad and usually unfinished "nature poems" in the Georgian style. I also, about twice, attempted a short story which was a ghastly failure. That was the total of the would-be serious work that I actually set down on paper during all those years.

However, throughout this time I did in a sense engage in literary activities. To begin with there was the made-to-order stuff which I produced quickly, easily and without much pleasure to myself. Apart from school work, I wrote *vers d'occasion,* semi-comic poems which I could turn out at what now seems to me astonishing speed—at fourteen I wrote a whole rhyming play, in imitation of Aristophanes, in about a week—and helped to edit school magazines, both printed and in manuscript. These magazines were the most pitiful burlesque stuff that you could imagine, and I took far less trouble with them than I now would with the cheapest journalism. But side by side with all this, for fifteen years or more, I was carrying out a literary exercise of a quite different kind: this was the making up of a continuous "story" about myself, a sort of diary existing only in the mind. I believe this is a common habit of children and adolescents. As a very small child I used to imagine that I was, say, Robin Hood, and picture myself as the hero of thrilling adventures, but quite soon my "story" ceased to be narcissistic in a crude way and became more and more a mere description of what I was doing and the things I saw. For minutes at a time this kind of thing would be running through my head: "He pushed the door open and entered the room. A yellow beam of sunlight, filtering through the muslin curtains, slanted on to the table, where a matchbox, half open, lay beside the inkpot. With his right hand in his pocket he moved across to the window. Down in the street a tortoiseshell cat was chasing a dead leaf," etc etc. This habit continued till I was about twenty-five, right through my non-literary years. Although I had to search, and did search, for the right words, I seemed to be making this descriptive effort almost against my will, under a kind of compulsion from outside. The "story" must, I suppose, have reflected the styles of the various writers I admired at different ages, but so far as I remember it always had the same meticulous descriptive quality.

When I was about sixteen I suddenly discovered the joy of mere words, i.e., the sounds and associations of words. The lines from *Paradise Lost,*

> So hee with difficulty and labour hard
> Moved on: with difficulty and labour hee,

which do not now seem to me so very wonderful, sent shivers down my backbone; and the spelling "hee" for "he" was an added pleasure. As for the need to describe things, I knew all about it already. So it is clear what kind of books I wanted to write, in so far as I could be said to want to write books at that time. I wanted to write enormous naturalistic novels with unhappy endings, full of detailed descriptions and arresting similes, and also full of purple passages in which words were used partly for the sake of their sound. And in fact my first completed novel, *Burmese Days,* which I wrote when I was thirty but projected much earlier, is rather that kind of book.

I give all this background information because I do not think one 5 can assess a writer's motives without knowing something of his early development. His subject matter will be determined by the age he lives in—at least this is true in tumultuous, revolutionary ages like our own— but before he ever begins to write he will have acquired an emotional attitude from which he will never completely escape. It is his job, no doubt, to discipline his temperament and avoid getting stuck at some immature stage, or in some perverse mood: but if he escapes from his early influences altogether, he will have killed his impulse to write. Putting aside the need to earn a living, I think there are four great motives for writing, at any rate for writing prose. They exist in different degrees in every writer, and in any one writer the proportions will vary from time to time, according to the atmosphere in which he is living. They are:

1. Sheer egoism. Desire to seem clever, to be talked about, to be remembered after death, to get your own back on grown-ups who snubbed you in childhood, etc. etc. It is humbug to pretend that this is not a motive, and a strong one. Writers share this characteristic with scientists, artists, politicians, lawyers, soldiers, successful businessmen—in short, with the whole top crust of humanity. The great mass of human beings are not acutely selfish. After the age of about thirty they abandon individual ambition—in many cases, indeed, they almost abandon the sense of being individuals at all—and live chiefly for others, or are simply smothered under drudgery. But there is also the minority of gifted, wilful people who are determined to live their own lives to the end, and writers belong in this class. Serious writers, I should say, are on the whole more vain and self-centered than journalists, though less interested in money.

2. Aesthetic enthusiasm. Perception of beauty in the external world, or, on the other hand, in words and their right arrangement. Pleasure in the impact of one sound on another, in the firmness of good prose or the rhythm of a good story. Desire to share an experience which one feels is valuable and ought not to be missed. The aesthetic motive is very feeble in a lot of writers, but even a pamphleteer or a writer of textbooks will have pet words and phrases which appeal to him for non-utilitarian reasons; or he may feel strongly about typography, width of margins, etc. Above the level of a railway guide, no book is quite free from aesthetic considerations.

3. Historical impulse. Desire to see things as they are, to find out true facts and store them up for the use of posterity.

4. Political purpose—using the word "political" in the widest possible sense. Desire to push the world in a certain direction, to alter other people's idea of the kind of society that they should strive after. Once again, no book is genuinely free from political bias. The opinion that art should have nothing to do with politics is itself a political attitude.

It can be seen how these various impulses must war against one another, and how they must fluctuate from person to person and from time to time. By nature—taking your "nature" to be the state you have attained when you are first adult—I am a person in whom the first three motives would outweigh the fourth. In a peaceful age I might have written ornate or merely descriptive books, and might have remained almost unaware of my political loyalties. As it is I have been forced into becoming a sort of pamphleteer. First I spent five years in an unsuitable profession (the Indian Imperial Police, in Burma), and then I underwent

10

poverty and the sense of failure. This increased my natural hatred of authority and made me for the first time fully aware of the existence of the working classes, and the job in Burma had given me some understanding of the nature of imperialism: but these experiences were not enough to give me an accurate political orientation. Then came Hitler, the Spanish civil war, etc. By the end of 1935 I had still failed to reach a firm decision. I remember a little poem that I wrote at that date, expressing my dilemma:

> A happy vicar I might have been
> Two hundred years ago,
> To preach upon eternal doom
> And watch my walnuts grow;
>
> But born, alas, in an evil time,
> I missed that pleasant haven,
> For the hair has grown on my upper lip
> And the clergy are all clean-shaven.
>
> And later still the times were good,
> We were so easy to please,
> We rocked our troubled thoughts to sleep
> On the bosoms of the trees.
>
> All ignorant we dared to own
> The joys we now dissemble;
> The greenfinch on the apple bough
> Could make my enemies tremble.
>
> But girls' bellies and apricots,
> Roach in a shaded stream,
> Horses, ducks in flight at dawn,
> All these are a dream.
>
> It is forbidden to dream again;
> We maim our joys or hide them;
> Horses are made of chromium steel
> And little fat men shall ride them.
>
> I am the worm who never turned,
> The eunuch without a harem;
> Between the priest and the commissar
> I walk like Eugene Aram;
>
> And the commissar is telling my fortune
> While the radio plays,
> But the priest has promised an Austin Seven,
> For Duggie always pays.
>
> I dreamed I dwelt in marble halls,
> And woke to find it true;
> I wasn't born for an age like this;
> Was Smith? Was Jones? Were you?

The Spanish war and other events in 1936–37 turned the scale and thereafter I knew where I stood. Every line of serious work that I have written since 1936 has been written, directly or indirectly, *against* totalitarianism and *for* democratic Socialism, as I understand it. It seems to me nonsense, in a period like our own, to think that one can avoid writing of such subjects. Everyone writes of them in one guise or another. It is simply a question of which side one takes and what approach one follows. And the more one is conscious of one's political bias, the more chance one has of acting politically without sacrificing one's aesthetic and intellectual integrity.

What I have most wanted to do throughout the past ten years is to make political writing into an art. My starting point is always a feeling of partisanship, a sense of injustice. When I sit down to write a book, I do not say to myself, "I am going to produce a work of art." I write it because there is some lie that I want to expose, some fact to which I want to draw attention, and my initial concern is to get a hearing. But I could not do the work of writing a book, or even a long magazine article, if it were not also an aesthetic experience. Anyone who cares to examine my work will see that even when it is downright propaganda it contains much that a full-time politician would consider irrelevant. I am not able, and I do not want, completely to abandon the world-view that I acquired in childhood. So long as I remain alive and well I shall continue to feel strongly about prose style, to love the surface of the earth, and to take pleasure in solid objects and scraps of useless information. It is no use trying to suppress that side of myself. The job is to reconcile my ingrained likes and dislikes with the essentially public, non-individual activities that this age forces on all of us.

It is not easy. It raises problems of construction and language, and it raises in a new way the problem of truthfulness. Let me give just one example of the cruder kind of difficulty that arises. My book about the Spanish civil war, *Homage to Catalonia,* is, of course, a frankly political book, but in the main it is written with a certain detachment and regard for form. I did try very hard in it to tell the whole truth without violating my literary instincts. But among other things it contains a long chapter, full of newspaper quotations and the like, defending the Trotskyists who were accused of plotting with Franco. Clearly such a chapter, which after a year or two would lose its interest for any ordinary reader, must ruin the book. A critic whom I respect read me a lecture about it. "Why did you put in all that stuff?" he said. "You've turned what might have been a good book into journalism." What he said was true, but I could not have done otherwise. I happened to know, what very few people in England had been allowed to know, that innocent men were being falsely accused. If I had not been angry about that I should never have written the book.

In one form or another this problem comes up again. The problem of language is subtler and would take too long to discuss. I will only say that of late years I have tried to write less picturesquely and more exactly. In any case I find that by the time you have perfected any style of writing, you have always outgrown it. *Animal Farm* was the first book in which I tried, with full consciousness of what I was doing, to fuse political purpose and artistic purpose into one whole. I have not written a novel for seven years, but I hope to write another fairly soon. It is bound to be a failure, every book is a failure, but I know with some clarity what kind of book I want to write.

Looking back through the last page or two, I see that I have made it appear as though my motives in writing were wholly public-spirited. I don't want to leave that as the final impression. All writers are vain, selfish and lazy, and at the very bottom of their motives there lies a mystery. Writing a book is a horrible, exhausting struggle, like a long bout of some painful illness. One would never undertake such a thing if one were not driven on by some demon whom one can neither resist nor understand. For all one knows that demon is simply the same instinct that makes a baby squall for attention. And yet it is also true that one can write nothing readable unless one constantly struggles to efface one's own personality. Good prose is like a window pane. I cannot say with certainty which of my motives are the strongest, but I know which of them deserve to be followed. And looking back through my work, I see that it is invariably where I lacked a *political* purpose that I wrote lifeless books and was betrayed into purple passages, sentences without meaning, decorative adjectives and humbug generally.

1946

Lines of Inquiry
"Why I Write"

Given the title and purpose of this piece, why do you suppose that Orwell does not restrict himself to listing, defining, illustrating, and explaining the four reasons for writing that he enumerates in paragraphs 6–9? How is the material that precedes and follows these paragraphs related to the purpose of his essay? How in particular is the surrounding material related to the points that he makes in these paragraphs?

After listing his four reasons for writing, Orwell says (at the beginning of paragraph 10) that "it can be seen how these various impulses must war against another, and how they must fluctuate from person to person and from time to time." Why does he believe they must war against one another? Why does he believe they must fluctuate from person to person and from time to time? Have you ever experienced conflicting impulses in your own writing? Have your reasons for writing fluctuated from time to time?

Which of the four reasons that Orwell lists do you consider to be the most important purpose for writing? What other reasons for writing can you think of beyond those that Orwell has defined? Why do you suppose he has not included them in his list? What are your reasons for writing? How do they compare with Orwell's?

Jonathan Swift
1667–1745

I have ever hated all nations, professions, and communities, and all my love is toward individuals. . . . But principally I hate and detest that animal called man, although I heartily love John, Peter, Thomas and so forth.

In this excerpt from a letter written in 1725, shortly after finishing *Gulliver's Travels,* Jonathan Swift defined the "system" that "governed" his thinking, not only in his most famous work, but in virtually all of his satiric writing. Though his outlook may seem extreme, it was the product of his eighteenth-century rationalism and his deeply religious conservatism. As a rationalist, he was devoted above all else to the virtues of good sense and reason, but as an Anglican clergyman, he believed human nature was flawed and thus inclined to act against its better judgment. As a realistic, rather than optimistic, observer of human affairs, he could not overlook the false learning, political corruption, and religious hypocrisy of his own time, nor could he ignore the folly, cruelty, perversity, and pride of humanity in general. So he did not consider man to be a rational animal, but merely an animal capable of reason—an animal that all too frequently failed to live up to its highest capabilities.

Born in Dublin seven months after the death of his father, Swift was the child of English parents who had emigrated to Ireland in 1660 when monarchy was restored to England. With the financial support of his uncle, he was educated at Kilkenny School, the finest grammar school in Ireland, and then at Trinity College in Dublin, from which he received a B.A. in 1686. His most influential schooling took place during a ten-year period after he moved to England in 1689 to become secretary to Sir William Temple, a retired diplomat and distinguished member of the Whig party. Under Temple's learned influence, Swift read widely and developed an interest in literature and writing that soon bore fruit in *The Battle of the Books* (1704), his witty defense of ancient over modern literature, and *A Tale of a Tub* (1704), his wide-ranging satiric attack on religious corruption, false learning, and human pride. Under Temple's influence, he also developed a knowledge of court affairs and an interest in politics that came to fruition in the brilliant political journalism and satire he produced between 1710 and 1735. At Temple's estate in Surrey, he also met Esther Johnson, then an eight-year-old girl, whom he was later to address as "Stella" in a remarkable series of letters and love poems. Though the exact nature of their relationship is unknown, they evidently remained devoted to each other until her death in 1728.

After Temple's death in 1699, Swift returned to Ireland, where he had previously been ordained in the Anglican Church. In 1700 he was appointed vicar of Laracor, a parish not far from Dublin, and in 1701 he took his Doctor of Divinity degree at Dublin. During the early 1700s he also became involved in the various political and religious issues of the period. As a Whig by birth and education, he supported parliamentary authority over the crown, but as an Anglican minister he was much more nearly allied with the conservative policies of the Tory party, which strongly supported allegiance to the legally established church against political encroachments from nonconformists. So when the Whigs sought to broaden their base of power by relaxing the laws against religious dissent, Swift found himself increasingly torn between his political and religious convictions. Ultimately, he chose to uphold his religious principles by speaking out against the policy of the Whigs, not only in several pamphlets, but also in his profoundly ironic and satiric essay *Against the Abolishing of Christianity* (1708). Thus when the Tories gained control of the government in 1710, he readily accepted the invitation to become their chief political writer.

As a Tory spokesman, Swift took up residence in London, became editor of the party newspaper, *The Examiner,* and soon found himself accepted within the most powerful circles of the day. The excitement of his life during that time is reflected in *The Journal to Stella,* Swift's vividly detailed, day-by-day record of his political and social activities from September 1710 to June 1711. By the time he settled in London, Swift had already become a well-known figure not only through the force of his religious and political essays, but also through the playfulness of his "Bickerstaff" papers (1708–1709), a series of pamphlets, written under the pseudonym of Isaac Bickerstaff, in which he undid a quack astrologer and prognosticator of the period by outdoing him at his own game. In fact, the name of Bickerstaff became so popular that Richard Steele borrowed it to attract interest in his newspaper, *The Tatler,* which he subtitled *The Lucubrations of Isaac Bickerstaff, Esq.*

Swift's reputation as a witty writer also led to friendships with some of the leading Tory literary figures of the day, most notably John Gay and Alexander Pope. Gay, Pope, Swift, and others subsequently formed a group called the Scriblerus Club, named after a fictitious character Martinus Scriblerus (Martin the Scribbler), whose learned pretensions they intended to record in a biography that would serve to satirize the learned follies of the day. Though they never completed the full-length project as planned, the playful and ingenious spirit of the club ultimately gave rise to some of the most powerful satires of the period— Gay's *Beggar's Opera* (1728), Pope's *Dunciad* (1728), and Swift's *Gulliver's Travels* (1726).

During the four years that the Tories remained in power, from 1710 to 1714, Swift served the party brilliantly, not only as a writer but also as a political counselor. For his service to the Tories, he was made dean of St. Patrick's, Dublin, in 1713—less than the English bishopric he might have hoped for, but a secure and important church position just the same. Thus when the Tories fell from power, Swift returned to Ireland. Initially shunned by Anglo-Irish Whigs and depressed at having to forsake the exciting and influential life he had enjoyed in London, Swift temporarily withdrew from all public affairs. Gradually, however, he became involved once again in political writing—this time on behalf of the Irish people, whose social and economic plight he sought to remedy in a scathing series of pamphlets and essays that he wrote between 1720 and 1735.

In the most famous of his Irish writings, *The Drapier's Letters* (1724) and *A Modest Proposal* (1729), Swift sought to call attention not only to English exploitation of the Irish, but also to the Irish people's exploitation of themselves. He relentlessly persisted in his attempts to improve the welfare of the Irish people throughout the remainder of his active life as a writer. So he was celebrated in his own time as a hero of Dublin and the conscience of Ireland. During the last several years of his life, he was increasingly beset by the dizziness and nausea that he had endured from his early adulthood, and during the last few years of his life, a stroke combined with the afflictions of aging gradually deprived him completely of his mental powers.

Indignant and scathing in virtually all of his satires, Swift rarely, if ever, conveyed his indignation directly. To do so would have been to forsake his rationalistic belief in the values of good sense and reason. So, the more gloomy, or pessimistic, or outraged he is about a specific subject or issue, the more artfully self-controlled he is likely to be in expressing his views of it. Sometimes, in fact, he conceals his actual point of view by putting on a mask, assuming a pose, or speaking in a voice that is an ironic variation of his own. But whatever his outlook and whatever his pose, he never forsakes "that simplicity" of style which he held to be "the best and truest ornament of most things in life." So his prose always fulfills his own very simple, but very challenging, stylistic rule of "proper words in proper places."

A Meditation upon
a Broomstick

This single stick, which you now behold ingloriously lying in that neglected corner, I once knew in a flourishing state in a forest. It was full of sap, full of leaves, and full of boughs, but now in vain does the busy art of man pretend to vie with nature by tying that withered bundle of twigs to its sapless trunk. It is now at best but the reverse of what it was: a tree turned upside down, the branches on the earth, and the root in the air. It is now handled by every dirty wench, condemned to do her drudgery, and by a capricious kind of fate destined to make other things clean and be nasty itself. At length, worn to the stumps in the service of the maids, it is either thrown out of doors or condemned to its last use of kindling a fire. When I beheld this, I sighed and said within myself, surely mortal man is a broomstick: nature sent him into the world strong and lusty, in a thriving condition, wearing his own hair on his head, the proper branches of this reasoning vegetable, 'til the axe of intemperance has lopped off his green boughs and left him a withered trunk; he then flies to art and puts on a perriwig, valuing himself upon an unnatural bundle of hairs, all covered with powder, that never grew on his head. But now should this our broomstick pretend to enter the scene, proud of those birchen spoils it never bore, and all covered with dust, though the sweepings of the finest lady's chamber, we should be apt to ridicule and despise its vanity, partial judges that we are of our own excellencies and other men's defaults.[1]

But a broomstick, perhaps you'll say, is an emblem of a tree standing on its head. And pray, what is man but a topsy-turvy creature, his animal faculties perpetually mounted on his rational, his head where his heels should be, grovelling on the earth? And yet with all his faults, he sets up to be an universal reformer and corrector of abuses, a remover of grievances; rakes into every slut's corner of nature, bringing hidden corruptions to the light; and raises a mighty dust where there was none before, sharing deeply all the while in the very same pollutions he pretends to sweep away. His last days are spent in slavery to women, and generally the least deserving, 'til worn to the stumps, like his brother bezom,[2] he's either kicked out of doors or made use of to kindle flames for others to warm themselves by.

---

[1] *defaults:* defects.
[2] *bezom:* broom.

Lines of Inquiry
"A Meditation upon a Broomstick"

In this brief essay, Swift develops a sustained comparison of a broomstick and its fate to man and man's fate. In what specific respects does the description and story of the broom that Swift offers in the first half of the first paragraph prepare for and connect to the situation of man that Swift describes in the remainder of that paragraph? In what specific respects does it apply to the situation of man that Swift offers in the second paragraph? How does the comparison in the second paragraph build on, and differ from, the comparison in the first paragraph?

What view of humanity does Swift seem to be expressing in this piece? How is this view implied by the basic terms of the comparison—i.e., of man to a broomstick? How is this view implied by the way that Swift develops the comparison? What specific aspect(s) of human nature and behavior does Swift satirize in each part of his meditation? What idea of human nature and human destiny does Swift convey in the climax of his comparison?

Swift is not the only author in this collection to develop an essay about human nature and behavior by means of a sustained comparison, as you can see by looking at Bacon's "Narcissus: or Self-Love," Dillard's "Living Like Weasels," Forster's "The Game of Life," or Thoreau's "War of the Ants." Read one or two of these essays on your own, and then consider how—and why—they differ from Swift's in their development of a sustained comparison.

The Art of Political Lying[1]

> Some fill idle ears
> With stories, others go far-off to tell
> What they have heard, and every story grows,
> And each new teller adds to what he hears.
> Here is Credulity, and reckless Error,
> Vain Joy, and panic Fear, sudden Sedition,
> Whispers that none can trace.
> (Ovid, *Metamorphosis,* XII, 56–62)

I am prevailed on, through the importunity of friends, to interrupt the scheme I had begun in my last paper, by an Essay upon the Art of Political Lying. We are told, "the Devil is the father of lies, and was a liar from the beginning"; so that, beyond contradiction, the invention is old: and which is more, his first essay of it was purely political, employed in undermining the authority of his Prince, and seducing a third part of the subjects from their obedience. For which he was driven down from Heaven, where (as Milton expresseth it) he had been viceroy of a great western province; and forced to exercise his talent in inferior regions among other fallen spirits or poor deluded men, whom he still daily tempts to his own sin, and will ever do so till he be chained in the bottomless pit.

But although the Devil be the father of lies, he seems, like other great inventors, to have lost much of his reputation by the continual improvements that have been made upon him.

Who first reduced lying into an art and adapted it to politics is not so clear from history, although I have made some diligent enquiries: I shall therefore consider it only according to the modern system, as it hath been cultivated these twenty years past in the southern part of our own island.

The poets tell us that after the giants were over-thrown by the gods, the earth in revenge produced her last offspring, which was Fame. And the fable is thus interpreted: that when tumults and seditions are quieted, rumours and false reports are plentifully spread through a nation. So that by this account, *lying* is the last relief of a routed, earth-born, rebellious party in a state. But here the moderns have made great additions, applying this art to the gaining of power, and preserving it,

---

[1] *The Examiner,* No. 14, November 9, 1710.

as well as revenging themselves after they have lost it: as the same instruments are made use of by animals to feed themselves when they are
hungry, and bite those that tread upon them.

But the same genealogy cannot always be admitted for *political lying*. 5
I shall therefore desire to refine upon it, by adding some circumstances
of its birth and parents. A political lie is sometimes born out of a discarded statesman's head, and thence delivered to be nursed and dandled
by the rabble. Sometimes it is produced a monster and *licked* into shape;
at other times it comes into the world completely formed and is spoiled
in the licking. It is often born an infant in the regular way and requires
time to mature it, and often it sees the light in its full growth, but
dwindles away by degrees. Sometimes it is of noble birth and sometimes the spawn of a stock-jobber. *Here,* it screams aloud at opening
the womb; and *there,* it is delivered with a whisper. I know a lie that
now disturbs half the kingdom with its noise, which although too proud
and great at present to own its parents, I can remember in its whisper-
hood. To conclude the nativity of this monster: when it comes into the
world without a *sting,* it is still-born; and whenever it loses its sting,
it dies.

No wonder if an infant so miraculous in its birth should be destined for great adventures: and accordingly we see it hath been the
guardian spirit of a prevailing party for almost twenty years. It can
conquer kingdoms without fighting, and sometimes with the loss of a
battle; it gives and resumes employments; can sink a mountain to a
mole-hill, and raise a mole-hill to a mountain; hath presided for many
years at committees of elections; can wash a blackamoor white; make a
saint of an atheist, and a patriot of a profligate; can furnish foreign
ministers with intelligence; and raise or let fall the credit of the nation.
This goddess flies with a huge looking-glass in her hands to dazzle the
crowd and make them see, according as she turns it, their ruin in their
interest, and their interest in their ruin. In this glass you will behold
your best friends clad in coats powdered with *flower-de-luces* and triple
crowns; their girdles hung round with chains, and beads, and wooden
shoes; and your worst enemies adorned with the ensigns of liberty,
property, indulgence, moderation, and a cornucopia in their hands. Her
large wings, like those of a flying fish, are of no use but while they are
moist; she therefore dips them in mud, and soaring aloft scatters it in
the eyes of the multitude, flying with great swiftness; but at every turn
is forced to stoop in dirty ways for new supplies.

I have been sometimes thinking, if a man had the art of the second
sight for seeing lies, as they have in Scotland for seeing spirits, how
admirably he might entertain himself in this town; to observe the different shapes, sizes and colours, of those swarms of lies which buzz
about the heads of some people, like flies about a horse's ears in summer; or those legions hovering every afternoon in Exchange Alley,

enough to darken the air; or over a club of discontented grandees, and thence sent down in cargoes to be scattered at elections.

There is one essential point wherein a political liar differs from others of the faculty: that he ought to have but a short memory, which is necessary according to the various occasions he meets with every hour, of differing from himself and swearing to both sides of a contradiction, as he finds the persons disposed with whom he hath to deal. In describing the virtues and vices of mankind, it is convenient upon every article to have some eminent person in our eye, from whence we copy our description. I have strictly observed this rule; and my imagination this minute represents before me a certain great man famous for this talent, to the constant practice of which he owes his twenty years' reputation of the most skilful head in England for the management of nice affairs. The superiority of his genius consists in nothing else but an inexhaustible fund of political lies, which he plentifully distributes every minute he speaks, and by an unparalleled generosity forgets and consequently contradicts the next half-hour. He never yet considered whether any proposition were true or false, but whether it were convenient for the present minute or company to affirm or deny it; so that if you think to refine upon him by interpreting every thing he says, as we do dreams by the contrary, you are still to seek, and will find yourself equally deceived, whether you believe or no: the only remedy is to suppose that you have heard some inarticulate sounds, without any meaning at all. And besides, that will take off the horror you might be apt to conceive at the oaths wherewith he perpetually tags both ends of every proposition: although at the same time I think he cannot with any justice be taxed for perjury, when he invokes God and Christ, because he hath often fairly given public notice to the world that he believes in neither.

Some people may think that such an accomplishment as this, can be of no great use to the owner or his party, after it hath been often practised, and is become notorious; but they are widely mistaken: few lies carry the inventor's mark; and the most prostitute enemy to truth may spread a thousand without being known for the author. Besides, as the vilest writer hath his readers, so the greatest liar hath his believers; and it often happens, that if a lie be believed only for an hour, it hath done its work, and there is no farther occasion for it. Falsehood flies, and Truth comes limping after it; so that when men come to be undeceived, it is too late, the jest is over, and the tale has had its effect: like a man who has thought of a good repartee when the discourse is changed, or the company parted: or, like a physician who hath found out an infallible medicine after the patient is dead.

Considering that natural disposition in many men to lie, and in   10 multitudes to believe, I have been perplexed what to do with that maxim, so frequent in everybody's mouth, that "Truth will at last prevail."

Here has this island of ours for the greatest part of twenty years lain under the influence of such counsels and persons, whose principle and interest it was to corrupt our managers, blind our understandings, drain our wealth, and in time destroy our constitution both in Church and State; and we at last were brought to the very brink of ruin; yet by the means of perpetual misrepresentations, have never been able to distinguish between our enemies and friends. We have seen a great part of the nation's money got into the hands of those, who by their birth, education and merit, could pretend no higher than to wear our liveries. While others, who by their credit, quality and fortune, were only able to give reputation and success to the Revolution, were not only laid aside as dangerous and useless, but loaden with the scandal of Jacobites, men of arbitrary principles, and pensioners to France; while Truth, who is said to lie in a well, seemed now to be buried there under a heap of stones. But I remember it was a usual complaint among the Whigs, that the bulk of landed men was not in their interests, which some of the wisest looked on as an ill omen; and we saw it was with the utmost difficulty that they could preserve a majority, while the court and ministry were on their side; till they had learned those admirable expedients for deciding elections, and influencing distant boroughs by *powerful motives* from the city. But all this was mere force and constraint, however upheld by most dexterous artifice and management; until the people began to apprehend their properties, their religion, and the monarchy itself in danger; then we saw them greedily laying hold on the first occasion to interpose. But of this mighty change in the dispositions of the people, I shall discourse more at large in some following paper; wherein I shall endeavour to undeceive or discover those deluded or deluding persons, who hope or pretend, it is only a short madness in the vulgar, from which they may soon recover. Whereas I believe it will appear to be very different in its causes, its symptoms, and its consequences; and prove a great example to illustrate the maxim I lately mentioned, that "Truth" (however sometimes late) "will at last prevail."

Lines of Inquiry
"The Art of Political Lying"

Although this essay was specifically directed against the Earl of Wharton, then viceroy of Ireland (referred to here as "viceroy of a great western province"), and against the Whig party (referred to here as "a prevailing party for almost twenty years"), Swift's observations also satirize a pervasive tendency among politicians. At what points does Swift's satire seem most topical, at what points most universal? How do you account for Swift's organization and placement of topical and universal passages? What techniques does Swift use to universalize his satire?

Though his topic here is political lying, Swift never assumes a tone of moral outrage or anything approaching it. How would you characterize his tone of voice and his apparent attitude in this piece? How are his tone and attitude determined, for example, by his pervasive reference to political lying as an "art" and by his attempt to provide a detailed "genealogy" of its origins and a record of its "great adventures"? What are the effects of his assuming such a tone rather than one of moral outrage?

Over the course of his essay, Swift makes a number of general assertions about the nature, the workings, and the effects of political lies and liars. Which of his assertions do you consider to be most valid? Which most questionable? Which do you consider to be most applicable to the contemporary political situation?

Hints Towards an Essay on Conversation

I have observed few obvious subjects to have been so seldom or, at least, so slightly handled as this, and, indeed, I know few so difficult to be treated as it ought, nor yet upon which there seemeth to be so much to be said.

Most things pursued by men for the happiness of public or private life, our wit or folly have so refined that they seldom subsist but in idea. A true friend, a good marriage, a perfect form of government, with some others, require so many ingredients, so good in their several kinds, and so much niceness in mixing them that for some thousands of years men have despaired of reducing their schemes to perfection. But in conversation, it is or might be otherwise, for here we are only to avoid a multitude of errors, which, although a matter of some difficulty, may be in every man's power, for want of which it remaineth as mere an idea as the other. Therefore, it seemeth to me that the truest way to understand conversation is to know the faults and errors to which it is subject, and from thence every man to form maxims to himself whereby it may be regulated, because it requireth few talents to which most men are not born, or least may not acquire without any great genius or study. For nature hath left every man a capacity of being agreeable, though not of shining in company, and there are an hundred men sufficiently qualified for both, who by a very few faults, that they might correct in half an hour, are not so much as tolerable.

I was prompted to write my thoughts upon this subject by mere indignation, to reflect that so useful and innocent a pleasure, so fitted for every period and condition of life, and so much in all men's power, should be so much neglected and abused.

And in this discourse, it will be necessary to note those errors that are obvious, as well as others which are seldomer observed, since there are few so obvious or acknowledged, into which most men some time or other are not apt to run.

For instance, nothing is more generally exploded than the folly of talking too much, yet I rarely remember to have seen five people together, where some one among them hath not been predominant in that kind, to the great constraint and disgust of all the rest. But among such as deal in multitudes of words, none are comparable to the sober, deliberate talker, who proceedeth with much thought and caution, maketh his preface, brancheth out into several digressions, findeth a hint that putteth him in mind of another story, which he promiseth to tell you when this is done, cometh back regularly to his subject, cannot readily call to mind some person's name, holdeth his head, complaineth of his memory—the whole company all this while in suspense—at length says, it is no matter, and so goes on. And, to crown the business, it perhaps proveth at last a story the company hath heard fifty times before, or, at best, some insipid adventure of the relater.

Another general fault in conversation is that of those who affect to talk of themselves. Some, without any ceremony, will run over the history of their lives, will relate the annals of their diseases, with the several symptoms and circumstances of them, will enumerate the hardships and unjustice they have suffered in court, in parliament, in love, or in law. Others are more dexterous, and with great art will lie on the watch to hook in their own praise. They will call a witness to remember they always foretold what would happen in such a case, but none would believe them: they advised such a man from the beginning, and told him the consequences just as they happened, but he would have his own way. Others make a vanity of telling their faults. They are the strangest men in the world: they cannot dissemble; they own it is a folly; they have lost abundance of advantages by it. But if you give them the world they cannot help it; there is something in their nature that abhors insincerity and constraint, with many other unsufferable topics of the same altitude.

Of such mighty importance every man is to himself, and ready to think he is so to others, without once making this easy and obvious reflection: that his affairs can have no more weight with other men than theirs have with him, and how little that is, he is sensible enough.

Where company hath met, I often have observed two persons discover by some accident that they were bred together at the same school or university, after which the rest are condemned to silence and to listen, while these two are refreshing each other's memory with the arch tricks and passages of themselves and their comrades.

I know a great officer of the army, who will sit for some time with a supercilious and impatient silence, full of anger and contempt for those who are talking; at length of a sudden demand audience, decide the matter in a short dogmatical way, then withdraw within himself again and vouchsafe to talk no more, until his spirits circulate again to the same point.

There are some faults in conversation, which none are so subject to 10 as the men of wit, nor ever so much as when they are with each other. If they have opened their mouths, without endeavoring to say a witty thing, they think it is so many words lost. It is a torment to the hearers, as much as to themselves, to see them upon the rack for invention, and in perpetual constraint, with so little success. They must do something extraordinary in order to acquit themselves and answer their character, else the standers-by may be disappointed and be apt to think them only like the rest of mortals. I have known two men of wit industriously brought together in order to entertain the company, where they have made a very ridiculous figure and provided all the mirth at their own expense.

I know a man of wit who is never easy but where he can be allowed to dictate and preside. He neither expecteth to be informed or entertained, but to display his own talents. His business is to be good company and not good conversation, and, therefore, he chooseth to frequent those who are content to listen and profess themselves his admirers. And, indeed, the worst conversation I ever remember to have heard in my life was that at Will's Coffee-house, where the wits, as they were called, used formerly to assemble. That is to say, five or six men, who had writ plays, or at least prologues, or had share in a miscellany, came thither and entertained one another with their trifling composures, in so important an air, as if they had been the noblest efforts of human nature, or that the fate of kingdoms depended on them. And they were usually attended with an humble audience of young students from the inns of court or the universities, who, at due distance, listened to these oracles and returned home with great contempt for their law and philosophy, their heads filled with trash, under the name of politeness, criticism, and belles lettres.

By these means, the poets for many years past were all overrun with pedantry. For, as I take it, the word is not properly used, because pedantry is the too frequent or unseasonable obtruding our own knowledge in common discourse and placing too great a value upon it, by which definition men of the court or the army may be as guilty of pedantry as a philosopher or a divine. And it is the same vice in women, when they are over-copious upon the subject of their petticoats, or their fans, or their china. For which reason, although it be a piece of prudence, as well as good manners, to put men upon talking on subjects they are best versed in, yet that is a liberty a wise man could hardly take, because, beside the imputation of pedantry, it is what he would never improve by.

This great town is usually provided with some player, mimic, or buffoon, who hath a general reception at the good tables, familiar and domestic with persons of the first quality, and usually sent for at every meeting to divert company, against which I have no objection. You go there as to a farce, or a puppet show: your business is only to laugh in season, either out of inclination or civility, while this merry companion is acting his part. It is a business he hath undertaken, and we are to suppose he is paid for his day's work. I only quarrel when in select and private meetings, where men of wit and learning are invited to pass an evening, this jester should be admitted to run over his circle of tricks and make the whole company unfit for any other's conversation, besides the indignity of confounding men's talents at so shameful a rate.

Raillery is the finest part of conversation, but as it is our usual custom to counterfeit and adulterate whatever is dear to us, so we have done with this and turned it all into what is generally called repartee, or being smart; just as when an expensive fashion cometh up, those who are not able to reach it content themselves with some paltry imitation. It now passeth for raillery to run a man down in discourse, to put him out of countenance, and make him ridiculous, sometimes to expose the defects of his person or understanding, on all which occasions he is obliged not to be angry, to avoid the imputation of not being able to take a jest. It is admirable to observe one who is dexterous at this art, singling out a weak adversary, getting the laugh on his side, and then carrying all before him. The French, from whom we borrow the word, have a quite different idea of the thing, and so had we in the politer age of our fathers. Raillery was to say something that at first appeared a reproach, or reflection, but, by some turn of wit unexpected and surprising, ended always in a compliment and to the advantage of the person it was addressed to. And, surely, one of the best rules in conversation is never to say a thing which any of the company can reasonably wish we had rather left unsaid. Nor can there anything be well more contrary to the ends for which people meet together than to part unsatisfied with each other or themselves.

There are two faults in conversation which appear very different, 15 yet arise from the same root and are equally blameable. I mean, an impatience to interrupt others and the uneasiness at being interrupted ourselves. The two chief ends of conversation are to entertain and improve those we are among, or to receive those benefits ourselves, which, whoever will consider, cannot easily run into either of those errors, because when any man speaketh in company, it is to be supposed he doth it for his hearer's sake and not his own. So that common discretion will teach us not to force their attention, if they are not willing to lend it, nor on the other side, to interrupt him who is in possession, because that is in the grossest manner to give the preference to our own good sense.

There are some people whose good manners will not suffer them to interrupt you, but what is almost as bad will discover abundance of impatience and lie upon the watch until you have done, because they have started something in their own thoughts which they long to be delivered of. Meantime, they are so far from regarding what passes that their imaginations are wholly turned upon what they have in reserve, for fear it should slip out of their memory. And thus they confine their invention, which might otherwise range over a hundred things full as good, and that might be much more naturally introduced.

There are some men excellent at telling a story and provided with a plentiful stock of them, which they can draw out upon occasion in all companies. And considering how low conversation runs among us, it is not altogether a contemptible talent. However, it is subject to two unavoidable defects: frequent repetition and being soon exhausted. So that whoever valueth this gift in himself hath need of a good memory and ought frequently to shift his company, that he may not discover the weakness of his fund, for those who are thus endowed have seldom any other revenue, but live upon the main stock.

Great speakers in public are seldom agreeable in private conversation, whether their faculty be natural or acquired by practice and often venturing. Natural elocution, although it may seem a paradox, usually springeth from a barrenness of invention and of words, by which men who have only one stock of notions upon every subject, and one set of phrases to express them in, they swim upon the superficies and offer themselves on every occasion. Therefore, men of much learning and who know the compass of a language are generally the worst talkers on a sudden, until much practice hath inured and emboldened them, because they are confounded with plenty of matter, variety of notions and of words, which they cannot readily choose, but are perplexed and entangled by too great a choice, which is no disadvantage in private conversation, where, on the other side, the talent of haranguing is, of all others, most insupportable.

Nothing hath spoiled men more for conversation than the character of being wits, to support which they never fail of encouraging a number of followers and admirers, who list themselves in their service, wherein they find their accounts on both sides by pleasing their mutual vanity. This hath given the former such an air of superiority, and made the latter so pragmatical, that neither of them are well to be endured. I say nothing here of the itch of dispute and contradiction, telling of lies, or of those who are troubled with the disease called the wandering of the thoughts, that they are never present in mind at what passeth in discourse, for whoever labors under any of these possessions is as unfit for conversation as a madman in Bedlam.

I think I have gone over most of the errors in conversation that have   20 fallen under my notice or memory, except some that are merely personal and others too gross to need exploding, such as lewd or profane talk. But I pretend only to treat the errors of conversation in general and not the several subjects of discourse, which would be infinite. Thus we see how human nature is most debased by the abuse of the faculty which is held the great distinction between men and brutes, and how little advantage we make of that which might be the greatest, the most lasting, and the most innocent, as well as useful, pleasure of life. In default of which, we are forced to take up with those poor amusements of dress and visiting, or the more pernicious ones of play, drink and vicious amours, whereby the nobility and gentry of both sexes are entirely corrupted both in body and mind, and have lost all notions of love, honor, friendship, and generosity, which under the name of fopperies have been for some time laughed out of doors.

This degeneracy of conversation, with the pernicious consequences thereof upon our humours and disposition, hath been owing, among other causes, to the custom arisen for some years past of excluding women from any share in our society, further than in parties at play, or dancing, or in the pursuit of an amour. I take the highest period of politeness in England (and it is of the same date in France) to have been the peaceable part of King Charles the First's reign. And from what we read of those times, as well as from the accounts I have formerly met with from some who lived in that court, the methods then used for raising and cultivating conversation were altogether different from ours. Several ladies, whom we find celebrated by the poets of that age, had assemblies at their houses, where persons of the best understanding, and of both sexes, met to pass the evenings in discoursing upon whatever agreeable subjects were occasionally started. And although we are apt to ridicule the sublime Platonic notions they had, or personated, in love and friendship, I conceive their refinements were grounded upon reason, and that a little grain of the romance is no ill ingredient to preserve and exalt the dignity of human nature, without which it is apt to degenerate into everything that is sordid, vicious, and low. If there were no other use in the conversation of ladies, it is sufficient that it would lay a restraint upon those odious topics of immodesty and indecencies into which the rudeness of our nothern genius is so apt to fall. And, therefore, it is observable in those spritely gentlemen about the town, who are so very dexterous at entertaining a vizard mask in the park or the playhouse, that in the company of ladies of virtue and honor they are silent and disconcerted and out of their element.

There are some people who think they sufficiently acquit themselves and entertain the company with relating of facts of no consequence, nor at all out of the road of such common incidents as happen every day. And this I have observed more frequently among the Scots than any other nation, who are very careful not to omit the minutest circumstances of time or place, which kind of discourse, if it were not a little relieved by the uncouth terms and phrases, as well as accent and gesture peculiar to that country, would hardly be tolerable. It is not a fault in company to talk much, but to continue it long is certainly one, for if the majority of those who are got together be naturally silent or cautious, the conversation will flag, unless it be renewed by one among them who can start new subjects, provided he doth not dwell upon them, but leaveth room for answers and replies.

Lines of Inquiry
"Hints Towards an Essay on Conversation"

The title of this piece suggests that it is a set of notes that Swift prepared for himself in anticipation of writing an essay. In what respects does this piece seem to be a set of "hints towards an essay"? In what respects does it seem to be a finished essay? To what extent, for example, does Swift seem to be noting down ideas and examples in a random order? To what extent does he seem to have organized his material in a coherent, clearly developed, and forceful way?

Over the course of this piece, Swift discusses numerous "faults in conversation." What common problems seem to be present in these different kinds of errors? What distinguishes the faults that he discusses at length from those that he deals with briefly or that he mentions only in passing? Given all the faults that he considers, what do you infer to be Swift's ideas about the nature, purpose, and practice of correct conversation?

Think about some irritating conversations that you have witnessed or been involved in recently. What faults did you find particularly bothersome? How does your list of faults square with Swift's? What is your idea of a good conversation?

A Modest Proposal
For Preventing the Children of Poor People
in Ireland From Being a Burden to Their
Parents or Country, and for Making
Them Beneficial to the Public

It is a melancholy object to those who walk through this great town, or travel in the country, when they see the streets, the roads and cabin-doors crowded with beggars of the female sex, followed by three, four, or six children, all in rags, and importuning every passenger for an alms. These mothers, instead of being able to work for their honest livelihood, are forced to employ all their time in strolling, to beg sustenance for their helpless infants, who, as they grow up, either turn thieves for want of work, or leave their dear native country to fight for the Pretender in Spain, or sell themselves to the Barbadoes.

I think it is agreed by all parties that this prodigious number of children, in the arms, or on the backs, or at the heels of their mothers, and frequently of their fathers, is in the present deplorable state of the kingdom a very great additional grievance; and therefore whoever could find out a fair, cheap, and easy method of making these children sound and useful members of the commonwealth would deserve so well of the public as to have his statue set up for a preserver of the nation.

But my intention is very far from being confined to provide only for the children of professed beggars; it is of a much greater extent, and shall take in the whole number of infants at a certain age who are born of parents in effect as little able to support them as those who demand our charity in the streets.

As to my own part, having turned my thoughts for many years upon this important subject, and maturely weighed the several schemes of other projectors, I have always found them grossly mistaken in their computation. It is true a child just dropped from its dam may be supported by her milk for a solar year with little other nourishment, at most not above the value of two shillings, which the mother may certainly get, or the value in scraps, by her lawful occupation of begging, and it is exactly at one year old that I propose to provide for them, in such a manner as, instead of being a charge upon their parents, or the parish, or wanting food and raiment for the rest of their lives, they shall, on the contrary, contribute to the feeding and partly to the clothing of many thousands.

There is likewise another great advantage in my scheme, that it will   5
prevent those voluntary abortions, and that horrid practice of women
murdering their bastard children, alas, too frequent among us, sacrificing the poor innocent babes, I doubt, more to avoid the expense than
the shame, which would move tears and pity in the most savage and
inhuman breast.

The number of souls in Ireland being usually reckoned one million
and a half, of these I calculate there may be about two hundred thousand couples whose wives are breeders, from which number I subtract
thirty thousand couples who are able to maintain their own children,
although I apprehend there cannot be so many under the present dis-
tresses of the kingdom, but this being granted, there will remain an
hundred and seventy thousand breeders. I again subtract fifty thousand
for those women who miscarry, or whose children die by accident or
disease within the year. There only remain an hundred and twenty
thousand children of poor parents annually born: the question therefore
is, how this number shall be reared, and provided for, which, as I have
already said, under the present situation of affairs is utterly impossible
by all the methods hitherto proposed, for we can neither employ them
in handicraft or agriculture; we neither build houses (I mean in the
country), nor cultivate land: they can very seldom pick up a livelihood
by stealing until they arrive at six years old, except where they are of
towardly parts, although I confess they learn the rudiments much earlier, during which time they can however be properly looked upon
only as probationers, as I have been informed by a principal gentleman
in the County of Cavan, who protested to me that he never knew above
one or two instances under the age of six, even in a part of the kingdom
so renowned for the quickest proficiency in that art.

I am assured by our merchants that a boy or a girl before twelve
years old, is no saleable commodity, and even when they come to this
age, they will not yield above three pounds, or three pounds and half-
a-crown at most on the Exchange, which cannot turn to account either
to the parents or the kingdom, the charge of nutriment and rags having
been at least four times that value.

I shall now therefore humbly propose my own thoughts, which I
hope will not be liable to the least objection.

I have been assured by a very knowing American of my acquaintance in London, that a young healthy child well nursed is at a year old
a most delicious, nourishing and wholesome food, whether stewed,
roasted, baked, or boiled, and I make no doubt that it will equally serve
in a fricassee, or a ragout.

I do therefore humbly offer it to public consideration, that of the   10
hundred and twenty thousand children already computed, twenty thousand may be reserved for breed, whereof only one fourth part to be
males, which is more than we allow to sheep, black-cattle, or swine,

and my reason is that these children are seldom the fruits of marriage, a circumstance not much regarded by our savages, therefore one male will be sufficient to serve four females. That the remaining hundred thousand may at a year old be offered in sale to the persons of quality, and fortune, through the kingdom, always advising the mother to let them suck plentifully in the last month, so as to render them plump, and fat for a good table. A child will make two dishes at an entertainment for friends, and when family dines alone, the fore or hind quarter will make a reasonable dish, and seasoned with a little pepper or salt will be very good boiled on the fourth day, especially in winter.

I have reckoned upon a medium, that a child just born will weigh twelve pounds, and in a solar year if tolerably nursed increaseth to twenty-eight pounds.

I grant this food will be somewhat dear, and therefore very proper for landlords, who, as they have already devoured most of the parents, seem to have the best title to the children.

Infant's flesh will be in season throughout the year, but more plentiful in March, and a little before and after, for we are told by a grave[1] author, an eminent French physician, that fish being a prolific diet, there are more children born in Roman Catholic countries about nine months after Lent than at any other season; therefore reckoning a year after Lent, the markets will be more glutted than usual, because the number of Popish infants is at least three to one in this kingdom, and therefore it will have one other collateral advantage by lessening the number of Papists among us.

I have already computed the charge of nursing a beggar's child (in which list I reckon all cottagers, labourers, and four-fifths of the farmers) to be about two shillings *per annum,* rags included, and I believe no gentleman would repine to give ten shillings for the carcass of a good fat child, which, as I have said, will make four dishes of excellent nutritive meat, when he hath only some particular friend or his own family to dine with him. Thus the Squire will learn to be a good landlord and grow popular among his tenants, the mother will have eight shillings net profit, and be fit for work until she produces another child.

Those who are more thrifty (as I must confess the times require) may flay the carcass; the skin of which artificially dressed, will make admirable gloves for ladies, and summer boots for fine gentlemen.

As to our city of Dublin, shambles may be appointed for this purpose, in the most convenient parts of it, and butchers we may be assured will not be wanting, although I rather recommend buying the children alive, and dressing them hot from the knife, as we do roasting pigs.

---

[1] Rabelais.

A very worthy person, a true lover of his country, and whose virtues I highly esteem, was lately pleased, in discoursing on this matter to offer a refinement upon my scheme. He said that many gentlemen of this kingdom, having of late destroyed their deer, he conceived that the want of venison might be well supplied by the bodies of young lads and maidens, not exceeding fourteen years of age, nor under twelve, so great a number of both sexes in every county being now ready to starve, for want of work and service: and these to be disposed of by their parents if alive, or otherwise by their nearest relations. But with due deference to so excellent a friend, and so deserving a patriot, I cannot be altogether in his sentiments. For as to the males, my American acquaintance assured me from frequent experience that their flesh was generally tough and lean, like that of our schoolboys, by continual exercise, and their taste disagreeable, and to fatten them would not answer the charge. Then as to the females, it would I think with humble submission, be a loss to the public, because they soon would become breeders themselves: and besides, it is not improbable that some scrupulous people might be apt to censure such a practice (although indeed very unjustly) as a little bordering upon cruelty, which I confess, hath always been with me the strongest objection against any project, howsoever well intended.

But in order to justify my friend, he confessed that this expedient was put into his head by the famous Psalmanazar, a native of the island Formosa, who came from thence to London, above twenty years ago, and in conversation told my friend that in his country when any young person happened to be put to death, the executioner sold the carcass to persons of quality, as a prime dainty, and that, in his time, the body of a plump girl of fifteen, who was crucified for an attempt to poison the emperor, was sold to his Imperial Majesty's Prime Minister of State, and other great Mandarins of the Court, in joints from the gibbet, at four hundred crowns. Neither indeed can I deny that if the same use were made of several plump young girls in this town who, without one single groat to their fortunes, cannot stir abroad without a chair, and appear at the playhouse and assemblies in foreign fineries, which they never will pay for, the kingdom would not be the worse.

Some persons of a desponding spirit are in great concern about that vast number of poor people, who are aged, diseased, or maimed, and I have been desired to employ my thoughts what course may be taken to ease the nation of so grievous an encumbrance. But I am not in the least pain upon that matter, because it is very well known that they are every day dying, and rotting, by cold, and famine, and filth, and vermin, as fast as can be reasonably expected. And as to the younger labourers they are now in almost as hopeful a condition. They cannot get work, and consequently pine away from want of nourishment, to a degree that if at any time they are accidentally hired to common labour, they have not strength to perform it; and thus the country and themselves are in a fair way of being soon delivered from the evils to come.

I have too long digressed, and therefore shall return to my subject. 20 I think the advantages by the proposal which I have made are obvious and many, as well as of the highest importance.

For first, as I have already observed, it would greatly lessen the number of Papists, with whom we are yearly over-run, being the principal breeders of the nation, as well as our most dangerous enemies, and who stay at home on purpose with a design to deliver the kingdom to the Pretender, hoping to take their advantage by the absence of so many good Protestants, who have chosen rather to leave their country than stay at home and pay tithes against their conscience to an idolatrous Episcopal curate.

Secondly, the poorer tenants will have something valuable of their own, which by law may be made liable to distress, and help to pay their landlord's rent, their corn and cattle being already seized, and money a thing unknown.

Thirdly, whereas the maintenance of an hundred thousand children, from two years old, and upwards, cannot be computed at less than ten shillings a piece *per annum,* the nation's stock will be thereby increased fifty thousand pounds *per annum,* besides the profit of a new dish, introduced to the tables of all gentlemen of fortune in the kingdom, who have any refinement in taste, and the money will circulate among ourselves, the goods being entirely of our own growth and manufacture.

Fourthly, the constant breeders, besides the gain of eight shillings sterling *per annum,* by the sale of their children, will be rid of the charge of maintaining them after the first year.

Fifthly, this food would likewise bring great custom to taverns, where 25 the vintners will certainly be so prudent as to procure the best receipts for dressing it to perfection, and consequently have their houses frequented by all the fine gentlemen, who justly value themselves upon their knowledge in good eating; and a skilful cook, who understands how to oblige his guests, will contrive to make it as expensive as they please.

Sixthly, this would be a great inducement to marriage, which all wise nations have either encouraged by rewards, or enforced by laws and penalties. It would increase the care and tenderness of mothers towards their children, when they were sure of a settlement for life to the poor babes, provided in some sort by the public to their annual profit instead of expense. We should soon see an honest emulation among the married women, which of them could bring the fattest child to the market. Men would become as fond of their wives during the time of their pregnancy, as they are now of their mares in foal, their cows in calf, or sows when they are ready to farrow, nor offer to beat or kick them (as it is too frequent a practice) for fear of a miscarriage.

Many other advantages might be enumerated. For instance, the addition of some thousand carcasses in our exportation of barrelled beef; the propagation of swine's flesh, and improvement in the art of making good bacon, so much wanted among us by the great destruction of pigs, too frequent at our tables, are no way comparable in taste or magnificence to a well-grown, fat yearling child, which roasted whole will make a considerable figure at a Lord Mayor's feast, or any other public entertainment. But this and many others I omit, being studious of brevity.

Supposing that one thousand families in this city would be constant customers for infants flesh, besides others who might have it at merry meetings, particularly weddings and christenings, I compute that Dublin would take off annually about twenty thousand carcasses, and the rest of the kingdom (where probably they will be sold somewhat cheaper) the remaining eighty thousand.

I can think of no one objection that will possibly be raised against this proposal, unless it should be urged that the number of people will be thereby much lessened in the kingdom. This I freely own, and it was indeed one principal design in offering it to the world. I desire the reader will observe, that I calculate my remedy *for this one individual Kingdom of* Ireland, *and for no other that ever was, is, or, I think, ever can be upon earth.* Therefore let no man talk to me of other expedients: *Of taxing our absentees at five shillings a pound: Of using neither clothes, nor household furniture, except what is of our own growth and manufacture: Of utterly rejecting the materials and instruments that promote foreign luxury: Of curing the expensiveness of pride, vanity, idleness, and gaming in our women: Of introducing a vein of parsimony, prudence, and temperance: Of learning to love our country, wherein we differ even from* Laplanders, *and the inhabitants of* Topinamboo: *Of quitting our animosities and factions, nor act any longer like the* Jews, *who were murdering one another at the very moment their city was taken: Of being a little cautious not to sell our country and consciences for nothing: Of teaching landlords to have at least one degree of mercy towards their tenants.* Lastly, *of putting a spirit of honesty, industry, and skill into our shopkeepers, who, if a resolution could now be taken to buy only our native goods, would immediately unite to cheat and exact upon us in the price, the measure and the goodness, nor could ever yet be brought to make one fair proposal of just dealing, though often and earnestly invited to it.*

Therefore I repeat, let no man talk to me of these and the like expedients, till he hath at least a glimpse of hope that there will ever be some hearty and sincere attempt to put them in practice.   30

But as to myself, having been wearied out for many years with offering vain, idle, visionary thoughts, and at length utterly despairing of success, I fortunately fell upon this proposal, which as it is wholly new, so it hath something solid and real, of no expense and little trouble, full in our own power, and whereby we can incur no danger in disobliging England. For this kind of commodity will not bear exportation, the flesh being of too tender a consistence to admit a long continuance in salt, *although perhaps I could name a country which would be glad to eat up our whole nation without it.*

After all I am not so violently bent upon my own opinion as to reject any offer, proposed by wise men, which shall be found equally innocent, cheap, easy and effectual. But before some thing of that kind shall be advanced in contradiction to my scheme, and offering a better, I desire the author, or authors, will be pleased maturely to consider two points. First, as things now stand, how they will be able to find food and raiment for a hundred thousand useless mouths and backs? And secondly, there being a round million of creatures in human figure, throughout this kingdom, whose whole subsistence put into a common stock would leave them in debt two millions of pounds sterling; adding those who are beggars by profession, to the bulk of farmers, cottagers, and labourers with their wives and children, who are beggars in effect; I desire those politicians who dislike my overture, and may perhaps be so bold to attempt an answer, that they will first ask the parents of these mortals whether they would not at this day think it a great happiness to have been sold for food at a year old, in the manner I prescribe, and thereby have avoided such a perpetual scene of misfortunes as they have since gone through, by the oppression of landlords, the impossibility of paying rent without money or trade, the want of common sustenance, with neither house nor clothes to cover them from the inclemencies of weather, and the most inevitable prospect of entailing the like, or greater miseries upon their breed for ever.

I profess in the sincerity of my heart that I have not the least personal interest in endeavouring to promote this necessary work, having no other motive than the *public good of my country, by advancing our trade, providing for infants, relieving the poor, and giving some pleasure to the rich.* I have no children by which I can propose to get a single penny; the youngest being nine years old, and my wife past child-bearing.

Lines of Inquiry
"A Modest Proposal"

In the process of reading this essay, you probably assumed, as have many other readers, that Swift does not in any respect endorse the "modest proposal." What do you think are Swift's actual views? What details in the essay helped you to identify them? What inferences, if any, did you make in order to identify them? Why do you suppose that Swift chose to convey his ideas in this ironic form? Why do you think he went to the trouble of creating an imaginary proposal that he did not actually endorse?

In reading this piece, you might also have assumed that Swift does not mean to be equated with the imaginary proposer. How would you characterize the proposer? What is your initial impression of his character? In what ways, if any, does your first impression of him change over the course of the essay? How is your impression affected by the content of his statements? By the style of his statements? By the structure of his presentation? On what bases are you able to distinguish between Swift and the proposer? Which do you consider to be more dangerous and disturbing—the proposer? Or his proposal?

In reflecting upon the proposer and his proposal, you probably could not help noticing his elaborately detailed mathematical calculations, which make him sound very much like the long-range economic and social planners of our own time. In what respects is his proposal comparable to any recent socio-economic proposals that you have read about or studied? In what respects does it differ from them?

Lewis Thomas
1913—

*It is no good standing on dignity in a situation like this, and better
not to try. It is a mystery.*

The mystery that Thomas affirms in this passage from *The Lives of a Cell* is the behavior of the submicroscopic mitochondria that inhabit the cells of his own body and those of every living thing on earth, producing and regulating the use of oxygen. Mitochondria are not the only natural things that have puzzled and fascinated him. Though an accomplished biochemist and cell biologist who has published over two hundred scientific articles, Thomas repeatedly celebrates in his essays the "astonishments," the "mysteries," of nature, from the intricate unities of a single cell to the complex ecologies of the earth as a whole. Often with wry humor and wit, sometimes with a poetic lyricism, Thomas demonstrates that much in our experience remains "unflattened by science," and he insists that this should encourage us: to respect our limits, to respect each other, to respect the world we inhabit and have the power to destroy.

Born in Flushing, New York, to a general practitioner and a former nurse, he grew up admiring his father's hard work and devotion to his patients. In *The Youngest Science* (1983), both an autobiography and a reflection on the recent history of medicine, Thomas portrays his father's dedication as representative of the medical profession at a time when it was "turning into a science, but the old art was still in place." Intent on becoming a doctor himself, he entered Princeton University, where he says he "turned into a moult of dullness and laziness, average or below average in the courses requiring real work," although an advanced course in biology his senior year awakened his interest in science. With the help of a family friend he was admitted to Harvard Medical School. After an internship at Boston City Hospital and residency at the Neurological Institute in New York, he was called into the Navy in 1941, for a tour of duty that led him into research on the origins of tropical diseases. After the war Thomas continued his research in the fields of immunology and pathology as a faculty member in the medical schools at Johns Hopkins, Tulane, and the University of Minnesota, gradually establishing a reputation as one of the premier cell biologists in the world. He has also established himself as a distinguished university and hospital administrator, first at New York University Medical School, then at Yale Medical School, and since 1973 at the Memorial Sloan-Kettering Cancer Center in New York, where he is currently chancellor.

Throughout his career as a scientist and researcher, Thomas has maintained an interest in literature and writing. At Princeton, the poetry of Eliot and Pound moved him to publish poems in the college literary magazine. While an intern and resident he published poems in the *Atlantic, Harper's Bazaar,* and *The Saturday Evening Post,* and he has continued writing poetry—"good bad verse" as he calls it. In *The Youngest Science* he admits that stylistically the scientific papers he wrote earlier in his career seem "hideous" as he reads them today, composed, as they had to be, "in the relentlessly flat style required for absolute unambiguity in every word."

In 1971 Thomas was given the opportunity to free himself from that style when he was invited to do an open-ended monthly column of 1200 words for one of the bastions of that style, *The New England Journal of Medicine.* Writing late at night, "usually on the weekend two days after [he'd] already passed the deadline," never outlining "or planning in advance," he started producing informal, personal essays, using scientific knowledge, particularly from the world of cell biology, as a source of metaphors for exploring relationships throughout the world of nature and human experience. The grace and humaneness of the column attracted such a large following outside the medical profession that a collection of them was published in 1974, *The Lives of a Cell,* which subsequently won the National Book Award. Two other collections followed, *The Medusa and the Snail* (1979) and *Late Night Thoughts on Listening to Mahler's Ninth Symphony* (1983).

As an essayist, Thomas' habit is to read the behavior of all organisms—mitochondria, sea slugs and jelly fish, ants, bees, beavers and otters—as metaphors of relationship and cooperation. "Every creature," Thomas says in *The Lives of a Cell,* "is, in some sense, connected to and dependent on the rest." Microbes "live together in dense, interdependent communities"; bacteria "live by collaboration, accommodation, exchange, and barter"—are "social animals." Human beings are part of this ecology, equally dependent upon other things, existing in various symbiotic relationships with microorganisms, animals, each other, the earth itself. For Thomas, in other words, nature is a cause for optimism, for celebration, although he worries throughout his essays about the ways in which human beings may violate the unity of nature. In the end he offers anthills and protozoan parasites and the generosity of mitochondria as hopeful alternatives to the suspicion, the violence, and the warfare of human beings. "There is something intrinsically good-natured about all symbiotic relations."

Nature is also, perhaps most of all, a cause of wonder. Though Thomas values the knowledge that science can bring us and insists on the integrity of the scientific method, symbiosis is only his favorite example of the mysteries science can never fully understand. "Things that used to seem clear and rational, matters of absolute certainty," he says, "have slipped through our fingers, and we are left with a new set of gigantic puzzles, cosmic uncertainties, ambiguities." So, like other essayists in the American naturalist tradition—such as Thoreau, White, Eiseley, Dillard, and Hoagland—Thomas's attitude is often one of wonder and amazement, of pleased astonishment. "The mind of a cat is an inscrutable mystery, beyond reach"; "bees are filled with astonishments, confounding anyone who studies them." In his view we understand almost nothing fully in our experience, from DNA, to language, to music, to our own behavior, to the ecological symmetry of the whole earth, functioning somehow as a giant cell, a "marvel." So, "illumination," according to Thomas, "comes in small bits, only from time to time, not ever in broad, bright flashes of public comprehension, and there can be no promise that we will ever emerge from the great depths of the mystery of being."

In the face of these mysteries and wonders, Thomas' stance as a writer is tentative, exploratory, personal, in the classic tradition of the essay. He tells about the events and experiences and places that stimulate his thinking—the music of Mahler, the behavior of germs, the physiology of warts—then tells about the ebb and flow of his thinking itself, digressing, juxtaposing images and ideas, seeming to revise as he goes, exclaiming, his language often down to earth and homey, often rich, textured, and evocative:

> I have been trying to think of the earth as a kind of organism, but it is no go. I cannot think of it this way. It is too big, too complex, with too many working parts lacking visible connections. The other night driving through a hilly, wooded part of southern New England, I wondered about this. If not like an organism, what is it like, what is it *most* like? Then satisfactorily for that moment, it came to me: it is *most* like a single cell.

Here as elsewhere, Thomas admits that he doesn't have the answers. So he lets us in on the drama of his thinking, sharing with us its origins and uncertainty. Like the essays of his hero and model Montaigne, Thomas' essays give the illusion of being "the easiest of conversations with a very old friend"—but they are conversations that challenge us even as they include us, that cause us to stop and consider both the wonders and the dangers around us.

The Iks

The small tribe of Iks, formerly nomadic hunters and gatherers in the mountain valleys of northern Uganda, have become celebrities, literary symbols for the ultimate fate of disheartened, heartless mankind at large. Two disastrously conclusive things happened to them: the government decided to have a national park, so they were compelled by law to give up hunting in the valleys and become farmers on poor hillside soil, and then they were visited for two years by an anthropologist who detested them and wrote a book about them.

The message of the book is that the Iks have transformed themselves into an irreversibly disagreeable collection of unattached, brutish creatures, totally selfish and loveless, in response to the dismantling of their traditional culture. Moreover, this is what the rest of us are like in our inner selves, and we will all turn into Iks when the structure of our society comes all unhinged.

The argument rests, of course, on certain assumptions about the core of human beings, and is necessarily speculative. You have to agree in advance that man is fundamentally a bad lot, out for himself alone, displaying such graces as affection and compassion only as learned habits. If you take this view, the story of the Iks can be used to confirm it. These people seem to be living together, clustered in small, dense villages, but they are really solitary, unrelated individuals with no evident use for each other. They talk, but only to make ill-tempered demands and cold refusals. They share nothing. They never sing. They turn the children out to forage as soon as they can walk, and desert the elders to starve whenever they can, and the foraging children snatch food from the mouths of the helpless elders. It is a mean society.

They breed without love or even casual regard. They defecate on each other's doorsteps. They watch their neighbors for signs of misfortune, and only then do they laugh. In the book they do a lot of laughing, having so much bad luck. Several times they even laughed at the anthropologist, who found this especially repellent (one senses, between the lines, that the scholar is not himself the world's luckiest man). Worse, they took him into the family, snatched his food, defecated on his doorstep, and hooted dislike at him. They gave him two bad years.

It is a depressing book. If, as he suggests, there is only Ikness at the center of each of us, our sole hope for hanging on to the name of humanity will be in endlessly mending the structure of our society, and it is changing so quickly and completely that we may never find the threads in time. Meanwhile, left to ourselves alone, solitary, we will become the same joyless, zestless, untouching lone animals. 5

But this may be too narrow a view. For one thing, the Iks are extraordinary. They are absolutely astonishing, in fact. The anthropologist has never seen people like them anywhere, nor have I. You'd think, if they were simply examples of the common essence of mankind, they'd seem more recognizable. Instead, they are bizarre, anomalous. I have known my share of peculiar, difficult, nervous, grabby people, but I've never encountered any genuinely, consistently detestable human beings in all my life. The Iks sound more like abnormalities, maladies.

I cannot accept it. I do not believe that the Iks are representative of isolated, revealed man, unobscured by social habits. I believe their behavior is something extra, something laid on. This unremitting, compulsive repellence is a kind of complicated ritual. They must have learned to act this way; they copied it, somehow.

I have a theory, then. The Iks have gone crazy.

The solitary Ik, isolated in the ruins of an exploded culture, has built a new defense for himself. If you live in an unworkable society you can make up one of your own, and this is what the Iks have done. Each Ik has become a group, a one-man tribe on its own, a constituency.

Now everything falls into place. This is why they do seem, after all, vaguely familiar to all of us. We've seen them before. This is precisely the way groups of one size or another, ranging from committees to nations, behave. It is, of course, this aspect of humanity that has lagged behind the rest of evolution, and this is why the Ik seems so primitive. In his absolute selfishness, his incapacity to give anything away, no matter what, he is a successful committee. When he stands at the door of his hut, shouting insults at his neighbors in a loud harangue, he is city addressing another city. 10

Cities have all the Ik characteristics. They defecate on doorsteps, in rivers and lakes, their own or anyone else's. They leave rubbish. They detest all neighboring cities, give nothing away. They even build institutions for deserting elders out of sight.

Nations are the most Iklike of all. No wonder the Iks seem familiar. For total greed, rapacity, heartlessness, and irresponsibility there is nothing to match a nation. Nations, by law, are solitary, self-centered, withdrawn into themselves. There is no such thing as affection between nations, and certainly no nation ever loved another. They bawl insults from their doorsteps, defecate into whole oceans, snatch all the food, survive by detestation, take joy in the bad luck of others, celebrate the death of others, live for the death of others.

That's it, and I shall stop worrying about the book. It does not signify that man is a sparse, inhuman thing at his center. He's all right. It only says what we've always known and never had enough time to worry about, that we haven't yet learned how to stay human when assembled in masses. The Ik, in his despair, is acting out this failure, and perhaps we should pay closer attention. Nations have themselves become too frightening to think about, but we might learn some things by watching these people.

Lines of Inquiry
"The Iks"

Each paragraph in this essay seems to be deliberately organized around a single controlling idea. Try to identify for yourself the main point of each paragraph. How does Thomas arrange his paragraphs so that they build towards the final idea, which happens to be the main point of the essay? How would your reaction to this idea be affected if Thomas had stated it at the beginning rather than delaying it until the end? How would the paragraphs have to be rearranged in this case?

Thomas out-and-out rejects the claim that the behavior of the Iks is representative of human nature. Why? What exactly are his arguments against the view that humans are "joyless, zestless, untouching lone animals" and how does he support these arguments? In particular, what does Thomas mean when he says that the "Iks have gone crazy," that each Ik is "a successful committee"?

For another view of primitive tribal cultures and general human behavior, consider Margaret Mead's "Warfare: An Invention—Not a Biological Necessity." Based on your reading of Mead's essay, how do you suppose that she would interpret the behavior of the Iks? Do you think she would agree with Thomas' view of them? Do you think she would side with the anthropologist whom Thomas attacks in his piece? Or do you think she would disagree with both of them and take an entirely different view? How representative do you consider the Iks to be of humans "when assembled in mass"?

On Cloning
a Human Being

It is now theoretically pos-
sible to recreate an identical creature from any animal or plant, from
the DNA contained in the nucleus of any somatic cell. A single plant
root-tip cell can be teased and seduced into conceiving a perfect copy
of the whole plant; a frog's intestinal epithelial cell possesses the complete instructions needed for a new, same frog. If the technology were
further advanced, you could do this with a human being, and there are
now startled predictions all over the place that this will in fact be done,
someday, in order to provide a version of immortality for carefully
selected, especially valuable people.

The cloning of humans is on most of the lists of things to worry
about from Science, along with behavior control, genetic engineering,
transplanted heads, computer poetry, and the unrestrained growth of
plastic flowers.

Cloning is the most dismaying of prospects, mandating as it does
the elimination of sex with only a metaphoric elimination of death as
compensation. It is almost no comfort to know that one's cloned, identical surrogate lives on, especially when the living will very likely involve edging one's real, now aging self off to the side, sooner or later.
It is hard to imagine anything like filial affection or respect for a single,
unmated nucleus; harder still to think of one's new, self-generated self
as anything but an absolute, desolate orphan. Not to mention the complex interpersonal relationship involved in raising one's self from infancy, teaching the language, enforcing discipline, instilling good
manners, and the like. How would you feel if you became an incorrigible juvenile delinquent by proxy, at the age of fifty-five?

The public questions are obvious. Who is to be selected, and on
what qualifications? How to handle the risks of misused technology,
such as self-determined cloning by the rich and powerful but socially
objectionable, or the cloning by governments of dumb, docile masses
for the world's work? What will be the effect on all the uncloned rest
of us of human sameness? After all, we've accustomed ourselves through
hundreds of millennia to the continual exhilaration of uniqueness; each
of us is totally different, in a fundamental sense, from all the other four
billion. Selfness is an essential fact of life. The thought of human non-
selfness, precise sameness, is terrifying, when you think about it.

Well, don't think about it, because it isn't a probable possibility,   5
not even as a long shot for the distant future, in my opinion. I agree

that you might clone some people who would look amazingly like their parental cell donors, but the odds are that they'd be almost as different as you or me, and certainly more different than any of today's identical twins.

The time required for the experiment is only one of the problems, but a formidable one. Suppose you wanted to clone a prominent, spectacularly successful diplomat, to look after the Middle East problems of the distant future. You'd have to catch him and persuade him, probably not very hard to do, and extirpate a cell. But then you'd have to wait for him to grow up through embryonic life and then for at least forty years more, and you'd have to be sure all observers remained patient and unmeddlesome through his unpromising, ambiguous childhood and adolescence.

Moreover, you'd have to be sure of recreating his environment, perhaps down to the last detail. "Environment" is a word which really means people, so you'd have to do a lot more cloning than just the diplomat himself.

This is a very important part of the cloning problem, largely overlooked in our excitement about the cloned individual himself. You don't have to agree all the way with B. F. Skinner to acknowledge that the environment does make a difference, and when you examine what we really mean by the word "environment" it comes down to other human beings. We use euphemisms and jargon for this, like "social forces," "cultural influences," even Skinner's "verbal community," but what is meant is the dense crowd of nearby people who talk to, listen to, smile or frown at, give to, withhold from, nudge, push, caress, or flail out at the individual. No matter what the genome says, these people have a lot to do with shaping a character. Indeed, if all you had was the genome, and no people around, you'd grow a sort of vertebrate plant, nothing more.

So, to start with, you will undoubtedly need to clone the parents. No question about this. This means the diplomat is out, even in theory, since you couldn't have gotten cells from both his parents at the time when he was himself just recognizable as an early social treasure. You'd have to limit the list of clones to people already certified as sufficiently valuable for the effort, with both parents still alive. The parents would need cloning and, for consistency, their parents as well. I suppose you'd also need the usual informed-consent forms, filled out and signed, not easy to get if I know parents, even harder for grandparents.

But this is only the beginning. It is the whole family that really influences the way a person turns out, not just the parents, according to current psychiatric thinking. Clone the family.   10

Then what? The way each member of the family develops has already been determined by the environment set around him, and this environment is more people, people outside the family, schoolmates, acquaintances, lovers, enemies, car-pool partners, even in special cir-cumstances, peculiar strangers across the aisle on the subway. Find them, and clone them.

But there is no end to the protocol. Each of the outer contacts has his own surrounding family, and his and their outer contacts. Clone them all.

To do the thing properly, with any hope of ending up with a gen-uine duplicate of a single person, you really have no choice. You must clone the world, no less.

We are not ready for an experiment of this size, nor, I should think, are we willing. For one thing, it would mean replacing today's world by an entirely identical world to follow immediately, and this means no new, natural, spontaneous, random, chancy children. No children at all, except for the manufactured doubles of those now on the scene. Plus all those identical adults, including all of today's politicians, all seen double. It is too much to contemplate.

Moreover, when the whole experiment is finally finished, fifty years   15
or so from now, how could you get a responsible scientific reading on the outcome? Somewhere in there would be the original clonee, prob-ably lost and overlooked, now well into middle age, but everyone around him would be precise duplicates of today's everyone. It would be to-day's same world, filled to overflowing with duplicates of today's peo-ple and their same, duplicated problems, probably all resentful at having had to go through our whole thing all over, sore enough at the clonee to make endless trouble for him, if they found him.

And obviously, if the whole thing were done precisely right, they would still be casting about for ways to solve the problem of universal dissatisfaction, and sooner or later they'd surely begin to look around at each other, wondering who should be cloned for his special value to society, to get us out of all this. And so it would go, in regular cycles, perhaps forever.

I once lived through a period when I wondered what Hell could be like, and I stretched my imagination to try to think of a perpetual sort of damnation. I have to confess, I never thought of anything like this.

I have an alternative suggestion, if you're looking for a way out. Set cloning aside, and don't try it. Instead, go in the other direction. Look for ways to get mutations more quickly, new variety, different songs. Fiddle around, if you must fiddle, but never with ways to keep things the same, no matter who, not even yourself. Heaven, some-where ahead, has got to be a change.

Lines of Inquiry
"On Cloning a Human Being"

Throughout this piece, Thomas often uses familiar, even conversational language, such as "all over the place," "things to worry about," and "long shot." What impression of Thomas do you get from such words and phrases? Is there a relationship between this impression and the kind of argument that Thomas is making here against cloning? What is the overall effect of mixing such down-to-earth language with the scientific terminology that Thomas also uses?

Thomas suggests that we should use the techniques of genetic engineering to "go in the other direction" from cloning, creating new mutations, "new variety, different songs." What exactly is he getting at in this alternative vision? Can you see any problems with it? What kind of world would result from his desire to "go in the other direction"? How consistent is his method of argument in this piece with the kind of world he argues for?

Many forces in our culture seem to work toward making people behave and think similarly if not identically. What pressures toward uniformity have you experienced within your own family? Within your home community? Within the school you're presently attending? Within your present writing course? What resources have you found in your studies—and in yourself—to resist such pressures?

The Tucson Zoo

Science gets most of its information by the process of reductionism, exploring the details, then the details of the details, until all the smallest bits of the structure, or the smallest parts of the mechanism, are laid out for counting and scrutiny. Only when this is done can the investigation be extended to encompass the whole organism or the entire system. So we say.

Sometimes it seems that we take a loss, working this way. Much of today's public anxiety about science is the apprehension that we may forever be overlooking the whole by an endless, obsessive preoccupation with the parts. I had a brief, personal experience of this misgiving one afternoon in Tucson, where I had time on my hands and visited the zoo, just outside the city. The designers there have cut a deep pathway between two small artificial ponds, walled by clear glass, so when you stand in the center of the path you can look into the depths of each pool, and at the same time you can regard the surface. In one pool, on the right side of the path, is a family of otters; on the other side, a family of beavers. Within just a few feet from your face, on either side, beavers and otters are at play, underwater and on the surface, swimming toward your face and then away, more filled with life than any creatures I have ever seen before, in all my days. Except for the glass, you could reach across and touch them.

I was transfixed. As I now recall it, there was only one sensation in my head: pure elation mixed with amazement at such perfection. Swept off my feet, I floated from one side to the other, swiveling my brain, staring astounded at the beavers, then at the otters. I could hear shouts across my corpus callosum, from one hemisphere to the other. I remember thinking, with what was left in charge of my consciousness, that I wanted no part of the science of beavers and otters; I wanted never to know how they performed their marvels; I wished for no news about the physiology of their breathing, the coordination of their muscles, their vision, their endocrine systems, their digestive tracts. I hoped never to have to think of them as collections of cells. All I asked for was the full hairy complexity, then in front of my eyes, of whole, intact beavers and otters in motion.

It lasted, I regret to say, for only a few minutes, and then I was back in the late twentieth century, reductionist as ever, wondering about the details by force of habit, but not, this time, the details of otters and beavers. Instead, me. Something worth remembering had happened in my mind, I was certain of that; I would have put it somewhere in the brain stem; maybe this was my limbic system at work. I became a behavioral scientist, an experimental psychologist, an ethologist, and in the instant I lost all the wonder and the sense of being overwhelmed. I was flattened.

But I came away from the zoo with something, a piece of news   5
about myself: I am coded, somehow, for otters and beavers. I exhibit instinctive behavior in their presence, when they are displayed close at hand behind glass, simultaneously below water and at the surface. I have receptors for this display. Beavers and otters possess a "release" for me, in the terminology of ethology, and the releasing was my experience. What was released? Behavior. What behavior? Standing, swiveling flabbergasted, feeling exultation and a rush of friendship. I could not, as the result of the transaction, tell you anything more about beavers and otters than you already know. I learned nothing new about them. Only about me, and I suspect also about you, maybe about human beings at large: we are endowed with genes which code out our reaction to beavers and otters, maybe our reaction to each other as well. We are stamped with stereotyped, unalterable patterns of response, ready to be released. And the behavior released in us, by such confrontations, is, essentially, a surprised affection. It is compulsory behavior and we can avoid it only by straining with the full power of our conscious minds, making up conscious excuses all the way. Left to ourselves, mechanistic and autonomic, we hanker for friends.

Everyone says, stay away from ants. They have no lessons for us; they are crazy little instruments, inhuman, incapable of controlling themselves, lacking manners, lacking souls. When they are massed together, all touching, exchanging bits of information held in their jaws like memoranda, they become a single animal. Look out for that. It is a debasement, a loss of individuality, a violation of human nature, an unnatural act.

Sometimes people argue this point of view seriously and with deep thought. Be individuals, solitary and selfish, is the message. Altruism, a jargon word for what used to be called love, is worse than weakness, it is sin, a violation of nature. Be separate. Do not be a social animal. But this is a hard argument to make convincingly when you have to depend on language to make it. You have to print up leaflets or publish books and get them bought and sent around, you have to turn up on television and catch the attention of millions of other human beings all at once, and then you have to say to all of them, all at once, all collected and paying attention: be solitary; do not depend on each other. You can't do this and keep a straight face.

Maybe altruism is our most primitive attribute, out of reach, beyond our control. Or perhaps it is immediately at hand, waiting to be released, disguised now, in our kind of civilization, as affection or friendship or attachment. I don't see why it should be unreasonable for all human beings to have strands of DNA coiled up in chromosomes, coding out instincts for usefulness and helpfulness. Usefulness may turn out to be the hardest test of fitness for survival, more important than aggression, more effective, in the long run, than grabbiness. If this is the sort of information biological science holds for the future, applying to us as well as to ants, then I am all for science.

One thing I'd like to know most of all: when those ants have made the Hill, and are all there, touching and exchanging, and the whole mass begins to behave like a single huge creature, and *thinks,* what on earth is that thought? And while you're at it, I'd like to know a second thing: when it happens, does any single ant know about it? Does his hair stand on end?

Lines of Inquiry
"The Tucson Zoo"

In paragraphs 3 and 4 of this essay, Thomas tells how his mind was "transfixed," as he watched the beavers and otters at play. Why does he let us in on his private thoughts like this, rather than simply presenting us with the polished and finished conclusions that he comes to in this piece? What is the effect of his telling us, as he does, about the ebb and flow of his thoughts on that occasion? Exactly how does this method of presentation differ from the scientific method that Thomas describes in the first paragraph?

Look closely at the different stages that Thomas goes through in the process of perceiving and reacting to the beavers and otters in paragraphs 2–5. Exactly what does he learn from looking at this display of the beavers and the otters? How does this knowledge challenge or confirm his identity as a scientist? Does Thomas end up in favor of scientific inquiry, or is he finally against such analysis? Or does he somehow arrive at a third position or no position at all?

In this essay Thomas describes what the romantic poet William Wordsworth called "a spot of time" or what the modern novelist James Joyce called an "epiphany"—an intense, private experience that stands out, because it involves a significant and memorable insight. Think about an epiphany that you've had. What was the occasion, the place, and the time? What happened to you on that occasion? What went on in your mind? What insight(s) did you have? Did your "hair stand on end"?

The Corner of the Eye

There are some things that human beings can see only out of the corner of the eye. The niftiest examples of this gift, familiar to all children, are small, faint stars. When you look straight at one such star, it vanishes; when you move your eyes to stare into the space nearby, it reappears. If you pick two faint stars, side by side, and focus on one of the pair, it disappears and now you can see the other in the corner of your eye, and you can move your eyes back and forth, turning off the star in the center of your retina and switching the other one on. There is a physiological explanation for the phenomenon: we have more rods, the cells we use for light perception, at the periphery of our retinas, more cones, for perceiving color, at the center.

Something like this happens in music. You cannot really hear certain sequences of notes in a Bach fugue unless at the same time there are other notes being sounded, dominating the field. The real meaning in music comes from tones only audible in the corner of the mind.

I used to worry that computers would become so powerful and sophisticated as to take the place of human minds. The notion of Artificial Intelligence used to scare me half to death. Already, a large enough machine can do all sorts of intelligent things beyond our capacities: calculate in a split second the answers to mathematical problems requiring years for a human brain, draw accurate pictures from memory, even manufacture successions of sounds with a disarming resemblance to real music. Computers can translate textbooks, write dissertations of their own for doctorates, even speak in machine-tooled, inhuman phonemes any words read off from a printed page. They can communicate with one another, holding consultations and committee meetings of their own in networks around the earth.

Computers can make errors, of course, and do so all the time in small, irritating ways, but the mistakes can be fixed and nearly always are. In this respect they are fundamentally inhuman, and here is the relaxing thought: computers will not take over the world, they cannot replace us, because they are not designed, as we are, for ambiguity.

Imagine the predicament faced by a computer programmed to make language, not the interesting communication in sounds made by vervets or in symbols by brilliant chimpanzee prodigies, but real human talk. The grammar would not be too difficult, and there would be no problem in constructing a vocabulary of etymons, the original, pure, unambiguous words used to name real things. The impossibility would   5 come in making the necessary mistakes we humans make with words instinctively, intuitively, as we build our kinds of language, changing the meanings to imply quite different things, constructing and elaborating the varieties of ambiguity without which speech can never become human speech.

Look at the record of language if you want to glimpse the special qualities of the human mind that lie beyond the reach of any machine. Take, for example, the metaphors we use in everyday speech to tell ourselves who we are, where we live, and where we come from.

The earth is a good place to begin. The word "earth" is used to name the ground we walk on, the soil in which we grow plants or dig clams, and the planet itself; we also use it to describe all of humanity ("the whole earth responds to the beauty of a child," we say to each other).

The earliest word for earth in our language was the Indo-European root *dhghem,* and look what we did with it. We turned it, by adding suffixes, into *humus* in Latin; today we call the complex polymers that hold fertile soil together "humic" acids, and somehow or other the same root became "humility." With another suffix the word became "human." Did the earth become human, or did the human emerge from the earth? One answer may lie in that nice cognate word "humble." "Humane" was built on, extending the meaning of both the earth and ourselves. In ancient Hebrew, *adamha* was the word for earth, *adam* for man. What computer could run itself through such manipulations as those?

We came at the same system of defining ourselves from the other direction. The word *wiros* was the first root for man; it took us in our vanity on to "virile" and "virtue," but also turned itself into the Germanic word *weraldh,* meaning the life of man, and thence in English to our word "world."

There is a deep hunch in this kind of etymology. The world of man 10 derives from this planet, shares origin with the life of the soil, lives in humility with all the rest of life. I cannot imagine programming a computer to think up an idea like that, not a twentieth-century computer, anyway.

The world began with what it is now the fashion to call the "Big Bang." Characteristically, we have assigned the wrong words for the very beginning of the earth and ourselves, in order to evade another term that would cause this century embarrassment. It could not, of course, have been a bang of any sort, with no atmosphere to conduct the waves of sound, and no ears. It was something else, occurring in the most absolute silence we can imagine. It was the Great Light.

We say it had been chaos before, but it was not the kind of place we use the word "chaos" for today, things tumbling over each other and bumping around. Chaos did not have that meaning in Greek; it simply meant empty.

We took it, in our words, from chaos to cosmos, a word that simply meant order, cosmetic. We perceived the order in surprise, and our cosmologists and physicists continue to find new and astonishing aspects of the order. We made up the word "universe" from the whole affair, meaning literally turning everything into one thing. We used to say it was a miracle, and we still permit ourselves to refer to the whole universe as a marvel, holding in our unconscious minds the original root meaning of these two words, miracle and marvel—from the ancient root word *smei,* signifying a smile. It immensely pleases a human being to see something never seen before, even more to learn something never known before, most of all to think something never thought before. The rings of Saturn are the latest surprise. All my physicist friends are enchanted by this phenomenon, marveling at the small violations of the laws of planetary mechanics, shocked by the unaccountable braids and spokes stuck there among the rings like graffiti. It is nice for physicists to see something new and inexplicable; it means that the laws of nature are once again about to be amended by a new footnote.

The greatest surprise of all lies within our own local, suburban solar system. It is not Mars; Mars was surprising in its way but not flabbergasting; it was a disappointment not to find evidences of life, and there was some sadness in the pictures sent back to earth from the Mars Lander, that lonely long-legged apparatus poking about with its jointed arm, picking up sample after sample of the barren Mars soil, looking for any flicker of life and finding none; the only sign of life on Mars was the Lander itself, an extension of the human mind all the way from earth to Mars, totally alone.

Nor is Saturn the great surprise, nor Jupiter, nor Venus, nor Mercury, nor any of the glimpses of the others.   15

The overwhelming astonishment, the queerest structure we know about so far in the whole universe, the greatest of all cosmological scientific puzzles, confounding all our efforts to comprehend it, is the earth. We are only now beginning to appreciate how strange and splendid it is, how it catches the breath, the loveliest object afloat around the sun, enclosed in its own blue bubble of atmosphere, manufacturing and breathing its own oxygen, fixing its own nitrogen from the air into its own soil, generating its own weather at the surface of its rain forests, constructing its own carapace from living parts: chalk cliffs, coral reefs, old fossils from earlier forms of life now covered by layers of new life meshed together around the globe, Troy upon Troy.

Seen from the right distance, from the corner of the eye of an extraterrestrial visitor, it must surely seem a single creature, clinging to the round warm stone, turning in the sun.

Lines of Inquiry
"The Corner of the Eye"

This essay begins with a clear thesis statement and then provides a paragraph of examples which support that thesis, followed by a paragraph that illustrates the same point by analogy. What strategies of diction, sentence rhythm, and organization does Thomas use to keep this initially straightforward organization and mode of presentation from becoming too mechanical and predictable? In other words, what makes this essay different from a strict and straightforward thesis–illustration type of theme? How does Thomas create in the form of this essay itself a sense of the "surprise" that he celebrates in nature?

In paragraphs 7–9, Thomas devotes himself primarily to discussing the derivation of various words. What leads him into this kind of etymological discussion? Do you notice any pattern or motif in the words that he chooses to discuss, or in their root meanings? What does this etymological exercise have to do with the overriding theme of this essay, namely with seeing things out of the corner of the eye?

Thomas says that "the record of language" reflects "the special qualities of the human mind that lie beyond the reach of any machine." If this statement is true, how is it possible that we can use computers to produce writing? Likewise, how is it possible that we can use computers to learn to read and write? Are there certain qualities of writing that cannot be grasped by computers, that can be seen, as it were, only out of the corner of the eye? If so, how can anyone learn to capture those qualities?

The Art of
Teaching Science

Everyone seems to agree that there is someting wrong with the way science is being taught these days. But no one is at all clear about when it went wrong or what is to be done about it. The term "scientific illiteracy" has become almost a cliché in educational circles. Graduate schools blame the colleges; colleges blame the secondary schools; the high schools blame the elementary schools, which, in turn, blame the family.

I suggest that the scientific community itself is partly, perhaps largely, to blame. Moreover, if there are disagreements between the world of the humanities and the scientific enterprise as to the place and importance of science in a liberal-arts education and the role of science in 20th-century culture, I believe that the scientists are themselves responsible for a general misunderstanding of what they are really up to.

During the last half-century, we have been teaching the sciences as though they were the same collection of academic subjects as always, and—here is what has really gone wrong—as though they would always be the same. Students learn today's biology, for example, the same way we learned Latin when I was in high school long ago: first, the fundamentals; then, the underlying laws; next, the essential grammar and, finally, the reading of texts. Once mastered, that was that: Latin was Latin and forever after would always be Latin. History, once learned, was history. And biology was precisely biology, a vast array of hard facts to be learned as fundamentals, followed by a reading of the texts.

Furthermore, we have been teaching science as if its facts were somehow superior to the facts in all other scholarly disciplines—more fundamental, more solid, less subject to subjectivism, immutable. English literature is not just one way of thinking; it is all sorts of ways; poetry is a moving target; the facts that underlie art, architecture and music are not really hard facts, and you can change them any way you like by arguing about them. But science, it appears, is an altogether different kind of learning: an unambiguous, unalterable and endlessly useful display of data that only needs to be packaged and installed somewhere in one's temporal lobe in order to achieve a full understanding of the natural world.

And, of course, it is not like this at all. In real life, every field of 5 science is incomplete, and most of them—whatever the record of accomplishment during the last 200 years—are still in their very earliest stages. In the fields I know best, among the life sciences, it is required that the most expert and sophisticated minds be capable of changing course—often with a great lurch—every few years. In some branches of biology the mind-changing is occurring with accelerating velocity. Next week's issue of any scientific journal can turn a whole field upside down, shaking out any number of immutable ideas and installing new bodies of dogma. This is an almost everyday event in physics, in chemistry, in materials research, in neurobiology, in genetics, in immunology.

On any Tuesday morning, if asked, a good working scientist will tell you with some self-satisfaction that the affairs of his field are nicely in order, that things are finally looking clear and making sense, and all is well. But come back again on another Tuesday, and the roof may have just fallen in on his life's work. All the old ideas—last week's ideas in some cases—are no longer good ideas. The hard facts have softened, melted away and vanished under the pressure of new hard facts. Something strange has happened. And it is this very strangeness of nature that makes science engrossing, that keeps bright people at it, and that ought to be at the center of science teaching.

The conclusions reached in science are always, when looked at closely, far more provisional and tentative than are most of the assumptions arrived at by our colleagues in the humanities. But we do not talk much in public about this, nor do we teach this side of science. We tend to say instead: These are the facts of the matter, and this is what the facts signify. Go and learn them, for they will be the same forever.

By doing this, we miss opportunity after opportunity to recruit young people into science, and we turn off a good many others who would never dream of scientific careers but who emerge from their education with the impression that science is fundamentally boring.

Sooner or later, we will have to change this way of presenting science. We might begin by looking more closely at the common ground that science shares with all disciplines, particularly with the humanities and with social and behavioral science. For there is indeed such a common ground. It is called bewilderment. There are more than seven times seven types of ambiguity in science, all awaiting analysis. The poetry of Wallace Stevens is crystal clear alongside the genetic code.

One of the complaints about science is that it tends to flatten everything. In its deeply reductionist way, it is said, science removes one mystery after another, leaving nothing in the place of mystery but data. I have even heard this claim as explanation for the drift of things in modern art and modern music: Nothing is left to contemplate except randomness and senselessness; God is nothing but a pair of dice, loaded at that. Science is linked somehow to the despair of the 20th-century mind. There is almost nothing unknown and surely nothing unknowable. Blame science.

I prefer to turn things around in order to make precisely the opposite case. Science, especially 20th-century science, has provided us with a glimpse of something we never really knew before, the revelation of human ignorance. We have been accustomed to the belief, from one century to another, that except for one or two mysteries we more or less comprehend everything on earth. Every age, not just the 18th century, regarded itself as the Age of Reason, and we have never lacked for explanations of the world and its ways. Now, we are being brought up short. We do not understand much of anything, from the episode we rather dismissively (and, I think, defensively) choose to call the "big bang," all the way down to the particles in the atoms of a bacterial cell. We have a wilderness of mystery to make our way through in the centuries ahead. We will need science for this but not science alone. In its own time, science will produce the data and some of the meaning in the data, but never the full meaning. For perceiving real significance when significance is at hand, we will need all sorts of brains outside the fields of science.

It is primarily because of this need that I would press for changes in the way science is taught. Although there is a perennial need to teach the young people who will be doing the science themselves, this will always be a small minority. Even more important, we must teach science to those who will be needed for thinking about it, and that means pretty nearly everyone else—most of all, the poets, but also artists, musicians, philosophers, historians and writers. A few of these people, at least, will be able to imagine new levels of meaning which may be lost on the rest of us.

In addition, it is time to develop a new group of professional thinkers, perhaps a somewhat larger group than the working scientists and the working poets, who can create a discipline of scientific criticism. We have had good luck so far in the emergence of a few people ranking as philosophers of science and historians and journalists of science, and I hope more of these will be coming along. But we have not yet seen specialists in the fields of scientific criticism who are of the caliber of the English literary and social critics F. R. Leavis and John Ruskin or the American literary critic Edmund Wilson. Science needs critics of this sort, but the public at large needs them more urgently.

I suggest that the introductory courses in science, at all levels from grade school through college, be radically revised. Leave the fundamentals, the so-called basics, aside for a while, and concentrate the attention of all students on the things that are not known. You cannot possibly teach quantum mechanics without mathematics, to be sure, but you can describe the strangeness of the world opened up by quantum theory. Let it be known, early on, that there are deep mysteries and profound paradoxes revealed in distant outline by modern physics. Explain that these can be approached more closely and puzzled over, once the language of mathematics has been sufficiently mastered.

At the outset, before any of the fundamentals, teach the still imponderable puzzles of cosmology. Describe as clearly as possible, for the youngest minds, that there are some things going on in the universe that lie still beyond comprehension, and make it plain how little is known. 15

Do not teach that biology is a useful and perhaps profitable science; that can come later. Teach instead that there are structures squirming inside each of our cells that provide all the energy for living. Essentially foreign creatures, these lineal descendants of bacteria were brought in for symbiotic living a billion or so years ago. Teach that we do not have the ghost of an idea how they got there, where they came from, or how they evolved to their present structure and function. The details of oxidative phosphorylation and photosynthesis can come later.

Teach ecology early on. Let it be understood that the earth's life is a system of interdependent creatures, and that we do not understand at all how it works. The earth's environment, from the range of atmospheric gases to the chemical constituents of the sea, has been held in an almost unbelievably improbable state of regulated balance since life began, and the regulation of stability and balance is somehow accomplished by the life itself, like the autonomic nervous system of an immense organism. We do not know how such a system works, much less what it means, but there are some nice reductionist details at hand, such as the bizarre proportions of atmospheric constituents, ideal for our sort of planetary life, and the surprising stability of the ocean's salinity, and the fact that the average temperature of the earth has remained quite steady in the face of at least a 25 percent increase in heat coming in from the sun since the earth began. That kind of thing: something to think about.

Go easy, I suggest, on the promises sometimes freely offered by science. Technology relies and depends on science these days, more than ever before, but technology is far from the first justification for doing research, nor is it necessarily an essential product to be expected from science. Public decisions about the future of technology are totally different from decisions about science, and the two enterprises should not be tangled together. The central task of science is to arrive, stage by stage, at a clearer comprehension of nature, but this does not at all mean, as it is sometimes claimed to mean, a search for mastery over nature.

Science may someday provide us with a better understanding of ourselves, but never, I hope, with a set of technologies for doing something or other to improve ourselves. I am made nervous by assertions that human consciousness will someday be unraveled by research, laid out for close scrutiny like the workings of a computer, and then—and *then . . . !* I hope with some fervor that we can learn a lot more than we now know about the human mind, and I see no reason why this strange puzzle should remain forever and entirely beyond us. But I would be deeply disturbed by any prospect that we might use the new knowledge in order to begin doing something about it—to improve it, say. This is a different matter from searching for information to use against schizophrenia or dementia, where we are badly in need of technologies, indeed likely one day to be sunk without them. But the ordinary, everyday, more or less normal human mind is too marvelous an instrument ever to be tampered with by anyone, science or no science.

The education of humanists cannot be regarded as complete, or even [20] adequate, without exposure in some depth to where things stand in the various branches of science, particularly, as I have said, in the areas of our ignorance. Physics professors, most of them, look with revulsion on assignments to teach their subject to poets. Biologists, caught up by the enchantment of their new power, armed with flawless instruments to tell the nucleotide sequences of the entire human genome, nearly matching the physicists in the precision of their measurements of living processes, will resist the prospect of broad survey courses; each biology professor will demand that any student in his path master every fine detail within that professor's research program.

The liberal-arts faculties, for their part, will continue to view the scientists with suspicion and apprehension. "What do the scientists want?" asked a Cambridge professor in Francis Cornford's wonderful "Microcosmographia Academica." "Everything that's going," was the quick answer. That was back in 1912, and scientists haven't much changed.

But maybe, just maybe, a new set of courses dealing systematically with ignorance in science will take hold. The scientists might discover in it a new and subversive technique for catching the attention of students driven by curiosity, delighted and surprised to learn that science is exactly as the American scientist and educator Vannevar Bush described it: an "endless frontier." The humanists, for their part, might take considerable satisfaction in watching their scientific colleagues confess openly to not knowing everything about everything. And the poets, on whose shoulders the future rests, might, late nights, thinking things over, begin to see some meanings that elude the rest of us. It is worth a try.

I believe that the worst thing that has happened to science education is that the fun has gone out of it. A great many good students look at it as slogging work to be got through on the way to medical school. Others are turned off by the premedical students themselves, embattled and bleeding for grades and class standing. Very few recognize science as the high adventure it really is, the wildest of all explorations ever taken by human beings, the chance to glimpse things never seen before, the shrewdest maneuver for discovering how the world works. Instead, baffled early on, they are misled into thinking that bafflement is simply the result of not having learned all the facts. They should be told that everyone else is baffled as well—from the professor in his endowed chair down to the platoons of postdoctoral students in the laboratories all night. Every important scientific advance that has come in looking like an answer has turned, sooner or later—usually sooner—into a question. And the game is just beginning.

If more students were aware of this, I think many of them would decide to look more closely and to try and learn more about what *is* known. That is the time when mathematics will become clearly and unavoidably recognizable as an essential, indispensable instrument for engaging in the game, and that is the time for teaching it. The calamitous loss of applied mathematics from what we might otherwise be calling higher education is a loss caused, at least in part, by insufficient incentives for learning the subject. Left by itself, standing there among curriculum offerings, it is not at all clear to the student what it is to be applied to. And there is all of science, next door, looking like an almost-finished field reserved only for chaps who want to invent or apply new technologies. We have had it wrong, and presented it wrong to class after class for several generations.

An appreciation of what is happening in science today, and how great a distance lies ahead for exploring, ought to be one of the rewards of a liberal-arts education. It ought to be good in itself, not something to be acquired on the way to a professional career but part of the cast of thought needed for getting into the kind of century that is now just down the road. Part of the intellectual equipment of an educated person, however his or her time is to be spent, ought to be a feel for the queernesses of nature, the inexplicable thing, the side of life for which informed bewilderment will be the best way of getting through the day.

Lines of Inquiry
"The Art of Teaching Science"

As an essayist, Thomas habitually summarizes a commonly held view or assumption and then disputes that view. Often he summarizes for several paragraphs at the beginning of a piece and then turns against the view he has summarized. Sometimes he moves back and forth throughout. Outline the structure that he uses in this essay. How does the pattern of summary and opposition compare to, and differ from, that of his other pieces in this book? What is the effect of the procedure that he uses in this essay?

Thomas says that the "common ground" of both science and the humanities is "bewilderment" and insists, therefore, that students should first be taught "the things that are not known," the "deep mysteries and profound paradoxes" that science reveals. How does this approach to education differ from the way both science and the humanities are generally taught today? What kind of people, what kind of citizens and professionals, does Thomas think the current method of education produces? What kind of people do you think would result from his alternative method of education?

As a student yourself, how do you react to Thomas' idea of education? How would you feel about going through a system where professors emphasized error and ambiguity and mystery, rather than clear-cut explanations and predictable structures? How would the educational philosophy that Thomas offers here apply to composition? What kinds of writing do you think he would assign? What qualities of style and form do you think he would most value?

Henry David Thoreau
1817–62

If a man does not keep pace with his companions, perhaps it is because he hears a different drummer.

In this resonant and famous sentence from *Walden,* Thoreau might well have been thinking of himself, for his life and his writing bear the marks of someone who evidently did hear "a different drummer." Indeed, he stands out as one of the most independent-minded figures of his time—and one of the most vigorous cultural critics to be heard from at any time in American history. As a critic of American culture, especially of its materialistic values, he is best known for *Walden, or Life in the Woods,* the work that grew out of his two-year experiment in living close to nature to "see if I could not learn what it had to teach, and not, when I came to die, discover that I had not lived." But long before the book appeared in 1854, or before the spring of 1845 when Thoreau "borrowed an axe and went down to the woods by Walden Pond," it was clear to all who knew him that his temperament, his inclinations, and his beliefs set him apart from most of his contemporaries.

He was born and grew up in Concord, Massachusetts. In fact, he spent almost his entire life in Concord, except for the four years of his undergraduate study at Harvard (1833–37), and for brief excursions to Canada, Cape Cod, Long Island, the Maine woods, Minnesota, and New Hampshire. He was "content," as he wrote his mother during one of those excursions, "to sit at the back door in Concord, under the poplar tree, henceforth forever." So he never really left home, and he never married. And though he worked sporadically in his father's pencil manufacturing business, he never did hold a regular job. Yet he was far from being idle or reclusive.

After graduating from Harvard, where he read widely in English poetry, classical literature, and mystical writing, he turned to teaching—briefly at the Concord town school during the fall of 1837, and then from 1838 to 1841 at a private school that he jointly founded and

developed with his brother John. He had quit the town school because
he objected to what was then the standard practice of disciplining students with a whip. So the school that he started up in his father's home
was a counter-cultural enterprise—the first of many such ventures that
he was to engage in throughout his life. Thoreau's school was radical
not only in its gentle form of discipline but also in its enterprising way
of teaching students about nature by taking them on field trips to observe it firsthand, a form of instruction that was then entirely new to
American education.

The act of observing nature was hardly something new to Thoreau.
From his childhood on, he had roamed the countryside around Concord—first looking for places to fish and hunt, then looking more closely
at things with the eye of a naturalist and the spirit of a transcendentalist.
His youthful attraction to nature had made him homesick throughout
his years at Harvard. His scientific interest in it subsequently led him
to carry out highly original studies in the succession of trees and in the
ecology of lakes and rivers. Indeed, his fascination with nature gave rise
to almost all of his major works. In 1839, for example, Thoreau and
his brother John took a two-week canoe trip down the Concord River
and then up the Merrimack River, which Thoreau transformed into his
first published book, *A Week on the Concord and Merrimack Rivers* (1849).
Then, as noted earlier, his two-year stay at Walden Pond led to *Walden,
or Life in the Woods* (1854). Finally, his several excursions to other points
of interest around the northeast provided the material for his posthumously published books, *The Maine Woods* (1864), *Cape Cod* (1865),
and *A Yankee in Canada* (1866).

Whether he reports on his bean field or describes the eye of a fish,
an exacting sense of detail always marks Thoreau's writing about nature. Thoreau achieved that sense of detail not only by observing nature
carefully, but by keeping a meticulous written record of his observations. He logged his perceptions in a journal that he began in 1834 as a
student at Harvard and that he maintained throughout the remaining
twenty-eight years of his life. In it he kept notes on his reading, personal reflections, and experiences, as well as records of his scientific
observations and investigations. Thus his journal, which ran to fourteen
volumes when it was first published in 1906, served him as the principal
source for most of his essays, lectures, and books. Indeed, Thoreau's
journal might well be considered the major occupation of his life.

Committed as he was to preserving and understanding the natural
world, Thoreau was just as intensely concerned with the quality of life
that prevailed among his neighbors in Concord and by extension among
his countrymen throughout the United States. Even during his two
years at Walden Pond, he did not by any means withdraw completely
from human companionship; in fact he received visitors at his cabin,
and made visits to friends and relatives in Concord. So *Walden* is not

just a paean to nature, but is an invocation to his countrymen, meant "to wake my neighbors up . . . to a higher life than we fell asleep from."

Thoreau himself had come to awareness of "a higher life," a world of transcendent moral and spiritual values, through his extensive reading in mystical literature, especially Hindu writing, and through his close friendship with Ralph Waldo Emerson, the leading member of a group of Concord intellectuals, known as transcendentalists, who aspired to reshape the beliefs and values of their time. In keeping with these aspirations, Thoreau went to Walden, not simply to observe nature, but to engage in philosophic meditation and to lead a life whose integrity and simplicity might constitute a challenge to the materialism of the times. Throughout *Walden* Thoreau's descriptions of nature are often resonant with philosophic implications—a lake "is earth's eye; looking into which the beholder measures the depth of his own nature." And his musings, in turn, often have social or political ramifications.

But the stands he took on the most pressing national issues of his time best reveal Thoreau's political consciousness. In 1845, the summer he went to settle at Walden, he refused to pay his poll tax as a form of protest against the Mexican War and against slavery. His protest landed him in jail, and the experience led him to write an essay, "Civil Disobedience" (1849), which came to be a guiding document for such eminent proponents of passive resistance as Mohandas K. Gandhi and Martin Luther King, Jr. In the early 1850s, he assisted fugitive slaves in escaping to Canada. In 1854, he delivered a passionate speech against the slavery in his home state of Massachusetts. And in 1859, his unyielding opposition to slavery gained him national attention when he became the first person to speak out in defense of the political martyr Captain John Brown. After the John Brown affair, he spent much of his time bedridden with tuberculosis, working on manuscripts of the several books that were published after his death.

As he lived, so he wrote in a style that was deliberately meant to awaken his readers, to get them to think about his ideas by expressing them in a provocative or surprising way. Thus, Thoreau's writing is always animated by a surprising play of language, by an arresting turn of speech. Sometimes the surprise comes from a striking allusion, sometimes from an unusual image or metaphor, sometimes from the power of a single word and the meanings that can be wrung out of it:

> I fear chiefly lest my expression may not be *extra-vagant* enough, may not wander far enough beyond the narrow limits of my daily experience, to be adequate to the truth of which I have been convinced. *Extra-vagance!* it depends on how you are yarded. The migrating buffalo, which seeks new pastures in another latitude, is not extravagant like the cow which kicks over the pail, leaps the cowyard fence, and runs after her calf, in

milking time. I desire to speak somewhere *without* bounds; like a man in a waking moment, to men in their waking moments; for I am convinced that I cannot exaggerate enough to lay the foundation of a true expression.

In this passage from *Walden,* the key word is "extravagant," and Thoreau playfully calls attention to it by putting it in italics and breaking it down into its Latin roots, *"extra-vagant,"* which mean literally "to wander outside." Then as if to confirm and emphasize this root meaning of the word, Thoreau repeatedly echoes it in such expressions as "may not wander far enough beyond" and *"without* bounds," as well as in such images as the "migrating buffalo" and the cow "which kicks over the pail, leaps the cowyard fence, and runs after her calf, in milking time." Thoreau's "expression" is not always so outlandish. But it usually does go beyond the "narrow limits" of standard usage and daily experience, inviting us to kick over a pail and leap a fence or two ourselves.

My House

Near the end of March, 1845, I borrowed an axe and went down to the woods by Walden Pond, nearest to where I intended to build my house, and began to cut down some tall arrowy white pines, still in their youth, for timber. It is difficult to begin without borrowing, but perhaps it is the most generous course thus to permit your fellow-men to have an interest in your enterprise. The owner of the axe, as he released his hold on it, said that it was the apple of his eye; but I returned it sharper than I received it. It was a pleasant hillside where I worked, covered with pine woods, through which I looked out on the pond, and a small open field in the woods where pines and hickories were springing up. The ice in the pond was all dark colored and saturated with water. There were some slight flurries of snow during the days that I worked there; but for the most part when I came out on to the railroad, on my way home, its yellow sand heap stretched away gleaming in the hazy atmosphere, and the rails shone in the spring sun, and I heard the lark and pewee and other birds already come to commence another year with us. They were pleasant spring days, in which the winter of man's discontent was thawing as well as the earth, and the life that had lain torpid began to stretch itself. One day, when my axe had come off and I had cut a green hickory for a wedge, driving it with a stone, and had placed the whole to soak in a pond hole in order to swell the wood, I saw a striped snake run into the water, and he lay on the bottom, apparently without inconvenience, as long as I staid there, or more than a quarter of an hour, perhaps because he had not yet fairly come out of the torpid state. It appeared to me that for a like reason men remain in their present low and primitive condition; but if they should feel the influence of the spring of springs arousing them, they would of necessity rise to a higher and more ethereal life. I had previously seen the snakes in frosty mornings in my path with portions of their bodies still numb and inflexible, waiting for the sun to thaw them. On the 1st of April it rained and melted the ice, and in the early part of the day, which was very foggy, I heard a stray goose groping about over the pond and cackling as if lost, or like the spirit of the fog.

So I went on for some days cutting and hewing timber, and also studs and rafters, all with my narrow axe, not having many communicable or scholar-like thoughts, singing to myself—

Men say they know many things;
But lo! they have taken wings,—

The arts and sciences,
And a thousand appliances;
The wind that blows
Is all that any body knows.

I hewed the main timbers six inches square, most of the studs on two sides only, and the rafters and floor timbers on one side, leaving the rest of the bark on, so that they were just as straight and much stronger than sawed ones. Each stick was carefully mortised or tenoned by its stump, for I had borrowed other tools by this time. My days in the woods were not very long ones; yet I usually carried my dinner of bread and butter, and read the newspaper in which it was wrapped, at noon, sitting amid the green pine boughs which I had cut off, and to my bread was imparted some of the fragrance, for my hands were covered with a thick coat of pitch. Before I had done I was more the friend than the foe of the pine tree, though I had cut down some of them, having become better acquainted with it. Sometimes a rambler in the wood was attracted by the sound of my axe, and we chatted pleasantly over the chips which I had made.

By the middle of April, for I made no haste in my work, but rather made the most of it, my house was framed and ready for the raising. I had already bought the shanty of James Collins, an Irishman who worked on the Fitchburg Railroad, for boards. James Collins' shanty was considered an uncommonly fine one. When I called to see it he was not at home. I walked about the outside, at first unobserved from within, the window was so deep and high. It was of small dimensions, with a peaked cottage roof, and not much else to be seen, the dirt being raised five feet all around as if it were a compost heap. The roof was the soundest part, though a good deal warped and made brittle by the sun. Doorsill there was none, but a perennial passage for the hens under the door board. Mrs. C. came to the door and asked me to view it from the inside. The hens were driven in by my approach. It was dark, and had a dirt floor for the most part, dank, clammy, and aguish, only here a board and there a board which would not bear removal. She lighted a lamp to show me the inside of the roof and the walls, and also that the board floor extended under the bed, warning me not to step into the cellar, a sort of dust hole two feet deep. In her own words, they were "good boards overhead, good boards all around and a good window,"—of two whole squares originally, only the cat had passed out that way lately. There was a stove, a bed, and a place to sit, an infant in the house where it was born, a silk parasol, gilt-framed looking-glass, and patent new coffee mill nailed to an oak sapling, all told. The bargain was soon concluded, for James had in the meanwhile returned. I to pay four dollars and twenty-five cents tonight, he to vacate at five tomorrow morning, selling to nobody else meanwhile: I to take possession at six. It were well, he said, to be there early, and anticipate certain indistinct but wholly unjust claims on the score of ground rent and fuel. This he assured me was the only encumbrance. At six I passed him and his family on the road. One large bundle held their all,—bed, coffee-mill, looking glass, hens,—all but the cat, she took to the woods and became a wild cat, and, as I learned afterward, trod in a trap set for woodchucks, and so became a dead cat at last.

I took down this dwelling the same morning, drawing the nails, and removed it to the pond side by small cart-loads, spreading the boards on the grass there to bleach and warp back again in the sun. One early thrush gave me a note or two as I drove along the woodland path. I was informed treacherously by a young Patrick that neighbor Seeley, an Irishman, in the intervals of the carting, transferred the still tolerable, straight, and drivable nails, staples, and spikes to his pocket and then stood when I came back to pass the time of day, and look freshly up, unconcerned, with spring thoughts, at the devastation; there being a dearth of work, as he said. He was there to represent spectatordom, and help make this seemingly insignificant event one with the removal of the gods of Troy.

I dug my cellar in the side of a hill sloping to the south, where a woodchuck had formerly dug his burrow, down through sumach and blackberry roots, and the lowest stain of vegetation, six feet square by seven deep, to a fine sand where potatoes would not freeze in any winter. The sides were left shelving, and not stoned; but the sun having never shone on them, the sand still keeps its place. It was but two hours' work. I took particular pleasure in this breaking of ground, for in almost all latitudes men dig into the earth for an equable temperature. Under the most splendid house in the city is still to be found the cellar where they store their roots as of old, and long after the superstructure has disappeared posterity remark its dent in the earth. The house is still but a sort of porch at the entrance of a burrow.

5

At length, in the beginning of May, with the help of some of my acquaintances, rather to improve so good an occasion for neighborliness than from any necessity, I set up the frame of my house. No man was ever more honored in the character of his raisers than I. They are destined, I trust, to assist at the raising of loftier structures one day. I began to occupy my house on the 4th of July, as soon as it was boarded and roofed, for the boards were carefully feather-edged and lapped, so that it was perfectly impervious to rain; but before boarding I laid the foundation of a chimney at one end, bringing two cartloads of stones up the hill from the pond in my arms. I built the chimney after my hoeing in the fall, before a fire became necessary for warmth, doing my cooking in the mean while out of doors on the ground, early in the morning: which mode I still think is in some respects more convenient and agreeable than the usual one. When it stormed before my bread was baked, I fixed a few boards over the fire, and sat under them to watch my loaf, and passed some pleasant hours in that way. In those days, when my hands were much employed, I read but little, but the least scraps of paper which lay on the ground, my holder, or table-cloth, afforded me as much entertainment, in fact answered the same purpose as the Iliad.

It would be worth the while to build still more deliberately than I did, considering, for instance, what foundation a door, a window, a cellar, a garret, have in the nature of man, and perchance never raising any superstructure until we found a better reason for it than our temporal necessities even. There is some of the same fitness in a man's building his own house that there is in a bird's building its own nest. Who knows but if men constructed their dwellings with their own hands, and provided food for themselves and families simply and honestly enough, the poetic faculty would be universally developed, as birds universally sing when they are so engaged? But alas! we do like cow-birds and cuckoos, which lay their eggs in nests which other birds have built, and cheer no traveller with their chattering and unmusical notes. Shall we forever resign the pleasure of construction to the carpenter? What does architecture amount to in the experience of the mass of men? I never in all my walks came across a man engaged in so simple and natural an occupation as building his house. We belong to the community. It is not the tailor alone who is the ninth part of a man, it is as much the preacher, and the merchant, and the farmer. Where is this division of labor to end? and what object does it finally serve? No doubt another *may* also think for me; but it is not therefore desirable that he should do so to the exclusion of my thinking for myself.

True, there are architects so called in this country, and I have heard of one at least possessed with the idea of making architectural ornaments have a core of truth, a necessity, and hence a beauty, as if it were a revelation to him. All very well perhaps from his point of view, but only a little better than the common dilettantism. A sentimental reformer in architecture, he began at the cornice, not at the foundation. It was only how to put a core of truth within the ornaments, that every sugar plum in fact might have an almond or caraway seed in it,—though I hold that almonds are most wholesome without the sugar—and not how the inhabitant, the indweller, might build truly within and without, and let the ornaments take care of themselves. What reasonable man ever supposed that ornaments were something outward and in the skin merely,—that the tortoise got his spotted shell, or the shellfish its mother-o'-pearl tints by such a contract as the inhabitants of Broadway their Trinity Church? But a man has no more to do with the style of architecture of his house than a tortoise with that of its shell: nor need the soldier be so idle as to try to paint the precise *color* of his virtue on his standard. The enemy will find it out. He may turn pale when the trial comes. This man seemed to me to lean over the cornice, and timidly whisper his half truth to the rude occupants who really knew it better than he. What of architectural beauty I now see, I know has gradually grown from within outward, out of the necessities and character of the indweller, who is the only builder—out of some unconscious truthfulness, and nobleness, without ever a thought for the appearance; and whatever additional beauty of this kind is destined to be produced will be preceded by a like unconscious beauty of life. The most interesting dwellings in this country, as the painter knows, are the most unpretending, humble log huts and cottages of the poor commonly; it is the life of the inhabitants whose shells they are, and not any peculiarity in their surfaces, merely, which makes them *picturesque;* and equally interesting will be the citizen's suburban box, when his life shall be as simple and as agreeable to the imagination, and there is as little straining after effect in the style of his dwelling. A great proportion of architectural ornaments are literally hollow, and a September gale would strip them off, like borrowed plumes, without injury to the substantials. They can do without *architecture* who have no olives nor wines in the cellar. What if an equal ado were made about the ornaments of style in literature, and the architects of our bibles spent as much time about their cornices as the architects of our churches do? So are made the *belles-lettres* and the *beaux-arts* and their professors. Much it concerns a man, forsooth, how a few sticks are slanted over him or under him and what colors are daubed upon his box. It would signify somewhat, if, in any earnest sense, *he* slanted them and daubed it; but the spirit having departed out of the tenant, it is of a piece with constructing his own coffin,—the architecture of the grave, and "carpenter," is but another name for "coffin-maker." One man says, in his despair or indifference to life, take up a handful of the earth at your feet, and paint your house that color. Is he thinking of his last and narrow house? Toss up a copper for it as well. What an abundance of leisure he must have! Why do you take up a handful of dirt? Better paint your house your own complexion; let it turn pale or blush for you. An enterprise to improve the style of cottage architecture! When you have got my ornaments ready I will wear them.

Before winter I built a chimney, and shingled the sides of my house, which were already impervious to rain, with imperfect and sappy shingles made of the first slice of the log, whose edges I was obliged to straighten with a plane.

I have thus a tight shingled and plastered house, ten feet wide by 10
fifteen long, and eight-feet posts, with a garret and a closet, a large window on each side, two trap doors, one door at the end, and a brick fireplace opposite. The exact cost of my house, paying the usual price for such materials as I used, but not counting the work, all of which

was done by myself, was as follows; and I give the details because very few are able to tell exactly what their houses cost, and fewer still, if any, the separate cost of the various materials which compose them:—

Boards	$8 03½,	mostly shanty boards.
Refuse shingles for roof and sides,	4 00	
Laths,	1 25	
Two second-hand windows with glass,	2 43	
One thousand old brick,	4 00	
Two casks of lime,	2 40	That was high.
Hair,	0 31	More than I needed.
Mantle-tree iron,	0 15	
Nails,	3 90	
Hinges and screws,	0 14	
Latch,	0 10	
Chalk,	0 01	
Transportation,	1 40	I carried a good part on my back.
In all,	$28 12½	

These are all the materials excepting the timber, stones and sand, which I claimed by squatter's right. I have also a small wood-shed adjoining made chiefly of the stuff which was left after building the house.

I intend to build me a house which will surpass any on the main street in Concord in grandeur and luxury, as soon as it pleases me as much and will cost me no more than my present one.

I thus found that the student who wishes for a shelter can obtain one for a lifetime at an expense not greater than the rent which he now pays annually. If I seem to boast more than is becoming, my excuse is that I brag for humanity rather than for myself; and my shortcomings and inconsistencies do not affect the truth of my statement. Notwithstanding much cant and hypocrisy,—chaff which I find it difficult to separate from my wheat, but for which I am sorry as any man,—I will breathe freely and stretch myself in this respect, it is such a relief to both the moral and physical system; and I am resolved that I will not through humility become the devil's attorney. I will endeavor to speak a good word for the truth. At Cambridge College the mere rent of a student's room, which is only a little larger than my own, is thirty dollars each year, though the corporation had the advantage of building thirty-two side by side and under one roof, and the occupant suffers the inconvenience of many and noisy neighbors, and perhaps a residence in the fourth story. I cannot but think that if we had more true wisdom in these respects, not only less education would be needed, because, forsooth, more would already have been acquired, but the pecuniary expense of getting an education would in a great measure vanish. Those conveniences which the student requires at Cambridge or elsewhere cost him or somebody else ten times as great a sacrifice of life as they would with proper management on both sides. Those things for which the most money is demanded are never the things which the student most wants. Tuition, for instance, is an important item in the term bill, while for the far more valuable education which he gets by associating with the most cultivated of his contemporaries no charge is made. The mode of founding a college is, commonly, to get up a subscription of dollars, and cents, and then following blindly the principles of a division of labor to its extreme, a principle which should never be followed but with circumspection,—to call in a contractor who makes this a subject of speculation, and he employs Irishmen or other operatives actually to lay the foundation, while the students that are to be are said to be fitting themselves for it; and for these oversights successive generations have to pay. I think that it would be *better than this,* for the students, or those who desire to be benefited by it, even to lay the foundation themselves. The student who secures his coveted leisure and retirement by systematically shirking any labor necessary to man obtains but an ignoble and unprofitable leisure, defrauding himself of the experience which alone can make leisure fruitful. "But," says one, "you do not mean that the students should go to work with their hands instead of their heads?" I do not mean that exactly, but I mean something which he might think a good deal like that; I mean that they should not *play* life, or *study* it merely, while the community supports them at this expensive game, but earnestly *live* it from beginning to end. How could youths better learn to live than by at once trying the experiment of living? Methinks this would exercise their minds as much as mathematics. If I wished a boy to know something about the arts and sciences, for instance, I would not pursue the common course, which is merely to send him into the neighborhood of some professor, where any thing is professed and practised but the art of life;—to survey the world through a telescope or a microscope, and never with his natural eye; to study chemistry, and not learn how his bread is made, or mechanics, and not learn how it is earned; to discover new satellites to Neptune, and not detect the motes in his eyes, or to what vagabond he is a satellite himself; or to be devoured by the monsters that swarm all around him, while contemplating the monsters in a drop of vinegar. Which would have advanced the most at the end of a month,—the boy who had made his own jackknife from the ore which he had dug and smelted, reading as much as would be necessary for this,—or the boy who had attended the lectures on metallurgy at the Institute in the mean while, and had received a Rogers' penknife from his father? Which would be most likely to cut his fingers? . . . To my astonishment I was informed on leaving college that I had studied navigation!—why, if I had taken one turn down the harbor I should have known more about it. Even the *poor* student studies and is taught only *political* economy, while that economy of living which is synonymous with philosophy is not even sincerely professed in our colleges. The consequence is, that while he is reading Adam Smith, Ricardo, and Say, he runs his father in debt irretrievably.

Lines of Inquiry
"My House"

Throughout this piece about building his house, Thoreau repeatedly digresses from his account, sometimes briefly, sometimes lengthily, to tell about or reflect upon other topics. Why do you suppose he doesn't keep himself focused entirely on the report of his house-building? Make a note of all the points at which he digresses. What seems to trigger each of these digressions? How does he move back and forth between his account and these other topics without losing an overall sense of continuity?

How are these digressions related to each other? How are they related to Thoreau's house-building account? For example, what is the relationship between his lengthy reflections on architecture and college education, and how are these, in turn, related to the detailed financial record of his house-building costs that comes in between them? What point do you think Thoreau is trying to convey through the interplay between the account of his house and the other topics he discusses?

At the end of this piece, Thoreau criticizes the scientific teaching in his own time. For other views of scientific teaching, look at Eiseley's "The Hidden Teacher" or Thomas' "The Art of Teaching Science." Based on your own experience in science courses, whose view of scientific instruction is most relevant to the problems you have observed?

Where I Lived, and What I Lived For

When first I took up my abode in the woods, that is, began to spend my nights as well as days there, which, by accident, was on Independence Day, or the Fourth of July, 1845, my house was not finished for winter, but was merely a defence against the rain, without plastering or chimney, the walls being of rough, weather-stained boards, with wide chinks, which made it cool at night. The upright white hewn studs and freshly planed door and window casings gave it a clean and airy look, especially in the morning, when its timbers were saturated with dew, so that I fancied that by noon some sweet gum would exude from them. To my imagination it retained throughout the day more or less of this auroral character, reminding me of a certain house on a mountain which I had visited a year before. This was an airy and unplastered cabin, fit to entertain a travelling god, and where a goddess might trail her garments. The winds which passed over my dwelling were such as sweep over the ridges of mountains, bearing the broken strains, or celestial parts only, of terrestrial music. The morning wind forever blows, the poem of creation is uninterrupted; but few are the ears that hear it. Olympus is but the outside of the earth everywhere.

The only house I had been the owner of before, if I except a boat, was a tent, which I used occasionally when making excursions in the summer, and this is still rolled up in my garret; but the boat, after passing from hand to hand, has gone down the stream of time. With this more substantial shelter about me, I had made some progress toward settling in the world. This frame, so slightly clad, was a sort of crystallization around me, and reacted on the builder. It was suggestive somewhat as a picture in outlines. I did not need to go out of doors to take the air, for the atmosphere within had lost none of its freshness. It was not so much within doors as being a door where I sat, even in the rainiest weather. The Harivansa[1] says, "An abode without birds is like a meat without seasoning." Such was not my abode, for I found myself suddenly neighbor to the birds; not by having imprisoned one, but having caged myself near them. I was not only nearer to some of those which commonly frequent the garden and the orchard, but to those wilder and more thrilling songsters of the forest which never, or rarely, serenade a villager,—the wood-thrush, the veery, the scarlet tanager, the field-sparrow, the whippoorwill, and many others.

---

[1] A fifth-century Hindu epic.

I was seated by the shore of a small pond, about a mile and half south of the village of Concord and somewhat higher than it, in the midst of an extensive wood between that town and Lincoln, and about two miles south of that our only field known to fame, Concord Battle Ground; but I was so low in the woods that the opposite shore, half a mile off, like the rest, covered with wood, was my most distant horizon. For the first week, whenever I looked out on the pond it impressed me like a tarn high up on the side of a mountain, its bottom far above the surface of other lakes, and, as the sun arose, I saw it throwing off its nightly clothing of mist, and here and there, by degrees, its soft ripples or its smooth reflecting surface was revealed, while the mists, like ghosts, were stealthily withdrawing in every direction into the woods, as at the breaking up of some nocturnal conventicle. The very dew seemed to hang upon the trees later into the day than usual, as on the sides of mountains.

This small lake was of most value as a neighbor in the intervals of a gentle rain-storm in August, when, both air and water being perfectly still, but the sky overcast, mid-afternoon had all the serenity of evening, and the wood thrush sang around, and was heard from shore to shore. A lake like this is never smoother than at such a time; and the clear portion of the air above it being shallow and darkened by clouds, the water, full of light and reflections, becomes a lower heaven itself so much the more important. From a hilltop near by, where the wood had been recently cut off, there was a pleasing vista southward across the pond, through a wide indentation in the hills which form the shore there, where their opposite sides sloping toward each other suggested a stream flowing out in that direction through a wooded valley, but stream there was none. That way I looked between and over the near green hills to some distant and higher ones in the horizon, tinged with blue. Indeed, by standing on tiptoe I could catch a glimpse of some of the peaks of the still bluer and more distant mountain ranges in the northwest, those true-blue coins from heaven's own mint, and also of some portion of the village. But in other directions, even from this point, I could not see over or beyond the woods which surrounded me. It is well to have some water in your neighborhood, to give buoyancy to and float the earth. One value even of the smallest well is, that when you look into it you see that earth is not continent but insular. This is as important as that it keeps butter cool. When I looked across the pond from this peak toward the Sudbury meadows, which in time of flood I distinguished elevated perhaps by a mirage in their seething valley, like a coin in a basin, all the earth beyond the pond appeared like a thin crust insulated and floated even by this small sheet of intervening water, and I was reminded that this on which I dwelt was but *dry land*.

Though the view from my door was still more contracted, I did not   5
feel crowded or confined in the least. There was pasture enough for my

imagination. The low shrub oak plateau to which the opposite shore arose stretched away toward the prairies of the West and the steppes of Tartary, affording ample room for all the roving families of men. "There are none happy in the world but beings who enjoy freely a vast horizon,"—said Damodara,[2] when his herds required new and larger pastures.

Both place and time were changed, and I dwelt nearer to those parts of the universe and to those eras in history which had most attracted me. Where I lived was as far off as many a region viewed nightly by astronomers. We are wont to imagine rare and delectable places in some remote and more celestial corner of the system, behind the constellation of Cassiopeia's Chair, far from noise and disturbance. I discovered that my house actually had its site in such a withdrawn, but forever new and unprofaned, part of the universe. If it were worth the while to settle in those parts near to the Pleiades or the Hyades, to Aldebaran or Altair,[3] then I was really there, or at an equal remoteness from the life which I had left behind, divided and twinkling with as fine a ray to my nearest neighbor, and to be seen only in moonless nights by him. Such was that part of creation where I had squatted;—

> "There was a shepherd that did live,
>   And held his thoughts as high
>   As were the mounts whereon his flocks
>   Did hourly feed him by."

What should we think of the shepherd's life if his flocks always wandered to higher pastures than his thoughts?

Every morning was a cheerful invitation to make my life of equal simplicity, and I may say innocence, with Nature herself. I have been as sincere a worshipper of Aurora[4] as the Greeks. I got up early and bathed in the pond; that was a religious exercise, and one of the best things which I did. They say that characters were engraven on the bathing tub of King Tchingthang[5] to this effect—"Renew thyself completely each day; do it again, and again, and forever again." I can understand that. Morning brings back the heroic ages. I was as much affected by the faint hum of a mosquito making its invisible and unimaginable tour through my apartment at earliest dawn, when I was sitting with door and windows open, as I could be by any trumpet that ever sang of fame. It was Homer's requiem; itself an Iliad and Odyssey in the air, singing its own wrath and wanderings. There was something

---

[2] Krishna, in the Hindu religion, is the incarnation of the God Vishnu.
[3] Names of stars and constellations.
[4] The classical goddess of dawn.
[5] Confucius (551–479 B.C.) was China's greatest sage.

cosmical about it; a standing advertisement, till forbidden, of the ever-lasting vigor and fertility of the world. The morning, which is the most memorable season of the day, is the awakening hour. Then there is least somnolence in us; and for an hour, at least, some part of us awakes which slumbers all the rest of the day and night. Little is to be expected of that day, if it can be called a day, to which we are not awakened by our Genius, but by the mechanical nudgings of some servitor, are not awakened by our own newly acquired force and aspirations from within, accompanied by the undulations of celestial music, instead of factory bells, and a fragrance filling the air—to a higher life than we fell asleep from; and thus the darkness bear its fruit, and prove itself to be good, no less than the light. The man who does not believe that each day contains an earlier, more sacred, and auroral hour than he has yet pro-faned, has despaired of life, and is pursuing a descending and darkening way. After a partial cessation of his sensuous life, the soul of man, or its organs rather, are reinvigorated each day, and his Genius tries again what noble life it can make. All memorable events, I should say, tran-spire in morning time and in a morning atmosphere. The Vedas[6] say, "All intelligences awake with the morning." Poetry and art, and the fairest and most memorable of the actions of men, date from such an hour. All poets and heroes, like Memmon,[7] are the children of Aurora, and emit their music at sunrise. To him whose elastic and vigorous thought keeps pace with the sun, the day is a perpetual morning. It matters not what the clocks say or the attitudes and labors of men. Morning is when I am awake and there is a dawn in me. Moral reform is the effort to throw off sleep. Why is it that men give so poor an account of their day if they have not been slumbering? They are not such poor calculators. If they had not been overcome with drowsiness, they would have performed something. The millions are awake enough for physical labor; but only one in a million is awake enough for effec-tive intellectual exertion, only one in a hundred millions to a poetic or divine life. To be awake is to be alive. I have never yet met a man who was quite awake. How could I have looked him in the face?

We must learn to reawaken and keep ourselves awake, not by me-chanical aids, but by an infinite expectation of the dawn, which does not forsake us in our soundest sleep. I know of no more encouraging fact than the unquestionable ability of man to elevate his life by a con-scious endeavor. It is something to be able to paint a particular picture, or to carve a statue, and so to make a few objects beautiful; but it is far more glorious to carve and paint the very atmosphere and medium through which we look, which morally we can do. To affect the qual-

---

[6] Ancient Hindu scriptures.
[7] At Thebes the statue of Memmon was said to emit music at dawn.

ity of the day, that is the highest of arts. Every man is tasked to make his life, even in its details, worthy of the contemplation of his most elevated and critical hour. If we refused, or rather used up, such paltry information as we get, the oracles would distinctly inform us how this might be done.

I went to the woods because I wished to live deliberately, to front only the essential facts of life, and see if I could not learn what it had to teach, and not, when I came to die, discover that I had not lived. I did not wish to live what was not life, living is so dear, nor did I wish to practice resignation, unless it was quite necessary. I wanted to live deep and suck out all the marrow of life, to live so sturdily and Spartan-like as to put to rout all that was not life, to cut a broad swath and shave close, to drive life into a corner, and reduce it to its lowest terms, and, if it proved to be mean, why then to get the whole and genuine meanness of it, and publish its meanness to the world; or it if were sublime, to know it by experience, and be able to give a true account of it in my next excursion. For most men, it appears to me, are in a strange uncertainty about it, whether it is of the devil or of God and have *somewhat hastily* concluded that it is the chief end of man here to "glorify God and enjoy him forever."

Still we live meanly, like ants; though the fable tells us that we were   10
long ago changed into men; like pygmies we fight with cranes; it is error upon error, and clout upon clout, and our best virtue has for its occasion a superfluous and evitable wretchedness. Our life is frittered away by detail. An honest man has hardly need to count more than his ten fingers, or in extreme cases he may add his ten toes, and lump the rest. Simplicity, simplicity, simplicity! I say, let your affairs be as two or three, and not a hundred or a thousand; instead of a million count half a dozen, and keep your accounts on your thumb-nail. In the midst of this chopping sea of civilized life, such are the clouds and storms and quicksands and thousand-and-one items to be allowed for, that a man has to live, if he would not founder and go to the bottom and not make his port at all, by dead reckoning, and he must be a great calculator indeed who succeeds. Simplify, simplify. Instead of three meals a day, if it be necessary eat but one; instead of a hundred dishes, five; and reduce other things in proportion. Our life is like a German Confederacy, made up of petty states, with its boundary forever fluctuating, so that even a German cannot tell you how it is bounded at any moment. The nation itself, with all its so-called internal improvements, which, by the way, are all external and superficial, is just such an unwieldy and overgrown establishment, cluttered with furniture and tripped up by its own traps, ruined by luxury and heedless expense, by want of calculation and a worthy aim, as the million households in the land; and the only cure for it, as for them, is in a rigid economy, a stern and more than Spartan simplicity of life and elevation of purpose. It lives too fast.

Men think that it is essential that the *Nation* have commerce, and export ice, and talk through a telegraph, and ride thirty miles an hour, without a doubt, whether *they* do or not; but whether we should live like baboons or like men, is a little uncertain. If we do not get out sleepers,[8] and forge rails, and devote days and nights to the work, but go to tinkering upon our *lives* to improve *them,* who will build railroads? And if railroads are not built, how shall we get to Heaven in season? But if we stay at home and mind our business, who will want railroads? We do not ride on the railroad; it rides upon us. Did you ever think what those sleepers are that underlie the railroad? Each one is a man, an Irishman, or a Yankee man. The rails are laid on them, and they are covered with sand, and the cars run smoothly over them. They are sound sleepers, I assure you. And every few years a new lot is laid down and run over; so that, if some have the pleasure of riding on a rail, others have the misfortune to be ridden upon. And when they run over a man that is walking in his sleep, a supernumerary sleeper in the wrong position, and wake him up, they suddenly stop the cars, and make a hue and cry about it, as if this were an exception. I am glad to know that it takes a gang of men for every five miles to keep the sleepers down and level in their beds as it is, for this is a sign that they may sometime get up again.

Why should we live with such hurry and waste of life? We are determined to be starved before we are hungry. Men say that a stitch in time saves nine, and so they take a thousand stitches to-day to save nine tomorrow. As for *work,* we haven't any of any consequence. We have the Saint Vitus' dance, and cannot possibly keep our heads still. If I should only give a few pulls at the parish bell-rope, as for a fire, that is, without setting the bell, there is hardly a man on his farm in the outskirts of Concord, notwithstanding that press of engagements which was his excuse so many times this morning, nor a boy, nor a woman, I might almost say, but would forsake all and follow that sound, not mainly to save property from the flames, but, if we will confess the truth, much more to see it burn, since burn it must, and we, be it known, did not set it on fire,—or to see it put out, and have a hand in it, if that is done as handsomely; yes, even if it were the parish church itself. Hardly a man takes a half-hour's nap after dinner, but when he wakes he holds up his head and asks, "What's the news?" as if the rest of mankind had stood his sentinels. Some give directions to be waked every half-hour, doubtless for no other purpose; and then, to pay for it, they tell what they have dreamed. After a night's sleep the news is as indispensable as the breakfast. "Pray tell me anything new that has happened to a man anywhere on this globe,"—and he reads it over his

---

[8]Railroad ties.

coffee and rolls, that a man has had his eyes gouged out this morning on the Wachito River, never dreaming the while that he lives in the dark unfathomed mammoth cave of this world, and has but the rudiment of an eye himself.

For my part, I could easily do without the post-office. I think that there are very few important communications made through it. To speak critically, I never received more than one or two letters in my life—I wrote this some years ago—that were worth the postage. The penny-post is, commonly, an institution through which you seriously offer a man that penny for his thoughts which is so often safely offered in jest. And I am sure that I never read any memorable news in a newspaper. If we read of one man robbed, or murdered, or killed by accident, or one house burned, or one vessel wrecked, or one steamboat blown up, or one cow run over on the Western Railroad, or one mad dog killed, or one lot of grasshoppers in the winter,—we never read of another. One is enough. If you are acquainted with the principle, what do you care for a myriad instances and applications? To a philosopher all *news,* as it is called, is gossip and they who edit and read it are old women over their tea. Yet not a few are greedy after this gossip. There was such a rush, as I hear, the other day at one of the offices to learn the foreign news by the last arrival, that several large squares of plate glass belonging to the establishment were broken by the pressure,—news which I seriously think a ready wit might write a twelvemonth, or twelve years, beforehand with sufficient accuracy. As for Spain, for instance, if you know how to throw in Don Carlos and the Infanta, and Don Pedro and Seville and Granada, from time to time in the right proportions,—they may have changed the names a little since I saw the papers,—and serve up a bull-fight when other entertainments fail, it will be true to the letter, and give us as good an idea of the exact state of ruin of things in Spain as the most succinct and lucid reports under this head in the newspapers: and as for England, almost the last significant scrap of news from that quarter was the revolution of 1649,[9] and if you have learned the history of her crops for an average year, you never need attend to that thing again, unless your speculations are of a merely pecuniary character. If one may judge who rarely looks into the newspapers, nothing new does ever happen in foreign parts, a French revolution not excepted.

What news! how much more important to know what that is which was never old! "Kieou-he-yu (great dignitary of the state of Wei) sent a man to Khoung-tseu to know his news. Khoung-tseu caused the messenger to be seated near him, and questioned him in these terms: What

---

[9]The English monarchy was overthrown and Charles I executed by the Puritans in 1649.

is your master doing? The messenger answered with respect: My master desires to diminish the number of his faults, but he cannot come to the end of them. The messenger being gone, the philosopher remarked: 'What a worthy messenger! What a worthy messenger!' " The preacher, instead of vexing the ears of drowsy farmers on their day of rest at the end of the week,—for Sunday is the fit conclusion of an ill-spent week, and not the fresh and brave beginning of a new one,—with this one other draggle-tail of a sermon, should shout with thundering voice, "Pause! Avast! Why so seeming fast, but deadly slow?"

Shams and delusions are esteemed for soundest truths, while reality is fabulous. If men would steadily observe realities only, and not allow themselves to be deluded, life, to compare it with such things as we know, would be like a fairy tale and the Arabian Nights' Entertainments. If we respected only what is inevitable and has a right to be, music and poetry would resound along the streets. When we are unhurried and wise, we perceive that only great and worthy things have any permanent and absolute existence, that petty fears and petty pleasures are but the shadow of the reality. This is always exhilarating and sublime. By closing the eyes and slumbering, and consenting to be deceived by shows, men establish and confirm their daily life of routine and habit everywhere, which still is built on purely illusory foundations. Children, who play life, discern its true law and relations more clearly than men, who fail to live it worthily, but who think that they are wiser by experience, that is, by failure. I have read in a Hindoo book, that "there was a king's son, who, being expelled in infancy from his native city, was brought up by a forester, and growing up to maturity in that state, imagined himself to belong to the barbarous race with which he lived. One of his father's ministers having discovered him, revealed to him what he was, and the misconception of his character was removed, and he knew himself to be a prince. So soul," continues the Hindoo philosopher, "from the circumstances in which it is placed, mistakes its own character, until the truth is revealed to it by some holy teacher, and then it knows itself to be *Brahma*." I perceive that we inhabitants of New England live this mean life that we do because our vision does not penetrate the surface of things. We think that that *is* which *appears* to be. If a man should walk through this town and see only the reality, where, think you, would the "Mill-dam" go to? If he should give us an account of the realities he beheld there, we should not recognize the place in his description. Look at a meeting-house, or a court-house, or a jail, or a shop, or a dwelling-house, and say what that thing really is before a true gaze, and they would all go to pieces in your account of them. Men esteem truth remote, in the outskirts of the system, behind the farthest star, before Adam and after the last man. In eternity there is indeed something true and sublime. But all these times and places and occasions are now and here. God himself culminates in the present moment, and will never be more divine in the lapse of all the ages. And we are enabled to apprehend at all what is sublime and noble only by the perpetual instilling and drenching of the reality that surrounds us. The universe constantly and obediently answers to our conceptions; whether we travel fast or slow, the track is laid for us. Let us spend our lives in conceiving then. The poet or the artist never yet had so fair and noble a design but some of his posterity at least could accomplish it.

Let us spend one day as deliberately as Nature, and not be thrown   15 off the track by every nutshell and mosquito's wing that falls on the rails. Let us rise early and fast, or break fast, gently and without perturbation; let company come and let company go, let the bells ring and the children cry,—determined to make a day of it. Why should we knock under and go with the stream? Let us not be upset and overwhelmed in that terrible rapid and whirlpool called a dinner, situated in the meridian shallows. Weather this danger and you are safe, for the rest of the way is down hill. With unrelaxed nerves, with morning vigor, sail by it, looking another way, tied to the mast like Ulysses. If the engine whistles, let it whistle till it is hoarse for its pains. If the bell rings, why should we run? We will consider what kind of music they are like. Let us settle ourselves, and work and wedge our feet downward through the mud and slush of opinion, and prejudice, and tradition, and delusion, and appearance, that alluvion which covers the globe, through Paris and London, through New York and Boston and Concord, through Church and State, through poetry and philosophy and religion, till we come to a hard bottom and rocks in place, which we can call *reality,* and say, This is, and no mistake; and then begin, having a *point d'appui,*[10] below freshet and frost and fire, a place where you might found a wall or a state, or set a lamp-post safely, or perhaps a gauge, not a Nilometer,[11] but a Realometer, that future ages might know how deep a freshet of shams and appearances had gathered from time to time. If you stand right fronting and face to face to a fact, you will see the sun glimmer on both its surfaces, as if it were a cimeter,[12] and feel its sweet edge dividing you through the heart and marrow, and so you will happily conclude your mortal career. Be it life or death, we crave only reality. If we are really dying, let us hear the rattle in our throats and feel cold in the extremities; if we are alive, let us go about our business.

Time is but the stream I go a-fishing in. I drink at it; but while I drink I see the sandy bottom and detect how shallow it is. Its thin

---

[10] A point of support or foundation.
[11] A device to measure the water level in the Nile River.
[12] A curved sword.

current slides away, but eternity remains. I would drink deeper; fish in the sky, whose bottom is pebbly with stars. I cannot count one. I know not the first letter of the alphabet. I have always been regretting that I was not as wise as the day I was born. The intellect is a cleaver; it discerns and rifts its way into the secret of things. I do not wish to be any more busy with my hands than is necessary. My head is hands and feet. I feel all my best faculties concentrated in it. My instinct tells me that my head is an organ for burrowing, as some creatures use their snout and fore paws, and with it I would mine and burrow my way through these hills. I think that the richest vein is somewhere hereabouts; so by the divining-rod and thin rising vapors I judge; and here I will begin to mine.

Lines of Inquiry
"Where I Lived, and What I Lived For"

In this piece, Thoreau contrasts his life in the woods with life elsewhere in mid-nineteenth-century America. Notice the various ways in which he organizes and develops this contrast. What kinds of details does he focus on in the first half of the piece when he describes his life in the woods; what kinds does he focus on in the second half when he describes life elsewhere? How would you characterize his style, tone of voice, and attitude in the first half? In the second half?

Notice all the instances in which "life," "to live," or some other form of these words appears in this piece, particularly in the second half. What do these words mean to Thoreau? What does he mean, for example, when he says, "I wished to live deliberately, to front only the essential facts of life, and see if I could not learn what it had to teach, and not, when I came to die, discover that I had not lived. I did not wish to live what was not life, living is so dear"? In other words, what is Thoreau's idea of life? What is his idea of not living?

This piece from the second chapter of *Walden* clearly relates to the previous piece about Thoreau's house-building from the first chapter of *Walden,* if only because his house in the woods figures in both selections. In what respects are they concerned with related topics and ideas, in what respects with different topics and ideas? In what respects do they involve similar styles of writing and modes of presentation, and in what respects different styles and modes of presentation? How do you account for the differences?

The War of the Ants

One day when I went out to my wood-pile, or rather my pile of stumps, I observed two large ants, the one red, the other much larger, nearly half an inch long, and black, fiercely contending with one another. Having once got hold they never let go, but struggled and wrestled and rolled on the chips incessantly. Looking farther, I was surprised to find that the chips were covered with such combatants, that it was not a *duellum,* but a *bellum,* a war between two races of ants, the red always pitted against the black, and frequently two red ones to one black. The legions of these Myrmidons covered all the hills and vales in my wood-yard, and the ground was already strewn with the dead and dying, both red and black. It was the only battle which I have ever witnessed, the only battle-field I ever trod while the battle was raging; internecine war; the red republicans on the one hand, and the black imperialists on the other. On every side they were engaged in deadly combat, yet without any noise that I could hear, and human soldiers never fought so resolutely. I watched a couple that were fast locked in each other's embraces, in a little sunny valley amid the chips, now at noonday prepared to fight till the sun went down, or life went out. The smaller red champion had fastened himself like a vise to his adversary's front, and through all the tumblings on that field never for an instant ceased to gnaw at one of his feelers near the root, having already caused the other to go by the board; while the stronger black one dashed him from side to side, and, as I saw on looking nearer, had already divested him of several of his members. They fought with more pertinacity than bulldogs. Neither manifested the least disposition to retreat. It was evident that their battle-cry was "Conquer or die." In the meanwhile there came along a single red ant on the hillside of this valley, evidently full of excitement, who either had despatched his foe, or had not yet taken part in the battle; probably the latter, for he had lost none of his limbs; whose mother had charged him to return with his shield or upon it. Or perchance he was some Achilles, who had nourished his wrath apart, and had now come to avenge or rescue his Patroclus. He saw this unequal combat from afar,—for the blacks were nearly twice the size of the red,—he drew near with rapid pace till he stood on his guard within half an inch of the combatants; then, watching his opportunity, he sprang upon the black warrior, and commenced his operations near the root of his right fore leg, leaving the foe to select among his own members; so there were three united for life, as if a new kind of attraction had been invented which put all other locks and cements to shame. I should not have wondered by this time to find that they had their respective musical bands stationed on some eminent chip, and playing their national airs the while, to excite the slow and cheer the dying combatants. I was myself excited somewhat even as if they had been men. The more you think of it, the less the difference. And certainly there is not the fight recorded in Concord history, at least, if in the history of America, that will bear a moment's comparison with this, whether for the numbers engaged in it, or for the patriotism and heroism displayed. For numbers and for carnage it was an Austerlitz or Dresden. Concord fight! Two killed on the patriots' side, and Luther Blanchard wounded! Why here every ant was a Buttrick,—"Fire! for God's sake fire!"—and thousands shared the fate of Davis and Hosmer. There was not one hireling there. I have no doubt that it was a principle they fought for, as much as our ancestors, and not to avoid a three-penny tax on their tea; and the results of this battle will be as important and memorable to those whom it concerns as those of the battle of Bunker Hill, at least.

I took up the chip on which the three I have particularly described were struggling, carried it into my house, and placed it under a tumbler on my window-sill, in order to see the issue. Holding a microscope to the first-mentioned red ant, I saw that, though he was assiduously gnawing at the near fore leg of his enemy, having severed his remaining feeler, his own breast was all torn away, exposing what vitals he had there to the jaws of the black warrior, whose breastplate was apparently too thick for his to pierce; and the dark carbuncles of the sufferer's eyes shone with ferocity such as war only could excite. They struggled half an hour longer under the tumbler, and when I looked again the black soldier had severed the heads of his foes from their bodies, and the still living heads were hanging on either side off him like ghastly trophies at his saddle-bow, still apparently as firmly fastened as ever, and he was endeavoring with feeble struggles, being without feelers, and with only the remnant of a leg, and I know not how many other wounds, to divest himself of them; which at length, after half an hour or more, he accomplished. I raised the glass, and he went off over the window-sill in that crippled state. Whether he finally survived that combat, and spent the remainder of his days in some Hôtel des Invalides, I do not know; but I thought that his industry would not be worth much thereafter. I never learned which party was victorious, nor the cause of the war; but I felt for the rest of that day as if I had had my feelings excited and harrowed by witnessing the struggle, the ferocity and carnage, of a human battle before my door.

Kirby and Spence tell us that the battles of ants have long been celebrated and the date of them recorded, though they say that Huber is the only modern author who appears to have witnessed them. "Æneas Sylvius," say they, "after giving a very circumstantial account of one contested with great obstinacy by a great and small species on the trunk of a pear tree," adds that " 'this action was fought in the pontificate of Eugenius the Fourth, in the presence of Nicholas Pistoriensis, an eminent lawyer, who related the whole history of the battle with the greatest fidelity.' A similar engagement between great and small ants is recorded by Olaus Magnus, in which the small ones, being victorious, are said to have buried the bodies of their own soldiers, but left those of their giant enemies a prey to the birds. This event happened previous to the expulsion of the tyrant Christiern the Second from Sweden." The battle which I witnessed took place in the Presidency of Polk, five years before the passage of Webster's Fugitive-Slave Bill.

Lines of Inquiry
"The War of the Ants"

Throughout this piece, Thoreau repeatedly compares the conflict among the ants to human warfare, alluding in the process to a variety of wars and warriors, from classical Greek literature to colonial American history. Examine the piece carefully in order to identify all of the words and phrases that contribute implicitly or explicitly to this extended analogy. What do you think he wanted to convey through this extended analogy? Why do you think he ends this piece about the ants by referring to other written accounts of warfare among ants?

Brief though it is, this piece on the ants offers a highly detailed description of conflict among creatures who are ordinarily considered to be highly social beings. What do you suppose was Thoreau's main purpose in making so detailed a description of the conflict? Do you think he was primarily concerned with making an observation about the behavior of ants? Or about the nature of war? Or about racial conflict? Or do you suppose he had some other subject uppermost in mind? Whatever you take his primary subject to be, what do you think he was trying to say about it through this description?

This essay-like piece is actually an excerpt from Chapter 12 of Thoreau's *Walden.* Read that chapter, and you will see that it includes detailed descriptions of activities not only among ants, but also among several other natural creatures—squirrels, otters, partridges, cats, and loons. Based on your reading of that chapter, what do you believe to be Thoreau's main purpose for describing the ants in the context of these other creatures?

Civil Disobedience[1]

I heartily accept the motto, "That government is best which governs least"; and I should like to see it acted up to more rapidly and systematically. Carried out, it finally amounts to this, which also I believe,—"That government is best which governs not at all"; and when men are prepared for it, that will be the kind of government which they will have. Government is at best but an expedient; but most governments are usually, and all governments are sometimes, inexpedient. The objections which have been brought against a standing army, and they are many and weighty, and deserve to prevail, may also at last be brought against a standing government. The standing army is only an arm of the standing government. The government itself, which is only the mode which the people have chosen to execute their will, is equally liable to be abused and perverted before the people can act through it. Witness the present Mexican war, the work of comparatively a few individuals using the standing government as their tool; for, in the outset, the people would not have consented to this measure.

This American government,—what is it but a tradition, though a recent one, endeavoring to transmit itself unimpaired to posterity, but each instant losing some of its integrity? It has not the vitality and force of a single living man; for a single man can bend it to his will. It is a sort of wooden gun to the people themselves. But it is not the less necessary for this; for the people must have some complicated machinery or other, and hear its din, to satisfy that idea of government which they have. Governments show thus how successfully men can be imposed on, even impose on themselves, for their own advantage. It is excellent, we must all allow. Yet this government never of itself furthered any enterprise, but by the alacrity with which it got out of its way. *It* does not keep the country free. *It* does not settle the West. *It* does not educate. The character inherent in the American people has done all that has been accomplished; and it would have done somewhat more, if the government had not sometimes got in its way. For government is an expedient by which men would fain succeed in letting one another alone; and, as has been said, when it is most expedient, the

---

[1]The episode that prompted this essay occurred in the summer of 1846. Thoreau had not paid his poll tax since 1841, apparently to make a test case of the poll-tax law, but his Aunt Maria paid the tax for him, so the only case left to Thoreau was rhetorical.—Ed.

governed are most let alone by it. Trade and commerce, if they were not made of india-rubber, would never manage to bounce over the obstacles which legislators are continually putting in their way; and, if one were to judge these men wholly by the effects of their actions and not partly by their intentions, they would deserve to be classed and punished with those mischievous persons who put obstructions on the railroads.

But, to speak practically and as a citizen, unlike those who call themselves no-government men, I ask for, not at once no government, but *at once* a better government. Let every man make known what kind of government would command his respect, and that will be one step toward obtaining it.

After all, the practical reason why, when the power is once in the hands of the people, a majority are permitted, and for a long period continue, to rule is not because they are most likely to be in the right, nor because this seems fairest to the minority, but because they are physically the strongest. But a government in which the majority rule in all cases cannot be based on justice, even as far as men understand it. Can there not be a government in which majorities do not virtually decide right and wrong, but conscience?—in which majorities decide only those questions to which the rule of expediency is applicable? Must the citizen ever for a moment, or in the least degree, resign his conscience to the legislator? Why has every man a conscience, then? I think that we should be men first, and subjects afterward. It is not desirable to cultivate a respect for the law, so much as for the right. The only obligation which I have a right to assume is to do at any time what I think right. It is truly enough said that a corporation has no conscience; but a corporation of conscientious men is a corporation *with* a conscience. Law never made men a whit more just; and, by means of their respect for it, even the well-disposed are daily made the agents of injustice. A common and natural result of an undue respect for law is, that you may see a file of soldiers, colonel, captain, corporal, privates, powder-monkeys, and all, marching in admirable order over hill and dale to the wars, against their wills, ay, against their common sense and consciences, which makes it very steep marching indeed, and produces a palpitation of the heart. They have no doubt that it is a damnable business in which they are concerned; they are all peaceably inclined. Now, what are they? Men at all? or small movable forts and magazines, at the service of some unscrupulous man in power? Visit the Navy-Yard, and behold a marine, such a man as an American government can make, or such as it can make a man with its black arts,—a mere shadow and reminiscence of humanity, a man laid out alive and standing, and already, as one may say, buried under arms with funeral accompaniments, though it may be,—

> "Not a drum was heard, not a funeral note,
>   As his corse to the rampart we hurried;
> Not a soldier discharged his farewell shot
>   O'er the grave where our hero we buried."

The mass of men serve the state thus, not as men mainly, but as   5
machines, with their bodies. They are the standing army, and the mi-
litia, jailers, constables, *posse comitatus,* etc. In most cases there is no free
exercise whatever of the judgment or of the moral sense; but they put
themselves on a level with wood and earth and stones; and wooden
men can perhaps be manufactured that will serve the purpose as well.
Such command no more respect than men of straw or a lump of dirt.
They have the same sort of worth only as horses and dogs. Yet such as
these even are commonly esteemed good citizens. Others—as most legislators, politicians, lawyers, ministers, and office-holders—serve the state
chiefly with their heads; and, as they rarely make any moral distinctions, they are as likely to serve the devil, without *intending* it, as God.
A very few—as heroes, patriots, martyrs, reformers in the great sense,
and *men*—serve the state with their consciences also, and so necessarily
resist it for the most part; and they are commonly treated as enemies
by it. A wise man will only be useful as a man, and will not submit to
be "clay," and "stop a hole to keep the wind away," but leave that
office to his dust at least:—

> "I am too high-born to be propertied,
>   To be a secondary at control,
>   Or useful serving-man and instrument
> To any sovereign state throughout the world."

He who gives himself entirely to his fellow-men appears to them
useless and selfish; but he who gives himself partially to them is pronounced a benefactor and philanthropist.

How does it become a man to behave toward this American government to-day? I answer, that he cannot without disgrace be associated
with it. I cannot for an instant recognize that political organization as
my government which is the *slave*'s government also.

All men recognize the right of revolution; that is, the right to refuse
allegiance to, and to resist, the government, when its tyranny or its
inefficiency are great and unendurable. But almost all say that such is
not the case now. But such was the case, they think, in the Revolution
of '75. If one were to tell me that this was a bad government because it
taxed certain foreign commodities brought to its port, it is most probable that I should not make an ado about it, for I can do without them.
All machines have their friction; and possibly this does enough good to
counterbalance the evil. At any rate, it is a great evil to make a stir
about it. But when the friction comes to have its machine, and oppres-

sion and robbery are organized, I say, let us not have such a machine any longer. In other words, when a sixth of the population of a nation which has undertaken to be the refuge of liberty are slaves, and a whole country is unjustly overrun and conquered by a foreign army, and subjected to military law, I think that it is not too soon for honest men to rebel and revolutionize. What makes this duty the more urgent is the fact that the country so overrun is not our own, but ours is the invading army.

Paley, a common authority with many on moral questions, in his chapter on the "Duty of Submission to Civil Government," resolves all civil obligation into expediency; and he proceeds to say that

> so long as the interest of the whole society requires it, that is, so long as the established government cannot be resisted or changed without public inconveniency, it is the will of God . . . that the established government be obeyed,—and no longer. This principle being admitted, the justice of every particular case of resistance is reduced to a computation of the quantity of the danger and grievance on the one side, and of the probability and expense of redressing it on the other.

Of this, he says, every man shall judge for himself. But Paley appears never to have contemplated those cases to which the rule of expediency does not apply, in which a people, as well as an individual, must do justice, cost what it may. If I have unjustly wrested a plank from a drowning man, I must restore it to him though I drown myself. This, according to Paley, would be inconvenient. But he that would save his life, in such a case, shall lose it. This people must cease to hold slaves, and to make war on Mexico, though it cost them their existence as a people.

In their practice, nations agree with Paley; but does any one think   10
that Massachusetts does exactly what is right at the present crisis?

> "A drab of state, a cloth-o'-silver slut,
>   To have her train borne up, and her soul trail in the dirt."

Practically speaking, the opponents to a reform in Massachusetts are not a hundred thousand politicians at the South, but a hundred thousand merchants and farmers here, who are more interested in commerce and agriculture than they are in humanity, and are not prepared to do justice to the slave and to Mexico, *cost what it may*. I quarrel not with far-off foes, but with those who, near at home, cooperate with, and do the bidding of, those far away, and without whom the latter would be harmless. We are accustomed to say, that the mass of men are unprepared; but improvement is slow, because the few are not materially wiser or better than the many. It is not so important that many should be as good as you, as that there be some absolute goodness somewhere;

for that will leaven the whole lump. There are thousands who are *in opinion* opposed to slavery and to the war, who yet in effect do nothing to put an end to them; who, esteeming themselves children of Washington and Franklin, sit down with their hands in their pockets, and say that they know not what to do, and do nothing; who even postpone the question of freedom to the question of free trade, and quietly read the prices-current along with the latest advices from Mexico, after dinner, and, it may be, fall asleep over them both. What is the price-current of an honest man and patriot to-day? They hesitate, and they regret, and sometimes they petition; but they do nothing in earnest and with effect. They will wait, well disposed, for others to remedy the evil, that they may no longer have it to regret. At most, they give only a cheap vote, and a feeble countenance and God-speed, to the right, as it goes by them. There are nine hundred and ninety-nine patrons of virtue to one virtuous man. But it is easier to deal with the real possessor of a thing than with the temporary guardian of it.

All voting is a sort of gaming, like checkers or backgammon, with a slight moral tinge to it, a playing with right and wrong, with moral questions; and betting naturally accompanies it. The character of the voters is not staked. I cast my vote, perchance, as I think right; but I am not vitally concerned that that right should prevail. I am willing to leave it to the majority. Its obligation, therefore, never exceeds that of expediency. Even voting *for the right* is *doing* nothing for it. It is only expressing to men feebly your desire that it should prevail. A wise man will not leave the right to the mercy of chance, nor wish it to prevail through the power of the majority. There is but little virtue in the action of masses of men. When the majority shall at length vote for the abolition of slavery, it will be because they are indifferent to slavery, or because there is but little slavery left to be abolished by their vote. *They* will then be the only slaves. Only *his* vote can hasten the abolition of slavery who asserts his own freedom by his vote.

I hear of a convention to be held at Baltimore, or elsewhere, for the selection of a candidate for the Presidency, made up chiefly of editors, and men who are politicians by profession; but I think, what is it to any independent, intelligent, and respectable man what decision they may come to? Shall we not have the advantage of his wisdom and honesty, nevertheless? Can we not count upon some independent votes? Are there not many individuals in the country who do not attend conventions? But no: I find that the respectable man, so called, has immediately drifted from his position, and despairs of his country, when his country has more reason to despair of him. He forthwith adopts one of the candidates thus selected as the only *available* one, thus proving that he is himself *available* for any purposes of the demagogue. His vote is of no more worth than that of any unprincipled foreigner or hireling native, who may have been bought. O for a man who is a *man,* and, as my neighbor says, has a bone in his back which you cannot pass your hand through! Our statistics are at fault: the population has been returned too large. How many *men* are there to a square thousand miles in this country? Hardly one. Does not America offer any inducement for men to settle here? The American has dwindled into an Odd Fellow,—one who may be known by the development of his organ of gregariousness, and a manifest lack of intellect and cheerful self-reliance; whose first and chief concern, on coming into the world, is to see that the almshouses are in good repair; and, before yet he has lawfully donned the virile garb, to collect a fund for the support of the widows and orphans that may be; who, in short, ventures to live only by the aid of the Mutual Insurance company, which has promised to bury him decently.

It is not a man's duty, as a matter of course, to devote himself to the eradication of any, even the most enormous, wrong; he may still properly have other concerns to engage him; but it is his duty, at least, to wash his hands of it, and, if he gives it no thought longer, not to give it practically his support. If I devote myself to other pursuits and contemplations, I must first see, at least, that I do not pursue them sitting upon another man's shoulders. I must get off him first, that he may pursue his contemplations too. See what gross inconsistency is tolerated. I have heard some of my townsmen say, "I should like to have them order me out to help put down an insurrection of the slaves, or to march to Mexico;—see if I would go"; and yet these very men have each, directly by their allegiance, and so indirectly, at least, by their money, furnished a substitute. The soldier is applauded who refuses to serve in an unjust war by those who do not refuse to sustain the unjust government which makes the war; is applauded by those whose own act and authority he disregards and sets at naught; as if the state were penitent to that degree that it hired one to scourge it while it sinned, but not to that degree that it left off sinning for a moment. Thus, under the name of Order and Civil Government, we are all made at last to pay homage to and support our own meanness. After the first blush of sin comes its indifference; and from immoral it becomes, as it were, *un*moral, and not quite unnecessary to that life which we have made.

The broadest and most prevalent error requires the most disinterested virtue to sustain it. The slight reproach to which the virtue of patriotism is commonly liable, the noble are most likely to incur. Those who, while they disapprove of the character and measures of a government, yield to it their allegiance and support are undoubtedly its most conscientious supporters, and so frequently the most serious obstacles to reform. Some are petitioning the State to dissolve the Union, to disregard the requisitions of the President. Why do they not dissolve it themselves,—the union between themselves and the State,—and refuse to pay their quota into its treasury? Do not they stand in the same relation to the State that the State does to the Union? And have not the same reasons prevented the State from resisting the Union which have prevented them from resisting the State?

How can a man be satisfied to entertain an opinion merely, and enjoy *it?* Is there any enjoyment in it, if his opinion is that he is aggrieved? If you are cheated out of a single dollar by your neighbor, you do not rest satisfied with knowing that you are cheated, or with saying that you are cheated, or even with petitioning him to pay you your due, but you take effectual steps at once to obtain the full amount, and see that you are never cheated again. Action from principle, the perception and the performance of right, changes things and relations; it is essentially revolutionary, and does not consist wholly with anything which was. It not only divides States and churches, it divides families; ay, it divides the *individual,* separating the diabolical in him from the divine.

Unjust laws exist: shall we be content to obey them, or shall we endeavor to amend them, and obey them until we have succeeded, or shall we transgress them at once? Men generally, under such a government as this, think that they ought to wait until they have persuaded the majority to alter them. They think that, if they should resist, the remedy would be worse than the evil. But it is the fault of the government itself that the remedy *is* worse than the evil. *It* makes it worse. Why is it not more apt to anticipate and provide for reform? Why does it not cherish its wise minority? Why does it cry and resist before it is hurt? Why does it not encourage its citizens to be on the alert to point out its faults, and *do* better than it would have them? Why does it always crucify Christ, and excommunicate Copernicus and Luther, and pronounce Washington and Franklin rebels?

One would think, that a deliberate and practical denial of its authority was the only offence never contemplated by government; else, why has it not assigned its definite, its suitable and proportionate, penalty? If a man who has no property refuses but once to earn nine shillings for the State, he is put in prison for a period unlimited by any law that I know, and determined only by the discretion of those who placed him there; but if he should steal ninety times nine shillings from the State, he is soon permitted to go at large again.

If the injustice is part of the necessary friction of the machine of government, let it go, let it go: perchance it will wear smooth,—certainly the machine will wear out. If the injustice has a spring, or a pulley, or a rope, or a crank, exclusively for itself, then perhaps you may consider whether the remedy will not be worse than the evil; but if it is of such a nature that it requires you to be the agent of injustice to another, then, I say, break the law. Let your life be a counter-friction to stop the machine. What I have to do is to see, at any rate, that I do not lend myself to the wrong which I condemn.

As for adopting the ways which the State has provided for remedying the evil, I know not of such ways. They take too much time, and a man's life will be gone. I have other affairs to attend to. I came into this world, not chiefly to make this a good place to live in, but to live in it, be it good or bad. A man has not everything to do, but something; and because he cannot do *everything,* it is not necessary that he should do *something* wrong. It is not my business to be petitioning the Governor or the Legislature any more than it is theirs to petition me; and if they should not hear my petition, what should I do then? But in this case the State has provided no way: its very Constitution is the evil. This may seem to be harsh and stubborn and unconciliatory; but it is to treat with the utmost kindness and consideration the only spirit that can appreciate or deserves it. So is all change for the better, like birth and death, which convulse the body.

I do not hesitate to say, that those who call themselves Abolitionists   20 should at once effectually withdraw their support, both in person and property, from the government of Massachusetts, and not wait till they constitute a majority of one, before they suffer the right to prevail through them. I think that it is enough if they have God on their side, without waiting for that other one. Moreover, any man more right than his neighbors constitutes a majority of one already.

I meet this American government, or its representative, the State government, directly, and face to face, once a year—no more—in the person of its tax-gatherer; this is the only mode in which a man situated as I am necessarily meets it; and it then says distinctly, Recognize me; and the simplest, the most effectual, and, in the present posture of affairs, the indispensablest mode of treating with it on this head, of expressing your little satisfaction with and love for it, is to deny it then. My civil neighbor, the tax-gatherer, is the very man I have to deal with,—for it is, after all, with men and not with parchment that I quarrel,—and he has voluntarily chosen to be an agent of the government. How shall he ever know well what he is and does as an officer of the government, or as a man, until he is obliged to consider whether he shall treat me, his neighbor, for whom he has respect, as a neighbor and well-disposed man, or as a maniac and disturber of the peace, and see if he can get over this obstruction to his neighborliness without a ruder and more impetuous thought or speech corresponding with his action. I know this well, that if one thousand, if one hundred, if ten men whom I could name,—if ten *honest* men only,—ay, if *one* HONEST man, in this State of Massachusetts, *ceasing to hold slaves,* were actually to withdraw from this copartnership, and be locked up in the county jail therefor, it would be the abolition of slavery in America. For it matters not how small the beginning may seem to be: what is once well done is done forever. But we love better to talk about it: that we say is our mission. Reform keeps many scores of newspapers in its service, but not one man. If my esteemed neighbor, the State's ambassador, who will devote his days to the settlement of the question of human rights in the Council Chamber, instead of being threatened with the prisons of Carolina, were to sit down the prisoner of Massachusetts, that State which is so anxious to foist the sin of slavery upon her sister,—though at present she can discover only an act of inhospitality to be the ground of a quarrel with her,—the Legislature would not wholly waive the subject the following winter.

Under a government which imprisons any unjustly, the true place for a just man is also a prison. The proper place to-day, the only place which Massachusetts has provided for her freer and less desponding spirits, is in her prisons, to be put out and locked out of the State by her own act, as they have already put themselves out by their principles. It is there that the fugitive slave, and the Mexican prisoner on parole, and the Indian come to plead the wrongs of his race should find them; on that separate, but more free and honorable, ground, where the State places those who are not *with* her, but *against* her,—the only house in a slave State in which a free man can abide with honor. If any think that their influence would be lost there, and their voices no longer afflict the ear of the State, that they would not be as an enemy within its walls, they do not know by how much truth is stronger than error, nor how much more eloquently and effectively he can combat injustice who has experienced a little in his own person. Cast your whole vote, not a strip of paper merely, but your whole influence. A minority is powerless while it conforms to the majority; it is not even a minority then; but it is irresistible when it clogs by its whole weight. If the alternative is to keep all just men in prison, or give up war and slavery, the State will not hesitate which to choose. If a thousand men were not to pay their tax-bills this year, that would not be a violent and bloody measure, as it would be to pay them, and enable the State to commit violence and shed innocent blood. This is, in fact, the definition of a peaceable revolution, if any such is possible. If the tax-gatherer, or any other public officer, asks me, as one has done, "But what shall I do?" my answer is, "If you really wish to do anything, resign your office." When the subject has refused allegiance, and the officer has resigned his office, then the revolution is accomplished. But even suppose blood should flow. Is there not a sort of blood shed when the conscience is wounded? Through this wound a man's real manhood and immortality flow out, and he bleeds to an everlasting death. I see this blood flowing now.

I have contemplated the imprisonment of the offender, rather than the seizure of his goods,—though both will serve the same purpose,—

because they who assert the purest right, and consequently are most dangerous to a corrupt State, commonly have not spent much time in accumulating property. To such the State renders comparatively small service, and a slight tax is wont to appear exorbitant, particularly if they are obliged to earn it by special labor with their hands. If there were one who lived wholly without the use of money, the State itself would hesitate to demand it of him. But the rich man—not to make any invidious comparison—is always sold to the institution which makes him rich. Absolutely speaking, the more money, the less virtue; for money comes between a man and his objects, and obtains them for him; and it was certainly no great virtue to obtain it. It puts to rest many questions which he would otherwise be taxed to answer; while the only new question which it puts is the hard but superfluous one, how to spend it. Thus his moral ground is taken from under his feet. The opportunities of living are diminished in proportion as what are called the "means" are increased. The best thing a man can do for his culture when he is rich is to endeavor to carry out those schemes which he entertained when he was poor. Christ answered the Herodians according to their condition. "Show me the tribute money," said he,— and one took a penny out of his pocket;—if you use money which has the image of Caesar on it, and which he has made current and valuable, that is, *if you are men of the State,* and gladly enjoy the advantages of Caesar's government, then pay him back some of his own when he demands it. "Render therefore to Caesar that which is Caesar's, and to God those things which are God's,"—leaving them no wiser than before as to which was which; for they did not wish to know.

When I converse with the freest of my neighbors, I perceive that, whatever they may say about the magnitude and seriousness of the question, and their regard for the public tranquillity, the long and the short of the matter is, that they cannot spare the protection of the existing government, and they dread the consequences to their property and families of disobedience to it. For my own part, I should not like to think that I ever rely on the protection of the State. But, if I deny the authority of the State when it presents its tax-bill, it will soon take and waste all my property, and so harass me and my children without end. This is hard. This makes it impossible for a man to live honestly, and at the same time comfortably, in outward respects. It will not be worth the while to accumulate property; that would be sure to go again. You must hire or squat somewhere, and raise but a small crop, and eat that soon. You must live within yourself, and depend upon yourself always tucked up and ready for a start, and not have many affairs. A man may grow rich in Turkey even, if he will be in all respects a good subject of the Turkish government. Confucius said: "If a state is governed by the principles of reason, poverty and misery are subjects of shame; if a state is not governed by the principles of reason, riches and honors are the subjects of shame." No: until I want the protection of Massachusetts to be extended to me in some distant Southern port, where my liberty is endangered, or until I am bent solely on building up an estate at home by peaceful enterprise, I can afford to refuse allegiance to Massachusetts, and her right to my property and life. It costs me less in every sense to incur the penalty of disobedience to the State than it would to obey. I should feel as if I were worth less in that case.

Some years ago, the State met me in behalf of the Church, and 25 commanded me to pay a certain sum toward the support of a clergyman whose preaching my father attended, but never I myself. "Pay," it said, "or be locked up in the jail." I declined to pay. But, unfortunately, another man saw fit to pay it. I did not see why the schoolmaster should be taxed to support the priest, and not the priest the schoolmaster; for I was not the State's schoolmaster, but I supported myself by voluntary subscription. I did not see why the lyceum should not present its tax-bill, and have the State to back its demand, as well as the Church. However, at the request of the selectmen, I condescended to make some such statement as this in writing:—"Know all men by these presents, that I, Henry Thoreau, do not wish to be regarded as a member of any incorporated society which I have not joined." This I gave to the town clerk; and he has it. The State, having thus learned that I did not wish to be regarded as a member of that church, has never made a like demand on me since; though it said that it must adhere to its original presumption that time. If I had known how to name them, I should then have signed off in detail from all the societies which I never signed on to; but I did not know where to find a complete list.

I have paid no poll-tax for six years. I was put into a jail once on this account, for one night; and, as I stood considering the walls of solid stone, two or three feet thick, the door of wood and iron, a foot thick, and the iron grating which strained the light, I could not help being struck with the foolishness of that institution which treated me as if I were mere flesh and blood and bones, to be locked up. I wondered that it should have concluded at length that this was the best use it could put me to, and had never thought to avail itself of my services in some way. I saw that, if there was a wall of stone between me and my townsmen, there was a still more difficult one to climb or break through before they could get to be as free as I was. I did not for a moment feel confined, and the walls seemed a great waste of stone and mortar. I felt as if I alone of all my townsmen had paid my tax. They plainly did not know how to treat me, but behaved like persons who are underbred. In every threat and in every compliment there was a blunder; for they thought that my chief desire was to stand the other side of that stone wall. I could not but smile to see how industriously they locked the door on my meditations, which followed them out again without let or hindrance, and *they* were really all that was dangerous. As they could not reach me, they had resolved to punish my body; just as boys, if they cannot come at some person against whom they have a spite, will abuse his dog. I saw that the State was half-witted, that it was timid as a lone woman with her silver spoons, and that it did not know its friends from its foes, and I lost all my remaining respect for it, and pitied it.

Thus the State never intentionally confronts a man's sense, intellectual or moral, but only his body, his senses. It is not armed with superior wit or honesty, but with superior physical strength. I was not born to be forced. I will breathe after my own fashion. Let us see who is the strongest. What force has a multitude? They only can force me who obey a higher law than I. They force me to become like themselves. I do not hear of *men* being *forced* to live this way or that by masses of men. What sort of life were that to live? When I meet a government which says to me, "Your money or your life," why should I be in haste to give it my money? It may be in a great strait, and not know what to do: I cannot help that. It must help itself; do as I do. It is not worth the while to snivel about it. I am not responsible for the successful working of the machinery of society. I am not the son of the engineer. I perceive that, when an acorn and a chestnut fall side by side, the one does not remain inert to make way for the other, but both obey their own laws, and spring and grow and flourish as best they can, till one, perchance, overshadows and destroys the other. If the plant cannot live according to its nature, it dies; and so a man.

The night in prison was novel and interesting enough. The prisoners in their shirt-sleeves were enjoying a chat and the evening air in the doorway, when I entered. But the jailer said, "Come, boys, it is time to lock up"; and so they dispersed, and I heard the sound of their steps returning into the hollow apartments. My room-mate was introduced to me by the jailer as "a first-rate fellow and a clever man." When the door was locked, he showed me where to hang my hat, and how he managed matters there. The rooms were whitewashed once a month; and this one, at least, was the whitest, most simply furnished, and probably the neatest apartment in the town. He naturally wanted to know where I came from, and what brought me there; and, when I had told him, I asked him in my turn how he came there, presuming him to be an honest man, of course; and, as the world goes, I believe he was. "Why," said he, "they accuse me of burning a barn; but I never did it." As near as I could discover, he had probably gone to bed in a barn when drunk, and smoked his pipe there; and so a barn was burnt. He had the reputation of being a clever man, had been there some three months waiting for his trial to come on, and would have to wait as much longer; but he was quite domesticated and contented, since he got his board for nothing, and thought that he was well treated.

He occupied one window, and I the other; and I saw that if one stayed there long, his principal business would be to look out the window. I had soon read all the tracts that were left there, and examined where former prisoners had broken out, and where a grate had been sawed off, and heard the history of the various occupants of that room; for I found that even here there was a history and a gossip which never circulated beyond the walls of the jail. Probably this is the only house in the town where verses are composed, which are afterward printed in a circular form, but not published. I was shown quite a long list of verses which were composed by some young men who had been detected in an attempt to escape, who avenged themselves by singing them.

I pumped my fellow-prisoner as dry as I could, for fear I should   30
never see him again; but at length he showed me which was my bed, and left me to blow out the lamp.

It was like traveling into a far country, such as I had never expected to behold, to lie there for one night. It seemed to me that I never had heard the town clock strike before, nor the evening sounds of the village; for we slept with the windows open, which were inside the grating. It was to see my native village in the light of the Middle Ages, and our Concord was turned into a Rhine stream, and visions of knights and castles passed before me. They were the voices of old burghers that I heard in the streets. I was an involuntary spectator and auditor of whatever was done and said in the kitchen of the adjacent village inn,— a wholly new and rare experience to me. It was a closer view of my native town. I was fairly inside of it. I never had seen its institutions before. This is one of its peculiar institutions; for it is a shire town. I began to comprehend what its inhabitants were about.

In the morning, our breakfasts were put through the hole in the door, in small oblong-square tin pans, made to fit, and holding a pint of chocolate, with brown bread, and an iron spoon. When they called for the vessels again, I was green enough to return what bread I had left; but my comrade seized it, and said that I should lay that up for lunch or dinner. Soon after he was let out to work at haying in a neighboring field, whither he went every day, and would not be back till noon; so he bade me good-day, saying that he doubted if he should see me again.

When I came out of prison,—for some one interfered, and paid that tax,—I did not perceive that great changes had taken place on the common, such as he observed who went in a youth and emerged a tottering and gray-headed man; and yet a change had to my eyes come over the scene,—the town, and State, and country,—greater than any that mere time could effect. I saw yet more distinctly the State in which I lived. I saw to what extent the people among whom I lived could be trusted as good neighbors and friends; that their friendship was for summer weather only; that they did not greatly propose to do right; that they were a distinct race from me by their prejudices and superstitions, as the Chinamen and Malays are; that in their sacrifices to humanity they ran no risks, not even to their property; that after all they were not so noble but they treated the thief as he had treated them, and hoped, by a certain outward observance and a few prayers, and by walking in a particular straight though useless path from time to time, to save their souls. This may be to judge my neighbors harshly; for I believe that many of them are not aware that they have such an institution as the jail in their village.

It was formerly the custom in our village, when a poor debtor came out of jail, for his acquaintances to salute him, looking through their fingers, which were crossed to represent the grating of a jail window, "How do ye do?" My neighbors did not thus salute me, but first looked at me, and then at one another, as if I had returned from a long journey. I was put into jail as I was going to the shoemaker's to get a shoe which was mended. When I was let out the next morning, I proceeded to finish my errand, and, having put on my mended shoe, joined a huckleberry party, who were impatient to put themselves under my conduct; and in half an hour,—for the horse was soon tackled,—was in the midst of a huckleberry field, on one of our highest hills, two miles off, and then the State was nowhere to be seen.

This is the whole history of "My Prisons." 35

I have never declined paying the highway tax, because I am as desirous of being a good neighbor as I am of being a bad subject; and as for supporting schools, I am doing my part to educate my fellow-countrymen now. It is for no particular item in the tax-bill that I refuse to pay it. I simply wish to refuse allegiance to the State, to withdraw and stand aloof from it effectually. I do not care to trace the course of my dollar, if I could, till it buys a man or a musket to shoot one with,— the dollar is innocent,—but I am concerned to trace the effects of my allegiance. In fact, I quietly declare war with the State, after my fashion, though I will still make what use and get what advantage of her I can, as is usual in such cases.

If others pay the tax which is demanded of me, from a sympathy with the State, they do but what they have already done in their own case, or rather they abet injustice to a greater extent than the State requires. If they pay the tax from a mistaken interest in the individual taxed, to save his property, or prevent his going to jail, it is because they have not considered wisely how far they let their private feelings interfere with the public good.

This, then, is my position at present. But one cannot be too much on his guard in such a case, lest his action be biased by obstinacy or an undue regard for the opinions of men. Let him see that he does only what belongs to himself and to the hour.

I think sometimes, Why, this people mean well, they are only ignorant; they would do better if they knew how: why give your neighbors this pain to treat you as they are not inclined to? But I think again,
This is no reason why I should do as they do, or permit others to suffer
much greater pain of a different kind. Again, I sometimes say to myself, When many millions of men, without heat, without ill will, without personal feeling of any kind, demand of you a few shillings only,
without the possibility, such is their constitution, of retracting or altering their present demand, and without the possibility, on your side, of
appeal to any other millions, why expose yourself to this overwhelming brute force? You do not resist cold and hunger, the winds
and the waves, thus obstinately; you quietly submit to a thousand similar necessities. You do not put your head into the fire. But just in
proportion as I regard this as not wholly a brute force, but partly a
human force, and consider that I have relations to those millions as to
so many millions of men, and not of mere brute or inanimate things, I
see that appeal is possible, first and instantaneously, from them to the
Maker of them, and, secondly, from them to themselves. But if I put
my head deliberately into the fire, there is no appeal to fire or to the
Maker of fire, and I have only myself to blame. If I could convince
myself that I have any right to be satisfied with men as they are, and
to treat them accordingly, and not according, in some respects, to my
requisitions and expectations of what they and I ought to be, then, like
a good Mussulman and fatalist, I should endeavor to be satisfied with
things as they are, and say it is the will of God. And, above all, there
is this difference between resisting this and a purely brute or natural
force, that I can resist this with some effect; but I cannot expect, like
Orpheus, to change the nature of the rocks and trees and beasts.

I do not wish to quarrel with any man or nation. I do not wish to   40
split hairs, to make fine distinctions, or set myself up as better than my
neighbors. I seek rather, I may say, even an excuse for conforming to
the laws of the land. I am but too ready to conform to them. Indeed, I
have reason to suspect myself on this head; and each year, as the tax-
gatherer comes round, I find myself disposed to review the acts and
position of the general and State governments, and the spirit of the
people, to discover a pretext for conformity.

> "We must affect our country as our parents,
>   And if at any time we alienate
>   Our love or industry from doing it honor,
>   We must respect effects and teach the soul
>   Matter of conscience and religion,
>   And not desire of rule or benefit."

I believe that the State will soon be able to take all my work of this
sort out of my hands, and then I shall be no better a patriot than my

fellow-countrymen. Seen from a lower point of view, the Constitution, with all its faults, is very good; the law and the courts are very respectable; even this State and this American government are, in many respects, very admirable, and rare things, to be thankful for, such as a great many have described them; but seen from a point of view a little higher, they are what I have described them; seen from a higher still, and the highest, who shall say what they are, or that they are worth looking at or thinking of at all?

However, the government does not concern me much, and I shall bestow the fewest possible thoughts on it. It is not many moments that I live under a government, even in this world. If a man is thought-free, fancy-free, imagination-free, that which *is not* never for a long time appearing *to be* to him, unwise rulers or reformers cannot fatally interrupt him.

I know that most men think differently from myself; but those whose lives are by profession devoted to the study of these or kindred subjects content me as little as any. Statesmen and legislators, standing so completely within the institution, never distinctly and nakedly behold it. They speak of moving society; but have no resting-place without it. They may be men of a certain experience and discrimination, and have no doubt invented ingenious and even useful systems, for which we sincerely thank them; but all their wit and usefulness lie within certain not very wide limits. They are wont to forget that the world is not governed by policy and expediency. Webster never goes behind government, and so cannot speak with authority about it. His words are wisdom to those legislators who contemplate no essential reform in the existing government; but for thinkers, and those who legislate for all time, he never once glances at the subject. I know of those whose serene and wise speculations on this theme would soon reveal the limits of his mind's range and hospitality. Yet, compared with the cheap professions of most reformers, and the still cheaper wisdom and eloquence of politicians in general, his are almost the only sensible and valuable words, and we thank Heaven for him. Comparatively, he is always strong, original, and, above all, practical. Still, his quality is not wisdom, but prudence. The lawyer's truth is not Truth, but consistency or a consistent expediency. Truth is always in harmony with herself, and is not concerned chiefly to reveal the justice that may consist with wrong-doing. He well deserves to be called, as he has been called, the Defender of the Constitution. There are really no blows to be given by him but defensive ones. He is not a leader, but a follower. His leaders are the men of '87. "I have never made an effort," he says, "and never propose to make an effort; I have never countenanced an effort, and never mean to countenance an effort, to disturb the arrangement as originally made, by which the various States came into the Union." Still thinking of the sanction which the Constitution gives to slavery, he says, "Because it was a part of the original compact,—let it stand." Notwithstanding his special acuteness and ability, he is unable to take a fact out of its merely political relations, and behold it as it lies absolutely to be disposed of by the intellect,—what, for instance, it behooves a man to do here in America to-day with regard to slavery,—but ventures, or is driven, to make some such desperate answer as the following, while professing to speak absolutely, and as a private man,—from which what new and singular code of social duties might be inferred? "The manner," says he,

> in which the governments of those States where slavery exists are to regulate it is for their own consideration, under their responsibility to their constituents, to the general laws of propriety, humanity, and justice, and to God. Associations formed elsewhere, springing from a feeling of humanity, or any other cause, have nothing whatever to do with it. They have never received any encouragement from me, and they never will.[2]

They who know of no purer sources of truth, who have traced up its stream no higher, stand, and wisely stand, by the Bible and the Constitution, and drink at it there with reverence and humility; but they who behold where it comes trickling into this lake or that pool, gird up their loins once more, and continue their pilgrimage toward its fountain-head.

No man with a genius for legislation has appeared in America. They are rare in the history of the world. There are orators, politicians, and eloquent men, by the thousand; but the speaker has not yet opened his mouth to speak who is capable of settling the much-vexed questions of the day. We love eloquence for its own sake, and not for any truth which it may utter, or any heroism it may inspire. Our legislators have not yet learned the comparative value of free trade and of freedom, of union, and of rectitude, to a nation. They have no genius or talent for comparatively humble questions of taxation and finance, commerce and manufactures and agriculture. If we were left solely to the wordy wit of legislators in Congress for our guidance, uncorrected by the seasonable experience and the effectual complaints of the people, America could not long retain her rank among the nations. For eighteen hundred years, though perchance I have no right to say it, the New Testament has been written; yet where is the legislator who has wisdom and practical talent enough to avail himself of the light which it sheds on the science of legislation?

The authority of government, even such as I am willing to submit   45 to,—for I will cheerfully obey those who know and can do better than I, and in many things even those who neither know nor can do so

---

[2] These extracts have been inserted since the lecture was read.

well,—is still an impure one: to be strictly just, it must have the sanction and consent of the governed. It can have no pure right over my person and property but what I concede to it. The progress from an absolute to a limited monarchy, from a limited monarchy to a democracy, is a progress toward a true respect for the individual. Even the Chinese philosopher was wise enough to regard the individual as the basis of the empire. Is a democracy, such as we know it, the last improvement possible in government? Is it not possible to take a step further toward recognizing and organizing the rights of man? There will never be a really free and enlightened State until the State comes to recognize the individual as a higher and independent power, from which all its own power and authority are derived, and treats him accordingly. I please myself with imagining a State at last which can afford to be just to all men, and to treat the individual with respect as a neighbor; which even would not think it inconsistent with its own repose if a few were to live aloof from it, not meddling with it, nor embraced by it, who fulfilled all the duties of neighbors and fellowmen. A State which bore this kind of fruit, and suffered it to drop off as fast as it ripened, would prepare the way for a still more perfect and glorious State, which also I have imagined, but not yet anywhere seen.

Lines of Inquiry
"Civil Disobedience"

Thoreau considers several issues in the course of this piece. How do you account for the selection and organization of material that he discusses? For example, why do you suppose that he begins by affirming the idea of a government "which governs least," when he makes clear in paragraph 3 that he is not a "no-government man"? Why does he discuss the issue of voting in paragraphs 11 and 12 rather than doing so immediately after paragraph 19, as one of "the ways which the State has provided for remedying the evil"? Why does he tell the lengthy story of his night in jail? Why does he single out Webster for attack near the end of the essay?

What exactly is Thoreau's idea of "civil disobedience"? For example, what assumptions does it entail about the relationship of citizens to the government? Under what type of circumstances does Thoreau believe that civil disobedience is necessary? Why does he consider other remedies inferior to it? Under what type of circumstances does he believe it is not required? What are the basic elements in any act of civil disobedience?

How does Thoreau's idea of civil disobedience relate to King's idea of nonviolent resistance as explained in "An Experiment in Love" and "A Letter from Birmingham Jail"? In what respects are these similar ideas, in what respects different?

Barbara Tuchman
1912—89

Should the historian be an artist? Certainly a conscious art should be part of his equipment. Macaulay describes him as half poet, half philosopher. I do not aspire to either of these heights. I think of myself as a storyteller, a narrator, who deals in true stories, not fiction. The distinction is not one of relative values; it is simply that history interests me more than fiction.

Barbara Tuchman, who has been called "America's foremost popular historian," frequently commented on the historian's responsibility as well as on her own historical practice. Describing herself as "a writer who happens to write history," she argued that historians, like any other artist, must make choices, select and omit, in order to shape their material into a *story*. "I believe that the material must precede the thesis," she said, "that chronological narrative is the spine and the bloodstream that bring history closer to 'how it really was.'"

Tuchman was born and raised in New York City, spending summers and holidays in Connecticut at her family's country estate, where she and her husband made their home for many years. In 1933, "the fateful year that saw the advent both of Franklin Roosevelt as President and Adolf Hitler as Chancellor," she graduated from Radcliffe College with a degree, appropriately enough, in both history and literature. It was the height of the Depression and paying jobs for young women with college degrees were hard to come by, so Tuchman took a volunteer position with the American Council of the Institute of Pacific Relations (IPR), as assistant to the international secretary. In 1934 the work of the IPR took her to Tokyo, where she began writing journalistic pieces which appeared in several small IPR magazines. Shortly after her return to America in 1935, she gained attention as a writer for a piece about her Japanese experience that appeared in the respected journal *Foreign Affairs*.

In 1936 she joined the staff of *The Nation,* a weekly political journal which her father, "a banker of rather eclectic interests," had bought "to save it from bankruptcy." There she honed her abilities as a political journalist, and in 1937 she went to cover the Spanish Civil War for both *The Nation* and another newsweekly, *War in Spain*. For Tuchman as for

Hemingway, Orwell, and so many other members of her generation, the outcome of that war was profoundly disillusioning: "With the defeat of the Republic in 1939 I met the event that cracked my heart, politically speaking, and replaced my illusions with a recognition of *realpolitik;* it was the beginning of adulthood." The Nazi war threat sent her back to the United States in 1939, but not before she had published her first book, *The Lost British Policy* (1938), a slim volume on the history of Britain's foreign policy towards Spain.

World War II, marriage, and motherhood combined to interrupt Tuchman's writing career for most of the next ten years. She married in June of 1940, "the day Hitler entered Paris," and her first child was born in 1941. While her husband served in the Army, she worked for a time as a writer for the Office of War Information, but when the war ended she took up the tasks of full-time domesticity and parenting. So, while she started work on her second book shortly after the birth of her third child in 1948, she did not complete it until eight years later. Of her efforts to pick up the threads of her career and to become a writer of history, she said that "it was a struggle. I had three small children and no status whatever. To come home, close a door and feel that it was your place to work, that was very difficult, particularly when you were—well, just a Park Avenue matron."

The publication of her second book, *The Bible and the Sword* (1956), a history of political relations between England and Palestine, evidently proved to be a great impetus for her, and she managed to quickly finish her next one, *The Zimmermann Telegram* (1958), an inquiry into the causes of World War I. Her fourth book, *The Guns of August* (1962), a detailed account of the first month of World War I, won her a Pulitzer Prize for nonfiction and permanently established her reputation as a writer who, according to one reviewer, "has the story-teller's knack for getting the maximum dramatic effect out of the events which crowd her pages." Her books continued to appear regularly: *The Proud Tower* (1966), concerning the state of affairs in the two decades before World War I; *Stilwell and the American Experience in China* (1970), which won her a second Pulitzer Prize; *Notes from China* (1972); *A Distant Mirror* (1980), concerning the fourteenth century and its haunting parallels to our own time; *Practicing History* (1981), a collection of her most outstanding articles, essays, and lectures; and *The March of Folly: From Troy to Vietnam* (1984), a detailed record of notable failures in leadership and their political consequences.

In all of these works she sought "to write history so as to enthrall the reader and make the subject as captivating and exciting to him as it is to me," and her lively style earned her a wide and devoted audience. Her books regularly gained recognition as book club selections, and *A Distant Mirror* became one of the top ten paperback sellers of all time. Academic historians, though, have not been so quick to praise her, probably because of her repeated insistence on writing not for scholars but for the public, seeking to convey her perception of "a historical truth . . . not by piling up a list of all the facts I have collected, which is the way of the Ph.D., but by exercising the artist's privilege of selection." She insisted, in fact, that it was her very lack of graduate training which enabled her to succeed as a writer: "I never took a Ph.D. It's what saved me. If I had taken a doctoral degree, it would have stifled any writing capacity." As she saw it, then, her status as both an independent scholar and a writer best allowed her to meet the dual demands of fidelity to historical fact and grace of presentation, she believed "there is no need to choose between accuracy and beauty: one should be clothed in the other."

She also insisted that "the historian cannot do without imagination," that imagination gives the writer of history "extra vision." So, her declared ambition was to write history as literature, which she referred to as "the literature of actuality." Given these views, she chafed at negative definitions of historical writing:

> I see no reason why the word ["artist"] should always be confined to writers of fiction and poetry while the rest of us are lumped together under that despicable term "Nonfiction"—as if we were some sort of remainder. I do not feel like a Non-something; I feel quite specific. I wish I could think of a name in place of "Nonfiction." In the hope of finding an antonym I looked up "Fiction" in Webster and found it defined as opposed to "Fact, Truth, and Reality." I thought for a while of adopting FTR, standing for Fact, Truth, and Reality, as my new term, but it is awkward to use. "Writers of Reality" is the nearest I could come to what I want, but I cannot very well call us "Realtors" because that has been pre-empted—although as a matter of fact I would like to. "Real Estate," when you come to think of it, is a very fine phrase and it is exactly the sphere that writers of nonfiction deal in: the real estate of man, of human conduct. I wish we could get it back from the dealers in land. The categories could be poets, novelists, and realtors.

Concerned though she was with the factual, artful, and imaginative presentation of history, Tuchman also felt keenly the tragedies of her own time and sought in the record of the past some wisdom to save the human race from itself. So, her belief that historical presentation must be rooted in the lively narration of events did not prevent her from taking quite strong political stands in her later works against American foreign policy from Vietnam to Central America, as well as against the preoccupation with image, rather than ideas, that now dominates political life not only in America but throughout the world. Thus she remained true to her belief in the moral responsibility of the historian: "To take no sides in history would be as false as to take no sides in life."

"Perdicaris Alive or Raisuli Dead"

On a scented Mediterranean May evening in 1904 Mr. Ion Perdicaris, an elderly, wealthy American, was dining with his family on the vine-covered terrace of the Place of Nightingales, his summer villa in the hills above Tangier. Besides a tame demoiselle crane and two monkeys who ate orange blossoms, the family included Mrs. Perdicaris; her son by a former marriage, Cromwell Oliver Varley, who (though wearing a great name backward) was a British subject; and Mrs. Varley. Suddenly a cacophony of shrieks, commands, and barking of dogs burst from the servants' quarters at the rear. Assuming the uproar to be a further episode in the chronic feud between their German housekeeper and their French-Zouave chef, the family headed for the servants' hall to frustrate mayhem. They ran into the butler flying madly past them, pursued by a number of armed Moors whom at first they took to be their own household guards. Astonishingly, these persons fell upon the two gentlemen, bound them, clubbed two of the servants with their gunstocks, knocked Mrs. Varley to the floor, drew a knife against Varley's throat when he struggled toward his wife, dragged off the housekeeper, who was screaming into the telephone, "Robbers! Help!," cut the wire, and shoved their captives out of the house with guns pressed in their backs.

Waiting at the villa's gate was a handsome, black-bearded Moor with blazing eyes and a Greek profile, who, raising his arm in a theatrical gesture, announced in the tones of Henry Irving playing King Lear, "I am the Raisuli!" Awed, Perdicaris and Varley knew they stood face to face with the renowned Berber chief, lord of the Rif and last of the Barbary pirates, whose personal struggle for power against his nominal overlord, the Sultan of Morocco, periodically erupted over Tangier in raids, rapine, and interesting varieties of pillage. He now ordered his prisoners hoisted onto their horses and, thoughtfully stealing Perdicaris' best mount, a black stallion, for himself, fired the signal for departure. The bandit cavalcade, in a mad confusion of shouts, rearing horses, and trampled bodies, scrambled off down the rocky hillside, avoiding the road, and disappeared into the night in the general direction of the Atlas Mountains.

A moment later Samuel R. Gummere, United States Consul General, was interrupted at dinner by the telephone operator, who passed on the alarm from the villa. After a hasty visit to the scene of the outrage, where he ascertained the facts, assuaged the hysterical ladies, and posted guards, Gummere returned to confer with his colleague Sir Arthur Nicolson, the British Minister. Both envoys saw alarming prospects of danger to all foreigners in Morocco as the result of Raisuli's latest pounce.

Morocco's already anarchic affairs had just been thrown into even greater turmoil by the month-old Anglo-French entente. Under this arrangement England, in exchange for a free hand in Egypt, had given France a free hand in Morocco, much to the annoyance of all Moroccans. The Sultan, Abdul-Aziz, was a well-meaning but helpless young man uneasily balanced on the shaky throne of the last independent Moslem country west of Constantinople. He was a puppet of a corrupt clique headed by Ben Sliman, the able and wicked old Grand Vizier. To keep his young master harmlessly occupied while he kept the reins, not to mention the funds, of government in his own hands, Ben Sliman taught the Sultan a taste for, and indulged him in all manner of, extravagant luxuries of foreign manufacture. But Abdul-Aziz's tastes got out of bounds. Not content with innumerable bicycles, six hundred cameras, twenty-five grand pianos, and a gold automobile (though there were no roads), he wanted Western reforms to go with them. These, requiring foreign loans, willingly supplied by the French, opened the age-old avenue of foreign penetration. The Sultan's Western tastes and Western debts roused resentment among his fanatic tribes. Rebellions and risings had kept the country in strife for some years past, and European rivalries complicated the chaos. France, already deep in Algeria, was pressing against Morocco's borders. Spain had special interests along the Mediterranean coast. Germany was eyeing Morocco for commercial opportunities and as a convenient site for naval coaling bases. England, eyeing Germany, determined to patch up old feuds with France and had just signed the entente in April. The Moroccan government, embittered by what it considered England's betrayal, hating France, harassed by rebellion, tottering on the brink of bankruptcy, had yet one more scourge to suffer. This was the Sherif Mulai Ahmed ibn-Muhammed er Raisuli, who now seized his moment. To show up the Sultan's weakness, proportionately increase his own prestige, and extract political concessions as ransom, he kidnapped the prominent American resident Mr. Perdicaris.

"Situation serious," telegraphed Gummere to the State Department on May 19. "Request man-of-war to enforce demands." No request could have been more relished by President Theodore Roosevelt. Not yet forty-six, bursting with vigor, he delighted to make the Navy the vehicle of his exuberant view of national policy. At the moment of Perdicaris' kidnapping he faced, within the next month, a nominating convention that could give him what he most coveted: a chance to be elected President "in my own right." Although there was no possibility

5

of the convention's nominating anyone else, Roosevelt knew it would be dominated by professional politicians and standpatters who were unanimous in their distaste for "that damned cowboy," as their late revered leader, Mark Hanna, had called him. The prospect did not intimidate Roosevelt. "The President," said his great friend Ambassador Jean Jules Jusserand of France, "is in his best mood." The President promptly ordered to Morocco not one warship but four, the entire South Atlantic Squadron—due shortly to coal at Tenerife in the Canaries, where it could receive its orders to proceed at once to Tangier. Roosevelt knew it to be under the command of a man exactly suited to the circumstances, Admiral French Ensor Chadwick, a decorated veteran of the Battle of Santiago and, like Roosevelt, an ardent disciple of Admiral Alfred Thayer Mahan's strenuous theories of naval instrumentality.

Roosevelt's second in foreign policy was that melancholy and cultivated gentleman and wit, John Hay, who had been Lincoln's private secretary, wanted only to be a poet, and was, often to his own disgust, Secretary of State. On the day of the kidnapping he was absent, delivering a speech at the St. Louis Fair. His subordinates, however, recognized Gummere, who was senior diplomatic officer in Tangier in the absence of any American minister and had six years' experience at that post, as a man to be listened to. The victim, Perdicaris, was also a man of some repute, whose name was known in the State Department through a public crusade he had waged back in 1886–7 against certain diplomatic abuses practiced in Tangier. His associate in that battle had been Gummere himself, then a junior member of the foreign service and Perdicaris' friend and fellow townsman from Trenton, New Jersey.

"Warships will be sent to Tangier as soon as possible," the Department wired Gummere. "May be three or four days before one arrives." "Ships" in the plural was gratifying, but the promised delay was not. Gummere feared the chances of rescuing Perdicaris and Varley were slim. Nicolson gloomily concurred. They agreed that the only hope was to insist upon the Sultan's government giving in to whatever demands Raisuli might make as his price for release of his prisoners. Most inconveniently, the government was split, its Foreign Minister, Mohammed Torres, being resident at Tangier, where the foreign legations were located, while the Sultan, Grand Vizier, and court were at Fez, which was three days' journey by camel or mule into the interior. Gummere and Nicolson told Mohammed Torres they expected immediate acquiescence to Raisuli's demands, whatever these might prove to be, and dispatched their vice-consuls to Fez to impress the same view urgently upon the Sultan.

The French Minister, St. René Taillandier, did likewise, but since the Anglo-French entente was still too new to have erased old jealousies, he acted throughout the affair more or less independently. France had her own reasons for wishing to see Perdicaris and Varley safely restored as quickly as possible. Their abduction had put the foreign colony in an uproar that would soon become panic if they were not rescued. The approach of the American fleet would seem to require equal action by France as the paramount power in the area, but France was anxious to avoid a display of force. She was "very nervous," Admiral Chadwick wrote later, at the prospect of taking over "the most fanatic and troublesome eight or ten millions in the world"; she had hoped to begin her penetration as unobtrusively as possible without stirring up Moroccan feelings any further against her. Hurriedly St. René Taillandier sent off two noble mediators to Raisuli; they were the young brother sherifs of the Wazan family, who occupied a sort of religious primacy among sherifs and whom France found it worthwhile to subsidize as her protégés.

While awaiting word from the mediators, Gummere and Nicolson anxiously conferred with an old Moroccan hand, Walter B. Harris, correspondent of the London *Times,* who had himself been kidnapped by Raisuli the year before. Raisuli had used that occasion to force the Bashaw, or local governor, of Tangier to call off a punitive expedition sent against him. This Bashaw, who played Sheriff of Nottingham to Raisuli's Robin Hood, was Raisuli's foster brother and chief hate; the two had carried on a feud ever since the Bashaw had tricked Raisuli into prison eight years before. The Bashaw sent troops to harass and tax Raisuli's tribes and burn his villages; at intervals he dispatched emissaries instructed to lure his enemy to parley. Raisuli ambushed and slaughtered the troops and returned the emissaries—or parts of them. The head of one was delivered in a basket of melons. Another came back in one piece, soaked in oil and set on fire. The eyes of another had been burned out with hot copper coins.

Despite such grisly tactics, Harris reported to Gummere and Nicolson, his late captor was a stimulating conversationalist who discoursed on philosophy in the accents of the Moorish aristocracy and denied interest in ransom for its own sake. "Men think I care about money," he had told Harris, "but, I tell you, it is only useful in politics." He had freed Harris in return for the release of his own partisans from government prisons, but since then more of these had been captured. This time Raisuli's demands would be larger and the Sultan less inclined to concede them. Sir Arthur recalled that on the last occasion Mohammed Torres had "behaved like an old brute" and shrugged off Harris' fate as being in the hands of the Lord, when in fact, as Nicolson had pointed out to him, Harris was "in the hands of a devil." Sir Arthur had suffered acutely. "I *boil,*" he confessed, "to have to humiliate myself and negotiate with these miserable brigands within three hours of Gibraltar." Gummere thought sadly of his poor friend Perdicaris. "I cannot

10

conceal from myself and the Department," he wrote that night, "that only by extremely delicate negotiations can we hope to escape from the most terrible consequences."

Back in America, the Perdicaris case provided a welcome sensation to compete in the headlines with the faraway fortunes of the Russo-Japanese War. A rich old gentleman held for ransom by a cruel but romantic brigand, the American Navy steaming to the rescue—here was personal drama more immediate than the complicated rattle of unpronounceable generals battling over unintelligible terrain. The President's instant and energetic action on behalf of a single citizen fallen among thieves in a foreign land made Perdicaris a symbol of America's new role on the world stage.

The man himself was oddly cast for the part. Digging up all available information, the press discovered that he was the son of Gregory Perdicaris, a native of Greece who had become a naturalized American, taught Greek at Harvard, married a lady of property from South Carolina, made a fortune in illuminating gas, settled in Trenton, New Jersey, and served for a time as United States Consul in his native land. The son entered Harvard with the class of 1860, but left in his sophomore year to study abroad. For a young man who was twenty-one at the opening of the Civil War, his history during the next few years was strangely obscure, a fact which the press ascribed to a conflict between his father, a Union sympathizer, and his mother, an ardent Confederate. Subsequently the son lived peripatetically in England, Morocco, and Trenton as a dilettante of literature and the arts, producing magazine articles, a verse play, and a painting called "Tent Life." He had built the now famous Villa Aidonia (otherwise Place of Nightingales) in 1877 and settled permanently in Tangier in 1884. There he lavishly entertained English and American friends among Oriental rugs, damasks, rare porcelains, and Moorish attendants in scarlet knee-pants and gold-embroidered jackets. He was known as a benefactor of the Moors and as a supporter of a private philanthropy that endowed Tangier with a modern sanitation system. He rode a splendid Arab steed—followed by his wife on a white mule—produced an occasional literary exercise or allegorical painting, and enjoyed an Edwardian gentleman's life amid elegant bric-a-brac.

A new telegram from the State Department desired Gummere to urge "energetic" efforts by the authorities to rescue Perdicaris and punish his captor—"if practicable," it added, with a bow to realities. Gummere replied that this was the difficulty: Raisuli, among his native crags, was immune from reprisal. The Sultan, who had a tatterdemalion army of some two thousand, had been trying vainly to capture him for years. Gummere became quite agitated. United action by the powers was necessary to prevent further abductions of Christians; Morocco was "fast drifting into a state of complete anarchy," the Sultan and his advisers were weak or worse, governors were corrupt, and very soon "neither life nor property will be safe."

On May 22 the younger Wazan returned with Raisuli's terms. They demanded everything: prompt withdrawal of government troops from the Rif; dismissal of the Bashaw of Tangier; arrest and imprisonment of certain officials who had harmed Raisuli in the past; release of Raisuli's partisans from prison; payment of an indemnity of $70,000 to be imposed personally upon the Bashaw, whose property must be sold to raise the amount; appointment of Raisuli as governor of two districts around Tangier that should be relieved of taxes and ceded to him absolutely; and, finally, safe-conduct for all Raisuli's tribesmen to come and go freely in the towns and markets.

Gummere was horrified; Mohammed Torres declared his government would never consent. Meanwhile European residents, increasingly agitated, were flocking in from outlying estates, voicing indignant protests, petitioning for a police force, guards, and gunboats. The local Moors, stimulated by Raisuli's audacity, were showing an aggressive mood. Gummere, scanning the horizon for Admiral Chadwick's smokestacks, hourly expected an outbreak. Situation "not reassuring," he wired; progress of talks "most unsatisfactory"; warship "anxiously awaited. Can it be hastened?"

The American public awaited Chadwick's arrival as eagerly as Gummere. Excitement rose when the press reported that Admiral Theodore F. Jewell, in command of the European Squadron, three days' sail behind Chadwick, would be ordered to reinforce him if the emergency continued.

Tangier received further word from the sherifs of Wazan that Raisuli had not only absolutely declined to abate his demands but had added an even more impossible condition: a British and American guarantee of fulfillment of the terms by the Moroccan government.

Knowing his government could not make itself responsible for the performance or non-performance of promises by another government, Gummere despairingly cabled the terms to Washington. As soon as he saw them, Roosevelt sent "in a hurry" for Secretary Hay (who had meanwhile returned to the capital). "I told him," wrote Hay that night in his diary, "I considered the demands of the outlaw Raisuli preposterous and the proposed guarantee of them by us and by England impossible of fulfillment." Roosevelt agreed. Two measures were decided upon and carried out within the hour: Admiral Jewell's squadron was ordered to reinforce Chadwick at Tangier, and France was officially requested to lend her good offices. (By recognizing France's special status in Morocco, this step, consciously taken, was of international significance in the train of crises that was to lead through Algeciras and Agadir to 1914.) Roosevelt and Hay felt they had done their utmost. "I hope they may not murder Mr. Perdicaris," recorded Hay none too hopefully,

15

"but a nation cannot degrade itself to prevent ill-treatment of a citizen."

An uninhibited press told the public that in response to Raisuli's "insulting" ultimatum, "all available naval forces" in European waters were being ordered to the spot. Inspired by memory of U.S. troops chasing Aguinaldo in the Philippines, the press suggested that "if other means fail," marines could make a forced march into the interior to "bring the outlaw to book for his crimes." Such talk terrified Gummere, who knew that leathernecks would have as much chance against Berbers in the Rif as General Braddock's redcoats against Indians in the Alleghenies; and besides, the first marine ashore would simply provoke Raisuli to kill his prisoners.

On May 29 the elder Wazan brought word that Raisuli threatened to do just that if all his demands were not met in two days. Two days! This was the twentieth century, but as far as communications with Fez were concerned it might as well have been the time of the Crusades. Nevertheless Gummere and Nicolson sent couriers to meet their vice-consuls at Fez (or intercept them if they had already left) with orders to demand a new audience with the Sultan and obtain his acceptance of Raisuli's terms.

At five-thirty next morning a gray shape slid into the harbor. Gummere, awakened from a troubled sleep, heard the welcome news that Admiral Chadwick had arrived at last aboard his flagship, the *Brooklyn.* Relieved, yet worried that the military mind might display more valor than discretion, he hurried down to confer with the Admiral. In him he found a crisp and incisive officer whose quick intelligence grasped the situation at once. Chadwick agreed that the point at which to apply pressure was Mohammed Torres. Although up in the hills the brigand's patience might be wearing thin, the niceties of diplomatic protocol, plus the extra flourishes required by Moslem practice, called for an exchange of courtesy calls before business could be done. Admiral and Consul proceeded at once to wait upon the Foreign Minister, who returned the call upon the flagship that afternoon. It was a sight to see, Chadwick wrote to Hay, his royal progress through the streets, "a mass of beautiful white wool draperies, his old calves bare and his feet naked but for his yellow slippers," while "these wild fellows stoop and kiss his shoulder as he goes by."

Mohammed Torres was greeted by a salute from the flagship's guns and a review of the squadron's other three ships, which had just arrived. Unimpressed by these attentions, he continued to reject Raisuli's terms. "Situation critical," reported Chadwick.

The situation was even more critical in Washington. On June 1 an extraordinary letter reached the State Department. Its writer, one A. H. Slocumb, a cotton broker of Fayetteville, North Carolina, said he had read with interest about the Perdicaris case and then, without warning, asked a startling question, "But is Perdicaris an American?" In the winter of 1863, Mr. Slocumb went on to say, he had been in Athens, and Perdicaris had come there "for the express purpose, as he stated, to become naturalized as a Greek citizen." His object, he had said, was to prevent confiscation by the Confederacy of some valuable property in South Carolina inherited from his mother. Mr. Slocumb could not be sure whether Perdicaris had since resumed American citizenship, but he was "positive" that Perdicaris had become a Greek subject forty years before, and he suggested that the Athens records would bear out his statement.

What blushes reddened official faces we can only imagine. Hay's diary for June 1 records that the President sent for him and Secretary of the Navy Moody "for a few words about Perdicaris," but, maddeningly discreet, Hay wrote no more. A pregnant silence of three days ensues between the Slocumb letter and the next document in the case. On June 4 the State Department queried our Minister in Athens, John B. Jackson, asking him to investigate the charge—"important if true," added the Department, facing bravely into the wind. Although Slocumb had mentioned only 1863, the telegram to Jackson asked him to search the records for the two previous years as well; apparently the Department had been making frenzied inquiries of its own during the interval. On June 7 Jackson telegraphed in reply that a person named Ion Perdicaris, described as an artist, unmarried, aged twenty-two, had indeed been naturalized as a Greek on March 19, 1862.

Posterity will never know what Roosevelt or Hay thought or said 25 at this moment, because the archives are empty of evidence. But neither the strenuous President nor the suave Secretary of State was a man easily rattled. The game must be played out. Already Admiral Jewell's squadron of three cruisers had arrived to reinforce Chadwick, making a total of seven American warships at Tangier. America's fleet, flag, and honor were committed. Wheels had been set turning in foreign capitals. Hay had requested the good offices of France. The French Foreign Minister, Théophile Delcassé, was himself bringing pressure. A British warship, the *Prince of Wales,* had also come to Tangier. Spain wanted to know if the United States was wedging into Morocco.

And just at this juncture the Sultan's government, succumbing to French pressure, ordered Mohammed Torres to accede to all Raisuli's demands. Four days later, on June 12, a French loan to the government of Morocco was signed at Fez in the amount of 62.5 million francs, secured by the customs of all Moroccan ports. It seemed hardly a tactful moment to reveal the fraudulent claim of Mr. Perdicaris.

He was not yet out of danger, for Raisuli refused to release him before all the demands were actually met, and the authorities were proving evasive. Washington was trapped. Impossible to reveal Perdicaris' status now; equally impossible to withdraw the fleet and leave him, whom the world still supposed to be an American, at the brigand's mercy.

During the next few days suspense was kept taut by a stream of telegrams from Gummere and Chadwick reporting one impasse after another in the negotiations with Raisuli. When the Sultan balked at meeting all the terms in advance of the release, Raisuli merely raised his ante, demanding that four districts instead of two be ceded to him and returning to the idea of an Anglo-American guarantee. "You see there is no end to the insolence of this blackguard," wrote Hay in a note to the President on June 15; Roosevelt, replying the same day, agreed that we had gone "as far as we possibly can go for Perdicaris" and could now only "demand the death of those that harm him if he is harmed." He dashed off an alarming postscript: 'I think it would be well to enter into negotiations with England and France looking to the possibility of an expedition to punish the brigands if Gummere's statement as to the impotence of the Sultan is true."

No further action was taken in pursuit of this proposal because Gummere's telegrams now grew cautiously hopeful; on the nineteenth he wired that all arrangements had been settled for the release to take place on the twenty-first. But on the twentieth all was off. Raisuli suspected the good faith of the government, a sentiment which Gummere and Chadwick evidently shared, for they blamed the delay on "intrigue of authorities here." Finally the exasperated Gummere telegraphed on the twenty-first that the United States position was "becoming humiliating." He asked to be empowered to deliver an ultimatum to the Moroccan government claiming an indemnity for each day's further delay, backed by a threat to land marines and seize the customs as security. Admiral Chadwick concurred in a separate telegram.

June 21 was the day the Republican National Convention met in Chicago. "There is a great deal of sullen grumbling," Roosevelt wrote that day to his son Kermit, "but they don't dare oppose me for the nomination. . . . How the election will turn out no one can tell." If a poll of Republican party leaders had been taken at any time during the past year, one newspaper estimated, it would have shown a majority opposed to Roosevelt's nomination. But the country agreed with Viscount Bryce, who said Roosevelt was the greatest President since Washington (prompting a Roosevelt friend to recall Whistler's remark when told he was the greatest painter since Velázquez: "Why drag in Velázquez?"). The country wanted Teddy and, however distasteful that fact was, the politicians saw the handwriting on the bandwagon. On the death of Mark Hanna four months before, active opposition had collapsed, and the disgruntled leaders were now arriving in Chicago prepared to register the inevitable as ungraciously as possible.

They were the more sullen because Roosevelt and his strategists, preparing against any possible slip-up, had so steamrollered and stage-managed the proceedings ahead of time that there was nothing left for the delegates to do. No scurrying, no back-room bargaining, no fights, no trades, no smoke-filled deals. *Harper's Weekly* reported an Alabama delegate's summation: "There ain't nobody who can do nothin' " and added: "It is not a Republican Convention, it is no kind of a convention; it is a Roosevelt."

The resulting listlessness and pervading dullness were unfortunate. Although Elihu Root, Henry Cabot Lodge, and other handpicked Roosevelt choices filled the key posts, most of the delegates and party professionals did not make even a pretense of enthusiasm. The ostentatious coldness of the delegation from New York, Roosevelt's home state, was such that one reporter predicted they would all go home with pneumonia. There were no bands, no parades, and for the first time in forty years there were hundreds of empty seats.

Roosevelt knew he had the nomination in his pocket, but all his life, like Lincoln, he had a haunting fear of being defeated in elections. He was worried lest the dislike and distrust of him so openly exhibited at Chicago should gather volume and explode at the ballot box. Something was needed to prick the sulks and dispel the gloom of the convention before it made a lasting impression upon the public.

At this moment came Gummere's plea for an ultimatum. Again we have no record of what went on in high councils, but President and Secretary must have agreed upon their historic answer within a matter of hours. The only relevant piece of evidence is a verbal statement made to Hay's biographer, the late Tyler Dennett, by Gaillard Hunt, who was chief of the State Department's Citizenship Bureau during the Perdicaris affair. Hunt said he showed the correspondence about Perdicaris' citizenship to Hay, who told him to show it to the President; on seeing it, the President decided to overlook the difficulty and instructed Hunt to tell Hay to send the telegram anyway, at once. No date is given for this performance, so one is left with the implication that Roosevelt was not informed of the facts until this last moment—a supposition which the present writer finds improbable.

When Roosevelt made up his mind to accomplish an objective, he 35
did not worry too much about legality of method. Before any unusual procedure he would ask an opinion from his Attorney General, Philander Knox, but Knox rather admired Roosevelt's way of overriding his advice. Once, when asked for his opinion, he replied, "Ah, Mr. President, why have such a beautiful action marred by any taint of legality?" Another close adviser, Admiral Mahan, when asked by Roosevelt how to solve the political problem of annexing the Hawaiian Islands, answered, "Do nothing unrighteous but . . . take the islands first and

solve afterward." It may be that the problem of Perdicaris seemed susceptible of the same treatment.

The opportunity was irresistible. Every newspaperman who ever knew him testified to Roosevelt's extraordinary sense of news value, to his ability to create news, to dramatize himself to the public. He had a genius for it. "Consciously or unconsciously," said the journalist Isaac Marcosson, "he was the master press agent of all time." The risk, of course, was great, for it would be acutely embarrassing if the facts leaked out during the coming campaign. It may have been the risk itself that tempted Roosevelt, for he loved a prank and loved danger for its own sake; if he could combine danger with what William Allen White called a "frolicking intrigue," his happiness was complete.

Next day, June 22, the memorable telegram "This Government wants Perdicaris alive or Raisuli dead" flashed across the Atlantic cable over Hay's signature and was simultaneously given to the press at home. It was not an ultimatum, because Hay deliberately deprived it of meaningfulness by adding to Gummere, "Do not land marines or seize customs without Department's specific instructions." But this sentence was not allowed to spoil the effect: It was withheld from the press.

At Chicago, Uncle Joe Cannon, the salty perennial Speaker of the House, who was convention chairman, rapped with his gavel and read the telegram. The convention was electrified. Delegates sprang upon their chairs and hurrahed. Flags and handkerchiefs waved. Despite Hay's signature, everyone saw the Roosevelt teeth, cliché of a hundred cartoons, gleaming whitely behind it. "Magnificent, magnificent!" pronounced Senator Depew. "The people want an administration that will stand by its citizens, even if it takes the fleet to do it," said Representative Dwight of New York, expressing the essence of popular feeling. "Roosevelt and Hay know what they are doing," said a Kansas delegate. "Our people like courage. We'll stand for anything those two men do." "Good hot stuff and echoes my sentiments," said another delegate. The genius of its timing and phrasing, wrote a reporter, "gave the candidate the maximum benefit of the thrill that was needed." Although the public was inclined to credit authorship to Roosevelt, the Baltimore *Sun* pointed out that Mr. Hay too knew how to make the eagle scream when he wanted to. Hay's diary agreed. "My telegram to Gummere," he noted comfortably the day afterward, "had an uncalled for success. It is curious how a concise impropriety hits the public."

After nominating Roosevelt by acclamation, the convention departed in an exhilarated mood. In Morocco a settlement had been reached before receipt of the telegram. Raisuli was ready at last to return his captives. Mounted on a "great, grey charger," he personally escorted Perdicaris and Varley on the ride down from the mountains, pointing out on the way the admirable effect of pink and violet shadows cast by the rising sun on the rocks. They met the ransom party, with thirty pack mules bearing boxes of Spanish silver dollars, half way down. Payment was made and prisoners exchanged, and Perdicaris took leave, as he afterward wrote, of "one of the most interesting and kindly-hearted native gentlemen" he had ever known, whose "singular gentleness and courtesy . . . quite endeared him to us." At nightfall, as he rode into Tangier and saw the signal lights of the American warships twinkling the news of his release, Perdicaris was overcome with patriotic emotion at "such proof of his country's solicitude for its citizens and for the honor of its flag!" Few indeed are the Americans, he wrote to Gummere in a masterpiece of understatement, "who can have appreciated as keenly as I did then what the presence of our Flag in foreign waters meant at such a moment and in such circumstances."

Only afterward, when it was all over, did the State Department 40 inform Gummere how keen indeed was Perdicaris' cause for appreciation. "Overwhelmed with amazement" and highly indignant, Gummere extracted from Perdicaris a full, written confession of his forty-year-old secret. He admitted that he had never in ensuing years taken steps to resume American citizenship because, as he ingenuously explained, having been born an American, he disliked the idea of having to become naturalized, and so "I continued to consider myself an American citizen." Since Perdicaris perfectly understood that the American government was in no position to take action against him, his letter made no great pretension of remorse.

Perdicaris retired to England for his remaining years. Raisuli duly became governor of the Tangier districts in place of the false-hearted Bashaw. The French, in view of recent disorders, acquired the right to police Morocco (provoking the Kaiser's notorious descent upon Tangier). The Sultan, weakened and humiliated by Raisuli's triumph, was shortly dethroned by a brother. Gummere was officially congratulated and subsequently appointed minister to Morocco and American delegate to the Algeciras Conference. Sir Arthur Nicolson took "a long leave of absence," the Wazan brothers received handsomely decorated Winchester rifles with suitable inscriptions from Mr. Roosevelt, Hay received the Grand Cross of the Legion of Honor, and Roosevelt was elected in November by the largest popular majority ever given to a presidential candidate.

"As to Paregoric or is it Pericarditis," wrote Hay to Assistant Secretary Adee on September 3, "it is a bad business. We must keep it excessively confidential for the present." They succeeded. Officials in the know held their breath during the campaign, but no hint leaked out either then or during the remaining year of Hay's lifetime or during Roosevelt's lifetime. As a result of the episode, Roosevelt's administration proposed a new citizenship law which was introduced in Congress in 1905 and enacted in 1907, but the name of the errant gentleman who inspired it was never mentioned during the debates. The truth about

Perdicaris remained unknown to the public until 1933, when Tyler Dennett gave it away—in one paragraph in his biography of John Hay.

August 1959

Lines of Inquiry
" 'Perdicaris Alive or Raisuli Dead' "

Tuchman's story of this brief historical incident includes quite a few characters, events, and significant details. What techniques does she use to introduce the characters and to distinguish the most important figures from the minor functionaries? How does she select and organize details in the telling of the story to keep it clear, suspenseful, and surprising? Why does she weave back and forth between details pertaining to the hostage incident and details about concurrent events such as the Republican Convention? Why doesn't she focus on the hostage incident alone?

The fact that Perdicaris turns out to have been a Greek rather than American citizen is one of many ironies in this story. Why does Tuchman make so much of this ironic fact in the middle and at the end of the story? Why doesn't she take note of his Greek citizenship at the beginning of the piece when she first introduces him? How does this irony contribute to the significance of the story? What does it suggest about the workings of history and the conduct of American foreign policy? What other ironic facts or surprising sidelights does Tuchman reveal in the process of the story? What do these facts and sidelights suggest about the workings of history and of American foreign policy?

How do historical views of an incident compare with a journalistic approach to it? For example, consult the *New York Times* accounts of the incident during the months of May and June, 1904, to see what similarities, what differences, you notice between their handling of the story and Tuchman's. Then consult the London *Times* for the same period. What are the most striking differences that you notice between Tuchman's account and the journalistic accounts, as well as between the American and English accounts? How do you explain these differences?

Mankind's Better Moments

For a change from prevailing pessimism, I should like to recall some of the positive and even admirable capacities of the human race. We hear very little of them lately. Ours is not a time of self-esteem or self-confidence—as was, for instance, the nineteenth century, when self-esteem may be seen oozing from its portraits. Victorians, especially the men, pictured themselves as erect, noble, and splendidly handsome. Our self-image looks more like Woody Allen or a character from Samuel Beckett. Amid a mass of worldwide troubles and a poor record for the twentieth century, we see our species—with cause—as functioning very badly, as blunderers when not knaves, as violent, ignoble, corrupt, inept, incapable of mastering the forces that threaten us, weakly subject to our worst instincts; in short, decadent.

The catalogue is familiar and valid, but it is growing tiresome. A study of history reminds one that mankind has its ups and downs and during the ups has accomplished many brave and beautiful things, exerted stupendous endeavors, explored and conquered oceans and wilderness, achieved marvels of beauty in the creative arts and marvels of science and social progress; has loved liberty with a passion that throughout history has led men to fight and die for it over and over again; has pursued knowledge, exercised reason, enjoyed laughter and pleasures, played games with zest, shown courage, heroism, altruism, honor, and decency; experienced love; known comfort, contentment, and occasionally happiness. All these qualities have been part of human experience, and if they have not had as important notice as the negatives nor exerted as wide and persistent an influence as the evils we do, they nevertheless deserve attention, for they are currently all but forgotten.

Among the great endeavors, we have in our own time carried men to the moon and brought them back safely—surely one of the most remarkable achievements in history. Some may disapprove of the effort as unproductive, too costly, and a wrong choice of priorities in relation to greater needs, all of which may be true but does not, as I see it, diminish the achievement. If you look carefully, all positives have a negative underside—sometimes more, sometimes less—and not all admirable endeavors have admirable motives. Some have sad consequences. Although most signs presently point from bad to worse, human capacities are probably what they have always been. If primitive man

could discover how to transform grain into bread, and reeds growing
by the riverbank into baskets; if his successors could invent the wheel,
harness the insubstantial air to turn a millstone, transform sheep's wool,
flax, and worms' cocoons into fabric—we, I imagine, will find a way
to manage the energy problem.

Consider how the Dutch accomplished the miracle of making land
out of sea. By progressive enclosure of the Zuider Zee over the last
sixty years, they have added half a million acres to their country, enlarging its area by eight percent and providing homes, farms, and towns
for close to a quarter of a million people. The will to do the impossible,
the spirit of can-do that overtakes our species now and then, was never
more manifest than in this earth-altering act by the smallest of the major European nations.

A low-lying, windswept, waterlogged land, partly below sea level,   5
pitted with marshes, rivers, lakes, and inlets, sliding all along its outer
edge into the stormy North Sea with only fragile sand dunes as nature's
barrier against the waves, Holland, in spite of physical disadvantages,
has made itself into one of the most densely populated, orderly, prosperous, and, at one stage of its history, dominant nations of the West.
For centuries, ever since the first inhabitants, fleeing enemy tribes, settled in the bogs where no one cared to bother them, the Dutch struggled against water and learned how to live with it: building on mounds,
constructing and reconstructing seawalls of clay mixed with straw, carrying mud in an endless train of baskets, laying willow mattresses
weighted with stones, repairing each spring the winter's damage, draining marshes, channeling streams, building ramps to their attics to save
the cattle in times of flood, gaining dike-enclosed land from the waves
in one place and losing as much to the revengeful ocean somewhere
else, progressively developing methods to cope with their eternal antagonist.

The Zuider Zee was a tidal gulf penetrating eighty miles into the
land over an area ten to thirty miles wide. The plan to close off the sea
by a dam across the entire mouth of the gulf had long been contemplated but never adopted, for fear of the cost, until a massive flood in
1916, which left saltwater standing on all the farmlands north of Am-
sterdam, forced the issue. The act for enclosure was passed unani-
mously by both houses of Parliament in 1918. As large in ambition as
the country was small, the plan called for a twenty-mile dike from shore
to shore, rising twenty feet above sea level, wide enough at the top to
carry an auto road and housing for the hydraulic works, and as much
as six hundred feet wide on the sea bottom. The first cartload of gravel
was dumped in 1920.

The dike was but part of the task. The inland sea it formed had to
be drained of its saltwater and transformed from salt to fresh by the
inflow from lower branches of the Rhine. Four polders, or areas rising

from the shallows, would be lifted by the draining process from under water into the open air. Secondary dikes, pumping stations, sluices, drainage ditches to control the inflow, as well as locks and inland ports for navigation, had to be built, the polder lands restored to fertility, trees planted, roads, bridges, and rural and urban housing constructed, the whole scheduled for completion in sixty years.

The best-laid plans of engineers met errors and hazards. During construction, gravel that had been painstakingly dumped within sunken frameworks would be washed away in a night by heavy currents or a capricious storm. Means proved vulnerable, methods sometimes unworkable. Yet slowly the dike advanced from each shore toward the center. As the gap narrowed, the pressure of the tidal current rushing through increased daily in force, carrying away material at the base, undermining the structure, and threatening to prevent a final closing. In the last days a herd of floating derricks, dredges, barges, and every piece of available equipment was mustered at the spot, and fill was desperately poured in before the next return of the tide, due in twelve hours. At this point, gale winds were reported moving in. The check dam to protect the last gap showed signs of giving way; operations were hurriedly moved thirty yards inward. Suspense was now extreme. Roaring and foaming with sand, the tide threw itself upon the narrowing passage; the machines closed in, filled the last space in the dike, and it held. Men stood that day in 1932 where the North Sea's waves had held dominion for seven hundred years.

As the dry land appeared, the first comers to take possession were the birds. Gradually, decade by decade, crops, homes, and civilization followed, and unhappily, too, man's destructive intervention. In World War II the retreating Germans blew up a section of the dike, completely flooding the western polder, but by the end of the year the Dutch had pumped it dry, resowed the fields in the spring, and over the next seven years restored the polder's farms and villages. Weather, however, is never conquered. The disastrous floods of 1953 laid most of coastal Holland under water. The Dutch dried themselves out and, while the work at Zuider Zee continued, applied its lessons elsewhere and lent their hydraulic skills to other countries. Today the *Afsluitdijk,* or Zuider Zee road, is a normal thoroughfare. To drive across it between the sullen ocean on one side and new land on the other is for that moment to feel optimism for the human race.

Great endeavor requires vision and some kind of compelling impulse, not necessarily practical as in the case of the Dutch, but sometimes less definable, more exalted, as the case of the Gothic cathedrals of the Middle Ages. The architectural explosion that produced this multitude of soaring vaults—arched, ribbed, pierced with jeweled light, studded with thousands of figures of the stone-carvers' art—represents in size, splen-   10 dor, and numbers one of the great, permanent artistic achievements of human hands. What accounts for it? Not religious fervor alone but the zeal of a dynamic age, a desire to outdo, an ambition for the biggest and the best. Only the general will, shared by nobles, merchants, guilds, artisans, and commoners, could command the resources and labor to sustain so great an undertaking. Each group contributed donations, especially the magnates of commerce, who felt relieved thereby from the guilt of money-making. Voluntary work programs involved all classes. "Who has ever seen or heard tell in times past," wrote an observer, "that powerful princes of the world, that men brought up in honors and wealth, that nobles—men and women—have bent their haughty necks to the harness of carts and, like beasts of burden, have dragged to the abode of Christ these wagons loaded with wines, grains, oil, stones, timber and all that is necessary for the construction of the church?"

Abbot Suger, whose renovation of St.-Denis is considered the start of Gothic architecture, embodied the spirit of the builders. Determined to create the most splendid basilica in Christendom, he supervised every aspect of the work from fund-raising to decoration, and caused his name to be inscribed for immortality on keystones and capitals. He lay awake worrying, as he tells us, where to find trees large enough for the beams, and went personally with his carpenters to the forest to question the woodcutters under oath. When they swore that nothing of the kind he wanted could be found in the area, he insisted on searching for them himself and, after nine hours of scrambling through thorns and thickets, succeeded in locating and marking twelve trees of the necessary size.

Mainly the compelling impulse lay in the towns, where, in those years, economic and political strengths and wealth were accumulating. Amiens, the thriving capital of Picardy, decided to build the largest church in France, "higher than all the saints, higher than all the kings." For the necessary space, the hospital and bishop's palace had to be relocated and the city walls moved back. At the same time Beauvais, a neighbor town, raised a vault over the crossing of transept and nave to an unprecedented height of 158 feet, the apogee of architects' daring in its day. It proved too daring, for the height of the columns and spread of the supporters caused the vault to collapse after twelve years. Repaired with undaunted purpose, it was defiantly topped by a spire rising 492 feet above ground, the tallest in France. Beauvais, having used up its resources, never built the nave, leaving a structure foreshortened but glorious. The interior is a fantasy of soaring space; to enter is to stand dazed in wonder, breathless in admiration.

The higher and lighter grew the buildings and the slenderer the columns, the more new expedients and techniques had to be devised to hold them up. Buttresses flew like angels' wings against the exteriors. This was a period of innovation and audacity, and a limitless spirit of excelsior. In a single century, from 1170 to 1270, six hundred cathedrals and major churches were built in France alone. In England in that period, the cathedral of Salisbury, with the tallest spire in the country, was completed in thirty-eight years. The spire of Freiburg in Germany was constructed entirely of filigree in stone as if spun by some supernatural spider. In the St.-Chapelle in Paris the fifteen miraculous windows swallow the walls; they have become the whole.

Embellishment was integral to the construction. Reims is populated by five thousand statues of saints, prophets, kings and cardinals, bishops, knights, ladies, craftsmen and commoners, devils, animals and birds. Every type of leaf known in northern France is said to appear in the decoration. In carving, stained glass, and sculpture the cathedrals displayed the art of medieval hands, and the marvel of these buildings is permanent even when they no longer play a central role in everyday life. Rodin said he could feel the beauty and presence of Reims even at night when he could not see it. "Its power," he wrote, "transcends the senses so that the eye sees what it sees not."

Explanations for the extraordinary burst that produced the cathedrals are several. Art historians will tell you that it was the invention of the ribbed vault. Religious historians will say it was the product of an age of faith which believed that with God's favor anything was possible; in fact it was not a period of untroubled faith, but of heresies and Inquisition. Rather, one can only say that conditions were right. Social order under monarchy and the towns was replacing the anarchy of the barons, so that existence was no longer merely a struggle to stay alive but allowed a surplus of goods and energies and greater opportunity for mutual effort. Banking and commerce were producing capital, roads were making possible wheeled transport, universities nourishing ideas and communication. It was one of history's high tides, an age of vigor, confidence, and forces converging to quicken the blood.

Even when the historical tide is low, a particular group of doers may emerge in exploits that inspire awe. Shrouded in the mists of the eighth century, long before the cathedrals, Viking seamanship was a wonder of daring, stamina and skill. Pushing relentlessly outward in open boats, the Vikings sailed south, around Spain to North Africa and Arabia, north to the top of the world, west across uncharted seas to American coasts. They hauled their boats overland from the Baltic to make their way down Russian rivers to the Black Sea. Why? We do not know what engine drove them, only that it was part of the human endowment.

What of the founding of our own country, America? We take the *Mayflower* for granted—yet think of the boldness, the enterprise, the determined independence, the sheer grit it took to leave the known and set out across the sea for the unknown where no houses or food, no stores, no cleared land, no crops or livestock, none of the equipment or settlement of organized living awaited.

Equally bold was the enterprise of the French in the northern forests of the American continent, who throughout the seventeenth century explored and opened the land from the St. Lawrence to the Mississippi, from the Great Lakes to the Gulf of Mexico. They came not for liberty like the Pilgrims, but for gain and dominion, whether in spiritual empire for the Jesuits or in land, glory, and riches for the agents of the King; and rarely in history have men willingly embraced such hardship, such daunting adventure, and persisted with such tenacity and endurance. They met hunger, exhaustion, frostbite, capture and torture by Indians, wounds and disease, dangerous rapids, swarms of insects, long portages, bitter weather, and hardly ever did those who suffered the experience fail to return, re-enter the menacing but bountiful forest, and pit themselves once more against danger, pain, and death.

Above all others, the perseverance of La Salle in his search for the mouth of the Mississippi was unsurpassed. While preparing in Quebec, he mastered eight Indian languages. From then on he suffered accidents, betrayals, desertions, losses of men and provisions, fever and snow blindness, the hostility and intrigues of rivals who incited the Indians against him and plotted to ambush or poison him. He was truly pursued, as Francis Parkman wrote, by "a demon of havoc." Paddling through heavy waves in a storm over Lake Ontario, he waded through freezing surf to beach the canoes each night, and lost guns and baggage when a canoe was swamped and sank. To lay foundations of a fort above Niagara, frozen ground had to be thawed by boiling water. When the fort was at last built, La Salle christened it Crèvecoeur—that is, Heartbreak. It earned the name when in his absence it was plundered and deserted by its half-starved mutinous garrison. Farther on, a friendly Indian village, intended as a destination, was found laid waste by the Iroquois with only charred stakes stuck with skulls standing among the ashes, while wolves and buzzards prowled through the remains.

When at last, after four months' hazardous journey down the Great 20
River, La Salle reached the sea, he formally took possession in the name of Louis XIV of all the country from the river's mouth to its source and of its tributaries—that is, of the vast basin of the Mississippi from the Rockies to the Appalachians—and named it Louisiana. The validity of the claim, which seems so hollow to us (though successful in its own time), is not the point. What counts is the conquest of fearful adversity by one man's extraordinary exertions and inflexible will.

Happily, man has a capacity for pleasure too, and in contriving ways to entertain and amuse himself has created brilliance and delight. Pageants, carnivals, festivals, fireworks, music, dancing and drama, parties and picnics, sports and games, the comic spirit and its gift of laughter—

all the range of enjoyment from grand ceremonial to the quiet solitude of a day's fishing has helped to balance the world's infelicity.

The original Olympic Games held every fourth year in honor of Zeus was the most celebrated festival of classic times, of such significance to the Greeks that they dated their history from the first games in 776 B.C. as we date ours from the birth of Christ. The crown of olive awarded to the winner in each contest was considered the crown of happiness. While the Romans took this to be a sign of the essential frivolity of the Greek character, the ancient games endured for twelve centuries, a longer span than the supremacy of Rome.

Homo ludens, man at play, is surely as significant a figure as man at war or at work. In human activity the invention of the ball may be said to rank with the invention of the wheel. Imagine America without baseball, Europe without soccer, England without cricket, the Italians without bocci, China without Ping-Pong, and tennis for no one. Even stern John Calvin, the examplar of Puritan self-denial, was once discovered playing bowls on Sunday, and in 1611 an English supply ship arriving at Jamestown found the starving colonists suppressing their misery in the same game. Cornhuskings, logrollings, barn-raisings, horseraces, and wrestling and boxing matches have engaged America as, somewhat more passively, the armchair watching of football and basketball does today.

Play was invented for diversion, exertion, and escape from routine cares. In colonial New York, sleighing parties preceded by fiddlers on horseback drove out to country inns, where, according to a participant, "we danced, sang, romped, ate and drank and kicked away care from morning to night." John Audubon, present at a barbecue and dance on the Kentucky frontier, wrote, "Every countenance beamed with joy, every heart leaped with gladness . . . care and sorrow were flung to the winds."

Play has its underside, too, in the gladiatorial games, in cockfights 20 and prizefights, which arouse one of the least agreeable of human characteristics, pleasure in blood and brutality, but in relation to play as a whole, this is minor.

Much of our pleasure derives from eating and sex, two components which have received an excess of attention in our time—allowing me to leave them aside as understood, except to note how closely they are allied. All those recipes, cuisines, exotic foods, and utensils of kitchen chic seem to proliferate in proportion to pornography, sex therapy, blue movies, and instructive tales for children on pederasty and incest. Whether this twin increase signifies decadence or liberation is disputable. Let us move on to other ground.

To the carnival, for instance. Mardi Gras in all its forms is an excuse for letting go; for uninhibited fun before the abstinence of Lent; for dressing up, play-acting, cavorting in costumes and masks, constructing imaginative floats; for noise, pranks, jokes, battles of flowers and confetti, balls and banquets, singing and dancing, and fireworks. In the Belgian carnival of Gilles-Binche, originating in the sixteenth century in honor of Charles V's conquest of Peru, the dancers are spectacular in superlatively tall feather headdresses representing the Incas, and brilliant costumes trimmed with gold lace and tinkling bells. They wear wooden shoes to stamp out the rhythm of their dance and carry baskets of oranges symbolizing the treasures of Peru with which they pelt the onlookers. In the celebrated Palio of Siena at harvest time, a horse and rider from each neighborhood race madly around a sloping cobblestoned course in the public square, while the citizens shriek in passionate rivalry. Walpurgis Night on the eve of May Day is an excuse for bacchanalia in the guise of witches' revels; winter's festival at Christmas is celebrated by gift-giving. Humanity has invented infinite ways to enjoy itself.

No people have invented more ways than have the Chinese, perhaps to balance floods, famine, warlords, and other ills of fate. The clang of gongs, clashing of cymbals, and beating of drums sound through their long history. No month is without fairs and theatricals when streets are hung with fantasies of painted lanterns and crowded with "carriages that flow like water, horses like roaming dragons." Night skies are illuminated by firecrackers—a Chinese invention—bursting in the form of peonies, flowerpots, fiery devils. The ways of pleasure are myriad. Music plays in the air through bamboo whistles of different pitch tied to the wings of circling pigeons. To skim a frozen lake in an ice sleigh with a group of friends on a day when the sun is warm is rapture, like "moving in a cup of jade." What more delightful than the ancient festival called "Half an Immortal," when everyone from palace officials to the common man took a ride on a swing? When high in the air, one felt like an Immortal; when back to earth once again, human—no more than to be for an instant a god.

In Europe's age of grandeur, princes devised pageants of dazzling splendor to express their magnificence, none more spectacular than the extravaganza of 1660 celebrating the marriage of Leopold I of Austria to the Infanta of Spain. As the climax to festivities lasting three months, an equestrian contest of the Four Elements was performed in the grand plaza, each element represented by a company of a thousand, gorgeously costumed. Water's company were dressed in blue and silver covered with fish scales and shells; Air's in gold brocade shaded in the colors of the rainbow; Earth's decorated with flowers; Fire's with curling flames. Neptune, surrounded by marine monsters and winds, rode in a car drawn by a huge whale spouting water. Earth's car contained a garden with Pan and shepherds, drawn by elephants with castles on their backs; Air rode a dragon escorted by thirty griffins; Fire was accompanied by Vulcan, thirty Cyclopes, and a flame-spouting salamander. A rather irrelevant ship carrying the Argonauts to the Golden Fleece was added for extras. The contest was resolved when a star-studded globe, arched by an artificial rainbow representing Peace, rolled across the plaza and opened to display a Temple of Immortality from which emerged riders impersonating the fifteen previous Hapsburg emperors, ending with Leopold in person. Dressed as Glory, in silver lace and diamonds, and wearing his crown, he rode in a silver seashell drawn by eight white horses and carrying seven singers in jeweled robes, who sere-naded the Infanta. Then followed the climactic equestrian ballet per-formed by four groups of eight cavaliers each, whose elaborate movements were marked by trumpet flourishes, kettledrums, and can-non salutes. In a grand finale a thousand rockets blazed from two arti-ficial mountains named Parnassus and Aetna, and the sky was lit in triumph by the Hapsburg acrostic AEIOU standing for *Austria Est Imper-are Omne Universo,* meaning, approximately, "Austria rules the world."

The motive may have been self-aggrandizement, but the results were 25 sumptuous and exciting; viewers were enthralled, performers proud, and the designer of the pageant was made a baron. It was a case of men and women engaged in the art of enjoyment, a function common to all times, although one would hardly know it from today's image of our-selves as wretched creatures forever agonizing over petty squalors of sex and drink as if we had no other recourse or destiny.

The greatest recourse, and mankind's most enduring achievement, is art. At its best, it reveals the nobility that coexists in human nature along with flaws and evils, and the beauty and truth it can perceive. Whether in music or architecture, literature, painting or sculpture, art opens our eyes, ears, and feelings to something beyond ourselves, something we cannot experience without the artist's vision and the ge-nius of his craft. The placing of Greek temples, like the Temple of Poseidon on the promontory at Sunion, outlined against the piercing blue of the Aegean Sea, Poseidon's home; the majesty of Michelange-lo's sculptured figures in stone; Shakespeare's command of language and knowledge of the human soul; the intricate order of Bach, the en-chantment of Mozart; the purity of Chinese monochrome pottery with its lovely names—celadon, oxblood, peach blossom, clair de lune; the exuberance of Tiepolo's ceilings where, without picture frames to limit movement, a whole world in exquisitely beautiful colors lives and moves in the sky; the prose and poetry of all the writers from Homer to Cer-vantes to Jane Austen and John Keats to Dostoevski and Chekhov—who made all these things? We—our species—did. The range is too vast and various to do justice to it in this space, but the random samples I have mentioned, and all the rest they suggest, are sufficient reason to honor mankind.

If we have (as I think) lost beauty and elegance in the modern world, we have gained much, through science and technology and democratic pressures, in the material well-being of the masses. The change in the lives of, and society's attitude toward, the working class marks the great divide between the modern world and the old regime. From the French Revolution through the brutal labor wars of the nineteenth and twentieth centuries, the change was earned mainly by force against fierce and often vicious opposition. While this was a harsh process, it developed and activated a social conscience hardly operative before. Slavery, beggary, unaided misery, and want have, on the whole, been eliminated in the developed nations of the West. That much is a credit in the human record, even if the world is uglier as a result of adapting to mass values. History generally arranges these things so that gain is balanced by loss, perhaps in order not to make the gods jealous.

The material miracles wrought by science and technology—from the harnessing of steam and electricity to anesthesia, antisepsis, antibiotics, and woman's liberator, the washing machine, and all the labor-savers that go with it—are too well recognized in our culture to need my emphasis. Pasteur is as great a figure in the human record as Michelangelo or Mozart—probably, as far as the general welfare is concerned, greater. We are more aware of his kind of accomplishment than of those less tangible. Ask anyone to suggest the credits of mankind and the answer is likely to start with physical things. Yet the underside of scientific progress is prominent and dark. The weaponry of war in its ever-widening capacity to kill is the deadly example, and who is prepared to state with confidence that the over-all effect of the automobile, airplane, telephone, television, and computer has been, on balance, beneficent?

Pursuit of knowledge for its own sake has been a more certain good. There was a springtime in the eighteenth century when, through knowledge and reason, everything seemed possible; when reason was expected to break through religious dogma like the sun breaking through fog, and man, armed with knowledge and reason, would be able at last to control his own fate and construct a good society. The theory that because this world exists it is the best of all possible worlds spread outward from Leibniz; the word "optimism" was used for the first time in 1737.

What a burst of intellectual energies shook these decades! In twenty years, 1735–55, Linnaeus named and classified all of known botany, Buffon systematized natural history in thirty-six volumes, and an American, John Bartram, scoured the wilderness for plants to send to correspondents in Europe. Voltaire, Montesquieu, and Hume investigated the nature of man and the moral foundations of law and society. Benjamin Franklin demonstrated electricity from lightning. Dr. Johnson by himself compiled the first dictionary of the English language; Diderot and the Encyclopedists of France undertook to present the whole of knowledge in enlightened terms. The Chinese secret of making porcelain having been uncovered by Europeans, its manufacture flourished at Meissen and Dresden. Clearing for the Place de la Concorde, to be the most majestic in Europe, was begun in Paris. No less than 150 newspapers and journals circulated in England. The novel was exuberantly born in the work of Richardson and Fielding. Chardin, a supreme artist, portrayed humanity with a loving brush in his gentle domestic scenes. Hogarth, seeing another creature, exposed the underside in all its ribaldry and squalor. It was an age of enthusiasm; at the first London performance of Handel's *Messiah* in 1743, George II was so carried away by the "Hallelujah Chorus" that he rose to his feet, causing the whole audience to stand with him and thereby establishing a custom still sometimes followed by *Messiah* audiences. The man in whom the spirit of the age was to flower, Thomas Jefferson, was born.

If the twenty-year period is stretched by another ten, it includes the reverberating voice of Rousseau's *Social Contract,* Beccaria's ground-breaking study *Essay on Crimes and Punishment,* Gibbon's beginning of the *Decline and Fall,* and, despite the Lisbon earthquake and *Candide,* the admission of "optimism" into the dictionary of the Académie Française.

Although the Enlightenment may have overestimated the power of reason to guide human conduct, it nevertheless opened to men and women a more humane view of their fellow passengers. Slowly the harshest habits gave way to reform—in treatment of the insane, reduction of death penalties, mitigation of the fierce laws against debtors and poachers, and in the passionately fought cause for abolition of the slave trade.

The humanitarian movement was not charity, which always carries an overtone of being done in the donor's interest, but a more disinterested benevolence or altruism, motivated by conscience. It was personified in William Wilberforce, who in the later eighteenth century stirred the great rebellion of the English conscience against the trade in human beings. In America the immorality of slavery had long troubled the colonies. By 1789 slavery had been legally abolished by the New England states followed by New York, New Jersey, and Pennsylvania, but the southern states, as their price for joining the Union, insisted that the subject be excluded from the Constitution.

In England, where the home economy did not depend on slave labor, Wilberforce had more scope. His influence could have carried him to the Prime Minister's seat if personal power had been his goal, but he channeled his life instead toward a goal for mankind. He instigated, energized, inspired a movement whose members held meetings, organized petitions, collected information on the horrors of the middle passage, showered pamphlets on the public, gathered Non-conformist middle-class sentiment into a swelling tide that, in Trevelyan's phrase, "melted the hard prudence of statesmen." Abolition of the slave trade under the British flag was won in 1807. The British Navy was used to enforce the ban by searches on the high seas and regular patrols of the African coast. When Portugal and Spain were persuaded to join in the prohibition, they were paid a compensation of £300,000 and £400,000 respectively by the British taxpayer. Violations and smuggling continued, convincing the abolitionists that, in order to stop the trade, slavery itself had to be abolished. Agitation resumed. By degrees over the next quarter-century, compensation reduced the opposition of the West Indian slave-owners and their allies in England until emancipation of all slaves in the British Empire was enacted in 1833. The total cost to the British taxpayer was reckoned at £20 million.

Through recent unpleasant experiences we have learned to expect   35
ambition, greed, or corruption to reveal itself behind every public act, but, as we have just seen, it is not invariably so. Human beings do possess better impulses, and occasionally act upon them, even in the twentieth century. Occupied Denmark, during World War II, outraged by Nazi orders for deportation of its Jewish fellow citizens, summoned the courage of defiance and transformed itself into a united underground railway to smuggle virtually all eight thousand Danish Jews out to Sweden, and Sweden gave them shelter. Far away and unconnected, a village in southern France, Le Chambon-sur-Lignon, devoted itself to rescuing Jews and other victims of the Nazis at the risk of the inhabitants' own lives and freedom. "Saving lives became a hobby of the people of Le Chambon," said one of them. The larger record of the time was admittedly collaboration, passive or active. We cannot reckon on the better impulses predominating in the world, only that they will always appear.

The strongest of these in history, summoner of the best in men, has been zeal for liberty. Time after time, in some spot somewhere on the globe, people have risen in what Swinburne called the "divine right of insurrection"—to overthrow despots, repel alien conquerors, achieve independence—and so it will be until the day power ceases to corrupt, which, I think, is not a near expectation.

The ancient Jews rose three times against alien rulers, beginning with the revolt of the Maccabees against the effort of Antiochus to outlaw observance of the Jewish faith. Mattathias the priest and his five sons, assembling loyal believers in the mountains, opened a guerrilla war which, after the father's death, was to find a leader of military genius in his son Judah, called Maccabee or the Hammer. Later honored in the Middle Ages as one of the Nine Worthies of the world, he defeated his enemies, rededicated the temple, and re-established the independence of Judea. In the next century the uprising of the Zealots against Roman rule was fanatically and hopelessly pursued through famines, sieges, the fall of Jerusalem and destruction of the temple until a last stand of fewer than a thousand on the rock of Masada ended in group suicide in preference to surrender. After sixty years as an occupied province, Judea rose yet again under Simon Bar Kochba, who regained

Jerusalem for a brief moment of Jewish control but could not withstand the arms of Hadrian. The rebellion was crushed, but the zeal for selfhood, smoldering in exile through eighteen centuries, was to revive and regain its home in our time.

The phenomenon continues in our day, in Algeria, in Vietnam, although, seen at close quarters and more often than not manipulated by outsiders, contemporary movements seem less pure and heroic than those polished by history's gloss—as, for instance, the Scots under William Wallace, the Swiss against the Hapsburgs, the American colonies against the mother country.

I have always cherished the spirited rejoinder of one of the great colonial landowners of New York, who, on being advised not to risk his property by signing the Declaration of Independence, replied, "Damn the property; give me the pen!" On seeking confirmation for purposes of this essay, I am deeply chagrined to report that the saying appears to be apocryphal. Yet not its spirit, for the signers well knew they were risking their property, not to mention their heads, by putting their names to the Declaration.

Nor did they escape. Left vulnerable by Washington's defeat on Long Island, their estates were deliberately wrecked by the British, their homes ransacked and looted, books and papers burned, furniture smashed, livestock and stores destroyed, tenants and servants driven out, a thousand acres of Lewis Morris' timberland left in stumps. All were reduced to living by the charity of friends during the war. Philip Livingston died without ever seeing his home and lands again; the rich merchant William Floyd was permanently ruined. Other affluent men who signed had much to lose—Hancock of Massachusetts, who wrote his name large so that no one would mistake it, Lee of Virginia, Carroll of Baltimore. George Washington himself epitomized the spirit later in the war when he wrote to reproach his overseer at Mount Vernon for supplying provisions to a British landing party that had sailed up to the Potomac and threatened to burn the estate unless their demands were met. It would have been "less painful," he wrote, to have learned that, as a result of refusal, "they had burnt my House and laid my plantation in ruins." Economic self-interest, as this illustrates, is not always our guiding instinct.

So far I have considered qualities of the group rather than of the individual—except for art, which in most cases is a product of the single spirit. Happiness, too, is an individual matter. It springs up here or there, haphazard, random, without origin or explanation. It resists study, laughs at sociology, flourishes, vanishes, reappears somewhere else. Take Izaak Walton, author of *The Compleat Angler,* that guide to contentment as well as fishing, of which Charles Lamb said, "It would sweeten any man's temper at any time to read it." Though Walton lived in distracted times of revolution and regicide, though he adhered to the losing side in the English Civil War, though he lost in their infancy all seven children by his first wife and the eldest son of his second marriage, though he was twice a widower, his misfortunes could not sour an essentially buoyant nature. "He passed through turmoil," in the words of a biographer, "ever accompanied by content."

Walton's secret was friendship. Born to a yeoman family and apprenticed in youth as an ironmonger, he managed to gain an education and, through sweetness of disposition and a cheerful religious faith, became a friend on equal terms of various learned clergymen and poets whose lives he wrote and works he prefaced—among them John Donne, George Herbert, and Michael Drayton. Another companion, Charles Cotton, wrote of Izaak, "In him I have the happiness to know the worthiest man, and to enjoy the best and truest friend any man ever had."

The Compleat Angler, published when the author was sixty, glows in the sunshine of his character. In it are humor and piety, grave advice on the idiosyncrasies of fish and the niceties of landing them, delight in nature and in music. Walton saw five editions reprinted in his lifetime, while unnumerable later editions secured him immortality. The surviving son by his second wife became a clergyman; the surviving daughter married one and gave her father a home among grandchildren. He wrote his last work at eighty-five and died at ninety after being celebrated in verse by one of his circle as a "happy old man" whose life "showed how to compass true felicity." Let us think of him when we grumble.

Is anything to be learned from my survey? I raise the question only because most people want history to teach them lessons, which I believe it can do, although I am less sure we can use them when needed. I gathered these examples not to teach but merely to remind people in a despondent era that the good in mankind operates even if the bad secures more attention. I am aware that selecting out the better moments does not result in a realistic picture. Turn them over and there is likely to be a darker side, as when Project Apollo, our journey to the moon, was authorized because its glamour could obtain subsidies for rocket and missile development that otherwise might not have been forthcoming. That is the way things are.

Whole philosophies have evolved over the question whether the human species is predominately good or evil. I only know that it is mixed, that you cannot separate good from bad, that wisdom, courage, and benevolence exist alongside knavery, greed, and stupidity; heroism and fortitude alongside vainglory, cruelty, and corruption.

It is a paradox of our time in the West that never have so many people been so relatively well off and never has society been more troubled. Yet I suspect that humanity's virtues have not vanished, although the experiences of our century seem to suggest that they are in abeyance. A century that took shape in the disillusion which followed the enormous effort and hopes of World War I, that saw revolution in Russia congeal into the same tyranny it overthrew, saw a supposedly civilized nation revert under the Nazis into organized and unparalleled savagery, saw the craven appeasement by the democracies, is understandably marked by suspicion of human nature. A literary historian, Van Wyck Brooks, discussing the 1920s and '30s, spoke of "an eschatological despair of the world." Whereas Whitman and Emerson, he wrote, "had been impressed by the worth and good sense of the people, writers of the new time" were struck by their lusts, cupidity, and violence, and had come to dislike their fellow men. The same theme reappeared in a recent play in which a mother struggled against her two "pitilessly contemptuous" children. Her problem was that she wanted them to be happy and they did not want to be. They preferred to watch horrors on television. In essence this is our epoch. It insists upon the flaws and corruptions, without belief in valor or virtue or the possibility of happiness. It keeps turning to look back on Sodom and Gommorah; it has no view of the Delectable Mountains.

We must keep a balance, and I know of no better prescription than a phrase from Condorcet's eulogy on the death of Benjamin Franklin: "He pardoned the present for the sake of the future."

April 1980

Lines of Inquiry
"Mankind's Better Moments"

Tuchman covers quite a wide range of human achievement in this piece. How do you account for her selection, arrangement, and proportioning of illustrative material? For example, why does she begin her survey of "mankind's better moments" with the story of the Dutch "making land out of sea" and end with the story of Izaak Walton's "happiness"? Why does she begin by moving from the present to the past—from the twentieth century Dutch to gothic cathedrals to Viking explorations? Why does she devote so much more space and detail to games, play, carnivals, and celebrations than to art, despite her claim that art is "mankind's most enduring achievement"? Why does she bring art, intellectual inquiry, "zeal for liberty," and happiness together within a single section at the end of the piece?

Though she begins her piece by claiming to seek "a change from prevailing pessimism" about the human race, Tuchman gradually includes details that reveal human beings to be "violent, ignoble, corrupt, inept," and so on. At what point in the essay did you first notice such details? At what point in the essay do such details figure most prominently in her discussion? Why do you suppose she includes them in her discussion? Given the mix of these details with the affirmative details that she emphasizes, how do you think Tuchman assesses human behavior and experience?

For other views of human nature and experience, look at Mead's "Warfare: An Invention—Not a Biological Necessity," Swift's "A Meditation upon a Broomstick," and Thomas' "The Iks." How do these authors differ from Tuchman in the way they write about human nature and behavior? How do they differ in their view of human nature and behavior? How do you account for the differences?

Is History a Guide to the Future?

The commonest question asked of historians by laymen is whether history serves a purpose. Is it useful? Can we learn from the lessons of history?

When people want history to be utilitarian and teach us lessons, that means they also want to be sure that it meets scientific standards. This, in my opinion, it cannot do, for reasons which I will come to in a moment. To practice history as a science is sociology, an altogether different discipline which I personally find antipathetic—although I suppose the sociologists would consider that my deficiency rather than theirs. The sociologists plod along with their noses to the ground assembling masses of statistics in order to arrive at some obvious conclusion which a reasonably perceptive historian, not to mention a large part of the general public, knows anyway, simply from observation—that social mobility is increasing, for instance, or that women have different problems from men. One wishes they would just cut loose someday, lift up their heads, and look at the world around them.

If history were a science, we should be able to get a grip on her, learn her ways, establish her patterns, know what will happen tomorrow. Why is it that we cannot? The answer lies in what I call the Unknowable Variable—namely, man. Human beings are always and finally the subject of history. History is the record of human behavior, the most fascinating subject of all, but illogical and so crammed with an unlimited number of variables that it is not susceptible of the scientific method nor of systematizing.

I say this bravely, even in the midst of the electronic age when computers are already chewing at the skirts of history in the process called Quantification. Applied to history, quantification, I believe, has its limits. It depends on a method called "data manipulation," which means that the facts, or data, of the historical past—that is, of human behavior—are manipulated into named categories so that they can be programmed into computers. Out comes—hopefully—a pattern. I can only tell you that for history "data manipulation" is a built-in invalidator, because to the degree that you manipulate your data to suit some extraneous requirement, in this case the requirements of the machine, to that degree your results will be suspect—and run the risk of being invalid. Everything depends on the naming of the categories and the assigning of facts to them, and this depends on the quantifier's individual judgment at the very base of the process. The categories are not revealed doctrine nor are the results scientific truth.

The hope for quantification, presumably, is that by processing a   5
vast quantity of material far beyond the capacity of the individual to
encompass, it can bring to light and establish reliable patterns. That
remains to be seen, but I am not optimistic. History has a way of escaping attempts to imprison it in patterns. Moreover, one of its basic
data is the human soul. The conventional historian, at least the one
concerned with truth, not propaganda, will try honestly to let his "data"
speak for themselves, but data which are shut up in prearranged boxes
are helpless. Their nuances have no voice. They must carry one fixed
meaning or another and weight the result accordingly. For instance, in
a quantification study of the origins of World War I which I have seen,
the operators have divided all the diplomatic documents, messages, and
utterances of the July crisis into categories labeled "hostility," "friendship," "frustration," "satisfaction," and so on, with each statement rated
for intensity on a scale from one to nine, including fractions. But no
pre-established categories could match all the private character traits and
public pressures variously operating on the nervous monarchs and ministers who were involved, The massive effort that went into this study
brought forth a mouse—the less than startling conclusion that the like-
lihood of war increased in proportion to the rise in hostility of the messages.

Quantification is really only a new approach to the old persistent
effort to make history fit a pattern, but *reliable* patterns, or what are
otherwise called the lessons of history, remain elusive.

For instance, suppose Woodrow Wilson had not been President of
the United States in 1914 but instead Theodore Roosevelt, who had
been his opponent in the election of 1912. Had that been the case, America
might have entered the war much earlier, perhaps at the time of the
Lusitania in 1915, with possible shortening of the war and incalculable
effects on history. Well, it happens that among the Anarchists in my
book *The Proud Tower* is an obscure Italian named Miguel Angiolillo,
whom nobody remembers but who shot dead Premier Canovas of Spain
in 1897. Canovas was a strong man who was just about to succeed in
quelling the rebels in Cuba when he was assassinated. Had he lived,
there might have been no extended Cuban insurrection for Americans
to get excited about, no Spanish-American War, no San Juan Hill, no
Rough Riders, no Vice-Presidency for Theodore Roosevelt to enable
him to succeed when another accident, another Anarchist, another unpredictable human being, killed McKinley. If Theodore had never been
President, there would have been no third party in 1912 to split the
Republicans, and Woodrow Wilson would not have been elected. The
speculations from that point on are limitless. To me it is comforting
rather than otherwise to feel that history is determined by the illogical
human record and not by large immutable scientific laws beyond our
power to deflect.

I know very little (a euphemism for "nothing") about laboratory science, but I have the impression that conclusions are supposed to be logical; that is, from a given set of circumstances a predictable result should follow. The trouble is that in human behavior and history it is impossible to isolate or repeat a given set of circumstances. Complex human acts cannot be either reproduced or deliberately initiated—or counted upon like the phenomena of nature. The sun comes up every day. Tides are so obedient to schedule that a timetable for them can be printed like that for trains, though more reliable. In fact, tides and trains sharply illustrate my point: One depends on the moon and is certain; the other depends on man and is uncertain.

In the absence of dependable recurring circumstance, too much confidence cannot be placed on the lessons of history.

There *are* lessons, of course, and when people speak of learning   10
from them, they have in mind, I think, two ways of applying past experience: One is to enable us to avoid past mistakes and to manage better in similar circumstances next time; the other is to enable us to anticipate a future course of events. (History could tell us something about Vietnam, I think, if we would only listen.) To manage better next time is within our means; to anticipate does not seem to be.

World War II, for example, with the experience of the previous war as an awful lesson, was certainly conducted, once we got into it, more intelligently than World War I. Getting into it was another matter. When it was important to anticipate the course of events, Americans somehow failed to apply the right lesson. Pearl Harbor is the classic example of failure to learn from history. From hindsight we now know that what we should have anticipated was surprise attack by Japan in the midst of negotiations. Merely because this was dishonorable, did that make it unthinkable? Hardly. It was exactly the procedure Japan had adopted in 1904 when she opened the Russo-Japanese War by surprise attack on the Russian fleet at Port Arthur.

In addition we had every possible physical indication. We had broken the Japanese code, we had warnings on radar, we had a constant flow of accurate intelligence. What failed? Not information but *judgment.* We had all the evidence and refused to interpret it correctly, just as the Germans in 1944 refused to believe the evidence of a landing in Normandy. Men will not believe what does not fit in with their plans or suit their prearrangements. The flaw in all military intelligence, whether twenty or fifty or one hundred percent accurate, is that it is no better than the judgment of its interpreters, and this judgment is the product of a mass of individual, social, and political biases, prejudgments, and wishful thinkings; in short, it is human and therefore fallible. If man can break the Japanese code and yet not believe what it tells him, how can he be expected to learn from the lessons of history?

Would a computer do better? In the case of Pearl Harbor, probably yes. If one could have fed all the pieces of intelligence available in November 1941 into a computer, it could have hardly failed to reply promptly, "Air attack, Hawaii, Philippines" and probably even "December 7." But will this work every time? Can we trust the lessons of history to computers? I think not, because history will fool them. They may make the right deductions and draw the right conclusions, but a twist occurs, someone sneezes, history swerves and takes another path. Had Cleopatra's nose been shorter, said Pascal, the whole aspect of the world would have been changed. Can a computer account for Cleopatra?

Once long ago when the eternal verities seemed clear—that is, during the Spanish Civil War—I thought the lessons of history were unmistakable. It appeared obvious beyond dispute that if fascism under Franco won, Spain in the foreshadowed European war would become a base for Hitler and Mussolini, the Mediterranean would become an Italian lake, Britain would lose Gibraltar and be cut off from her empire east of Suez. The peril was plain, the logic of the thing implacable, every sensible person saw it, and I, just out of college, wrote a small book published in England to point it up, all drawn from the analogy of history. The book showed how, throughout the eighteenth and nineteenth centuries, Britain had consistently interposed herself against the gaining of undue influence over Spain by whatever power dominated the continent. The affair of the Spanish marriages, the campaigns of Wellington, the policies of Castlereagh, Canning, and Palmerston all were directed toward the same objective: The strongest continental power must be prevented from controlling Spain. My treatise was, I thought, very artful and very telling. It did not refer to the then current struggle, but let the past speak for itself and make the argument. It was an irrefutable one—until history refuted it. Franco, assisted by Hitler and Mussolini, *did* win, European war *did* follow, yet unaccountably Spain remained neutral—at least nominally. Gibraltar did not fall, the portals of the Mediterranean did *not* close. I, not to mention all the other "premature" anti-fascists, as we were called, while morally right about the general danger of fascism, had been wrong about a particular outcome. The lessons of history I had so carefully set forth simply did not operate. History misbehaved.

Pearl Harbor and Spain demonstrate two things: One, that man fails to profit from the lessons of history because his prejudgments prevent him from drawing the indicated conclusions; and, two, that history will often capriciously take a different direction from that in which her lessons point. Herein lies the flaw in systems of history.   15

When it comes to systems, history played her greatest betrayal on Karl Marx. Never was a prophet so sure of his premises, never were believers so absolutely convinced of a predicted outcome, never was there an interpretation of history that seemed so foolproof. Analyzing the effects of the Industrial Revolution, Marx exposed the terrible riddle of the nineteenth century: that the greater the material progress, the wider and deeper the resulting poverty, a process which could only end, he decided, in the violent collapse of the existing order brought on by revolution. From this he formulated the doctrine of *Verelendung* (progressive impoverishment) and *Zusammenbruch* (collapse) and decreed that since working-class self-consciousness increased in proportion to industrialization, revolution would come first in the most industrialized country.

Marx's analysis was so compelling that it seemed impossible history could follow any other course. His postulates were accepted by followers of his own and later generations as if they had been graven on the tablets of Sinai. Marxism as the revealed truth of history was probably the most convincing dogma ever enunciated. Its influence was tremendous, incalculable, continuing. The founder's facts were correct, his thinking logical and profound; he was right in everything but his conclusions. Developing events did not bear him out. The working class grew progressively better, not worse, off. Capitalism did not collapse. Revolution came in the least, not the most, industrialized country. Under collectivism the state did not wither but extended itself in power and function and in its grip on society. History, ignoring Marx, followed her own mysterious logic, and went her own way.

When it developed that Marx was wrong, men in search of determinism rushed off to submit history to a new authority—Freud. His hand is now upon us. The Unconscious is king. At least it was. There are new voices, I believe, claiming that the Unconscious is a fraud— iconoclasm has reached even Freud. Nevertheless, in his effect on the modern outlook, Freud, I believe, unquestionably was the greatest influence for change between the nineteenth and twentieth centuries. It may well be that our time may one day be named for him and the Freudian Era be said to have succeeded the Victorian Era. Our understanding of human motivation has taken on a whole new dimension since his ideas took hold. Yet it does not seem to me that unconscious sexual and psychological drives are as relevant in all circumstances as they are said to be by the Freudians, who have become as fixed in their system as were the orthodox Marxists. They can supply historians with insights but not with guidance to the future because man *en masse* cannot be relied upon to behave according to pattern. All salmon swim back to spawn in the headwaters of their birth; that is universal for salmon. But man lives in a more complicated world than a fish. Too many influences are at work on him to make it applicable that every man is driven by an unconscious desire to swim back to the womb.

It has always seemed to me unfortunate, for instance, that Freud chose the experiences of two royal families to exemplify his concept of the Oedipus and Elektra complexes. Royalty lives under special circumstances, particularly as regards the issue of power between the sovereign and his heir, which are not valid as universal experience. The legend of Oedipus killing his father may have derived from the observed phenomenon that every royal heir has always hated his father, not because he wants to sleep with his mother but because he wants to ascend the throne. If the parental sovereign happens to be his mother, he hates her just as much. She will dislike him equally from birth because she knows he is destined to take her place, as in the case of Queen Victoria and her eldest son, who became Edward VII. That is not Freudian, it is simply dynastic.

As for Elektra, it is hard to know what to make of that tale. The 20 House of Atreus was a very odd family indeed. More was going on there than just Elektra being in love with her father. How about Orestes, who helped her to kill their mother, or killed her himself, according to another version? Was not that the wrong parent? How come he did not kill his father? How about Iphigenia, the sister, whom Agememnon killed as a sacrifice? What is the Freudian explanation for that? They do not say, which is not being historical. A historian cannot pick and choose his facts; he must deal with all the evidence.

Or take Martin Luther. As you know, Professor Erik Erikson of Harvard has discovered that Luther was constipated from childhood and upon this interesting physiological item he has erected a system which explains everything about his man. This is definitely the most camp thing that has happened to history in years. It even made Broadway. Nevertheless I do not think Luther pinned the 95 Theses on the church door at Wittenberg solely or even mainly because of the activity, or inactivity rather, of his anal muscle. His personal motive for protest may have had an anal basis for all I know, but what is important historically is the form the protest took, and this had to do with old and deep social grievances concerned with the worldliness of the church, the sale of indulgences, corruption of the clergy, and so on. If it had not been Luther who protested, it would have been someone else; Protestantism would have come with or without him, and its causes had nothing whatever to do with his private physiological impediment. Professor Erikson, I am sure, was attempting to explain Luther, not Protestantism, but his book has started a fad for psycho-history among those without the adequate knowledge or training to use it.

Following Freud there flourished briefly a minor prophet, Oswald Spengler, who proclaimed the Decline of the West, based on an elaborate study of the lessons of history. Off and on since then people have been returning to his theme, especially since World War II and the end of colonialism. The rise of China and the rash of independence movements in Asia and Africa have inspired many nervous second looks at Spengler. Europe is finished, say the knowing ones; the future belongs to the colored races and all that.

People have been burying Europe for quite some time. I remember a political thinker for whom I had great respect telling me in the thirties that Europe's reign was over; the future belonged to America, Russia, and China. It was a new and awful thought to me then and I was immensely impressed. As I see it now, his grouping has not been justified. I do not think Russia and America can be dissociated from Europe; rather, we are extensions of Europe. I hesitate to be dogmatic about Russia, but I am certain about the United States. American culture stems from Europe, our fortunes are linked with hers, in the long run we are aligned. My impression is that Europe, and by extension the white race, is far from finished. Europe's vitality keeps reviving; as a source of ideas she is inexhaustible. Nuclear fission, the most recent, if unwanted, advance, came from the work of a whole series of Europeans: Max Planck, the Curies, Einstein, Rutherford, Fermi, Nils Bohr, Szilard. Previously the three great makers of the modern mind, Darwin, Marx, and Freud, were Europeans. I do not know of an original idea to have importantly affected the *modern* world which has come from Asia or Africa (except perhaps for Gandhi's concept of non-violent resistance or civil disobedience, and, after all, Thoreau had the same idea earlier).

It does not seem to me a passing phenomenon or an accident that the West, in ideas and temporal power, has been dominant for so long. Far from falling behind, it seems to be extending its lead, except in the fearful matter of mere numbers and I like to think the inventiveness of the West will somehow eventually cope with that. What is called the emergence of the peoples of Asia and Africa is taking place in Western terms and is measured by the degree to which they take on Western forms, political, industrial, and otherwise. That they are losing their own cultures is sad, I think, but I suppose it cannot be helped. The new realm is space, and that too is being explored by the West. So much for Spengler.

Theories of history go in vogues which, as is the nature of vogues, soon fade and give place to new ones. Yet this fails to discourage the systematizers. They believe as firmly in this year's as last year's, for, as Isaiah Berlin says, the "obstinate craving for unity and symmetry at the expense of experience" is always with us. When I grew up, the economic interpretation of history, as formulated with stunning impact by Charles Beard, was the new gospel—as incontrovertible as if it had been revealed to Beard in a burning bush. Even to question that financial interests motivated our Founding Fathers in the separation from Britain, or that equally mercenary considerations decided our entrance into

25

the First World War, was to convict oneself of the utmost naïveté. Yet lately the fashionable—indeed, what appears to be the required—exercise among historians has been jumping on Beard with both feet. He and the considerable body of his followers who added to his system and built it up into a dogma capable of covering any historical situation have been knocked about, analyzed, dissected, and thoroughly disposed of. Presently the historical establishment has moved on to dispose of Frederick Jackson Turner and his theory of the Frontier. I do not know what the new explanation is, but I am sure there must be some thesis, for, as one academic historian recently ruled, the writing of history requires a "large organizing idea."

I visualize the "large organizing idea" as one of those iron chain mats pulled behind by a tractor to smooth over a plowed field. I see the professor climbing up on the tractor seat and away he goes, pulling behind his large organizing idea over the bumps and furrows of history until he has smoothed it out to a nice, neat, organized surface—in other words, into a system.

The human being—you, I, or Napoleon—is unreliable as a scientific factor. In combination of personality, circumstance, and historical moment, each man is a package of variables impossible to duplicate. His birth, his parents, his siblings, his food, his home, his school, his economic and social status, his first job, his first girl, and the variables inherent in all of these, make up that mysterious compendium, personality—which then combines with another set of variables: country, climate, time, and historical circumstance. Is it likely, then, that all these elements will meet again in their exact proportions to reproduce a Moses, or Hitler, or De Gaulle, or for that matter Lee Harvey Oswald, the man who killed Kennedy?

So long as man remains the Unknowable Variable—and I see no immediate prospect of his ever being pinned down in every facet of his infinite variety—I do not see how his actions can be usefully programmed and quantified. The eager electronic optimists will go on chopping up man's past behavior into the thousands of little definable segments which they call Input, and the machine will whirr and buzz and flash its lights and in no time at all give back Output. But will Output be dependable? I would lay ten to one that history will pay no more attention to Output than it did to Karl Marx. It will still need historians. Electronics will have its uses, but it will not, I am confident, transform historians into button-pushers or history into a system.

October 1966

Lines of Inquiry
"Is History a Guide to the Future?"

One of Tuchman's main purposes in this essay is to show history as being "so crammed with an unlimited number of variables that it is not susceptible of the scientific method nor of systematizing." How does she attempt to make a case for this view of history? What assumption(s) does she base it on? What kinds of evidence and logic does she use to show that history is not susceptible of the scientific method? What kinds of evidence and logic does she use to show "it is not susceptible . . . of systematizing?"

Given her attempt to disassociate history not only from the scientific method but from systematizing of any kind, it seems appropriate to consider exactly what she does believe to be the nature of history and the appropriateness of her methods of gathering and analyzing historical information. Given her view that "too much confidence cannot be placed on the lessons of history," what relevance does she attribute to history? Given her mocking attitude towards "systems of history" or any "large organizing idea," what do you think of her claim on p. 630 that no original ideas from Asia or Africa "have importantly affected the *modern* world" or American culture?

How consistent is Tuchman's idea of history with her own historical writing? For example, how closely does she seem to follow her definition of history in " 'Perdicaris Alive or Raisuli Dead' "? How closely does she seem to follow it in "Mankind's Better Moments"?

History by the Ounce

At a party given for its re-opening last year, the Museum of Modern Art in New York served champagne to five thousand guests. An alert reporter for the *Times,* Charlotte Curtis, noted that there were eighty cases, which, she informed her readers, amounted to 960 bottles or 7,680 three-ounce drinks. Somehow through this detail the Museum's party at once becomes alive; a fashionable New York occasion. One sees the crush, the women eyeing each other's clothes, the exchange of greetings, and feels the gratifying sense of elegance and importance imparted by champagne—even if, at one and a half drinks per person, it was not on an exactly riotous scale. All this is conveyed by Miss Curtis' detail. It is, I think, the way history as well as journalism should be written. It is what Pooh-Bah, in *The Mikado,* meant when, telling how the victim's head stood on its neck and bowed three times to him at the execution of Nanki-Poo, he added that this was "corroborative detail intended to give artistic verisimilitude to an otherwise bald and unconvincing narrative." Not that Miss Curtis' narrative was either bald or unconvincing; on the contrary, it was precise, factual, and a model in every way. But what made it excel, made it vivid and memorable, was her use of corroborative detail.

Pooh-Bah's statement of the case establishes him in my estimate as a major historian or, at least, as the formulator of a major principle of historiography. True, he invented his corroborative detail, which is cheating if you are a historian and fiction if you are not; nevertheless, what counts is his recognition of its importance. He knew that it supplies verisimilitude, that without it a narrative is bald and unconvincing. Neither he nor I, of course, discovered the principle; historians have for long made use of it, beginning with Thucydides, who insisted on details of topography, "the appearance of cities and localities, the description of rivers and harbors, the peculiar features of seas and countries and their relative distances."

Corroborative detail is the great corrective. Without it historical narrative and interpretation, both, may slip easily into the invalid. It is a disciplinarian. It forces the historian who uses and respects it to cleave to the truth, or as much as he can find out of the truth. It keeps him from soaring off the ground into theories of his own invention. On those Toynbeean heights the air is stimulating and the view is vast, but people and houses down below are too small to be seen. However persuaded the historian may be of the validity of the theories he conceives, if they are not supported and illustrated by corroborative detail they are of no more value as history than Pooh-Bah's report of the imagined execution.

It is wiser, I believe, to arrive at theory by way of the evidence rather than the other way around, like so many revisionists today. It is more rewarding, in any case, to assemble the facts first and, in the process of arranging them in narrative form, to discover a theory or a historical generalization emerging of its own accord. This to me is the excitement, the built-in treasure hunt, of writing history. In the book I am working on now, which deals with the twenty-year period before 1914 (and the reader must forgive me if all my examples are drawn from my own work, but that, after all, is the thing one knows best), I have been writing about a moment during the Dreyfus Affair in France when on the day of the reopening of Parliament everyone expected the Army to attempt a *coup d'état*. English observers predicted it, troops were brought into the capital, the Royalist pretender was summoned to the frontier, mobs hooted and rioted in the streets, but when the day had passed, nothing had happened; the Republic still stood. By this time I had assembled so much corroborative detail pointing to a *coup d'état* that I had to explain why it had not occurred. Suddenly I had to stop and think. After a while I found myself writing, "The Right lacked that necessary chemical of a coup—a leader. It had its small, if loud, fanatics; but to upset the established government in a democratic country requires either foreign help or the stuff of a dictator." That is a historical generalization, I believe; a modest one, to be sure, but my size. I had arrived at it out of the necessity of the material and felt immensely pleased and proud. These moments do not occur every day; sometimes no more than one a chapter, if that, but when they do they leave one with a lovely sense of achievement.

I am a disciple of the ounce because I mistrust history in gallon jugs   5 whose purveyors are more concerned with establishing the meaning and purpose of history than with what happened. Is it necessary to insist on a purpose? No one asks the novelist why he writes novels or the poet what is his purpose in writing poems. The lilies of the field, as I remember, were not required to have a demonstrable purpose. Why cannot history be studied and written and read for its own sake, as the record of human behavior, the most fascinating subject of all? Insistence on a purpose turns the historian into a prophet—and that is another profession.

To return to my own: Corroborative detail will not produce a generalization every time, but it will often reveal a historical truth, besides keeping one grounded in historical reality. When I was investigating General Mercier, the Minister of War who was responsible for the original condemnation of Dreyfus and who in the course of the Affair became the hero of the Right, I discovered that at parties of the *haut monde* ladies rose to their feet when General Mercier entered the room. That is the kind of detail which to me is worth a week of research. It illustrates the society, the people, the state of feeling at the time more vividly than anything I could write and in shorter space, too, which is an additional advantage. It epitomizes, it crystallizes, it visualizes. The reader can see it; moreover, it sticks in his mind; it is memorable.

The same is true, verbally though not visually, of a statement by President Eliot of Harvard in 1896 in a speech on international arbitration, a great issue of the time. In this chapter I was writing about the founding tradition of the United States as an anti-militarist, anti-imperialist nation, secure within its own shores, having nothing to do with the wicked armaments and standing armies of Europe, setting an example of unarmed strength and righteousness. Looking for material to illustrate the tradition, I found in a newspaper report these words of Eliot, which I have not seen quoted by anyone else: "The building of a navy," he said, "and the presence of a large standing army mean . . . the abandonment of what is characteristically American. . . . The building of a navy and particularly of battleships is English and French policy. It should never be ours."

How superb that is! Its assurance, its conviction, its Olympian authority—what does it not reveal of the man, the time, the idea? In those words I saw clearly for the first time the nature and quality of the American anti-militarist tradition, of what has been called the American dream—it was a case of detail not merely corroborating but revealing an aspect of history.

Failing to know such details, one can be led astray. In 1890 Congress authorized the building of the first three American battleships and, two years later, a fourth. Shortly thereafter, in 1895, this country plunged into a major quarrel with Great Britain, known as the Venezuelan crisis, in which there was much shaking of fists and chauvinist shrieking for war. Three years later we were at war with Spain. She was no longer a naval power equal to Britain, of course, but still not negligible. One would like to know what exactly was American naval strength at the time of both these crises. How many, if any, of the battleships authorized in 1890 were actually at sea five years later? When the jingoes were howling for war in 1895, what ships did we have to protect our coasts, much less to take the offensive? It seemed to me this was a piece of information worth knowing.

To my astonishment, on looking for the answer in textbooks on 10 the period, I could not find it. The historians of America's rise to world power, of the era of expansion, of American foreign policy, or even of the navy have not concerned themselves with what evidently seems to them an irrelevant detail. It was hardly irrelevant to policymakers of the time who bore the responsibility for decisions of peace or war. Text after text in American history is published every year, each repeating on this question more or less what his predecessor has said before, with no further enlightenment. To find the facts I finally had to write to the Director of Naval History at the Navy Department in Washington.

My point is not how many battleships we had on hand in 1895 and '98 (which I now know) but why this hard, physical fact was missing from the professional historians' treatment. "Bald and unconvincing," said Pooh-Bah of narrative without fact, a judgment in which I join.

When I come across a generalization or a general statement in history unsupported by illustration I am instantly on guard; my reaction is, "Show me." If a historian writes that it was raining heavily on the day war was declared, that is a detail corroborating a statement, let us say, that the day was gloomy. But if he writes merely that it was a gloomy day without mentioning the rain, I want to know what is his evidence; what made it gloomy. Or if he writes, "The population was in a belligerent mood," or, "It was a period of great anxiety," he is indulging in general statements which carry no conviction to me if they are not illustrated by some evidence. I write, for example, that fashionable French society in the 1890s imitated the English in manners and habits. Imagining myself to be my own reader—a complicated fugue that goes on all the time at my desk—my reaction is of course, "Show me." The next two sentences do. I write, "The Greffulhes and Breteuils were intimates of the Prince of Wales, *le betting* was the custom at Longchamps, *le Derby* was held at Chantilly, *le steeplechase* at Auteuil and an unwanted member was *black-boulé* at the Jockey Club. Charles Haas, the original of Swann, had 'Mr' engraved on his calling cards."

Even if corroborative detail did not serve a valid historical purpose, its use makes a narrative more graphic and intelligible, more pleasurable to read, in short more readable. It assists communication, and communication is, after all, the major purpose. History written in abstract terms communicates nothing to me. I cannot comprehend the abstract and since a writer tends to create the reader in his own image, I assume my reader cannot comprehend it either. No doubt I underestimate him. Certainly many serious thinkers write in the abstract and many people read them with interest and profit and even, I suppose, pleasure. I respect this ability, but I am unable to emulate it.

My favorite visible detail in *The Guns of August,* for some inexplicable reason, is the one about the Grand Duke Nicholas, who was so tall (six foot six) that when he established headquarters in a railroad car his aide pinned up a fringe of white paper over the doorway to remind him to duck his head. Why this insignificant item, after several years' work and out of all the material crammed into a book of 450 pages, should be the particular one to stick most sharply in my mind I cannot explain, but it is. I was so charmed by the white paper fringe that I constructed a whole paragraph describing Russian headquarters at Baranovici in order to slip it in logically.

In another case the process failed. I had read that the Kaiser's birth-   15 day gift to his wife was the same every year: twelve hats selected by himself which she was obliged to wear. There you see the value of corroborative detail in revealing personality; this one is worth a whole book about the Kaiser—or even about Germany. It represents, however, a minor tragedy of *The Guns,* for I never succeeded in working it in at all. I keep my notes on cards, and the card about the hats started out with those for the first chapter. Not having been used, it was moved forward to a likely place in Chapter 2, missed again, and continued on down through all the chapters until it emerged to a final resting place in a packet marked "Unused."

A detail about General Sir Douglas Haig, equally revealing of personality or at any rate of contemporary customs and conditions in the British officer corps, did find a place. This was the fact that during the campaign in the Sudan in the nineties he had "a camel laden with claret" in the personal pack train that followed him across the desert. Besides being a vivid bit of social history, the phrase itself, "a camel laden with claret," is a thing of beauty, a marvel of double and inner alliteration. That, however, brings up another whole subject, the subject of language, which needs an article of its own for adequate discussion.

Having inadvertently reached it, I will only mention that the independent power of words to affect the writing of history is a thing to be watched out for. They have an almost frightening autonomous power to produce in the mind of the reader an image or idea that was not in the mind of the writer. Obviously they operate this way in all forms of writing, but history is particularly sensitive because one has a duty to be accurate, and careless use of words can leave a false impression one had not intended. Fifty percent at least of the critics of *The Guns* commented on what they said was my exposé of the stupidity of the generals. Nothing of the kind was in my mind when I wrote. What I meant to convey was that the generals were in the trap of the circumstances, training, ideas, and national impulses of their time and their individual countries. I was not trying to convey stupidity but tragedy, fatality. Many reviewers understood this, clearly intelligent perceptive persons (those who understand one always are), but too many kept coming up with the word "stupidity" to my increasing dismay.

This power of words to escape from a writer's control is a fascinating problem which, since it was not what I started out to discuss, I can only hint at here. One more hint before I leave it: For me the problem lies in the fact that the art of writing interests me as much as the art of history (and I hope it is not provocative to say that I think of history as an art, not a science). In writing I am seduced by the sound of words and by the interaction of their sound and sense. Recently at the start of a paragraph I wrote, "Then occurred the intervention which irretrievably bent the twig of events." It was intended as a kind of signal to the reader. (Every now and then in a historical narrative, after one has been explaining a rather complicated background, one feels the need of waving a small red flag that says, "Wake up, Reader; something is going to happen.") Unhappily, after finishing the paragraph, I was forced to admit that the incident in question had *not* irretrievably bent the twig of events. Yet I hated to give up such a well-made phrase. Should I leave it in because it was good writing or take it out because it was not good history? History governed and it was lost to posterity (although, you notice, I have rescued it here). Words are seductive and dangerous material, to be used with caution. Am I writer first or am I historian? The old argument starts inside my head. Yet there need not always be dichotomy or dispute. The two functions need not be, in fact should not be, at war. The goal is fusion. In the long run the best writer is the best historian.

In quest of that goal I come back to the ounce. The most effective ounce of visual detail is that which indicates something of character or circumstance in addition to appearance. Careless clothes finished off by drooping white socks corroborate a description of Jean Jaurès as looking like the expected image of a labor leader. To convey both the choleric looks and temper and the cavalry officer's snobbism of Sir John French, it helps to write that he affected a cavalryman's stock in place of collar and tie, which gave him the appearance of being perpetually on the verge of choking.

The best corroborative detail I ever found concerned Lord Shaftes- 20 bury, the eminent Victorian social reformer, author of the Factory Act and child-labor laws, who appeared in my first book, *Bible and Sword.* He was a man, wrote a contemporary, of the purest, palest, stateliest exterior in Westminster, on whose classic head "every separate dark lock of hair seemed to curl from a sense of duty." For conveying both appearance and character of a man and the aura of his times, all in one, that line is unequaled.

Novelists have the advantage that they can invent corroborative detail. Wishing to portray, let us say, a melancholy introspective character, they make up physical qualities to suit. The historian must make do with what he can find, though he may sometimes point up what he finds by calling on a familiar image in the mental baggage of the reader. To say that General Joffre looked like Santa Claus instantly conveys a picture which struck me as peculiarly apt when I wrote it. I was thinking of Joffre's massive paunch, fleshy face, white mustache, and bland and benevolent appearance, and I forgot that Santa Claus wears a beard, which Joffre, of course, did not. Still, the spirit was right. One must take care to choose a recognizable image for this purpose. In my current book I have a melancholy and introspective character, Lord Salisbury, Prime Minister in 1895, a supreme, if far from typical, product of the British aristocracy, a heavy man with a curly beard and big, bald forehead, of whom I wrote that he was called the Hamlet of English politics and looked like Karl Marx. I must say that I was really rather pleased with that phrase, but my editor was merely puzzled. It developed that he did not know what Karl Marx looked like, so the comparison conveyed no image. If it failed its first test, it would certainly not succeed with the average reader and so, sadly, I cut it out.

Sources of corroborative detail must of course be contemporary with the subject. Besides the usual memoirs, letters, and autobiographies, do not overlook novelists and newspapers. The inspired bit about the ladies rising to their feet for General Mercier comes from Proust, as do many other brilliant details; for instance, that during the Affair ladies had *"A bas les juifs"* printed on their parasols. Proust is invaluable not only because there is so much of him but because it is all confined to a narrow segment of society which he knew personally and intimately; it is like a woman describing her own living room. On the other hand, another novel set in the same period, *Jean Barois* by Roger Martin du Gard, considered a major work of fiction on the Affair, gave me nothing I could use, perhaps because visual detail—at least the striking and memorable detail—was missing. It was all talk and ideas, interesting, of course, but for source material I want something I can *see*. When you have read Proust you can see Paris of the nineties, horse cabs and lamplight, the clubman making his calls in white gloves stitched in black and gray top hat lined in green leather.

Perhaps this illustrates the distinction between a major and a less gifted novelist which should hold equally true, I believe, for historians. Ideas alone are not flesh and blood. Too often, scholarly history is written in terms of ideas rather than acts; it tells what people wrote instead of what they performed. To write, say, a history of progressivism in America or of socialism in the era of the Second International by quoting the editorials, books, articles, speeches, and so forth of the leading figures is easy. They were the wordiest people in history. If, however, one checks what they said and wrote against what actually was happening, a rather different picture emerges. At present I am writing a chapter on the Socialists and I feel like someone in a small rowboat under Niagara. To find and hold on to anything hard and factual under their torrent of words is an epic struggle. I suspect the reason is that people out of power always talk more than those who have power. The historian must be careful to guard against this phenomenon—weight it, as the statisticians say—lest his result be unbalanced.

Returning to novels as source material, I should mention *The Edwardians* by V. Sackville-West, which gave me precise and authoritative information on matters on which the writers of memoirs remain discreet. Like Proust, this author was writing of a world she knew. At the great house parties, one learns, the hostess took into consideration established liaisons in assigning the bedrooms and each guest had his name on a card slipped into a small brass frame outside his door. The poets too serve. Referring in this chapter on Edwardian England to the central role of the horse in the life of the British aristocracy, and describing the exhilaration of the hunt, I used a line from a sonnet by Wilfrid Scawen Blunt, "My horse a thing of wings, myself a god." Anatole France supplied, through the mouth of a character in *M. Bergeret,* the words to describe a Frenchman's feeling about the Army at the time of the Affair, that it was "all that is left of our glorious past. It consoles us for the present and gives us hope of the future." Zola expressed the fear of the bourgeoisie for the working class through the manager's wife in *Germinal,* who, watching the march of the striking miners, saw "the red vision of revolution . . . when on some somber evening at the end of the century the people, unbridled at last, would make the blood of the middle class flow." In *The Guns* there is a description of the retreating French Army after the Battle of the Frontiers with their red trousers faded to the color of pale brick, coats ragged and torn, cavernous eyes sunk in unshaven faces, gun carriages with once-new gray paint now blistered and caked with mud. This came from Blasco Ibáñez's novel *The Four Horsemen of the Apocalypse.* From H. G. Wells's *Mr. Britling Sees It Through* I took the feeling in England at the outbreak of war that it contained an "enormous hope" of something better afterward, a chance to end war, a "tremendous opportunity" to remake the world.

I do not know if the professors would allow the use of such sources 25 in a graduate dissertation, but I see no reason why a novelist should not supply as authentic material as a journalist or a general. To determine what may justifiably be used from a novel, one applies the same criterion as for any nonfictional account: If a particular item fits with what one knows of the time, the place, the circumstances, and the people, it is acceptable; otherwise not. For myself, I would rather quote Proust or Sackville-West or Zola than a professional colleague as is the academic habit. I could never see any sense whatever in referring to one's neighbor in the next university as a source. To me that is no source at all; I want to know where a given fact came from originally, not who used it last. As for referring to an earlier book of one's own as a source, this seems to me the ultimate absurdity. I am told that graduate students are required to cite the secondary historians in order to show they are familiar with the literature, but if I were granting degrees I would demand primary familiarity with primary sources. The secondary histories are necessary when one starts out ignorant of a subject and I am greatly in their debt for guidance, suggestion, bibliography, and outline of events, but once they have put me on the path I like to go the rest of the way myself. If I were a teacher I would disqualify anyone who was content to cite a secondary source as his reference for a fact. To trace it back oneself to its origin means to discover all manner of fresh material from which to make one's own selection instead of being content to re-use something already selected by someone else.

Though it is far from novels, I would like to say a special word for *Who's Who*. For one thing, it is likely to be accurate because its entries are written by the subjects themselves. For another, it shows them as they wish to appear and thus often reveals character and even something of the times. H. H. Rogers, a Standard Oil partner and business tycoon of the 1890s, listed himself simply and succinctly as "Capitalist," obviously in his own eyes a proud and desirable thing to be. The social history of a period is contained in that self-description. Who would call himself by that word today?

As to newspapers, I like them for period flavor perhaps more than for factual information. One must be wary in using them for facts, because an event reported one day in a newspaper is usually modified or denied or turns out to be rumor on the next. It is absolutely essential to take nothing from a newspaper without following the story through for several days or until it disappears from the news. For period flavor, however, newspapers are unsurpassed. In the *New York Times* for August 10, 1914, I read an account of the attempt by German officers disguised in British uniforms to kidnap General Leman at Liège. The reporter wrote that the General's staff, "maddened by the dastardly violation of the rules of civilized warfare, spared not but slew."

This sentence had a tremendous effect on me. In it I saw all the difference between the world before 1914 and the world since. No reporter could write like that today, could use the word "dastardly," could take as a matter of course the concept of "civilized warfare," could write unashamedly, "spared not but slew." Today the sentence is embarrassing; in 1914 it reflected how people thought and the values they believed in. It was this sentence that led me back to do a book on the world before the war.

Women are a particularly good source for physical detail. They seem to notice it more than men or at any rate to consider it more worth reporting. The contents of the German soldier's knapsack in 1914, including thread, needles, bandages, matches, chocolate, tobacco, I found in the memoirs of an American woman living in Germany. The Russian moose who wandered over the frontier to be shot by the Kaiser at Rominten came from a book by the English woman who was governess to the Kaiser's daughter. Lady Warwick, mistress for a time of the Prince of Wales until she regrettably espoused socialism, is indispensable for Edwardian society, less for gossip than for habits and behavior. Princess Daisy of Pless prattles endlessly about the endless social rounds of the nobility, but every now and then supplies a dazzling nugget of information. One, which I used in *The Zimmermann Telegram,* was her description of how the Kaiser complained to her at dinner of the ill-treatment he had received over the *Daily Telegraph* affair and of how, in the excess of his emotion, "a tear fell on his cigar." In the memoirs of Edith O'Shaughnessy, wife of the First Secretary of the American Embassy in Mexico, is the description of the German Ambassador, von

Hintze, who dressed and behaved in all things like an Englishman except that he wore a large sapphire ring on his little finger which gave him away. No man would have remarked on that.

In the end, of course, the best place to find corroborative detail is   30
on the spot itself, if it can be visited, as Herodotus did in Asia Minor or Parkman on the Oregon Trail. Take the question of German atrocities in 1914. Nothing requires more careful handling because, owing to post-war disillusions, "atrocity" came to be a word one did not believe in. It was supposed because the Germans had not, after all, cut off the hands of Belgian babies, neither had they shot hostages nor burned Louvain. The results of this disbelief were dangerous because when the Germans became Nazis people were disinclined to believe they were as bad as they seemed and appeasement became the order of the day. (It strikes me that here is a place to put history to use and that a certain wariness might be in order today.) In writing of German terrorism in Belgium in 1914 I was at pains to use only accounts by Germans themselves or in a few cases by Americans, then neutral. The most telling evidence, however, was that which I saw forty-five years later: the rows of gravestones in the churchyard of a little Belgian village on the Meuse, each inscribed with a name and a date and the legend *"fusillé par les Allemands."* Or the stone marker on the road outside Senlis, twenty-five miles from Paris, engraved with the date September 2, 1914, and the names of the mayor and six other civilian hostages shot by the Germans. Somehow the occupations engraved opposite the names— baker's apprentice, stonemason, *garçon de café*—carried extra conviction. This is the verisimilitude Pooh-Bah and I too have been trying for.

The desire to find the significant detail plus the readiness to open his mind to it and let it report to him are half the historian's equipment. The other half, concerned with idea, point of view, the reason for writing, the "Why" of history, has been left out of this discussion although I am not unconscious that it looms in the background. The art of writing is the third half. If that list does not add up, it is because history is human behavior, not arithmetic.

July 1965

Lines of Inquiry
"History by the Ounce"

In making a case for corroborative detail, Tuchman relies heavily on such details. Make a list of all the corroborative details that she uses in her first sixteen paragraphs. In what respects are these details similar? In what respects different? How long on the average does she stick with one detail? How often on the average does she introduce a new detail? Given all the different details that she uses in this piece, how does she prevent it from becoming a hodge-podge of detail?

In the course of her discussion, Tuchman offers several reasons for her belief in the value of detail. Make a list of all the reasons she considers and try to arrange them in an order that reflects their relative importance to her in the writing of history. In the latter part of her discussion, Tuchman also considers several different types of source material for obtaining historical detail. Make a list of the different types she considers and try to arrange them in an order that reflects their relative importance to her. What do these rank-ordered lists suggest to you about Tuchman's idea of history and the historian's responsibility?

Though Tuchman does not explicitly acknowledge any dangers in relying so heavily on detail, she does mention some of the problems that might come from relying too heavily on the "power of words." To what extent might there be similar dangers in the allure of details, especially when the details are drawn from novels rather than "on the spot" factual sources? In what respect might it be argued that just as science is "not a catalog of facts," as Gould says in "Women's Brains," so history is not a catalog of details?

Mark Twain
(Samuel Langhorne Clemens)
1835–1910

The most permanent lessons in morals are those which come not of booky teaching, but of experience.

Samuel Clemens (who took the pen name of Mark Twain in 1862) was undoubtedly moved to this observation by the force of his own firsthand experience, for his experiences were extraordinarily wide-ranging, and he drew on them throughout his career as a journalist, humorist, lecturer, novelist, and essayist. In fact, by the time he wrote this maxim in 1880, Mark Twain not only had worked his way around much of the United States, Hawaii (then an independent monarchy), and Europe, but also had turned his adventures into four remarkably successful books. So it is hardly surprising that he came to think of experience as "an author's most valuable asset . . . the thing that puts the muscle and the breath and the warm blood into the book he writes."

The itch to travel came early—from his boyhood in the river town of Hannibal, Missouri, where his family moved when he was four years old. There on the Mississippi, in the heyday of river traffic, he grew up with the steamboat whistle sounding in his ears, and the steamboat pilots, the riverboat gamblers, the adventurers, and the speculators passing before his eyes. There, too, when he was twelve years old and his father had just died, he dropped out of school and became a "printer's devil" for the local newspaper. At eighteen he left Hannibal and for the next fifteen years traveled around the country trying his hand at a variety of occupations—journeyman printer, steamboat pilot, secretary, and gold miner—before turning once again to the newspaper business in 1862, but this time as a reporter for the Virginia City *Territorial Enterprise* in Nevada.

The job of reporting, especially in a frontier mining town, brought out his natural talent for humorous storytelling, and Twain refined it when he moved to San Francisco in 1864 and met up with a group of humorous writers and lecturers, most notably Artemus Ward, from whom he learned the "high and delicate art" of "how a story ought to be told." His mastery of that art in "The Celebrated Jumping Frog of Calaveras County" (1865) brought him widespread attention, and the attention brought him further opportunities to display it—as a roving reporter in Hawaii for the Sacramento *Union,* as a public lecturer on the west coast, in the Rocky Mountains, and in New York City, and as a reporter on a tour of Europe and the Holy Land for the San Francisco *Alta California.* His vividly detailed and amusing travel stories, which he later incorporated in *Innocents Abroad* (1869) and *Roughing It* (1872), were so widely read and distributed that soon after he returned from his Mediterranean tour in 1867 he had become one of the most popular authors in America.

In 1870, he married Olivia Langdon, the socially cultivated daughter of a well-to-do mine owner from upstate New York, and in 1872 they moved to Hartford, where Twain made his home for most of the next thirty years. During that period, he continued to lecture and travel extensively throughout Europe and the United States, yet he also managed to produce virtually all of his major works, most notably *The Adventures of Tom Sawyer* (1876), *The Prince and the Pauper* (1882), *Life on the Mississippi* (1883), *The Adventures of Huckleberry Finn* (1884), and *A Connecticut Yankee in King Arthur's Court* (1889). During that period, too, he invested heavily in several business ventures, among them a publishing house and a typesetting machine, all of which failed, leaving him bankrupt and badly in debt by the early 1890s. Though he managed to work off the debt by lecturing around the world and recording his experiences in *Following the Equator* (1897), the last ten years of his life were darkened by the deaths of his wife and two of his daughters.

Well before the misfortunes of his later years, Twain began to develop a distinctly cynical set of views about human nature and religious belief, epitomized by his reference to the "damned human race." In an essay on "The Character of Man" (1885), for example, he described man as "the most detestable" [of all the creatures], "the only one—the solitary one—that possesses malice." Thus, in one of the sardonic maxims that opens each chapter of *Following the Equator,* he was moved to observe that "Man is the Only Animal that blushes. Or needs to." In the years that followed, his increasingly pessimistic and deterministic views were embodied in *The Man That Corrupted Hadleyburg* (1900), *What Is Man?* (privately printed, 1906), and other writings so philosophically somber and so much at odds with the prevailing view of him as a humorist that he chose not to publish them during his lifetime.

Given the reach of his experience and the length of his career, Twain's essays cover a wide range of subject matter—personal, literary, social, political, religious, and philosophical. Whatever their subject, his essays typically reflect his interest in story telling, whether a brief anecdote or a full-fledged account. The style of his essays reflects his experience as a lecturer, keenly aware that a good "talker" can "persuade a fish to come out and take a walk with him." His language, in turn, is meant for the ear, so it generally stays close to the American idiom of his time. The "right word," as he knew, "tastes as tart and crisp and good as the autumn butter that creams the sumac berry." But above all, his essays, no matter how serious their subject, are almost always tinged with humor, for humor, as he believed, "is the great thing, the saving thing, after all."

"S-t-e-a-m-boat a-comin'!"

When I was a boy there was but one permanent ambition among my comrades in our village[1] on the west bank of the Mississippi River. That was to be a steamboatman. We had transient ambitions of other sorts but they were only transient. When a circus came and went, it left us all burning to become clowns; the first Negro minstrel show that ever came to our section left us all suffering to try that kind of life; now and then we had a hope that, if we lived and were good, God would permit us to be pirates. These ambitions faded out, each in its turn; but the ambition to be a steam-boatman always remained.

Once a day a cheap, gaudy packet arrived upward from St Louis, and another downward from Keokuk. Before these events, the day was glorious with expectancy; after them, the day was a dead and empty thing. Not only the boys but the whole village felt this. After all these years I can picture that old time to myself now, just as it was then: the white town drowsing in the sunshine of a summer's morning; the streets empty or pretty nearly so; one or two clerks sitting in front of the Water Street stores, with their splint-bottomed chairs tilted back against the walls, chins on breasts, hats slouched over their faces, asleep—with shingle-shavings enough around to show what broke them down; a sow and a litter of pigs loafing along the sidewalk, doing a good business in watermelon rinds and seeds; two or three lonely little freight piles scattered about the "levee"; a pile of "skids" on the slope of the stone-paved wharf, and the fragrant town drunkard asleep in the shadow of them; two or three wood flats at the head of the wharf but nobody to listen to the peaceful lapping of the wavelets against them; the great Mississippi, the majestic, the magnificent Mississippi, rolling its mile-wide tide along, shining in the sun; the dense forest away on the other side; the "point" above the town, and the "point" below, bounding the river-glimpse and turning it into a sort of sea, and withal a very still and brilliant and lonely one. Presently a film of dark smoke appears above one of those remote "points"; instantly a Negro drayman, famous for his quick eye and prodigious voice, lifts up the cry, "S-t-e-a-m-boat a-comin'!" and the scene changes! The town drunkard stirs, the clerks wake up, a furious clatter of drays follows, every house and store

---

[1] Hannibal, Missouri.

pours out a human contribution, and all in a twinkling the dead town is alive and moving. Drays, carts, men, boys, all go hurrying from many quarters to a common center, the wharf. Assembled there, the people fasten their eyes upon the coming boat as upon a wonder they are seeing for the first time. And the boat *is* rather a handsome sight, too. She is long and sharp and trim and pretty; she has two tall, fancy-topped chimneys, with a gilded device of some kind swung between them; a fanciful pilot-house, all glass and "gingerbread," perched on top of the "texas" deck behind them; the paddle-boxes are gorgeous with a picture or with gilded rays above the boat's name; the boiler-deck, the hurricane-deck, and the texas deck are fenced and ornamented with clean white railings; there is a flag gallantly flying from the jack-staff; the furnace doors are open and the fires glaring bravely; the upper decks are black with passengers; the captain stands by the big bell, calm, imposing, the envy of all; great volumes of the blackest smoke are rolling and tumbling out of the chimneys—a husbanded grandeur created with a bit of pitch-pine just before arriving at a town; the crew are grouped on the forecastle; the broad stage is run far out over the port bow and an envied deck-hand stands picturesquely on the end of it with a coil of rope in his hand; the pent steam is screaming through the gauge-cocks; the captain lifts his hand, a bell rings, the wheels stop; then they turn back, churning the water to foam, and the steamer is at rest. Then such a scramble as there is to get aboard and to get ashore, and to take in freight and to discharge freight, all at one and the same time; and such a yelling and cursing as the mates facilitate it all with! Ten minutes later the steamer is under way again, with no flag on the jack-staff and no black smoke issuing from the chimneys. After ten more minutes the town is dead again and the town drunkard asleep by the skids once more.

Lines of Inquiry
" 'S-t-e-a-m-boat a-comin'!' "

The fourth and eighth sentences of paragraph 2 each run on for an extraordinarily long time, each accumulating quite a few details along the way. What effects are produced in each case by including all of those details in a single sentence, rather than in a series of shorter ones? How does Twain keep each sentence moving clearly and emphatically from beginning to end? How has he selected the organized details in the fourth sentence to lead up to the coming of the steamboat? How has he selected and organized details in the eighth sentence to give a comprehensive, vivid, and dramatic impression of the steamboat?

Immediately after the steamboat is announced, "the scene changes," according to Twain, as if to suggest that the arrival and departure of the steamboat are something like a dramatic production. In what particular ways does

Twain depict these events as being like a theatrical performance and the townspeople like theatrical spectators? What does this analogy imply about Twain's attitude toward the steamboat? Toward the quality of life in the village?

For a description of life in a different kind of village culture, look at Mead's "A Day in Samoa." What similarities, what differences, do you notice in the ways that Mead and Twain select, organize, and present details about life in each village? How do you account for both the similarities and the differences in their methods of description?

Corn-Pone Opinions

Fifty years ago, when I was a boy of fifteen and helping to inhabit a Missourian village on the banks of the Mississippi, I had a friend whose society was very dear to me because I was forbidden by my mother to partake of it. He was a gay and impudent and satirical and delightful young black man—a slave—who daily preached sermons from the top of his master's woodpile, with me for sole audience. He imitated the pulpit style of the several clergymen of the village, and did it well, and with fine passion and energy. To me he was a wonder. I believed he was the greatest orator in the United States, and would some day be heard from. But it did not happen; in the distribution of rewards he was overlooked. It is the way, in this world.

He interrupted his preaching, now and then, to saw a stick of wood; but the sawing was a pretence—he did it with his mouth; exactly imitating the sound the buck-saw makes in shrieking its way through the wood. But it served its purpose: it kept his master from coming out to see how the work was getting along. I listened to the sermons from the window of a lumber-room at the back of our house. One of his texts was this:

"You tell me whar a man gits his corn-pone, en I'll tell you what his 'pinions is."

I can never forget it. It was deeply impressed upon me. By my mother. Not upon my memory, but elsewhere. She had slipped in upon me while I was absorbed and not watching. The black philosopher's idea was, that a man is not independent, and cannot afford views which might interfere with his bread and butter. If he would prosper, he must train with the majority; in matters of large moment, like politics and religion, he must think and feel with the bulk of his neighbors, or suffer damage in his social standing and in his business prosperities. He must restrict himself to corn-pone opinions—at least on the surface. He must get his opinions from other people; he must reason out none for himself; he must have no first-hand views.

I think Jerry was right, in the main, but I think he did not go far enough.

5

1. It was his idea that a man conforms to the majority-view of his locality by calculation and intention. This happens, but I think it is not the rule.

2. It was his idea that there is such a thing as a first-hand opinion; an original opinion; an opinion which is coldly reasoned out in a man's head, by a searching analysis of facts involved, with the heart uncon-

sulted, and the jury-room closed against outside influences. It may be that such an opinion has been born somewhere, at some time or other, but I suppose it got away before they could catch it and stuff it and put it in the museum.

I am persuaded that a coldly thought-out and independent verdict upon a fashion in clothes, or manners, or literature, or politics, or religion, or any other matter that is projected into the field of our notice and interest, is a most rare thing—if it has indeed ever existed.

A new thing in costume appears—the flaring hoop-skirt, for example—and the passers-by are shocked, and the irreverent laugh. Six months later everybody is reconciled; the fashion has established itself; it is admired, now, and no one laughs. Public opinion resented it before, public opinion accepts it now, and is happy in it. Why? Was the resentment reasoned out? Was the acceptance reasoned out? No. The instinct that moves to conformity did the work. It is our nature to conform; it is a force which not many can successfully resist. What is its seat? The inborn requirement of Self-Approval. We all have to bow to that; there are no exceptions. Even the woman who refuses from first to last to wear the hoop-skirt comes under that law and is its slave; she could not wear the skirt and have her own approval; and that she *must* have, she cannot help herself. But as a rule our self-approval has its source in but one place and not elsewhere—the approval of other people. A person of vast consequence can introduce any kind of novelty in dress and the general world will presently adopt it—moved to do it, in the first place, by the natural instinct to passively yield to that vague something recognized as authority, and in the second place by the human instinct to train with the multitude and have its approval. An Empress introduced the hoop-skirt, and we know the result. A nobody introduced the bloomer, and we know the result. If Eve should come again, in her ripe renown, and reintroduce her quaint styles—well, we know what would happen. And we should be cruelly embarrassed, along at first.

The hoop-skirt runs its course, and disappears. Nobody reasons about 10 it. One woman abandons the fashion; her neighbor notices this and follows her lead; this influences the next woman; and so on and so on, and presently the skirt has vanished out of the world, no one knows how nor why; nor cares, for that matter. It will come again, by and by; and in due course will go again.

Twenty-five years ago, in England, six or eight wine glasses stood grouped by each person's plate at a dinner party, and they were used, not left idle and empty; to-day there are but three or four in the group, and the average guest sparingly uses about two of them. We have not adopted this new fashion yet, but we shall do it presently. We shall not think it out, we shall merely conform, and let it go at that. We get our notions and habits and opinions from outside influences, we do not have to study them out.

Our table manners, and company manners, and street manners change from time to time, but the changes are not reasoned out; we merely notice and conform. We are creatures of outside influences; as a rule we do not think, we only imitate. We cannot invent standards that will stick; what we mistake for standards are only fashions, and perishable. We may continue to admire them, but we drop the use of them. We notice this in literature. Shakespeare is a standard, and fifty years ago we used to write tragedies which he couldn't tell from—from somebody else's; but we don't do it any more, now. Our prose standard, three-quarters of a century ago, was ornate and diffuse; some authority or other changed it in the direction of compactness and simplicity, and conformity followed, without argument. The historical novel starts up suddenly, and sweeps the land. Everybody writes one, and the nation is glad. We had historical novels before; but nobody read them, and the rest of us conformed—without reasoning it out. We are conforming in the other way, now, because it is another case of everybody.

The outside influences are always pouring in upon us, and we are always obeying their orders and accepting their verdicts. The Smiths like the new play; the Joneses go to see it, and they copy the Smith verdict. Morals, religions, politics, get their following from surrounding influences and atmospheres, almost entirely; not from study, not from thinking. A man must and will have his own approval first of all, in each and every moment and circumstance of his life—even if he must repent of a self-approved act the moment after its commission, in order to get his self-approval *again;* but, speaking in general terms, a man's self-approval, in the large concerns of life, has its source in the approval of the people about him, and not in a searching personal examination of the matter. Mohammedans are Mohammedans because they are born and reared among that sect, not because they have thought it out and can furnish sound reasons for being Mohammedans; we know why Catholics are Catholics; why Presbyterians are Presbyterians; why Baptists are Baptists; why Mormons are Mormons; why thieves are thieves; why monarchists are monarchists; why republicans are republicans, and democrats democrats. We know it is a matter of association and sympathy, not reasoning and examination; that hardly a man in the world has an opinion upon morals, politics or religion which he got otherwise than through his associations and sympathies. Broadly speaking, there are none but corn-pone opinions. And broadly speaking, Corn-Pone stands for Self-Approval. Self-approval is acquired mainly from the approval of other people. The result is Conformity. Sometimes Conformity has a sordid business interest—the bread-and-butter interest—but not in most cases, I think. I think that in the majority of cases it is unconscious and not calculated; that it is born of the human being's natural yearning to stand well with his fellows, and have their inspiring approval and praise—a yearning which is commonly so strong and so insistent that it cannot be effectually resisted, and must have its way.

A political emergency brings out the corn-pone opinion in fine force in its two chief varieties—the pocket-book variety, which has its origin in self-interest, and the bigger variety, the sentimental variety—the one which can't bear to be outside the pale; can't bear to be in disfavor; can't endure the averted face and the cold shoulder; wants to stand well with the friends, wants to be smiled upon, wants to be welcome, wants to hear the precious words *"he's* on the right track!" Uttered, perhaps, by an ass, but still an ass of high degree, an ass whose approval is gold and diamonds to a smaller ass, and confers glory, and honor and happiness, and membership in the herd. For these gauds many a man will dump his life-long principles into the street, and his conscience along with them. We have seen it happen. In some millions of instances.

Men think they think upon great political questions, and they do; but they think with their party, not independently; they read its literature, but not that of the other side; they arrive at convictions, but they are drawn from a partial view of the matter in hand and are of no particular value. They swarm with their party, they feel with their party, they are happy in their party's approval; and where the party leads they will follow, whether for right and honor, or through blood and dirt and a mush of mutilated morals.   15

In our late canvas half of the nation passionately believed that in silver lay salvation, the other half as passionately believed that that way lay destruction. Do you believe that a tenth part of the people, on either side, had any rational excuse for having an opinion about the matter at all? I studied that mighty question to the bottom—and came out empty. Half of our people passionately believe in high tariff, the other half believe otherwise. Does this mean study and examination, or only feeling? The latter, I think. I have deeply studied that question, too—and didn't arrive. We all do no end of feeling, and we mistake it for thinking. And out of it we get an aggregation which we consider a Boon. Its name is Public Opinion. It is held in reverence. It settles everything. Some think it the Voice of God. Pr'aps.

I suppose that in more cases than we should like to admit, we have two sets of opinions: one private, the other public; one secret and sincere, the other corn-pone, and more or less tainted.

1901

Lines of Inquiry
"Corn-Pone Opinions"

Twain begins this piece about public opinion with a detailed little story of himself and Jerry, a slave. Why doesn't he begin, instead, with a more direct statement of his topic and point, such as appears in paragraph 9? In what respects is the story particularly relevant to his point about the power of public opinion? How does your view of this story compare with the comments that Hoagland makes about it in "What I Think, What I Am"?

Twain views public opinion quite negatively. What kinds of evidence does he offer to support his contention about the rareness of original opinion? What assumptions about human nature, human behavior, and human motives does Twain bring to the discussion in support of his contention about public opinion and belief? In what respects does Twain seem more concerned with voicing his ideas about the weakness of human nature than with arguing his point about the rarity of original ideas?

According to Twain, public opinion exerts its dominating influence in all areas of human existence—in clothes, manners, morals, art, politics, and religion. In which of these respects does he seem most convincing? In which respects, least convincing? What do you suppose would be the most effective way(s) of challenging Twain's contentions about public opinion and human nature?

Was the World Made
for Man?

*"Alfred Russell Wallace's revival of the theory that this earth is
at the centre of the stellar universe, and is the only habitable globe,
has aroused great interest in the world."*—Literary Digest.
    *"For ourselves we do thoroughly believe that man, as he lives
just here on this tiny earth, is in essence and possibilities the most
sublime existence in all the range of non-divine being—the chief
love and delight of God."*—Chicago "Interior," *(Presb.)*

I seem to be the only scientist and theologian still remaining to be heard from on this important matter of whether the world was made for man or not. I feel that it is time for me to speak.

I stand almost with the others. They believe the world was made for man, I believe it likely that it was made for man; they think there is proof, astronomical mainly, that it was made for man, I think there is evidence only, not proof, that it was made for him. It is too early, yet, to arrange the verdict, the returns are not all in. When they are all in, I think they will show that the world was made for man; but we must not hurry, we must patiently wait till they are all in.

Now as far as we have got, astronomy is on our side. Mr. Wallace[1] has clearly shown this. He has clearly shown two things: that the world was made for man, and that the universe was made for the world—to stiddy it, you know. The astronomy part is settled, and cannot be challenged.

We come now to the geological part. This is the one where the evidence is not all in, yet. It is coming in, hourly, daily, coming in all the time, but naturally it comes with geological carefulness and deliberation, and we must not be impatient, we must not get excited, we must be calm, and wait. To lose our tranquillity will not hurry geology; nothing hurries geology.

It takes a long time to prepare a world for man, such a thing is not done in a day. Some of the great scientists, carefully ciphering the evidences furnished by geology, have arrived at the conviction that our world is prodigiously old, and they may be right, but Lord Kelvin[2] is not of their opinion. He takes a cautious, conservative view, in order

5

---

[1] *Mr. Wallace:* Alfred Russell Wallace, English naturalist, 1823–1913
[2] *Lord Kelvin:* William Thomson Kelvin, British mathematician and physicist, 1824–1907.

to be on the safe side, and feels sure it is not so old as they think. As Lord Kelvin is the highest authority in science now living, I think we must yield to him and accept his view. He does not concede that the world is more than a hundred million years old. He believes it is that old, but not older. Lyell[3] believed that our race was introduced into the world 31,000 years ago, Herbert Spencer[4] makes it 32,000. Lord Kelvin agrees with Spencer.

Very well. According to these figures it took 99,968,000 years to prepare the world for man, impatient as the Creator doubtless was to see him and admire him. But a large enterprise like this has to be conducted warily, painstakingly, logically. It was foreseen that man would have to have the oyster. Therefore the first preparation was made for the oyster. Very well, you cannot make an oyster out of whole cloth, you must make the oyster's ancestor first. This is not done in a day. You must make a vast variety of invertebrates, to start with—belemnites, trilobites, jebusites, amalekites, and that sort of fry, and put them to soak in a primary sea, and wait and see what will happen. Some will be a disappointment—the belemnites, the ammonites and such; they will be failures, they will die out and become extinct, in the course of the 19,000,000 years covered by the experiment, but all is not lost, for the amalekites will fetch the home-stake; they will develop gradually into encrinites, and stalactites, and blatherskites, and one thing and another as the mighty ages creep on and the Archaean and the Cambrian Periods pile their lofty crags in the primordial seas, and at last the first grand stage in the preparation of the world for man stands completed, the Oyster is done. An oyster has hardly any more reasoning power than a scientist has; and so it is reasonably certain that this one jumped to the conclusion that the nineteen-million years was a preparation for *him;* but that would be just like an oyster, which is the most conceited animal there is, except man. And anyway, this one could not know, at that early date, that he was only an incident in a scheme, and that there was some more to the scheme, yet.

The oyster being achieved, the next thing to be arranged for in the preparation of the world for man, was fish. Fish, and coal—to fry it with. So the Old Silurian seas were opened up to breed the fish in, and at the same time the great work of building Old Red Sandstone mountains 80,000 feet high to cold-storage their fossils in was begun. This latter was quite indispensable, for there would be no end of failures again, no end of extinctions—millions of them—and it would be cheaper and less trouble to can them in the rocks than keep tally of them in a book. One does not build the coal beds and 80,000 feet of perpendicular Old

[3] *Lyell:* Sir Charles Lyell, British geologist, 1797–1875.
[4] *Spencer:* Herbert Spencer, English philosopher, 1820–1903.

Red Sandstone in a brief time—no, it took twenty million years. In the first place, a coal bed is a slow and troublesome and tiresome thing to construct. You have to grow prodigious forests of tree-ferns and reeds and calamites and such things in a marshy region; then you have to sink them under out of sight and let them rot; then you have to turn the streams on them, so as to bury them under several feet of sediment, and the sediment must have time to harden and turn to rock; next you must grow another forest on top, then sink it and put on another layer of sediment and harden it; then more forest and more rock, layer upon layer, three miles deep—ah, indeed it is a sickening slow job to build a coal-measure and do it right!

So the millions of years drag on; and meantime the fish-culture is lazying along and frazzling out in a way to make a person tired. You have developed ten thousand kinds of fishes from the oyster; and come to look, you have raised nothing but fossils, nothing but extinctions. There is nothing left alive and progressive but a ganoid or two and perhaps half a dozen asteroids. Even the cat wouldn't eat such.

Still, it is no great matter; there is plenty of time, yet, and they will develop into something tasty before man is ready for them. Even a ganoid can be depended on for that, when he is not going to be called on for sixty million years.

The Palaeozoic time-limit having now been reached, it was neces-   10
sary to begin the next stage in the preparation of the world for man, by opening up the Mesozoic Age and instituting some reptiles. For man would need reptiles. Not to eat, but to develop himself from. This being the most important detail of the scheme, a spacious liberality of time was set apart for it—thirty million years. What wonders followed! From the remaining ganoids and asteroids and alkaloids were developed by slow and steady and pains-taking culture those stupendous saurians that used to prowl about the steamy world in those remote ages, with their snaky heads reared forty feet in the air and sixty feet of body and tail racing and thrashing after. All gone, now, alas—all extinct, except the little handful of Arkansawrians left stranded and lonely with us here upon this far-flung verge and fringe of time.

Yes, it took thirty million years and twenty million reptiles to get one that would stick long enough to develop into something else and let the scheme proceed to the next step.

Then the Pterodactyl burst upon the world in all his impressive solemnity and grandeur, and all Nature recognized that the Cainozoic threshold was crossed and a new Period open for business, a new stage begun in the preparation of the globe for man. It may be that the Pterodactyl thought the thirty million years had been intended as a prepa-ration for himself, for there was nothing too foolish for a Pterodactyl to imagine, but he was in error, the preparation was for man. Without doubt the Pterodactyl attracted great attention, for even the least obser-

vant could see that there was the making of a bird in him. And so it
turned out. Also the makings of a mammal, in time. One thing we
have to say to his credit, that in the matter of picturesqueness he was
the triumph of his Period; he wore wings and had teeth, and was a
starchy and wonderful mixture altogether, a kind of long-distance premonitory symptom of Kipling's marine:

> 'E isn't one o' the reg'lar Line, nor 'e isn't one of the crew,
> 'E's a kind of a giddy harumfrodite—soldier an' sailor too!

From this time onward for nearly another thirty million years the preparation moved briskly. From the Pterodactyl was developed the bird;
from the bird the kangaroo, from the kangaroo the other marsupials;
from these the mastodon, the megatherium, the giant sloth, the Irish
elk, and all that crowd that you make useful and instructive fossils out
of—then came the first great Ice Sheet, and they all retreated before it
and crossed over the bridge at Behring's strait and wandered around
over Europe and Asia and died. All except a few, to carry on the preparation with. Six Glacial Periods with two million years between Periods chased these poor orphans up and down and about the earth, from
weather to weather—from tropic swelter at the poles to Arctic frost at
the equator and back again and to and fro, they never knowing what
kind of weather was going to turn up next; and if ever they settled
down anywhere the whole continent suddenly sank under them without the least notice and they had to trade places with the fishes and
scramble off to where the seas had been, and scarcely a dry rag on
them; and when there was nothing else doing a volcano would let go
and fire them out from wherever they had located. They led this unset-
tled and irritating life for twenty-five million years, half the time afloat,
half the time aground, and always wondering what it was all for, they
never suspecting, of course, that it was a preparation for man and had
to be done just so or it wouldn't be any proper and harmonious place
for him when he arrived.

And at last came the monkey, and anybody could see that man
wasn't far off, now. And in truth that was so. The monkey went on
developing for close upon 5,000,000 years, and then turned into a man—
to all appearances.

Such is the history of it. Man has been here 32,000 years. That it
took a hundred million years to prepare the world for him is proof that
that is what it was done for. I suppose it is. I dunno. If the Eiffel tower
were now representing the world's age, the skin of paint on the pinna-
cle-knob at its summit would represent man's share of that age; and
anybody would perceive that that skin was what the tower was built
for. I reckon they would, I dunno.

1903

Lines of Inquiry
"Was the World Made for Man?"

The speaker in this piece refers to himself as a "scientist and theologian." How scientific and theological do his information and ideas seem to be in paragraphs 6 and 7, when he explains what was required "to prepare the world for man"? How scientific and theological does his style seem to be in those same paragraphs—in such expressions as "make an oyster out of whole cloth" or "the amalekites will fetch the home-stake"? How would you describe the style of such expressions or characterize the personality that comes across as a result of them? To what extent do you associate that personality with Twain?

The story of geological, natural, and human evolution that comes across in this piece is quite preposterous. In what respect(s), if any, does it seem intended to mock scientific theories of evolution? Or theological explanations of evolution? What exactly do you think is the point of Twain's mock story of evolution? What is the point of his analogy in the final paragraph between the world and the Eiffel tower?

For another story of evolution, look at Eiseley's "How Flowers Changed the World." What similarities, what differences, do you notice between these two explanations? Assuming that you did not know of Twain and of his typically humorous and satiric approach to experience, and that you did not know about Eiseley and his scientific background, how would you know to take one piece humorously and the other straight-forwardly? What do you suppose Twain would think about Eiseley's story of how flowers changed the world? What do you think Eiseley would think about Twain's story?

"The Turning Point of
My Life"

If I understand the idea, the *Bazar* invites several of us to write upon the above text. It means the change in my life's course which introduced what must be regarded by me as the most *important* condition of my career. But it also implies— without intention, perhaps—that that turning point was *itself,* individually, the creator of the new condition. This gives it too much distinction, too much prominence, too much credit. It is only the *last* link in a very long chain of turning points commissioned to produce the weighty result; it is not any more important than the humblest of its ten thousand predecessors. Each of the ten thousand did its appointed share, on its appointed date, in forwarding the scheme, and they were all necessary; to have let out any one of them would have defeated the scheme and brought about *some other* result. I know we have a fashion of saying "such and such an event was *the* turning point of my life," but we shouldn't say it. We should merely grant that its place as *last* link in the chain makes it the most *conspicuous* link; in real importance it has no advantage over any one of its predecessors.

Perhaps the most celebrated turning point recorded in history was the crossing of the Rubicon. Suetonius says:

> Coming up with his troops on the banks of the Rubicon, he halted for a while, and, revolving in his mind the importance of the step he was on the point of taking, he turned to those about him and said, "We may still retreat; but if we pass this little bridge, nothing is left for us but to fight it out in arms."

This was a stupendously important moment. And all the incidents, big and little, of Caesar's previous life had been leading up to it, stage by stage, link by link. This was the *last* link—merely the last one, and no bigger than the others; but as we gaze back at it through the inflating mists of our imagination, it looks as big as the orbit of Neptune.

You, the reader, have a *personal* interest in that link, and so have I; so has the rest of the human race. It was one of the links in your life-chain, and it was one of the links in mine. We may wait, now, with bated breath, while Caesar reflects. Your fate and mine are involved in his decision.

> While he was thus hesitating, the following incident occurred. A person remarkable for his noble mien and graceful aspect, appeared close at hand,

sitting and playing upon a pipe. When not only the shepherds, but a number of soldiers also, flocked to listen to him, and some trumpeters among them, he snatched a trumpet from one of them, ran to the river with it, and sounding the advance with a piercing blast, crossed to the other side. Upon this, Caesar exclaimed, "Let us go whither the omens of the gods and the iniquity of our enemies call us. *The die is cast.*"

So he crossed—and changed the future of the whole human race, 5 for all time. But that stranger was a link in Caesar's life-chain, too; and a necessary one. We don't know his name, we never hear of him again, he was very casual, he acts like an accident; but he was no accident, he was there by compulsion of *his* life-chain, to blow the electrifying blast that was to make up Caesar's mind for him, and thence go piping down the aisles of history forever.

If the stranger hadn't been there! But he *was.* And Caesar crossed. With such results! Such vast events—each a link in the *human race's* life-chain; each event producing the next one, and that one the next one, and so on: the destruction of the republic; the founding of the empire; the breaking up of the empire; the rise of Christianity upon its ruins; the spread of the religion to other lands—and so on: link by link took its appointed place at its appointed time, the discovery of America being one of them; our Revolution another; the inflow of English and other immigrants another; their drift westward (my ancestors among them) another; the settlement of certain of them in Missouri—which resulted in *me.* For I was one of the unavoidable results of the crossing of the Rubicon. If the stranger, with his trumpet blast, had stayed away (which he *couldn't,* for he was an appointed link), Caesar would not have crossed. What would have happened, in that case, we can never guess. We only know that the things that did happen would not have happened. They might have been replaced by equally prodigious things, of course, but their nature and results are beyond our guessing. But the matter that interests me personally is, that I would not be *here,* now, but somewhere else; and probably black—there is no telling. Very well, I am glad he crossed. And very really and thankfully glad, too, though I never cared anything about it before.

II

To me, the most important feature of my life is its literary feature. I have been professionally literary something more than forty years. There have been many turning points in my life, but the one that was the last link in the chain appointed to conduct me to the literary guild is the most *conspicuous* link in that chain. *Because* it was the last one. It was not any more important than its predecessors. All the other links have an inconspicuous look, except the crossing of the Rubicon; but as factors in making me literary they are all of the one size, the crossing of the Rubicon included.

I know how I came to be literary, and I will tell the steps that led up to it and brought it about.

The crossing of the Rubicon was not the first one, it was hardly even a recent one; I should have to go back ages before Caesar's day to find the first one. To save space I will go back only a couple of generations, and start with an incident of my boyhood. When I was twelve and a half years old, my father died. It was in the spring. The summer came, and brought with it an epidemic of measles. For a time, a child died almost every day. The village was paralysed with fright, distress, despair. Children that were not smitten with the disease were imprisoned in their homes to save them from the infection. In the homes there were no cheerful faces, there was no music, there was no singing but of solemn hymns, no voice but of prayer, no romping was allowed, no noise, no laughter, the family moved spectrally about on tiptoe, in a ghostly hush. I was a prisoner. My soul was steeped in this awful dreariness—and in fear. At some time or other every day and every night a sudden shiver shook me to the marrow, and I said to myself, "There, I've got it! and I shall die." Life on these miserable terms was not worth living, and at last I made up my mind to get the disease and have it over, one way or the other. I escaped from the house and went to the house of a neighbor where a playmate of mine was very ill with the malady. When the chance offered I crept into his room and got into bed with him. I was discovered by his mother and sent back into captivity. But I had the disease; they could not take that from me. I came near to dying. The whole village was interested, and anxious, and sent for news for me every day; and not only once a day, but several times. Everybody believed I would die; but on the fourteenth day a change came for the worse and they were disappointed.

This was a turning point of my life. (Link number one.) For when 10 I got well my mother closed my school career and apprenticed me to a printer. She was tired of trying to keep me out of mischief, and the adventure of the measles decided her to put me into more masterful hands than hers.

I became a printer, and began to add one link after another to the chain which was to lead me into the literary profession. A long road, but I could not know that; and as I did not know what its goal was, or even that it had one, I was indifferent. Also contented.

A young printer wanders around a good deal, seeking and finding work; and seeking again, when necessity commands. N. B. Necessity is a *Circumstance;* Circumstance is man's master—and when Circumstance commands, he must obey; he may argue the matter—that is his privilege, just as it is the honorable privilege of a falling body to argue with the attraction of gravitation—but it won't do any good, he must *obey.* I wandered for ten years, under the guidance and dictatorship of Circumstance, and finally arrived in a city of Iowa, where I worked several months. Among the books that interested me in those days was one about the Amazon. The traveler told an alluring tale of his long voyage up the great river from Para to the sources of the Madeira, through the heart of an enchanted land, a land wastefully rich in tropical wonders, a romantic land where all the birds and flowers and animals were of the museum varieties, and where the alligator and the crocodile and the monkey seemed as much at home as if they were in the Zoo. Also, he told an astonishing tale about *coca,* a vegetable product of miraculous powers; asserting that it was so nourishing and so strength-giving that the native of the mountains of the Madeira region would tramp up-hill and down all day on a pinch of powdered coca and require no other sustenance.

I was fired with a longing to ascend the Amazon. Also with a longing to open up a trade in coca with all the world. During months I dreamed that dream, and tried to contrive ways to get to Para and spring that splendid enterprise upon an unsuspecting planet. But all in vain. A person may *plan* as much as he wants to, but nothing of consequence is likely to come of it until the magician *Circumstance* steps in and takes the matter off his hands. At last Circumstance came to my help. It was in this way. Circumstance, to help or hurt another man, made him lose a fifty-dollar bill in the street; and to help or hurt me, made me find it. I advertised the find, and left for the Amazon the same day. This was another turning point, another link.

Could Circumstance have ordered another dweller in that town to go to the Amazon and open up a world-trade in coca on a fifty-dollar basis and been obeyed? No, I was the only one. There were other fools there—shoals and shoals of them—but they were not of my kind. I was the only one of my kind.

Circumstance is powerful, but it cannot work alone, it has to have 15 a partner. Its partner is man's *temperament*—his natural disposition. His temperament is not his invention, it is *born* in him, and he has no authority over it, neither is he responsible for its acts. He cannot change it, nothing can change it, nothing can modify it,—except temporarily. But it won't stay modified. It is permanent; like the color of the man's eyes and the shape of his ears. Blue eyes are gray, in certain unusual lights; but they resume their natural color when that stress is removed.

A Circumstance that will coerce one man, will have no effect upon a man of a different temperament. If Circumstance had thrown the bank note in Caesar's way, his temperament would not have made him start for the Amazon. His temperament would have compelled him to do something with the money, but not that. It might have made him advertise the note—and *wait.* We can't tell. Also, it might have made him go to New York and buy into the government; with results that would leave Tweed nothing to learn when it came his turn.

Very well, Circumstance furnished the capital, and my temperament told me what to do with it. Sometimes a temperament is an ass.

When that is the case the owner of it is an ass, too, and is going to remain one. Training, experience, association, can temporarily so elevate him that people will think he is a mule, but they will be mistaken. Artificially he *is* a mule, for the time being, but at bottom he is an ass yet, and will remain one.

By temperament I was the kind of person that *does* things. Does them, and reflects afterwards. So I started for the Amazon, without reflecting, and without asking any questions. That was more than fifty years ago. In all that time my temperament has not changed, by even a shade. I have been punished many and many a time, and bitterly, for doing things first and reflecting afterward, but these tortures have been of no value to me; I still do the thing commanded by Circumstance and Temperament, and reflect afterward. Always violently. When I am reflecting, on those occasions, even deaf persons can hear me think.

I went by the way of Cincinnati, and down the Ohio and Mississippi. My idea was to take ship, at New Orleans, for Para. In New Orleans I inquired, and found there was no ship leaving for Para. Also, that there never had *been* one leaving for Para. I reflected. A policeman came and asked me what I was doing, and I told him. He made me move on; and said if he caught me reflecting in the public street again he would run me in.

After a few days I was out of money. Then Circumstance arrived,   20 with another turning point of my life—a new link. On my way down, I had made the acquaintance of a pilot; I begged him to teach me the river, and he consented. I became a pilot.

By and by Circumstance came again—introducing the Civil War, this time, in order to push me ahead a stage or two toward the literary profession. The boats stopped running, my livelihood was gone.

Circumstance came to the rescue with a new turning point and a fresh link. My brother was appointed secretary to the new Territory of Nevada, and he invited me to go with him and help him in his office. I accepted.

In Nevada, Circumstance furnished me the silver fever and I went into the mines to make a fortune and enter the ministry. As I supposed; but that was not the idea. The idea was, to move me another step toward literature. For amusement I scribbled things for the Virginia City *Enterprise*. One isn't a printer ten years without setting up acres of good and bad literature, and learning—unconsciously at first, consciously later—to discriminate between the two, within his mental limitations; and meantime he is unconsciously acquiring what is called a "style." One of my efforts attracted attention, and the *Enterprise* sent for me, and put me on its staff.

And so I became a journalist—another link. By and by Circumstance and the Sacramento *Union* sent me to the Sandwich Islands for five or six months, to write up sugar. I did it; and threw in a good deal of extraneous matter that hadn't anything to do with sugar. But it was this extraneous matter that helped me to another link.

It made me notorious, and San Francisco invited me to lecture. Which   25
I did. And profitably. I had long had a desire to travel and see the world, and now the platform had furnished me the means. So I joined the "Quaker City Excursion."

When I returned to America, Circumstance was waiting on the pier—with the *last* link: I was asked to *write a book,* and I did it, and called it *The Innocents Abroad.* Thus at last I became a member of the literary guild. That was forty-two years ago, and I have been a member ever since. Leaving the Rubicon incident away back where it belongs, I can say with truth that the reason I am in the literary profession is because I had the measles when I was twelve years old.

III

Now what interests me, as regards these details, is not the details themselves, but the fact that none of them was foreseen by me, none of them was planned by me, I was the author of none of them. Circumstance, working in harness with my temperament, created them all and compelled them all. I often offered help, and with the best intentions, but it was rejected: as a rule, uncourteously. I could never plan a thing and get it to come out the way I planned it. It came out some other way—some way I had not counted upon.

And so I do not admire the human being—as an intellectual marvel—as much as I did when I was young, and got him out of books, and did not know him personally. When I used to read that such and such a general did a certain brilliant thing, I believed it. Whereas it was not so. Circumstance did it, by help of his temperament. The circumstances would have failed of effect with a general of another temperament: he might see the chance, but lose the advantage by being by nature too slow or too quick or too doubtful. Once General Grant was asked a question about a matter which had been much debated by the public and the newspapers; he answered the question without any hesitancy: "General, who planned the march through Georgia?" "The enemy!" He added that the enemy usually makes your plans for you. He meant that the enemy, by neglect or through force of circumstances, leaves an opening for you, and you see your chance and take advantage of it.

Circumstances do the planning for us all, no doubt, by help of our temperaments. I see no great difference between a man and a watch, except that the man is conscious and the watch isn't, and the man *tries* to plan things and the watch doesn't. The watch doesn't wind itself, and doesn't regulate itself—these things are done exteriorly. Outside influences, outside circumstances, wind the *man* and regulate him. Left to himself he wouldn't get regulated at all, and the sort of time he would keep would not be valuable. Some rare men are wonderful watches, with gold case, compensation balance, and all those things, and some men are only simple and sweet and humble Waterburys. I am a Waterbury. A Waterbury of that kind, some say.

A nation is only an individual, multiplied. It makes plans, and Circumstance comes and upsets them—or enlarges them. A gang of patriots throws the tea overboard; it destroys a Bastile. The plans stop there; then Circumstance comes in, quite unexpectedly, and turns these modest riots into a revolution. 30

And there was poor Columbus. He elaborated a deep plan to find a new route to an old country. Circumstance revised his plan for him, and he found a new *world.* And *he* gets the credit of it, to this day. He hadn't anything to do with it.

Necessarily the scene of the real turning point of my life (and of yours) was the Garden of Eden. It was there that the first link was forged of the chain that was ultimately to lead to the emptying of me into the literary guild. Adam's *temperament* was the first command the Deity ever issued to a human being on this planet. And it was the only command Adam would *never* be able to disobey. It said, "Be weak, be water, be characterless, be cheaply persuadable." The later command, to let the fruit alone, was certain to be disobeyed. Not by Adam himself, but by his *temperament*—which he did not create and had no authority over. For the *temperament* is the man; the thing tricked out with clothes and named Man, is merely its Shadow, nothing more. The law of the tiger's temperament is, Thou shalt kill; the law of the sheep's temperament is, Thou shalt not kill. To issue later commands requiring the tiger to let the fat stranger alone, and requiring the sheep to imbue its hands in the blood of the lion is not worth while, for those commands *can't* be obeyed. They would invite to violations of the law of *temperament,* which is supreme, and takes precedence of all other authorities. I cannot help feeling disappointed in Adam and Eve. That is, in their temperaments. Not in *them,* poor helpless young creatures—afflicted with temperaments made out of butter; which butter was commanded to get into contact with fire and *be melted.* What I cannot help wishing is, that Adam and Eve had been postponed, and Martin Luther and Joan of Arc put in their place—that splendid pair equipped with temperaments not made of butter, but of asbestos. By neither sugary persuasions nor by hellfire could Satan have beguiled *them* to eat the apple.

There would have been results! Indeed yes. The apple would be intact to-day: there would be no human race; there would be no *you;* there would be no *me.* And the old, old creation-dawn scheme of ultimately launching me into the literary guild would have been defeated.

1910

Lines of Inquiry
" 'The Turning Point of My Life' "

Twain claims that no single event in a person's life is of more "real importance" than "any one of its predecessors," yet he tells what he considers to be
the most important events that led to his becoming a writer. How do you
account for this apparent contradiction? Given his mocking attitude towards the
idea of a turning point in life, why doesn't he confine himself instead to the
story of Caesar crossing the Rubicon? Or to the story of Adam and Eve? What
purpose is served by telling the story of his life from the age of twelve to thirty-
four? What purposes are served by preceding it with the story of Caesar and
following it with the story of Adam?

From the beginning to the end of this piece, Twain states several of his
beliefs concerning the course of human affairs. Note down or underline the
ones that seem to be most important in his thinking, and then try to produce
an outline showing how these ideas are logically interrelated. Check your analysis
of his ideas against the essay as a whole in order to determine what you consider to be the major idea that he is trying to convey in this piece.

In this essay, Twain considers "Circumstance" to be the decisive influence
in human affairs, whereas in "Corn-Pone Opinions," he regards "Conformity"
as the decisive influence. How do you make sense of this apparent contradiction? Which of these influences do you consider to be most decisive in human
affairs? Which one has been most influential in your own life?

Alice Walker
1944—

I believe that the truth about any subject only comes when all the sides of the story are put together, and all their different meanings make one new one. Each writer writes the missing parts to the other writer's story. And the whole story is what I'm after.

Alice Walker's contribution to American writing has been to add a black woman's "side of the story" and to challenge any version of the American experience that has pretended to be the "whole story" but which has, in fact, been constructed around the silence of that "missing part." As a writer, she has consistently supported the interests of her "affinity groups," black people and women, yet her work has never been narrowly political. Ultimately, her artistic quest is also a spiritual one: "One thing I try to have in my life and my fiction is an awareness of and openness to mystery, which, to me, is deeper than any politics, race, or geographical location."

The youngest of eight children, Walker was born in Eatonton, Georgia, a town "which passes for the Walker ancestral home." Her "four-greats" grandmother on her father's side had been forced in the early nineteenth century to walk all the way from Virginia to Georgia, a baby on each hip, and Walker has chosen to keep and use her family name to honor this grandmother and that walk. By the time she was born, Walker's father, a sharecropper, was a defeated, sickly, and emotionally distant man. But her mother was a "large, soft, loving-eyed woman" who "adorned with flowers whatever shabby house we were forced to live in" and sustained her large family with her patient industry. In addition to teaching by example the "womanist" tradition of black women who grow up knowing they can "do anything," Walker's mother gave her three symbolically significant gifts: a sewing machine, suggesting "independence and self-sufficiency"; a suitcase, representing "permission to travel"; and a typewriter, supporting her interest in writing.

Throughout her childhood, Walker read avidly: "Books became my world because the world I was in was very hard." From the age of eight, when she was accidentally blinded in her right eye, Walker kept a detailed personal notebook. While in many ways profoundly connected to her family, she felt herself to be also profoundly different:

> Sometimes I thought I'd gotten into the family by mistake. I always seemed to need more peace and quiet than anybody else. That's very difficult when you're living with ten people in three or four rooms. So I found what privacy I had by walking in the fields. We had to get our water from a spring, so that was a time to be alone, too.

Walker's early love affair with nature was also an escape from the harsh reality of her hometown, where before integration blacks were not permitted to swim in the public pool, where they could enter the local drug store to buy ice cream but were not allowed to stay inside to eat it, and where stories of lynchings and other forms of racial violence perpetually filled the air. Completely segregated from the white population, in schools as in neighborhoods, blacks took care of each other's needs, fostering the education of the young, nursing the sick, sharing food and clothes, burying the dead. That interdependence gave Walker a rich experience of community, but "I was an exile in my own town," she writes, "and grew to despise its white citizens as much as I loved the Georgia countryside where I fished and swam and walked through fields of black-eyed Susans. . . ."

Walker struggled with the hatred, and like James Baldwin and Martin Luther King before her, came to realize that it would finally destroy not her enemies but herself: "Once spread about . . . [hatred] becomes a web in which I would sit caught and paralyzed like the fly who stepped into the parlor." Walker has said that King gave the South back to its black sons and daughters and inspired her to hope rather than hate. Nevertheless, the memory of her poverty-stricken and racially oppressed heritage remains vivid: "It is memory, more than anything else, that sours the sweetness of what has been accomplished in the South. What we cannot forget and will never forget."

Walker left home in 1961 to attend Spelman College for black women in Atlanta, but after two years became frustrated with its strict social rules and regulations, so in search of greater "freedom" she transferred to Sarah Lawrence, an academically elite, predominantly white woman's college, where she graduated in 1965. While in college she traveled to the Soviet Union, Europe, and Africa on fellowships, and began to develop the global consciousness that has characterized her later writing. And at Sarah Lawrence, encouraged by her writing teachers, particularly the poet Muriel Rukeyser, she completed her first book, *Once,* a collection of poems that was published in 1968.

After graduating from college, Walker married an activist lawyer in 1967 (from whom she was divorced in 1976) and moved with him to

Mississippi, where he went to take part in the civil rights movement. Back in the South, she taught black studies at Jackson State College, and she thus came to discover a wealth of black literature of which her education had left her ignorant. So, she entered "still another college," this one "simply a college of books," and became acquainted with her literary forbears. Having read widely in the work of white writers throughout her school years, she sought to correct the imbalance by immersing herself in the work of black poets and novelists, many of them out of print and forgotten. Her discoveries inspired her to begin a crusade to restore black writing into the mainstream of American literature. In her essays she has repeatedly made known the work of black American and African writers, and she has also written a children's biography of Langston Hughes, as well as having edited a collection of works by Zora Neale Hurston.

Walker herself has been a prolific writer, publishing twelve books—novels, short stories, poems, and essays—and numerous magazine pieces since 1968. Her work has won her wide recognition and many awards, though she is probably best known for her novel of southern black experience, *The Color Purple* (1983), which received both the Pulitzer Prize and the National Book Award before being made into a highly successful motion picture. She has served for a number of years as a contributing editor of *Ms* magazine, as well as having taught writing and literature at schools in Mississippi, Boston, and New York, before settling in California, where she lives with her family in the countryside near San Francisco.

Her essays have been collected in two volumes, *In Search of Our Mothers' Gardens* (1983) and *Living by the Word* (1988), both of which represent significant contributions to the self-defining process of her race and her gender. Her growing vision, though, has led her increasingly to resist race as a category for definition:

> I have not labeled myself yet. I would like to call myself revolutionary, for I am always changing, and growing, it is hoped for the good of more black people. I do call myself black when it seems necessary to call myself anything, especially since I believe one's work rather than one's appearance adequately labels one.

In this respect, Walker follows the precedent of Baldwin, among others, in calling into question the designations of "white" and "black." Indeed, in her most recent essays, Walker has pressed on her readers a mystical vision of oneness, not only of all the world's people but also of humankind with everything else in creation. Following in the tradition of ancient African and Native American belief, she celebrates a vision affirming that "everything is inhabited by spirit." So, in historical times filled with doubt and with the fear of annihilation, she has taken upon herself the task of urging the need for the "survival whole" of the human race and the planet which is its home. "The truest and most enduring impulse I have is simply to write," she says, and she is clear about what it is she hopes to accomplish through her writing:

> I am trying to arrive at that place where black music already is; to arrive at that unself-conscious sense of collective oneness; that naturalness, that (even when anguished) grace.

Beauty: When the Other Dancer Is the Self

It is a bright summer day in 1947. My father, a fat, funny man with beautiful eyes and a subversive wit, is trying to decide which of his eight children he will take with him to the county fair. My mother, of course, will not go. She is knocked out from getting most of us ready: I hold my neck stiff against the pressure of her knuckles as she hastily completes the braiding and then beribboning of my hair.

My father is the driver for the rich old white lady up the road. Her name is Miss Mey. She owns all the land for miles around, as well as the house in which we live. All I remember about her is that she once offered to pay my mother thirty-five cents for cleaning her house, raking up piles of her magnolia leaves, and washing her family's clothes, and that my mother—she of no money, eight children, and a chronic earache—refused it. But I do not think of this in 1947. I am two and a half years old. I want to go everywhere my daddy goes. I am excited at the prospect of riding in a car. Someone has told me fairs are fun. That there is room in the car for only three of us doesn't faze me at all. Whirling happily in my starchy frock, showing off my biscuit-polished patent-leather shoes and lavender socks, tossing my head in a way that makes my ribbons bounce, I stand, hands on hips, before my father. "Take me, Daddy," I say with assurance; "I'm the prettiest!"

Later, it does not surprise me to find myself in Miss Mey's shiny black car, sharing the back seat with the other lucky ones. Does not surprise me that I thoroughly enjoy the fair. At home that night I tell the unlucky ones all I can remember about the merry-go-round, the man who eats live chickens, and the teddy bears, until they say: that's enough, baby Alice. Shut up now, and go to sleep.

It is Easter Sunday, 1950. I am dressed in a green, flocked, scalloped-hem dress (handmade by my adoring sister, Ruth) that has its own smooth satin petticoat and tiny hot-pink roses tucked into each scallop. My shoes, new T-strap patent leather, again highly biscuit-polished. I am six years old and have learned one of the longest Easter speeches to be heard that day, totally unlike the speech I said when I was two: "Easter lilies/pure and white/blossom in/the morning light." When I rise to give my speech I do so on a great wave of love and pride and expectation. People in the church stop rustling their new crinolines. They seem to hold their breath. I can tell they admire my dress, but it is my spirit, bordering on sassiness (womanishness), they secretly applaud.

"That girl's a little *mess*," they whisper to each other, pleased.   5

Naturally I say my speech without stammer or pause, unlike those who stutter, stammer, or, worst of all, forget. This is before the word "beautiful" exists in people's vocabulary, but "Oh, isn't she the *cutest* thing!" frequently floats my way. "And got so much sense!" they gratefully add . . . for which thoughtful addition I thank them to this day.

It was great fun being cute. But then, one day, it ended.

I am eight years old and a tomboy. I have a cowboy hat, cowboy boots, checkered shirt and pants, all red. My playmates are my brothers, two and four years older than I. Their colors are black and green, the only difference in the way we are dressed. On Saturday nights we all go to the picture show, even my mother; Westerns are her favorite kind of movie. Back home, "on the ranch," we pretend we are Tom Mix, Hopalong Cassidy, Lash LaRue (we've even named one of our dogs Lash LaRue); we chase each other for hours rustling cattle, being outlaws, delivering damsels from distress. Then my parents decide to buy my brothers guns. These are not "real" guns. They shoot "BBs," copper pellets my brothers say will kill birds. Because I am a girl, I do not get a gun. Instantly I am relegated to the position of Indian. Now there appears a great distance between us. They shoot and shoot at everything with their new guns. I try to keep up with my bow and arrows.

One day while I am standing on top of our makeshift "garage"— pieces of tin nailed across some poles—holding my bow and arrow and looking out toward the fields, I feel an incredible blow in my right eye. I look down just in time to see my brother lower his gun.

Both brothers rush to my side. My eye stings, and I cover it with   10
my hand. "If you tell," they say, "we will get a whipping. You don't want that to happen, do you?" I do not. "Here is a piece of wire," says the older brother, picking it up from the roof; "say you stepped on one end of it and the other flew up and hit you." The pain is beginning to start. "Yes," I say. "Yes, I will say that is what happened." If I do not say this is what happened, I know my brothers will find ways to make me wish I had. But now I will say anything that gets me to my mother.

Confronted by our parents we stick to the lie agreed upon. They place me on a bench on the porch and I close my left eye while they examine the right. There is a tree growing from underneath the porch that climbs past the railing to the roof. It is the last thing my right eye sees. I watch as its trunk, its branches, and then its leaves are blotted out by the rising blood.

I am in shock. First there is intense fever, which my father tries to break using lily leaves bound around my head. Then there are chills: my mother tries to get me to eat soup. Eventually, I do not know how, my parents learn what has happened. A week after the "accident" they take me to see a doctor. "Why did you wait so long to come?" he asks, looking into my eye and shaking his head. "Eyes are sympathetic," he says. "If one is blind, the other will likely become blind too."

This comment of the doctor's terrifies me. But it is really how I look that bothers me most. Where the BB pellet struck there is a glob of whitish scar tissue, a hideous cataract, on my eye. Now when I stare at people—a favorite pastime, up to now—they will stare back. Not at the "cute" little girl, but at her scar. For six years I do not stare at anyone, because I do not raise my head.

Years later, in the throes of a mid-life crisis, I ask my mother and sister whether I changed after the "accident." "No," they say, puzzled. "What do you mean?"

What do I mean?   15

I am eight, and, for the first time, doing poorly in school, where I have been something of a whiz since I was four. We have just moved to the place where the "accident" occurred. We do not know any of the people around us because this is a different county. The only time I see the friends I knew is when we go back to our old church. The new school is the former state penitentiary. It is a large stone building, cold and drafty, crammed to overflowing with boisterous, ill-disciplined children. On the third floor there is a huge circular imprint of some partition that has been torn out.

"What used to be here?" I ask a sullen girl next to me on our way past it to lunch.

"The electric chair," says she.

At night I have nightmares about the electric chair, and about all the people reputedly "fried" in it. I am afraid of the school, where all the students seem to be budding criminals.

"What's the matter with your eye?" they ask, critically.   20

When I don't answer (I cannot decide whether it was an "accident" or not), they shove me, insist on a fight.

My brother, the one who created the story about the wire, comes to my rescue. But then brags so much about "protecting" me, I become sick.

After months of torture at the school, my parents decide to send me back to our old community, to my old school. I live with my grandparents and the teacher they board. But there is no room for Phoebe, my cat. By the time my grandparents decide there *is* room, and I ask for my cat, she cannot be found. Miss Yarborough, the boarding teacher, takes me under her wing, and begins to teach me to play the piano. But soon she marries an African—a "prince," she says—and is whisked away to his continent.

At my old school there is at least one teacher who loves me. She is the teacher who "knew me before I was born" and bought my first baby clothes. It is she who makes life bearable. It is her presence that finally helps me turn on the one child at the school who continually calls me "one-eyed bitch." One day I simply grab him by his coat and beat him until I am satisfied. It is my teacher who tells me my mother is ill.

My mother is lying in bed in the middle of the day, something I have never seen. She is in too much pain to speak. She has an abscess in her ear. I stand looking down on her, knowing that if she dies, I cannot live. She is being treated with warm oils and hot bricks held against her cheek. Finally a doctor comes. But I must go back to my grandparents' house. The weeks pass but I am hardly aware of it. All I know is that my mother might die, my father is not so jolly, my brothers still have their guns, and I am the one sent away from home.

"You did not change," they say.   25

Did I imagine the anguish of never looking up?

I am twelve. When relatives come to visit I hide in my room. My cousin Brenda, just my age, whose father works in the post office and whose mother is a nurse, comes to find me. "Hello," she says. And then she asks, looking at my recent school picture, which I did not want taken, and on which the "glob," as I think of it, is clearly visible, "You still can't see out of that eye?"

"No," I say, and flop back on the bed over my book.

That night, as I do almost every night, I abuse my eye. I rant and rave at it, in front of the mirror. I plead with it to clear up before morning. I tell it I hate and despise it. I do not pray for sight. I pray for beauty.

"You did not change," they say.   30

I am fourteen and baby-sitting for my brother Bill, who lives in Boston. He is my favorite brother and there is a strong bond between us. Understanding my feelings of shame and ugliness he and his wife take me to a local hospital, where the "glob" is removed by a doctor named O. Henry. There is still a small bluish crater where the scar tissue was, but the ugly white stuff is gone. Almost immediately I become a different person from the girl who does not raise her head. Or so I think. Now that I've raised my head I win the boyfriend of my dreams. Now that I've raised my head I have plenty of friends. Now that I've raised my head classwork comes from my lips as faultlessly as Easter speeches did, and I leave high school as valedictorian, most popular student, and *queen,* hardly believing my luck. Ironically, the girl who was voted most beautiful in our class (and was) was later shot twice through the chest by a male companion, using a "real" gun, while she was pregnant. But that's another story in itself. Or is it?

"You did not change," they say.

It is now thirty years since the "accident." A beautiful journalist comes to visit and to interview me. She is going to write a cover story for her magazine that focuses on my latest book. "Decide how you want to look on the cover," she says. "Glamorous, or whatever."

Never mind "glamorous," it is the "whatever" that I hear. Suddenly all I can think of is whether I will get enough sleep the night before the photography session: if I don't, my eye will be tired and wander, as blind eyes will.

At night in bed with my lover I think up reasons why I should not appear on the cover of a magazine. "My meanest critics will say I've sold out," I say. "My family will now realize I write scandalous books." 35

"But what's the real reason you don't want to do this?" he asks.

"Because in all probability," I say in a rush, "my eye won't be straight."

"It will be straight enough," he says. Then, "Besides, I thought you'd made your peace with that."

And I suddenly remember that I have.

I remember: 40

I am talking to my brother Jimmy, asking if he remembers anything unusual about the day I was shot. He does not know I consider that day the last time my father, with his sweet home remedy of cool lily leaves, chose me, and that I suffered and raged inside because of this. "Well," he says, "all I remember is standing by the side of the highway with Daddy, trying to flag down a car. A white man stopped, but when Daddy said he needed somebody to take his little girl to the doctor, he drove off."

I remember:

I am in the desert for the first time. I fall totally in love with it. I am so overwhelmed by its beauty, I confront for the first time, consciously, the meaning of the doctor's words years ago: "Eyes are sympathetic. If one is blind, the other will likely become blind too." I realize I have dashed about the world madly, looking at this, looking at that, storing up images against the fading of the light. *But I might have missed seeing the desert!* The shock of that possibility—and gratitude for over twenty-five years of sight—sends me literally to my knees. Poem after poem comes—which is perhaps how poets pray.

ON SIGHT

I am so thankful I have seen
The Desert
And the creatures in the desert
And the desert Itself.

The desert has its own moon
Which I have seen
With my own eye.
There is no flag on it.

Trees of the desert have arms
All of which are always up
That is because the moon is up
The sun is up
Also the sky
The stars
Clouds
None with flags.

If there *were* flags, I doubt
the trees would point.
Would you?

But mostly, I remember this:
I am twenty-seven, and my baby daughter is almost three. Since   40
her birth I have worried about her discovery that her mother's eyes are
different from other people's. Will she be embarrassed? I think. What
will she say? Every day she watches a television program called "Big
Blue Marble." It begins with a picture of the earth as it appears from
the moon. It is bluish, a little battered-looking, but full of light, with
whitish clouds swirling around it. Every time I see it I weep with love,
as if it is a picture of Grandma's house. One day when I am putting
Rebecca down for her nap, she suddenly focuses on my eye. Something
inside me cringes, gets ready to try to protect myself. All children are
cruel about physical differences, I know from experience, and that they
don't always mean to be is another matter. I assume Rebecca will be
the same.

But no-o-o-o. She studies my face intently as we stand, her inside
and me outside her crib. She even holds my face maternally between
her dimpled little hands. Then, looking every bit as serious and law-
yerlike as her father, she says, as if it may just possibly have slipped
my attention: "Mommy, there's a *world* in your eye." (As in, "Don't
be alarmed, or do anything crazy.") And then, gently, but with great
interest: "Mommy, where did you *get* that world in your eye?"

For the most part, the pain left then. (So what if my brothers grew
up to buy even more powerful pellet guns for their sons and to carry
real guns themselves. So what, if a young "Morehouse man" once nearly

fell off the steps of Trevor Arnett Library because he thought my eyes were blue.) Crying and laughing I ran to the bathroom, while Rebecca mumbled and sang herself off to sleep. Yes indeed, I realized, looking into the mirror. There *was* a world in my eye. And I saw that it was possible to love it: that in fact, for all it had taught me of shame and anger and inner vision, I *did* love it. Even to see it drifting out of orbit in boredom, or rolling up out of fatigue, not to mention floating back at attention in excitement (bearing witness, a friend has called it), deeply suitable to my personality, and even characteristic of me.

That night I dream I am dancing to Stevie Wonder's song "Always" (the name of the song is really "As," but I hear it as "Always"). As I dance, whirling and joyous, happier than I've ever been in my life, another bright-faced dancer joins me. We dance and kiss each other and hold each other through the night. The other dancer has obviously come through all right, as I have done. She is beautiful, whole and free. And she is also me.

1983

Lines of Inquiry
"Beauty: When the Other Dancer Is the Self"

In this narrative essay, Walker tells her story in a number of unusual ways. For example, what do you consider to be the effect(s) of her telling about the past in present tense? Why do you suppose she divides the story into a series of short segments, separated from each other by some extra space, rather than telling it and presenting it on the page in a continuously connected manner? And why does she depart from chronological order in the last two segments, first telling about a time "thirty years since the 'accident' " and then about an episode when she was twenty-seven? Imagine how the piece might work out if these episodes were reversed.

Though Walker never announces the point of this essay, it seems clear that she is not just telling about herself because she wants to divulge an aspect of her private life. So, what do you infer about the significance of this piece from her unusual ways of telling her story? What do you infer about the significance of the piece from the lines that she has singled out for emphasis either by italics or by indentation, such as her poem "On Sight"? What do you infer about the significance of the piece from the title and the echoes of it throughout the essay, particularly in the final paragraph?

Think about an especially painful accident or loss that you suffered earlier in your life that has been difficult for you to come to terms with. What was the nature of your accident or loss? In what specific way(s) did it affect you and your attitude towards yourself? At what points in your subsequent life can you remember being particularly troubled by its effects or at ease with them? What has been most helpful for you in coming to terms with it? In what respects, if any, did your reading about Walker's experience help to shed light on your own?

The Civil Rights Movement: What Good Was It?[1]

Someone said recently to an old black lady from Mississippi, whose legs had been badly mangled by local police who arrested her for "disturbing the peace," that the Civil Rights Movement was dead, and asked, since it was dead, what she thought about it. The old lady replied, hobbling out of his presence on her cane,. that the Civil Rights Movement was like herself, "if it's dead, it shore ain't ready to lay down!"

This old lady is a legendary freedom fighter in her small town in the Delta. She has been severely mistreated for insisting on her rights as an American citizen. She has been beaten for singing Movement songs, placed in solitary confinement in prisons for talking about freedom, and placed on bread and water for praying aloud to God for her jailers' deliverance. For such a woman the Civil Rights Movement will never be over as long as her skin is black. It also will never be over for twenty million others with the same "affliction," for whom the Movement can never "lay down," no matter how it is killed by the press and made dead and buried by the white American public. As long as one black American survives, the struggle for equality with other Americans must also survive. This is a debt we owe to those blameless hostages we leave to the future, our children.

Still, white liberals and deserting Civil Rights sponsors are quick to justify their disaffection from the Movement by claiming that it is all over. "And since it is over," they will ask, "would someone kindly tell me what has been gained by it?" They then list statistics supposedly showing how much more advanced segregation is now than ten years ago—in schools, housing, jobs. They point to a gain in conservative politicians during the last few years. They speak of ghetto riots and of the survey that shows that most policemen are admittedly too anti-Negro to do their jobs in ghetto areas fairly and effectively. They speak

---

[1] I wrote the following essay in the winter of 1966–67 while sharing one room above Washington Square Park in New York with a struggling young Jewish law student who became my husband. It was my first published essay and won the three-hundred-dollar first prize in the annual *American Scholar* essay contest. The money was almost magically reassuring to us in those days of dissaffected parents, outraged friends, and one-item meals, and kept us in tulips, peonies, daisies, and lamb chops for several months.

of every area that has been touched by the Civil Rights Movement as somehow or other going to pieces.

They rarely talk, however, about human attitudes among Negroes that have undergone terrific changes just during the past seven to ten years (not to mention all those years when there was a Movement and only the Negroes knew about it). They seldom speak of changes in personal lives because of the influence of people in the Movement. They see general failure and few, if any, individual gains.

They do not understand what it is that keeps the Movement from   5 "laying down" and Negroes from reverting to their former *silent* second-class status. They have apparently never stopped to wonder why it is always the white man—on his radio and in his newspaper and on his television—who says that the Movement is dead. If a Negro were audacious enough to make such a claim, his fellows might hanker to see him shot. The Movement is dead to the white man because it no longer interests him. And it no longer interests him because he can afford to be uninterested: he does not have to live by it, with it, or for it, as Negroes must. He can take a rest from the news of beatings, killings, and arrests that reach him from North and South—if his skin is white. Negroes cannot now and will never be able to take a rest from the injustices that plague them, for they—not the white man—are the target.

Perhaps it is naïve to be thankful that the Movement "saved" a large number of individuals and gave them something to live for, even if it did not provide them with everything they wanted. (Materially, it provided them with precious little that they wanted.) When a movement awakens people to the possibilities of life, it seems unfair to frustrate them by then denying what they had thought was offered. But what was offered? What was promised? What was it all about? What good did it do? Would it have been better, as some have suggested, to leave the Negro people as they were, unawakened, unallied with one another, unhopeful about what to expect for their children in some future world?

I do not think so. If knowledge of my condition is all the freedom I get from a "freedom movement," it is better than unawareness, forgottenness, and hopelessness, the existence that is like the existence of a beast. Man only truly lives by knowing; otherwise he simply performs, copying the daily habits of others, but conceiving nothing of his creative possibilities as a man, and accepting someone else's superiority and his own misery.

When we are children, growing up in our parents' care, we await the spark from the outside world. Sometimes our parents provide it— if we are lucky—sometimes it comes from another source far from home. We sit, paralyzed, surrounded by our anxiety and dread, hoping we will not have to grow up into the narrow world and ways we see about us. We are hungry for a life that turns us on; we yearn for a knowledge of living that will save us from our innocuous lives that resemble death. We look for signs in every strange event; we search for heroes in every unknown face.

It was just six years ago that I began to be alive. I had, of course, been living before—for I am now twenty-three—but I did not really know it. And I did not know it because nobody told me that I—a pensive, yearning, typical high-school senior, but Negro—existed in the minds of others as I existed in my own. Until that time my mind was locked apart from the outer contours and complexion of my body as if it and the body were strangers. The mind possessed both thought and spirit—I wanted to be an author or a scientist—which the color of the body denied. I had never seen myself and existed as a statistic exists, or as a phantom. In the white world I walked, less real to them than a shadow; and being young and well hidden among the slums, among people who also did not exist—either in books or in films or in the government of their own lives—I waited to be called to life. And, by a miracle, I was called.

There was a commotion in our house that night in 1960. We had   10 managed to buy our first television set. It was battered and overpriced, but my mother had gotten used to watching the afternoon soap operas at the house where she worked as maid, and nothing could satisfy her on days when she did not work but a continuation of her "stories." So she pinched pennies and bought a set.

I remained listless throughout her "stories," tales of pregnancy, abortion, hypocrisy, infidelity, and alcoholism. All these men and women were white and lived in houses with servants, long staircases that they floated down, patios where liquor was served four times a day to "relax" them. But my mother, with her swollen feet eased out of her shoes, her heavy body relaxed in our only comfortable chair, watched each movement of the smartly coiffed women, heard each word, pounced upon each innuendo and inflection, and for the duration of these "stories" she saw herself as one of them. She placed herself in every scene she saw, with her braided hair turned blond, her two hundred pounds compressed into a sleek size-seven dress, her rough dark skin smooth and *white*. Her husband became "dark and handsome," talented, witty, urbane, charming. And when she turned to look at my father sitting near her in his sweat shirt with his smelly feet raised on the bed to "air," there was always a tragic look of surprise on her face. Then she would sigh and go out to the kitchen looking lost and unsure of herself. My mother, a truly great woman who raised eight children of her own and half a dozen of the neighbors' without a single complaint, was convinced that she did not exist compared to "them." She subordinated her soul to theirs and became a faithful and timid supporter of the

"Beautiful White People." Once she asked me, in a moment of vicarious pride and despair, if I didn't think that "they" were "jest naturally smarter, prettier, better." My mother asked this: a woman who never got rid of any of her children, never cheated on my father, was never a hypocrite if she could help it, and never even tasted liquor. She could not even bring herself to blame "them" for making her believe what they wanted her to believe: that if she did not look like them, think like them, be sophisticated and corrupt-for-comfort's sake like them, she was a nobody. Black was not a color on my mother; it was a shield that made her invisible.

Of course, the people who wrote the soap-opera scripts always made the Negro maids in them steadfast, trusty, and wise in a home-remedial sort of way; but my mother, a maid for nearly forty years, never once identified herself with the scarcely glimpsed black servant's face beneath the ruffled cap. Like everyone else, in her daydreams at least, she thought she was free.

Six years ago, after half-heartedly watching my mother's soap operas and wondering whether there wasn't something more to be asked of life, the Civil Rights Movement came into my life. Like a good omen for the future, the face of Dr. Martin Luther King, Jr., was the first black face I saw on our new television screen. And, as in a fairy tale, my soul was stirred by the meaning for me of his mission—at the time he was being rather ignominiously dumped into a police van for having led a protest march in Alabama—and I fell in love with the sober and determined face of the Movement. The singing of "We Shall Overcome"—that song betrayed by nonbelievers in it—rang for the first time in my ears. The influence that my mother's soap operas might have had on me became impossible. The life of Dr. King, seeming bigger and more miraculous than the man himself, because of all he had done and suffered, offered a pattern of strength and sincerity I felt I could trust. He had suffered much because of his simple belief in nonviolence, love, and brotherhood. Perhaps the majority of men could not be reached through these beliefs, but because Dr. King kept trying to reach them in spite of danger to himself and his family, I saw in him the hero for whom I had waited so long.

What Dr. King promised was not a ranch-style house and an acre of manicured lawn for every black man, but jail and finally freedom. He did not promise two cars for every family, but the courage one day for all families everywhere to walk without shame and unafraid on their own feet. He did not say that one day it will be us chasing prospective buyers out of our prosperous well-kept neighborhoods, or in other ways exhibiting our snobbery and ignorance as all other ethnic groups before us have done; what he said was that we had a right to live anywhere in this country we chose, and a right to a meaningful well-paying job to provide us with the upkeep of our homes. He did not say we had to become carbon copies of the white American middle class; but he did say we had the right to become whatever we wanted to become.

Because of the Movement, because of an awakened faith in the   15
newness and imagination of the human spirit, because of "black and white together"—for the first time in our history in some human relationship on and off TV—because of the beatings, the arrests, the hell of battle during the past years, I have fought harder for my life and for a chance to be myself, to be something more than a shadow or a number, than I had ever done before in my life. Before, there had seemed to be no real reason for struggling beyond the effort for daily bread. Now there was a chance at that other that Jesus meant when He said we could not live by bread alone.

I have fought and kicked and fasted and prayed and cursed and cried myself to the point of existing. It has been like being born again, literally. Just "knowing" has meant everything to me. Knowing has pushed me out into the world, into college, into places, into people.

Part of what existence means to me is knowing the difference between what I am now and what I was then. It is being capable of looking after myself intellectually as well as financially. It is being able to tell when I am being wronged and by whom. It means being awake to protect myself and the ones I love. It means being a part of the world community, and being *alert* to which part it is that I have joined, and knowing how to change to another part if that part does not suit me. To know is to exist: to exist is to be involved, to move about, to see the world with my own eyes. This, at least, the Movement has given me.

The hippies and other nihilists would have me believe that it is all the same whether the people in Mississippi have a movement behind them or not. Once they have their rights, they say, they will run all over themselves trying to be just like everybody else. They will be well fed, complacent about things of the spirit, emotionless, and without that marvelous humanity and "soul" that the Movement has seen them practice time and time again. "What has the Movement done," they ask, "with the few people it has supposedly helped?" "Got them white-collar jobs, moved them into standardized ranch houses in white neighborhoods, given them nondescript gray flannel suits?" "What are these people now?" they ask. And then they answer themselves, "Nothings!"

I would find this reasoning—which I have heard many, many times from hippies and nonhippies alike—amusing if I did not also consider it serious. For I think it is a delusion, a cop-out, an excuse to disassociate themselves from a world in which they feel too little has been changed or gained. The real question, however, it appears to me, is not whether poor people will adopt the middle-class mentality once they are well fed; rather, it is whether they will ever be well fed enough to be able to choose whatever mentality they think will suit them. The lack of a movement did not keep my mother from *wishing* herself bourgeois in her daydreams.

There is widespread starvation in Mississippi. In my own state of Georgia there are more hungry families than Lester Maddox would like to admit—or even see fed. I went to school with children who ate red dirt. The Movement has prodded and pushed some liberal senators into pressuring the government for food so that the hungry may eat. Food stamps that were two dollars and out of the reach of many families not long ago have been reduced to fifty cents. The price is still out of the reach of some families, and the government, it seems to a lot of people, could spare enough free food to feed its own people. It angers people in the Movement that it does not; they point to the billions in wheat we send free each year to countries abroad. Their government's slowness while people are hungry, its unwillingness to believe that there are Americans starving, its stingy cutting of the price of food stamps, make many Civil Rights workers throw up their hands in disgust. But they do not give up. They do not withdraw into the world of psychedelia. They apply what pressure they can to make the government give away food to hungry people. They do not plan so far ahead in their disillusionment with society that they can see these starving families buying identical ranch-style houses and sending their snobbish children to Bryn Mawr and Yale. They take first things first and try to get them fed.

They do not consider it their business, in any case, to say what kind of life the people they help must lead. How one lives is, after all, one of the rights left to the individual—when and if he has opportunity to choose. It is not the prerogative of the middle class to determine what is worthy of aspiration. There is also every possibility that the middle-class people of tomorrow will turn out ever so much better than those of today. I even know some middle-class people of today who are not *all* bad.

I think there are so few Negro hippies because middle-class Negroes, although well fed, are not careless. They are required by the treacherous world they live in to be clearly aware of whoever or whatever might be trying to do them in. They are middle class in money and position, but they cannot afford to be middle class in complacency. They distrust the hippie movement because they know that it can do nothing for Negroes as a group but "love" them, which is what all paternalists claim to do. And since the only way Negroes can survive (which they cannot do, unfortunately, on love alone) is with the support of the group, they are wisely wary and stay away.

A white writer tried recently to explain that the reason for the relatively few Negro hippies is that Negroes have built up a "super-cool"

20

that cracks under LSD and makes them have a "bad trip." What this writer doesn't guess at is that Negroes are needing drugs less than ever these days for any kind of trip. While the hippies are "tripping," Negroes are going after power, which is so much more important to their survival and their children's survival than LSD and pot.

Everyone would be surprised if the Israelis ignored the Arabs and took up "tripping" and pot smoking. In this country we are the Israelis. Everybody who can do so would like to forget this, of course. But for us to forget it for a minute would be fatal. "We Shall Overcome" is just a song to most Americans, *but we must do it.* Or die.

What good was the Civil Rights Movement? If it had just given this country Dr. King, a leader of conscience, for once in our lifetime, it would have been enough. If it had just taken black eyes off white television stories, it would have been enough. If it had fed one starving child, it would have been enough.

If the Civil Rights Movement is "dead," and if it gave us nothing else, it gave us each other forever. It gave some of us bread, some of us shelter, some of us knowledge and pride, all of us comfort. It gave us our children, our husbands, our brothers, our fathers, as men reborn and with a purpose for living. It broke the pattern of black servitude in this country. It shattered the phony "promise" of white soap operas that sucked away so many pitiful lives. It gave us history and men far greater than Presidents. It gave us heroes, selfless men of courage and strength, for our little boys and girls to follow. It gave us hope for tomorrow. It called us to life.

Because we live, it can never die.

1967

Lines of Inquiry
"The Civil Rights Movement: What Good Was It?"

In the course of this piece, Walker tells stories not only about herself, but also about her mother and about "an old black lady from Mississippi." Why doesn't she focus just on her own behavior and experience? Why does she tell about those other two women and go into such detail about her mother? In the course of this piece she also talks about the behavior of "white liberals and deserting Civil Rights sponsors," as well as about "hippies and other nihilists," but she never refers to any one of them specifically. Why do you suppose she concentrates on individuals in one case and groups in the other? Why do you suppose she begins by attacking one pair of groups but ends by attacking a different pair?

In trying to make clear "what good was" served by the movement, Walker explicitly pits her value system against some others. Define her value system and explain how it differs from the others that she attacks. Why do you think she attacks those other systems? Why doesn't she just answer the question that she puts in the title by telling directly what good she thinks the movement did? According to Walker, what was its greatest good?

Here, as in "Beauty: When the Other Dancer Is the Self," Walker writes about herself and her mother, but the tone she takes in each piece and the way her personality comes across in each piece is quite different. How would you describe her style and characterize the way she comes across in each piece? How do you account for the differences?

The Black Writer and the Southern Experience

My mother tells of an incident that happened to her in the thirties during the Depression. She and my father lived in a small Georgia town and had half a dozen children. They were sharecroppers, and food, especially flour, was almost impossible to obtain. To get flour, which was distributed by the Red Cross, one had to submit vouchers signed by a local official. On the day my mother was to go into town for flour she received a large box of clothes from one of my aunts who was living in the North. The clothes were in good condition, though well worn, and my mother needed a dress, so she immediately put on one of those from the box and wore it into town. When she reached the distribution center and presented her voucher she was confronted by a white woman who looked her up and down with marked anger and envy.

"What'd you come up here for?" the woman asked.

"For some flour," said my mother, presenting her voucher.

"Humph," said the woman, looking at her more closely and with unconcealed fury. "Anybody dressed up as good as you don't need to come here *begging* for food."

"I ain't begging," said my mother; "the government is giving away   5
flour to those that need it, and I need it. I wouldn't be here if I didn't. And these clothes I'm wearing was given to me." But the woman had already turned to the next person in line, saying over her shoulder to the white man who was behind the counter with her, "The *gall* of niggers coming in here dressed better than me!" This thought seemed to make her angrier still, and my mother, pulling three of her small children behind her and crying from humiliation, walked sadly back into the street.

"What did you and Daddy do for flour that winter?" I asked my mother.

"Well," she said, "Aunt Mandy Aikens lived down the road from us and she got plenty of flour. We had a good stand of corn so we had plenty of meal. Aunt Mandy would swap me a bucket of flour for a bucket of meal. We got by all right."

Then she added thoughtfully, "And that old woman that turned me off so short got down so bad in the end that she was walking on *two* sticks." And I knew she was thinking, though she never said it: Here I am today, my eight children healthy and grown and three of them in college and me with hardly a sick day for years. Ain't Jesus wonderful?

In this small story is revealed the condition and strength of a people. Outcasts to be used and humiliated by the larger society, the Southern black sharecropper and poor farmer clung to his own kind and to a religion that had been given to pacify him as a slave but which he soon transformed into an antidote against bitterness. Depending on one another, because they had nothing and no one else, the sharecroppers often managed to come through "all right." And when I listen to my mother tell and retell this story I find that the white woman's vindictiveness is less important than Aunt Mandy's resourceful generosity or my mother's ready stand of corn. For their lives were not about that pitiful example of Southern womanhood, but about themselves.

What the black Southern writer inherits as a natural right is a sense   10
of *community*. Something simple but surprisingly hard, especially these days, to come by. My mother, who is a walking history of our community, tells me that when each of her children was born the midwife accepted as payment such home-grown or homemade items as a pig, a quilt, jars of canned fruits and vegetables. But there was never any question that the midwife would come when she was needed, whatever the eventual payment for her services. I consider this each time I hear of a hospital that refuses to admit a woman in labor unless she can hand over a substantial sum of money, cash.

Nor am I nostalgic, as a French philosopher once wrote, for lost poverty. I am nostalgic for the solidarity and sharing a modest existence can sometimes bring. We knew, I suppose, that we were poor. Somebody knew; perhaps the landowner who grudgingly paid my father three hundred dollars a year for twelve months' labor. But we never considered ourselves to be poor, unless, of course, we were deliberately humiliated. And because we never believed we were poor, and therefore worthless, we could depend on one another without shame. And always there were the Burial Societies, the Sick-and-Shut-in Societies, that sprang up out of spontaneous need. And no one seemed terribly upset that black sharecroppers were ignored by white insurance companies. It went without saying, in my mother's day, that birth and death required assistance from the community, and that the magnitude of these events was lost on outsiders.

As a college student I came to reject the Christianity of my parents, and it took me years to realize that though they had been force-fed a white man's palliative, in the form of religion, they had made it into something at once simple and noble. True, even today, they can never successfully picture a God who is not white, and that is a major cruelty, but their lives testify to a greater comprehension of the teachings of Jesus than the lives of people who sincerely believe a God *must* have a color and that there can be such a phenomenon as a "white" church.

The richness of the black writer's experience in the South can be remarkable, though some people might not think so. Once, while in college, I told a white middle-aged Northerner that I hoped to be a poet. In the nicest possible language, which still made me as mad as I've ever been, he suggested that a "farmer's daughter" might not be the stuff of which poets are made. On one level, of course, he had a point. A shack with only a dozen or so books is an unlikely place to discover a young Keats. But it is narrow thinking, indeed, to believe that a Keats is the only kind of poet one would want to grow up to be. One wants to write poetry that is understood by one's people, not by the Queen of England. Of course, should she be able to profit by it too, so much the better, but since that is not likely, catering to her tastes would be a waste of time.

For the black Southern writer, coming straight out of the country, as Wright did—Natchez and Jackson are still not as citified as they like to think they are—there is the world of comparisons; between town and country, between the ugly crowding and griminess of the cities and the spacious cleanliness (which actually seems impossible to dirty) of the country. A country person finds the city confining, like a too tight dress. And always, in one's memory, there remain all the rituals of one's growing up: the warmth and vividness of Sunday worship (never mind that you never quite believed) in a little church hidden from the road, and houses set so far back into the woods that at night it is impossible for strangers to find them. The daily dramas that evolve in such a private world are pure gold. But this view of a strictly private and hidden existence, with its triumphs, failures, grotesqueries, is not nearly as valuable to the socially conscious black Southern writer as his double vision is. For not only is he in a position to see his own world, and its close community ("Homecomings" on First Sundays, barbecues to raise money to send to Africa—one of the smaller ironies—the simplicity and eerie calm of a black funeral, where the beloved one is buried way in the middle of a wood with nothing to mark the spot but perhaps a wooden cross already coming apart), but also he is capable of knowing, with remarkably silent accuracy, the people who make up the larger world that surrounds and suppresses his own.

It is a credit to a writer like Ernest J. Gaines, a black writer who writes mainly about the people he grew up with in rural Louisiana, that he can write about whites and blacks exactly as he sees them and *knows* them, instead of writing of one group as a vast malignant lump and of the other as a conglomerate of perfect virtues. 15

In large measure, black Southern writers owe their clarity of vision to parents who refused to diminish themselves as human beings by succumbing to racism. Our parents seemed to know that an extreme negative emotion held against other human beings for reasons they do not control can be blinding. Blindness about other human beings, especially for a writer, is equivalent to death. Because of this blindness, which is, above all, racial, the works of many southern writers have died. Much that we read today is fast expiring.

My own slight attachment to William Faulkner was rudely broken by realizing, after reading statements he made in *Faulkner in the University,* that he believed whites superior morally to blacks; that whites had a duty (which at their convenience they would assume) to "bring blacks along" politically, since blacks, in Faulkner's opinion, were "not ready" yet to function properly in a democratic society. He also thought that a black man's intelligence is directly related to the amount of white blood he has.

For the black person coming of age in the sixties, where Martin Luther King stands against the murderers of Goodman, Chaney, and Schwerner, there appears no basis for such assumptions. Nor was there any in Garvey's day, or in Du Bois's or in Douglass's or in Nat Turner's. Nor at any other period in our history, from the very founding of the country; for it was hardly incumbent upon slaves to be slaves and saints too. Unlike Tolstoy, Faulkner was not prepared to struggle to change the structure of the society he was born in. One might concede that in his fiction he did seek to examine the reasons for its decay, but unfortunately, as I have learned while trying to teach Faulkner to black students, it is not possible, from so short a range, to separate the man from his works.

One reads Faulkner knowing that his "colored" people had to come through "Mr. William's" back door, and one feels uneasy, and finally enraged that Faulkner did not burn the whole house down. When the provincial mind starts out *and continues* on a narrow and unprotesting course, "genius" itself must run on a track.

Flannery O'Connor at least had the conviction that "reality" is at   20
best superficial and that the puzzle of humanity is less easy to solve than that of race. But Miss O'Connor was not so much of Georgia, as in it. The majority of Southern writers have been too confined by prevailing social customs to probe deeply into mysteries that the Citizens Councils insist must never be revealed.

Perhaps my Northern brothers will not believe me when I say there is a great deal of positive material I can draw from my "underprivileged" background. But they have never lived, as I have, at the end of a long road in a house that was faced by the edge of the world on one side and nobody for miles on the other. They have never experienced the magnificent quiet of a summer day when the heat is intense and one is so very thirsty, as one moves across the dusty cotton fields, that one learns forever that water is the essence of all life. In the cities it cannot be so clear to one that he is a creature of the earth, feeling the soil between the toes, smelling the dust thrown up by the rain, loving the earth so much that one longs to taste it and sometimes does.

Nor do I intend to romanticize the Southern black country life. I can recall that I hated it, generally. The hard work in the fields, the shabby houses, the evil greedy men who worked my father to death and almost broke the courage of that strong woman, my mother. No, I am simply saying that Southern black writers, like most writers, have a heritage of love and hate, but that they also have enormous richness and beauty to draw from. And, having been placed, as Camus says, "halfway between misery and the sun," they, too, know that "though all is not well under the sun, history is not everything."

No one could wish for a more advantageous heritage than that bequeathed to the black writer in the South: a compassion for the earth, a trust in humanity beyond our knowledge of evil, and an abiding love of justice. We inherit a great responsibility as well, for we must give voice to centuries not only of silent bitterness and hate but also of neighborly kindness and sustaining love.

1970

Lines of Inquiry
"The Black Writer and the Southern Experience"

Walker opens this piece with a vividly detailed story about her mother, a story that she offers to illustrate "the condition and strength of a people." Though she does not refer specifically to the story later on in her essay, she clearly intends it to echo throughout the remainder of the essay. What details does she use, what assertions does she make, that echo in the story? In what respects might it also be said that Walker's own way of thinking and talking in this piece echoes the behavior of her mother?

The "black Southern writer" is uniquely endowed, according to Walker, by virtue of inheriting "a sense of *community*." What exactly does she mean by community that makes it so special? In what respect(s) does she believe that the black Southern writer's sense of community differs from that of anyone else? Why does she believe that this sense of community is so important to a writer? To what extent do you think she displays that sense of community in her own writing?

A sense of community, particularly the kind of community that prevails in a rural or village setting, might also be seen in Baker's "A Visit with the Folks" or Baldwin's "Stranger in the Village" or Mead's "A Day in Samoa" or Twain's "S-t-e-a-m-boat a-comin'!" Read or reread a couple of these pieces, and then consider whether the communities depicted in them share any qualities with the community Walker portrayed.

Am I Blue?

*"**A**in't these tears in these eyes tellin' you?"*[1]

For about three years my companion and I rented a small house in the country that stood on the edge of a large meadow that appeared to run from the end of our deck straight into the mountains. The mountains, however, were quite far away, and between us and them there was, in fact, a town. It was one of the many pleasant aspects of the house that you never really were aware of this.

It was a house of many windows, low, wide, nearly floor to ceiling in the living room, which faced the meadow, and it was from one of these that I first saw our closest neighbor, a large white horse, cropping grass, flipping its mane, and ambling about—not over the entire meadow, which stretched well out of sight of the house, but over the five or so fenced-in acres that were next to the twenty-odd that we had rented. I soon learned that the horse, whose name was Blue, belonged to a man who lived in another town, but was boarded by our neighbors next door. Occasionally, one of the children, usually a stocky teen-ager, but sometimes a much younger girl or boy, could be seen riding Blue. They would appear in the meadow, climb up on his back, ride furiously for ten or fifteen minutes, then get off, slap Blue on the flanks, and not be seen again for a month or more.

There were many apple trees in our yard, and one by the fence that Blue could almost reach. We were soon in the habit of feeding him apples, which he relished, especially because by the middle of summer the meadow grasses—so green and succulent since January—had dried out from lack of rain, and Blue stumbled about munching the dried stalks half-heartedly. Sometimes he would stand very still just by the apple tree, and when one of us came out he would whinny, snort loudly, or stamp the ground. This meant, of course: I want an apple.

It was quite wonderful to pick a few apples, or collect those that had fallen to the ground overnight, and patiently hold them, one by one, up to his large, toothy mouth. I remained as thrilled as a child by his flexible dark lips, huge, cubelike teeth that crunched the apples, core and all, with such finality, and his high, broad-breasted *enormity;* beside which, I felt small indeed. When I was a child, I used to ride horses,

---

and was especially friendly with one named Nan until the day I was riding and my brother deliberately spooked her and I was thrown, head first, against the trunk of a tree. When I came to, I was in bed and my mother was bending worriedly over me; we silently agreed that perhaps horseback riding was not the safest sport for me. Since then I have walked, and prefer walking to horseback riding—but I had forgotten the depth of feeling one could see in horses' eyes.

I was therefore unprepared for the expression in Blue's. Blue was   5
lonely. Blue was horribly lonely and bored. I was not shocked that this should be the case; five acres to tramp by yourself, endlessly, even in the most beautiful of meadows—and his was—cannot provide many interesting events, and once rainy season turned to dry that was about it. No, I was shocked that I had forgotten that human animals and nonhuman animals can communicate quite well; if we are brought up around animals as children we take this for granted. By the time we are adults we no longer remember. However, the animals have not changed. They are in fact *completed* creations (at least they seem to be, so much more than we) who are not likely *to* change; it is their nature to express themselves. What else are they going to express? And they do. And, generally speaking, they are ignored.

After giving Blue the apples, I would wander back to the house, aware that he was observing me. Were more apples not forthcoming then? Was that to be his sole entertainment for the day? My partner's small son had decided he wanted to learn how to piece a quilt; we worked in silence on our respective squares as I thought . . .

Well, about slavery: about white children, who were raised by black people, who knew their first all-accepting love from black women, and then, when they were twelve or so, were told they must "forget" the deep levels of communication between themselves and "mammy" that they knew. Later they would be able to relate quite calmly, "My old mammy was sold to another good family." "My old mammy was——
——." Fill in the blank. Many more years later a white woman would say: "I can't understand these Negroes, these blacks. What do they want? They're so different from us."

And about the Indians, considered to be "like animals" by the "settlers" (a very benign euphemism for what they actually were), who did not understand their description as a compliment.

And about the thousands of American men who marry Japanese, Korean, Filipina, and other non-English-speaking women and of how happy they report they are, *"blissfully,"* until their brides learn to speak English, at which point the marriages tend to fall apart. What then did the men see, when they looked into the eyes of the women they married, before they could speak English? Apparently only their own reflections.

I thought of society's impatience with the young. "Why are they   10
playing the music so loud?" Perhaps the children have listened to much

of the music of oppressed people their parents danced to before they were born, with its passionate but soft cries for acceptance and love, and they have wondered why their parents failed to hear.

I do not know how long Blue had inhabited his five beautiful, boring acres before we moved into our house; a year after we had arrived—and had also traveled to other valleys, other cities, other worlds—he was still there.

But then, in our second year at the house, something happened in Blue's life. One morning, looking out the window at the fog that lay like a ribbon over the meadow, I saw another horse, a brown one, at the other end of Blue's field. Blue appeared to be afraid of it, and for several days made no attempt to go near. We went away for a week. When we returned, Blue had decided to make friends and the two horses ambled or galloped along together, and Blue did not come nearly as often to the fence underneath the apple tree.

When he did, bringing his new friend with him, there was a different look in his eyes. A look of independence, of self-possession, of inalienable *horse*ness. His friend eventually became pregnant. For months and months there was, it seemed to me, a mutual feeling between me and the horses of justice, of peace. I fed apples to them both. The look in Blue's eyes was one of unabashed "this is *it*ness."

It did not, however, last forever. One day, after a visit to the city, I went out to give Blue some apples. He stood waiting, or so I thought, though not beneath the tree. When I shook the tree and jumped back from the shower of apples, he made no move. I carried some over to him. He managed to half-crunch one. The rest he let fall to the ground. I dreaded looking into his eyes—because I had of course noticed that Brown, his partner, had gone—but I did look. If I had been born into slavery, and my partner had been sold or killed, my eyes would have looked like that. The children next door explained that Blue's partner had been "put with him' (the same expression that old people used, I had noticed, when speaking of an ancestor during slavery who had been impregnated by her owner) so that they could mate and she conceive. Since that was accomplished, she had been taken back by her owner, who lived somewhere else.

Will she be back? I asked.   15

They didn't know.

Blue was like a crazed person. Blue *was*, to me, a crazed person. He galloped furiously, as if he were being ridden, around and around his five beautiful acres. He whinnied until he couldn't. He tore at the ground with his hooves. He butted himself against his single shade tree. He looked always and always toward the road down which his partner had gone. And then, occasionally, when he came up for apples, or I took apples to him, he looked at me. It was a look so piercing, so full of grief, a look so *human*, I almost laughed (I felt too sad to cry) to think there are people who do not know that animals suffer. People like me who have forgotten, and daily forget, all that animals try to tell us. "Everything you do to us will happen to you; we are your teachers, as you are ours. We are one lesson" is essentially it, I think. There are those who never once have even considered animals' rights: those who have been taught that animals actually want to be used and abused by us, as small children "love" to be frightened, or women "love" to be mutilated and raped. . . . They are the great-grandchildren of those who honestly thought, because someone taught them this: "Women can't think," and "niggers can't faint." But most disturbing of all, in Blue's large brown eyes was a new look, more painful than the look of despair: the look of disgust with human beings, with life; the look of hatred. And it was odd what the look of hatred did. It gave him, for the first time, the look of a beast. And what that meant was that he had put up a barrier within to protect himself from further violence; all the apples in the world wouldn't change that fact.

And so Blue remained, a beautiful part of our landscape, very peaceful to look at from the window, white against the grass. Once a friend came to visit and said, looking out on the soothing view: "And it *would* have to be a *white* horse; the very image of freedom." And I thought, yes, the animals are forced to become for us merely "images" of what they once so beautifully expressed. And we are used to drinking milk from containers showing "contented" cows, whose real lives we want to hear nothing about, eating eggs and drumsticks from "happy" hens, and munching hamburgers advertised by bulls of integrity who seem to command their fate.

As we talked of freedom and justice one day for all, we sat down to steaks. I am eating misery, I thought, as I took the first bite. And spit it out.

1986

Lines of Inquiry
"Am I Blue?"

Notice the descriptive and narrative techniques that Walker uses to make her point in this essay. For example, what descriptive details does she emphasize and endow with special significance? Why does she interrupt her description of Blue, first to tell about her childhood horseback riding accident, then to tell about the thoughts that ran through her mind as she was quilting with the son of her partner? What do these apparent digressions have to do with her initial description of Blue, with the subsequent story of Blue, or with the point of her piece? Why doesn't she focus just on the story of Blue and Brown?

Why do you think Walker focuses as she does on Blue? To what extent do you think she intends him to be suggestive of the mistreated and misunderstood persons that she thinks about in the middle of her piece? To what extent do you think she intends him to be a symbol of the inhumane treatment of animals? To what extent do you think she is concerned with the interdependency of animals and human beings and thus with inhumanity in general? Or is she concerned with some other issue?

The situation of animals and their relationship to human beings is also explored in Dillard's "The Deer at Providencia," in Eiseley's "The Bird and the Machine," and in Hoagland's "Dogs and the Tug of Life." Read or reread one of these and consider what ideas and concerns Walker shares with that essayist, as well as what issues are of special interest to her alone.

E. B. White
1899–1985

The whole duty of a writer is to please and satisfy himself, and the true writer always plays to an audience of one. Let him start sniffing the air, or glancing at the Trend Machine, and he is as good as dead, although he may make a nice living.

Throughout his career, E. B. White remained just as staunchly self-reliant as he is in this uncompromising statement of principle. Yet in writing "to please and satisfy himself," he attracted an audience of millions. His readers followed him through a surprisingly varied body of writing, for White was not willing either to glance at the "Trend Machine" or to work in a single, narrowly established vein. Indeed, during his most active years as a professional writer, from 1920 to 1970, he won recognition for his witty poems and sketches, his personal essays, his reflections on world government, his children's stories, and his advice to young writers. Varied as it is, White's writing embodies a clear-cut and persistent set of values that can be seen in his "intoxication" with nature, his "love affair" with freedom, his desire for world peace, and his belief "in the truth and worth of the scrawl."

The youngest of six children of a wealthy piano manufacturer, Elwyn Brooks White was born and raised in the New York City suburb of Mount Vernon. There, in his father's stable, in his friends' backyards, and in the nearby woods and ponds, he first experienced his long felt "sense of living somewhat freely in a natural world," a feeling that that was intensified for him at the "large and undisturbed lake" in Maine where his family vacationed each August. As a youngster, he also started keeping a daily journal—a record of his experiences, observations, and early literary efforts—that he maintained for the next twenty years. As a teenager, he not only wrote for the school literary journal, but also entered and won a handful of national magazine contests for aspiring writers.

White's commitment to writing grew even stronger during his undergraduate days at Cornell University. Throughout his four years there (1917–21), he worked on the *Cornell Daily Sun*, first as a reporter, finally as editor-in-chief. So, too, one of his favorite professors was William Strunk, whose lessons in how to be "clear, brief, bold" touched White so deeply that forty years later he resurrected Strunk's writing manual, *The Elements of Style*, and turned it into a best-selling textbook. After graduation, he turned halfheartedly to the world of practical writing, but the business of getting out news reports, press releases, and advertising copy was evidently far less interesting to White than the pleasure of writing his own witty poems and sketches. Far less interesting, too, than a cross-country trip in his Model T Ford during the spring and summer of 1922, or a one-way ticket on a cruise ship to Alaska and Siberia in the summer of 1923.

Not until 1925, when *The New Yorker* magazine was launched, did White find a publication congenial to the witty writing that he had been working at for several years. From 1926 to 1937, he was continuously affiliated with *The New Yorker*, bringing to it a wryly humorous voice and a common-sensical view of affairs for which the magazine came to be very well known. White's wide-ranging contributions during those years included not only editorials and sketches in its "Talk of the Town" section, but also poems, cartoon captions, and witty taglines that appeared elsewhere in the magazine. During those years, he also published several humorous books, most notably *Is Sex Necessary? or Why You Feel the Way You Do* (1929), a parody of various sexual studies, done jointly with his office mate and fellow humorist, James Thurber.

But by the mid-thirties, the complex pressures of "the weekly gaiety field" and the complex pressures, too, of living amid "the spiky ruins of New York" had begun to weigh heavily upon White. So, in the spirit of Thoreau, he decided "to simplify" his life by giving up his full-time job at *The New Yorker* and moving his family to a saltwater farm in Maine. Though he continued to do occasional work for *The New Yorker*, the bulk of his writing between 1938 and 1943 was devoted to a monthly column that he produced for *Harper's Magazine* under the general heading of "One Man's Meat." As its title suggests, the column was "a personal record," a "description or narration" based on his experience in Maine, or wherever else he happened to be. His personal experience, in turn, invariably provided him with an occasion to reflect upon a broad range of ideas, issues, and concerns—from "A Shepherd's Life" to "The World of Tomorrow," from "Children's Books" to the "Second World War."

"One Man's Meat," by his own admission, "turned out to be one of the luckiest things that ever happened" to White, for it gave him the opportunity to write in "the first person singular." Given the freedom and directness of that perspective, White achieved a rare blend of description and reflection, of seriousness and humor, of personal and public testimony that gradually led to his being widely recognized as the most distinguished American essayist of his time. But by 1943, White's desire to be more directly and frequently involved in writing about the war—and about the need for world government after the war—led him to give up his monthly column at *Harper's* and devote himself once again to writing weekly editorials for *The New Yorker*. His "Notes and Comments" about war, peace, and the politics of world government were subsequently collected and published in *The Wild Flag* (1946).

Busy as he was at *The New Yorker*, as well as in moving back and forth between an apartment in New York City and his farm in Maine, he managed during the forties and early-fifties to produce two best-selling children's books—*Stuart Little* (1945) and *Charlotte's Web* (1952). In these classic works, as in his numerous essays about the barnyard life on his farm, White drew on his affection for animals, transforming them into enchanting characters whose experiences embody his personal ideas about life and human experience. By the mid-fifties, the weekly deadlines at *The New Yorker* had once again become too much of a burden both for White and for his wife, Katherine Angell, who for many years had been fiction editor of the magazine. So in 1957, they both resigned their positions and returned to their permanent home in Maine. Between the mid-fifties and the mid-seventies, White wrote occasional "Letters" to *The New Yorker*, very much in the manner of his pieces for "One Man's Meat," and in 1970 his last children's book appeared, *The Trumpet of the Swan*.

White's wide-ranging essays, editorials, and sketches can be found in several collections, most notably *One Man's Meat* (1944), *The Second Tree from the Corner* (1954), *The Points of My Compass* (1962), *Essays of E. B. White* (1977), and *Poems and Sketches of E. B. White* (1981). Given the variety of his subjects and moods, his essays present him in an equally wide array of "attitudes or poses"—as "philosopher, scold, jester, raconteur, confidant, pundit, devil's advocate, enthusiast." Each of his essays "differs from the last," if only because each is a "new excursion," "a new 'attempt' " that "takes him into a new country." Still, in all of his writing he remains true to his first principles—"to please and satisfy himself." So, he never wavers from his personal convictions. So, too, he never wavers from his personal voice, which above all else remains true to his belief in the value of "plainness, simplicity, orderliness, sincerity."

Once More to the Lake

One summer, along about 1904, my father rented a camp on a lake in Maine and took us all there for the month of August. We all got ringworm from some kittens and had to rub Pond's Extract on our arms and legs at night and morning, and my father rolled over in a canoe with all his clothes on; but outside of that the vacation was a success and from then on none of us ever thought there was any place in the world like that lake in Maine. We returned summer after summer—always on August 1 for one month. I have since become a salt-water man, but sometimes in summer there are days when the restlessness of the tides and the fearful cold of the sea water and the incessant wind that blows across the afternoon and into the evening make me wish for the placidity of a lake in the woods. A few weeks ago this feeling got so strong I bought myself a couple of bass hooks and a spinner and returned to the lake where we used to go, for a week's fishing and to revisit old haunts.

I took along my son, who had never had any fresh water up his nose and who had seen lily pads only from train windows. On the journey over to the lake I began to wonder what it would be like. I wondered how time would have marred this unique, this holy spot— the coves and streams, the hills that the sun set behind, the camps and the paths behind the camps. I was sure that the tarred road would have found it out, and I wondered in what other ways it would be desolated. It is strange how much you can remember about places like that once you allow your mind to return into the grooves that lead back. You remember one thing, and that suddenly reminds you of another thing. I guess I remembered clearest of all the early mornings, when the lake was cool and motionless, remembered how the bedroom smelled of the lumber it was made of and of the wet woods whose scent entered through the screen. The partitions in the camp were thin and did not extend clear to the top of the rooms, and as I was always the first up I would dress softly so as not to wake the others, and sneak out into the sweet outdoors and start out in the canoe, keeping close along the shore in the long shadows of the pines. I remembered being very careful never to rub my paddle against the gunwale for fear of disturbing the still-ness of the cathedral.

The lake had never been what you would call a wild lake. There were cottages sprinkled around the shores, and it was in farming coun-try although the shores of the lake were quite heavily wooded. Some of the cottages were owned by nearby farmers, and you would live at the shore and eat your meals at the farmhouse. That's what our family did. But although it wasn't wild, it was a fairly large and undisturbed lake and there were places in it that, to a child at least, seemed infinitely remote and primeval.

I was right about the tar: it led to within half a mile of the shore. But when I got back there, with my boy, and we settled into a camp near a farmhouse and into the kind of summertime I had known, I could tell that it was going to be pretty much the same as it had been before—I knew it, lying in bed the first morning, smelling the bedroom and hearing the boy sneak quietly out and go off along the shore in a boat. I began to sustain the illusion that he was I, and therefore, by simple transposition, that I was my father. This sensation persisted, kept cropping up all the time we were there. It was not an entirely new feeling, but in this setting it grew much stronger. I seemed to be living a dual existence. I would be in the middle of some simple act, I would be picking up a bait box or laying down a table fork, or I would be saying something, and suddenly it would be not I but my father who was saying the words or making the gesture. It gave me a creepy sensation.

We went fishing the first morning. I felt the same damp moss covering the worms in the bait can, and saw the dragonfly alight on the tip of my rod as it hovered a few inches from the surface of the water. It was the arrival of this fly that convinced me beyond any doubt that everything was as it always had been, that the years were a mirage and that there had been no years. The small waves were the same, chucking the rowboat under the chin as we fished at anchor, and the boat was the same boat, the same color green and the ribs broken in the same places, and under the floorboards the same fresh-water leavings and débris—the dead helgramite, the wisps of moss, the rusty discarded fishhook, the dried blood from yesterday's catch. We stared silently at the tips of our rods, at the dragonflies that came and went. I lowered the tip of mine into the water, tentatively, pensively dislodging the fly, which darted two feet away, poised, darted two feet back, and came to rest again a little farther up the rod. There had been no years between the ducking of this dragonfly and the other one—the one that was part of memory. I looked at the boy, who was silently watching his fly, and it was my hands that held his rod, my eyes watching. I felt dizzy and didn't know which rod I was at the end of.

We caught two bass, hauling them in briskly as though they were mackerel, pulling them over the side of the boat in a businesslike manner without any landing net, and stunning them with a blow on the back of the head. When we got back for a swim before lunch, the lake was exactly where we had left it, the same number of inches from the dock, and there was only the merest suggestion of a breeze. This seemed an utterly enchanted sea, this lake you could leave to its own devices for a few hours and come back to, and find that it had not stirred, this constant and trustworthy body of water. In the shallows, the dark, water-soaked sticks and twigs, smooth and old, were undulating in clusters on the bottom against the clean ribbed sand, and the track of the mussel was plain. A school of minnows swam by, each minnow with its small individual shadow, doubling the attendance, so clear and sharp in the sunlight. Some of the other campers were in swimming, along the shore, one of them with a cake of soap, and the water felt thin and clear and unsubstantial. Over the years there had been this person with the cake of soap, this cultist, and here he was. There had been no years.

Up to the farmhouse to dinner through the teeming, dusty field, the road under our sneakers was only a two-track road. The middle track was missing, the one with the marks of the hooves and the splotches of dried, flaky manure, There had been three tracks to choose from in choosing which track to walk in; now the choice was narrowed down to two. For a moment I missed terribly the middle alternative. But the way led past the tennis court, and something about the way it lay there in the sun reassured me; the tape had loosened along the backline, the alleys were green with plantains and other weeds, and the net (installed in June and removed in September) sagged in the dry noon, and the whole place steamed with midday heat and hunger and emptiness. There was a choice of pie for dessert, and one was blueberry and one was apple, and the waitresses were the same country girls, there having been no passage of time, only the illusion of it as in a dropped curtain—the waitresses were still fifteen; their hair had been washed, that was the only difference—they had been to the movies and seen the pretty girls with clean hair.

Summertime, oh, summertime, pattern of life indelible, the fade-proof lake, the woods unshatterable, the pasture with the sweetfern and the juniper forever and ever, summer without end; this was the background, and the life along the shore was the design, the cottagers with their innocent and tranquil design, their tiny docks with the flagpole and the American flag floating against the white clouds in the blue sky, the little paths over the roots of the trees leading from camp to camp and the paths leading back to the outhouses and the can of lime for sprinkling, and at the souvenir counters at the store the miniature birch-bark canoes and the postcards that showed things looking a little better than they looked. This was the American family at play, escaping the city heat, wondering whether the newcomers in the camp at the head of the cove were "common" or "nice," wondering whether it was true that the people who drove up for Sunday dinner at the farmhouse were turned away because there wasn't enough chicken.

It seemed to me, as I kept remembering all this, that those times and those summers had been infinitely precious and worth saving. There had been jollity and peace and goodness. The arriving (at the beginning of August) had been so big a business in itself, at the railway station the farm wagon drawn up, the first smell of the pine-laden air, the first glimpse of the smiling farmer, and the great importance of the trunks and your father's enormous authority in such matters, and the feel of the wagon under you for the long ten-mile haul, and at the top of the last long hill catching the first view of the lake after eleven months of not seeing this cherished body of water. The shouts and cries of the other campers when they saw you, and the trunks to be unpacked, to give up their rich burden. (Arriving was less exciting nowadays, when you sneaked up in your car and parked it under a tree near the camp and took out the bags and in five minutes it was all over, no fuss, no loud wonderful fuss about trunks.)

Peace and goodness and jollity. The only thing that was wrong now, really, was the sound of the place, an unfamiliar nervous sound of the outboard motors. This was the note that jarred, the one thing that would sometimes break the illusion and set the years moving. In those other summertimes all motors were inboard; and when they were at a little distance, the noise they made was a sedative, an ingredient of summer sleep. They were one-cylinder and two-cylinder engines, and some were make-and-break and some were jump-spark, but they all made a sleepy sound across the lake. The one-lungers throbbed and fluttered, and the twin-cylinder ones purred and purred, and that was a quiet sound, too. But now the campers all had outboards. In the daytime, in the hot mornings, these motors made a petulant, irritable sound; at night, in the still evening when the afterglow lit the water, they whined about one's ears like mosquitoes. My boy loved our rented outboard, and his great desire was to achieve single-handed mastery over it, and authority, and he soon learned the trick of choking it a little (but not too much), and the adjustment of the needle valve. Watching him I would remember the things you could do with the old one-cylinder engine with the heavy flywheel, how you could have it eating out of your hand if you got really close to it spiritually. Motorboats in those days didn't have clutches, and you would make a landing by shutting off the motor at the proper time and coasting in with a dead rudder. But there was a way of reversing them, if you learned the trick, by cutting the switch and putting it on again exactly on the final dying revolution of the flywheel, so that it would kick back against compression and begin reversing. Approaching a dock in a strong following breeze, it was difficult to slow up sufficiently by the ordinary coasting method, and if a boy felt he had complete mastery over his motor, he was tempted to keep it running beyond its time and then reverse it a few feet from the dock. It took a cool nerve, because if you threw the switch a twentieth of a second too soon you would catch the flywheel when it still had speed enough to go up past center, and the boat would leap ahead, charging bull-fashion at the dock.

We had a good week at the camp. The bass were biting well and the sun shone endlessly, day after day. We would be tired at night and lie down in the accumulated heat of the little bedrooms after the long

10

hot day and the breeze would stir almost imperceptibly outside and the smell of the swamp drift in through the rusty screens. Sleep would come easily and in the morning the red squirrel would be on the roof, tapping out his gay routine. I kept remembering everything, lying in bed in the mornings—the small steamboat that had a long rounded stern like the lip of a Ubangi, and how quietly she ran on the moonlight sails, when the older boys played their mandolins and the girls sang and we ate doughnuts dipped in sugar, and how sweet the music was on the water in the shining night, and what it had felt like to think about girls then. After breakfast we would go up to the store and the things were in the same place—the minnows in a bottle, the plugs and spinners disarranged and pawed over by the youngsters from the boys' camp, the Fig Newtons and the Beeman's gum. Outside, the road was tarred and cars stood in front of the store. Inside, all was just as it had always been, except there was more Coca-Cola and not so much Moxie and root beer and birch beer and sarsaparilla. We would walk out with the bottle of pop apiece and sometimes the pop would backfire up our noses and hurt. We explored the streams, quietly, where the turtles slid off the sunny logs and dug their way into the soft bottom; and we lay on the town wharf and fed worms to the tame bass. Everywhere we went I had trouble making out which was I, the one walking at my side, the one walking in my pants.

One afternoon while we were there at that lake a thunderstorm came up. It was like the revival of an old melodrama that I had seen long ago with childish awe. The second-act climax of the drama of the electrical disturbance over a lake in America had not changed in any important respect. This was the big scene, still the big scene. The whole thing was so familiar, the first feeling of oppression and heat and a general air around camp of not wanting to go very far away. In mid-afternoon (it was all the same) a curious darkening of the sky, and a lull in everything that had made life tick; and then the way the boats suddenly swung the other way at their moorings with the coming of a breeze out of the new quarter, and the premonitory rumble. Then the kettle drum, then the snare, then the bass drum and cymbals, then crackling light against the dark, and the gods grinning and licking their chops in the hills. Afterward the calm, the rain steadily rustling in the calm lake, the return of light and hope and spirits, and the campers running out in joy and relief to go swimming in the rain, their bright cries perpetuating the deathless joke about how they were getting simply drenched, and the children screaming with delight at the new sensation of bathing in the rain, and the joke about getting drenched linking the generations in a strong indestructible chain. And the comedian who waded in carrying an umbrella.

When the others went swimming, my son said he was going in, too. He pulled his dripping trunks from the line where they had hung all through the shower and wrung them out. Languidly, and with no thought of going in, I watched him, his hard little body, skinny and bare, saw him wince slightly as he pulled up around his vitals the small, soggy, icy garment. As he buckled the swollen belt, suddenly my groin felt the chill of death.

August 1941

Lines of Inquiry
"Once More to the Lake"

Early in the essay, White remarks that "it is strange how much you can remember about places like that once you allow your mind to return into the grooves that lead back." How does White organize the story of his visit to show the "strange" experience he went through when he allowed his mind to return into the grooves that lead back? How does White organize his material to clarify not only the memories of his past experience but also the details of his present experience, as well as the interplay between the two?

On his journey back to the lake, White "wondered how time would have marred this unique, this holy spot." How do his memories of the place compare with the place as he finds it during the visit with his son? In what ways has it changed? In what ways has it stayed the same? How does the presence of his son affect White's memories and perceptions of the lake, the camps, the cottagers, the surroundings, and himself?

Think about a place that was important during your earlier life and that you revisited after having been away from it for a period of time. In what ways did it change? In what ways did it stay the same? What particular memories about the place stand out for you when you allow your mind to return into the grooves that lead back? Did your visit turn out to be as haunting and disturbing to you as White's was to him, or did it prove to be just an ordinary visit without anything noteworthy to distinguish it? Or did it have a special twist that you associate with the place itself?

The Ring of Time

Fiddler Bayou, March 22, 1956

After the lions had returned to their cages, creeping angrily through the chutes, a little bunch of us drifted away and into an open doorway nearby, where we stood for a while in semidarkness, watching a big brown circus horse go harumphing around the practice ring. His trainer was a woman of about forty, and the two of them, horse and woman, seemed caught up in one of those desultory treadmills of afternoon from which there is no apparent escape. The day was hot, and we kibitzers were grateful to be briefly out of the sun's glare. The long rein, or tape, by which the woman guided her charge counterclockwise in his dull career formed the radius of their private circle, of which she was the revolving center; and she, too, stepped a tiny circumference of her own, in order to accommodate the horse and allow him his maximum scope. She had on a short-skirted costume and a conical straw hat. Her legs were bare and she wore high heels, which probed deep into the loose tanbark and kept her ankles in a state of constant turmoil. The great size and meekness of the horse, the repetitious exercise, the heat of the afternoon, all exerted a hypnotic charm that invited boredom; we spectators were experiencing a languor—we neither expected relief nor felt entitled to any. We had paid a dollar to get into the grounds, to be sure, but we had got our dollar's worth a few minutes before, when the lion trainer's whiplash had got caught around a toe of one of the lions. What more did we want for a dollar?

Behind me I heard someone say, "Excuse me, please," in a low voice. She was halfway into the building when I turned and saw her—a girl of sixteen or seventeen, politely threading her way through us onlookers who blocked the entrance. As she emerged in front of us, I saw that she was barefoot, her dirty little feet fighting the uneven ground. In most respects she was like any of two or three dozen showgirls you encounter if you wander about the winter quarters of Mr. John Ringling North's circus, in Sarasota—cleverly proportioned, deeply browned by the sun, dusty, eager, and almost naked. But her grave face and the naturalness of her manner gave her a sort of quick distinction and brought a new note into the gloomy octagonal building where we had all cast our lot for a few moments. As soon as she had squeezed through the crowd, she spoke a word or two to the older woman, whom I took to be her mother, stepped to the ring, and waited while the horse coasted to a stop in front of her. She gave the animal a couple of affectionate swipes on his enormous neck and then swung herself aboard. The horse immediately resumed his rocking canter, the woman goading him on, chanting something that sounded like "Hop! Hop!"

In attempting to recapture this mild spectacle, I am merely acting as recording secretary for one of the oldest of societies—the society of those who, at one time or another, have surrendered, without even a show of resistance, to the bedazzlement of a circus rider. As a writing man, or secretary, I have always felt charged with the safekeeping of all unexpected items of worldly or unworldly enchantment, as though I might be held personally responsible if even a small one were to be lost. But it is not easy to communicate anything of this nature. The circus comes as close to being the world in microcosm as anything I know; in a way, it puts all the rest of show business in the shade. Its magic is universal and complex. Out of its wild disorder comes order; from its rank smell rises the good aroma of courage and daring; out of its preliminary shabbiness comes the final splendor. And buried in the familiar boasts of its advance agents lies the modesty of most of its people. For me the circus is at its best before it has been put together. It is at its best at certain moments when it comes to a point, as through a burning glass, in the activity and destiny of a single performer out of so many. One ring is always bigger than three. One rider, one aerialist, is always greater than six. In short, a man has to catch the circus unawares to experience its full impact and share its gaudy dream.

The ten-minute ride the girl took achieved—as far as I was concerned, who wasn't looking for it, and quite unbeknownst to her, who wasn't even striving for it—the thing that is sought by performers everywhere, on whatever stage, whether struggling in the tidal currents of Shakespeare or bucking the difficult motion of a horse. I somehow got the idea she was just cadging a ride, improving a shining ten minutes in the diligent way all serious artists seize free moments to hone the blade of their talent and keep themselves in trim. Her brief tour included only elementary postures and tricks, perhaps because they were all she was capable of, perhaps because her warmup at this hour was unscheduled and the ring was not rigged for a real practice session. She swung herself off and on the horse several times, gripping his mane. She did a few knee-stands—or whatever they are called—dropping to her knees and quickly bouncing back up on her feet again. Most of the time she simply rode in a standing position, well aft on the beast, her hands hanging easily at her sides, her head erect, her straw-colored ponytail lightly brushing her shoulders, the blood of exertion showing faintly through the tan of her skin. Twice she managed a one-foot stance—a sort of ballet pose, with arms outstretched. At one point the neck strap of her bathing suit broke and she went twice around the ring in the classic·attitude of a woman making minor repairs to a garment. The fact that she was standing on the back of a moving horse while doing this invested the matter with a clownish significance that perfectly fitted the spirit of the circus—jocund, yet charming. She just rolled the strap into a neat ball and stowed it inside her bodice while the horse rocked and rolled beneath her in dutiful innocence. The bathing suit proved as self-reliant as its owner and stood up well enough without benefit of strap.

The richness of the scene was in its plainness, its natural condition— 5
of horse, of ring, of girl, even to the girl's bare feet that gripped the bare back of her proud and ridiculous mount. The enchantment grew not out of anything that happened or was performed but out of something that seemed to go round and around and around with the girl, attending her, a steady gleam in the shape of a circle—a ring of ambition, of happiness, of youth. (And the positive pleasures of equilibrium under difficulties.) In a week or two, all would be changed, all (or almost all) lost: the girl would wear makeup, the horse would wear gold, the ring would be painted, the bark would be clean for the feet of the horse, the girl's feet would be clean for the slippers that she'd wear. All, all would be lost.

As I watched with the others, our jaws adroop, our eyes alight, I became painfully conscious of the element of time. Everything in the hideous old building seemed to take the shape of a circle, conforming to the course of the horse. The rider's gaze, as she peered straight ahead, seemed to be circular, as though bent by force of circumstance; then time itself began running in circles, and so the beginning was where the end was, and the two were the same, and one thing ran into the next and time went round and around and got nowhere. The girl wasn't so young that she did not know the delicious satisfaction of having a perfectly behaved body and the fun of using it to do a trick most people can't do, but she was too young to know that time does not really move in a circle at all. I thought: "She will never be as beautiful as this again"—a thought that made me acutely unhappy—and in a flash my mind (which is too much of a busybody to suit me) had projected her twenty-five years ahead, and she was now in the center of the ring, on foot, wearing a conical hat and high-heeled shoes, the image of the older woman, holding the long rein, caught in the treadmill of an afternoon long in the future. "She is at that enviable moment in life [I thought] when she believes she can go once around the ring, make one complete circuit, and at the end be exactly the same age as at the start." Everything in her movements, her expression, told you that for her the ring of time was perfectly formed, changeless, predictable, without beginning or end, like the ring in which she was traveling at this moment with the horse that wallowed under her. And then I slipped back into my trance, and time was circular again—time, pausing quietly with the rest of us, so as not to disturb the balance of a performer.

Her ride ended as casually as it had begun. The older woman stopped the horse, and the girl slid to the ground. As she walked toward us to leave, there was a quick, small burst of applause. She smiled broadly, in surprise and pleasure; then her face suddenly regained its gravity and she disappeared through the door.

It has been ambitious and plucky of me to attempt to describe what is indescribable, and I have failed, as I knew I would. But I have discharged my duty to my society; and besides, a writer, like an acrobat, must occasionally try a stunt that is too much for him. At any rate, it is worth reporting that long before the circus comes to town, its most notable performances have already been given. Under the bright lights of the finished show, a performer need only reflect the electric candle power that is directed upon him; but in the dark and dirty old training rings and in the makeshift cages, whatever light is generated, whatever excitement, whatever beauty, must come from original sources—from internal fires of professional hunger and delight, from the exuberance and gravity of youth. It is the difference between planetary light and the combustion of stars.

The South is the land of the sustained sibilant. Everywhere, for the appreciative visitor, the letter "s" insinuates itself in the scene: in the sound of sea and sand, in the singing shell, in the heat of sun and sky, in the sultriness of the gentle hours, in the siesta, in the stir of birds and insects. In contrast to the softness of its music, the South is also cruel and hard and prickly. A little striped lizard, flattened along the sharp green bayonet of a yucca, wears in its tiny face and watchful eye the pure look of death and violence. And all over the place, hidden at the bottom of their small sandy craters, the ant lions lie in wait for the ant that will stumble into their trap. (There are three kinds of lions in this region: the lions of the circus, the ant lions, and the Lions of the Tampa Lions Club, who roared their approval of segregation at a meeting the other day—all except one, a Lion named Monty Gurwit, who declined to roar and thereby got his picture in the paper.)

The day starts on a note of despair: the sorrowing dove, alone on 10 its telephone wire, mourns the loss of night, weeps at the bright perils of the unfolding day. But soon the mockingbird wakes and begins an early rehearsal, setting the dove down by force of character, running through a few slick imitations, and trying a couple of original numbers into the bargain. The redbird takes it from there. Despair gives way to good humor. The Southern dawn is a pale affair, usually, quite different from our northern daybreak. It is a triumph of gradualism; night turns to day imperceptibly, softly, with no theatrics. It is subtle and undisturbing. As the first light seeps in through the blinds I lie in bed half awake, despairing with the dove, sounding the A for the brothers

Alsop. All seems lost, all seems sorrowful. Then a mullet jumps in the bayou outside the bedroom window. It falls back into the water with a smart smack. I have asked several people why the mullet incessantly jump and I have received a variety of answers. Some say the mullet jump to shake off a parasite that annoys them. Some say they jump for the love of jumping—as the girl on the horse seemed to ride for the love of riding (although she, too, like all artists, may have been shaking off some parasite that fastens itself to the creative spirit and can be got rid of only by fifty turns around a ring while standing on a horse).

In Florida at this time of year, the sun does not take command of the day until a couple of hours after it has appeared in the east. It seems to carry no authority at first. The sun and the lizard keep the same schedule; they bide their time until the morning has advanced a good long way before they come fully forth and strike. The cold lizard waits astride his warming leaf for the perfect moment; the cold sun waits in his nest of clouds for the crucial time.

On many days, the dampness of the air pervades all life, all living. Matches refuse to strike. The towel, hung to dry, grows wetter by the hour. The newspaper, with its headlines about integration, wilts in your hand and falls limply into the coffee and the egg. Envelopes seal themselves. Postage stamps mate with one another as shamelessly as grasshoppers. But most of the time the days are models of beauty and wonder and comfort, with the kind sea stroking the back of the warm sand. At evening there are great flights of birds over the sea, where the light lingers; the gulls, the pelicans, the terns, the herons stay aloft for half an hour after land birds have gone to roost. They hold their ancient formations, wheel and fish over the Pass, enjoying the last of day like children playing outdoors after suppertime.

To a beachcomber from the North, which is my present status, the race problem has no pertinence, no immediacy. Here in Florida I am a guest in two houses—the house of the sun, the house of the State of Florida. As a guest, I mind my manners and do not criticize the customs of my hosts. It gives me a queer feeling, though, to be at the center of the greatest social crisis of my time and see hardly a sign of it. Yet the very absence of signs seems to increase one's awareness. Colored people do not come to the public beach to bathe, because they would not be made welcome there; and they don't fritter away their time visiting the circus, because they have other things to do. A few of them turn up at the ballpark, where they occupy a separate but equal section of the left-field bleachers and watch Negro players on the visiting Braves team using the same bases as the white players, instead of separate (but equal) bases. I have had only two small encounters with "color." A colored woman named Viola, who had been a friend of my wife's sister years ago, showed up one day with some laundry of ours that she had consented to do for us, and with the bundle she brought a bunch of nasturtiums, as a sort of natural accompaniment to the delivery of clean clothes. The flowers seemed a very acceptable thing and I was touched by them. We asked Viola about her daughter, and she said she was at Kentucky State College, studying voice.

The other encounter was when I was explaining to our cook, who is from Finland, the mysteries of bus travel in the American Southland. I showed her the bus stop, armed her with a timetable, and then, as a matter of duty, mentioned the customs of the Romans. "When you get on the bus," I said, "I think you'd better sit in one of the front seats—the seats in back are for colored people." A look of great weariness came into her face, as it does when we use too many dishes, and she replied, "Oh, I know—isn't it silly!"

Her remark, coming as it did all the way from Finland and landing on this sandbar with a plunk, impressed me. The Supreme Court said nothing about silliness, but I suspect it may play more of a role than one might suppose. People are, if anything, more touchy about being thought silly than they are about being thought unjust. I note that one of the arguments in the recent manifesto of Southern Congressmen in support of the doctrine of "separate but equal" was that it had been founded on "common sense." The sense that is common to one generation is uncommon to the next. Probably the first slave ship, with Negroes lying in chains on its decks, seemed commonsensical to the owners who operated it and to the planters who patronized it. But such a vessel would not be in the realm of common sense today. The only sense that is common, in the long run, is the sense of change—and we all instinctively avoid it, and object to the passage of time, and would rather have none of it.

The Supreme Court decision is like the Southern sun, laggard in its early stages, biding its time. It has been the law in Florida for two years now, and the years have been like the hours of the morning before the sun has gathered its strength. I think the decision is as incontrovertible and warming as the sun, and, like the sun, will eventually take charge.

But there is certainly a great temptation in Florida to duck the passage of time. Lying in warm comfort by the sea, you receive gratefully the gift of the sun, the gift of the South. This is true seduction. The day is a circle—morning, afternoon, and night. After a few days I was clearly enjoying the same delusion as the girl on the horse—that I could ride clear around the ring of day, guarded by wind and sun and sea and sand, and be not a moment older.

P.S. (April, 1962).   When I first laid eyes on Fiddler Bayou, it was wild land, populated chiefly by the little crabs that gave it its name, visited by wading birds and by an occasional fisherman. Today, houses ring the bayou, and part of the mangrove shore has been bulkheaded with a concrete wall. Green lawns stretch from patio to water's edge, and sprinklers make rainbows in the light. But despite man's encroachment, Nature manages to hold her own and assert her authority: high tides and high winds in the gulf sometimes send the sea crashing across the sand barrier, depositing its wrack on lawns and ringing everyone's front door bell. The birds and the crabs accommodate themselves quite readily to the changes that have taken place; every day brings herons to hunt around among the roots of the mangroves, and I have discovered that I can approach to within about eight feet of a Little Blue Heron simply by entering the water and swimming slowly toward him. Apparently he has decided that when I'm in the water, I am without guile—possibly even desirable, like a fish.

The Ringling circus has quit Sarasota and gone elsewhere for its hibernation. A few circus families still own homes in the town, and every spring the students at the high school put on a circus, to let off steam, work off physical requirements, and provide a promotional spectacle for Sarasota. At the drugstore you can buy a postcard showing the bed John Ringling slept in. Time has not stood still for anybody but the dead, and even the dead must be able to hear the acceleration of little sports cars and know that things have changed.

From the all-wise *New York Times,* which has the animal kingdom ever in mind, I have learned that one of the creatures most acutely aware of the passing of time is the fiddler crab himself. Tiny spots on his body enlarge during daytime hours, giving him the same color as the mudbank he explores and thus protecting him from his enemies. At night the spots shrink, his color fades, and he is almost invisible in the light of the moon. These changes are synchronized with the tides, so that each day they occur at a different hour. A scientist who experimented with the crabs to learn more about the phenomenon discovered that even when they are removed from their natural environment and held in confinement, the rhythm of their bodily change continues uninterrupted, and they mark the passage of time in their laboratory prison, faithful to the tides in their fashion.

20

Lines of Inquiry
"The Ring of Time"

Though this essay consists of two separate sections, and a P.S. that White added several years after its initial publication, anthologizers usually truncate it, reprinting only the first section, which focuses on the scene at the circus. What do you think is lost, what do you think is gained, by reprinting only the first section? What images and themes from the first section are carried over and developed in the second section and the P.S.? What new images and themes are developed in the second section and the P.S.?

At various spots in this essay, White seems to be reflecting on several topics—on the circus, on writing, on artistic performance, on time, on the southern landscape, climate, and culture, on segregation, and on the ways of nature. Which of these do you consider to be White's primary center of interest in this piece? What point do you think White is trying to develop through his focus on this topic? How are his other topics of interest related to the development of this idea?

In this piece as in "Once More to the Lake," White focuses on specific places that are important to him, not just because they are vacation spots, but because they involve images and experiences that are endowed with special significance and value for him. Based on your reading of these two essays, what issues and themes are of special interest to White? What do you consider to be the most striking similarities and differences in the way that White develops and conveys his thoughts in these two pieces?

The Age of Dust

On a sunny morning last week, I went out and put up a swing for a little girl, age three, under an apple tree—the tree being much older than the girl, the sky being blue, the clouds white. I pushed the little girl for a few minutes, then returned to the house and settled down to an article on death dust, or radiological warfare, in the July *Bulletin of the Atomic Scientists,* Volume VI, No. 7.

The article ended on a note of disappointment. "The area that can be poisoned with the fission products available to us today is disappointingly small; it amounts to not more than two or three major cities per month." At first glance, the sentence sounded satirical, but a rereading convinced me that the scientist's disappointment was real enough—that it had the purity of detachment. The world of the child in the swing (the trip to the blue sky and back again) seemed, as I studied the ABC of death dust, more and more a dream world with no true relation to things as they are or to the real world of discouragement over the slow rate of the disappearance of cities.

Probably the scientist-author of the death-dust article, if he were revising his literary labors with a critical eye, would change the wording of that queer sentence. But the fact is, the sentence got written and published. The terror of the atom age is not the violence of the new power but the speed of man's adjustment to it—the speed of his acceptance. Already, bombproofing is on approximately the same level as mothproofing. Two or three major cities per month isn't much of an area, but it is a start. To the purity of science (which hopes to enlarge the area) there seems to be no corresponding purity of political thought, never the same detachment. We sorely need, from a delegate in the Security Council, a statement as detached in its way as the statement of the scientist on death dust. This delegate (and it makes no difference what nation he draws his pay from) must be a man who has not adjusted to the age of dust. He must be a person who still dwells in the mysterious dream world of swings, and little girls in swings. He must be more than a good chess player studying the future; he must be a memoirist remembering the past.

I couldn't seem to separate the little girl from radiological warfare—she seemed to belong with it, although inhabiting another sphere. The article kept getting back to her. "This is a novel type of warfare, in that it produces no destruction, except to life." The weapon, said the author, can be regarded as a horrid one, or, on the other hand, it "can be regarded as a remarkably humane one. In a sense, it gives each member of the target population [including each little girl] a choice of whether he will live or die." It turns out that the way to live—if that be your choice—is to leave the city as soon as the dust arrives, holding "a folded, dampened handkerchief" over your nose and mouth. I went outdoors again to push the swing some more for the little girl, who is always forgetting her handkerchief. At lunch I watched her try to fold her napkin. It seemed to take forever.

As I lay in bed that night, thinking of cities and target populations,   5
I saw the child again. This time she was with the other little girls in the subway. When the train got to 242nd Street, which is as far as it goes into unreality, the children got off. They started to walk slowly north. Each child had a handkerchief, and every handkerchief was properly moistened and folded neatly—the way it said in the story.

Lines of Inquiry
"The Age of Dust"

At the opening of paragraph 4, White says that he "couldn't seem to separate the little girl from radiological warfare—she seemed to belong with it, although inhabiting another sphere." In what sense(s) does she inhabit "another sphere"? Given that White regards her as existing in another sphere, why does he think that "she seemed to belong with radiological warfare"? Consider how this piece might work if it focused exclusively on the article about radiological warfare without any reference to the little girl.

In paragraph 2, White speaks of the sentence that he quotes from the article as being "queer." What exactly is queer about it? How would you "change the wording" of it, so that it would not seem queer? Though White doesn't make any explicit judgments about the sentences that he quotes in paragraph 4, he evidently also considers them to be queer. But are they queer in the same way as the one in paragraph 2? How would you change these sentences to make them less queer? In what sense(s) is the queer wording of the article reflective of the larger problem that concerns White in this piece?

White is not the only author in this collection to be concerned with queer language, as you can see by looking at Goodman's "Sinking the Relationship" or Orwell's "Politics and the English Language." In what ways is White's concern with queer language similar to that of Goodman and Orwell? In what ways is it different?

A Slight Sound
at Evening

In his journal for July 10–12, 1841, Thoreau wrote: "A slight sound at evening lifts me up by the ears, and makes life seem inexpressibly serene and grand. It may be in Uranus, or it may be in the shutter." The book into which he later managed to pack both Uranus and the shutter was published in 1854, and now, a hundred years having gone by, *Walden,* its serenity and grandeur unimpaired, still lifts us up by the ears, still translates for us that language we are in danger of forgetting, "which all things and events speak without metaphor, which alone is copious and standard."

Walden is an oddity in American letters. It may very well be the oddest of our distinguished oddities. For many it is a great deal too odd, and for many it is a particular bore. I have not found it to be a well-liked book among my acquaintances, although usually spoken of with respect, and one literary critic for whom I have the highest regard can find no reason for anyone's giving *Walden* a second thought. To admire the book is, in fact, something of an embarrassment, for the mass of men have an indistinct notion that its author was a sort of Nature Boy.

I think it is of some advantage to encounter the book at a period in one's life when the normal anxieties and enthusiasms and rebellions of youth closely resemble those of Thoreau in that spring of 1845 when he borrowed an ax, went out to the woods, and began to whack down some trees for timber. Received at such a juncture, the book is like an invitation to life's dance, assuring the troubled recipient that no matter what befalls him in the way of success or failure he will always be welcome at the party—that the music is played for him, too, if he will but listen and move his feet. In effect, that is what the book is—an invitation, unengraved; and it stirs one as a young girl is stirred by her first big party bid. Many think it a sermon; many set it down as an attempt to rearrange society; some think it an exercise in nature-loving; some find it a rather irritating collection of inspirational puffballs by an eccentric show-off. I think it none of these. It still seems to me the best youth's companion yet written by an American, for it carries a solemn warning against the loss of one's valuables, it advances a good argument for traveling light and trying new adventures, it rings with the power of positive adoration, it contains religious feeling without religious images, and it steadfastly refuses to record bad news. Even its pantheistic note is so pure as to be noncorrupting—pure as the flute-note blown across the pond on those faraway summer nights. If our colleges and universities were alert, they would present a cheap pocket edition of the book to every senior upon graduating, along with his sheepskin, or instead of it. Even if some senior were to take it literally and start felling trees, there could be worse mishaps: the ax is older than the Dictaphone and it is just as well for a young man to see what kind of chips he leaves before listening to the sound of his own voice. And even if some were to get no farther than the table of contents, they would learn how to name eighteen chapters by the use of only thirty-nine words and would see how sweet are the uses of brevity.

If Thoreau had merely left us an account of a man's life in the woods or if he had simply retreated to the woods and there recorded his complaints about society, or even if he had contrived to include both records in one essay, *Walden* would probably not have lived a hundred years. As things turned out, Thoreau, very likely without knowing quite what he was up to, took man's relation to Nature and man's dilemma in society and man's capacity for elevating his spirit and he beat all these matters together, in a wild free interval of self-justification and delight, and produced an original omelette from which people can draw nourishment in a hungry day. *Walden* is one of the first of the vitamin-enriched American dishes. If it were a little less good than it is, or even a little less queer, it would be an abominable book. Even as it is, it will continue to baffle and annoy the literal mind and all those who are unable to stomach its caprices and imbibe its theme. Certainly the plodding economist will continue to have rough going if he hopes to emerge from the book with a clear system of economic thought. Thoreau's assault on the Concord society of the mid-nineteenth century has the quality of a modern Western: he rides into the subject at top speed, shooting in all directions. Many of his shots ricochet and nick him on the rebound, and throughout the melee there is a horrendous cloud of inconsistencies and contradictions, and when the shooting dies down and the air clears, one is impressed chiefly by the courage of the rider and by how splendid it was that somebody should have ridden in there and raised all that ruckus.

When he went to the pond, Thoreau struck an attitude and did so   5
deliberately, but his posturing was not to draw the attention of others to him but rather to draw his own attention more closely to himself. "I learned this at least by my experiment: that if one advances confidently in the direction of his dreams, and endeavors to live the life which he has imagined, he will meet with a success unexpected in common hours." The sentence has the power to resuscitate the youth drowning in his sea of doubt. I recall my exhilaration upon reading it, many years ago, in a time of hesitation and despair. It restored me to health. And now in 1954 when I salute Henry Thoreau on the hundredth birthday of his book, I am merely paying off an old score—or an installment on it.

In his journal for May 3–4, 1838—Boston to Portland—he wrote: "Midnight—head over the boat's side—between sleeping and waking— with glimpses of one or more lights in the vicinity of Cape Ann. Bright moonlight—the effect heightened by seasickness." The entry illuminates the man, as the moon the sea on that night in May. In Thoreau the natural scene was heightened, not depressed, by a disturbance of the stomach, and nausea met its match at last. There was a steadiness in at least one passenger if there was none in the boat. Such steadiness (which in some would be called intoxication) is at the heart of *Walden*—confidence, faith, the discipline of looking always at what is to be seen, undeviating gratitude for the life-everlasting that he found growing in his front yard. "There is nowhere recorded a simple and irrepressible satisfaction with the gift of life, any memorable praise of God." He worked to correct that deficiency. *Walden* is his acknowledgement of the gift of life. It is the testament of a man in a high state of indignation because (it seemed to him) so few ears heard the uninterrupted poem of creation, the morning wind that forever blows. If the man sometimes wrote as though all his readers were male, unmarried, and well-connected, it is because he gave his testimony during the callow years. For that matter, he never really grew up. To reject the book because of the immaturity of the author and the bugs in the logic is to throw away a bottle of good wine because it contains bits of the cork.

Thoreau said he required of every writer, first and last, a simple and sincere account of his own life. Having delivered himself of this chesty dictum, he proceeded to ignore it. In his books and even in his enormous journal, he withheld or disguised most of the facts from which an understanding of his life could be drawn. *Walden,* subtitled "Life in the Woods," is not a simple and sincere account of a man's life, either in or out of the woods; it is an account of a man's journey into the mind, a toot on the trumpet to alert the neighbors. Thoreau was well aware that no one can alert his neighbors who is not wide-awake himself, and he went to the woods (among other reasons) to make sure that he would stay awake during his broadcast. What actually took place during the years 1845–47 is largely unrecorded, and the reader is excluded from the private life of the author, who supplies almost no gossip about himself, a great deal about his neighbors and about the universe.

As for me, I cannot in this short ramble give a simple and sincere account of my own life, but I think Thoreau might find it instructive to know that this memorial essay is being written in a house that, through no intent on my part, is the same size and shape as his own domicile on the pond—about ten by fifteen, tight, plainly finished, and at a little distance from my Concord. The house in which I sit this morning was built to accommodate a boat, not a man, but by long experience I have learned that in most respects it shelters me better than the larger dwelling where my bed is, and which, by design, is a manhouse not a boathouse. Here in the boathouse I am a wilder and, it would appear, a healthier man, by a safe margin. I have a chair, a bench, a table, and I can walk into the water if I tire of the land. My house fronts a cove. Two fishermen have just arrived to spot fish from the air—an osprey and a man in a small yellow plane who works for the fish company. The man, I have noticed, is less well equipped than the hawk, who can dive directly on his fish and carry it away, without telephoning. A mouse and a squirrel share the house with me. The building is, in fact, a multiple dwelling, a semidetached affair. It is because I am semidetached while here that I find it possible to transact this private business with the fewest obstacles.

There is also a woodchuck here, living forty feet away under the wharf. When the wind is right, he can smell my house; and when the wind is contrary, I can smell his. We both use the wharf for sunning, taking turns, each adjusting his schedule to the other's convenience. Thoreau once ate a woodchuck. I think he felt he owed it to his readers, and that it was little enough, considering the indignities they were suffering at his hands and the dressing-down they were taking. (Parts of *Walden* are pure scold.) Or perhaps he ate the woodchuck because he believed every man should acquire strict business habits, and the woodchuck was destroying his market beans. I do not know. Thoreau had a strong experimental streak in him. It is probably no harder to eat a woodchuck than to construct a sentence that lasts a hundred years. At any rate, Thoreau is the only writer I know who prepared himself for his great ordeal by eating a woodchuck; also the only one who got a hangover from drinking too much water. (He was drunk the whole time, though he seldom touched wine or coffee or tea.)

Here in this compact house where I would spend one day as deliberately as Nature if I were not being pressed by the editor of a magazine, and with a woodchuck (as yet uneaten) for neighbor, I can feel the companionship of the occupant of the pond-side cabin in Walden woods, a mile from the village, near the Fitchburg right of way. Even my immediate business is no barrier between us: Thoreau occasionally batted out a magazine piece, but was always suspicious of any sort of purposeful work that cut into his time. A man, he said, should take care not to be thrown off the track by every nutshell and mosquito's wing that falls on the rails.

There has been much guessing as to why he went to the pond. To set it down to escapism is, of course, to misconstrue what happened. Henry went forth to battle when he took to the woods, and *Walden* is the report of a man torn by two powerful and opposing drives—the desire to enjoy the world (and not be derailed by a mosquito wing) and the urge to set the world straight. One cannot join these two successfully, but sometimes, in rare cases, something good or even great results from the attempt of the tormented spirit to reconcile them. Henry

10

went forth to battle, and if he set the stage himself, if he fought on his own terms and with his own weapons, it was because it was his nature to do things differently from most men, and to act in a cocky fashion. If the pond and the woods seemed a more plausible site for a house than an in-town location, it was because a cowbell made for him a sweeter sound than a churchbell. *Walden,* the book, makes the sound of a cowbell, more than a churchbell, and proves the point, although both sounds are in it, and both remarkably clear and sweet. He simply preferred his churchbell at a little distance.

I think one reason he went to the woods was a perfectly simple and commonplace one—and apparently he thought so, too. "At a certain season of our life," he wrote, "we are accustomed to consider every spot as the possible site of a house." There spoke the young man, a few years out of college, who had not yet broken away from home. He hadn't married, and he had found no job that measured up to his rigid standards of employment, and like any young man, or young animal, he felt uneasy and on the defensive until he had fixed himself a den. Most young men, of course, casting about for a site, are content merely to draw apart from their kinfolks. Thoreau, convinced that the greater part of what his neighbors called good was bad, withdrew from a great deal more than family: he pulled out of everything for a while, to serve everybody right for being so stuffy, and to try his own prejudices on the dog.

The house-hunting sentence above, which starts the chapter called "Where I Lived, and What I Lived For," is followed by another passage that is worth quoting here because it so beautifully illustrates the offbeat prose that Thoreau was master of, a prose at once strictly disciplined and wildly abandoned. "I have surveyed the country on every side within a dozen miles of where I live," continued this delirious young man. "In imagination I have bought all the farms in succession, for all were to be bought, and I knew their price. I walked over each farmer's premises, tasted his wild apples, discoursed on husbandry with him, took his farm at his price, at any price, mortgaging it to him in my mind; even put a higher price on it—took everything but a deed of it—took his word for his deed, for I dearly love to talk—cultivated it, and him too to some extent, I trust, and withdrew when I had enjoyed it long enough, leaving him to carry it on." A copy-desk man would get a double hernia trying to clean up that sentence for the management, but the sentence needs no fixing, for it perfectly captures the meaning of the writer and the quality of the ramble.

"Wherever I sat, there I might live, and the landscape radiated from me accordingly." Thoreau, the home-seeker, sitting on his hummock with the entire State of Massachusetts radiating from him, is to me the most humorous of the New England figures, and *Walden* the most humorous of the books, though its humor is almost continuously subsurface and there is nothing deliberately funny anywhere, except a few weak jokes and bad puns that rise to the surface like the perch in the pond that rose to the sound of the maestro's flute. Thoreau tended to write in sentences, a feat not every writer is capable of, and *Walden* is, rhetorically speaking, a collection of certified sentences, some of them, it would now appear, as indestructible as they are errant. The book is distilled from the vast journals, and this accounts for its intensity: he picked out bright particles that pleased his eye, whirled them in the kaleidoscope of his content, and produced the pattern that has endured—the color, the form, the light.

On this its hundredth birthday, Thoreau's *Walden* is pertinent and timely. In our uneasy season, when all men unconsciously seek a retreat from a world that has got almost completely out of hand, his house in the Concord woods is a haven. In our culture of gadgetry and the multiplicity of convenience, his cry "Simplicity, simplicity, simplicity!" has the insistence of a fire alarm. In the brooding atmosphere of war and the gathering radioactive storm, the innocence and serenity of his summer afternoons are enough to burst the remembering heart, and one gazes back upon that pleasing interlude—its confidence, its purity, its deliberateness—with awe and wonder, as one would look upon the face of a child asleep. 15

"This small lake was of most value as a neighbor in the intervals of a gentle rain-storm in August, when, both air and water being perfectly still, but the sky overcast, midafternoon had all the serenity of evening, and the wood-thrush sang around, and was heard from shore to shore." Now, in the perpetual overcast in which our days are spent, we hear with extra perception and deep gratitude that song, tying century to century.

I sometimes amuse myself by bringing Henry Thoreau back to life and showing him the sights. I escort him into a phone booth and let him dial Weather. "This is a delicious evening," the girl's voice says, "when the whole body is one sense, and imbibes delight through every pore." I show him the spot in the Pacific where an island used to be, before some magician made it vanish. "We know not where we are," I murmur. "The light which puts out our eyes is darkness to us. Only that day dawns to which we are awake." I thumb through the latest copy of *Vogue* with him. "Of two patterns which differ only by a few threads more or less of a particular color," I read, "the one will be sold readily, the other lie on the shelf, though it frequently happens that, after the lapse of a season, the latter becomes the most fashionable." Together we go outboarding on the Assabet, looking for what we've lost—a hound, a bay horse, a turtledove. I show him a distracted farmer who is trying to repair a hay baler before the thunder shower breaks. "This farmer," I remark, "is endeavoring to solve the problem of a livelihood by a formula more complicated than the problem itself. To get his shoestrings he speculates in herds of cattle."

I take the celebrated author to Twenty-One for lunch, so the waiters may study his shoes. The proprietor welcomes us. "The gross feeder," remarks the proprietor, sweeping the room with his arm, "is a man in the larva stage." After lunch we visit a classroom in one of those schools conducted by big corporations to teach their superannuated executives how to retire from business without serious injury to their health. (The shock to men's systems these days when relieved of the exacting routine of amassing wealth is very great and must be cushioned.) "It is not necessary," says the teacher to his pupils, "that a man should earn his living by the sweat of his brow, unless he sweats easier than I do. We are determined to be starved before we are hungry."

I turn on the radio and let Thoreau hear Winchell beat the red hand around the clock. "Time is but the stream I go a-fishing in," shouts Mr. Winchell, rattling his telegraph key. "Hardly a man takes a half hour's nap after dinner, but when he wakes he holds up his head and asks, 'What's the news?' If we read of one man robbed, or murdered, or killed by accident, or one house burned, or one vessel wrecked, or one steamboat blown up, or one cow run over on the Western Railroad, or one mad dog killed, or one lot of grasshoppers in the winter— we need never read of another. One is enough."

I doubt that Thoreau would be thrown off balance by the fantastic   20
sights and sounds of the twentieth century. "The Concord nights," he once wrote, "are stranger than the Arabian nights." A four-engined airliner would merely serve to confirm his early views on travel. Everywhere he would observe, in new shapes and sizes, the old predicaments and follies of men—the desperation, the impedimenta, the meanness— along with the visible capacity for elevation of the mind and soul. "This curious world which we inhabit is more wonderful than it is convenient; more beautiful than it is useful; it is more to be admired and enjoyed than used." He would see that today ten thousand engineers are busy making sure that the world shall be convenient even if it is destroyed in the process, and others are determined to increase its usefulness even though its beauty is lost somewhere along the way.

At any rate, I'd like to stroll about the countryside in Thoreau's company for a day, observing the modern scene, inspecting today's snowstorm, pointing out the sights, and offering belated apologies for my sins. Thoreau is unique among writers in that those who admire him find him uncomfortable to live with—a regular hairshirt of a man. A little band of dedicated Thoreauvians would be a sorry sight indeed: fellows who hate compromise and have compromised, fellows who love wildness and have lived tamely, and at their side, censuring them and chiding them, the ghostly figure of this upright man, who long ago gave corroboration to impulses they perceived were right and issued warnings against the things they instinctively knew to be their enemies. I should hate to be called a Thoreauvian, yet I wince every time I walk into the barn I'm pushing before me, seventy-five feet by forty, and the author of *Walden* has served as my conscience through the long stretches of my trivial days.

Hairshirt or no, he is a better companion than most, and I would not swap him for a soberer or more reasonable friend even if I could. I can reread his famous invitation with undiminished excitement. The sad thing is that not more acceptances have been received, that so many decline for one reason or another, pleading some previous engagement or ill health. But the invitation stands. It will beckon as long as this remarkable book stays in print—which will be as long as there are August afternoons in the intervals of a gentle rainstorm, as long as there are ears to catch the faint sounds of the orchestra. I find it agreeable to sit here this morning, in a house of correct proportions, and hear across a century of time his flute, his frogs, and his seductive summons to the wildest revels of them all.

Allen Cove, Summer, 1954

Lines of Inquiry
"A Slight Sound at Evening"

White has divided this essay into two sections, marked by a space break between paragraphs 16 and 17. What is the purpose of that second section, in which White imagines himself "bringing Henry Thoreau back to life and showing him the sights"? What relationship, if any, does it have to the first section, in which White is concerned with commemorating the hundredth anniversary of *Walden?* Why doesn't White simply end his essay with paragraph 16, especially since that paragraph ends with a sentence that seems to be a fitting conclusion to the piece as a whole?

In paragraphs 3–7, White lists numerous reasons for his admiration of *Walden.* What connection do you see between all of these reasons and the ones that he cites in paragraphs 15–16, having to do with the contemporary relevance of *Walden?* What overriding values seem to be guiding White in his enumeration of all these reasons? How are these values reflected by White's description in paragraphs 8–10 of the house where he wrote "this memorial essay"?

For another, quite different, memorial essay dealing with Thoreau and *Walden,* you might find it interesting to look at Woolf's *Thoreau,* which also appears in this collection. What are the most striking differences that you notice between the views that White and Woolf offer of Thoreau and his work? How do you account for these differences? Based on your own reading of Thoreau's pieces in this collection, whose view do you think is more reliable?

The Essayist and the Essay

The essayist is a self-liberated man, sustained by the childish belief that everything he thinks about, everything that happens to him, is of general interest. He is a fellow who thoroughly enjoys his work, just as people who take bird walks enjoy theirs. Each new excursion of the essayist, each new "attempt," differs from the last and takes him into new country. This delights him. Only a person who is congenitally self-centered has the effrontery and the stamina to write essays.

There are as many kinds of essays as there are human attitudes or poses, as many essay flavors as there are Howard Johnson ice creams. The essayist arises in the morning and, if he has work to do, selects his garb from an unusually extensive wardrobe: he can pull on any sort of shirt, be any sort of person, according to his mood or his subject matter—philosopher, scold, jester, raconteur, confidant, pundit, devil's advocate, enthusiast. I like the essay, have always liked it, and even as a child was at work, attempting to inflict my young thoughts and experiences on others by putting them on paper. I early broke into print in the pages of *St. Nicholas.* I tend still to fall back on the essay form (or lack of form) when an idea strikes me, but I am not fooled about the place of the essay in twentieth-century American letters—it stands a short distance down the line. The essayist, unlike the novelist, the poet, and the playwright, must be content in his self-imposed role of second-class citizen. A writer who has his sights trained on the Nobel Prize or other earthly triumphs had best write a novel, a poem, or a play, and leave the essayist to ramble about, content with living a free life and enjoying the satisfactions of a somewhat undisciplined existence. (Dr. Johnson called the essay "an irregular, undigested piece"; this happy practitioner has no wish to quarrel with the good doctor's characterization.)

There is one thing the essayist cannot do, though—he cannot indulge himself in deceit or in concealment, for he will be found out in no time. Desmond MacCarthy, in his introductory remarks to the 1928 E. P. Dutton & Company edition of Montaigne, observes that Montaigne "had the gift of natural candour. . . ." It is the basic ingredient. And even the essayist's escape from discipline is only a partial escape: the essay, although a relaxed form, imposes its own disciplines, raises its own problems, and these disciplines and problems soon become apparent and (we all hope) act as a deterrent to anyone wielding a pen merely because he entertains random thoughts or is in a happy or wandering mood.

I think some people find the essay the last resort of the egoist, a much too self-conscious and self-serving form for their taste; they feel that it is presumptuous of a writer to assume that his little excursions or his small observations will interest the reader. There is some justice in their complaint. I have always been aware that I am by nature self-absorbed and egoistical; to write of myself to the extent I have done indicates a too great attention to my own life, not enough to the lives of others. I have worn many shirts, and not all of them have been a good fit. But when I am discouraged or downcast I need only fling open the door of my closet, and there, hidden behind everything else, hangs the mantle of Michel de Montaigne, smelling slightly of camphor.

Lines of Inquiry
"The Essayist and the Essay"

In his second paragraph, White claims that "there are as many kinds of essays as there are human attitudes or poses," and that the essayist can "be any sort of person, according to his mood or his subject matter." What "sort of person" does White appear to be in this piece? How would you characterize his "mood" and his "attitudes"? How is your impression of him shaped by his ideas? By the way he develops his ideas? By the way he words his ideas? What relationship do you see between the kind of person he appears to be and the subject matter he discusses?

In his third paragraph, White maintains that the essayist "cannot indulge himself in deceit or in concealment." How do you square this assertion with his previous statement about all of the "poses" that are available to the essayist? How is it possible to assume a pose in writing without engaging "in deceit or in concealment?" How is it possible to assume a pose while also being "self-centered"? What exactly do you think White believes about the relationship between the sort of person an essayist appears to be in writing and the sort of person an essayist actually is?

White is not the only essayist to be concerned with the personality that comes across in an essay, as you can see by looking at Hoagland's "What I Think, What I Am" and Woolf's "The Modern Essay." How does White's idea about the "poses" of an essayist compare with Hoagland's assertion that "the artful 'I' of an essay can be as chameleon as any narrator in fiction"? How does White's idea compare with Woolf's belief that the "problem" for every essayist is "never to be yourself and yet always" to be yourself? What relationship do you think exists between the sort of person you are and the sort of person you appear to be in your writing?

Tom Wolfe
1931—

Readers were bored to tears without understanding why. When they came upon that pale beige tone, it began to signal to them, unconsciously, that a well-known bore was here again, "the journalist," a phlegmatic spirit, a faded personality, and there was no way to get rid of the pallid little troll, short of ceasing to read.

In this passage from his essay, "The New Journalism," Tom Wolfe criticizes the "calm," "cultivated," "genteel" voice that characterized nonfiction writing in the early sixties. To avoid such a "beige" and "faded" style in his own writing, Wolfe says, "I would try anything," and he does: imitating the voices of his subjects, inhabiting their minds, stretching sentences to their limits with modifiers and intensifiers—using a whole battery of amplifying strategies that have come to define the "new journalism." For him, these strategies are not simply matters of prose style alone. In his view, only writing with "personality, energy, drive, bravura" can capture the intensity of American experience, particularly the exuberance and excesses of popular culture since the sixties, the object of his most brilliant satire.

Born in Richmond, Virginia, a graduate of Washington and Lee University, Wolfe left the South for graduate school at Yale, where he received a PhD in American Studies in 1957. The atmosphere of Yale was "poisonous," and "morbid," Wolfe says, and he longed to escape it for the "real world" of newspaper reporting. After stints with the *Springfield Union* and *Washington Post,* he left for "the hulking carnival" of New York City and the staffs of *The New York Herald Tribune* and *New York Times Sunday Magazine.* There, working under the pressure of deadlines and the competition of his fellow reporters, Wolfe developed his signature techniques for bringing feature writing alive.

The breakthrough came in 1963 on a story Wolfe was doing for *Esquire* on the custom car culture in California. He'd done all the research but didn't know how to shape or analyze it. "I couldn't pull the thing together," he says, so he just sat down and started "typing away," "recording it all, and inside of a couple of hours, typing along like a madman, I could tell something was beginning to happen." The spontaneity and immediacy of the result impressed the editors at *Esquire,* who published the piece exactly as it was—as "The Kandy-Kolored Tangerine-Flake Streamline Baby"—even though Wolfe intended it to begin simply as a memo noting first impressions. He had found his style, his voice, his way of making things happen in prose.

Since then Wolfe has written a series of controversial social portraits and cultural critiques. In 1965 he published his first collection of essays—also entitled *The Kandy-Kolored Tangerine-Flake Streamline Baby*—revelling in the "freer forms" of popular culture, from the "electronic jollification" of Las Vegas to the down-home heroism of stock car racing to the "marvelous" tackiness of youth culture figures like Murray the K and Muhammed Ali. But Wolfe satirizes even as he celebrates. In *The Electric Kool Aid Acid Test* (1968), he zestfully recreates the manic energy of novelist Ken Kesey and the Merry Pranksters, a group of hippies dedicated to LSD and the psychedelic experience, yet he questions their undisciplined ways and their solemn elevation of a life-style into a "theology," an experience of "the holy." In *Radical Chic and Mau-Mauing the Flak Catchers* (1970), one of his most controversial books, Wolfe caricatures Leonard Bernstein and other "radically chic" liberals who raise money for groups like the Black Panthers at high society cocktail parties. In *The Painted Word* (1975) and *From Bauhaus to Our House* (1981) he satirizes the self-important obscurity of modern painting and architecture. And in his most widely known and highly praised book, *The Right Stuff* (1979), Wolfe offers a detailed study of "the righteous fraternities" of fighter pilots and astronauts in the early years of the American space program. Again, he is attracted by energy and talent and uniqueness, in this case by the "ineffable" quality of "the right stuff," a mysterious amalgam of bravery and skill possessed by every successful pilot. Yet he remains skeptical of the romanticizing, the mystifying, and the pomposity inherent in the very idea of "the right stuff."

Like many other satirists, Wolfe takes as his targets excessiveness and pretentiousness. His concern is that the various trends and consciousness-raising movements of the sixties and seventies oversimplify complex experience. So, he is always on the lookout for the holier-than-thou, for people who take themselves too seriously and look down on everyone else. He also cautions us about the dangers of self-indulgence. In a famous and much quoted essay, "The Me Decade and the Third Great Awakening," he writes with great irony about "the luxury enjoyed by so many millions of middling folk, of dwelling upon the self."

Wolfe's satire is not often so direct. Indeed, he rarely comes out in his own voice and tells us what he thinks. Instead, he relies on the technique of third-person omniscient narration, looking at experience through "the eye sockets" of the people involved, speaking in their own voices, as if he knows their thoughts and feelings. Through the hard work of "saturation reporting," of interviewing and researching and living with the subject, a reporter, he believes, can learn enough about an individual to re-create his or her thoughts accurately and fairly. Saturation reporting is one of the four basic techniques of the "new journalism," according to Wolfe, the one most attacked by other journalists as "subjective" and "biased." Another technique is what Wolfe calls "scene-by-scene reconstruction," "telling the story by moving from scene to scene and resorting as little as possible to sheer historical narrative." A third technique uses "status details," bits and pieces of everyday life—gestures, habits, manners, "modes of behaving"—that help evoke the textures of an experience. The fourth is dialogue, which Wolfe says "involves the reader more completely than any other device." In other words, Wolfe shows, rarely tells. So his essays and books are often hard to distinguish from fiction, made up as they are of stories and events and descriptions of experience.

On the sentence level Wolfe pulls out all the stops. He exclaims, digresses, interrupts, writing often in the present tense, as if the event is happening before our eyes, even as we are reading about it. So his phrases expand and develop excitedly. His punctuation abounds with ellipses, dashes, parentheses, italics. He plays with the sound of words, mimicking, repeating. His goal, he says, "is to give the illusion not only of a person talking but of a person thinking":

> My God—to be a part of Edwards in the late forties and early fifties!— even to be on the ground and hear one of those incredible explosions from 35,000 feet and know that some True Brother had commenced his rocket launch . . . in the X–1, the X–1A, the X–2, the D558–1, the horrible XF–92A, the beautiful D–558-2 . . . and to know that he would seem to be at an altitude, in the thin air at the edge of space, where the stars and the moon came out at noon, in an atmosphere so thin that the ordinary laws of aerodynamics no longer applied and a plane could skid into a flat spin like a cereal bowl on a waxed Formica counter and then start tumbling, not spinning and not diving, but tumbling, end over end like a brick. . . .

Wolfe has said in an interview that he wanted the writing in *The Right Stuff* to appear "buoyant, free and easy, spontaneous," but the paradox is that "creating the effect of spontaneity in writing is one of the most difficult things you can do." It requires revision and discipline. Like the fighter-jocks themselves, who "push the outside of the envelope" whenever they set a new speed or altitude record, Wolfe pushes the outside of the envelope of language, but only through hard work, painstaking control, and the risk of "tumbling, end over end like a brick. . . ."

O Rotten Gotham— Sliding down into the Behavioral Sink

I just spent two days with Edward T. Hall, an anthropologist, watching thousands of my fellow New Yorkers short-circuiting themselves into hot little twitching death balls with jolts of their own adrenalin. Dr. Hall says it is overcrowding that does it. Overcrowding gets the adrenalin going, and the adrenalin gets them hyped up. And here they are, hyped up, turning bilious, nephritic, queer, autistic, sadistic, barren, batty, sloppy, hot-in-the-pants, chancred-on-the-flankers, leering, puling, numb—the usual in New York, in other words, and God knows what else. Dr. Hall has the theory that overcrowding has already thrown New York into a state of behavioral sink. Behavioral sink is a term from ethology, which is the study of how animals relate to their environment. Among animals, the sink winds up with a "population collapse" or "massive die-off." O rotten Gotham.

It got to be easy to look at New Yorkers as animals, especially looking down from some place like a balcony at Grand Central at the rush hour Friday afternoon. The floor was filled with the poor white humans, running around, dodging, blinking their eyes, making a sound like a pen full of starlings or rats or something.

"Listen to them skid," says Dr. Hall.

He was right. The poor old etiolate animals were out there skidding on their rubber soles. You could hear it once he pointed it out. They stop short to keep from hitting somebody or because they are disoriented and they suddenly stop and look around, and they skid on their rubber-sole shoes, and a screech goes up. They pour out onto the floor down the escalators from the Pan-Am Building, from 42nd Street, from Lexington Avenue, up out of subways, down into subways, railroad trains, up into helicopters—

"You can also hear the helicopters all the way down here," says Dr. Hall. The sound of the helicopters using the roof of the Pan-Am Building nearly fifty stories up beats right through. "If it weren't for this ceiling"—he is referring to the very high ceiling in Grand Central—"this place would be unbearable with this kind of crowding. And yet they'll probably never 'waste' space like this again."

They screech! And the adrenal glands in all those poor white animals enlarge, micrometer by micrometer, to the size of cantaloupes. Dr. Hall pulls a Minox camera out of a holster he has on his belt and starts shooting away at the human scurry. The Sink!

5

Dr. Hall has the Minox up to his eye—he is a slender man, calm, 52 years old, young-looking, an anthropologist who has worked with Navajos, Hopis, Spanish-Americans, Negroes, Trukese. He was the most important anthropologist in the government during the crucial years of the foreign aid program, the 1950's. He directed both the Point Four training program and the Human Relations Area Files. He wrote *The Silent Language* and *The Hidden Dimension,* two books that are picking up the kind of "underground" following his friend Marshall McLuhan started picking up about five years ago. He teaches at the Illinois Institute of Technology, lives with his wife, Mildred, in a high-ceilinged town house on one of the last great residential streets in downtown Chicago, Astor Street; has a grown son and daughter, loves good food, good wine, the relaxed, civilized life—but comes to New York with a Minox at his eye to record—perfect!—The Sink.

We really got down in there by walking down into the Lexington Avenue line subway stop under Grand Central. We inhaled those nice big fluffy fumes of human sweat, urine, effluvia, and sebaceous secretions. One old female human was already stroked out on the upper level, on a stretcher, with two policemen standing by. The other humans barely looked at her. They rushed into line. They bellied each other, haunch to paunch, down the stairs. Human heads shone through the gratings. The species North European tried to create bubbles of space around themselves, about a foot and a half in diameter—

"See, he's reacting against the line," says Dr. Hall.

—but the species Mediterranean presses on in. The hell with bub-   10 bles of space. The species North European resents that, this male human behind him presses forward toward the booth . . . *breathing* on him, he's disgusted, he pulls out of the line entirely, the species Mediterranean resents him for resenting it, and neither of them realizes what the hell they are getting irritable about exactly. And in all of them the old adrenals grow another micrometer.

Dr. Hall whips out the Minox. Too perfect! The bottom of The Sink.

It is the sheer overcrowding, such as occurs in the business sections of Manhattan five days a week and in Harlem, Bedford-Stuyvesant, southeast Bronx every day—sheer overcrowding is converting New Yorkers into animals in a sink pen. Dr. Hall's argument runs as follows: all animals, including birds, seem to have a built-in, inherited requirement to have a certain amount of territory, space, to lead their lives in. Even if they have all the food they need, and there are no predatory animals threatening them, they cannot tolerate crowding beyond a certain point. No more than two hundred wild Norway rats can survive on a quarter acre of ground, for example, even when they are given all the food they can eat. They just die off.

But why? To find out, ethologists have run experiments on all sorts of animals, from stickleback crabs to Sika deer. In one major experiment, an ethologist named John Calhoun put some domesticated white Norway rats in a pen with four sections to it, connected by ramps. Calhoun knew from previous experiments that the rats tend to split up into groups of ten to twelve and that the pen, therefore, would hold forty to forty-eight rats comfortably, assuming they formed four equal groups. He allowed them to reproduce until there were eighty rats, balanced between male and female, but did not let it get any more crowded. He kept them supplied with plenty of food, water, and nesting materials. In other words, all their more obvious needs were taken care of. A less obvious need—space—was not. To the human eye, the pen did not even look especially crowded. But to the rats, it was crowded beyond endurance.

The entire colony was soon plunged into a profound behavioral sink. "The sink," said Calhoun, "is the outcome of any behavioral process that collects animals together in unusually great numbers. The unhealthy connotations of the term are not accidental: a behavioral sink does act to aggravate all forms of pathology that can be found within a group."

For a start, long before the rat population reached eighty, a status   15
hierarchy had developed in the pen. Two dominant male rats took over the two end sections, acquired harems of eight to ten females each, and forced the rest of the rats into the two middle pens. All the overcrowding took place in the middle pens. That was where the "sink" hit. The aristocrat rats at the ends grew bigger, sleeker, healthier, and more secure the whole time.

In The Sink, meanwhile, nest building, courting, sex behavior, reproduction, social organization, health—all of it went to pieces. Normally, Norway rats have a mating ritual in which the male chases the female, the female ducks down into a burrow and sticks her head up to watch the male. He performs a little dance outside the burrow, then she comes out, and he mounts her, usually for a few seconds. When The Sink set in, however, no more than three males—the dominant males in the middle sections—kept up the old customs. The rest tried everything from satyrism to homosexuality or else gave up on sex altogether. Some of the subordinate males spent all their time chasing females. Three or four might chase one female at the same time, and instead of stopping at the burrow entrance for the ritual, they would charge right in. Once mounted, they would hold on for minutes instead of the usual seconds.

Homosexuality rose sharply. So did bisexuality. Some males would mount anything—males, females, babies, senescent rats, anything. Still other males dropped sexual activity altogether, wouldn't fight and, in fact, would hardly move except when the other rats slept. Occasionally a female from the aristocrat rats' harems would come over the ramps and into the middle sections to sample life in The Sink. When she had had enough, she would run back up the ramp. Sink males would give chase up to the top of the ramp, which is to say, to the very edge of the aristocratic preserve. But one glance from one of the king rats would stop them cold and they would return to The Sink.

The slumming females from the harems had their adventures and then returned to a placid, healthy life. Females in The Sink, however, were ravaged, physically and psychologically. Pregnant rats had trouble continuing pregnancy. The rate of miscarriages increased significantly, and females started dying from tumors and other disorders of the mammary glands, sex organs, uterus, ovaries, and Fallopian tubes. Typically, their kidneys, livers, and adrenals were also enlarged or diseased or showed other signs associated with stress.

Child-rearing became totally disorganized. The females lost the interest or the stamina to build nests and did not keep them up if they did build them. In the general filth and confusion, they would not put themselves out to save offspring they were momentarily separated from. Frantic, even sadistic competition among the males was going on all around them and rendering their lives chaotic. The males began unprovoked and senseless assaults upon one another, often in the form of tail-biting. Ordinarily, rats will suppress this kind of behavior when it crops up. In The Sink, male rats gave up all policing and just looked out for themselves. The "pecking order" among males in The Sink was never stable. Normally, male rats set up a three-class structure. Under the pressure of overcrowding, however, they broke up into all sorts of unstable subclasses, cliques, packs—and constantly pushed, probed, explored, tested one another's power. Anyone was fair game, except for the aristocrats in the end pens.

Calhoun kept the population down to eighty, so that the next stage, "population collapse" or "massive die-off," did not occur. But the autopsies showed that the pattern—as in the diseases among the female rats—was already there.

The classic study of die-off was John J. Christian's study of Sika deer on James Island in the Chesapeake Bay, west of Cambridge, Maryland. Four or five of the deer had been released on the island, which was 280 acres and uninhabited, in 1916. By 1955 they had bred freely into a herd of 280 to 300. The population density was only about one deer per acre at this point, but Christian knew that this was already too high for the Sikas' inborn space requirements, and something would give before long. For two years the number of deer remained 280 to 300. But suddenly, in 1958, over half the deer died; 161 carcasses were recovered. In 1959 more deer died and the population steadied at about 80.

In two years, two-thirds of the herd had died. Why? It was not starvation. In fact, all the deer collected were in excellent condition,

20

with well-developed muscles, shining coats, and fat deposits between the muscles. In practically all the deer, however, the adrenal glands had enlarged by 50 percent. Christian concluded that the die-off was due to "shock following severe metabolic disturbance, probably as a result of prolonged adrenocortical hyperactivity. . . . There was no evidence of infection, starvation, or other obvious cause to explain the mass mortality." In other words, the constant stress of overpopulation, plus the normal stress of the cold of the winter, had kept the adrenalin flowing so constantly in the deer that their systems were depleted of blood sugar and they died of shock.

Well, the white humans are still skidding and darting across the floor of Grand Central. Dr. Hall listens a moment longer to the skidding and the darting noises, and then says, "You know, I've been on commuter trains here after everyone has been through one of these rushes, and I'll tell you, there is enough acid flowing in the stomachs in every car to dissolve the rails underneath."

Just a little invisible acid bath for the linings to round off the day. The ulcers the acids cause, of course, are the one disease people have already been taught to associate with the stress of city life. But overcrowding, as Dr. Hall sees it, raises a lot more hell with the body than just ulcers. In everyday life in New York—just the usual, getting to work, working in massively congested areas like 42nd Street between Fifth Avenue and Lexington, especially now that the Pan-Am Building is set in there, working in cubicles such as those in the editorial offices at Time-Life, Inc., which Dr. Hall cites as typical of New York's poor handling of space, working in cubicles with low ceilings and, often, no access to a window, while construction crews all over Manhattan drive everybody up the Masonite wall with air-pressure generators with noises up to the boil-a-brain decibel levels, then rushing to get home, piling into subways and trains, fighting for time and for space, the usual day in New York—the whole now-normal thing keeps shooting jolts of adrenalin into the body, breaking down the body's defenses and winding up with the work-a-daddy human animal stroked out at the breakfast table with his head apoplexed like a cauliflower out of his $6.95 semispread Pima-cotton shirt, and nosed over into a plate of No-Klo-resto egg substitute, signing off with the black thrombosis, cancer, kidney, liver, or stomach failure, and the adrenals ooze to a halt, the size of eggplants in July.

One of the people whose work Dr. Hall is interested in on this score is Rene Dubos at the Rockefeller Institute. Dubos's work indicates that specific organisms, such as the tuberculosis bacillus or a pneumonia virus, can seldom be considered "the cause" of a disease. The germ or virus, apparently, has to work in combination with other things that have already broken the body down in some way—such as the old adrenal hyperactivity. Dr. Hall would like to see some autopsy studies made to record the size of adrenal glands in New York, especially of

25

people crowded into slums and people who go through the full rush-hour-work-rush-hour cycle every day. He is afraid that until there is some clinical, statistical data on how overcrowding actually ravages the human body, no one will be willing to do anything about it. Even in so obvious a thing as air pollution, the pattern is familiar. Until people can actually see the smoke or smell the sulphur or feel the sting in their eyes, politicans will not get excited about it, even though it is well known that many of the lethal substances polluting the air are invisible and odorless. For one thing, most politicans are like the aristocrat rats. They are insulated from The Sink by practically sultanic buffers—limousines, chauffeurs, secretaries, aides-de-camp, doormen, shuttered houses, high-floor apartments. They almost never ride subways, fight rush hours, much less live in the slums or work in the Pan-Am Building.

We took a cab from Grand Central to go up to Harlem, and by 48th Street we were already socked into one of those great, total traffic jams on First Avenue on Friday afternoon. Dr. Hall motions for me to survey the scene, and there they all are, humans, male and female, behind the glass of their automobile windows, soundlessly going through the torture of their own adrenalin jolts. This male over here contracts his jaw muscles so hard that they bunch up into a great cheese Danish pattern. He twists his lips, he bleeds from the eyeballs, he shouts . . . soundlessly behind glass . . . the fat corrugates on the back of his neck, his whole body shakes as he pounds the heel of his hand into the steering wheel. The female human in the car ahead of him whips her head around, she bares her teeth, she screams . . . soundlessly behind glass . . . she throws her hands up in the air, Whaddya expect me—Yah, yuh stupid—and they all sit there, trapped in their own congestion, bleeding hate all over each other, shorting out the ganglia and—goddam it—

Dr. Hall sits back and watches it all. This is it! The Sink! And where is everybody's wandering boy?

Dr. Hall says, "We need a study in which drivers who go through these rush hours every day would wear GSR bands."

GSR?

"Galvanic skin response. It measures the electric potential of the skin, which is a function of sweating. If a person gets highly nervous, his palms begin to sweat. It is an index of tension. There are some other fairly simple devices that would record respiration and pulse. I think everybody who goes through this kind of experience all the time should take his own pulse—not literally—but just be aware of what's happening to him. You can usually tell when stress is beginning to get you physically."

In testing people crowded into New York's slums, Dr. Hall would like to take it one step further—gather information on the plasma hydrocortisone level in the blood or the corticosteroids in the urine. Both

30

have been demonstrated to be reliable indicators of stress, and testing procedures are simple.

The slums—we finally made it up to East Harlem. We drove into 101st Street, and there was a new, avant-garde little church building, the Church of the Epiphany, which Dr. Hall liked—and, next to it, a pile of rubble where a row of buildings had been torn down, and from the back windows of the tenements beyond several people were busy "airmailing," throwing garbage out the window, into the rubble, beer cans, red shreds, the No-Money-Down Eames roller stand for a TV set, all flying through the air onto the scaggy sump. We drove around some more in Harlem, and a sequence was repeated, trash, buildings falling down, buildings torn down, rubble, scaggy sumps or, suddenly, a cluster of high-rise apartment projects, with fences around the grass.

"You know what this city looks like?" Dr. Hall said. "It looks bombed out. I used to live at Broadway and 124th Street back in 1946 when I was studying at Columbia. I can't tell you how much Harlem has changed in twenty years. It looks bombed out. It's broken down. People who live in New York get used to it and don't realize how filthy the city has become. The whole thing is typical of a behaviorial sink. So is something like the Kitty Genovese case—a girl raped and murdered in the courtyard of an apartment complex and forty or fifty people look on from their apartments and nobody even calls the police. That kind of apathy and anomie is typical of the general psychological deterioration of The Sink."

He looked at the high-rise housing projects and found them mainly testimony to how little planners know about humans' basic animal requirements for space.

"Even on the simplest terms," he said, "it is pointless to build one of these blocks much over five stories high. Suppose a family lives on the fifteenth floor. The mother will be completely cut off from her children if they are playing down below, because the elevators are constantly broken in these projects, and it often takes half an hour, literally half an hour, to get the elevator if it is running. That's very common. A mother in that situation is just as much a victim of overcrowding as if she were back in the tenement block. Some Negro leaders have a bitter joke about how the white man is solving the slum problem by stacking Negroes up vertically, and there is a lot to that."

For one thing, says Dr. Hall, planners have no idea of the different space requirements of people from different cultures, such as Negroes and Puerto Ricans. They are all treated as if they were minute, compact middle-class whites. As with the Sika deer, who are overcrowded at one per acre, overcrowding is a relative thing for the human animal, as well. Each species has its own feeling for space. The feeling may be "subjective," but it is quite real.

Dr. Hall's theories on space and territory are based on the same information, gathered by biologists, ethologists, and anthropologists, 35 chiefly, as Robert Ardrey's. Ardrey has written two well-publicized books, *African Genesis* and *The Territorial Imperative. Life* magazine ran big excerpts from *The Territorial Imperative,* all about how the drive to acquire territory and property and add to it and achieve status is built into all animals, including man, over thousands of centuries of genetic history, etc., and is a more powerful drive than sex. *Life*'s big display prompted Marshall McLuhan to crack, "They see this as a great historic justification for free enterprise and Republicanism. If the birds do it and the stickle-back crabs do it, then it's right for man." To people like Hall and McLuhan, and Ardrey, for that matter, the right or wrong of it is irrelevant. The only thing they find inexcusable is the kind of thinking, by influential people, that isn't even aware of all this. Such as the thinking of most city planners.

"The planners always show you a bird's-eye view of what they are doing," he said. "You've seen those scale models. Everyone stands around the table and looks down and says that's great. It never occurs to anyone that they are taking a bird's-eye view. In the end, these projects do turn out fine, when viewed from an airplane."

As an anthropologist, Dr. Hall has to shake his head every time he hears planners talking about fully integrated housing projects for the year 1980 or 1990, as if by then all cultural groups will have the same feeling for space and will live placidly side by side, happy as the happy burghers who plan all the good clean bird's-eye views. According to his findings, the very fact that every cultural group does have its own peculiar, unspoken feeling for space is what is responsible for much of the uneasiness one group feels around the other.

It is like the North European and the Mediterranean in the subway line. The North European, without ever realizing it, tries to keep a bubble of space around himself, and the moment a stranger invades that sphere, he feels threatened. Mediterranean peoples tend to come from cultures where everyone is much more involved physically, publicly, with one another on a day-to-day basis and feels no uneasiness about mixing it up in public, but may have very different ideas about space inside the home. Even Negroes brought up in America have a different vocabulary of space and gesture from the North European Americans who, historically, have been their models, according to Dr. Hall. The failure of Negroes and whites to communicate well often boils down to things like this: some white will be interviewing a Negro for a job; the Negro's culture has taught him to show somebody you are interested by looking right at him and listening intently to what he has to say. But the species North European requires something more. He expects his listener to nod from time to time, as if to say, "Yes, keep going." If he doesn't get this nodding, he feels anxious, for fear the listener doesn't agree with him or has switched off. The Negro may learn that the white expects this sort of thing, but he isn't used to the precise kind of nodding that is customary, and so he may start overresponding, nodding like mad, and at this point the North European is liable to think he has some kind of stupid Uncle Tom on his hands, and the guy still doesn't get the job.

The whole handling of space in New York is so chaotic, says Dr. Hall, that even middle-class housing now seems to be based on the bird's-eye models for slum projects. He took a look at the big Park West Village development, set up originally to provide housing in Manhattan for families in the middle-income range, and found its handling of space very much like a slum project with slightly larger balconies. He felt the time has come to start subsidizing the middle class in New York on its own terms—namely, the kind of truly "human" spaces that still remain in brownstones.

"I think New York City should seriously consider a program of encouraging the middle-class development of an area like Chelsea, which is already starting to come up. People are beginning to renovate houses there on their own, and I think if the city would subsidize that sort of thing with tax reliefs and so forth, you would be amazed at what would result. What New York needs is a string of minor successes in the housing field, just to show everyone that it can be done, and I think the middle class can still do that for you. The alternative is to keep on doing what you're doing now, trying to lift a very large lower class up by main force almost and finding it a very slow and discouraging process."

"But before deciding how to redesign space in New York," he said, "people must first simply realize how severe the problem already is. And the handwriting is already on the wall."

"A study published in 1962," he said, "surveyed a representative sample of people living in New York slums and found only 18 percent of them free from emotional symptoms. Thirty-eight percent were in need of psychiatric help, and 23 percent were seriously disturbed or incapacitated. Now, this study was published in 1962, which means the work probably went on from 1955 to 1960. There is no telling how bad it is now. In a behavioral sink, crises can develop rapidly."

Dr. Hall would like to see a large-scale study similar to that undertaken by two sociopsychologists, Chombart de Lauwe and his wife, in a French working-class town. They found a direct relationship between crowding and general breakdown. In families where people were crowded into the apartment so that there was less than 86 to 108 square feet per person, social and physical disorders doubled. That would mean that for four people the smallest floor space they could tolerate would be an apartment, say, 12 by 30 feet.

What would one find in Harlem? "It is fairly obvious," Dr. Hall wrote in *The Hidden Dimension,* "that the American Negroes and people of Spanish culture who are flocking to our cities are being very seriously stressed. Not only are they in a setting that does not fit them, but they have passed the limits of their own tolerance of stress. The United States is faced with the fact that two of its creative and sensitive peoples are in the process of being destroyed and like Samson could bring down the structure that houses us all."

Dr. Hall goes out to the airport, to go back to Chicago, and I am coming back in a cab, along the East River Drive. It is four in the afternoon, but already the damned drive is clogging up. There is a 1959 Oldsmobile just to the right of me. There are about eight people in there, a lot of popeyed silhouettes against a leopard-skin dashboard, leopard-skin seats—and the driver is classic. He has a mustache, sideburns down to his jaw socket, and a tattoo on his forearm with a Rossetti painting of Jane Burden Morris with her hair long. All right; it is even touching, like a postcard photo of the main drag in San Pedro, California. But suddenly Sideburns guns it and cuts in front of my cab so that my driver has to hit the brakes, and then hardly 100 feet ahead Sideburns hits a wall of traffic himself and has to hit his brakes, and then it happens. A stuffed white Angora animal, a dog, no, it's a Pekingese cat, is mounted in his rear window—as soon as he hits the brakes its *eyes* light up, Nighttown pink. To keep from ramming him, my driver has to hit the brakes again, too, and so here I am, out in an insane, jammed-up expressway at four in the afternoon, shuddering to a stop while a stuffed Pekingese grows bigger and bigger and brighter in the eyeballs directly in front of me. Jolt! Nighttown pink! Hey—that's me the adrenalin is hitting, *I* am this white human sitting in a projectile heading amid a mass of clotted humans toward a white Angora stuffed goddam leopard-dash Pekingese freaking cat— kill that damned Angora—Jolt!—got me—another micrometer on the old adrenals—

Lines of Inquiry
"O Rotten Gotham—Sliding down into the Behavioral Sink"

Wolfe's style differs greatly from that of Edward Hall and the other anthropologists he writes about here. Hall, for example, speaks of "galvanic skin response" in "humans," whereas Wolfe notes that New Yorkers in Grand Central Station "screech" and their adrenal glands enlarge "to the size of cantaloupes." How would you describe such differences in the diction and sentence structure of Wolfe and Hall? What are the effects of these stylistic differences? What are the advantages in Wolfe's style of communicating Hall's idea of "behavioral sink"? What are the disadvantages?

"Behavioral sink" is clearly the most important concept in this piece, so you might find it useful to summarize what it means in your own words. What does this phenomenon have to do with the other concepts that are central in Hall's studies, namely "status hierarchy" and the "territorial imperative"? How does the research of Calhoun, Christian, and Dubos support Hall's theories? How does Wolfe's cab ride illustrate Hall's theories? How does life in a college dormitory illustrate Hall's theories?

In "The Iks," Lewis Thomas also writes about the damaging effects of people coming together in groups. What similarities and what differences do you see in the way that Hall and Thomas attempt to account for group behavior? In what respects is Ik behavior comparable to the behavior of people in Grand Central Station? In what respects is Ik behavior comparable to the behavior of rats in overcrowded cages? In what respects are the situation and behavior of the Iks most notably different from caged rats or overcrowded people?

The Pump House Gang

Our boys never hair out. The black panther has black feet. Black feet on the crumbling black panther. Pan-thuh. Mee-dah. Pam Stacy, 16 years old, a cute girl here in La Jolla, California, with a pair of orange bell-bottom hip-huggers on, sits on a step about four steps down the stairway to the beach and she can see a pair of revolting black feet without lifting her head. So she says it out loud, "The black panther."

Somebody farther down the stairs, one of the boys with the *major* hair and khaki shorts, says, "The black feet of the black panther."

"Mee-dah," says another kid. This happens to be the cry of a, well, *underground* society known as the Mac Meda Destruction Company.

"The pan-thuh."

"The poon-thuh." 5

All these kids, seventeen of them, members of the Pump House crowd, are lollygagging around the stairs down to Windansea Beach, La Jolla, California, about 11 a.m., and they all look at the black feet, which are a woman's pair of black street shoes, out of which stick a pair of old veiny white ankles, which lead up like a senile cone to a fudge of tallowy, edematous flesh, her thighs, squeezing out of her bathing suit, with old faded yellow bruises on them, which she probably got from running eight feet to catch a bus or something. She is standing with her old work-a-hubby, who has on *sandals:* you know, a pair of navy-blue anklet socks and these sandals with big, wide, new-smelling tan straps going this way and that, *for keeps.* Man, they look like orthopedic sandals, if one can imagine that. Obviously, these people come from Tucson or Albuquerque or one of those hincty adobe towns. All these hincty, crumbling black feet come to La Jolla-by-the-sea from the adobe towns for the weekend. They even drive in cars all full of thermos bottles and mayonnaisey sandwiches and some kind of latticework wooden-back support for the old crock who drives and Venetian blinds on the back window.

"The black panther."

"Pan-thuh."

"Poon-thuh."

"Mee-dah." 10

Nobody says it to the two old crocks directly. God, they must be practically 50 years old. Naturally, they're carrying every piece of garbage imaginable: the folding aluminum chairs, the newspapers, the lending-library book with the clear plastic wrapper on it, the sunglasses, the sun ointment, about a vat of goo—

It is a Mexican standoff. In a Mexican standoff, both parties narrow their eyes and glare but nobody throws a punch. Of course, nobody in the Pump House crowd would ever even jostle these people or say anything right to them; they are too cool for that.

Everybody in the Pump House crowd looks over, even Tom Coman, who is a cool person. Tom Coman, 16 years old, got thrown out of his garage last night. He is sitting up on top of the railing, near the stairs, up over the beach, with his legs apart. Some nice long willowy girl in yellow slacks is standing on the sidewalk but leaning into him with her arms around his body, just resting. Neale Jones, 16, a boy with great lank perfect surfer's hair, is standing nearby with a Band-Aid on his upper lip, where the sun has burnt it raw. Little Vicki Ballard is up on the sidewalk. Her older sister, Liz, is down the stairs by the Pump House itself, a concrete block, 15 feet high, full of machinery for the La Jolla water system. Liz is wearing her great "Liz" styles, a hulking rabbit-fur vest and black-leather boots over her Levis, even though it is about 85 out here and the sun is plugged in up there like God's own dentist lamp and the Pacific is heaving in with some fair-to-middling surf. Kit Tilden is lollygagging around, and Tom Jones, Connie Carter, Roger Johnson, Sharon Sandquist, Mary Beth White, Rupert Fellows, Glenn Jackson, Dan Watson from San Diego, they are all out here, and everybody takes a look at the panthers.

The old guy, one means, you know, he must be practically 50 years old, he says to his wife, "Come on, let's go farther up," and he takes her by her fat upper arm as if to wheel her around and aim her away from here.

But she says, "No! We have just as much right to be here as   15 they do."

"That's *not the point*—"

"Are you going to—"

"*Mrs. Roberts,*" the work-a-hubby says, calling his own wife by her official married name, as if to say she took a vow once and his word is law, even if he is not testing it with the blond kids here—"farther up, *Mrs. Roberts.*"

They start to walk up the sidewalk, but one kid won't move his feet, and, oh, god, her work-a-hubby breaks into a terrible shaking Jello smile as she steps over them, as if to say, Excuse me, sir, I don't mean to make trouble, please, and don't you and your colleagues rise up and jump me, screaming *Gotcha*—

Mee-dah!   20

But exactly! This beach *is* verboten for people practically 50 years old. This is a segregated beach. They can look down on Windansea Beach and see nothing but lean tan kids. It is posted "no swimming" (for safety reasons), meaning surfing only. In effect, it is segregated by age. From Los Angeles on down the California coast, this is an era of age segregation. People have always tended to segregate themselves by age, teenagers hanging around with teenagers, old people with old people, like the old men who sit on the benches up near the Bronx Zoo and smoke black cigars. But before, age segregation has gone on within a larger community. Sooner or later during the day everybody has melted back into the old community network that embraces practically everyone, all ages.

But in California today surfers, not to mention rock 'n' roll kids and the hot-rodders or Hair Boys, named for their fanciful pompadours—all sorts of sets of kids—they don't merely hang around together. They establish whole little societies for themselves. In some cases they live with one another for months at a time. The "Sunset Strip" on Sunset Boulevard used to be a kind of Times Square for Hollywood hot dogs of all ages, anyone who wanted to promenade in his version of the high life. Today "The Strip" is almost completely the preserve of kids from about 16 to 25. It is lined with go-go clubs. One of them, a place called It's Boss, is set up for people 16 to 25 and won't let in anybody over 25, and there are some terrible I'm-dying-a-thousand-deaths scenes when a girl comes up with her boyfriend and the guy at the door at It's Boss doesn't think she looks under 25 and tells her she will have to produce some identification proving she is young enough to come in here and live The Strip kind of life and—she's *had* it, because she can't get up the I.D. and nothing in the world is going to make a woman look stupider than to stand around trying to argue *I'm younger than I look, I'm younger than I look.* So she practically shrivels up like a Peruvian shrunken head in front of her boyfriend and he trundles her off, looking for some place you can get an old doll like this into. One of the few remaining clubs for "older people," curiously, is the Playboy Club. There are apartment houses for people 20 and 30 only, such as the Sheri Plaza in Hollywood and the E'Questre Inn in Burbank. There are whole suburban housing developments, mostly private developments, where only people over 45 or 50 can buy a house. Whole towns, meantime, have become identified as "young": Venice, Newport Beach, Balboa—or "old": Pasadena, Riverside, Coronado Island.

Behind much of it—especially something like a whole nightclub district of a major city, "The Strip," going teenage—is, simply, money. World War II and the prosperity that followed pumped incredible amounts of money into the population, the white population at least, at every class level. All of a sudden here is an area with thousands of people from 16 to 25 who can get their hands on enough money to support a whole nightclub belt and to have the cars to get there and to set up autonomous worlds of their own in a fairly posh resort community like La Jolla—

—Tom Coman's garage. Some old bastard took Tom Coman's garage away from him, and that means eight or nine surfers are out of a place to stay.

"I went by there this morning, you ought to see the guy," Tom   25
Coman says. Yellow Stretch Pants doesn't move. She has him around the waist. "He was out there painting and he had this brush and about a thousand gallons of ammonia. He was really going to scrub me out of there."

"What did he do with the furniture?"

"I don't know. He threw it out."

"What are you going to do?"

"I don't know."

"Where are you going to stay?"   30

"I don't know. I'll stay on the beach. It wouldn't be the first time. I haven't had a place to stay for three years, so I'm not going to start worrying now."

Everybody thinks that over awhile. Yellow Stretch just hangs on and smiles. Tom Coman, 16 years old, piping fate again. One of the girls says, "You can stay at my place, Tom."

"Um. Who's got a cigarette?"

Pam Stacy says, "You can have these."

Tom Coman lights a cigarette and says, "Let's have a destructo."   35
A destructo is what can happen in a garage after eight or 10 surfers are kicked out of it.

"Mee-dah!"

"Wouldn't that be bitchen?" says Tom Coman. Bitchen is a surfer's term that means "great," usually.

"Bitchen!"

"Mee-dah!"

It's incredible—that old guy out there trying to scour the whole   40
surfing life out of that garage. He's a pathetic figure. His shoulders are hunched over and he's dousing and scrubbing away and the sun doesn't give him a tan, it gives him these . . . *mottles* on the back of his neck. But never mind! The hell with destructo. One only has a destructo spontaneously, a Dionysian . . . *bursting out,* like those holes through the wall during the Mac Meda Destruction Company Convention at Manhattan Beach—Mee-dah!

Something will pan out. It's a magic economy—yes!—all up and down the coast from Los Angeles to Baja California kids can go to one of these beach towns and live the complete surfing life. They take off from home and get to the beach, and if they need a place to stay, well, somebody rents a garage for twenty bucks a month and everybody moves in, girls and boys. Furniture—it's like, one means, you know, one *appropriates* furniture from here and there. It's like the Volkswagen buses a lot of kids now use as beach wagons instead of woodies. Woodies are old station wagons, usually Fords, with wooden bodies, from back before 1953. One of the great things about a Volkswagen bus is that one can . . . *exchange* motors in about three minutes. A good VW motor exchanger can go up to a parked Volkswagen, and a few ratchets of the old wrench here and it's up and out and he has a new motor. There must be a few nice old black panthers around wondering why their nice hubby-mommy VW's don't run so good anymore—but—then—they—are—probably—puzzled—about—a—lot of things. Yes.

Cash—it's practically in the air. Around the beach in La Jolla a guy can walk right out in the street and stand there, stop cars and make the candid move. Mister, I've got a quarter, how about 50 cents so I can get a *large* draft. Or, I need some after-ski boots. And the panthers give one a Jello smile and hand it over. Or a guy who knows how to do it can get $40 from a single night digging clams, and it's nice out there. Or he can go around and take up a collection for a keg party, a keg of beer. Man, anybody who won't kick in a quarter for a keg is a jerk. A couple of good keg collections—that's a trip to Hawaii, which is the surfer's version of a trip to Europe: there is a great surf and great everything there. Neale spent three weeks in Hawaii last year. He got $30 from a girl friend, he scrounged a little here and there and got $70 more and he headed off for Hawaii with $100.02, that being the exact plane fare, and borrowed 25 cents when he got there to . . . blast the place up. He spent the 25 cents in a photo booth, showed the photos to the people on the set of *Hawaii* and got a job in the movie. What's the big orgy about money? It's warm, nobody even wears shoes, nobody is starving.

All right, Mother gets worried about all this, but it is limited worry, as John Shine says. Mainly, Mother says, *Sayonara,* you all, and you head off for the beach.

The thing is, everybody, practically everybody, comes from a good family. Everyone has been . . . *reared well,* as they say. Everybody is very upper-middle, if you want to bring it down to that. It's just that this is a new order. Why hang around in the hubby-mommy household with everybody getting neurotic hang-ups with each other and slamming doors and saying, Why can't they have some privacy? Or, it doesn't mean anything that I have to work for a living, does it? It doesn't mean a thing to you. All of you just lie around here sitting in the big orange easy chair smoking cigarettes. I'd hate for you to have to smoke standing up, you'd probably get phlebitis from it—Listen to me, Sarah—

—why go through all that? It's a good life out here. Nobody is   45 mugging everybody for money and affection. There are a lot of bright people out here, and there are a lot of interesting things. One night there was a toga party in a garage, and everybody dressed in sheets, like togas, boys and girls and they put on the appropriated television set to an old Deanna Durbin movie and turned off the sound and put on Rolling Stones records, and you should have seen Deanna Durbin opening her puckered kumquat mouth with Mick Jagger's voice bawling out, *I ain't got no satisfaction.* Of course, finally everybody started pulling the togas off each other, but that is another thing. And one time they had a keg party down on the beach in Mission Bay and the lights from the amusement park were reflected all over the water and that, the whole design of the thing, those nutty lights, that was part of the party. Liz put out the fire throwing a "sand potion" or something on it. One can laugh at Liz and her potions, her necromancy and everything, but there is a lot of thought going into it, a lot of, well, mysticism.

You can even laugh at mysticism if you want to, but there is a kid like Larry Alderson, who spent two years with a monk, and he learned a lot of stuff, and Artie Nelander is going to spend next summer with some Outer Mongolian tribe; he really means to do that. Maybe the "mysterioso" stuff is a lot of garbage, but still, it is interesting. The surfers around the Pump House use that word, mysterioso, quite a lot. It refers to the mystery of the Oh Mighty Hulking Pacific Ocean and everything. Sometimes a guy will stare at the surf and say, "Mysterioso." They keep telling the story of Bob Simmons' wipeout, and somebody will say "mysterioso."

Simmons was a fantastic surfer. He was fantastic even though he had a bad leg. He rode the really big waves. One day he got wiped out at Windansea. When a big wave overtakes a surfer, it drives him right to the bottom. The board came in but he never came up and they never found his body. Very mysterioso. The black panthers all talked about what happened to "the Simmons boy." But the mysterioso thing was how he could have died at all. If he had been one of the old pan-thuhs, hell, sure he could have got killed. But Simmons was, well, one's own age, he was the kind of guy who could have been in the Pump House gang, he was . . . *immune,* he was plugged into the whole pattern, he could feel the whole Oh Mighty Hulking Sea, he didn't have to think it out step by step. But he got wiped out and killed. Very mysterioso.

Immune! If one is in the Pump House gang and really keyed in to this whole thing, it's— well, one is . . . *immune,* one is not full of black pan-thuh panic. Two kids, a 14-year-old girl and a 16-year-old boy, go out to Windansea at dawn, in the middle of winter, cold as hell, and take on 12-foot waves all by themselves. The girl, Jackie Haddad, daughter of a certified public accountant, wrote a composition about it, just for herself, called "My Ultimate Journey":

"It was six o'clock in the morning, damp, foggy and cold. We could feel the bitter air biting at our cheeks. The night before, my friend Tommy and I had seen one of the greatest surf films, *Surf Classics.* The film had excited us so much we made up our minds to go surfing the following morning. That is what brought us down on the cold, wet, soggy sand of Windansea early on a December morning.

"We were the first surfers on the beach. The sets were rolling in at eight to 10, filled with occasional 12-footers. We waxed up and waited for a break in the waves. The break came, neither of us said a word, but instantly grabbed our boards and ran into the water. The paddle out was difficult, not being used to the freezing water.

"We barely made it over the first wave of the set, a large set. Suddenly Tommy put on a burst of speed and shot past me. He cleared the biggest wave of the set. It didn't hit me hard as I rolled under it. It dragged me almost 20 yards before exhausting its strength. I climbed on my board gasping for air. I paddled out to where Tommy was resting. He laughed at me for being wet already. I almost hit him but I began laughing, too. We rested a few minutes and then lined up our position with a well known spot on the shore.

"I took off first. I bottom-turned hard and started climbing up the wave. A radical cut-back caught me off balance and I fell, barely hanging onto my board. I recovered in time to see Tommy go straight over the falls on a 10-footer. His board shot nearly 30 feet in the air. Luckily, I could get it before the next set came in, so Tommy didn't have to make the long swim in. I pushed it to him and then laughed. All of a sudden Tommy yelled, 'Outside!'

"Both of us paddled furiously. We barely made it up to the last wave, it was a monster. In precision timing we wheeled around and I took off. I cut left in reverse stance, then cut back, driving hard toward the famous Windansea bowl. As I crouched, a huge wall of energy came down over me, covering me up. I moved toward the nose to gain more speed and shot out of the fast-flowing suction just in time to kick out as the wave closed out.

"As I turned around I saw Tommy make a beautiful drop-in, then the wave peaked and fell all at once. Miraculously he beat the suction. He cut back and did a spinner, which followed with a reverse kick-up.

"Our last wave was the biggest. When we got to shore, we rested, neither of us saying a word, but each lost in his own private world of thoughts. After we had rested, we began to walk home. We were about half way and the rain came pouring down. That night we both had bad colds, but we agreed it was worth having them after the thrill and satisfaction of an extra good day of surfing."

John Shine and Artie Nelander are out there right now. They are just "outside," about one fifth of a mile out from the shore, beyond where the waves start breaking. They are straddling their surfboards with their backs to the shore, looking out toward the horizon, waiting for a good set. Their backs look like some kind of salmon-colored porcelain shells, a couple of tiny shells bobbing up and down as the swells roll under them, staring out to sea like Phrygian sacristans looking for a sign.

John and Artie! They are—they are what one means when one talks about the surfing life. It's like, you know, one means, they have this life all of their own; it's like a glass-bottom boat, and it floats over the "real" world, or the square world or whatever one wants to call it. They are not exactly off in a world of their own, they are and they aren't. What it is, they float right through the real world, but it can't touch them. They do these things, like the time they went to Malibu, and there was this party in some guy's apartment, and there wasn't enough *legal* parking space for everybody, and so somebody went out and painted the red curbs white and everybody parked. Then the cops came. Everybody ran out. Artie and John took an airport bus to the Los Angeles Airport, just like they were going to take a plane, in khaki shorts and T-shirts with Mac Meda Destruction Company stenciled on them. Then they took a helicopter to Disneyland. At Disneyland crazy Ditch had his big raincoat on and a lot of flasks strapped onto his body underneath, Scotch, bourbon, all kinds of stuff. He had plastic tubes from the flasks sticking out of the flyfront of his raincoat and everybody was sipping whiskey through the tubes—

—Ooooo-eeee—Mee-dah! They chant this chant, Mee-dah, in a real fakey deep voice, and it *really bugs people*. They don't know what the hell it is. It is the cry of the Mac Meda Destruction Company. The Mac Meda Destruction Company is . . . an *underground* society that started in La Jolla about three years ago. Nobody can remember exactly how; they have arguments about it. Anyhow, it is mainly something to *bug* people with and organize huge beer orgies with. They have their own complete, bogus phone number in La Jolla. They have Mac Meda Destruction Company decals. They stick them on phone booths, on cars, any place. Some mommy-hubby will come out of the shopping plaza and walk up to his Mustang, which is supposed to make him a hell of a tiger now, and he'll see a sticker on the side of it saying, "Mac Meda Destruction Company," and for about two days or something he'll think the sky is going to fall in.

But the big thing is the parties, the "conventions." Anybody can join, any kid, anybody can come, as long as they've heard about it, and they can only hear about it by word of mouth. One was in the Sorrento Valley, in the gulches and arroyos, and the fuzz came, and so the older guys put the young ones and the basket cases, the ones just too stoned out of their gourds, into the tule grass, and the cops shined their searchlights and all they saw was tule grass, while the basket cases moaned scarlet and oozed on their bellies like reptiles and everybody else ran down the arroyos, yelling Mee-dah.

The last one was at Manhattan Beach, inside somebody's poor hulking house. The party got *very Dionysian* that night and somebody put a hole through one wall, and everybody else decided to see if they could make   60 it bigger. Everybody was stoned out of their hulking gourds, and it got to be about 3:30 a.m. and everybody decided to go see the riots. These were the riots in Watts. The Los Angeles *Times* and the San Diego *Union* were all saying, WATTS NO-MAN'S LAND and STAY WAY FROM WATTS YOU GET YO' SE'F KILLED, but naturally nobody believed that. Watts was a blast, and the Pump House gang was immune to the trembling gourd panic rattles of the L.A. *Times* black pan-thuhs. Immune!

So John Shine, Artie Nelander and Jerry Sterncorb got in John's VW bus, known as the Hog of Steel, and they went to Watts. Gary Wickham and some other guys ran into an old man at a bar who said he owned a house in Watts and had been driven out by the drunk niggers. So they drove in a car to save the old guy's house from the drunk niggers. Artie and John had a tape recorder and decided they were going to make a record called "Random Sounds from the Watts Riots." They drove right into Watts in the Hog of Steel and there was blood on the streets and roofs blowing off the stores and all these apricot flames and drunk Negroes falling through the busted plate glass of the liquor stores. Artie got a nice recording of a lot of Negroes chanting "Burn, baby, burn." They all got out and talked to some Negro kids in a gang going into a furniture store, and the Negro kids didn't say Kill Whitey or Geed'um or any of that. They just said, Come on, man, it's a party and it's free. After they had been in there for about three hours talking to Negroes and watching drunks collapse in the liquor stores, some cop with a helmet on came roaring up and said, "Get the hell out of here, you kids, we cannot and will not provide protection."

Meantime, Gary Wickham and his friends drove in in a car with the old guy, and a car full of Negroes *did* stop them and say, Whitey, Geed'um, and all that stuff, but one of the guys in Gary's car just draped a pistol he had out the window and the colored guys drove off. Gary and everybody drove the old guy to his house and they all walked in and had a great raunchy time drinking beer and raising hell. A couple of Negroes, the old guy's neighbors, came over and told the old guy to cut out the racket. There were flames in the sky and ashes coming down with little rims of fire on them, like apricot crescents. The old guy got very cocky about all his "protection" and went out on the front porch about dawn and started yelling at some Negroes across the street, telling them "No more drunk niggers in Watts" and a lot of other unwise slogans. So Gary Wickham got up and everybody left. They were there about four hours altogether and when they drove out, they had to go through a National Guard checkpoint, and a lieutenant from the San Fernando Valley told them he could not and would not provide protection.

But exactly! Watts just happened to be what was going on at the time, as far as the netherworld of La Jolla surfing was concerned, and so one goes there and sees what is happening and comes back and tells everybody about it and laughs at the L.A. *Times.* That is what makes it so weird when all these black pan-thuhs come around to pick up "surfing styles," like the clothing manufacturers. They don't know what any of it means. It's like archaeologists discovering hieroglyphics of something, and they say, god, that's neat—Egypt!—but they don't know what the hell it is. They don't know anything about . . . *The Life.* It's great to think of a lot of old emphysematous pan-thuhs in the Garment District in New York City struggling in off the street against a gummy 15-mile-an-hour wind full of soot and coffee-brown snow and gasping in the elevator to clear their old nicotine-phlegm tubes on the way up-stairs to make out the invoices on a lot of surfer stuff for 1966, the big nylon windbreakers with the wide, white horizontal competition stripes, nylon swimming trunks with competition stripes, bell-bottom slacks for girls, the big hairy sleeveless jackets, vests, the blue "tennies," meaning tennis shoes, and the . . . *look,* the Major Hair, all this long lank blond hair, the plain face kind of tanned and bleached out at the same time, but with big eyes. It all starts in a few places, a few strategic groups, the Pump House gang being one of them, and then it moves up the beach, to places like Newport Beach and as far up as Malibu.

Well, actually there is a kind of back-and-forth thing with some of the older guys, the old heroes of surfing, like Bruce Brown, John Sev-erson, Hobie Alter and Phil Edwards. Bruce Brown will do one of those incredible surfing movies and he is out in the surf himself filming Phil Edwards coming down a 20-footer in Hawaii, and Phil has on a pair of nylon swimming trunks, which he has had made in Hawaii, because they dry out fast—and it is like a grapevine. Everybody's got to have a pair of nylon swimming trunks, and then the manufacturers move in, and everybody's making nylon swimming trunks, boxer trunk style, and pretty soon every kid in Utica, N.Y., is buying a pair of them, with the competition stripe and the whole thing, and they never heard of Phil Edwards. So it works back and forth—but so what? Phil Edwards is part of it. He may be an old guy, he is 28 years old, but he and Bruce Brown, who is even older, 30, and John Severson, 32, and Hobie Alter, 29, never haired out to the square world even though they make thousands. Hair refers to courage. A guy who "has a lot of hair" is courageous; a guy who "hairs out" is yellow.

Bruce Brown and Severson and Alter are known as the "surfing millionaires." They are not millionaires, actually, but they must be among the top businessmen south of Los Angeles. Brown grossed something around $500,000 in 1965 even before his movie *Endless Summer* became a hit nationally; and he has only about three people working for him. He goes out on a surfboard with a camera encased in a plastic shell and

65

takes his own movies and edits them himself and goes around showing them himself and narrating them at places like the Santa Monica Civic Auditorium, where 24,000 came in eight days once, at $1.50 a person, and all he has to pay is for developing the film and hiring the hall. John Severson has the big surfing magazine, *Surfer*. Hobie Alter is the biggest surfboard manufacturer, all hand-made boards. He made 5,000 boards in 1965 at $140 a board. He also designed the "Hobie" skate boards and gets 25 cents for every one sold. He grossed between $900,000 and $1 million in 1964.

God, if only everybody could grow up like these guys and know that crossing the horror dividing line, 25 years old, won't be the end of everything. One means, keep on living *The Life* and not get sucked into the ticky-tacky life with some insurance salesman sitting forward in your stuffed chair on your wall-to-wall telling you that life is like a football game and you sit there and take that stuff. The hell with that! Bruce Brown has the money and *The Life*. He has a great house on a cliff about 60 feet above the beach at Dana Point. He is married and has two children, but it is not that hubby-mommy you're-breaking-my-gourd scene. His office is only two blocks from his house and he doesn't even have to go on the streets to get there. He gets on his Triumph scrambling motorcycle and cuts straight across a couple of vacant lots and one can see him . . . *bounding* to work over the vacant lots. The Triumph hits ruts and hummocks and things and Bruce Brown bounces into the air with the motor—*thragggggh*—moaning away, and when he gets to the curbing in front of his office, he just leans back and pulls up the front wheel and hops it and gets off and walks into the office barefooted. *Barefooted;* why not? He wears the same things now that he did when he was doing nothing but surfing. He has on a faded gray sweatshirt with the sleeves cut off just above the elbows and a pair of faded corduroys. His hair is the lightest corn yellow imaginable, towheaded, practically white, from the sun. Even his eyes seem to be bleached. He has a rainbarrel old-apple-tree Tom-Sawyer little-boy roughneck look about him, like Bobby Kennedy.

Sometimes he carries on his business right there at the house. He has a dugout room built into the side of the cliff, about 15 feet down from the level of the house. It is like a big pale green box set into the side of the cliff, and inside is a kind of upholstered bench or settee you can lie down on if you want to and look out at the Pacific. The surf is crashing like a maniac on the rocks down below. He has a telephone in there. Sometimes it will ring, and Bruce Brown says hello, and the surf is crashing away down below, roaring like mad, and the guy on the other end, maybe one of the TV networks calling from New York or some movie hair-out from Los Angeles, says:

"What is all that noise? It sounds like you're sitting out in the surf."

"That's right," says Bruce Brown, "I have my desk out on the beach now. It's nice out here."

The guy on the other end doesn't know what to think. He is an-   70
other Mr. Efficiency who just got back from bloating his colon up at a
three-hour executive lunch somewhere and now he is Mr.-Big-Time-
Let's-Get-This-Show-on-the-Road.

"On the beach?"

"Yeah. It's cooler down here. And it's good for you, but it's not so
great for the desk. You know what I have now? A warped leg."

"A warped leg?"

"Yeah, and this is an $800 desk."

Those nutball California kids—and he will still be muttering that   75
five days after Bruce Brown delivers his film, on time, and Mr. Efficiency is still going through memo thickets or heaving his way into the
bar car to Darien—in the very moment that Bruce Brown and Hobie
Alter are both on their motorcycles out on the vacant lot in Dana Point.
Hobie Alter left his surfboard plant about two in the afternoon because
the wind was up and it would be good catamaranning and he wanted
to go out and see how far he could tip his new catamaran without
going over, and he did tip it over, about half a mile out in high swells
and it was hell getting the thing right side up again. But he did, and he
got back in time to go scrambling on the lot with Bruce Brown. They
are out there, roaring over the ruts, bouncing up in the air, and every
now and then they roar up the embankment so they can . . . fly, going
up in the air about six feet off the ground as they come up off the
embankment—*thraaagggggh*—all these people in the houses around there
come to the door and look out. These two . . . nuts are at it again.
Well, they can only fool around there for 20 minutes, because that is
about how long it takes the cops to get there if anybody gets burned
up enough and calls, and what efficient business magnate wants to get
hauled off by the Dana Point cops for scrambling on his motorcycle in
a vacant lot.

Bruce Brown has it figured out so no one in the whole rubber-
bloated black pan-thuh world can trap him, though. He bought a forest
in the Sierras. There is nothing on it but trees. His own wilds: no house,
no nothing, just Bruce Brown's forest. Beautiful things happen up there.
One day, right after he bought it, he was on the edge of his forest,
where the road comes into it, and one of these big rancher king moth-
eroos with the broad belly and the $70 lisle Safari shirt comes tooling
up in a Pontiac convertible with a funnel of dust pouring out behind.
He gravels it to a great flashy stop and yells:

"Hey! You!"

Of course, what he sees is some towheaded barefooted kid in a
torn-off sweatshirt fooling around the edge of the road.

"Hey! You!"

"Yeah?" says Bruce Brown.   80

"Don't you know this is private property?"

"Yeah," says Bruce Brown.

"Well, then, why don't you get your ass off it?"

"Because it's mine, it's my private property," says Bruce Brown. "Now you get *yours* off it."

And Safari gets a few rays from that old apple-tree rainbarrel don't-cross-that-line look and doesn't say anything and roars off, slipping gravel, the dumb crumbling pan-thuh.   85

But . . . perfect! It is like, one means, you know, poetic justice for all the nights Bruce Brown slept out on the beach at San Onofre and such places in the old surfing days and would wake up with some old crock's black feet standing beside his head and some phlegmy black rubber voice saying:

"All right, kid, don't you know this is private property?"

And he would prop his head up and out there would be the Pacific Ocean, a kind of shadowy magenta-mauve, and one thing, *that* was nobody's private property—

But how many Bruce Browns can there be? There is a built-in trouble with age segregation. Eventually one *does* reach the horror age of 25, the horror dividing line. Surfing and the surfing life have been going big since 1958, and already there are kids who—well, who aren't kids anymore, they are pushing 30, and they are stagnating on the beach. Pretty soon the California littoral will be littered with these guys, stroked out on the beach like beached white whales, and girls, too, who can't give up the mystique, the mysterioso mystique, Oh Mighty Hulking Sea, who can't *conceive* of living any other life. It is pathetic when they are edged out of groups like the Pump House gang. Already there are some guys who hang around with the older crowd around the Shack who are stagnating on the beach. Some of the older guys, like Gary Wickham, who is 24, are still in *The Life,* they still have it, but even Gary Wickham will be 25 one day and then 26 and then. . . . and then even pan-thuh age. Is one really going to be pan-thuh age one day? Watch those black feet go. And Tom Coman still snuggles with Yellow Slacks, and Liz still roosts moodily in her rabbit fur at the bottom of the Pump House and Pam still sits on the steps contemplating the mysterioso mysteries of Pump House ascension and John and Artie still bob, tiny pink porcelain shells, way out there waiting for godsown bitchen *set,* and godsown sun still turned on like a dentist's lamp and so far—

—the panthers scrape on up the sidewalk. They are at just about the   90 point Leonard Anderson and Donna Blanchard got that day, December 6, 1964, when Leonard said, Pipe it, and fired two shots, one at her and one at himself. Leonard was 18 and Donna was 21—21!—god, for a girl in the Pump House gang that is almost the horror line right there.

But it was all so mysterioso. Leonard was just lying down on the beach at the foot of the Pump House, near the stairs, just talking to John K. Weldon down there, and then Donna appeared at the top of the stairs and Leonard got up and went up the stairs to meet her, and they didn't say anything, they weren't *angry* over anything, they never had been, although the police said they had, they just turned and went a few feet down the sidewalk, away from the Pump House and—blam blam!—these two shots. Leonard fell dead on the sidewalk and Donna died that afternoon in Scripps Memorial Hospital. Nobody knew what to think. But one thing it seemed like—well, it seemed like Donna and Leonard thought they had lived *The Life* as far as it would go and now it was running out. All that was left to do was—but that is an *insane* idea. It can't be like that, *The Life* can't run out, people can't change all that much just because godsown chronometer runs on and the body packing starts deteriorating and the fudgy tallow shows up at the thighs where they squeeze out of the bathing suit—

Tom, boy! John, boy! Gary, boy! Neale, boy! Artie, boy! Pam, Liz, Vickie, Jackie Haddad! After all this—just a pair of bitchen black panther bunions inching down the sidewalk away from the old Pump House stairs?

Lines of Inquiry
"The Pump House Gang"

Throughout much of this piece, Wolfe mimics the language of the pump house gang, speaking as if he is one of them, recreating the experience from inside their heads. Why do you suppose that he engages in this mimicry? Does it help you to understand the surfers? Does it lead you to sympathize with them? Does it leave you confused about Wolfe's attitude toward them? What do you suppose is his attitude toward them? What words or phrases, what details or scenes, suggest his attitude?

Wolfe says that "there is a built-in trouble with age segregation." What exactly does he mean by "age segregation"? How is this segregation reflected in styles of clothing and language, in patterns of behavior, in values and beliefs? What is the "built-in trouble" with such segregation? Why is such segregation always temporary? Why is it potentially tragic?

Though this essay is rooted in scenes and situations from the sixties, it might be considered just the same in relation to contemporary experience. What recent versions of age segregation have you noticed in American culture? What styles of behavior, what patterns of belief, most clearly reflect such segregation today? Do you think that your generation is more—or less—respectful of age and the values of the "shiny black shoe masses"? Do you think that age segregation is inevitable?

Honks and Wonks

"Dja do da chem-yet?"

Dja do da chem-yet?

—this being the voice of a freshman on the campus of C.C.N.Y. at 139 Street and Convent Avenue the other day asking the question: "Have you done the chemistry assignment yet?" The irony of it is that here is a boy who will probably *do da chem* and God knows how many other assignments extremely well and score about a 3.5 academic average over four years and then go to law school at N.Y.U. and get his LL.B— and then for some reason he can't quite figure out, he never does land the great glistening job he was thinking of at Sullivan & Cromwell or Cravath Swain & Moore. Instead, he ends up in . . . *the neighborhood,* on the south side of Northern Boulevard in Bayside, Queens, in an office he shares with a real-estate man, an old friend of his from here in Bayside—which some of the local wiseacres call Brayside, because of all the "Brooklyn" and "Bronx" accents you hear here in Queens now—

Whaddyamean it's his voice? He's upgraded the *da* with *the* by now, hasn't he? And hasn't he replaced the *r*'s he's been dropping all these years—well, a few of them, anyway: "This is the first house we evuh owned. We have a gahden an my wife is the gahd*neh* . . ."

. . . here in Brayside . . .

The same day, in the little exotic knickknacks boutique on the ground floor of Henri Bendel, on Fifty-seventh Street just west of Fifth: a nice New York girl home from St. Timothy's, St. Tim's, the boarding school in Maryland. She and a girlfriend of hers are walking around town *checking boys,* among other things. It's true! They can tell just by looking at him whether a boy goes to an Eastern prep school or not. Not only that, they can tell *which prep school,* usually St. Paul's or Hotchkiss or Groton or Exeter or Andover, or whatever; just by checking his hair and his clothes. And *certainly* if they can get just one sentence out of him—

—like this gorgeous boy here, a tall milk-fed stud in a Brooks yellow shirt and tasseled loafers fumbling over a Cameroons egret-skin hassock with his tweedy-thatchy Prince Charles hanging over his brow and— He's Exeter, or possibly Andover. That is obvious immediately from the tie. His tie is tied properly at the throat, but the ends are slung over his left shoulder, after the fashion. And their eyes meet, and then his eyes shift to her shoes, naturally, and then he looks into her eyes again, into her soul, as it were, and says:

"Those are real Guccis, aren't they?"

Bliss! It's all there! Past, present, future! Certified! The Guccis, of course, being her loafers, bought at Gucci's, 699 Fifth Avenue, with the

authentic Gucci gold chain across the tongue and not any of the countless imitations of the Gucci loafer. A shorthand! A very metonymy! For
the whole Eastern boarding-school thing, but more than that—the *honk!*
He has it, the Eastern boy's boarding-school *honk,* lifting every vowel—
Those are real Guccis, aren't they?—up over the roof of his palate and
sticking them into his nose and honking them out without moving his
lower jaw. And there in one sentence he has said it all, announced that
he belongs in the world of the New York *honks,* of the honks who rule
and possess all and who every day sound the secret honk of New York
wealth and position; the nasal knighthood of the Bobby Kennedys, the
Robert Dowlings, Huntington Hartfords, Nelson Rockefellers, Thomas
Hovings, Averell Harrimans—for in New York the world is sheerly
but secretly divided into the *honks* and the wonks[1]—*Dja do da chem-
yet?*—and this fumbling milk-fed Exeter stud will carry a C-plus straight
to Wall Street or mid-Manhattan, for he is *one of us,* you understand—

Very ironic—the way New Yorkers at every class level delighted   10
for years in *My Fair Lady* on stage and screen. *My Fair Lady,* of course,
is the musical version of Shaw's play *Pygmalion,* about a linguistics professor, Henry Higgins, turning a Cockney flower seller into a lady of
Society by upgrading her accent. That silly, stuffy English class system!—whereupon we all settled back and just enjoyed the Cinderella
love story. It was just as well. It is probably a good thing that no Henry
Higgins has come along to wake up New York to the phonetic truth
about class and status in this city . . .

I have been talking to a man who could do it if he chose to, however—
Professor Marshall D. Berger of C.C.N.Y. Berger is one of the country's leading geographical linguists, one of those extraordinary people,
like Henry Lee Smith of the old radio days, who can listen to a man
for thirty seconds and tell what part of what state he was raised in.
Berger is a big husky man. He is fifty-five years old and has lived in
New York since he was thirteen. His family moved from Buffalo to

---

[1] "Honk" is a term of Eastern prep-school derivation, connoting both the
nasal quality of the upper-class voice and its presumably authoritative sound,
commanding obedience, like the horn of a large 1936 Packard. It is not to be
confused with "honkie," the black slang word for "white man," which is apparently a variation on a still older slang word, "hunky," originally a term of
opprobrium for Hungarian immigrants to the U.S. "Wonk" is an Eastern prep-
school term referring to all those who do not have the "honk" voice, i.e., all
who are non-aristocratic. There is some conjecture that the term is derived in
the natural Anglophile bias of Eastern social life from the English adjective
"wonky," meaning un-steady, shaky, feeble, awry, off. In current use, however, "wonk" is a vague, all-inclusive term, closely akin to the terms "wog"
and "wop," which are sometimes used at Eastern prep schools to refer to all
the rest of humanity.

Liberty Avenue in the East New York section of Brooklyn, where the kids all thought it was odd to the point of *weird* that he said things like *core*-respondence instead of *cah*-respondence and referred to the well-known game of *go'f* as *gawlf*. He wrote an honors thesis at C.C.N.Y. in 1941 on "The Sources of New York Speech," and then a doctoral dissertation at Columbia on "American-English Pronunciations of Russian-born Immigrants." And so for the past three decades he has been doomed by his own specialty to listen, day in and day out, to New Yorkers unconsciously confessing their ancestry, their status, their social yearnings, every time they open their struggling lips.

"This is a very sensitive area you're asking me about," he tells me. "The first thing you'll notice is that people in New York always invent euphemisms when they get on the subject of speech. They don't want to talk about ethnic background or class. So they invent euphemisms. They talk about a 'Brooklyn' accent or a 'Bronx' accent, when what they're really talking about are working-class and lower-middle-class accents found all over the city. Years ago, when Brooklyn was still a big farm, they talked about the 'Bowery' accent."

Berger's own voice sounds to me like Radio Announcer Rugged, if you know that sound. In any case—

"Even the newspapers, at this late date, observe the taboo. I remember the *Post*'s biographical sketch of a local college president. 'His speech betrays his Bronx origins,' they wrote. They were talking about 'lower class' and I suppose the readers get the point, but everyone observes the taboo.

"The same goes for 'New York accent.' Nothing pleases most New Yorkers more than to be told that they've 'lost their New York accent.' This is ironic, on the face of it, since New York is one of the great cosmopolitan centers of the world. But what they're thinking about, of course, is class. 'I've lost my lower-class accent,' they're thinking. Incidentally, people who tell you 'I've lost this or that accent' or 'I really don't have any accent any more' are almost invariably fooling themselves. What they've done in most cases is change a couple of obvious vowels or consonants—they may have changed their pronunciation of *example* from *ex-EHM-ple,* which is lower class or lower middle class, to ex-AM-ple, or something of the sort—but they've seldom changed their basic pattern. Even broadcasters." 15

The glorious New York accent!

In 'is town deh's nuh-uhn doin at da foist of da week, so I was lookin at a likka avatisement an I bought a bah-uhl an relaxed.

All this glorious dropping of *r*'s and *g*'s and *d*'s and muffing of the "voiceless linguadental fricative" (turning the *th* sound into *d*) and reducing vowels until they almost disappear—the usual explanation has been the waves of immigrants to New York in the 1890's and early 1900's. New York, of course, had had waves of immigrants before. But they were chiefly northern Europeans, Irish, German, Dutch, English, and they were middle as well as lower class. The new immigrants were chiefly from Eastern and Southern Europe, and they were lower class; Italians, Ukrainians, Poles, Russians, Greeks, Eastern European Jews, speaking Italian, Greek, Yiddish, Russian, and other Slavic tongues. Part of the "New York accent" that developed was a blend of the new speech patterns with English words.

For example, of the new tongues only Greek had the *th* sound. The result was millions of New Yorkers saying *wid* for *with* and *dis* for *this.* Or: in Yiddish a *t* in the middle of a word, like *winter,* was pronounced much more emphatically than it is in English. To this day, the New Yorker who says win-*ta* or fundamen-*tal* is usually someone from a home where Yiddish was spoken. Likewise, the heavily accented *g,* as in *sing-ga* for *singer* and *Lon Gy-land* for *Long Island.* Other innovations were in rhythm. Some of the most flamboyant came from Southern Italian and Sicilian lower-class speech, with the old . . . *So I says to my brudd'n'law, "Awriiide, so whaddya wan me to do, I says to him, whaddya whaddya or sump'm?"*

These were all foreign flavors coming into New York English, but   20
many of the elements of the "New York accent" had been here for years before the 1890 wave of immigrants; notably, such things as *dis* for *this* and *foist* for *first.* Berger's theory hits on a far more subtle point. Namely, street masculinity. Here were millions of working-class people massed into lower Manhattan, and their sons fell into the street life. On the street the big thing was physical competition, even if it was only stickball or, today, rock 'em games of basketball on a concrete slab shooting for a basket with a metal backboard and a rim with no net on it . . . In any case, the emphasis was always on the large muscles.

For a start, the street thing led to rapid speech in which words are swallowed whole, *r*'s are dropped, vowels are reduced to the vanishing point, and even some hard consonants disappear. A three-syllable word like *memory* gets reduced to one and a half or less: *m'm'r. Bottle* becomes *bah-uhl, little* becomes *lih-uhl.* A pronunciation like *lih-uhl* is what is known as a glottal stop, in which the double *t* is replaced by what is in fact a miniature cough. It is common in New York City, although in England, among the lower classes, the glottal stop sometimes replaces *p*'s and *k*'s as well as *t*'s. Street masculinity has also led New Yorkers to carry their tongues low in their mouths like dockworker's forearms. The result is some heavy handling of many consonants: *t*'s and *d*'s get dropped or mushed around. Most people's speech patterns are set between the ages of five and fifteen, and they are not likely to revamp them in any thorough way after that without something on the order of dramatic training. Often not even that will do it. A boy growing up on the street may unconsciously scorn the kind of delicate muscle play an upper-class boy learns in articulating words. The fancy work with the tip of the tongue in pronouncing *portraiture,* for example, may strike him as effete, even girlish. It seems to me that when it comes to prep-school *honks* like Averell Harriman, or Thomas Hoving—well, it doesn't matter how many worlds they have conquered or how old they are. As soon as they open their mouths, a bell goes off in the brains of most local-bred New York males: *sissy.* Here are a coupla kids who woulda got *mashed* in the street life. John Lindsay (St. Paul's) suffered continually from this disability when he was mayor of New York; also Bobby Kennedy (Milton Academy). Kennedy took the edge off his Bugs Bunny delicacy with public displays of masculinity of various sorts.

Women generally try much harder than men in New York to escape from the rock-bottom working-class accents, but they are often unaware of where the true . . . *honk-wonk* divide lies. They tug and pull on their accents, but often only get them into a form that the upper orders can laugh at in musical comedies. There is the musical-comedy working girl, for example, who is always saying,

Oh, Mr. Steiiiiiin, I had such a foiiiiin toiiiime, pronouncing the *i* as if she has wrapped it around a perfume bottle. In real life she is not a lower-class girl at all, but lower middle class.

The lower-middle-class girl who says *toiiiime* may also be aware, instinctively, that the muscle-bound tongue accounts for much of the lower-class sound. So she begins using her tongue in a vigorous way in pronouncing all sorts of things—only she overdoes it. She shoves her words all over the place but still doesn't hit them cleanly. This is the common phenomenon of the beautiful girl—"but she ruined it as soon as she opened her mouth." Here she is with her Twiggy eyes, Eve Nelson curly look, a wool jersey mini from Plymouth's, patent-leather pseudo-Guccis from A. S. Beck—and a huge rosy lingual blob rolling around between her orthodontic teeth.

The *oi* sound in *toiiiime,* by the way, is not to be confused with the so-called Brooklyn *oi* sound comedians always used to mimic: "Da oily boid gets da woim," "She read da New Yoik *Woild,*" "She lives on Toity-toid Street." These are all examples of dropping *r*'s and substituting *oi* for the *er* sound. Today you are only likely to hear it from older working-class people, such as some of the old cab drivers. This is one lower-class sound that dates back well before 1890 and is not even a peculiarly New York pronunciation. The same sound—it is actually closer to *ui* than *oi,* more like *fuist* than *foist*—can be heard today in two Southern port cities, Charleston, S.C., and New Orleans, among both upper- and lower-class people. A century ago upper-class New Yorkers used the same pronunciation, only with a slightly flutier intonation. About half a century ago upper-class New Yorkers began changing their pronunciation of *first* from a fluty *fuist* to a Boston or English *fuhst.*

This is all *r*-dropping, as I say, and it is one of the most subtle and vital matters in phonetic social climbing in New York. This is where strivers get caught out. The New Yorker who has risen above *wid* and ex*ehm*ple and even *toiiiime* and aspires to true bourgeois status will next start to replace all the *r*'s he or his family have been dropping all his life.

The *first* pahty I went to was in my senya year*r*—and so forth—not realizing that in the upper orders he envies everybody is busy dropping *r*'s like mad, in the ancient English mode.

Many New Yorkers have taken conscious pains to upgrade their accents socially and confidently believe that they now have the neutral accent of a "radio announcer." Three pronunciations almost invariably give them away: *owies* for *always* (lower-class *l*-dropping); *fo'ud* for *forward* (dropping the *r* and the *w*); frank*footer* for *frank-furter* and *footer moment* for *for the moment* (lower-class *r*-dropping).

"The fact is," Berger tells me, "that a person who tries to change one or two elements in his speech pattern may end up in worse shape than he thought he was in to begin with. His original pattern may not be prestigious, but it may be very good in terms of its internal arrangements, and he may succeed only in upsetting the equilibrium. Frankly, I like to hear people like Vito Battista and Jimmy Breslin talk. They have working-class accents and they don't care who knows it. They're very confident, that's the main thing. 'Dis is da way I tawk an dis is da way I'm *gonna* tawk, an you betta lissen.' A person's speech pattern is bound up with so many things, his personality, his role, his ambitions, that you can't deal with in isolation or simply in terms of some 'ideal.' "

Yes . . . but! . . . suppose your ideal is to get your daughter's picture on the first page of the Wedlock Section of the Sunday *Times,* and not in one of those scrimy little one-paragraphers at the bottom of the page, either—you know those little one-paragraphers, the ones hog-to-jowl up against the Arnold Constable ad with a little headlinette over the paragraph saying

Horlek-Klotkin

Suppose you're after the pole position, up at the top of the page, with a big three-column picture all downy silk with backlighting rising up behind her head like a choir of angels are back there singing and glowing, and a true headline proclaiming:

Satterthwaite-Klotkin
Betrothal Announced

One option is to do what Mrs. Bouvier did with her daughter Jacqueline. Namely, pack her off to a Virginia boarding school, whence she can return to New York bearing what the press chooses to call a "little girl voice" but which is known in the secret *honk* world as the "Southern 45-degree Upturn," in which your daughter turns her mouth up 45 degrees at either end, then her eyeballs, and says:

Ah you rilly an ahkitect?

Ah you rilly a docta?

Ah you rilly a senata?

And travel *fuhst* class forever after.

The British broad *a* has no social cachet in New York. Quite the opposite, in fact. Unless it is being used by an Englishman, it is taken as a sign of striving for a naïve or Schrafft's Mid-afternoon gentility. The great hangout of the American broad *a* used to be a vast L-shaped Schrafft's restaurant that had entrances on both Madison Avenue and East Fifty-eighth Street. The most genteel-looking matrons imaginable, dressed up in outfits such as three-piece peach wool suits with fur trim at the collars and cuffs and hats with enormous puffed-up crowns of cream-colored velvet, over apricot-colored hair, used to gather in Schrafft's throughout the afternoon. Much of the conversation had to do with stock quotations. You would hear the ladies say to one another:

"Ackshewly, I think Automatex is rahther pahst its peak."

"Oh, I know. It opened higher this mawning, but ahfter hahlf an hour it was down by two."

Such a conversation indicated that they had spent the morning in the spectator seats of the midtown street-level offices of the brokerage houses, in the board rooms, as they are called. This does *not* indicate wealth and position. For one thing, the E.S.A. (Eastern Socially Attractive) way for a woman to refer to her investments (if at all) is to make them seem as if they are *way out there* somewhere and she hasn't the vaguest idea what happens to them. For another, the old parties who hang out in the spectator seats of the midtown brokerage houses are referred to by the brokerage house employees as "board-room bums."

For still another, Schrafft's was not exactly the most prestigious place for a woman to eat. But eating at Schrafft's did have a certain secret beauty to it: the much underestimated beauty of American Comfort. The ladies' typical meal at Schrafft's was a cheeseburger, coffee, and a sundae. But such sundaes! Sundaes with towers of ice cream and nuts and sauces and fudge and maraschino cherries of a quality and buttery beauty such as the outside world has never dreamed of! And the secret art of the mid-afternoon at Schrafft's was *pacing* and the *final shape*. It was not enough merely to consume the sundae. No, the idea was to pace one's consumption along with everyone else's at the table, so that one did not finish up more than thirty seconds ahead of anyone else and, furthermore, so that one's very last bite—*the final shape*—would

35

be a *perfect miniature* of the original cheeseburger or of the original sundae, with precisely the same proportions of hamburger, cheese, and
bread, or of ice cream, whipped cream, sauce, nuts, and fruit dressing,
as the cheeseburger or the sundae had at the outset when it was first
served. And . . . they were *served so beautifully!* The waitresses at
Schrafft's, who seemed to be women who had immigrated from Europe as adults, were perhaps the most considerate and sensitive waitresses in the history of America. They understood, tacitly, from long
observation, about the final shape and its importance. If a woman had
eaten two thirds of her cheeseburger but had eaten it incorrectly, so
that the bread and the hamburger were left in the form of a perfect
final shape, as if there were a perfect mini-burger two inches in diameter on the plate, except that the cheese was all gone—she had only to
ask for more cheese, and one of these waitresses, these angels, these
nurses sent by Our Lady of Comfort, would take the cheeseburger,
two thirds eaten, back to the kitchen and have a perfectly proportioned
two-inch slab of cheese placed—but not merely *placed*—no!—*broiled!*—
broiled onto the remains!—and they would bring it back with a smile, as
if to say, "There! We understand, you and I!"
   "Oh, I cahn't thank you enough, my dear!"
   Now there, I submit, is Beauty. It is not, however, prestige.
   The true social competitors among New York's older women gather
earlier, about 1 p.m., for the Status Lunch, and the accents are quite
different. The Status Lunch is a peculiarly New York institution in this
country, although the same thing goes on in a less manic way in Paris
and London. At the Status Lunch women who have reached the upper
social orders gather during the week so that they may demonstrate and
celebrate their position. They may be at the top through family background or marriage or other good fortune. In any case, they are mostly
in their late thirties or in their forties or early fifties, starving themselves to near perfection in order to retain . . . *the look* . . . with just
a few piano wires showing in their necks and fore-arms and the backs
of their hands, owing to the deterioration of the body packing. Or
perhaps they have begun to let themselves go into that glorious creamy
Camembert look in which the flesh on the shoulders and the upper back
and the backs of their arms looks like it could be shaped with a butter
knife. They are Pucci'd and Gucci'd up to their temporal fossae, Pucci
in the dress, Gucci in the shoes and handbag—the Pucci-Gucci girls!—
yes. They start pulling into Status Lunch restaurants in the East and
West Fifties, such as La Grenouille, Lutèce, Orsini's, about 1 p.m. and
make a great point of calling the maître d' by his first name, which at
La Grenouille is Paul, then peer into that ocher golden mirrored gloom
to case the important tables, which are along the walls in the front
room, by way of weighing the social weight of today's gathering, as it
were. Then they suck in their cheeks—near perfection!—and begin the

entrance, looking straight ahead, as if they couldn't be more oblivious of who else is there, but waiting, hopefully, for the *voice*—

Dah-ling dah-ling dah-ling.   40

There it is!—the *dah-ling* voice, a languid weak baritone, not a man's voice, you understand, but a woman's, *The New York Social Baritone,* like that of a forty-eight-year-old male dwarf who just woke up after smoking three packs of Camels the day before, and then the social kisses, right out in the middle of the restaurant, with everybody locking heads, wincing slightly from the concentration on not actually pressing the lips, which would smudge the lipstick, or maybe even the powder covering the electrolysis lines above the lips, with the Social Baritone *dahling* voices beginning to bray softly in each other's ears, like an ensemble of cellos—*we are all here!* This voice cannot be achieved without some ten or fifteen years of smoking cigarettes and drinking whiskey or gin, which literally smoke-cures and pickles the vocal cords and changes them from soprano to the golden richness of baritone. It takes, on the average, at least 13,000 cigarettes over a ten-year period. In pronunciation, the *dah-ling* voice seeks to set itself off from both the urgency (what's going to hit the fan next?) of the lower-class female voice and the usual efficiency (must pronounce everything *correctly*) of the middle-class female voice with a languor and a nasal *honk,* connoting ease, leisure, insouciance. Two techniques are the most vital: dropping *r*'s, as in *dahling,* and pronouncing most accented vowels with a sigh thrown in, particularly the *a*'s and the *o*'s, as in—

Dahling, I caaaaan't [but not *cahnt*]. I just did the Mehhhht and, you know, the sets were stunnnnnning, Myron le Poove I think he is, but it was the most booooooring-sawt-of-thing—with the vowels coming out of the nose in gasps as if she is going to run out of gas at any moment.

And *yet!* She has worked on this voice for ten years, producing her deep rich pre-cancerous vocal cords, but it gives off the deadly odor: *parvenu.* The *dahling* voice, heard so often at Status Lunches and country weekends and dinner parties where two wineglasses are used, is almost invariably that of the striver who has come upon the upper-class *honk* voice too late in life. She has picked up a number of key principles: the nasality, the languor, the oiliness, the *r*-dropping. But she does not understand the underlying principle, which is historical. Her attention is fixed upon New York, and as a result her voice takes on a New York theatrical manner, a staginess, in the Tallulah Bankhead mode, which is show-business upper class, not *honk* upper class. The certified *honk* upper-class woman in New York has her attention fixed, phonetically although unconsciously, on Boston and the Richmond-Charleston social axis of the South.

The secret here, as among New York male *honks,* is the boarding school. The outstanding girls' boarding schools are oriented, socially, toward the nineteenth-century upper-class traditions of Boston and the South, which, until after World War I, had far more social clout than the upper-class world of New York. Miss Hall's, Miss Porter's, Westover, and Dana Hall are all girls' boarding schools where an old Boston upper-class tradition dominates, just as Foxcroft (Jackie Kennedy's school), Madeira, Chatham Hall, Garrison Forest, and St. Catherine's are still schools where the Richmond-Charleston tradition dominates. New York girls bring back the Boston or Southern sound in a somewhat crude form, but nevertheless it is not a New York sound. It is neither a street sound nor a theatrical sound nor an English sound. Its components are nasality, languor, oiliness, *r*-dropping—but with shorter, clearer, more open vowels than the *dahling* voice. If the girl has gone to a Southern school, like Jackie Kennedy, she will tend to have a soft, childish voice. If she has gone to a "Boston" school, the speech will be much brisker and yet still languid and oily, as if lubricated ball bearings were pouring out of both nostrils.

In the nineteenth century, the New York upper classes were much   45
more directly influenced by Boston and the South. Boston overshadowed New York in many phases of business, finance, and law and was unquestionably New York's social superior in the area of Culture and the Arts. The New York upper classes had close ties with the Southern upper classes because of the shipping trade. Southern planters came to New York continually for financing, and packet boats loaded with cotton came to New York on the way to England. About 1940, linguists at C.C.N.Y. made recordings of the voices of old New Yorkers, people in their seventies and eighties, most of them upper-middle-class, in order to get an idea of what speech patterns were like in New York in the nineteenth century. They tended to speak in a medley of Boston and Southern accents. One old party reminisced about an old structure on Twenty-third Street as "the old struk-cha on Twenty-thuid Street," with *struk-cha* a combination of the clipped Boston accent of *struk* and the Boston *r*-dropping of *cha;* and *Twenty-thuid* a case of Southern-style upper-class *r*-dropping, substituting a diphthong vowel sound, *ui,* for the standard *er* sound in *third*. Socially, New York was considered an exciting but crude town, and New York's upper classes felt the sense of inferiority and preferred to sound as if they came from some better spot. Even today some *honks* still use the Southern upper-class pronunciation of *thuid* for *third,* although most have shifted over the past half century to a more Bostonian *thuhd*. They still drop the *r* in any case.

Boys as well as girls, of course, learn the *honk* voice in prep school, and the same principle applies: the voice should suggest a languor that will separate one from the lower orders. The lower jaw is moved much less than in ordinary speech and the words are lifted up over the palate and secreted through the nose rather than merely blurted out of the mouth. The rigidity of the jaw may resemble an affliction to a person who has never watched someone speak this way before. In fact, the E.S.A. accent that is often heard on the north shore of Long Island in communities such as Huntington and Oyster Bay is known as Locust Valley Lockjaw. The same voice is known in Riverdale as Spotted Bostonian. Socially ambitious people in Riverdale may even try to keep their voices up by spending their summers in the select vacation communities of the Boston upper orders on the Maine shore.

Honk voices may fall anywhere in a range from Boston-Honk to New York-Honk. Leaning toward the Boston-Honk would be the late Bobby Kennedy (Milton Academy), Averell Harriman (Groton), the late Christian Herter (St. Paul's), and the late John F. Kennedy (Choate). The worst liabilities of the *honk* voice to a politician, quite aside from the class overtones, are the monotony and the delicacy and weakness brought about by this sort of voice's emphasis on languor and refinement. Bobby Kennedy, like his brother John, had great difficulty in conventional oratory from a rostrum. His voice was trained in delicacy rather than strength and tended to turn shrill at the very moment when the heavy chord should have been hit. He always sounded like a seventeen-year-old valedictorian with the goslings. In the case of Harriman and Herter, it was the nerve-gas monotony of the *honk* voice that caused them trouble as much as anything else.

The perfect New York *honk* voice is Huntington Hartford's (St. Paul's). Other notable New York *honks:* Nelson Rockefeller and the late Robert Dowling, the real-estate and investment tycoon. Their type of voice has the nasality of the *honk* voice without the delicacy of the same voice as practiced by Bobby Kennedy or even former New York Mayor John Lindsay (St. Paul's). The explanation, most likely, is that both Rockefeller and Dowling went to prep school in the city, Rockefeller at the Lincoln School and Dowling at Cutler. Rockefeller has gradually coarsened his voice for his public appearances. It is a kind of *honk* with a knish jammed in it, although he uses much more a conventional soft *honk* in private conversation. One of the ironies of the 1962 race for governor was that Rockefeller's upper-class voice with a knish in it was so much more effective among Low Rent voters in New York than that of his upper-middle-class opponent, Robert Morgenthau. As a result of his time at Deerfield Academy, Morgenthau's voice had taken on a kind of *honk* subtlety and delicacy that made him, not Rockefeller, sound like the Fauntleroy in the plot.

Lindsay tried to come down off the *honk* accent somewhat by inserting *r*'s where they would ordinarily be dropped, making his speech sound almost middle-class at points. He also referred to St. Paul's as his "high school" from time to time, as if it were nothing more than a kind of Stuyvesant or DeWitt Clinton unaccountably set out in

Concord, New Hampshire. This was a laugh and a half to all old "Pau-
lies," who are generally fond of St. Paul's reputation as the most snobbish school in America.

Even Amy Vanderbilt tried to roughen up her female *honk* accent   50
by adding middle-class *r*'s, perhaps in an unconscious rub-off from the
various bourgeois commercial interests with which she was involved.
In general, the public spotlight tends to make *honks* nervous about their
voices, whether they are politicians or performers or merely celebrities.
Very few have the self-assurance to just keep pouring it on, the way
Roosevelt did:

I hate wooouugggggggghawwwwwwwwwwwggggggghhhhhhhh—meaning *war.*

Boys today at St. Paul's, Groton, Middlesex, Hotchkiss, Deerfield,
St. Mark's, St. George's, Exeter, Andover, and the rest of them are
strangely goosy about it themselves. They are apparently hung up on
the masculinity thing, as they might put it, rather preferring to have
both the social certification of the languid, delicate *honk* voice and the
ruggedness and virility of various street voices. The upshot has been
that they have kept the *honk* voice but picked up the dope argot of
Greenwich Village, the Lower East Side, and other lower-middle-class
bohemias, studding the most improbable conversations with the inarticulate litany of "like-I-mean-you-know-man" intoned in a kind of Bugs
Bunny Bobby Kennedy *honk* spew of lubricated BB's:

Laiike, nyew nyeoow, man, ai mean, Fisha's Island is a groove and
a gas compaaaiiihed to Deeah Island and, like, now, ai mean, Wild-
wood, Nyew Juhsey, is prackly a mind-blowagggh . . .

And the whole *honk* world sinks, *wonking,* into a vast gummy Welt-
smeared nostalgia for the mud.

Lines of Inquiry
"Honks and Wonks"

In this piece, Wolfe relies heavily on spelling, punctuation, and typography
to convey the distinctive pronunciations and voices of honks and wonks. Which
of these devices do you think is most important in conveying how they sound?
Which is least important? Do you think Wolfe gives an accurate or exaggerated
impression of how they sound? How can you tell the difference? How does
Wolfe himself sound in this piece?

Wolfe says that "it is probably a good thiing that no Henry Higgins has
come along to wake up New York to the phonetic truth about class and status
in this city"? What is the "phonetic truth about class and status"? Why wouldn't
it be a good idea for people to be aware of this truth, this issue of class and
status? Do you think that Wolfe really believes people should remain ignorant

of such a truth? In what respects do you suppose their behavior might change if they were aware of this truth?

If you are not from New York City or from the East Coast, this essay may at first seem alien to your experience. But think again. What is the class structure in your own city, your own neighborhood, your own school? What "status details"—styles of clothing, ways of talking, and the like—indicate membership in the "in" group? Do you need to be a member of this in-group to succeed, or is it possible to succeed just on your own merits and abilities?

The Right Stuff

A young man might go into military flight training believing that he was entering some sort of technical school in which he was simply going to acquire a certain set of skills. Instead, he found himself all at once enclosed in a fraternity. And in this fraternity, even though it was military, men were not rated by their outward rank as ensigns, lieutenants, commanders, or whatever. No, herein the world was divided into those who had it and those who did not. This quality, this *it,* was never named, however, nor was it talked about in any way.

As to just what this ineffable quality was . . . well, it obviously involved bravery. But it was not bravery in the simple sense of being willing to risk your life. The idea seemed to be that any fool could do that, if that was all that was required, just as any fool could throw away his life in the process. No, the idea here (in the all-enclosing fraternity) seemed to be that a man should have the ability to go up in a hurtling piece of machinery and put his hide on the line and then have the moxie, the reflexes, the experience, the coolness, to pull it back in the last yawning moment—and then to go up again *the next day,* and the next day, and every next day, even if the series should prove infinite—and, ultimately, in its best expression, do so in a cause that means something to thousands, to a people, a nation, to humanity, to God. Nor was there *a test* to show whether or not a pilot had this righteous quality. There was, instead, a seemingly infinite series of tests. A career in flying was like climbing one of those ancient Babylonian pyramids made up of a dizzy progression of steps and ledges, a ziggurat, a pyramid extraordinarily high and steep; and the idea was to prove at every foot of the way up that pyramid that you were one of the elected and anointed ones who had *the right stuff* and could move higher and higher and even— ultimately, God willing, one day—that you might be able to join that special few at the very top, that elite who had the capacity to bring tears to men's eyes, the very Brotherhood of the Right Stuff itself.

None of this was to be mentioned, and yet it was acted out in a way that a young man could not fail to understand. When a new flight (i.e., a class) of trainees arrived at Pensacola, they were brought into an auditorium for a little lecture. An officer would tell them: "Take a look at the man on either side of you." Quite a few actually swiveled their heads this way and that, in the interest of appearing diligent. Then the officer would say: "One of the three of you is not going to make it!"— meaning, not get his wings. That was the opening theme, the *motif* of primary training. We already know that one-third of you do not have the right stuff—it only remains to find out who.

Furthermore, that was the way it turned out. At every level in one's progress up that staggeringly high pyramid, the world was once more divided into those men who had the right stuff to continue the climb and those who had to be *left behind* in the most obvious way. Some were eliminated in the course of the opening classroom work, as either not smart enough or not hardworking enough, and were left behind. Then came the basic flight instruction in single-engine, propeller-driven trainers, and a few more—even though the military tried to make this stage easy—were washed out and left behind. Then came more demanding levels, one after the other, formation flying, instrument flying, jet training, all-weather flying, gunnery, and at each level more were washed out and left behind. By this point easily a third of the original candidates had been, indeed, eliminated . . . from the ranks of those who might prove to have the right stuff.

In the Navy, in addition to the stages that Air Force trainees went through, the neophyte always had waiting for him, out in the ocean, a certain grim gray slab; namely, the deck of an aircraft carrier; and with it perhaps the most difficult routine in military flying, carrier landings. He was shown films about it, he heard lectures about it, and he knew that carrier landings were hazardous. He first practiced touching down on the shape of a flight deck painted on an airfield. He was instructed to touch down and gun right off. This was safe enough—the shape didn't move, at least—but it could do terrible things to, let us say, the gyroscope of the soul. *That shape!—it's so damned small!* And more candidates were washed out and left behind. Then came the day, without warning, when those who remained were sent out over the ocean for the first of many days of reckoning with the slab. The first day was always a clear day with little wind and a calm sea. The carrier was so steady that it seemed, from up there in the air, to be resting on pilings, and the candidate usually made his first carrier landing successfully, with relief and even *élan*. Many young candidates looked like terrific aviators up to that very point—and it was not until they were actually standing on the carrier deck that they first began to wonder if they had the proper stuff, after all. In the training film the flight deck was a grand piece of gray geometry, perilous, to be sure, but an amazing abstract shape as one looks down upon it on the screen. And yet once the newcomer's two feet were on it . . . *Geometry*—my God, man, this is a . . . skillet! It *heaved,* it moved up and down underneath his feet, it pitched up, it pitched down, it rolled to port (this great beast *rolled!*) and it rolled to starboard, as the ship moved into the wind and, therefore, into the waves, and the wind kept sweeping across, sixty feet up in the air out in the open sea, and there were no railings whatsoever. This was a *skillet!*—a frying pan!—a short-order grill!—not gray but black, smeared

5

with skid marks from one end to the other and glistening with pools of hydraulic fluid and the occasional jet-fuel slick, all of it still hot, sticky, greasy, runny, virulent from God knows what traumas—still ablaze!—consumed in detonations, explosions, flames, combustion, roars, shrieks, whines, blasts, horrible shudders, fracturing impacts, as little men in screaming red and yellow and purple and green shirts with black Mickey Mouse helmets over their ears skittered about on the surface as if for their very lives (you've said it now!), hooking fighter planes onto the catapult shuttles so that they can explode their afterburners and be slung off the deck in a red-mad fury with a *kaboom!* that pounds through the entire deck—a procedure that seems absolutely controlled, orderly, sublime, however, compared to what he is about to watch as aircraft return to the ship for what is known in the engineering stoicisms of the military as "recovery and arrest." To say that an F–4 was coming back onto this heaving barbecue from out of the sky at a speed of 135 knots . . . that might have been the truth in the training lecture, but it did not begin to get across the idea of what the newcomer saw from the deck itself, because it created the notion that perhaps the plane was gliding in. On the deck one knew differently! As the aircraft came closer and the carrier heaved on into the waves and the plane's speed did not diminish and the deck did not grow steady—indeed, it pitched up and down five or ten feet per greasy heave—one experienced a neural alarm that no lecture could have prepared him for: This is not an *airplane* coming toward me, it is a brick with some poor sonofabitch riding it *(someone much like myself!),* and it is not *gliding,* it is *falling,* a thirty-thousand-pound brick, headed not for a stripe on the deck but for *me*— and with a horrible *smash!* it hits the skillet, and with a blur of momentum as big as a freight train's it hurtles toward the far end of the deck— another blinding storm!—another roar as the pilot pushes the throttle up to full military power and another smear of rubber screams out over the skillet—and this is nominal!—quite okay!—for a wire stretched across the deck has grabbed the hook on the end of the plane as it hit the deck tail down, and the smash was the rest of the fifteen-ton brute slamming onto the deck, as it tripped up, so that it is now straining against the wire at full throttle, in case it hadn't held and the plane had "boltered" off the end of the deck and had to struggle up into the air again. And already the Mickey Mouse helmets are running toward the fiery monster . . .

And the candidate, looking on, begins to *feel* that great heaving sun-blazing deathboard of a deck wallowing in his own vestibular system— and suddenly he finds himself backed up against his own limits. He ends up going to the flight surgeon with so-called conversion symptoms. Overnight he develops blurred vision or numbness in his hands and feet or sinusitis so severe that he cannot tolerate changes in altitude. On one level the symptom is real. He really cannot see too well or use his fingers or stand the pain. But somewhere in his subconscious he knows it is a plea and a beg-off; he shows not the slightest concern (the flight surgeon notes) that the condition might be permanent and affect him in whatever life awaits him outside the arena of the right stuff.

Those who remained, those who qualified for carrier duty—and even more so those who later on qualified for *night* carrier duty—began to feel a bit like Gideon's warriors. *So many have been left behind!* The young warriors were now treated to a deathly sweet and quite unmentionable sight. They could gaze at length upon the crushed and wilted pariahs who had washed out. They could inspect those who did not have that righteous stuff.

The military did not have very merciful instincts. Rather than packing up these poor souls and sending them home, the Navy, like the Air Force and the Marines, would try to make use of them in some other role, such as flight controller. So the washout has to keep taking classes with the rest of his group, even though he can no longer touch an airplane. He sits there in the classes staring at sheets of paper with cataracts of sheer human mortification over his eyes while the rest steal looks at him . . . this man reduced to an ant, this untouchable, this poor sonofabitch. And in what test had he been found wanting? Why, it seemed to be nothing less than *manhood* itself. Naturally, this was never mentioned, either. Yet there it was. *Manliness, manhood, manly courage* . . . there was something ancient, primordial, irresistible about the challenge of this stuff, no matter what a sophisticated and rational age one might think he lived in.

Perhaps because it could not be talked about, the subject began to take on superstititous and even mystical outlines. A man either had it or he didn't! There was no such thing as having *most* of it . Moreover, it could blow at any seam. One day a man would be ascending the pyramid at a terrific clip, and the next—bingo!— he would reach his own limits in the most unexpected way. Conrad and Schirra met an Air Force pilot who had had a great pal at Tyndall Air Force Base in Florida. This man had been the budding ace of the training class; he had flown the hottest fighter-style trainer, the T–38, like a dream; and then he began the routine step of being checked out in the T–33. The T–33 was not nearly as hot an aircraft as the T–38; it was essentially the old P–80 jet fighter. It had an exceedingly small cockpit. The pilot could barely move his shoulders. It was the sort of airplane of which everybody said, "You don't get into it, you *wear* it." Once inside a T–33 cockpit this man, this budding ace, developed claustrophobia of the most paralyzing sort. He tried everything to overcome it. He even went to a psychiatrist, which was a serious mistake for a military officer if his superiors learned of it. But nothing worked. He was shifted over to flying jet transports, such as the C–135. Very demanding and necessary aircraft they were, too, and he was still spoken of as an excellent pilot.

But as everyone knew—and, again, it was never explained in so many words—only those who were assigned to fighter squadrons, the "fighter jocks," as they called each other with a self-satisfied irony, remained in the true fraternity. Those assigned to transports were not humiliated like washouts—*somebody* had to fly those planes—nevertheless, they, too, had been *left behind* for lack of the right stuff.

Or a man could go for a routine physical one fine day, feeling like a million dollars, and be grounded for *fallen arches*. It happened!—just like that! (And try raising them.) Or for breaking his wrist and losing only *part* of its mobility. Or for a minor deterioration of eyesight, or for any of hundreds of reasons that would make no difference to a man in an ordinary occupation. As a result all fighter jocks began looking upon doctors as their natural enemies. Going to see a flight surgeon was a no-gain proposition; a pilot could only hold his own or lose in the doctor's office. To be grounded for a medical reason was no humiliation, looked at objectively. But it was a humiliation, nonetheless!—for it meant you no longer had that indefinable, unutterable, integral stuff. (It could blow at *any* seam.) 10

All the hot young fighter jocks began trying to test the limits themselves in a superstitious way. They were like believing Presbyterians of a century before who used to probe their own experience to see if they were truly among *the elect*. When a fighter pilot was in training, whether in the Navy or the Air Force, his superiors were continually spelling out strict rules for him, about the use of the aircraft and conduct in the sky. They repeatedly forbade so-called hot-dog stunts, such as outside loops, buzzing, flat-hatting, hedgehopping and flying under bridges. But somehow one got the message that the man who truly *had* it could ignore those rules—not that he should make a point of it, but that he *could*—and that after all there was only one way to find out—and that in some strange unofficial way, peeking through his fingers, his instructor halfway expected him to challenge all the limits. They would give a lecture about how a pilot should never fly without a good solid breakfast—eggs, bacon, toast, and so forth—because if he tried to fly with his blood-sugar level too low, it could impair his alertness. Naturally, the next day every hot dog in the unit would get up and have a breakfast consisting of one cup of black coffee and take off and go up into a vertical climb until the weight of the ship exactly canceled out the upward thrust of the engine and his air speed was zero, and he would hang there for one thick adrenal instant—and then fall like a rock, until one of three things happened: he keeled over nose first and regained his aerodynamics and all was well, he went into a spin and fought his way out of it, or he went into a spin and had to eject or crunch it, which was always supremely possible.

Likewise, "hassling"—mock dogfighting—was strictly forbidden, and so naturally young fighter jocks could hardly wait to go up in, say, a pair of F–100s and start the duel by making a pass at each other at 800 miles an hour, the winner being the pilot who could slip in behind the other one and get locked in on his tail ("wax his tail"), and it was not uncommon for some eager jock to try too tight an outside turn and have his engine flame out, whereupon, unable to restart it, he has to eject . . . and he shakes his fist at the victor as he floats down by parachute and his million–dollar aircraft goes *kaboom!* on the palmetto grass or the desert floor, and he starts thinking about how he can get together with the other guy back at the base in time for the two of them to get their stories straight before the investigation: "I don't know what happened, sir. I was pulling up after a target run, and it just flamed out on me." Hassling was forbidden, and hassling that led to the destruction of an aircraft was a serious court-martial offense, and the man's superiors knew that the engine hadn't *just flamed out,* but every unofficial impulse on the base seemed to be saying: "Hell, we wouldn't give you a nickel for a pilot who hasn't done some crazy rat-racing like that. It's all part of the right stuff."

The other side of this impulse showed up in the reluctance of the young jocks to admit it when they had maneuvered themselves into a bad corner they couldn't get out of. There were two reasons why a fighter pilot hated to declare an emergency. First, it triggered a complex and very public chain of events at the field: all other incoming flights were held up, including many of one's comrades who were probably low on fuel; the fire trucks came trundling out to the runway like yellow toys (as seen from way up there), the better to illustrate one's hapless state; and the bureaucracy began to crank up the paper monster for the investigation that always followed. And second, to declare an emergency, one first had to reach that conclusion in his own mind, which to the young pilot was the same as saying: "A minute ago I still *had* it—now I need your help!" To have a bunch of young fighter pilots up in the air thinking this way used to drive flight controllers crazy. They would see a ship beginning to drift off the radar, and they couldn't rouse the pilot on the microphone for anything other than a few meaningless mumbles, and they would know he was probably out there with engine failure at a low altitude, trying to reignite by lowering his auxilliary generator rig, which had a little propeller that was supposed to spin in the slipstream like a child's pinwheel.

"Whiskey Kilo Two Eight, do you want to declare an emergency?"

This would rouse him!—to say: "Negative, negative, Whiskey Kilo 15 Two Eight is not declaring an emergency."

Kaboom. Believers in the right stuff would rather crash and burn.

One fine day, after he had joined a fighter squadron, it would dawn on the young pilot exactly how the losers in the great fraternal competition were now being left behind. Which is to say, not by instructors or other superiors or by failures at prescribed levels of competence, but by death. At this point the essence of the enterprise would begin to dawn on him. Slowly, step by step, the ante had been raised until he was now involved in what was surely the grimmest and grandest gamble of manhood. Being a fighter pilot—for that matter, simply taking off in a single-engine jet fighter of the Century series, such as an F–102, or any of the military's other marvelous bricks with fins on them—presented a man, on a perfectly sunny day, with more ways to get himself killed than his wife and children could imagine in their wildest fears. If he was barreling down the runway at two hundred miles an hour, completing the takeoff run, and the board started lighting up red, should he (a) abort the takeoff (and try to wrestle with the monster, which was gorged with jet fuel, out in the sand beyond the end of the runway) or (b) eject (and hope that the goddamned human cannonball trick works at zero altitude and he doesn't shatter an elbow or a knee-cap on the way out) or (c) continue the takeoff and deal with the problem aloft (knowing full well that the ship may be on fire and therefore seconds away from exploding)? He would have one second to sort out the options and act, and this kind of little workaday decision came up all the time. Occasionally a man would look coldly at the binary problem he was now confronting every day—Right Stuff/Death—and decide it wasn't worth it and voluntarily shift over to transports or reconnaissance or whatever. And his comrades would wonder, for a day or so, what evil virus had invaded his soul . . . as they left him behind. More often, however, the reverse would happen. Some college graduate would enter Navy aviation through the Reserves, simply as an alternative to the Army draft, fully intending to return to civilian life, to some waiting profession or family business; would become involved in the obsessive business of ascending the ziggurat pyramid of flying; and, at the end of his enlistment, would astound everyone back home and very likely himself as well by signing up for another one. What on earth got into him? He couldn't explain it. After all, the very words for it had been amputated. A Navy study showed that two-thirds of the fighter pilots who were rated in the top rungs of their groups—i.e., the hottest young pilots—reenlisted when the time came, and practically all were college graduates. By this point, a young fighter jock was like the preacher in *Moby Dick* who climbs up into the pulpit on a rope ladder and then pulls the ladder up behind him; except the pilot could not use the words necessary to express the vital lessons. Civilian life, and even home and hearth, now seemed not only far away but far *below,* back down many levels of the pyramid of the right stuff.

A fighter pilot soon found he wanted to associate only with other fighter pilots. Who else could understand the nature of the little proposition (right stuff/death) they were all dealing with? And what other subject could compare with it? It was riveting! To talk about it in so many words was forbidden, of course. The very words *death, danger, bravery, fear* were not to be uttered except in the occasional specific instance or for ironic effect. Nevertheless, the subject could be adumbrated in *code* or *by example*. Hence the endless evenings of pilots huddled together talking about flying. On these long and drunken evenings (the bane of their family life) certain theorems would be propounded and demonstrated—and all by *code* and *example*. One theorem was: There are no *accidents* and no fatal flaws in the machines; there are only pilots with the wrong stuff. (I.e., blind Fate can't kill me.) When Bud Jennings crashed and burned in the swamps at Jacksonville, the other pilots in Pete Conrad's squadron said: *How could he have been so stupid?* It turned out that Jennings had gone up in the SNJ with his cockpit canopy opened in a way that was expressly forbidden in the manual, and carbon monoxide had been sucked in from the exhaust, and he passed out and crashed. All agreed that Bud Jennings was a good guy and a good pilot, but his epitaph on the ziggurat was: *How could he have been so stupid?* This seemed shocking at first, but by the time Conrad had reached the end of that bad string at Pax River, he was capable of his own corollary to the theorem: viz., no single factor ever killed a pilot; there was always a chain of mistakes. But what about Ted Whelan, who fell like a rock from 8,100 feet when his parachute failed? Well, the parachute was merely part of the chain: first, someone should have caught the structural defect that resulted in the hydraulic leak that triggered the emergency; second, Whelan did not check out his seat-parachute rig, and the drogue failed to separate the main parachute from the seat; but even after those two mistakes, Whelan had fifteen or twenty seconds, as he fell, to disengage himself from the seat and open the parachute manually. Why just stare at the scenery coming up to smack you in the face! And everyone nodded. (He failed—but I wouldn't have!) Once the theorem and the corollary were understood, the Navy's statistics about one in every four Navy aviators dying meant nothing. The figures were averages, and averages applied to those with average stuff.

A riveting subject, especially if it were one's own hide that was on the line. Every evening at bases all over America, there were military pilots huddled in officers clubs eagerly cutting the right stuff up in coded slices so they could talk about it. What more compelling topic of conversation was there in the world? In the Air Force there were even pilots who would ask the tower for priority landing clearance so that they could make the beer call on time, at 4 p.m. sharp, at the Officers Club. They would come right out and state the reason. The drunken rambles began at four and sometimes went on for ten or twelve hours. Such conversations! They diced that righteous stuff up into little bits, bowed ironically to it, stumbled blindfolded around it, groped, lurched, belched, staggered, bawled, sang, roared, and feinted at it with self-deprecating humor. Nevertheless!—they never mentioned it by name. No, they used the approved codes, such as: "Like a jerk I got myself into a hell of a corner today." They told of how they "lucked out of it." To get across the extreme peril of his exploit, one would use certain oblique cues. He would say, "I looked over at Robinson"—who would be known to the listeners as a non-com who sometimes rode backseat to read radar— "and he wasn't talking any more, he was just staring at the radar, like this, giving it that *zombie* look. Then I *knew* I was in trouble!" Beautiful! Just right! For it would also be known to the listeners that the non-coms advised one another: "*Never* fly with a lieutenant. *Avoid* captains and majors. Hell, man, do yourself a favor: don't fly with anybody below colonel." Which in turn said: "Those young bucks shoot dice with death!" And yet once in the air the non-com had his own standards. He was determined to remain as outwardly cool as the pilot, so that when the pilot did something that truly petrified him, he would say nothing; instead, he would turn silent, catatonic, like a zombie. Perfect! *Zombie.* There you had it, compressed into a single word, all of the foregoing. I'm a hell of a pilot! I shoot dice with death! And now all you fellows know it! And I haven't spoken of that unspoken stuff even once!

The talking and drinking began at the beer call, and then the boys would break for dinner and come back afterward and get more wasted and more garrulous or else more quietly fried, drinking good cheap PX booze until 2 a.m. The night was young! Why not get the cars and go out for a little proficiency run? It seemed that every fighter jock thought himself an ace driver, and he would do anything to obtain a hot car, especially a sports car, and the drunker he was, the more convinced he would be about his driving skills, as if the right stuff, being indivisible, carried over into any enterprise whatsoever, under any conditions. A little proficiency run, boys! (There's only one way to find out!) And they would roar off in close formation from, say, Nellis Air Force Base, down Route 15, into Las Vegas, barreling down the highway, ratracing, sometimes four abreast, jockeying for position, piling into the most listless curve in the desert flats as if they were trying to root each other out of the groove at the Rebel 500—and then bursting into downtown Las Vegas with a rude fraternal roar like the Hell's Angels—and the natives chalked it up to youth and drink and the bad element that the Air Force attracted. They knew nothing about the right stuff, of course.

More fighter pilots died in automobiles than in airplanes. Fortunately, there was always some kindly soul up the chain to certify the papers "line of duty," so that the widow could get a better break on the insurance. That was okay and only proper because somehow the system itself had long ago said *Skol!* and *Quite right!* to the military cycle of Flying & Drinking and Drinking & Driving, as if there were no other way. Every young fighter jock knew the feeling of getting two or three hours' sleep and then waking up at 5:30 a.m. and having a few cups of coffee, a few cigarettes, and then carting his poor quiv-

20

ering liver out to the field for another day of flying. There were those who arrived not merely hungover but still drunk, slapping oxygen tank cones over their faces and trying to burn the alcohol out of their systems, and then going up, remarking later: "I don't *advise* it, you understand, but it *can* be done." (Provided you have the right stuff, you miserable pudknocker.)

Air Force and Navy airfields were usually on barren or marginal stretches of land and would have looked especially bleak and Low Rent to an ordinary individual in the chilly light of dawn. But to a young pilot there was an inexplicable bliss to coming out to the flight line while the sun was just beginning to cook up behind the rim of the horizon, so that the whole field was still in shadow and the ridges in the distance were in silhouette and the flight line was a monochrome of Exhaust Fume Blue, and every little red light on top of the water towers or power stanchions looked dull, shriveled, congealed, and the runway lights, which were still on, looked faded, and even the landing lights on a fighter that had just landed and was taxiing in were no longer dazzling, as they would be at night, and looked instead like shriveled gobs of candlepower out there—and yet it was beautiful, exhilarating!—for he was revved up with adrenalin, anxious to take off before the day broke, to burst up into the sunlight over the ridges before all those thousands of comatose souls down there, still dead to the world, snug in home and hearth, even came to their senses. To take off in an F–100 at dawn and cut in the afterburner and hurtle twenty-five thousand feet up into the sky so suddenly that you felt not like a bird but like a trajectory, yet with full control, full control of *five tons* of thrust, all of which flowed from your will and through your fingertips, with the huge engine right beneath you, so close that it was as if you were riding it bareback, until you leveled out and went supersonic, an event registered on earth by a tremendous cracking boom that shook windows, but up here only by the fact that you now felt utterly free of the earth—to describe it, even to wife, child, near ones and dear ones, seemed impossible. So the pilot kept it to himself, along with an even more indescribable . . . an even more sinfully inconfessable . . . feeling of superiority, appropriate to him and to his kind, lone bearers of the right stuff.

From *up here* at dawn the pilot looked down upon poor hopeless Las Vegas (or Yuma, Corpus Christi, Meridian, San Bernardino, or Dayton) and began to wonder: How can all of them down there, those poor souls who will soon be waking up and trudging out of their minute rectangles and inching along their little noodle highways toward whatever slots and grooves make up their everyday lives—how could they live like that, with such earnestness, if they had the faintest idea of what it was like up here in this righteous zone?

But of course! Not only the washed-out, grounded, and dead pilots had been left behind—but also all of those millions of sleepwalking souls who never even attempted the great gamble. The entire world below . . . *left behind.* Only at this point can one begin to understand just how big, how titanic, the ego of the military pilot could be. The world was used to enormous egos in artists, actors, entertainers of all sorts, in politicians, sports figures, and even journalists, because they had such familiar and convenient ways to show them off. But that slim young man over there in uniform, with the enormous watch on his wrist and the withdrawn look on his face, that young officer who is so shy that he can't even open his mouth unless the subject is flying—that young pilot—well, my friends, his ego is even *bigger!*—so big, it's *breathtaking!* Even in the 1950's it was difficult for civilians to comprehend such a thing, but *all* military officers and many enlisted men tended to feel superior to civilians. It was really quite ironic, given the fact that for a good thirty years the rising business classes in the cities had been steering their sons away from the military, as if from a bad smell, and the officer corps had never been held in lower esteem. Well, career officers returned the contempt in trumps. They looked upon themselves as men who lived by higher standards of behavior than civilians, as men who were the bearers and protectors of the most important values of American life, who maintained a sense of discipline while civilians abandoned themselves to hedonism, who maintained a sense of honor while civilians lived by opportunism and greed. Opportunism and greed: there you had your much-vaunted corporate business world. Khrushchev was right about one thing: when it came time to hang the capitalist West, an American businessman would sell him the rope. When the showdown came—and the showdowns always came—not all the wealth in the world or all the sophisticated nuclear weapons and radar and missile systems it could buy would take the place of those who had the uncritical willingness to face danger, those who, in short, had the right stuff.

In fact, the feeling was so righteous, so exalted, it could become   25
religious. Civilians seldom understood this, either. There was no one to teach them. It was no longer the fashion for serious writers to describe the glories of war. Instead, they dwelt upon its horrors, often with cynicism or disgust. It was left to the occasional pilot with a literary flair to provide a glimpse of the pilot's self-conception in its heavenly or spiritual aspect. When a pilot named Robert Scott flew his P–43 over Mount Everest, quite a feat at the time, he brought his hand up and snapped a salute to his fallen adversary. He thought he had *defeated* the mountain, surmounting all the forces of nature that had made it formidable. And why not? "God is my co-pilot," he said—that became the title of his book—and he meant it. So did the most gifted of all the pilot authors, the Frenchman Antoine de Saint-Exupéry. As he gazed down upon the world . . . from up there . . . during trans-

continental flights, the good Saint-Ex saw civilization as a series of tiny fragile patches clinging to the otherwise barren rock of Earth. He felt like a lonely sentinel, a protector of those vulnerable little oases, ready to lay down his life in their behalf, if necessary; a saint, in short, true to his name, flying up here at the right hand of God. The good Saint-Ex! And he was not the only one. He was merely the one who put it into words most beautifully and anointed himself before the altar of the right stuff.

Lines of Inquiry
"The Right Stuff"

Wolfe relies heavily in this piece on a deliberate repetition of the term "the right stuff" and several other key phrases. How often and at what special points does he repeat these phrases? What variations, if any, do you note in his wording of these phrases? Why do you suppose that he engages in such repetitions? How did they affect you?

In his discussion of the right stuff, Wolfe also relies heavily on religious terminology, comparing the test pilots to the righteous "elect" and calling the right stuff itself "mystical" and "ineffable." In what ways, according to Wolfe, do the astronauts behave like members of a religious group or sect? How is their own language religious? Why do you think Wolfe makes these comparisons?

Think about the field or profession that you plan to enter. Does it call just for hard work and preparation or does success depend on some special talent—the right stuff—that you either have or don't have? How do you know when something calls for such a special quality? Do you think that successful writing depends on having the right stuff, or can anyone learn to write well?

Virginia Woolf
1882–1941

But literature is stern; it is no use being charming, virtuous, or even learned and brilliant into the bargain, unless, she seems to reiterate, you fulfill her first condition—to know how to write.

Few writers of her generation were quite so charming, virtuous, learned, and brilliant as Virginia Woolf herself, and few were quite so keenly aware that these admirable qualities do not themselves give rise to literature. Writing for her was evidently a very "stern" and challenging discipline—"each day's work like a fence which I have to ride at. . . ." And the fences she rode at were especially challenging because as a critic, novelist, and essayist she self-consciously sought to alter not only the imaginative world of fiction but also the actual world of women's experience. So while she took great pleasure in entertaining a circle of remarkably gifted artists, writers, and intellectuals, she also realized that "if one wishes to better the world, one must paradoxically enough, withdraw and spend more and more time fashioning one's sentences to perfection in solitude." Though she was self-evidently a perfectionist, she managed over the course of her career to produce nine novels, four collections of short stories, two biographies, two books of feminist commentary, more than three hundred articles, essays, and reviews, six volumes of correspondence, and an extensive diary.

Born and raised in London, she was the third of four children of her father's second marriage. She did not attend school, but was educated at home under the highly cultured influence of her father, Leslie Stephen, a distinguished biographer, critic, editor, and philosopher. From her father she learned "to read what one liked because one liked it . . ." and "to write in the fewest possible words, as clearly as possible, exactly what one meant." From her father, too, she learned that "all the rest must be learnt for oneself." So she immersed herself in his extensive collection of English and classical literature, as well as in his dazzling array of literary acquaintances, and therefore grew up to be an extraordinarily cultured person herself. She also grew up in touch with the life and rhythm of the sea at her father's summer house in Cornwall.

After her father's death in 1904, her mother having died in 1895, she took up residence with her sister, Vanessa, and her brothers, Thoby and Adrian, at a house in the Bloomsbury area of London, conveniently located near the British Museum. Bloomsbury, in turn, soon became a gathering place for Thoby's friends from Cambridge University—a place to carry on the lively discussions of art, literature, politics, and society that had occupied them during their college years. After the death of Thoby and the marriage of Vanessa in 1906, Virginia and Adrian moved to another house in Bloomsbury, where they continued to hold the gatherings that Thoby had started, attracting over the years such well-known figures as the art critic Roger Fry, the biographer and historian Lytton Strachey, the economist John Maynard Keynes, the novelist E. M. Forster, and the political activist Leonard Woolf, whom she married in 1912. This remarkable array of progressive artists and intellectuals, which came to be known as the Bloomsbury Group, provided a uniquely stimulating atmosphere for Woolf, an ambiance that encouraged her to pursue her own progressive literary and social interests.

Shortly after moving to Bloomsbury, she began to pursue her own interests by writing literary reviews and articles, an activity that she was to continue from 1905 through the rest of her life, not simply out of a desire to convey her impressions of individual works, but also out of "an instinct to create . . . a portrait of a man, a sketch of an age, a theory of the art of writing." Her "instinct to create" also provoked her to begin writing her own fiction, which led in 1915 to the publication of her first novel, *The Voyage Out.* Two years later, when she and her husband bought a hand press and started up their own publishing house, the Hogarth Press, her creative instincts found another outlet in the form of literary editing. The Hogarth Press turned out, in fact, to be a very successful business, publishing the writing of such eminent figures as T. S. Eliot, E. M. Forster, Sigmund Freud, Robert Graves, Katherine Mansfield, and H. G. Wells.

The press also gave Woolf the freedom to follow her own creative bent, knowing she would have an outlet for her fiction no matter how experimental it might be. During the last twenty years of her career, she directly challenged the long-standing fictional emphasis on materialistic circumstances—on clear-cut settings, characters, and events—preferring instead to focus on the complex flow of mental experience, which she considered to be the essence of "life itself." "The mind," she believed, "receives a myriad impressions—trivial, fantastic, evanescent, or engraved with the sharpness of steel. From all sides they come, an incessant show of innumerable atoms. . . ." So, she set out "to record the atoms as they fall upon the mind," and she did so in a series of increasingly interiorized novels—*Jacob's Room* (1922), *Mrs. Dalloway*

(1925), *To the Lighthouse* (1927), *The Waves* (1931), *The Years* (1937), and *Between the Acts* (1941). Her focus on the interior life of her characters—on their sensations, associations, memories, and expectations—enabled her, in turn, to explore the complex nature of personal awareness, personal identity, and personal relationships.

Her own personal life was evidently far more complex than it seemed to be to her friends and acquaintances. Though she appeared on most occasions to be a very buoyant and vivacious person, she was, in fact, during most of her life afflicted by periods of severe depression, especially after completing a novel. Whatever the cause of her depressions and nervous breakdowns, she felt "certain" in March 1941 that she was "going mad again," and rather than put herself and her husband "through another of those terrible times," she put an end to her life by drowning herself in the river near the cottage where she had just finished her last novel.

Her personal essays and critical pieces cover a wide range of subjects from the death of a moth to the status of women, from the lives of the obscure to the works of the famous. They also embody a wide range of modes from description, narration, and reflection to explanation, evaluation, and argument. But whatever their subject or mode, they are always marked by "some fierce attachment to an idea . . . something believed in with conviction or seen with precision," which she believed to be the "backbone" of writing. Whatever the source of their backbone, they are always permeated by the sound of a human voice, the sense of a human presence—by the "spirit of personality," which she considered to be "the essayist's most proper but most dangerous and delicate tool."

The Death of the Moth

Moths that fly by day are not properly to be called moths; they do not excite that pleasant sense of dark autumn nights and ivy-blossom which the commonest yellow-underwing asleep in the shadow of the curtain never fails to rouse in us. They are hybrid creatures, neither gay like butterflies nor sombre like their own species. Nevertheless the present specimen, with his narrow hay-coloured wings, fringed with a tassel of the same colour, seemed to be content with life. It was a pleasant morning, mid-September, mild, benignant, yet with a keener breath than that of the summer months. The plough was already scoring the field opposite the window, and where the share had been, the earth was pressed flat and gleamed with moisture. Such vigour came rolling in from the fields and the down beyond that it was difficult to keep the eyes strictly turned upon the book. The rooks too were keeping one of their annual festivities; soaring round the tree tops until it looked as if a vast net with thousands of black knots in it had been cast up into the air; which, after a few moments sank slowly down upon the trees until every twig seemed to have a knot at the end of it. Then, suddenly, the net would be thrown into the air again in a wider circle this time, with the utmost clamour and vociferation, as though to be thrown into the air and settle slowly down upon the tree tops were a tremendously exciting experience.

The same energy which inspired the rooks, the ploughmen, the horses, and even, it seemed, the lean bare-backed downs, sent the moth fluttering from side to side of his square of the window-pane. One could not help watching him. One was, indeed, conscious of a queer feeling of pity for him. The possibilities of pleasure seemed that morning so enormous and so various that to have only a moth's part in life, and a day moth's at that, appeared a hard fate, and his zest in enjoying his meagre opportunities to the full, pathetic. He flew vigorously to one corner of his compartment, and, after waiting there a second, flew across to the other. What remained for him but to fly to a third corner and then to a fourth? That was all he could do, in spite of the size of the downs, the width of the sky, the far-off smoke of houses, and the romantic voice, now and then, of a steamer out at sea. What he could do he did. Watching him, it seemed as if a fibre, very thin, but pure, of the enormous energy of the world had been thrust into his frail and diminutive body. As often as he crossed the pane, I could fancy that a thread of vital light became visible. He was little or nothing but life.

Yet, because he was so small, and so simple a form of the energy that was rolling in at the open window and driving its way through so many narrow and intricate corridors in my own brain and in those of other human beings, there was something marvellous as well as pathetic about him. It was as if someone had taken a tiny bead of pure life and decking it as lightly as possible with down and feathers, had set it dancing and zigzagging to show us the true nature of life. Thus displayed one could not get over the strangeness of it. One is apt to forget all about life, seeing it humped and bossed and garnished and cumbered so that it has to move with the greatest circumspection and dignity. Again, the thought of all that life might have been had he been born in any other shape caused one to view his simple activities with a kind of pity.

After a time, tired by his dancing apparently, he settled on the window ledge in the sun, and, the queer spectacle being at an end, I forgot about him. Then, looking up, my eye was caught by him. He was trying to resume his dancing, but seemed either so stiff or so awkward that he could only flutter to the bottom of the window-pane; and when he tried to fly across it he failed. Being intent on other matters I watched these futile attempts for a time without thinking, unconsciously waiting for him to resume his flight, as one waits for a machine, that has stopped momentarily, to start again without considering the reason of its failure. After perhaps a seventh attempt he slipped from the wooden ledge and fell, fluttering his wings, on to his back on the window sill. The helplessness of his attitude roused me. It flashed upon me that he was in difficulties; he could no longer raise himself; his legs struggled vainly. But, as I stretched out a pencil, meaning to help him to right himself, it came over me that the failure and awkwardness were the approach of death. I laid the pencil down again.

The legs agitated themselves once more. I looked as if for the enemy against which he struggled. I looked out of doors. What had happened there? Presumably it was mid-day, and work in the fields had stopped. Stillness and quiet had replaced the previous animation. The birds had taken themselves off to feed in the brooks. The horses stood still. Yet the power was there all the same, massed outside indifferent, impersonal, not attending to anything in particular. Somehow it was opposed to the little hay-coloured moth. It was useless to try to do anything. One could only watch the extraordinary efforts made by those tiny legs against an oncoming doom which could, had it chosen, have submerged an entire city, not merely a city, but masses of human beings; nothing, I knew, had any chance against death. Nevertheless after a pause of exhaustion the legs fluttered again. It was superb this last protest, and so frantic that he succeeded at last in righting himself. One's sympathies, of course, were all on the side of life. Also, when there was nobody to care or to know, this gigantic effort on the part of an insignificant little moth, against a power of such magnitude, to retain what no one else valued or desired to keep, moved one strangely. Again,

5

somehow, one saw life, a pure bead. I lifted the pencil again, useless though I knew it to be. But even as I did so, the unmistakable tokens of death showed themselves. The body relaxed, and instantly grew stiff. The struggle was over. The insignificant little creature now knew death. As I looked at the dead moth, this minute wayside triumph of so great a force over so mean an antagonist filled me with wonder. Just as life had been strange a few minutes before, so death was now as strange. The moth having righted himself now lay most decently and uncomplainingly composed. O yes, he seemed to say, death is stronger than I am.

Lines of Inquiry
"The Death of the Moth"

Woolf begins her essay using a third-person point of view, but in the fourth paragraph she shifts to a predominantly first-person point of view. In the fifth paragraph, she moves back and forth between these two points of view. Why do you suppose that she combines these two very different points of view in a single essay? Why do you suppose that she shifts from one to the other at each point that such a shift occurs? How did the changing point of view affect your thoughts and feelings abut the moth? About Woolf?

Moths are such ordinary creatures that at first thought they seem to be an unlikely subject for an essay. What is it about this particular moth that catches the attention of Woolf? And once she takes note of the creature, why does she become absorbed in following its movements? Why does she come to see the "spectacle" of the moth as being so "queer," so "extraordinary," and so significant?

Virginia Woolf is not the only essayist in this collection to be concerned with the existence of moths, as you can see by looking at Annie Dillard's "The Death of a Moth." Given the very close connection in the titles of Dillard's and Woolf's essays, what other similarities do you see in their pieces? What are the most notable differences in the way they approach the death of a moth?

On a Faithful Friend

There is some impertinence as well as some foolhardiness in the way in which we buy animals for so much gold and silver and call them ours. One cannot help wondering what the silent critic on the hearthrug thinks of our strange conventions—the mystic Persian, whose ancestors were worshipped as gods whilst we, their masters and mistresses, grovelled in caves and painted our bodies blue. She has a vast heritage of experience, which seems to brood in her eyes, too solemn and too subtle for expression; she smiles, I often think, at our late-born civilisation, and remembers the rise and fall of dynasties. There is something, too, profane in the familiarity, half contemptuous, with which we treat our animals. We deliberately transplant a little bit of simple wild life, and make it grow up beside ours, which is neither simple nor wild. You may often see in a dog's eyes a sudden look of the primitive animal, as though he were once more a wild dog hunting in the solitary places of his youth. How have we the impertinence to make these wild creatures forego their nature for ours, which at best they can but imitate? It is one of the refined sins of civilization, for we know not what wild spirit we are taking from its purer atmosphere, or who it is—Pan, or Nymph, or Dryad—that we have trained to beg for a lump of sugar at tea.

I do not think that in domesticating our lost friend Shag we were guilty of any such crime; he was essentially a sociable dog, who had his near counterpart in the human world. I can see him smoking a cigar at the bow window of his club, his legs extended comfortably, whilst he discusses the latest news on the Stock Exchange with a companion. His best friend could not claim for him any romantic or mysterious animal nature, but that made him all the better company for mere human beings. He came to us, however, with a pedigree that had all the elements of romance in it; he, when, in horror at his price, his would-be purchaser pointed to his collie head and collie body, but terribly Skye-terrier legs—he, we were assured, was no less a dog than the original Skye—a chieftain of the same importance as the O'Brien or the O'Connor Don in human aristocracy. The whole of the Skye-terrier tribe—who, that is, inherited the paternal characteristics—had somehow been swept from the earth; Shag, the sole scion of true Skye blood, remained in an obscure Norfolk village, the property of a low-born blacksmith, who, however, cherished the utmost loyalty for his person, and pressed the claims of his royal birth with such success that we had the honour of buying him for a very substantial sum. He was too great a gentleman to take part in the plebeian work of killing rats for which he was originally needed, but he certainly added, we felt, to the respectability of the family. He seldom went for a walk without punishing the impertinence of middle-class dogs who neglected the homage due to his rank, and we had to enclose the royal jaws in a muzzle long after that restriction was legally unnecessary. As he advanced in middle life he became certainly rather autocratic, not only with his own kind, but with us, his masters and mistresses; such a title though was absurd where Shag was concerned, so we called ourselves his uncles and aunts. The solitary occasion when he found it necessary to inflict marks of his displeasure on human flesh was once when a visitor rashly tried to treat him as an ordinary pet-dog and tempted him with sugar and called him "out of his name" by the contemptible lap-dog title of "Fido." Then Shag, with characteristic independence, refused the sugar and took a satisfactory mouthful of calf instead. But when he felt that he was treated with due respect he was the most faithful of friends. He was not demonstrative; but failing eyesight did not blind him to his master's face, and in his deafness he could still hear his master's voice.

The evil spirit of Shag's life was introduced into the family in the person of an attractive young sheep-dog puppy—who, though of authentic breed, was unhappily without a tail—a fact which Shag could not help remarking with satisfaction. We deluded ourselves into the thought that the young dog might take the place of the son of Shag's old age, and for a time they lived happily together. But Shag had ever been contemptuous of social graces, and had relied for his place in our hearts upon his sterling qualities of honesty and independence; the puppy, however, was a young gentleman of most engaging manners, and, though we tried to be fair, Shag could not help feeling that the young dog got most of our attention. I can see him now, as in a kind of blundering and shamefaced way he lifted one stiff old paw and gave it me to shake, which was one of the young dog's most successful tricks. It almost brought the tears to my eyes. I could not help thinking, though I smiled, of old King Lear. But Shag was too old to acquire new graces; no second place should be his, and he determined that the matter should be decided by force. So after some weeks of growing tension the battle was fought; they went for each other with white teeth gleaming—Shag was the aggressor—and rolled round and round on the grass, locked in each other's grip. When at last we got them apart, blood was running, hair was flying, and both dogs bore scars. Peace after that was impossible; they had but to see each other to growl and stiffen; the question was—Who was the conqueror? Who was to stay and who to go? The decision we came to was base, unjust, and yet, perhaps, excusable. The old dog has had his day, we said, he must give place to the new generation. So old Shag was deposed, and sent to a kind of dignified dower-house at Parson's-green, and the young dog reigned in his stead. Year after year passed, and we never saw the old friend who had known us in the days of our youth; but in the summer holidays he revisited the house in our absence with the caretaker. And so time went on till this last year, which, though we did not know it, was to be the last year of his life. Then, one winter's night, at a time of great sickness and anxiety, a dog was heard barking repeatedly, with the bark of a dog who waits to be let in, outside our kitchen-door. It was many years since that bark had been heard, and only one person in the kitchen was able to recognise it now. She opened the door, and in walked Shag, now almost quite blind and stone deaf, as he had walked in many times before, and, looking neither to right nor left, went to his old corner by the fireside, where he curled up and fell asleep without a sound. If the usurper saw him he slunk guiltily away, for Shag was past fighting for his rights any more. We shall never know—it is one of the many things that we can never know—what strange wave of memory or sympathetic instinct it was that drew Shag from the house where he had lodged for years to seek again the familiar doorstep of his master's home. And it befell that Shag was the last of the family to live in the old house, for it was in crossing the road which leads to the gardens where he was taken for his first walks as a puppy, and bit all the other dogs and frightened all the babies in their perambulators, that he met his death. The blind, deaf dog neither saw nor heard a hansom; and the wheel went over him and ended instantly a life which could not have been happily prolonged. It was better for him to die thus out among the wheels and the horses than to end in a lethal-chamber or be poisoned in a stable-yard.

So we say farewell to a dear and faithful friend, whose virtues we remember—and dogs have few faults.

January 1905

Lines of Inquiry
"On a Faithful Friend"

Given Woolf's avowed purpose to write on her "faithful friend," Shag, it seems a bit unusual that she does not actually focus on him until the second paragraph of the essay. How does the opening paragraph affect your response to the story of Shag's life? How does it shape your impression of Woolf herself? How do you suppose you might respond to Woolf and her treatment of Shag without the first paragraph?

In what specific ways does Woolf portray Shag's "faithful" character? What other characteristics of Shag does she reveal in the course of telling about his life? What aspects of herself does she reveal? What attitude(s) did you develop toward Shag in the process of reading about him? What attitude(s) did you develop towards Woolf? Aside from eulogizing her "faithful friend," what other purposes do you think she achieves in this essay?

Woolf is not the only essayist in this collection to write about dogs and human beings, as you can see by reading Hoagland's "Dogs, and the Tug of Life." Given his approach to understanding dogs, how do you suppose Hoagland would account for Shag's "faithful" behavior? For Shag's relationship with the young sheepdog? For Shag's return home? For Shag's relationship with Woolf? In what respects do you think he would agree—in what respects do you think he would disagree—with Woolf's opening views about the way "we treat our animals"?

Thoreau

A hundred years ago, on July 12, 1817, was born Henry David Thoreau, the son of a pencil maker in Concord, Massachusetts. He has been lucky in his biographers, who have been attracted to him not by his fame so much as by their sympathy with his views, but they have not been able to tell us a great deal about him that we shall not find in the books themselves. His life was not eventful; he had, as he says, "a real genius for staying at home." His mother was quick and voluble, and so fond of solitary rambling that one of her children narrowly escaped coming into the world in an open field. The father, on the other hand, was a "small, quiet, plodding man," with a faculty for making the best lead pencils in America, thanks to a secret of his own for mixing levigated plumbago with fuller's earth and water, rolling it into sheets, cutting it into strips, and burning it. He could at any rate afford, with much economy and a little help, to send his son to Harvard, although Thoreau himself did not attach much importance to this expensive opportunity. It is at Harvard, however, that he first becomes visible to us. A class mate saw much in him as a boy that we recognize later in the grown man, so that instead of a portrait we will quote what was visible about the year 1837 to the penetrating eye of the Rev. John Weiss:

> He was cold and unimpressible. The touch of his hand was moist and indifferent, as if he had taken up something when he saw your hand coming, and caught your grasp on it. How the prominent grey-blue eyes seemed to rove down the path, just in advance of his feet, as his grave Indian stride carried him down to University Hall. He did not care for people; his class-mates seemed very remote. This reverie hung always about him, and not so loosely as the odd garments which the pious household care furnished. Thought had not yet awakened his countenance; it was serene, but rather dull, rather plodding. The lips were not yet firm; there was almost a look of smug satisfaction lurking round their corners. It is plain now that he was preparing to hold his future views with great setness and personal appreciation of their importance. The nose was prominent, but its curve fell forward without firmness over the upper lip, and we remember him as looking very much like some Egyptian sculpture of faces, large-featured, but brooding, immobile, fixed in a mystic egoism. Yet his eyes were sometimes searching, as if he had dropped, or expected to find, something. In fact his eyes seldom left the ground, even in his more earnest conversations with you. . . .

He goes on to speak of the "reserve and inaptness" of Thoreau's life at college.

Clearly the young man thus depicted, whose physical pleasures took the form of walking and camping out, who smoked nothing but "dried lily stems," who venerated Indian relics as much as Greek classics, who in early youth had formed the habit of "settling accounts" with his own mind in a diary, where his thoughts, feelings, studies, and experiences had daily to be passed under review by that Egyptian face and searching eye—clearly this young man was destined to disappoint both parents and teachers and all who wished him to cut a figure in the world and become a person of importance. His first attempt to earn his living in the ordinary way by becoming a schoolmaster was brought to an end by the necessity of flogging his pupils. He proposed to talk morals to them instead. When the committee pointed out that the school would suffer from this "undue leniency" Thoreau solemnly beat six pupils and then resigned, saying that school-keeping "interfered with his arrangements." The arrangements that the penniless young man wished to carry out were probably assignations with certain pine trees, pools, wild animals, and Indian arrowheads in the neighbourhood, which had already laid their commands upon him.

But for a time he was to live in the world of men, at least in that very remarkable section of the world of which Emerson was the centre and which professed the Transcendentalist doctrines. Thoreau took up his lodgings in Emerson's house and very soon became, so his friends said, almost indistinguishable from the prophet himself. If you listened to them both talking with your eyes shut you could not be certain where Emerson left off and Thoreau began ". . . in his manners, in the tones of his voice, in his modes of expression, even in the hesitations and pauses of his speech, he had become the counterpart of Mr Emerson." This may well have been so. The strongest natures, when they are influenced, submit the most unreservedly: it is perhaps a sign of their strength. But that Thoreau lost any of his own force in the process, or took on permanently any colours not natural to himself the readers of his books will certainly deny.

The Transcendentalist movement, like most movements of vigour, represented the effort of one or two remarkable people to shake off the old clothes which had become uncomfortable to them and fit themselves more closely to what now appeared to them to be the realities. The desire for readjustment had, as Lowell has recorded and the Memoirs of Margaret Fuller bear witness, its ridiculous symptoms and its grotesque disciples. But of all the men and women who lived in an age when thought was remoulded in common, we feel that Thoreau was the one who had least to adapt himself, who was by nature most in harmony with the new spirit. He was by birth among those people, as Emerson expresses it, who have "silently given in their several adherence to a new hope, and in all companies do signify a greater trust in the nature and resources of man than the laws of the popular opinion will well allow." There were two ways of life which seemed to the leaders of the movement to give scope for the attainment of these new hopes; one in some cooperative community, such as Brook Farm; the other in solitude with nature. When the time came to make his choice Thoreau decided emphatically in favour of the second. "As for the communities," he wrote in his journal, "I think I had rather keep bachelor's quarters in hell than go to board in heaven." Whatever the theory might be, there was deep in his nature "a singular yearning to all wildness" which would have led him to some such experiment as that recorded in "Walden," whether it seemed good to others or not. In truth he was to put in practice the doctrines of the Transcendentalists more thoroughly than any one of them, and to prove what the resources of man are by putting his entire trust in them. Thus, having reached the age of 27, he chose a piece of land in a wood on the brink of the clear deep green waters of Walden Pond, built a hut with his own hands, reluctantly borrowing an axe for some part of the work, and settled down, as he puts it, "to front only the essential facts of life, and see if I could not learn what it had to teach, and not, when I came to die, discover that I had not lived."

And now we have a chance of getting to know Thoreau as few   5
people are known, even by their friends. Few people, it is safe to say, take such an interest in themselves as Thoreau took in himself; for if we are gifted with an intense egoism we do our best to suffocate it in order to live on decent terms with our neighbours. We are not sufficiently sure of ourselves to break completely with the established order. This was Thoreau's adventure; his books are the record of that experiment and its results. He did everything he could to intensify his own understanding of himself, to foster whatever was peculiar, to isolate himself from contact with any force that might interfere with his immensely valuable gift of personality. It was his sacred duty, not to himself alone but to the world; and a man is scarcely an egoist who is an egoist on so grand a scale. When we read "Walden," the record of his two years in the woods, we have a sense of beholding life through a very powerful magnifying glass. To walk, to eat, to cut up logs, to read a little, to watch the bird on the bough, to cook one's dinner—all these occupations when scraped clean and felt afresh prove wonderfully large and bright. The common things are so strange, the usual sensations so astonishing that to confuse or waste them by living with the herd and adopting habits that suit the greater number is a sin—an act of sacrilege. What has civilization to give, how can luxury improve upon these simple facts? "Simplicity, simplicity, simplicity!" is his cry. "Instead of three meals a day, if it be necessary eat but one; instead of a hundred dishes, five; and reduce other things in proportion."

But the reader may ask, what is the value of simplicity? Is Thoreau's simplicity simplicity for its own sake, and not rather a method of intensification, a way of setting free the delicate and complicated machinery of the soul, so that its results are the reverse of simple? The most remarkable men tend to discard luxury because they find that it hampers the play of what is much more valuable to them. Thoreau himself was an extremely complex human being, and he certainly did not achieve simplicity by living for two years in a hut and cooking his own dinner. His achievement was rather to lay bare what was within him—to let life take its own way unfettered by artificial constraints. "I did not wish to live what was not life, living is so dear; nor did I wish to practice resignation, unless it was quite necessary. I wanted to live deep and suck out all the marrow of life. . . ." "Walden"—all his books, indeed—are packed with subtle, conflicting, and very fruitful discoveries. They are not written to prove something in the end. They are written as the Indians turn down twigs to mark their path through the forest. He cuts his way through life as if no one had ever taken that road before, leaving these signs for those who come after, should they care to see which way he went. But he did not wish to leave ruts behind him, and to follow is not an easy process. We can never lull our attention asleep in reading Thoreau by the certainty that we have now grasped his theme and can trust our guide to be consistent. We must always be ready to try something fresh; we must always be prepared for the shock of facing one of those thoughts in the original which we have known all our lives in reproductions. "All health and success does me good, however far off and withdrawn it may appear; all disease and failure helps to make me sad and do me evil, however much sympathy it may have with me or I with it." "Distrust all enterprises that require new clothes." "You must have a genius for charity as well as for anything else." That is a handful, plucked almost at random, and of course there are plenty of wholesome platitudes.

As he walked his woods, or sat for hours almost motionless like the sphinx of college days upon a rock watching the birds, Thoreau defined his own position to the world not only with unflinching honesty, but with a glow of rapture at his heart. He seems to hug his own happiness. Those years were full of revelations—so independent of other men did he find himself, so perfectly equipped by nature not only to keep himself housed, fed, and clothed, but also superbly entertained without any help from society. Society suffered a good many blows from his hand. He sets down his complaints so squarely that we cannot help suspecting that society might one of these days have come to terms with so noble a rebel. He did not want churches or armies, post-offices or newspapers, and very consistently he refused to pay his tithes and went into prison rather than pay his poll tax. All getting together in crowds for doing good or procuring pleasure was an intolerable infliction to him. Philanthropy was one of the sacrifices, he said, that he had made to a sense of duty. Politics seemed to him "unreal, incredible, insignificant," and most revolutions not so important as the drying up of a river or the death of a pine. He wanted only to be left alone tramping the woods in his suit of Vermont grey, unhampered even by those two pieces of limestone which lay upon his desk until they proved guilty of collecting the dust, and were at once thrown out of the window.

And yet this egoist was the man who sheltered runaway slaves in his hut; this hermit was the first man to speak out in public in defence of John Brown; this self-centred solitary could neither sleep nor think when Brown lay in prison. The truth is that anyone who reflects as much and as deeply as Thoreau reflected about life and conduct is possessed of an abnormal sense of responsibility to his kind, whether he chooses to live in a wood or to become President of the Republic. Thirty volumes of diaries which he would condense from time to time with infinite care into little books prove, moreover, that the independent man who professed to care so little for his fellows was possessed with an intense desire to communicate with them. "I would fain," he writes, "communicate the wealth of my life to men, would really give them what is most precious in my gift. . . . I have no private good unless it be my peculiar ability to serve the public. . . . I wish to communicate those parts of my life which I would gladly live again." No one can read him and remain unaware of this wish. And yet it is a question whether he ever succeeded in imparting his wealth, in sharing his life. When we have read his strong and noble books, in which every word is sincere, every sentence wrought as well as the writer knows how, we are left with a strange feeling of distance; here is a man who is trying to communicate but who cannot do it. His eyes are on the ground or perhaps on the horizon. He is never speaking directly to us; he is speaking partly to himself and partly to something mystic beyond our sight. "Says I to myself," he writes, "should be the motto to my journal," and all his books are journals. Other men and women were wonderful and very beautiful, but they were distant; they were different; he found it very hard to understand their ways. They were as "curious to him as if they had been prairie dogs." All human intercourse was infinitely difficult; the distance between one friend and another was unfathomable; human relationships were very precarious and terribly apt to end in disappointment. But, although concerned and willing to do what he could short of lowering his ideals, Thoreau was aware that the difficulty was one that could not be overcome by taking pains. He was made differently from other people. "If a man does not keep pace with his companions, perhaps it is because he hears a different drummer. Let him step to the music which he hears, however measured or far away." He was a wild man, and he would never submit to be a tame one. And for us here lies his peculiar charm. He hears a different drummer. He is a man into whom nature has breathed other instincts than ours, to whom she has whispered, one may guess, some of her secrets.

"It appears to be a law," he says, "that you cannot have a deep sympathy with both man and nature. Those qualities which bring you near to the one estrange you from the other." Perhaps that is true. The greatest passion of his life was his passion for nature. It was more than a passion, indeed; it was an affinity; and in this he differs from men like White and Jefferies. He was gifted, we are told, with an extraordinary keenness of the senses; he could see and hear what other men could not; his touch was so delicate that he could pick up a dozen pencils accurately from a box holding a bushel; he could find his way alone through thick woods at night. He could lift a fish out of the stream with his hands; he could charm a wild squirrel to nestle in his coat; he could sit so still that the animals went on with their play round him. He knew the look of the country so intimately that if he had waked in a meadow he could have told the time of year within a day or two from the flowers at his feet. Nature had made it easy for him to pick up a living without effort. He was so skilled with his hands that by labouring forty days he could live at leisure for the rest of the year. We scarcely know whether to call him the last of an older race of men, or the first of one that is to come. He had the toughness, the stoicism, the unspoilt senses of an Indian, combined with the self-consciousness, the exacting discontent, the susceptibility of the most modern. At times he seems to reach beyond our human powers in what he perceives upon the horizon of humanity. No philanthropist ever hoped more of mankind, or set higher and nobler tasks before him, and those whose ideal of passion and of service is the loftiest are those who have the greatest capacities for giving, although life may not ask of them all that they can give, and forces them to hold in reserve rather than to lavish. However much Thoreau had been able to do he would still have seen possibilities beyond; he would always have remained, in one sense, unsatisfied. That is one of the reasons why he is able to be the companion of a younger generation.

He died when he was in the full tide of life, and had to endure long 10
illness within doors. But from nature he had learnt both silence and stoicism. He had never spoken of the things that had moved him most in his private fortunes. But from nature, too, he had learnt to be content, not thoughtlessly or selfishly content, and certainly not with resignation, but with a healthy trust in the wisdom of nature, and in nature, as he says, there is no sadness. "I am enjoying existence as much as ever," he wrote from his deathbed, "and regret nothing." He was talking to himself of moose and Indian when, without a struggle, he died.

July 1917

Lines of Inquiry
"Thoreau"

In the opening paragraph of her essay, Woolf notes that Thoreau's biographers "have not been able to tell us a great deal about him" that we cannot find in his own writing, yet later in that same paragraph she quotes extensively from a biographical description of him. Why do you suppose Woolf gives so much space to that description of Thoreau, whereas throughout the remainder of her essay she relies almost completely on passages from Thoreau himself? What qualities does that early portrait of Thoreau reveal about him? What qualities do the passages from Thoreau's own writing reveal about him?

Early on in her piece, Woolf claims that Thoreau's "life was not eventful." Why, then, is she interested in telling us so many notable things about his life—for example, that "he sheltered runaway slaves in his hut," that he "was the first man to speak out in public in defence of John Brown," that "he could lift a fish out of the stream with his hands," and that "he could charm a wild squirrel to nestle in his coat"? Why is she interested in our "getting to know Thoreau"? Why doesn't she confine herself to explaining his ideas?

In this essay, as in "The Death of the Moth" and "On a Faithful Friend," Woolf displays her skill as a biographical essayist—her ability to sketch the life and death of someone or something in a significant and suggestive way. In what ways is her sketch of Thoreau similar to those of the moth and of Shag? In what ways is it different? How does she manage to make each sketch significant and suggestive?

Women and Fiction

The title of this article can be read in two ways: it may allude to women and the fiction that they write, or to women and the fiction that is written about them. The ambiguity is intentional, for in dealing with women as writers, as much elasticity as possible is desirable; it is necessary to leave oneself room to deal with other things besides their work, so much has that work been influenced by conditions that have nothing whatever to do with art.

The most superficial inquiry into women's writing instantly raises a host of questions. Why, we ask at once, was there no continuous writing done by women before the eighteenth century? Why did they then write almost as habitually as men, and in the course of that writing produce, one after another, some of the classics of English fiction? And why did their art then, and why to some extent does their art still, take the form of fiction?

A little thought will show us that we are asking questions to which we shall get, as answer, only further fiction. The answer lies at present locked in old diaries, stuffed away in old drawers, half-obliterated in the memories of the aged. It is to be found in the lives of the obscure—in those almost unlit corridors of history where the figures of generations of women are so dimly, so fitfully perceived. For very little is known about women. The history of England is the history of the male line, not of the female. Of our fathers we know always some fact, some distinction. They were soldiers or they were sailors; they filled that office or they made that law. But of our mothers, our grandmothers, our great-grandmothers, what remains? Nothing but a tradition. One was beautiful; one was red-haired; one was kissed by a Queen. We know nothing of them except their names and the dates of their marriages and the number of children they bore.

Thus, if we wish to know why at any particular time women did this or that, why they wrote nothing, why on the other hand they wrote masterpieces, it is extremely difficult to tell. Anyone who should seek among those old papers, who should turn history wrong side out and so construct a faithful picture of the daily life of the ordinary woman in Shakespeare's time, in Milton's time, in Johnson's time, would not only write a book of astonishing interest, but would furnish the critic with a weapon which he now lacks. The extraordinary woman depends on the ordinary woman. It is only when we know what were the conditions of the average woman's life—the number of her children, whether she had money of her own, if she had a room to herself, whether she had help in bringing up her family, if she had servants, whether part of the housework was her task—it is only when we can measure the way of life and the experience of life made possible to the ordinary woman that we can account for the success or failure of the extraordinary woman as a writer.

Strange spaces of silence seem to separate one period of activity   5 from another. There was Sappho and a little group of women all writing poetry on a Greek island six hundred years before the birth of Christ. They fall silent. Then about the year 1000 we find a certain court lady, the Lady Murasaki, writing a very long and beautiful novel in Japan. But in England in the sixteenth century, when the dramatists and poets were most active, the women were dumb. Elizabethan literature is exclusively masculine. Then, at the end of the eighteenth century and in the beginning of the nineteenth, we find women again writing—this time in England—with extraordinary frequency and success.

Law and custom were of course largely responsible for these strange intermissions of silence and speech. When a woman was liable, as she was in the fifteenth century, to be beaten and flung about the room if she did not marry the man of her parents' choice, the spiritual atmosphere was not favourable to the production of works of art. When she was married without her own consent to a man who thereupon became her lord and master, "so far at least as law and custom could make him," as she was in the time of the Stuarts, it is likely she had little time for writing, and less encouragement. The immense effect of environment and suggestion upon the mind, we in our psychoanalytical age are beginning to realize. Again, with memoirs and letters to help us, we are beginning to understand how abnormal is the effort needed to produce a work of art, and what shelter and what support the mind of the artist requires. Of those facts the lives and letters of men like Keats and Carlyle and Flaubert assure us.

Thus it is clear that the extraordinary outburst of fiction in the beginning of the nineteenth century in England was heralded by innumerable slight changes in law and customs and manners. And women of the nineteenth century had some leisure; they had some education. It was no longer the exception for women of the middle and upper classes to choose their own husbands. And it is significant that of the four great women novelists—Jane Austen, Emily Brontë, Charlotte Brontë, and George Eliot—not one had a child, and two were unmarried.

Yet, though it is clear that the ban upon writing had been removed, there was still, it would seem, considerable pressure upon women to write novels. No four women can have been more unlike in genius and character than these four. Jane Austen can have had nothing in common with George Eliot; George Eliot was the direct opposite of Emily Brontë. Yet all were trained for the same profession; all, when they wrote, wrote novels.

Fiction was, as fiction still is, the easiest thing for a woman to write. Nor is it difficult to find the reason. A novel is the least concentrated form of art. A novel can be taken up or put down more easily than a play or a poem. George Eliot left her work to nurse her father. Charlotte Brontë put down her pen to pick the eyes out of the potatoes. And living as she did in the common sitting-room, surrounded by people, a woman was trained to use her mind in observation and upon the analysis of character. She was trained to be a novelist and not to be a poet.

Even in the nineteenth century, a woman lived almost solely in her home and her emotions. And those nineteenth-century novels, remarkable as they were, were profoundly influenced by the fact that the women who wrote them were excluded by their sex from certain kinds of experience. That experience has a great influence upon fiction is indisputable. The best part of Conrad's novels, for instance, would be destroyed if it had been impossible for him to be a sailor. Take away all that Tolstoi knew of war as a soldier, of life and society as a rich young man whose education admitted him to all sorts of experience, and *War and Peace* would be incredibly impoverished.

Yet *Pride and Prejudice, Wuthering Heights, Villette,* and *Middlemarch* were written by women from whom was forcibly withheld all experience save that which could be met with in a middle-class drawing-room. No first-hand experience of war or seafaring or politics or business was possible for them. Even their emotional life was strictly regulated by law and custom. When George Eliot ventured to live with Mr. Lewes without being his wife, public opinion was scandalized. Under its pressure she withdrew into a suburban seclusion which, inevitably, had the worst possible effects upon her work. She wrote that unless people asked of their own accord to come and see her, she never invited them. At the same time, on the other side of Europe, Tolstoi was living a free life as a soldier, with men and women of all classes, for which nobody censured him and from which his novels drew much of their astonishing breadth and vigour.

But the novels of women were not affected only by the necessarily narrow range of the writer's experience. They showed, at least in the nineteenth century, another characteristic which may be traced to the writer's sex. In *Middlemarch* and in *Jane Eyre* we are conscious not merely of the writer's character, as we are conscious of the character of Charles Dickens, but we are conscious of a woman's presence—of someone resenting the treatment of her sex and pleading for its rights. This brings into women's writing an element which is entirely absent from a man's, unless, indeed, he happens to be a working-man, a negro, or one who for some other reason is conscious of disability. It introduces a distortion and is frequently the cause of weakness. The desire to plead some personal cause or to make a character the mouthpiece of some personal

10

discontent or grievance always has a distressing effect, as if the spot at which the reader's attention is directed were suddenly twofold instead of single.

The genius of Jane Austen and Emily Brontë is never more convincing than in their power to ignore such claims and solicitations and to hold on their way unperturbed by scorn or censure. But it needed a very serene or a very powerful mind to resist the temptation to anger. The ridicule, the censure, the assurance of inferiority in one form or another which were lavished upon women who practised an art, provoked such reactions naturally enough. One sees the effect in Charlotte Brontë's indignation, in George Eliot's resignation. Again and again one finds it in the work of the lesser women writers—in their choice of a subject, in their unnatural self-assertiveness, in their unnatural docility. Moreover, insincerity leaks in almost unconsciously. They adopt a view in deference to authority. The vision becomes too masculine or it becomes too feminine; it loses its perfect integrity and, with that, its most essential quality as a work of art.

The great change that has crept into women's writing is, it would seem, a change of attitude. The woman writer is no longer bitter. She is no longer angry. She is no longer pleading and protesting as she writes. We are approaching, if we have not yet reached, the time when her writing will have little or no foreign influence to disturb it. She will be able to concentrate upon her vision without distraction from outside. The aloofness that was once within the reach of genius and originality is only now coming within the reach of ordinary women. Therefore the average novel by a woman is far more genuine and far more interesting to-day than it was a hundred or even fifty years ago.

But it is still true that before a woman can write exactly as she 15 wishes to write, she has many difficulties to face. To begin with, there is the technical difficulty—so simple, apparently; in reality, so baffling—that the very form of the sentence does not fit her. It is a sentence made by men; it is too loose, too heavy, too pompous for a woman's use. Yet in a novel, which covers so wide a stretch of ground, an ordinary and usual type of sentence has to be found to carry the reader on easily and naturally from one end of the book to the other. And this a woman must make for herself, altering and adapting the current sentence until she writes one that takes the natural shape of her thought without crushing or distorting it.

But that, after all, is only a means to an end, and the end is still to be reached only when a woman has the courage to surmount opposition and the determination to be true to herself. For a novel, after all, is a statement about a thousand different objects—human, natural, divine; it is an attempt to relate them to each other. In every novel of merit these different elements are held in place by the force of the writer's vision. But they have another order also, which is the order imposed upon them by convention. And as men are the arbiters of that convention, as they have established an order of values in life, so too, since fiction is largely based on life, these values prevail there also to a very great extent.

It is probable, however, that both in life and in art the values of a woman are not the values of a man. Thus, when a woman comes to write a novel, she will find that she is perpetually wishing to alter the established values—to make serious what appears insignificant to a man, and trivial what is to him important. And for that, of course, she will be criticized; for the critic of the opposite sex will be genuinely puzzled and surprised by an attempt to alter the current scale of values, and will see in it not merely a difference of view, but a view that is weak, or trivial, or sentimental, because it differs from his own.

But here, too, women are coming to be more independent of opinion. They are beginning to respect their own sense of values. And for this reason the subject matter of their novels begins to show certain changes. They are less interested, it would seem, in themselves; on the other hand, they are more interested in other women. In the early nineteenth century, women's novels were largely autobiographical. One of the motives that led them to write was the desire to expose their own suffering, to plead their own cause. Now that this desire is no longer so urgent, women are beginning to explore their own sex, to write of women as women have never been written of before; for of course, until very lately, women in literature were the creation of men.

Here again there are difficulties to overcome for, if one may generalize, not only do women submit less readily to observation than men, but their lives are far less tested and examined by the ordinary processes of life. Often nothing tangible remains of a woman's day. The food that has been cooked is eaten; the children that have been nursed have gone out into the world. Where does the accent fall? What is the salient point for the novelist to seize upon? It is difficult to say. Her life has an anonymous character which is baffling and puzzling in the extreme. For the first time, this dark country is beginning to be explored in fiction; and at the same moment a woman has also to record the changes in women's minds and habits which the opening of the professions has introduced. She has to observe how their lives are ceasing to run underground; she has to discover what new colours and shadows are showing in them now that they are exposed to the outer world.

If, then, one should try to sum up the character of women's fiction 20 at the present moment, one would say that it is courageous; it is sincere; it keeps closely to what women feel. It is not bitter. It does not insist upon its femininity. But at the same time, a woman's book is not written as a man would write it. These qualities are much commoner than they were, and they give even to second- and third-rate work the value of truth and the interest of sincerity.

But in addition to these good qualities, there are two that call for a word more of discussion. The change which has turned the English woman from a nondescript influence, fluctuating and vague, to a voter, a wage-earner, a responsible citizen, has given her both in her life and in her art a turn toward the impersonal. Her relations now are not only emotional; they are intellectual, they are political. The old system which condemned her to squint askance at things through the eyes or through the interests of husband or brother, has given place to the direct and practical interests of one who must act for herself, and not merely influence the acts of others. Hence her attention is being directed away from the personal centre which engaged it exclusively in the past to the impersonal, and her novels naturally become more critical of society, and less analytical of individual lives.

We may expect that the office of gadfly to the state, which has been so far a male prerogative, will now be discharged by women also. Their novels will deal with social evils and remedies. Their men and women will not be observed wholly in relation to each other emotionally, but as they cohere and clash in groups and classes and races. That is one change of some importance. But there is another more interesting to those who prefer the butterfly to the gadfly—that is to say, the artist to the reformer. The greater impersonality of women's lives will encourage the poetic spirit, and it is in poetry that women's fiction is still weakest. It will lead them to be less absorbed in facts and no longer content to record with astonishing acuteness the minute details which fall under their own observation. They will look beyond the personal and political relationships to the wider questions which the poet tries to solve—of our destiny and the meaning of life.

The basis of the poetic attitude is of course largely founded upon material things. It depends upon leisure, and a little money, and the chance which money and leisure give to observe impersonally and dispassionately. With money and leisure at their service, women will naturally occupy themselves more than has hitherto been possible with the craft of letters. They will make a fuller and a more subtle use of the instrument of writing. Their technique will become bolder and richer.

In the past, the virtue of women's writing often lay in its divine spontaneity, like that of the blackbird's song or the thrush's. It was untaught; it was from the heart. But it was also, and much more often, chattering and garrulous—mere talk spilt over paper and left to dry in pools and blots. In future, granted time and books and a little space in the house for herself, literature will become for women, as for men, an art to be studied. Women's gift will be trained and strengthened. The novel will cease to be the dumping-ground for the personal emotions. It will become, more than at present, a work of art like any other, and its resources and its limitations will be explored.

From this it is a short step to the practice of the sophisticated arts, 25 hitherto so little practised by women—to the writing of essays and criticism, of history and biography. And that, too, if we are considering the novel, will be of advantage; for besides improving the quality of the novel itself, it will draw off the aliens who have been attracted to fiction by its accessibility while their hearts lay elsewhere. Thus will the novel be rid of those excrescences of history and fact which, in our time, have made it so shapeless.

So, if we may prophesy, women in time to come will write fewer novels, but better novels; and not novels only, but poetry and criticism and history. But in this, to be sure, one is looking ahead to that golden, that perhaps fabulous, age when women will have what has so long been denied them—leisure, and money, and a room to themselves.

March 1929

Lines of Inquiry
"Women and Fiction"

In the second paragraph of her essay, Woolf asks a series of pointed questions about "women's writing," but then at the opening of her third paragraph she says "that we are asking questions to which we shall get, as answer, only further fiction." What do you think she means by describing the answers as "only further fiction"? During most of the essay that follows, Woolf gives herself over to answering those very same questions. In what respects do her answers seem to be only further fiction? In what respects do they seem to be something other than fiction, such as fact, or inference, or surmise, or common sense? In what ways does she manage to give her answers an air of credibility?

In paragraph 6, Woolf notes "how abnormal is the effort needed to produce a work of art." Later in the same sentence she speaks about the "shelter" and "support the mind of the artist requires," as if to suggest that these needs are also "abnormal." Why do you suppose Woolf believes that such an abnormal state of affairs is necessary to "produce a work of art"? Why does she believe that this abnormal situation has normally been available to men, but not to women? What kind of social and economic changes would be necessary to make this abnormal state of affairs available to women?

In her final paragraph, Woolf imagines a golden age, when women write "not novels only, but poetry and criticism and history." Given the careers of the recent women writers represented in this collection, and any others you may be familiar with, how do you think Woolf would characterize the current situation? What do you think about the current situation for women's writing?

The Modern Essay

As Mr. Rhys truly says, it is unnecessary to go profoundly into the history and origin of the essay—whether it derives from Socrates or Siranney the Persian—since, like all living things, its present is more important than its past. Moreover, the family is widely spread; and while some of its representatives have risen in the world and wear their coronets with the best, others pick up a precarious living in the gutter near Fleet Street. The form, too, admits variety. The essay can be short or long, serious or trifling, about God and Spinoza, or about turtles and Cheapside. But as we turn over the pages of these five little volumes,[1] containing essays written between 1870 and 1920, certain principles appear to control the chaos, and we detect in the short period under review something like the progress of history.

Of all forms of literature, however, the essay is the one which least calls for the use of long words. The principle which controls it is simply that it should give pleasure; the desire which impels us when we take it from the shelf is simply to receive pleasure. Everything in an essay must be subdued to that end. It should lay us under a spell with its first word, and we should only wake, refreshed, with its last. In the interval we may pass through the most various experiences of amusement, surprise, interest, indignation; we may soar to the heights of fantasy with Lamb or plunge to the depths of wisdom with Bacon, but we must never be roused. The essay must lap us about and draw its curtain across the world.

So great a feat is seldom accomplished, though the fault may well be as much on the reader's side as on the writer's. Habit and lethargy have dulled his palate. A novel has a story, a poem rhyme; but what art can the essayist use in these short lengths of prose to sting us wide awake and fix us in a trance which is not sleep but rather an intensification of life—a basking, with every faculty alert, in the sun of pleasure? He must know—that is the first essential—how to write. His learning may be as profound as Mark Pattison's, but in an essay it must be so fused by the magic of writing that not a fact juts out, not a dogma tears the surface of the texture. Macaulay in one way, Froude in another, did this superbly over and over again. They have blown more knowledge into us in the course of one essay than the innumerable chapters of a hundred text-books. But when Mark Pattison has to tell

---

[1] *Modern English Essays,* edited by Ernest Rhys, five volumes (Dent).

us, in the space of thirty-five little pages, about Montaigne, we feel that he had not previously assimilated M. Grün. M. Grün was a gentleman who once wrote a bad book. M. Grün and his book should have been embalmed for our perpetual delight in amber. But the process is fatiguing; it requires more time and perhaps more temper than Pattison had at his command. He served M. Grün up raw, and he remains a crude berry among the cook meats, upon which our teeth must grate for ever. Something of the sort applies to Matthew Arnold and a certain translator of Spinoza. Literal truth-telling and finding fault with a culprit for his good are out of place in an essay, where everything should be for our good and rather for eternity than for the March number of the *Fortnightly Review*. But if the voice of the scold should never be heard in this narrow plot, there is another voice which is as a plague of locusts—the voice of a man stumbling drowsily among loose words, clutching aimlessly at vague ideas, the voice, for example, of Mr. Hutton in the following passage:

> Add to this that his married life was very brief, only seven years and a half, being unexpectedly cut short, and that his passionate reverence for his wife's memory and genius—in his own words, "a religion"—was one which, as he must have been perfectly sensible, he could not make to appear otherwise than extravagant, not to say an hallucination, in the eyes of the rest of mankind, and yet that he was possessed by an irresistible yearning to attempt to embody it in all the tender and enthusiastic hyperbole of which it is so pathetic to find a man who gained his fame by his "dry-light" a master, and it is impossible not to feel that the human incidents in Mr. Mill's career are very sad.

A book could take that blow, but it sinks an essay. A biography in two volumes is indeed the proper depositary; for there, where the licence is so much wider, and hints and glimpses of outside things make part of the feast (we refer to the old type of Victorian volume), these yawns and stretches hardly matter, and have indeed some positive value of their own. But that value, which is contributed by the reader, perhaps illicitly, in his desire to get as much into the book from all possible sources as he can, must be ruled out here.

There is no room for the impurities of literature in an essay. Somehow or other, by dint of labour or bounty of nature, or both combined, the essay must be pure—pure like water or pure like wine, but pure from dullness, deadness, and deposits of extraneous matter. Of all writers in the first volume, Walter Pater best achieves this arduous task, because before setting out to write his essay ("Notes on Leonardo da Vinci") he has somehow contrived to get his material fused. He is a learned man, but it is not knowledge of Leonardo that remains with us, but a vision, such as we get in a good novel where everything contributes to bring the writer's conception as a whole before us. Only here, in the essay, where the bounds are so strict and facts have to be used in their nakedness, the true writer like Walter Pater makes these limitations yield their own quality. Truth will give it authority; from its narrow limits he will get shape and intensity; and then there is no more fitting place for some of those ornaments which the old writers loved and we, by calling them ornaments, presumably despise. Nowadays nobody would have the courage to embark on the once famous description of Leonardo's lady who has

> learned the secrets of the grave; and has been a diver in deep seas and keeps their fallen day about her; and trafficked for strange webs with Eastern merchants; and, as Leda, was the mother of Helen of Troy, and, as Saint Anne, the mother of Mary . . .

The passage is too thumb-marked to slip naturally into the context. But when we come unexpectedly upon "the smiling of women and the motion of great waters," or upon "full of the refinement of the dead, in sad, earth-coloured raiment, set with pale stones," we suddenly remember that we have ears and we have eyes, and that the English language fills a long array of stout volumes with innumerable words, many of which are of more than one syllable. The only living Englishman who ever looks into these volumes is, of course, a gentleman of Polish extraction. But doubtless our abstention saves us much gush, much rhetoric, much high-stepping and cloud-prancing, and for the sake of the prevailing sobriety and hard-headedness we should be willing to barter the splendour of Sir Thomas Browne and the vigour of Swift.

Yet, if the essay admits more properly than biography or fiction of sudden boldness and metaphor, and can be polished till every atom of its surface shines, there are dangers in that too. We are soon in sight of ornament. Soon the current, which is the life-blood of literature, runs slow; and instead of sparkling and flashing or moving with a quieter impulse which has a deeper excitement, words coagulate together in frozen sprays which, like the grapes on a Christmas-tree, glitter for a single night, but are dusty and garish the day after. The temptation to decorate is great where the theme may be of the slightest. What is there to interest another in the fact that one has enjoyed a walking tour, or has amused oneself by rambling down Cheapside and looking at the turtles in Mr. Sweeting's shop window? Stevenson and Samuel Butler chose very different methods of exciting our interest in these domestic themes. Stevenson, of course, trimmed and polished and set out his matter in the traditional eighteenth-century form. It is admirably done, but we cannot help feeling anxious, as the essay proceeds, lest the material may give out under the craftsman's fingers. The ingot is so small, the manipulation so incessant. And perhaps that is why the peroration—

> To sit still and contemplate—to remember the faces of women without desire, to be pleased by the great deeds of men without envy, to be everything and everywhere in sympathy and yet content to remain where and what you are—

has the sort of insubstantiality which suggests that by the time he got to the end he had left himself nothing solid to work with. Butler adopted the very opposite method. Think your own thoughts, he seems to say, and speak them as plainly as you can. These turtles in the shop window which appear to leak out of their shells through heads and feet suggest a fatal faithfulness to a fixed idea. And so, striding unconcernedly from one idea to the next, we traverse a large stretch of ground; observe that a wound in the solicitor is a very serious thing; that Mary Queen of Scots wears surgical boots and is subject to fits near the Horse Shoe in Tottenham Court Road; take it for granted that no one really cares about Aeschylus; and so, with many amusing anecdotes and some profound reflections, reach the peroration, which is that, as he had been told not to see more in Cheapside than he could get into twelve pages of the *Universal Review,* he had better stop. And yet obviously Butler is at least as careful of our pleasure as Stevenson; and to write like oneself and call it not writing is a much harder exercise in style than to write like Addison and call it writing well.

But, however much they differ individually, the Victorian essayists yet had something in common. They wrote at greater length than is now usual, and they wrote for a public which had not only time to sit down to its magazine seriously, but a high, if peculiarly Victorian, standard of culture by which to judge it. It was worth while to speak out upon serious matters in an essay; and there was nothing absurd in writing as well as one possibly could when, in a month or two, the same public which had welcomed the essay in a magazine would carefully read it once more in a book. But a change came from a small audience of cultivated people to a larger audience of people who were not quite so cultivated. The change was not altogether for the worse. In volume III we find Mr. Birrell and Mr. Beerbohm. It might even be said that there was a reversion to the classic type, and that the essay by losing its size and something of its sonority was approaching more nearly the essay of Addison and Lamb. At any rate, there is a great gulf between Mr. Birrell on Carlyle and the essay which one may suppose that Carlyle would have written upon Mr. Birrell. There is little similarity between *A Cloud of Pinafores,* by Max Beerbohm, and *A Cynic's Apology,* by Leslie Stephen. But the essay is alive; there is no reason to despair. As the conditions change so the essayist, most sensitive of all plants to public opinion, adapts himself, and if he is good makes the best of the change, and if he is bad the worst. Mr. Birrell is certainly good; and so we find that, though he has dropped a considerable amount of weight, his attack is much more direct and his movement more supple. But what did Mr. Beerbohm give to the essay and what did he take from it? That is a much more complicated question, for here we have an essayist who has concentrated on the work and is without doubt the prince of his profession.

What Mr. Beerbohm gave was, of course, himself. This presence, which has haunted the essay fitfully from the time of Montaigne, had been in exile since the death of Charles Lamb. Matthew Arnold was never to his readers Matt, nor Walter Pater affectionately abbreviated in a thousand homes to Wat. They gave us much, but that they did not give. Thus, some time in the 'nineties, it must have surprised readers accustomed to exhortation, information, and denunciation to find themselves familiarly addressed by a voice which seemed to belong to a man no larger than themselves. He was affected by private joys and sorrows, and had no gospel to preach and no learning to impart. He was himself, simply and directly, and himself he has remained. Once again we have an essayist capable of using the essayist's most proper but most dangerous and delicate tool. He has brought personality into literature, not unconsciously and impurely, but so consciously and purely that we do not know whether there is any relation between Max the essayist and Mr. Beerbohm the man. We only know that the spirit of personality permeates every word that he writes. The triumph is the triumph of style. For it is only by knowing how to write that you can make use in literature of your self; that self which, while it is essential to literature, is also its most dangerous antagonist. Never to be yourself and yet always—that is the problem. Some of the essayists in Mr. Rhys' collection, to be frank, have not altogether succeeded in solving it. We are nauseated by the sight of trivial personalities decomposing in the eternity of print. As talk, no doubt, it was charming, and certainly the writer is a good fellow to meet over a bottle of beer. But literature is stern; it is no use being charming, virtuous, or even learned and brilliant into the bargain, unless, she seems to reiterate, you fulfil her first condition—to know how to write.

This art is possessed to perfection by Mr. Beerbohm. But he has not searched the dictionary for polysyllables. He has not moulded firm periods or seduced our ears with intricate cadences and strange melodies. Some of his companions—Henley and Stevenson, for example—are momentarily more impressive. But *A Cloud of Pinafores* had in it that indescribable inequality, stir, and final expressiveness which belong to life and to life alone. You have not finished with it because you have read it, any more than friendship is ended because it is time to part. Life wells up and alters and adds. Even things in a book-case change if they are alive; we find ourselves wanting to meet them again; we find them altered. So we look back upon essay after essay by Mr. Beerbohm, knowing that, come September or May, we shall sit down with them and talk. Yet it is true that the essayist is the most sensitive of all writers to public opinion. The drawing-room is the place where a great deal of reading is done nowadays, and the essays of Mr. Beerbohm lie, with an exquisite appreciation of all that the position exacts, upon the drawing-room table. There is no gin about; no strong tobacco; no puns, drunkenness, or insanity. Ladies and gentlemen talk together, and some things, of course, are not said.

But if it would be foolish to attempt to confine Mr. Beerbohm to one room, it would be still more foolish, unhappily, to make him, the artist, the man who gives us only his best, the representative of our age. There are no essays by Mr. Beerbohm in the fourth or fifth volumes of the present collection. His age seems already a little distant, and the drawing-room table, as it recedes, begins to look rather like an altar where, once upon a time, people deposited offerings—fruit from their own orchards, gifts carved with their own hands. Now once more the conditions have changed. The public needs essays as much as ever, and perhaps even more. The demand for the light middle not exceeding fifteen hundred words, or in special cases seventeen hundred and fifty, much exceeds the supply. Where Lamb wrote one essay and Max perhaps writes two, Mr. Belloc at a rough computation produces three hundred and sixty-five. They are very short, it is true. Yet with what dexterity the practised essayist will utilise his space—beginning as close to the top of the sheet as possible, judging precisely how far to go, when to turn, and how, without sacrificing a hair's breadth of paper, to wheel about and alight accurately upon the last word his editor allows! As a feat of skill it is well worth watching. But the personality upon which Mr. Belloc, like Mr. Beerbohm, depends suffers in the process. It comes to us not with the natural richness of the speaking voice, but strained and thin and full of mannerisms and affectations, like the voice of a man shouting through a megaphone to a crowd on a windy day. "Little friends, my readers," he says in the essay called "An Unknown Country," and he goes on to tell us how—

> There was a shepherd the other day at Findon Fair who had come from the east by Lewes with sheep, and who had in his eyes that reminiscence of horizons which makes the eyes of shepherds and of mountaineers different from the eyes of other men. . . . I went with him to hear what he had to say, for shepherds talk quite differently from other men.

Happily this shepherd had little to say, even under the stimulus of the inevitable mug of beer, about the Unknown Country, for the only remark that he did make proves him either a minor poet, unfit for the care of sheep, or Mr. Belloc himself masquerading with a fountain pen. That is the penalty which the habitual essayist must now be prepared to face. He must masquerade. He cannot afford the time either to be himself or to be other people. He must skim the surface of thought and dilute the strength of personality. He must give us a worn weekly halfpenny instead of a solid sovereign once a year.

But it is not Mr. Belloc only who has suffered from the prevailing conditions. The essays which bring the collection to the year 1920 may not be the best of their authors' work, but, if we except writers like Mr. Conrad and Mr. Hudson, who have strayed into essay writing accidentally, and concentrate upon those who write essays habitually, we shall find them a good deal affected by the change in their circumstances. To write weekly, to write daily, to write shortly, to write for busy people catching trains in the morning or for tired people coming home in the evening, is a heartbreaking task for men who know good writing from bad. They do it, but instinctively draw out of harm's way anything precious that might be damaged by contact with the public, or anything sharp that might irritate its skin. And so, if one reads Mr. Lucas, Mr. Lynd, or Mr. Squire in the bulk, one feels that a common greyness silvers everything. They are as far removed from the extravagant beauty of Walter Pater as they are from the intemperate candour of Leslie Stephen. Beauty and courage are dangerous spirits to battle in a column and a half; and thought, like a brown paper parcel in a waistcoat pocket, has a way of spoiling the symmetry of an article. It is a kind, tired, apathetic world for which they write, and the marvel is that they never cease to attempt, at least, to write well.

But there is no need to pity Mr. Clutton Brock for this change in the essayist's conditions. He has clearly made the best of his circumstances and not the worst. One hesitates even to say that he has had to make any conscious effort in the matter, so naturally has he effected the transition from the private essayist to the public, from the drawing-room to the Albert Hall. Paradoxically enough, the shrinkage in size has brought about a corresponding expansion of individuality. We have no longer the "I" of Max and of Lamb, but the "we" of public bodies and other sublime personages. It is "we" who go to hear the *Magic Flute;* "we" who ought to profit by it; "we," in some mysterious way, who, in our corporate capacity, once upon a time actually wrote it. For music and literature and art must submit to the same generalisation or they will not carry to the farthest recesses of the Albert Hall. That the voice of Mr. Clutton Brock, so sincere and so disinterested, carries such a distance and reaches so many without pandering to the weakness of the mass or its passions must be a matter of legitimate satisfaction to us all. But while "we" are gratified, "I," that unruly partner in the human fellowship, is reduced to despair. "I" must always think things for himself, and feel things for himself. To share them in a diluted form with the majority of well-educated and well-intentioned men and women is for him sheer agony; and while the rest of us listen intently and profit profoundly, "I" slips off to the woods and the fields and rejoices in a single blade of grass or a solitary potato.

In the fifth volume of modern essays, it seems, we have got some way from pleasure and the art of writing. But in justice to the essayists of 1920 we must be sure that we are not praising the famous because they have been praised already and the dead because we shall never meet them wearing spats in Piccadilly. We must know what we mean when we say that they can write and give us pleasure. We must compare them; we must bring out the quality. We must point to this and say it is good because it is exact, truthful, and imaginative:

> Nay, retire men cannot when they would; neither will they, when it were Reason; but are impatient of Privateness, even in age and sickness, which require the shadow: like old Townsmen: that will still be sitting at their street door, though thereby they offer Age to Scorn . . .

and to this, and say it is bad because it is loose, plausible, and commonplace:

> With courteous and precise cynicism on his lips, he thought of quiet virginal chambers, of waters singing under the moon, of terraces where taintless music sobbed into the open night, of pure maternal mistresses with protecting arms and vigilant eyes, of fields slumbering in the sunlight, of leagues of ocean heaving under warm tremulous heavens, of hot ports, gorgeous and perfumed. . . .

It goes on, but already we are bemused with sound and neither feel nor hear. The comparison makes us suspect that the art of writing has for backbone some fierce attachment to an idea. It is on the back of an idea, something believed in with conviction or seen with precision and thus compelling words to its shape, that the diverse company which included Lamb and Bacon, and Mr. Beerbohm and Hudson, and Vernon Lee and Mr. Conrad, and Leslie Stephen and Butler and Walter Pater reaches the farther shore. Very various talents have helped or hindered the passage of the idea into words. Some scrape through painfully; others fly with every wind favouring. But Mr. Belloc and Mr. Lucas and Mr. Lynd and Mr. Squire are not fiercely attached to anything in itself. They share the contemporary dilemma—that lack of an obstinate conviction which lifts ephemeral sounds through the misty sphere of anybody's language to the land where there is a perpetual marriage, a perpetual union. Vague as all definitions are, a good essay must have this permanent quality about it; it must draw its curtain round us, but it must be a curtain that shuts us in, not out.

Lines of Inquiry
"The Modern Essay"

As indicated in the first footnote, this essay is a review of a five-volume collection of essays that appeared in 1920; but as indicated by the title, it is also a set of reflections on the modern essay; and as the piece itself makes clear, it is also an attempt by Woolf to define her idea of the essay. How does Woolf organize her essay to deal with all of these purposes in a clear, coherent, and developed way? Given the organization, proportioning, and detailing of her essay, which of these purposes do you think is most important to Woolf?

In paragraph 2, Woolf asserts that "the principle which controls" the essay "is simply that it should give pleasure"? What kind of pleasure do you think she has in mind? Why does Woolf think that knowing "how to write" is so important to producing this sense of pleasure? What does knowing how to write have to do with evoking "the spirit of personality," which Woolf refers to in paragraph 8 as the essayist's "most proper but most dangerous and delicate tool"? Given her emphasis on the pleasure of the essay, as well as on the proper style and personality of the essayist, how do you account for Woolf's statement in her final paragraph that "the art of writing has for backbone some fierce attachment to an idea"? Exactly what idea of the essay is Woolf most fiercely attached to in this essay?

Which of Woolf's essays in this collection do you believe most effectively exemplifies her ideas about the essay? Which least effectively? What specific aspects of each essay account for your ratings?

Copyrights and Acknowledgments

E. B. White. Reprinted by permission of Harper & Row, Publishers, Inc. "The Essayist and the Essay" (pages vii–viii) from *Essays of E. B. White* by E. B. White. Copyright © 1977 by E. B. White. Reprinted by permission of Harper & Row, Publishers, Inc.

Tom Wolfe   "O Rotten Gotham—Sliding down into the Behavioral Sink" and "The Pump House Gang" from *The Pump House Gang* by Tom Wolfe. Copyright © 1968 by Tom Wolfe. Reprinted by permission of Farrar, Straus and Giroux, Inc. "Honks and Wonks" from *Mauve Gloves & Madmen, Clutter & Vine* by Tom Wolfe. Copyright © 1967, 1968, 1969, 1973, 1974, 1975, 1976 by Tom Wolfe. Reprinted by permission of Farrar, Straus and Giroux, Inc. "The Right Stuff" a selection from *The Right Stuff* by Tom Wolfe. Copyright © 1979 by Tom Wolfe. Reprinted by permission of Farrar, Straus and Giroux, Inc.

Virginia Woolf   "The Death of the Moth" from *The Death of the Moth and Other Essays* by Virginia Woolf. Copyright © 1942 by Harcourt Brace Jovanovich, Inc., renewed 1970 by Marjorie T. Parsons, Executrix. Reprinted by permission of the publisher. "On a Faithful Friend" from *Books and Portraits* by Virginia Woolf. Copyright © 1977 by Harcourt Brace Jovanovich, Inc. Reprinted by permission of the publisher. "Thoreau" from *Books and Portraits* by Virginia Woolf. Copyright © 1977 by Harcourt Brace Jovanovich, Inc. Reprinted by permission of the publisher. "Women and Fiction" from *Granite and Rainbow* by Virginia Woolf. Copyright © 1958 by Leonard Woolf, renewed 1986 by M. T. Parsons. Reprinted by permission of Harcourt Brace Jovanovich, Inc. "The Modern Essay" from *The Common Reader* by Virginia Woolf. Copyright © 1925 by Harcourt Brace Jovanovich, Inc., renewed 1953 by Leonard Woolf. Reprinted by permission of the publisher.

Illustration Credits

Pages **100, 102, 103,** and **104** from "Joey: A 'Mechanical Boy,' " by Bruno Bettelheim, 1959, *Scientific American* 200:116–127. Reprinted by permission of Bruno Bettelheim.

Pages **291, 296,** and **297** copyright © The Walt Disney Company.

Pages **294** from *Studies in Animal and Human Behavior,* vol. 2, by Konrad Lorenz, 1971. Reprinted by permission of Methuen & Co. Ltd.

Rhetorical Index

Titles under each category refer to essays that exhibit the rhetorical feature in whole or in significant part.

Analogy

Baldwin, "Stranger in the Village,"   *66*
Bettelheim, "Joey: A 'Mechanical Boy,' "   *95*
Dillard, "Living Like Weasels,"   *186*
Eiseley, "The Hidden Teacher,"   *232*
Forster, "The Game of Life,"   *248*
Goodman, "Anxiety Is the Class Uniform,"   *276*
Gould, "The Corner of the Eye,"   *536*
King, "I Have a Dream,"   *390*
Orwell, "Politics and the English Language,"   *478*
Swift "A Meditation upon a Broomstick,"   *500*
    "The Art of Political Lying,"   *502*
Thomas, "The Iks,"   *526*
Thoreau, "Civil Disobedience,"   *574*
    "The War of the Ants,"   *571*
    "Where I Lived, and What I Lived For,"   *561*
Twain, " 'The Turning Point of My Life,' "   *661*
White, "The Ring of Time,"   *704*
Wolfe, "O Rotten Gotham—Sliding Down into the Behavioral
    Sink,"   *734*
    "The Right Stuff,"   *772*

Argument

Baldwin, "If Black English Isn't a Language, Then Tell Me
    What Is,"   *85*
    "Stranger in the Village,"   *66*
Bettelheim, "The Ignored Lesson of Anne Frank,"   *122*
Dillard, "Singing with the Fundamentalists,"   *194*
Forster, "Anonymity: An Enquiry,"   *262*
    "What I Believe,"   *254*
Goodman, "Protection from the Prying Camera,"   *278*
    "Sinking the Relationship,"   *281*
Gould, "On Heroes and Fools in Science,"   *305*
    "Women's Brains,"   *299*
King, "Black Power,"   *394*
    "I Have a Dream,"   *390*
    "Letter from Birmingham Jail,"   *375*

Mead, "Warfare: An Invention—Not a Biological Necessity," *430*
Orwell, "Politics and the English Language," *478*
Swift, "A Modest Proposal," *514*
Thomas, "The Art of Teaching Science," *540*
   "The Iks," *526*
   "On Cloning a Human Being," *529*
Thoreau, "Civil Disobedience," *574*
   "Where I Lived, and What I Lived For," *561*
Tuchman, "Is History a Guide to the Future?," *624*
Twain, "Corn-Pone Opinions," *651*
   " 'The Turning Point of My Life,' " *661*
Walker, "The Civil Rights Movement: What Good Was It?," *682*

Associative Form

Didion, "Georgia O'Keeffe," *157*
   "On Keeping a Notebook," *171*
   "On the Road," *166*
Dillard, "The Death of a Moth," *183*
   "Living Like Weasels," *186*
Eiseley, "The Bird and the Machine," *218*
Hemingway, "The Clark's Fork Valley, Wyoming," *326*
Orwell, "Some Thoughts on the Common Toad," *474*
Swift, "Hints Toward an Essay on Conversation," *507*
Thoreau, "My House," *553*
   "Where I Lived, and What I Lived For," *561*
Walker, "Am I Blue?," *695*

Cause-and-Effect Analysis

Bacon, "Of Studies," *35*
Baldwin, "If Black English Isn't a Language, Then Tell Me What Is," *85*
   "Stranger in the Village," *66*
Bettelheim, "Growing Up Female," *106*
   "The Ignored Lesson of Anne Frank," *122*
   "Joey: A 'Mechanical Boy,' " *95*
   "Some Comments on Privacy," *133*
Didion, "On Keeping a Notebook," *171*
Forster, "My Wood," *251*
Gould, "On Heroes and Fools in Science," *305*
   "Women's Brains," *299*
Hoagland, "Dogs, and the Tug of Life," *343*
   "The Problem of the Golden Rule," *352*
King, "Black Power," *394*
Orwell, "Politics and the English Language," *478*
   "Shooting an Elephant," *461*

"Why I Write,"   *490*
Swift,   "A Modest Proposal,"   *514*
Thomas,   "The Tucson Zoo,"   *533*
Tuchman,   "Is History a Guide to the Future?,"   *624*
Twain,   "Corn-Pone Opinions,"   *651*
      " 'The Turning Point of My Life,' "   *661*
      "Was the World Made for Man?,"   *650*
Walker,   "The Civil Rights Movement: What Good Was It?,"   *682*
Wolfe,   "Honks and Wonks,"   *759*

Comparison and Contrast

Bacon,   "Of Youth and Age,"   *32*
Baldwin,   "Stranger in the Village,"   *66*
Bettelheim,   "Growing Up Female,"   *106*
      "Some Comments on Privacy,"   *133*
Eiseley,   "The Long Loneliness,"   *226*
Gould,   "A Biological Homage to Mickey Mouse,"   *290*
      "On Heroes and Fools in Science,"   *305*
Hoagland,   "Dogs, and the Tug of Life,"   *343*
      "What I Think, What I Am,"   *362*
King,   "I Have a Dream,"   *390*
      "Letter from Birmingham Jail,"   *375*
Mead,   "Adolescents,"   *436*
      "New Superstitions for Old,"   *446*
Thomas,   "The Art of Teaching Science,"   *540*
White,   "Once More to the Lake,"   *704*
Wolfe,   "Honks and Wonks,"   *759*
      "The Pump House Gang,"   *745*
Woolf,   "Women and Fiction,"   *802*

Definition

Baldwin,   "If Black English Isn't a Language, Then Tell Me
      What Is,"   *85*
Didion,   "On the Mall,"   *161*
Forster,   "The Game of Life,"   *248*
Goodman,   "Sinking the Relationship,"   *281*
Gould,   "Darwin's Dilemma: The Odyssey of Evolution,"   *309*
      "On Heroes and Fools in Science,"   *305*
Hemingway,   "The Three Acts of a Bullfight,"   *318*
Hoagland,   "What I Think, What I Am,"   *362*
King,   "Black Power,"   *394*
      "An Experiment in Love: Nonviolent Resistance,"   *370*
Mead,   "New Superstitions for Old,"   *436*
      "Warfare: An Invention—Not a Biological Necessity,"   *430*
Orwell,   "Politics and the English Language,"   *478*

Thomas,   "The Corner of the Eye,"   *536*
Twain,   "Corn-Pone Opinions,"   *651*
     " 'The Turning Point of My Life,' "   *661*
Walker,   "The Black Writer and the Southern Experience,"   *690*
White,   "The Essayist and the Essay,"   *728*
Wolfe,   "Honks and Wonks,"   *759*
     "The Right Stuff,"   *772*
Woolf,   "The Modern Essay,"   *809*

Description

Baker,   "A Visit with the Folks,"   *47*
Baldwin,   "Stranger in the Village,"   *66*
Didion,   "Georgia O'Keeffe,"   *157*
     "John Wayne: A Love Song,"   *149*
     "On Keeping a Notebook,"   *171*
     "On the Road,"   *166*
Dillard,   "The Death of a Moth,"   *183*
     "The Deer at Providencia,"   *190*
     "Living Like Weasels,"   *186*
     "Singing with the Fundamentalists,"   *194*
Eiseley,   "The Bird and the Machine,"   *218*
     "The Hidden Teacher,"   *232*
Hemingway,   "The Clark's Fork Valley, Wyoming,"   *326*
     "A New Kind of War,"   *321*
Hoagland,   "Dogs, and the Tug of Life,"   *343*
Mead,   "A Day in Samoa,"   *426*
Orwell,   "A Hanging,"   *456*
     "Marrakech,"   *468*
     "Shooting an Elephant,"   *461*
     "Some Thoughts on the Common Toad,"   *474*
Swift,   "An Essay upon the Art of Political Lying,"   *502*
     "A Meditation upon a Broomstick,"   *500*
Thomas,   "The Iks,"   *526*
Thoreau,   "The War of the Ants,"   *571*
     "Where I Lived, and What I Lived For,"   *561*
Tuchman,   "History by the Ounce,"   *633*
     " 'Perdicaris Alive or Raisuli Dead,' "   *596*
Twain,   " 'S-t-e-a-m-boat a-comin'!,' "   *648*
Walker,   "Am I Blue?,"   *695*
     "Beauty: When the Other Dancer Is the Self,"   *675*
Wolfe,   "Honks and Wonks,"   *759*
     "The Pump House Gang,"   *745*
     "The Right Stuff,"   *772*

Woolf, "The Death of the Moth,"   *788*
    "On a Faithful Friend,"   *791*
    "Thoreau,"   *795*

Dialogue

Baker, "Marriage à la Mode,"   *50*
    "A Visit with the Folks,"   *47*
Didion, "John Wayne: A Love Song,"   *149*
    "On the Road,"   *166*
Baldwin, "A Fly in Buttermilk,"   *77*
Hemingway, "Monologue to the Maestro: A High Seas
    Letter,"   *329*
    "A New Kind of War,"   *321*
Wolfe, "Honks and Wonks,"   *759*
    "The Pump House Gang,"   *745*

Explanation

Bacon, "Narcissus; or Self-Love,"   *30*
    "Of Negotiating,"   *37*
    "Of Studies,"   *35*
    "Of Youth and Age,"   *32*
Bettelheim, "Growing Up Female,"   *106*
    "Joey: A 'Mechanical Boy,' "   *95*
Didion, "Georgia O'Keeffe,"   *157*
    "On the Mall,"   *161*
Eiseley, "The Hidden Teacher," *232*
    "How Flowers Changed the World,"   *209*
    "The Long Loneliness,"   *226*
Goodman, "Anxiety Is the Class Uniform,"   *276*
Gould, "A Biological Homage to Mickey Mouse,"   *290*
    "Darwin's Dilemma: The Odyssey of Evolution,"   *309*
Hemingway, "Monologue to the Maestro: A High Seas
    Letter,"   *329*
    "The Three Acts of a Bullfight,"   *318*
Hoagland, "Dogs, and the Tug of Life,"   *343*
    "What I Think, What I Am,"   *362*
Mead, "Adolescents,"   *436*
    "New Superstitions for Old,"   *446*
    "Warfare: An Invention—Not a Biological Necessity,"   *430*
Orwell, "Why I Write,"   *490*
Swift, "Hints Toward an Essay on Conversation,"   *507*
Thomas, "The Corner of the Eye,"   *536*
Tuchman, "History by the Ounce,"   *633*
    " 'Perdicaris Alive or Raisuli Dead,' "   *596*

Twain,   "Corn-Pone Opinions,"   *654*
Walker,   "The Black Writer and the Southern Experience,"   *690*
White,   "The Essayist and the Essay,"   *728*
Wolfe,   "Honks and Wonks,"   *759*
    "O Rotten Gotham—Sliding down into the Behavioral
    Sink,"   *734*
    "The Right Stuff,"   *772*
Woolf,   "The Modern Essay,"   *809*
    "Thoreau,"   *795*
    "Women and Fiction,"   *802*

Narration

Bacon,   "Narcissus; or Self-Love,"   *30*
Baker,   "The Cruelest Month,"   *44*
    "Marriage à la Mode,"   *50*
    "A Visit with the Folks,"   *47*
Baldwin,   "Autobiographical Notes,"   *61*
    "A Fly in Buttermilk,"   *77*
    "Stranger in the Village,"   *66*
Bettelheim,   "Joey: A 'Mechanical Boy,' "   *95*
Didion,   "John Wayne: A Love Song,"   *149*
    "On the Road,"   *166*
Dillard,   "The Death of a Moth,"   *183*
    "The Deer at Providencia,"   *190*
    "Living Like Weasels,"   *186*
    "Singing with the Fundamentalists,"   *194*
Eiseley,   "The Bird and the Machine,"   *218*
    "The Hidden Teacher,"   *232*
Hemingway,   "A New Kind of War,"   *321*
Hoagland,   "A Run of Bad Luck,"   *340*
King,   "Black Power,"   *394*
Mead,   "A Day in Samoa,"   *426*
Orwell,   "A Hanging,"   *456*
    "Marrakech,"   *468*
    "Shooting an Elephant,"   *461*
Thoreau,   "My House,"   *553*
    "The War of the Ants,"   *571*
Tuchman,   "Mankind's Better Moments,"   *609*
    " 'Perdicaris Alive or Raisuli Dead,' "   *596*
Twain,   " 'S-t-e-a-m-boat a-comin'!,' "   *648*
    " 'The Turning Point of My Life,' "   *661*
Walker,   "Am I Blue?,"   *695*
    "Beauty: When the Other Dancer Is the Self,"   *675*
    "The Black Writer and the Southern Experience,"   *690*

Wolfe, "The Pump House Gang," *745*
   "The Right Stuff," *772*
Woolf, "The Death of the Moth," *788*
   "On a Faithful Friend," *791*

Parody

Allen, "A Brief, Yet Helpful, Guide to Civil Disobedience," *19*
   "The Early Essays," *22*
   "My Speech to the Graduates," *16*
   "Spring Bulletin," *12*
Baker, "Completely Different," *53*
Twain, "Was the World Made for Man?," *656*
Wolfe, "The Pump House Gang," *745*

Process Analysis

Bettelheim, "Growing Up Female," *106*
Eiseley, "How Flowers Changed the World," *209*
Gould, "A Biological Homage to Mickey Mouse," *290*
   "Darwin's Dilemma: The Odyssey of Evolution," *309*
Hemingway, "The Three Acts of a Bullfight," *318*
Mead, "A Day in Samoa," *426*
Swift, "The Art of Political Lying," *502*
Thomas, "The Art of Teaching Science," *540*
   "On Cloning a Human Being," *529*
Twain, "Was the World Made for Man?," *656*
Wolfe, "The Right Stuff," *772*

Reflection

Baker, "The Cruelest Month," *44*
   "A Visit with the Folks,' *47*
Baldwin, "Autobiographical Notes," *61*
   "Stranger in the Village," *66*
Didion, "John Wayne: A Love Song," *149*
   "On Keeping a Notebook," *171*
   "On the Mall," *161*
   "On the Road," *166*
Dillard, "The Death of a Moth," *183*
   "The Deer at Providencia," *190*
   "Living Like Weasels," *186*
Eiseley, "The Bird and the Machine," *218*
   "The Hidden Teacher," *232*
Forster, "The Game of Life," *248*
   "My Wood," *251*

Hemingway, "The Clark's Fork Valley, Wyoming," 326
Hoagland, "A Run of Bad Luck," 340
Orwell, "Some Thoughts on the Common Toad," 474
    "Why I Write," 490
Swift, "A Meditation upon a Broomstick," 500
Thomas, "The Corner of the Eye," 536
    "The Tucson Zoo," 533
Thoreau, "My House," 553
    "Where I Lived, and What I Lived For," 561
Walker, "Am I Blue?," 695
    "Beauty: When the Other Dancer Is the Self," 675
White, "The Age of Dust," 718
    "Once More to the Lake," 704
    "The Ring of Time," 710
    "A Slight Sound at Evening," 720
Woolf, "The Death of the Moth," 788
    "On a Faithful Friend," 791

Theme and Variation

Baker, "Completely Different," 53
Didion, "On the Road," 166
Dillard, "The Deer at Providencia," 190
    "Living Like Weasels," 186
Eiseley, "The Bird and the Machine," 218
    "The Hidden Teacher," 232
Goodman, "Sinking the Relationship," 281
Hemingway, "The Three Acts of a Bullfight," 318
King, "I Have a Dream," 390
Orwell, "Marrakech," 468
Swift, "A Meditation upon a Broomstick," 500
Thomas, "The Corner of the Eye," 536
Thoreau, "Civil Disobedience," 574
    "My House," 553
    "Where I Lived, and What I Lived For," 561
Tuchman, "Mankind's Better Moments," 609
Twain, " 'The Turning Point of My Life,' " 661
White, "The Ring of Time," 710
    "A Slight Sound at Evening," 720
Woolf, "The Death of the Moth," 788

Author–Title Index

Adolescents, 436
Age of Dust, The, 718
Allen, Woody, 8
Am I Blue?, 695
Anonymity: An Enquiry, 262
Anxiety Is the Class Uniform, 276
Art of Political Lying, The, 502
Art of Teaching Science, The, 540
Autobiographical Notes, 61

Bacon, Francis, 26
Baker, Russell, 40
Baldwin, James, 56
Beauty: When the Other Dancer Is the Self, 675
Bettelheim, Bruno, 90
Biological Homage to Mickey Mouse, A, 290
Bird and the Machine, The, 218
Black Writer and the Southern Experience, The, 690
Black Power, 394
Brief, Yet Helpful, Guide to Disobedience, A, 19

Civil Disobedience, 574
Civil Rights Movement: What Good Was It?, The, 682
Clark's Fork Valley, Wyoming, The, 326
Completely Different, 53
Corner of the Eye, The, 536
Corn-Pone Opinions, 651
Cruelest Month, The, 44

Darwin's Dilemma: The Odyssey of Evolution, 309
Day in Samoa, A, 426
Death of a Moth, The, 183
Death of the Moth, The, 788

Deer at Providencia, The, 190
Didion, Joan, 144
Dillard, Annie, 178
Dogs, and the Tug of Life, 343

Early Essays, The, 22
Eiseley, Loren, 204
Essayist and the Essay, The, 728
Experiment in Love: Nonviolent Resistance, An, 370

Fly in Buttermilk, A, 77
Forster, E. M., 244

Game of Life, The, 248
Georgia O'Keeffe, 157
Goodman, Ellen, 272
Gould, Stephen Jay, 286
Growing Up Female, 106

Hanging, A, 456
Hemingway, Ernest, 314
Hidden Teacher, The, 232
Hints Toward an Essay on Conversation, 507
History by the Ounce, 633
Hoagland, Edward, 336
Honks and Wonks, 759
How Flowers Changed the World, 209

If Black English Isn't a Language, Then Tell Me What Is?, 85
Ignored Lesson of Anne Frank, The, 122
I Have a Dream, 390
Iks, The, 526
In the Male Direction, 283
Is History a Guide to the Future?, 624

Joey: A "Mechanical Boy," 95
John Wayne: A Love Song, 149

King, Martin Luther, Jr.,   *366*

Letter from Birmingham Jail,   375
Living Like Weasels,   186
Long Loneliness, The,   226

Mankind's Better Moments,   609
Marrakech,   468
Marriage à la Mode,   50
Mead, Margaret,   *422*
*Meditation upon a Broomstick,
    A,   500*
Modern Essay, The,   809
Modest Proposal, A,   514
*Monologue to the Maestro: A High
    Seas Letter,   329*
My House,   553
My Speech to the Graduates,   16
My Wood,   251

Narcissus; or Self-Love,   30
New Kind of War, A,   321
New Superstitions for Old,   446

Of Negotiating,   37
Of Studies,   35
Of Youth and Age,   32
On a Faithful Friend,   791
Once More to the Lake,   704
On Cloning a Human Being,   529
*On Heroes and Fools in Sci-
    ence,   305*
On Keeping a Notebook,   171
On the Mall,   161
On the Road,   166
*O Rotten Gotham—Sliding down
    into the Behavioral Sink,   734*
Orwell, George,   *452*

*"Perdicaris Alive or Raisuli
    Dead,"   596*
*Politics and the English Lan-
    guage,   478*
*Problem of the Golden Rule,
    The,   352*
*Protection from the Prying
    Camera,   278*
Pump House Gang, The,   745

Right Stuff, The,   772
Ring of Time, The,   710
Run of Bad Luck, A,   340

Shooting an Elephant,   461
*Singing with the Fundamental-
    ists,   194*
Sinking the Relationship,   281
Slight Sound at Evening, A,   720
Some Comments on Privacy,   133
*Some Thoughts on the Common
    Toad,   474*
Spring Bulletin,   12
"S-t-e-a-m-boat a-comin'!,"   648
Stranger in the Village,   66
Swift, Jonathan,   *496*

Thomas, Lewis,   *522*
Thoreau,   795
Thoreau, Henry David,   *548*
*Three Acts of a Bullfight,
    The,   318*
Tuchman, Barbara,   *592*
Tucson Zoo, The,   533
*"Turning Point of My Life,
    The,"   661*
Twain, Mark,   *644*

Visit with the Folks, A,   47

Walker, Alice,   *670*
War of the Ants, The,   571
*Warfare: An Invention—Not a
    Biological Necessity,   430*
*Was the World Made for
    Man?,   656*
What I Believe,   254
What I Think, What I Am,   362
*Where I Lived, and What I Lived
    For,   561*
White, E. B.,   *700*
Why I Write,   490
Wolfe, Tom,   *730*
Women and Fiction,   802
Women's Brains,   299
Woolf, Virginia,   *784*

B   0
C   1
D   2
E   3
F   4
G   5
H   6
I   7
J   8